READINGS IN AMERICAN GOVERNMENT AND POLITICS

READINGS IN AMERICAN GOVERNMENT AND POLITICS

THIRD EDITION

EDITED BY
RANDALL B. RIPLEY AND **ELLIOT E. SLOTNICK**

The Ohio State University

Longman

New York   San Francisco   Boston
London   Toronto   Sydney   Tokyo   Singapore   Madrid
Mexico City   Munich   Paris   Cape Town   Hong Kong   Montreal

Vice President: Paul A. Smith
Editorial Assistant: Kathy Rubino
Marketing Manager: Jeff Lasser
Editorial Production Service: Chestnut Hill Enterprises
Manufacturing Buyer: Megan Cochran
Cover Administrator: Jennifer Hart

Library of Congress Cataloging-in-Publication Data

Readings in American government and politics / edited by Randall B.
    Ripley and Elliot E. Slotnick. — 3rd ed.
        p. cm.
    Includes bibliographical references.
    ISBN 0-205-18880-X (pbk.)
    1. United States—Politics and government.   I. Ripley, Randall B.
II. Slotnick, Elliot E.
JK21.R383   1998
320.973—dc21   98-13173
                                                CIP

Printed in the United States of America

10 9 8 7 6 5 4 3 2 1   RRD-VA   03 02 01 00 99 98

CONTENTS

The glare of media attention on the contemporary presidency far exceeds the wildest imaginations of earlier chief executives. While the president serves as "master of ceremonies presiding over the public will," he is diverted from pursuing policy goals.

The freedom of speech protected by the First Amendment sometimes requires us to be subjected to messages that we find distasteful or worse. This case involves the emotionally laden issue of the right to burn an American flag, the most sacred symbol of our democracy, as part and parcel of the enjoyment of freedom of expression.

Not all of the Court's landmark rulings fall in the realm of civil rights and liberties. In this critical case the Court refused to recognize Richard Nixon's claim of "executive privilege." Nixon acquiesced in the Court's ruling, thereby avoiding a constitutional crisis of great urgency. He released the secret White House Tapes that underscored his role in the Watergate conspiracy and led to his swift resignation from office.

PREFACE

This collection of readings on American government and politics contains selections that are factually informative, raises broad normative questions about the fundamental nature of American government and politics, and displays a variety of political scientists, historians, journalists, and other professionals at work analyzing what they observe.

Each selection is intended to stand on its own. At the same time, we have chosen a range of readings in each chapter that are intended to present several different facets of a topic. Our chapter introductions weave together those facets and also comment briefly on some aspects of the topic not directly addressed by the readings. Each brief headnote sets the stage for the piece that follows, but it would be a mistake to think that the headnote captures the richness of the reading itself. The readings are meant to be read!

The organization of the book parallels the organization of a typical course in introductory American government or a textbook used in such a course. Naturally, any individual instructor may prefer a different order for the topics. That presents no problem because the order of the chapters can be changed without loss of information or perspective.

We start with three chapters on the American Political Tradition. These set the constitutional and federalistic context for the entire American system of government. Second, we have five chapters on The Environment for Governmental Activity. In these chapters we explore the impact of public opinion, the media, political parties, elections, and interest groups on how government addresses public problems. Third, we present five chapters on National Institutions and Policy. Four of these chapters focus on the basic institutions of national government: Congress, the presidency, the bureaucracy, and the judiciary. The fifth chapter in this final part returns to the constitutional theme by including some recent significant constitutional decisions by the Supreme Court. Such decisions continue to shape the nature of our political system, as they have throughout our history.

We have sought to make the selections highly readable through choosing well-written pieces in the first place, editing them where necessary to keep them succinct, and omitting scholarly citations, footnotes, and bibliographies.

We are grateful to a number of people for helping us with this project. Janet E. Franz, University of Southwestern Louisiana; Thomas A. Kazee, Davidson College; Janet M. Martin, Bowdoin College; Mark C. Miller, Clark University; Hoyt D. Gardner, Indiana University Southeast; Scott R. Furlong, University of Wisconsin–Green Bay; and Lisa Langenback, Middle Tennessee State University. We are particularly indebted to Lisa Campoli, a graduate student in political science at Ohio State, who performed a number of demanding tasks very well over several years.

Randall B. Ripley
Elliot E. Slotnick

Randall B. Ripley is Dean of the College of Social and Behavioral Sciences and Professor of Political Science at The Ohio State University, where he has taught since 1967. Prior to that, he spent five years in Washington at the Brookings Institution. He also served as an intern in the U.S. House of Representatives. He earned his B.A. from DePauw University and his Ph.D. from Harvard University. He has written extensively, in both books and articles, on Congress, public policy processes and substance, and bureaucracy. He has taught a range of courses in American government and politics.

Elliot E. Slotnick is Associate Dean of the Graduate School and Associate Professor of Political Science at The Ohio State University, where he has taught since 1977. He earned his B.A. from Brooklyn College and his Ph.D. from the University of Minnesota. He has taught a range of courses in American government and politics and was the recipient of the Outstanding Teaching Award at OSU. He has written extensively on judicial politics in numerous political science and law-related journals, edited *Judicial Politics: Readings From Judicature* (American Judicature Society), and recently co-authored *Television News and the Supreme Court: All the News That's Fit to Air?* (Cambridge University Press).

CHAPTER 1

CONSTITUTIONAL CREATION

Constitutional systems may be characterized as those in which the contours of governmental powers are well articulated and understood, while the rights and liberties of the populace with respect to the government are equally well established. While autocratic governmental systems (such as, for example, the former Soviet Union) may have elaborately written constitutional shells, when the power relationships established by the constitution and the rights and liberties recognized for the polity are breached in practice, one can hardly make an argument that a functioning constitutional system is in place. Conversely, there may be instances in which no single written document can be identified as a country's "constitution" (as is the case, for example, in Great Britain), yet the operation of the country's governmental system would clearly be characterized as a working constitutional order.

In the case of the American polity, fidelity to a concrete, written document, the United States Constitution, holds a uniquely revered place in the nation's self-understanding, while serving as an inspiration to and a model for many nations throughout the world, including the emerging democracies of Eastern Europe, Latin America, Africa, and elsewhere. While it remains easy and, perhaps, somewhat justifiable to place the U.S. Constitution on a pedestal for worldwide admiration, it is critical to examine our constitutional system from the perspective of the times in which it was created. By doing so we may understand more fully just what kind of system the framers were attempting to create and why they made the critical and, often, difficult choices that they did.

The articles in this chapter offer such an exploration of the Constitution's founding and they demonstrate, collectively, that things are often considerably more complex and less clear cut than they seem at first blush. At the outset, historian Gordon Wood argues in *Eighteenth-Century American Constitutionalism* that Americans were the first to establish the idea that a meaningful written constitution could be framed, distinguishable from and superior to the government and, in particular, the legislative majority's judgments of the moment. Further distinguishing the U.S. constitutional system from its English heritage, where entrenched customs and parliamentary decisions take on constitutional status, was the notion that the Constitution would be adaptable and subject to interpretation. Indeed, Wood offers us our first look at judicial review (a subject we will return to in Chapter 2) which, combined with the elements of a written constitution, the creation of conventions for authorizing and altering constitutions, and establishment of procedures for ratifying constitutions through popular mechanisms, has resulted in the development of a constitutional order that "institutionalized and legitimized revolution."

While Wood's article is suggestive of the unique nature of the U.S. Constitution, other articles in this chapter offer somewhat alternative perspectives on the motivations that led to the document's framing. Clearly, the most idealistic view is offered by another historian, Lance Banning, in *From Confederation to Constitution: The Revolutionary Context of the Great Convention.* While not arguing, in any sense, that our constitutional system was totally responsive to democratic ideals Banning does, nevertheless, underscore that one must understand the work of the framers in the context of the broad social revolution in which they were participating. In Banning's view, they sought to transform society while offering a model for governance that "dreamed revolutionary dreams of perfection."

While Banning recognizes that at the time of the Constitution's writing, just as now, "perfection" might be defined rather differently by different segments of society, his vision of the Constitution's framing remains a relatively sunny and optimistic one. Such is patently not the case in the selection we offer from Charles Beard's classic study, *An Economic Interpretation of the Constitution,* in which the author asserts that it was the propertied interests who were most supportive of the Constitution because of its ability to free the most well-off members of society from the excesses, whims, and caprices of popular majorities. Beard's thesis was first published in 1913, and it is easy to see how his conceptualization of our country's founding was affected by the Marxist tide that was swelling in parts of Europe, while also undergoing protracted discussion among critical masses of the American populace as well at this time.

Somewhat less overtly cynical in their orientation, *The Federalist Papers* authored by Alexander Hamilton, James Madison, and John Jay offer their own abundance of rationales to the voters of New York State regarding why it is in their own clear self-interest, a theme not too distant from Beard's, to abandon the Articles of Confederation and support the ratification of the new U.S. Constitution. *The Federalist*'s critique of the Articles and proffered justifications for adopting the Constitution underscore the uniquely pragmatic and self-consciously non-ideological tone that might be said to characterize the American polity's approach to governing. If, indeed, *The Federalist Papers* represent the primary statement of American political thought at the time of the Constitution's founding, it is important to recognize that their deification of self-interested ratifying behavior is a far cry from the more impassioned ideological pleas of the French Revolution for liberty, equality, and fraternity, and the Russian Revolution's imploring of the workers of the world to unite and throw off their chains.

Importantly, however, such a pragmatic approach to politics and governance that lies at the heart of our Constitution's founding may hold a key to our constitutional system's longevity and stability, particularly when compared with the turbulence we witness in almost every other corner of the globe. Such a theme is developed further in political scientist Martin Landau's contribution to this chapter, *A Self-Correcting*

System: The Constitution of the United States. Landau traces the success of our constitutional system to the Constitution's fundamental simplicity. While well aware of the frustrations and criticisms often associated with a system that seems to welcome and support the status quo, a policymaking process characterized by disjointed half steps that are generally easy to block, Landau concludes that efficiency was not the goal our Constitution's framers strove for. Rather, they sought a "self-regulating" and "high-reliability" system characterized by balance, equilibrium, and stability, the very checks and balances to minimize the risks of human error in governance explored in *The Federalist.*

READING 1

Eighteenth-Century American Constitutionalism

Gordon Wood

The period of our country's founding has been characterized as the most innovative and important age for the development of constitutionalism in American and, perhaps, world history. Here, historian Gordon Wood of Brown University argues that Americans established the idea of a meaningful, written constitution that served as fundamental law, yet was adaptable and subject to interpretation. Of primary importance, the American Constitution was distinguishable from and superior to the government per se. Wood's analysis explores the notion that constitutions are not simply reflections of transitory majority will, but organic acts ordained by the people and superior to legislative choices. This is, of course, fundamentally at variance with our English political heritage, which dictated that entrenched

---

customs and Parliament, not a parchment constitution, were the primary protectors of the people's liberties and that laws passed by Parliament were, by definition, legal and, consequently, constitutional. Importantly, the American version of constitutionalism differed in distinguishing the legality of the processes through which laws were passed from their constitutionality.

Interestingly, Wood notes, in colonial and post-Independence America the distinction between "fundamental" constitutions and contemporary legislative enactments tended to break down in practice and, over time, legislatures became feared at least as much as governors. Desires for fundamental constitutions necessitated their creation by groups truly independent of the government, and the impetus existed for constitutional formulation by conventions established for that specific purpose, to be ratified by the people, not their representatives.

This method of generating a fundamental constitution does not solve, in any sense, the problem of how to interpret such a document and how to decide who speaks for "the people" when disputes arise. Wood foreshadows the unique political role played by the American judiciary in which judges exercising judicial review (the power to declare the acts and actions of other governmental agents unconstitutional) serve as the oracle of the people's will.

The era of the American Revolution was the greatest and most creative age of constitutionalism in American history. During the last part of the eighteenth century Americans established the modern idea of a written constitution. There had been written constitutions before in Western history, but Americans did something new and different. They made written constitutions a practical and everyday part of governmental life. They showed the world not only how written constitutions could be made truly fundamental, distinguishable from ordinary legislation, but also how such constitutions could be interpreted on a regular basis and altered when necessary. Further, they offered the world concrete and usable governmental institutions for the carrying out of these con-

stitutional tasks. All in all it was an extraordinary achievement, scarcely duplicated by any modern country in such a brief period of time.

Before the era of the American Revolution a constitution was rarely ever distinguished from the government and its operations. Traditionally in English culture a constitution referred not only to fundamental rights but also to the way the government was put together or constituted. A constitution was the disposition of the government; it even had medical or physiological connotations, like the constitution of the human body. "By constitution," wrote Lord Bolingbroke in 1733, "we mean, whenever we speak with propriety and exactness, that assemblage of laws, institutions and customs, derived from certain fixed principles of reason, directed to certain fixed objects of public good, that compose the general system, according to which the community hath agreed to be governed." The English constitution, in other words, included both fundamental principles and rights and the existing arrangement of governmental laws, customs, and institutions.

By the end of the Revolutionary era, however, the Americans' idea of a constitution had become very different from that of the English. A constitution was now seen to be no part of the government at all. A constitution was a written document distinct from and superior to all the operations of government. It was, as Thomas Paine said in 1791, "a thing *antecedent* to a government; and a government is only the creature of a constitution." And, said Paine, it was "not a thing in name only; but in fact." For Americans a constitution was like a bible, possessed by every family and every member of government. "It is the body of elements, to which you can refer, and quote article by article; and which contains... everything that relates to the complete organization of a civil government, and the principles on which it shall act, and by which it shall be bound." A constitution thus could never be an act of a legislature or of a government; it had to be the act of the people themselves, declared James Wilson in 1790, one of the principal framers of the federal Constitution of 1787; and "in their hands it is clay in the hands of a potter; they have the right to mould, to preserve, to improve, to refine, and to furnish it as they please." If the English thought this American idea of a constitution was, as Arthur Young caustically suggested in 1792, like "a pudding made by a recipe," the Americans had become convinced the English no longer had a constitution at all.

It was a momentous transformation of meaning. It involved not just a change in the Americans' political vocabulary but an upheaval in their whole political culture. In the short span of less than three decades Americans created a whole new way of looking at government.

The colonists began the imperial crisis in the early 1760s thinking about constitutional issues in much the same way as their fellow Britons. Like the English at home they believed that the principal threat to the people's ancient rights and liberties had always been the prerogative powers of the king, those vague and discretionary but equally ancient rights of authority that the king possessed in order to carry out his responsibility for governing the realm. Indeed, eighteenth-century English citizens saw their history as essentially a struggle between these conflicting rights, between a centralizing monarchy on one hand and localist-minded nobles and people on the other. Eighteenth-century colonists had no reason to think about government much differently. Time and again in the colonial period the colonists had been forced to defend themselves against the intrusions of royal prerogative power. They relied for defense on their colonial assemblies, their rights as Englishmen, and what they called their ancient charters. In the seventeenth century many of the colonies had been established by crown charters, corporate or proprietary grants made by the king to groups like the Massachusetts Puritans or to individuals like William Penn and Lord Baltimore to found colonies in the New World. In subsequent years these written charters gradually lost their original purpose in the eyes of the colonists and took on a new importance, both as prescriptions for government and as devices guaranteeing the rights of the people against their royal governors. In fact, the whole of the colonists' past was littered with such charters and other written documents of various sorts to which the colonial assemblies had repeatedly appealed in their squabbles with royal power.

In appealing to written documents as confirmations of their liberties the colonists acted no differ-

ently from other Englishmen. From almost the beginning of their history, Britons had continually invoked written documents and charters in defense of their rights against the crown's power. "Anxious to preserve and transmit" their liberties "unimpaired to posterity," the English people, observed one colonist on the eve of the Revolution, had repeatedly "caused them to be reduced to writing, and in the most solemn manner to be recognized, ratified and confirmed," first by King John with Magna Carta, then by Henry III and Edward I, and "afterwards by a multitude of corroborating acts, reckoned in all, by Lord Cook, to be thirty-two from Edw. 1st to Hen. 4th, and since, in a great variety of instances, by the bills of rights and acts of settlement." All of these documents, from Magna Carta to the Bill of Rights of the Glorious Revolution of 1689, were merely written evidence of those "fixed principles of reason" from which Bolingbroke had said the English constitution was derived.

Although eighteenth-century Englishmen talked about the fixed principles and the fundamental law of the English constitution, few of them doubted that Parliament, as the representative of the nobles and people and as the sovereign law-making body of the nation, was the supreme guarantor and interpreter of these fixed principles and fundamental law. Parliament was in fact the bulwark of the people's liberties against the crown's encroachments; it alone defended and confirmed the people's rights. The Petition of Right, the act of Habeus Corpus, the Bill of Rights were all acts of Parliament, statutes not different in form from other laws passed by Parliament.

For Englishmen therefore, as William Blackstone, the great eighteenth-century jurist pointed out, there could be no distinction between the "constitution or frame of government" and "the system of laws." All were of a piece: every act of Parliament was part of the English constitution and all law, customary and statute, was thus constitutional. "Therefore," concluded the English theorist William Paley, "the terms *constitutional* and *unconstitutional,* mean *legal* and *illegal.*"

Nothing could be more strikingly different from what Americans came to believe. Indeed, it was precisely on this distinction between "legal" and "constitutional" that the American and the British constitutional traditions diverged at the Revolution. During the 1760s and seventies the colonists came to realize that although acts of Parliament, like the Stamp Act of 1765, might be legal, that is, in accord with the acceptable way of making law, such acts could not thereby be automatically considered constitutional, that is, in accord with the basic principles of rights and justice that made the English constitution what it was. It was true that the English Bill of Rights and the act of settlement in 1689 were only statutes of Parliament, but surely, the colonists insisted, they were of "a nature more sacred than those which established a turnpike road." Under this pressure of events the Americans came to believe that the fundamental principles of the English constitution had to be lifted out of the lawmaking and other institutions of government and set above them. "In all free States," said Samuel Adams in 1768, "the Constitution is fixed; and as the supreme Legislature derives its Powers and Authority from the Constitution, it cannot overleap the Bounds of it without destroying its own foundation." Thus in 1776, when Americans came to make their own constitutions for their newly independent states, it was inevitable that they would seek to make them fundamental and explicitly write them out in documents.

It was one thing, however, to define the constitution as fundamental law, different from ordinary legislation and circumscribing the institutions of government; it was quite another to make such a distinction effective. In the years following the Declaration of Independence, many Americans paid lip service to the fundamental character of their state constitutions, but like eighteenth-century Britons they continued to believe that their legislatures were the best instruments for interpreting and changing these constitutions. The state legislatures were the representatives of the people, and the people, it seemed, could scarcely tyrannize themselves. Thus in the late 1770s and early eighties, several state legislatures, acting on behalf of the people, set aside parts of their constitutions by statute and interpreted and altered them, as one American observed, "upon any occasion to serve a purpose." Time and again the legislatures interfered with the governors' legitimate powers, rejected judicial decisions, disregarded individual liberties and

property rights, and in general, as one victim complained, violated "those fundamental principles which first induced men to come into civil compact."

By the mid-1780s many American leaders had come to believe that the state legislatures, not the governors as they had thought in 1776, were the political authority to be most feared. Legislators were supposedly the representatives of the people who annually elected them; but "173 despots would surely be as oppressive as one," wrote Thomas Jefferson. "An *elective despotism* was not the government we fought for." It increasingly seemed to many that the idea of a constitution as fundamental law had no real meaning after all. "If it were possible it would be well to define the extent of the Legislative power, but," concluded a discouraged James Madison in 1785, "the nature of it seems in many respects to be indefinite."

No one wrestled more persistently with this problem of distinguishing between statutory and fundamental law than did Jefferson. In 1779 Jefferson knew from experience that no legislature "elected by the people for the ordinary purposes of legislation only" could restrain the acts of succeeding legislatures. Thus he realized that to declare his great act for Establishing Religious Freedom in Virginia to be "irrevocable would be of no effect in law; yet we are free," he wrote into the bill in frustration, "to declare, and do declare, that...if any act shall be hereafter passed to repeal the present or to narrow its operation, such act will be an infringement of natural right." But such a paper declaration was obviously not enough; he realized that something more was needed. By the 1780s both he and Madison were eager "to form a real constitution" for Virginia; the existing one was merely an "ordinance" with "no higher authority than the other ordinances of the same session." They wanted a constitution that would be "perpetual" and "unalterable by other legislatures." But how? That was the rub. Somehow or other, if the constitution were to be truly fundamental and immune from legislative tampering, it would have to be created, as Jefferson put it, "by a power superior to that of the legislature."

By the time Jefferson came to write his *Notes on the State of Virginia* in the early 1780s the answer had become clear. "To render a form of government unalterable by ordinary acts of assembly," said Jefferson, "the people must delegate persons with special powers. They have accordingly chosen special conventions to form and fix their governments." In 1775–76 conventions or congresses had been legally deficient legislatures made necessary by the refusal of the royal governors to call together the regular and legal representations of the people. Now, however, these conventions were seen to be special alternative representations of the people with the exclusive authority to frame or amend constitutions. When Massachusetts and New Hampshire wrote new constitutions in the early 1780s, the proper pattern of constitution-making and constitution-altering was set: constitutions were formed by specially elected conventions and then placed before the people for ratification. Thus in 1787 those who wished to change the federal government knew precisely what to do: they called a convention in Philadelphia and sent the resultant document to the states for approval. Even the French in their own revolution several years later followed the American pattern. Conventions and the process of ratification made the people the actual constituent power. Such institutions, historian R. R. Palmer has said, were the most distinctive contributions the American Revolution made to Western politics.

But these were not the only contributions. With the idea of a constitution as fundamental law immune from legislative encroachment more firmly in hand, some state judges during the 1780s began cautiously moving in isolated cases to impose restraints on what the assemblies were enacting as law. In effect they said to the legislatures, as George Wythe, judge of the Virginia supreme court did in 1782, "Here is the limit of your authority; and hither shall you go, but no further." These were the hesitant beginnings of what would come to be called judicial review—that remarkable American practice by which judges in the ordinary courts of law have the authority to determine the constitutionality of acts of the state and federal legislatures. There is nothing quite like it anywhere else in the world.

The development of judicial review came slowly. It was not easy for people in the eighteenth century, even those who were convinced that many of the acts of the state legislatures in the 1780s were unjust and unconstitutional, to believe that unelected judges could set aside acts of the popularly-elected legislatures; this prerogative seemed to be an undemocratic judicial usurpation of power. But as early as 1787 James Iredell of North Carolina, soon to be appointed a justice of the newly-created Supreme Court of the United States, saw that the new meaning Americans had given to a constitution had clarified the responsibility of judges to determine the law. A constitution in America, said Iredell, was not only "a fundamental law" but also a special popularly-created "law in writing…limiting the powers of the Legislature, and with which every exercise of those powers must necessarily be compared." Judges were not arbiters of the constitution or usurpers of legislative power. They were, said Iredell, merely judicial officials fulfilling their duty of applying the proper law. When faced with a decision between "the *fundamental unrepealable* law" made specially by the people and an ordinary statute enacted by a legislature contrary to the constitution, they must simply determine which law was superior. Judges could not avoid exercising this authority, concluded Iredell, for in America a constitution was not "a mere imaginary thing, about which ten thousand different opinions may be formed, but a written document to which all may have recourse, and to which, therefore, the judges cannot witfully blind themselves." Although Iredell may have been wrong about the number of different opinions that could be formed over a constitution, he was certainly right about the direction judicial authority in America would take. Through the subsequent development of the doctrine of judicial review judges in America came to exercise a power over governmental life unparalleled by any other judiciary in the world.

These then were the great contributions to constitutionalism that Americans in the Revolutionary era made to the world—the modern idea of a constitution as a written document, the device of a convention for creating and amending constitutions, the process of popular ratification, and the practice of judicial review. The sources of these constitutional contributions went back deep in Western history. For centuries people had talked about fundamental law and the placing of limits on the operations of government. But not until the American Revolution had anyone ever developed such regular and everyday institutions not only for controlling government and protecting the rights of individuals but also for changing the very framework by which the government operated. Americans in 1787 and in numerous state constitutional conventions thereafter demonstrated to the world how a people could fundamentally and yet peaceably alter their forms of government. In effect they had institutionalized and legitimized revolution. After these American achievements, discussions of constitutionalism could never again be quite the same.

From Confederation to Constitution: The Revolutionary Context of the Great Convention

Lance Banning

Analysts of our nation's beginnings continually debate the motives of those who framed our governmental system. Were they primarily democratic visionaries or, alternatively, self-interested men motivated largely by greed? University of Kentucky historian Lance Banning clearly opts for the more charitable view in his discussion of the period leading to the constitutional convention.

Beginning from the premise that revolutions need not, necessarily, be characterized by violence and upheaval, Banning views the Constitution's framing as a revolutionary act. A good deal more than simply the war against Great Britain, the American Revolution was started a decade prior to independence and would last another quarter century. Beyond seeking independence, the Revolution sought "a new example for mankind." While relatively tame in retrospect, it was radical in

the context of its time as Americans "dreamed revolutionary visions of perfection." Thus, Banning asserts, the war for independence was largely a war about ideas concerning the relationship of a polity with its government. By the time of our independence, Americans believed in republicanism—support for a government in which both liberty and representative democracy could coexist with majority rule tempered by minority rights.

Banning offers a balanced view of the Articles of Confederation, demonstrating that they accomplished a great deal while recognizing that they failed to solve the critical problems of "squabbling" states and the nation's revenue needs. He concludes that changes in the Articles were needed because they endangered liberty and appeared incapable of accomplishing the envisioned Revolution. While conceding that the Revolution would fail any modern test of democracy and that the founders were, above all else, eighteenth-century thinkers, the assertion that "the revolutionary air was full of popular awareness of people's rights" should be given close scrutiny. The issue remains paramount of whose liberty was being endangered and whose rights were on the agenda at the time of the constitutional convention.

From "From Confederation to Constitution: The Revolutionary Context of the Great Convention" by L. Banning, 1985, *This Constitution*, no. 6, Spring, 1985, Project '87, pp. 12–18. Copyright © 1985 by the American Political Science Association. Reprinted by permission.

Most Americans recall our Revolution in decidedly selective ways. As a people, we are not as eager as we used to be to recollect how truly revolutionary are our roots. Our Bicentennial celebration, for example, focused overwhelmingly on independence and the war with Britain, not on the genuinely revolutionary facets of the struggle. Too often, we commemorated even independence with hoary myths about tyrannical King George and clever minutemen who used the woods and fences to defeat the British regulars. Perhaps, then, it is not so inexcusable as it would first appear for some Americans to think that Thomas Jefferson wrote the Constitution as well as the Declaration of Independence in 1776. If we think of the American Revolution as no more than a sudden, brave attempt to shake off English rule, perverse consistency leads easily to a mistake that lumps together all the documents and incidents connected with the Founding. For a better understanding... we would do well to fit the Constitution back into the revolutionary process from which it emerged.

As John Adams said, the American Revolution was not the war against Great Britain; it should not be confused with independence. The Revolution started in the people's minds at least ten years before the famous shots at Lexington and Concord. It was well advanced before the colonies declared their independence. It continued for perhaps a quarter of a century after the fighting came to an end. It dominated the entire life experience of America's greatest generation of public men. And it was fully revolutionary in many of the strictest definitions of that term. The men who made it wanted not just independence, but a change that would transform their own societies and set a new example for mankind. They wanted to create, as they put it on the Great Seal of the United States, "a new order of the ages" which would become a foundation for the happiness of all of their descendents and a model for the other peoples of the world. To their minds, the federal Constitution was a Revolutionary act, an episode in their experimental quest for such an order.

A REPUBLICAN EXPERIMENT

From a twentieth-century perspective, the American Revolution may appear conservative and relatively tame. There were no mass executions. Social relationships and political arrangements were not turned upside down in an upheaval of scattering violence, as they would be later on in France or Russia or any of a dozen other countries we might name. To people living through it, nonetheless—or watching it from overseas—the American Revolution seemed very radical indeed. It was not self-evident in 1776 that all men are created equal, that governments derive their just authority from popular consent, or that good governments exist in order to protect God-given rights. These concepts are not undeniable in any age. From the point of view of eighteenth-century Europeans, they contradicted common sense. The notions that a sound society could operate without the natural subordination customary where men were either commoners or nobles or that a stable government could be based entirely on elections seemed both frighten-

ing and ridiculously at odds with the obvious lessons of the past. A republican experiment had been attempted once before on something like this scale—in England during the 1640s and 1650s—and the ultimate result had been a Cromwellian dictatorship and a quick return to the ancient constitution of King, Lords, and Commons.

Nevertheless, the Americans dreamed revolutionary visions of perfection, comparable in many ways to revolutionary visions of later times. They sought a new beginning, a rebirth, in which hereditary privilege would disappear and all political authority would derive exclusively from talent, public service, and the people's choice. And their commitment to the principles of liberty and equal rights did touch and change most aspects of their common life.

No essay of this length can possibly describe all of the ways in which the Revolution altered American society. To understand the Constitution, though, we have to realize, at minimum, that as they fought the War for Independence, Americans were equally involved in a fundamental transformation of political beliefs and thus of political institutions. The decision to separate from England was also a decision that Americans were a people different from the English, a separate nation with a special mission in the world. This people had no way to understand their new identity except in terms of their historical mission, no way to define or perfect their national character except by building their new order. To be an American, by 1776, was to be a republican, and to become consistently republican required a thorough reconstruction of existing institutions.

A republican experiment, in fact, required rebuilding governments afresh. For in the months between the clash at Lexington and the Declaration of Independence, formal governments dissolved in one American colony after another. The people, who had ordinarily elected only one branch of their local governments, simply transferred their allegiance from their legal governmental institutions to extralegal revolutionary committees, state conventions, and the Continental Congress. Through the first months of the fighting, the conventions and committees managed very well. Power rested with the people in a wholly literal sense, the people followed the directives of these revolutionary bodies, and those bodies turned the popular determination into armies and materials of war.

Some revolutionaries might have been content to see their states continue indefinitely under governmental bodies of this sort. Many patriots were intensely localistic, and they had learned a fierce distrust of any power much beyond the people's easy reach. Other patriots, however, many more of those who exercised great influence, never saw the revolutionary agencies as anything but temporary. A structure that depended so immediately on the people was good enough for an emergency, but hardly suitable for the longer term. For permanence, most patriots admired a governmental structure that balanced and divided power between different and independent parts, not one that concentrated it in single bodies which performed both legislative and executive functions.

The revolutionaries had been reared as Englishmen, in a tradition that instructed them that liberty was incompatible with the unchecked rule of the majority or with a government composed of only a single branch. Proper constitutions, they believed, depended on consent, but governments existed in order to protect the liberties of all. The revolutionaries had decided that good governments should have no place for aristocrats or kings, but they continued to believe that immediate and undiluted rule by the majority could not provide the wisdom and stability that governments require, nor could it offer proper safeguards for the rights of all. Thus, as they moved toward independence, the revolutionaries started a long search for a governmental structure in which liberty and representative democracy could be combined. This was what they meant by a "republic."

Most of the revolutionary states established written constitutions before the end of 1776. Although they differed greatly in details, these constitutions tended to be similar in broader lines. The colonial experience, together with the quarrel with Great Britain, had taught a powerful fear of the executive and of the executive's ability to undermine the independence of the other parts of government by use of patronage or "influence." Accordingly, most states created governors too weak to do such harm. Most stripped the governors of the majority of their traditional powers of appointment and deprived them of the traditional right to veto legislation. Most provided for election of the governors by the legislative branch. Most confined the chief executives, in short, to the job of enforcing the legislatures' wills.

According to these constitutions, the legislative power would remain within the people's hardy grip. The concept of a balance required two legislative houses, but hostility to privilege was far too sharp to let the second house become a bastion for any special group, in imitation of the English House of Lords. Moreover, in societies without hereditary ranks, it was difficult to reach agreement on a genuinely republican method for selecting the few men of talent and leisure whose superior wisdom, lodged in an upper house, was traditionally supposed to check the passions of the multitude. The revolutionary senates differed relatively little in their makeup from the lower houses of assembly. Democratic Pennsylvania did without an upper house at all and placed executive authority in the hands of a council, rather than a single man, though this was such a radical departure from general ideas that it quickly created an anti-constitutional party in that state.

Nearly all the revolutionaries would have failed a modern test of loyalty to democratic standards. Even the most dedicated patriots were eighteenth-century men, and eighteenth-century thinking normally excluded many portions of the people from participation in the politics of a republic: adherents to unpopular religions, women, blacks, and even very poor white males.

Accordingly, not even Pennsylvania departed so far from tradition as to give the vote to every male adult. And yet most states moved noticeably in that direction. Most lowered the amount of property one had to own in order to possess the franchise. Several gave the vote to every man who paid a tax. All the states provided for annual elections of the lower house of legislature and, often, for annual elections of the senate and governor as well. Every part of these new governments would be chosen by the people or by those the people had elected. And the legislatures in particular were filled with men whose modest means and ordinary social rank would have excluded them from higher office in colonial times. In a variety of ways, these governments were far more responsive to the people than the old colonial governments had been. They were also far more closely watched. The revolutionary air was full of popular awareness of the people's rights.

The revolutionary movement disestablished churches, altered attitudes toward slavery, and partly redefined the role of women in American society. Eventually, of course, revolutionary concepts paved the way for an extension of the rights of citizens to all the groups that eighteenth-century patriots excluded. But whatever else the Revolution was or would become, its essence lay originally in these thirteen problematic experiments in constructing republican regimes. It would succeed or fail, in revolutionary minds, according to the success of these regimes in raising the new order and fulfilling expectations that republicanism would defend and perfect this special people and the democratic social structure that they hoped would become the envy of the world.

A PERMANENT CONFEDERATION

Americans did not intend, at the beginning, to extend the revolutionary experiment in republican government from the states to the nation as a whole. Republics were expected to be small. The Revolution had begun as an attempt to protect the old colonial governments from external interference by a distant Parliament and king. Traditional loyalties and revolutionary ideas were both keyed to the states.

Still, the argument with Britain taught Americans to think that they were a single people, and the War for Independence built a growing sense of nationhood. There was a Continental Congress before there were any independent states. *Congress* declared American independence and recommended that new state governments be formed. *Congress* assumed the direction of the war.

The Continental Congress was an extralegal body. It had simply emerged in the course of the imperial quarrel and continued to exert authority with the approval of the people and the states, all of which sent an unspecified number of delegates to help take care of common concerns. As early as June 12, 1776, these delegates initiated consideration of a plan to place their authority on formal grounds. But the experiences that had led to independence made Americans powerfully suspicious of any central government, and there were many disagreements in the Congress.

Meanwhile, there was also the necessity of managing a war.

Not until November 17, 1777 did Congress finally present a formal proposal to the states. This plan, the Articles of Confederation, called upon the sovereign states to join in a permanent confederation presided over by a Congress whose authority would be confined to matters of interest to all: war and peace; foreign relations; trade with the Indians; disputes between states; and other common concerns. Each state would continue to have a single vote in Congress. In matters of extreme importance, such as war and peace, Congress would act only when nine of the thirteen states agreed, Since Congress would not directly represent the people, troops or money could be raised only by requisitioning the states.

The Articles of Confederation did not issue from a systematic, theoretical consideration of the problems of confederation government. For the most part, they only codified the structure and procedures that had emerged in practice in the years since 1774. Most of the country scarcely noticed when they finally went into effect, which was not until February, 1781—three years after they were first proposed. Maryland, which had a definite western border, refused its consent until Virginia and the other giant states, whose colonial charters gave them boundaries which might stretch from coast to coast, agreed to cede their lands beyond the mountains to the Confederation as a whole. Then, for most of the rest of the 1780s, Americans lived in a confederation of this sort.

Historians have long since given up the old idea that the Confederation years were a period of governmental folly and unmixed disaster. The Articles established a genuine federal government, not merely a league of states. The union was to be permanent, and Congress was granted many of the usual attributes of sovereign authority. Great things were accomplished. The states secured their independence and won a generous treaty of peace, which placed their western border at the Mississippi River. The country weathered a severe postwar depression, Congress organized the area northwest of the Ohio for settlement and eventual statehood. In fact, the Northwest Ordinance of 1787 established the pattern for all the rest of the continental expansion of the United States, providing that new territories would eventually enter the union on terms of full equality with its original members and thus assuring that America would manage to escape most of the problems usually confronted by an expanding empire. It was not an unimpressive record.

THIRTEEN SQUABBLING STATES

Nevertheless, the Articles of Confederation came under increasing criticism from an influential minority even before they formally went into practice. This minority was centered in the Congress itself and around the powerful executive officials created by the Congress, especially Robert Morris, a Philadelphia merchant who was appointed Superintendent of Finance in 1781. Morris and his allies were necessarily concerned with the Confederation as a whole, and they found it almost impossible to meet their responsibilities under this kind of government. By the time the war was over, the Confederation's paper money was entirely worthless—"not worth a Continental," as the phrase still goes. The Confederation owed huge debts to army veterans, to citizens who had lent supplies or money during the war, and to foreign governments and foreign subjects who had purchased American bonds. Dependent on the states for revenues, Congress could not even pay the interest on these obligations. All the states had war debts of their own, and in the midst of a depression, their citizens were seldom willing or even able to pay taxes high enough to make it possible for the republics to handle their own needs and meet their congressional requisitions as well. By 1783, Morris, Alexander Hamilton, James Madison, and many other continental-minded men were insisting on reform. They demanded, at the very least, that Congress be granted the authority to levy a tax on foreign imports, which might provide it with a steady, independent source of revenue.

The need for revenue, however, was only the most urgent of several concerns. Lacking a direct connection with the people, Congress had to work through and depend on the states for nearly everything. Unable to compel cooperation, its members watched in futile anger as the sovereign republics went their separate ways. Some states quarreled over boundaries. Troubled by the depression, others passed competitive duties on foreign imports. The states ignored Confederation treaties,

fought separate wars with Indians, and generally neglected congressional pleas for money.

As this happened, American ambassadors in foreign lands—John Adams in England and Thomas Jefferson in France—discovered that the European nations treated the American confederation with contempt. The European powers refused to make commercial treaties that would lower their barriers to freer trade and ease America's commercial problems. England refused to remove her soldiers from forts in the American northwest, insisting that she would abide by the treaty of peace only when the states began to meet their own obligations to cease persecuting returning loyalists and to open their courts to British creditors who wanted to collect their debts.

Nevertheless, the nationalists in Congress were frustrated in their desire for reform. The Articles of Confederation could be amended only by unanimous consent, but when Congress recommended an amendment that would give it the authority to levy a 5 percent duty on imports, little Rhode Island refused to agree. When Congress asked for power to retaliate against Great Britain's navigation laws, the states again could not concur.

Repeatedly defeated in their efforts at reform, increasingly alarmed by mutual antagonisms between the states, which had grown serious enough by 1786 to threaten an immediate fragmentation of the union into several smaller confederacies, the men of continental vision turned their thoughts to fundamentals. A much more sweeping change, they now suspected, might be necessary to resolve the pressing problems of the current central government. And if the change went far enough, a few of them began to think, it might accomplish something more. It might restore the Revolution to its proper course.

The Revolution, after all, involved a dream of national greatness; and the dream was going wrong. A people who had hoped to be a model for the world was fragmented into thirteen petty, squabbling states. The states would not—or could not—subordinate their separate interests to the good of the Confederation as a whole. Even worse, too many of the states fell short of fulfilling revolutionary expectations within their individual bounds. The early revolutionary constitutions had delivered overwhelming power to the people's immediate representatives in the lower houses of assembly. As these lower houses struggled to protect the people from hard times, they frequently neglected private rights and seldom seemed to give a due consideration to the long-term good. As clashing groups in different states competed to control their house of representatives, nobody could feel certain what the law might be next year, when one majority replaced another. The lower houses of assembly were essentially unchecked by the other parts of government, and to many revolutionaries it appeared that the assemblies proceeded on their ways with slight regard for justice and little thought about tomorrow. The rule of law appeared to be collapsing into a kind of anarchy in which the liberty and property of everyone might depend on the good will of whichever temporary majority happened to control his state. No one could feel secure in the enjoyment of his rights.

LIBERTY IN PERIL

During the 1780s, in other words, the feeling grew that liberty was once again in peril. Alarm was most intense among the men whose duties, education, or experience encouraged them to pin their patriotic feelings on the continent as a whole: certain members of Congress; most of the best-known revolutionary thinkers; most of the former officers of the continental army; many merchants, public creditors, and other men of wealth. Men of social standing were distressed with the way in which the revolutionary principles of liberty and equality seemed to slide into a popular contempt for talent or distinction. Too often, to their minds, the best men lost elections in the states to self-serving, scrambling demagogues, and the revolutionary constitutions made it far too easy for these demagogues to set an ill-considered course or even to oppress the propertied minority in order to secure the people's favor. Continued confiscations of the property of people who had sympathized with Britain and continued use of paper money, which threatened men's investments and their right to hold their property secure, were grievances of particular importance to those who had investments and positions to defend.

And yet the sense of fading hopes and failing visions was not exclusively confined to men of wealth. Anyone whose life had been immersed in revolution-

ary expectations might share in the concern. Every state seemed full of quarrels. Every individual seemed to be on the scrape for himself. No one seemed to have a real regard for common interests, a willingness to recognize that selfish interests must be limited by some consideration for the good of all. Public virtue, to use the phrase the revolutionaries used, seemed to be in danger of completely disappearing as every man and every social group sought private goods at the expense of harmony and other people's rights. But virtue, revolutionaries thought, was the indispensable foundation for republics, without which they could not survive. If public virtue was collapsing, then the Revolution was about to fail. It would degenerate into a kind of chaos, from which a tyrant might emerge, or else the people, in disgust, might eventually prefer to return to hereditary rule.

So, at least, did many fear. Guided by the same ideas that had impelled them into independence, they saw a second crisis, as dangerous to liberty as the crisis that had led them into Revolution. As they had done in 1776, they blamed their discontents on governments that lacked the character to mold a virtuous people and fit them for their special role. Once more, they turned to constitutional reform. They saw in the problems of the Confederation government not merely difficulties that would have to be corrected, but an opportunity that might be seized for even greater ends, an opportunity to rescue revolutionary hopes from their decay.

The constitutional reformers of the 1780s had several different motives and several different goals. Some had an economic interest in a constitutional reform that would enable the central government to pay its debts and act to spur the economic revival. All wanted to make the government adequate to its tasks and able to command more respect from the rest of the world. Some wanted more: to reconstruct the central government in such a way that its virtues might override the mistakes that had been made in some of the states. They wanted to redeem the reputation of democracy and save the republican experiment from a process of degeneration which threatened to destroy all that they had struggled for.

Shays' Rebellion handed them their chance. Out in western Massachusetts, hard times, large debts, and the high taxes prompted by the state's attempt to handle its revolutionary debt drove many farmers to distress. They first petitioned for relief, but when the legislature refused to issue paper money or to pass the laws required to protect their property from seizure, petitions gave way to rebellion. Farmers forced the courts to close in several counties, and Daniel Shays, a revolutionary captain, organized an armed resistance. The rebels were defeated with surprising ease. The state called out the militia during the winter of 1786, and Shays' forces disintegrated after a minor fight. The incident was nonetheless, for many, the final straw atop a growing load of fears. Armed resistance to a republican government seemed the ultimate warning of a coming collapse.

Earlier in 1786, delegates from five states had met at Annapolis, Maryland to consider better means of replacing interstate and international trade. Nationalist sentiment was strong among the delegates. Hamilton and Madison were there. The participants quickly agreed that little could be done about commercial problems without a revision of the Articles of Confederation. They said as much in a report to Congress and their states, and Congress endorsed their recommendation for the meeting of a national convention to consider ways to make the central government "adequate to the exigencies of the union." Badly frightened by events in Massachusetts, whose constitution was widely thought to be among the best, every state except Rhode Island answered the call. From this context and in hope that it might save both liberty and union, the Constitutional Convention emerged.

An Economic Interpretation of the Constitution

Charles A. Beard

Historian Charles A. Beard's classic book, An Economic Interpretation of the Constitution, *offers a sharp contrast to the idealistic vision of constitutional creation seen in Lance Banning's analysis. In his*

book, Beard, who taught at Columbia before helping to found the New School for Social Research, utilizes much documentary evidence to demonstrate that identifiable economic interests were most supportive of and benefited the most from the new Constitution. In the following selection we have included several snippets of Beard's work that serve to unveil the flavor of his argument. Several themes associated with Beard's analysis emerge clearly. For one, identifiable economic interests were hurt under the Articles of Confederation. Second, the Constitutional Convention was not the result of a popular movement and it did not represent the "large propertyless mass" that was excluded under contemporary suffrage requirements. Third, the Constitution was an economic document that protected property interests from popular majorities as is plainly evident, Beard contends, in The Federalist Papers *(Reading 4). Finally, the ratification process for the new Constitution was not based on the consent of popular majorities.*

Much of Beard's argument seems fairly commonplace now, but was considered considerably more radical in the context of the time in which it was written. In pondering arguments such as those offered by Banning and Beard it is important to recognize that while motivations underlying our Constitution's framing are important concerns, even more important for understanding the contemporary workings of our constitutional system is a sense of what the document means today. Clearly, the idealistic tone of Banning's analysis and Beard's more cynical view have had an impact on contemporary interpretations of the Constitution. Yet, just as clearly, as revealed in Chapter Two's selections on constitutional interpretation, considerable discretion remains in the hands of those responsible for applying the Constitution's dictates, whatever the motivations underlying the document's framing, to real-world political problems and controversies.

The requirements for an economic interpretation of the formation and adoption of the Constitution may be stated in a hypothetical proposition which, although it cannot be verified absolutely from ascertainable data, will at once illustrate the problem and furnish a guide to research and generalization.

It will be admitted without controversy that the Constitution was the creation of a certain number of men, and it was opposed by a certain number of men. Now, if it were possible to have an economic biography of all those connected with its framing and adoption—perhaps about 160,000 men altogether—the materials for scientific analysis and classification would be available. Such an economic biography would include a list of the real and personal property owned by all of these men and their families: lands and houses, with incumbrances, money at interest, slaves, capital invested in shipping and manufacturing, and in state and continental securities.

Suppose it could be shown from the classification of the men who supported and opposed the Constitution that there was no line of property division at all; that is, that men owning substantially the same amounts of the same kinds of property were equally divided on the matter of adoption or rejection—it would then become apparent that the Constitution had no ascertainable relation to economic groups or classes, but was the product of some abstract causes remote from the chief business of life—gaining a livelihood.

Suppose, on the other hand, that substantially all of the merchants, money lenders, security holders, manufacturers, shippers, capitalists, and financiers and their professional associates are to be found on one side in support of the Constitution and that substantially all or the major portion of the opposition came from the non-slaveholding farmers and the debtors—would it not be pretty conclusively demonstrated that our fundamental law was not the product of an abstraction known as "the whole people," but of a group of economic interests which must have expected beneficial results from its adoption? Obviously all the facts here desired cannot be discovered, but the data presented in the following chapters bear out the latter hypothesis, and thus a reasonable presumption in favor of the theory is created. . . .

THE MOVEMENT FOR THE CONSTITUTION

Did the system of government prevailing in the United States in 1787 affect adversely any . . . economic interests? . . . Furthermore, were the leaders in the movement which led to the adoption of the Constitution representatives of the interests so affected?

Fortunately, it is not necessary to devote any considerable attention to the first of these questions. . . . [A]ll of the standard treatises show conclusively that the legal system prevailing at the opening of 1787 was unfavorable to the property rights of . . . powerful groups. . . . That system was, in brief, as follows. There was a loose union of thirteen sovereign states under the Articles of Confederation. The national government consisted of a legislature of one house in which the states had an equal voting power. There was no executive department and no general judiciary. The central government had no power to regulate commerce or to tax directly; and in the absence of these powers all branches of the government were rendered helpless. Particularly, money could not be secured to pay the holders of public securities, either their interest or principal. Under this system, the state legislatures were substantially without restrictions or judicial control; private rights in property were continually attacked by stay laws, legal tender laws, and a whole range of measures framed in behalf of debtors: and in New England open rebellion had broken out.

That the economic groups in question looked to a new national government as the one source of relief and advantage, is shown in a hundred contemporary pamphlets and newspaper articles. It was in fact the topic of the times.

For example, a letter from Philadelphia, under date of August 29, 1787, sums up concisely the interests which were turning to the new Constitution: "The states neglect their roads and canals, till they see whether those necessary improvements will not become the objects of a national government. Trading and manufacturing companies suspend their voyages and manufactures till they see how far their commerce will be protected and promoted by a national system of commercial regulations. The lawful usurer locks up or buries his specie till he sees whether the new frame of government will deliver him from the curse or fear of paper money and the tender laws.... The public creditor, who, from the deranged state of finances in every state and their total inability to support their partial funding systems, has reason to fear that his certificates will perish in his hands, now places all his hopes of justice in an enlightened and stable national government. The embarrassed farmer and the oppressed tenant, who wishes to become free ... by emigrating to a frontier country, wait to see whether they shall be protected by a national force from the Indians."

A final answer to the second question propounded above would require an exhaustive analysis of the movement for the Constitution...."

In the present state of our historical materials, therefore, all that can be attempted here is a superficial commentary on some of the outward aspects of the movement for the Constitution which are described in the conventional works on the subject. Many of the eminent men prominently identified with the events which led up to the Convention of 1787 were themselves members of that Assembly, and their economic interests are considered below.... But it is not without significance to discover that some of the leading men outside of the Convention who labored for an overthrow of the old system were also directly interested in the results of their labors....

Certain...conclusions emerge at this point.

Large and important groups of economic interests were adversely affected by the system of government under the Articles of Confederation, namely, those of public securities, shipping and manufacturing, money at interest; in short, capital as opposed to land.

The representatives of these important interests attempted through the regular legal channels to secure amendments to the Articles of Confederation which would safeguard their rights in the future, particularly those of the public creditors.

Having failed to realize their great purposes through the regular means, the leaders in the movement set to work to secure by a circuitous route the assemblying of a Convention to "revise" the Articles of Confederation with the hope of obtaining, outside of the existing legal framework, the adoption of a revolutionary programme.

Ostensibly, however, the formal plan of approval by Congress and the state legislatures was to be preserved....

THE CONSTITUTION AS AN ECONOMIC DOCUMENT

It is difficult for the superficial student of the Constitution, who has read only the commentaries of the legists, to conceive of that instrument as an economic document. It places no property qualifications on voters or officers; it gives no outward recognition of any economic groups in society; it mentions no special privileges to be conferred upon any class. It betrays no feeling, such as vibrates through the French constitution of 1791; its language is cold, formal, and severe.

The true inwardness of the Constitution is not revealed by an examination of its provisions as simple propositions of law, but by a long and careful study of the voluminous correspondence of the period, contemporary newspapers and pamphlets, the records of the debates in the Convention at Philadelphia and in the several state conventions, and particularly, *The Federalist,* which was widely circulated during the struggle over ratification. The correspondence shows the exact character of the evils which the Constitution was intended to remedy; the records of the proceedings in the Philadelphia Convention reveal the successive steps in the building of the framework of the government under the pressure of economic interests; the pamphlets and newspapers disclose the ideas of the contestants over the ratification; and *The Federalist* presents the political science of the new system as conceived by three of the profoundest thinkers of the period, Hamilton, Madison, and Jay....

The Federalist ... presents in a relatively brief and systematic form an economic interpretation of the Constitution by the men best fitted, through an intimate knowledge of the ideals of the framers, to expound the political science of the new government. This wonderful piece of argumentation by Hamilton, Madison, and Jay is in fact the finest study in the economic interpretation of politics which exists in any language; and whoever would understand the Constitution as an economic document need hardly go beyond it. It is true that the tone of the writers is somewhat modified on account of the fact that they are appealing to the voters to ratify the Constitution, but at the same time they are, by the force of circumstances, compelled to convince large economic groups that safety and strength lie in the adoption of the new system.

Indeed, every fundamental appeal in it is to some material and substantial interest. Sometimes it is to the people at large in the name of protection against invading armies and European coalitions. Sometimes it is to the commercial classes whose business is represented as prostrate before the follies of the Confederation. Now it is to creditors seeking relief against paper money and the assaults of the agrarians in general; now it is to the holders of federal securities which are depreciating toward the vanishing point. But above all, it is to the owners of personalty anxious to find a foil against the attacks of levelling democracy, that the authors of *The Federalist* address their most cogent arguments in favor of ratification. It is true there is much discussion of the details of the new framework of government, to which even some friends of reform took exceptions; but Madison and Hamilton both knew that these were incidental matters when compared with the sound basis upon which the superstructure rested.

In reading the pages of this remarkable work as a study in political economy, it is important to bear in mind that the system, which the authors are describing, consisted of two fundamental parts—one positive, the other negative:

1. A government endowed with certain positive powers, but so constructed as to break the force of majority rule and prevent invasions of the property rights of minorities.

2. Restrictions on the state legislatures which had been so vigorous in their attacks on capital. . . .

CONCLUSIONS

At the close of this long and arid survey. . . . it seems worth while to bring together the important conclusions for political science which the data presented appear to warrant.

The movement for the Constitution of the United States was originated and carried through principally by four groups of personalty interests which had been adversely affected under the Articles of Confederation: money, public securities, manufactures, and trade and shipping.

The first firm steps toward the formation of the Constitution were taken by a small and active group of men immediately interested through their personal possessions in the outcome of their labors.

No popular vote was taken directly or indirectly on the proposition to call the Convention which drafted the Constitution.

A large propertyless mass was, under the prevailing suffrage qualifications, excluded at the outset from participation (through representatives) in the work of framing the Constitution.

The members of the Philadelphia Convention which drafted the Constitution were, with a few exceptions, immediately, directly, and personally interested in, and derived economic advantages from, the establishment of the new system.

The Constitution was essentially an economic document based upon the concept that the fundamental private rights of property are anterior to government and morally beyond the reach of popular majorities.

The major portion of the members of the Convention are on record as recognizing the claim of property to a special and defensive position in the Constitution.

In the ratification of the Constitution, about three-fourths of the adult males failed to vote on the question, having abstained from the elections at which delegates to the state conventions were chosen, either on account of their indifference or their disfranchisement by property qualifications.

The Constitution was ratified by a vote of probably not more than one-sixth of the adult males.

It is questionable whether a majority of the voters participating in the elections for the state conventions in New York, Massachusetts, New Hampshire, Virginia, and South Carolina, actually approved the ratification of the Constitution.

The leaders who supported the Constitution in the ratifying conventions represented the same economic groups as the members of the Philadelphia Convention; and in a large number of instances they were also directly and personally interested in the outcome of their efforts.

In the ratification, it became manifest that the line of cleavage for and against the Constitution was between substantial personalty interests on the one hand and the small farming and debtor interests on the other.

The Constitution was not created by "the whole people" as the jurists have said; neither was it created by "the states" as Southern nullifiers long contended; but it was the work of a consolidated group whose interests knew no state boundaries and were truly national in their scope.

READING 4

The Federalist Papers

Alexander Hamilton, John Jay, and James Madison

Those supporting passage of the new Constitution formulated in 1787 felt that failure to ratify the document would doom the new republic. New York, where Governor Clinton opposed the new governmental charter, was a major ratification battleground. In an effort to sway his home state, Alexander Hamilton initiated a series of essays that explained and defended the new governmental plan. Hamilton was joined by James Madison and John Jay, and their essays were published under the pseudonym of "Publius" in New York City newspapers. Hamilton authored about two-thirds of the papers, although history has judged Madison's contributions to be at least as important. The Federalist Papers *clearly occupy a place in the American political heritage surpassed, perhaps, only by the Declaration of Independence and the Constitution itself. Interestingly, one finds in* The Federalist *a good deal of internal inconsistency, strained logic, lengthy, repetitive, and sometimes obtuse writing. It must never be forgotten that these essays represent the viewpoint of advocates seeking*

to win an ongoing political battle. The authors wrote with a pragmatic pen, attempting to convince readers it was in their self-interest to adopt the new Constitution. It is, perhaps, this pragmatic thrust of The Federalist Papers *that is their greatest legacy and a commentary on the underlying ideology supporting the new Constitution.*

We begin with Hamilton's introductory essay Number 1 *where the reader is warned to be wary of the exhortations of constitutional critics not motivated by the common good. Hamilton concludes by asserting point-blank that the electorate faces two choices: adopt the Constitution or dismember the Union.* Number 10, *Madison's initial contribution, is perhaps the most famous paper in the series. Here, Madison explores the nature, causes, and effects of factions (e.g., interest groups and/or political parties) on the operation of government. Factions are characterized as the product and price of liberty. They should not be suppressed but, rather, controlled. In Madison's view, the key to fostering such control is a large nation with an extended and representative form of government—the very type of system the new Constitution would create. Madison's portrait of controlled competition among factions in the envisioned republic offers an early perspective on a pluralist model of public policymaking in the United States. Among* The Federalist Papers, Hamilton's Number 15 *represents one of the more polemical entries and serves to document some of the problems associated with the Articles of Confederation that threatened the continued existence of the Union.*

In a series of essays authored by Madison, The Federalist *examined the nature and implications of several fundamental features of the proposed new governmental system. The division of powers between the Federal government and the states portrayed in* Number 45 *clearly does not represent the way in which American federalism has developed. In an effort to allay the fears of the states, Madison significantly downplayed the scope of national powers and centralization under the new Constitution, predicting that the states would hold the upper hand. In* Numbers 47 and 48 *the separation of powers principle is analyzed with an eye towards documenting the impracticality, impossibility, and*

From *The Federalist Papers* by A. Hamilton, J. Jay, and J. Madison. Taken from numbers 1, 10, 15, 45, 47, 48, 51.

lack of wisdom in absolute and inviolable separation. Here, Madison attempts to meld the principles of separation of powers and checks and balances into a coherent whole. In Number 51, Madison continues the melding process returning to a consideration of factions. He concludes that the new constitutional order will secure civil rights for the citizenry because of the multitude of interests subsumed in the republic. Separation of powers will, in practice, be maintained by effective governmental checks and balances. Throughout the essay, the pluralist assumptions emphasizing elite competition and compromise that guide Madison's views of the policy processes that will result from the new republic are clearly evident.

NUMBER 1 (ALEXANDER HAMILTON)

After an unequivocal experience of the inefficacy of the subsisting federal government, you are called upon to deliberate on a new Constitution for the United States of America. The subject speaks its own importance; comprehending in its consequences nothing less than the existence of the UNION, the safety and welfare of the parts of which it is composed, the fate of an empire in many respects the most interesting in the world. It has been frequently remarked that it seems to have been reserved to the people of this country, by their conduct and example, to decide the important question, whether societies of men are really capable or not of establishing good government from reflection and choice, or whether they are forever destined to depend for their political constitutions on accident and force. If there be any truth in the remark, the crisis at which we are arrived may with propriety be regarded as the era in which that decision is to be made; and a wrong election of the part we shall act may, in this view, deserve to be considered as the general misfortune of mankind....

Happy will it be if our choice should be directed by a judicious estimate of our true interests, unperplexed and unbiased by considerations not connected with the public good. But this is a thing more ardently to be wished than seriously to be expected. The plan offered to our deliberations affects too many particular interests, innovates upon too many local institutions,

not to involve in its discussion a variety of objects foreign to its merits, and of views, passions, and prejudices little favorable to the discovery of truth.

Among the most formidable of the obstacles which the new Constitution will have to encounter may readily be distinguished the obvious interest of a certain class of men in every State to resist all changes which may hazard a diminution of the power, emolument, and consequence of the offices they hold under the State establishments; and the perverted ambition of another class of men, who will either hope to aggrandize themselves by the confusions of their country, or will flatter themselves with fairer prospects of elevation from the subdivision of the empire into several partial confederacies than from its union under one government.

It is not, however, my design to dwell upon observations of this nature. I am well aware that it would be disingenuous to resolve indiscriminately the opposition of any set of men (merely because their situations might subject them to suspicion) into interested or ambitious views. Candor will oblige us to admit that even such men may be actuated by upright intentions, and it cannot be doubted that much of the opposition which has made its appearance, or may hereafter make its appearance, will spring from sources, blameless at least if not respectable—the honest errors of minds led astray by preconceived jealousies and fears. So numerous indeed and so powerful are the causes which serve to give a false bias to the judgment, that we, upon many occasions, see wise and good men on the wrong as well as on the right side of questions of the first magnitude to society. This circumstance, if duly attended to, would furnish a lesson of moderation to those who are ever so thoroughly persuaded of their being in the right in any controversy. And a further reason for caution, in this respect, might be drawn from the reflection that we are not always sure that those who advocate the truth are influenced by purer principles than their antagonists. Ambition, avarice, personal animosity, party opposition, and many other motives not more laudable than these, are apt to operate as well upon those who support as those who oppose the right side of a question....

In the course of the preceding observations, I have had an eye, my fellow-citizens, to putting you upon your guard against all attempts, from whatever quarter, to influence your decision in a matter of the utmost moment to your welfare by any impressions other than those which may result from the evidence of truth. You will, no doubt, at the same time have collected from the general scope of them that they proceed from a source not unfriendly to the new Constitution. Yes, my countrymen, I own to you that after having given it an attentive consideration, I am clearly of opinion it is your interest to adopt it. I am convinced that this is the safest course for your liberty, your dignity, and your happiness. I affect not reserves which I do not feel. I will not amuse you with an appearance of deliberation when I have decided. I frankly acknowledge to you my convictions, and I will freely lay before you the reasons on which they are founded. The consciousness of good intentions disdains ambiguity.... My arguments will be open to all and may be judged of by all. They shall at least be offered in a spirit which will not disgrace the cause of truth.

I propose, in a series of papers, to discuss the following interesting particulars:—*The utility of the UNION to your political prosperity—The insufficiency of the present Confederation to preserve that Union—The necessity of a government at least equally energetic with the one proposed, to the attainment of this object—The conformity of the proposed Constitution to the true principles of republican government—Its analogy to your own State constitution—and lastly, The additional security which its adoption will afford to the preservation of that species of government, to liberty, and to property.*

In the progress of this discussion I shall endeavor to give a satisfactory answer to all the objections which shall have made their appearance, that may seem to have any claim to your attention.

It may perhaps be thought superfluous to offer arguments to prove the utility of the UNION, a point, no doubt, deeply engraved on the hearts of the great body of the people in every State, and one which, it may be imagined, has no adversaries. But the fact is that we already hear it whispered in the private circles of those who oppose the new Constitution, that the thirteen States are of too great extent for any general system, and that we must of necessity resort to separate confederacies of distinct portions of the

whole. This doctrine will, in all probability, be gradually propagated, till it has votaries enough to countenance an open avowal of it. For nothing can be more evident to those who are able to take an enlarged view of the subject than the alternative of an adoption of the new Constitution or a dismemberment of the Union. It will therefore be of use to begin by examining the advantages of that Union, the certain evils, and the probable dangers, to which every State will be exposed from its dissolution....

NUMBER 10 (JAMES MADISON)

Among the numerous advantages promised by a well-constructed Union, none deserves to be more accurately developed than its tendency to break and control the violence of faction. The friend of popular governments never finds himself so much alarmed for their character and fate as when he contemplates their propensity to this dangerous vice. He will not fail, therefore, to set a due value on any plan which, without violating the principles to which he is attached, provides a proper cure for it. The instability, injustice, and confusion introduced into the public councils have, in truth, been the mortal diseases under which popular governments have everywhere perished, as they continue to be the favorite and fruitful topics from which the adversaries to liberty derive their most specious declamations. The valuable improvements made by the American constitutions on the popular models, both ancient and modern, cannot certainly be too much admired; but it would be an unwarrantable partiality to contend that they have as effectually obviated the danger on this side, as was wished and expected. Complaints are everywhere heard from our most considerate and virtuous citizens, equally the friends of public and private faith and of public and personal liberty, that our governments are too unstable, that the public good is disregarded in the conflicts of rival parties, and that measures are too often decided, not according to the rules of justice and the rights of the minor party, but by the superior force of an interested and overbearing majority. However anxiously we may wish that these complaints had no foundation, the evidence of known facts will not permit us to deny that they are in some degree true. It will be found, indeed, on a candid review of our situation, that some of the distresses under which we labor have been erroneously charged on the operation of our governments, but it will be found, at the same time, that other causes will not alone account for many of our heaviest misfortunes; and, particularly, for that prevailing and increasing distrust of public engagements and alarm for private rights which are echoed from one end of the continent to the other. These must be chiefly, if not wholly, effects of the unsteadiness and injustice with which a factious spirit has tainted our public administration.

By a faction I understand a number of citizens, whether amounting to a majority or minority of the whole, who are united and actuated by some common impulse of passion, or of interest, adverse to the rights of other citizens, or to the permanent and aggregate interests of the community.

There are two methods of curing the mischiefs of faction: the one, by removing its causes; the other, by controlling its effects.

There are again two methods of removing the causes of faction: the one, by destroying the liberty which is essential to its existences; the other, by giving to every citizen the same opinions, the same passions, and the same interests.

It could never be more truly said than of the first remedy that it was worse than the disease. Liberty is to faction what air is to fire, an aliment without which it instantly expires. But it could not be a less folly to abolish liberty, which is essential to political life, because it nourishes faction than it would be to wish the annihilation of air, which is essential to animal life, because it imparts to fire its destructive agency.

The second expedient is as impracticable as the first would be unwise. As long as the reason of man continues fallible, and he is at liberty to exercise it, different opinions will be formed....

The latent causes of faction are thus sown in the nature of man; and we see them everywhere brought into different degrees of activity, according to the different circumstances of civil society. A zeal for different opinions concerning religion, concerning government, and many other points, as well of speculation as of practice; an attachment to different leaders ambitiously contending for pre-eminence and power; or to

persons of other descriptions whose fortunes have been interesting to the human passions, have, in turn, divided mankind into parties, inflamed them with mutual animosity, and rendered them much more disposed to vex and oppress each other than to co-operate for their common good. So strong is this propensity of mankind to fall into mutual animosities that where no substantial occasion presents itself the most frivolous and fanciful distinctions have been sufficient to kindle their unfriendly passions and excite their most violent conflicts. But the most common and durable source of factions has been the various and unequal distribution of property. Those who hold and those who are without property have ever formed distinct interests in society. Those who are creditors, and those who are debtors, fall under a like discrimination. A landed interest, a manufacturing interest, a mercantile interest, a moneyed interest, with many lesser interests, grow up of necessity in civilized nations, and divide them into different classes, actuated by different sentiments and views. The regulation of these various and interfering interests forms the principal task of modern legislation and involves the spirit of party and faction in the necessary and ordinary operations of government.

No man is allowed to be a judge in his own cause, because his interest would certainly bias his judgment, and, not improbably, corrupt his integrity. With equal, nay with greater reason, a body of men are unfit to be both judges and parties at the same time; yet what are many of the most important acts of legislation but so many judicial determinations, not indeed concerning the rights of single persons, but concerning the rights of large bodies of citizens? And what are the different classes of legislators but advocates and parties to the causes which they determine? Is a law proposed concerning private debts? It is a question to which the creditors are parties on one side and the debtors on the other. Justice ought to hold the balance between them. Yet the parties are, and must be, themselves the judges; and the most numerous party, or in other words, the most powerful faction must be expected to prevail. Shall domestic manufacturers be encouraged, and in what degree, by restrictions on foreign manufacturers? are questions which would be differently decided by the landed and the manufacturing classes, and probably by neither with a sole regard to justice and the public good. The apportionment of taxes on the various descriptions of property is an act which seems to require the most exact impartiality; yet there is, perhaps, no legislative act in which greater opportunity and temptation are given to a predominant party to trample on the rules of justice. Every shilling with which they overburden the inferior number is a shilling saved to their own pockets.

It is in vain to say that enlightened statesmen will be able to adjust these clashing interests and render them all subservient to the public good. Enlightened statesmen will not always be at the helm. Nor, in many cases, can such an adjustment be made at all without taking into view indirect and remote considerations, which will rarely prevail over the immediate interest which one party may find in disregarding the rights of another or the good of the whole.

The inference to which we are brought is that the *causes* of faction cannot be removed and that relief is only to be sought in the means of controlling its *effects*

If a faction consists of less than a majority, relief is supplied by the republican principle, which enables the majority to defeat its sinister views by regular vote. It may clog the administration, it may convulse the society; but it will be unable to execute and mask its violence under the forms of the Constitution. When a majority is included in a faction, the form of popular government, on the other hand, enables it to sacrifice to its ruling passion or interest both the public good and the rights of other citizens. To secure the public good and private rights against the danger of such a faction, and at the same time to preserve the spirit and the form of popular government, is then the great object to which our inquiries are directed....

By what means is this object attainable? Evidently by one of two only. Either the existence of the same passion or interest in a majority at the same time must be prevented, or the majority, having such coexistent passion or interest, must be rendered, by their number and local situation, unable to concert and carry into effect schemes of oppression. If the impulse and the opportunity be suffered to coincide, we well know that neither moral nor religious motives can be relied on as an adequate control. They are not found to be such on the injustice and violence of individuals, and lose their efficacy in proportion to

the number combined together, that is, in proportion as their efficacy becomes needful.

From this view of the subject it may be concluded that a pure democracy, by which I mean a society consisting of a small number of citizens, who assemble and administer the government in person, can admit of no cure for the mischiefs of faction. A common passion or interest will, in almost every case, be felt by a majority of the whole; a communication and concert results from the form of government itself; and there is nothing to check the inducements to sacrifice the weaker party or an obnoxious individual. Hence it is that such democracies have ever been spectacles of turbulence and contention; have ever been found incompatible with personal security or the rights of property; and have in general been as short in their lives as they have been violent in their deaths. Theoretic politicians, who have patronized this species of government, have erroneously supposed that by reducing mankind to a perfect equality in their political rights, they would at the same time be perfectly equalized and assimilated in their possessions, their opinions, and their passions.

A republic, by which I mean a government in which the scheme of representation takes place, opens a different prospect and promises the cure for which we are seeking. Let us examine the points in which it varies from pure democracy, and we shall comprehend both the nature of the cure and the efficacy which it must derive from the Union.

The two great points of difference between a democracy and a republic are: first, the delegation of the government, in the latter, to a small number of citizens elected by the rest; secondly, the greater number of citizens and greater sphere of country over which the latter may be extended.

The effect of the first difference is, on the one hand, to refine and enlarge the public views by passing them through the medium of a chosen body of citizens, whose wisdom may best discern the true interest of their country and whose patriotism and love of justice will be least likely to sacrifice it to temporary or partial considerations. Under such a regulation it may well happen that the public voice, pronounced by the representatives of the people, will be more consonant to the public good than if pronounced by the people themselves, convened for the purpose. On the other hand, the effect may be inverted. Men of factious tempers, of local prejudices, or of sinister designs, may, by intrigue, by corruption, or by other means, first obtain the suffrages, and then betray the interests of the people. The question resulting is, whether small or extensive republics are most favorable to the election of proper guardians of the public weal; and it is clearly decided in favor of the latter by two obvious considerations.

In the first place it is to be remarked that however small the republic may be the representatives must be raised to a certain number in order to guard against the cabals of a few; and that however large it may be they must be limited to a certain number in order to guard against the confusion of a multitude. Hence, the number of representatives in the two cases not being in proportion to that of the constituents, and being proportionally greatest in the small republic, it follows that if the proportion of fit characters be not less in the large than in the small republic, the former will present a greater option, and consequently a greater probability of a fit choice.

In the next place, as each representative will be chosen by a greater number of citizens in the large than in the small republic, it will be more difficult for unworthy candidates to practise with success the vicious arts by which elections are too often carried; and the suffrages of the people being more free, will be more likely to center on men who possess the most attractive merit and the most diffusive and established characters.

It must be confessed that in this, as in most other cases, there is a mean, on both sides of which inconveniencies will be found to lie. By enlarging too much the number of electors, you render the representative too little acquainted with all their local circumstances and lesser interests; as by reducing it too much, you render him unduly attached to these, and too little fit to comprehend and pursue great and national objects. The federal Constitution forms a happy combination in this respect; the great and aggregate interests being referred to the national, the local and particular to the State legislatures,

The other point of difference is the greater number of citizens and extent of territory which may be brought within the compass of republican than of democratic government; and it is this circumstance principally which renders factious combinations less to be dreaded in the former than in the latter. The smaller the society, the fewer probably will be the distinct parties and interests composing it; the fewer the distinct parties and interests, the more frequently will a majority be found of the same party; and the smaller the number of individuals composing a majority, and the smaller the compass within which they are placed, the more easily will they concert and execute their plans of oppression. Extend the sphere and you take in a greater variety of parties and interests; you make it less probable that a majority of the whole will have a common motive to invade the rights of other citizens; or if such a common motive exists, it will be more difficult for all who feel it to discover their own strength and to act in unison with each other....

Hence, it clearly appears that the same advantage which a republic has over a democracy in controlling the effects of faction is enjoyed by a large over a small republic—is enjoyed by the Union over the States composing it. Does this advantage consist in the substitution of representatives whose enlightened views and virtuous sentiments render them superior to local prejudices and to schemes of injustice? It will not be denied that the representation of the Union will be most likely to possess these requisite endowments. Does it consist in the greater security afforded by a greater variety of parties, against the event of any one party being able to outnumber and oppress the rest? In an equal degree does the increased variety of parties comprised within the Union increase this security. Does it, in fine, consist in the greater obstacles opposed to the concert and accomplishment of the secret wishes of an unjust and interested majority? Here again the extent of the Union gives it the most palpable advantage.

The influence of factious leaders may kindle a flame within their particular States but will be unable to spread a general conflagration through the other States. A religious sect may degenerate into a political faction in a part of the Confederacy; but the variety of sects dispersed over the entire face of it must secure the national councils against any danger from that source. A rage for paper money, for an abolition of debts, for an equal division of property, or for any other improper or wicked project, will be less apt to pervade the whole body of the Union than a particular member of it, in the same proportion as such a malady is more likely to taint a particular county or district than an entire State.

In the extent and proper structure of the Union, therefore, we behold a republican remedy for the diseases most incident to republican government. And according to the degree of pleasure and pride we feel in being republicans ought to be our zeal in cherishing the spirit and supporting the character of federalists.

NUMBER 15 (ALEXANDER HAMILTON)

In the course of the preceding papers I have endeavored, my fellow-citizens, to place before you in a clear and convincing light the importance of Union to your political safety and happiness. I have unfolded to you a complication of dangers to which you would be exposed, should you permit that sacred knot which binds the people of America together to be severed or dissolved by ambition or by avarice, by jealousy or by misrepresentation. In the sequel of the inquiry through which I propose to accompany you, the truths intended to be inculcated will receive further confirmation from facts and arguments hitherto unnoticed. If the road over which you will still have to pass should in some places appear to you tedious or irksome, you will recollect that you are in quest of information on a subject the most momentous which can engage the attention of a free people, that the field through which you have to travel is in itself spacious, and that the difficulties of the journey have been unnecessarily increased by the mazes with which sophistry has beset the way. It will be my aim to remove the obstacles to your progress in as compendious a manner as it can be done, without sacrificing utility to dispatch.

In pursuance of the plan which I have laid down for the discussion of the subject, the point next in order to be examined is the "insufficiency of the present Confederation to the preservation of the Union." It may perhaps be asked what need there is of reasoning or proof to illustrate a position which is not either con-

troverted or doubted, to which the understandings and feelings of all classes of men assent, and which in substance is admitted by the opponents as well as by the friends of the new Constitution. It must in truth be acknowledged that, however these may differ in other respects, they in general appear to harmonize in this sentiment at least: that there are material imperfections in our national system and that something is necessary to be done to rescue us from impending anarchy. The facts that support this opinion are no longer objects of speculation. They have forced themselves upon the sensibility of the people at large, and have at length extorted from those, whose mistaken policy has had the principal share in precipitating the extremity at which we are arrived, a reluctant confession of the reality of those defects in the scheme of our federal government which have been long pointed out and regretted by the intelligent friends of the Union.

We may indeed with propriety be said to have reached almost the last stage of national humiliation. There is scarcely anything that can wound the pride or degrade the character of an independent nation which we do not experience. Are there engagements to the performance of which we are held by every tie respectable among men? These are the subjects of constant and unblushing violation. Do we owe debts to foreigners and to our own citizens contracted in a time of imminent peril for the preservation of our political existence? These remain without any proper or satisfactory provision for their discharge. Have we valuable territories and important posts in the possession of a foreign power which, by express stipulations, ought long since to have been surrendered? These are still retained to the prejudice of our interests, not less than of our rights. Are we in a condition to resent or to repel the aggression? We have neither troops, nor treasury, nor government.* Are we even in a condition to remonstrate with dignity? The just amputations on our own faith in respect to the same treaty ought first to be removed. Are we entitled by nature and compact to a free participation in the navigation of the Mississippi? Spain excludes us from it.

---

*"I mean for the Union."

Is public credit an indispensable resource in time of public danger? We seem to have abandoned its cause as desperate and irretrievable. Is commerce of importance to national wealth? Ours is at the lowest point of declension. Is respectability in the eyes of foreign powers a safeguard against foreign encroachments? The imbecility of our government even forbids them to treat with us. Our ambassadors abroad are the mere pageants of mimic sovereignty. Is a violent and unnatural decrease in the value of land a symptom of national distress? The price of improved land in most parts of the country is much lower than can be accounted for by the quantity of waste land at market, and can only be fully explained by that want of private and public confidence, which are so alarmingly prevalent among all ranks and which have a direct tendency to depreciate property of every kind. Is private credit the friend and patron of industry? That most useful kind which relates to borrowing and lending is reduced within the narrowest limits, and this still more from an opinion of insecurity than from a scarcity of money. To shorten an enumeration of particulars which can afford neither pleasure nor instruction, it may in general be demanded, what indication is there of national disorder, poverty, and insignificance that could befall a community so peculiarly blessed with natural advantages as we are, which does not form a part of the dark catalogue of our public misfortunes?

This is the melancholy situation to which we have been brought by those very maxims and counsels which would now deter us from adopting the proposed Constitution; and which, not content with having conducted us to the brink of a precipice, seem resolved to plunge us into the abyss that awaits us below. Here, my countrymen, impelled by every motive that ought to influence an enlightened people, let us make a firm stand for our safety, our tranquillity, our dignity, our reputation. Let us at last break the fatal charm which has too long seduced us from the paths of felicity and prosperity. . . .

NUMBER 45 (JAMES MADISON)

Having shown that no one of the powers transferred to the federal government is unnecessary or im-

proper, the next question to be considered is, whether the whole mass of them will be dangerous to the portion of authority left in the several States.

The adversaries to the plan of the convention, instead of considering in the first place what degree of power was absolutely necessary for the purposes of the federal government, have exhausted themselves in a secondary inquiry into the possible consequences of the proposed degree of power to the governments of the particular States. But if the Union . . . be essential to the security of the people of America against foreign danger; if it be essential to their security against contentions and wars among the different States; if it be essential to guard them against those violent and oppressive factions which embitter the blessings of liberty, and against those military establishments which must gradually poison its very fountain: if, in a word, the Union be essential to the happiness of the people of America, is it not preposterous to urge as an objection to a government, without which the objects of the Union cannot be attained, that such a government may derogate from the importance of the governments of the individual States? Was, then, the American Revolution effected, was the American Confederacy formed, was the precious blood of thousands spilt, and the hard-earned substance of millions lavished, not that the people of America should enjoy peace, liberty, and safety, but that the government of the individual States, that particular municipal establishments, might enjoy a certain extent of power and be arrayed with certain dignities and attributes of sovereignty? We have heard of the impious doctrine in the Old World, that the people were made for kings, not kings for the people. Is the same doctrine to be revived in the New in another shape—that the solid happiness of the people is to be sacrificed to the views of political institutions of a different form? It is too early for politicians to presume on our forgetting that the public good, the real welfare of the great body of the people, is the supreme object to be pursued; and that no form of government whatever has any other value than as it may be fitted for the attainment of this object. Were the plan of the convention adverse to the public happiness, my voice would be, reject the plan. Were the Union itself inconsistent with the public happiness, it would be, abolish the Union. In like manner, as far as the sovereignty of the States cannot be reconciled to the happiness of the people, the voice of every good citizen must be, let the former be sacrificed to the latter. How far the sacrifice is necessary, has been shown. How far the unsacrificed residue will be endangered, is the question before us.

Several important considerations have been touched in the course of these papers, which discountenance the supposition that the operation of the federal government will by degrees prove fatal to the State governments....

The State governments will have the advantage of the federal government, whether we compare them in respect to the immediate dependence of the one on the other; to the weight of personal influence which each side will possess; to the powers respectively vested in them; to the predilection and probable support of the people; to the disposition and faculty of resisting and frustrating the measures of each other.

The State governments may be regarded as constituent and essential parts of the federal government; whilst the latter is nowise essential to the operation or organization of the former. Without the intervention of the State legislatures, the President of the United States cannot be elected at all. They must in all cases have a great share in his appointment, and will, perhaps, in most cases, of themselves determine it. The Senate will be elected absolutely and exclusively by the State legislatures. Even the House of Representatives, though drawn immediately from the people, will be chosen very much under the influence of that class of men, whose influence over the people obtains for themselves an election into the State legislatures. Thus, each of the principal branches of the federal government will owe its existence more or less to the favor of the State governments, and must consequently feel a dependence, which is much more likely to beget a disposition too obsequious than too overbearing towards them. On the other side, the component parts of the State governments will in no instance be indebted for their appointment to the direct agency of the federal government, and very little, if at all, to the local influence of its members.

The number of individuals employed under the Constitution of the United States will be much smaller than the number employed under the particular States. There will consequently be less of personal influence on the side of the former than of the latter. The members of the legislative, executive, and judiciary departments of thirteen and more States, the justices of peace, officers of militia, ministerial officers of justice, with all the county, corporation, and town officers, for three millions and more of people, intermixed, and having particular acquaintance with every class and circle of people, must exceed, beyond all proportion, both in number and influence, those of every description who will be employed in the administration of the federal system. Compare the members of the three great departments of the thirteen States, excluding from the judiciary department the justices of peace, with the members of the corresponding departments of the single government of the Union; compare the militia officers of three millions of people with the military and marine officers of any establishment which is within the compass of probability, or ... of possibility, and in this view alone, we may pronounce the advantage of the States to be decisive. If the federal government is to have collectors of revenue, the State governments will have theirs also. And as those of the former will be principally on the seacoast and not very numerous, whilst those of the latter will be spread over the face of the country and will be very numerous, the advantage in this view also lies on the same side. It is true that the Confederacy is to possess and may exercise the power of collecting internal as well as external taxes throughout the States, but it is probable that this power will not be resorted to, except for supplemental purposes of revenue; that an option will then be given to the States to supply their quotas by previous collections of their own; and that the eventual collection, under the immediate authority of the Union, all generally be made by the officers, and according to the rules, appointed by the several States. Indeed it is extremely probable that in other instances, particularly in the organization of the judicial power, the officers of the States will be clothed with the correspondent authority of the Union. Should it happen, however, that separate collectors of internal revenue should be appointed under the federal government, the influence of the whole number would not bear a comparison with that of the multitude of State officers in the opposite scale. Within every district to which a federal collector would be allotted, there would not be less than thirty or forty, or even more, officers of different descriptions, and many of them persons of character and weight, whose influence would lie on the side of the State.

The powers delegated by the proposed Constitution to the federal government are few and defined. Those which are to remain in the State governments are numerous and indefinite. The former will be exercised principally on external objects, as war, peace, negotiation, and foreign commerce; with which last the power of taxation will, for the most part, be connected. The powers reserved to the several States will extend to all the objects which, in the ordinary course of affairs, concern the lives, liberties, and properties of the people, and the internal order, improvement, and prosperity of the State.

The operations of the federal government will be most extensive and important in times of war and danger, those of the State governments in times of peace and security. As the former periods will probably bear a small proportion to the latter, the State governments will here enjoy another advantage over the federal government. The more adequate, indeed, the federal powers may be rendered to the national defence, the less frequent will be those scenes of danger which might favor their ascendancy over the governments of the particular States.

If the new Constitution be examined with accuracy and candor, it will be found that the change which it proposes consists much less in the addition of NEW POWERS to the Union, than in the invigoration of its ORIGINAL POWERS. The regulation of commerce, it is true, is a new power; but that seems to be an addition which few oppose and from which no apprehensions are entertained. The powers relating to war and peace, armies and fleets, treaties and finance, with the other more considerable powers, are all vested in the existing Congress by the articles of Confederation. The proposed change does not enlarge these powers; it only substitutes a more effectual mode of administering them. The change relating to taxation may be regarded as the most important; and yet the present Congress have as complete authority to REQUIRE of the States indefinite supplies of money for the common

defence and general welfare as the future Congress will have to require them of individual citizens; and the latter will be no more bound than the States themselves have been to pay the quotas respectively taxed on them. Had the States complied punctually with the articles of Confederation or could their compliance have been enforced by as peaceable means as may be used with success towards single persons, our past experience is very far from countenancing an opinion, that the State governments would have lost their constitutional powers, and have gradually undergone an entire consolidation. To maintain that such an event would have ensued, would be to say at once, that the existence of the State governments is incompatible with any system whatever that accomplishes the essential purposes of the Union.

NUMBER 47 (JAMES MADISON)

Having reviewed the general form of the proposed government and the general mass of power allotted to it, I proceed to examine the particular structure of this government, and the distribution of this mass of power among its constituent parts.

One of the principal objections inculcated by the more respectable adversaries to the Constitution is its supposed violation of the political maxim that the legislative, executive, and judiciary departments ought to be separate and distinct. In the structure of the federal government no regard, it is said, seems to have been paid to this essential precaution in favor of liberty. The several departments of power are distributed and blended in such a manner as at once to destroy all symmetry and beauty of form, and to expose some of the essential parts of the edifice to the danger of being crushed by the disproportionate weight of other parts.

No political truth is certainly of greater intrinsic value, or is stamped with the authority of more enlightened patrons of liberty than that on which the objection is founded. The accumulation of all powers, legislative, executive, and judiciary, in the same hands, whether of one, a few, or many, and whether hereditary, self-appointed, or elective, may justly be pronounced the very definition of tyranny. Were the federal Constitution, therefore, really chargeable with this accumulation of power, or with a mixture of powers, having a dangerous tendency to such an accumulation, no further arguments would be necessary to inspire a universal reprobation of the system. I persuade myself, however, that it will be made apparent to everyone that the charge cannot be supported, and that the maxim on which it relies has been totally misconceived and misapplied. In order to form correct ideas on this important subject it will be proper to investigate the sense in which the preservation of liberty requires that the three great departments of power should be separate and distinct.

The oracle who is always consulted and cited on this subject is the celebrated Montesquieu. If he be not the author of this invaluable precept in the science of politics, he has the merit at least of displaying and recommending it most effectually to the attention of mankind. Let us endeavor, in the first place, to ascertain his meaning on this point.

The British Constitution was to Montesquieu what Homer has been to the didactic writers on epic poetry. As the latter have considered the work of the immortal bard as the perfect model from which the principles and rules of the epic art were to be drawn, and by which all similar works were to be judged, so this great political critic appears to have viewed the Constitution of England as the standard, or to use his own expression, as the mirror of political liberty. . . .

On the slightest view of the British Constitution, we must perceive that the legislative, executive, and judiciary departments are by no means totally separate and distinct from each other. The executive magistrate forms an integral part of the legislative authority. He alone has the prerogative of making treaties with foreign sovereigns which, when made, have, under certain limitations, the force of legislative acts. All the members of the judiciary department are appointed by him, can be removed by him on the address of the two Houses of Parliament, and form, when he pleases to consult them, one of his constitutional councils. One branch of the legislative department forms also a great constitutional council to the executive chief, as, on another hand, it is the sole depositary of judicial power in cases of impeachment, and is invested with the supreme appellate jurisdiction in all other cases. The judges, again, are so far connected with the legislative department as often to attend and participate in its deliberations, though not admitted to a legislative vote.

From these facts, by which Montesquieu was guided, it may clearly be inferred that in saying "There can be no liberty where the legislative and executive powers are united in the same person, or body of magistrates," or, "if the power of judging be not separated from the legislative and executive powers," he did not mean that these departments ought to have no *partial agency* in, or no *control over,* the acts of each other. His meaning, as his own words import, and still more conclusively as illustrated by the example in his eye, can amount to no more than this, that where the *whole* power of one department is exercised by the same hands which possess the *whole* power of another department, the fundamental principles of a free constitution are subverted. This would have been the case in the constitution examined by him, if the king, who is the sole executive magistrate, had possessed also the complete legislative power, or the supreme administration of justice; or if the entire legislative body had possessed the supreme judiciary, or the supreme executive authority. This, however, is not among the vices of that constitution. The magistrate in whom the whole executive power resides cannot of himself make a law, though he can put a negative on every law; nor administer justice in person, though he has the appointment of those who do administer it. The judges can exercise no executive prerogative, though they are shoots from the executive stock; nor any legislative function, though they may be advised by the legislative councils. The entire legislature can perform no judiciary act, though by the joint act of two of its branches the judges may be removed from their offices, and though one of its branches is possessed of the judicial power in the last resort. The entire legislature, again, can exercise no executive prerogative, though one of its branches constitutes the supreme executive magistracy, and another, on the impeachment of a third, can try and condemn all the subordinate officers in the executive department.

The reasons on which Montesquieu grounds his maxim are a further demonstration of his meaning. "When the legislative and executive powers are united in the same person or body," says he, "there can be no liberty, because apprehensions may arise lest *the same* monarch or senate should *enact* tyrannical laws to *execute* them in a tyrannical manner." Again: "Were the power of judging joined with the legislative, the life and liberty of the subject would be exposed to arbitrary control, for *the judge* would then be *the legislator.* Were it joined to the executive power, *the judge* might behave with all the violence of *an oppressor.*" Some of these reasons are more fully explained in other passages; but briefly stated as they are here they sufficiently establish the meaning which we have put on this celebrated maxim of this celebrated author.

If we look into the constitutions of the several States we find that, notwithstanding the emphatical and, in some instances, the unqualified terms in which this axiom has been laid down, there is not a single instance in which the several departments of power have been kept absolutely separate and distinct. New Hampshire, whose constitution was the last formed, seems to have been fully aware of the impossibility and inexpediency of avoiding any mixture whatever of these departments, and has qualified the doctrine by declaring "that the legislative, executive, and judiciary powers ought to be kept as separate from, and independent of, each other *as the nature of a free government will admit; or as is consistent with that chain connection that binds the whole fabric of the constitution in one indissoluble bond of unity and amity.*" Her constitution accordingly mixes these departments in several respects. The Senate, which is a branch of the legislative department, is also a judicial tribunal for the trial of impeachments. The President, who is the head of the executive department, is the presiding member also of the Senate; and, besides an equal vote in all cases, has a casting vote in case of a tie. The executive head is himself eventually elective every year by the legislative department, and his council is every year chosen by and from the members of the same department. Several of the officers of state are also appointed by the legislature. And the members of the judiciary department are appointed by the executive department.

The constitution of Massachusetts has observed a sufficient though less pointed caution in expressing this fundamental article of liberty. It declares "that the legislative department shall never exercise the execu-

tive and judicial powers, or either of them; the executive shall never exercise the legislative and judicial powers, or either of them; the judicial shall never exercise the legislative and executive powers, or either of them." This declaration corresponds precisely with the doctrine of Montesquieu, as it has been explained, and is not in a single point violated by the plan of the convention. It goes no farther than to prohibit any one of the entire departments from exercising the powers of another department. In the very Constitution to which it is prefixed, a partial mixture of powers has been admitted. The executive magistrate has a qualified negative on the legislative body, and the Senate, which is a part of the legislature, is a court of impeachment for members both of the executive and judiciary departments. The members of the judiciary department, again, are appointable by the executive department, and removable by the same authority on the address of the two legislative branches. Lastly, a number of the officers of government are annually appointed by the legislative department. As the appointment to offices, particularly executive offices, is in its nature an executive function, the compilers of the Constitution have, in this last point at least, violated the rule established by themselves....

The constitution of New York contains no declaration on this subject, but appears very clearly to have been framed with an eye to the danger of improperly blending the different departments. It gives, nevertheless, to the executive magistrate, a partial control over the legislative department; and, what is more, gives a like control to the judiciary department; and even blends the executive and judiciary departments in the exercise of this control. In its council of appointment members of the legislative are associated with the executive authority, in the appointment of officers, both executive and judiciary. And its court for the trial of impeachments and correction of errors is to consist of one branch of the legislature and the principal members of the judiciary department.

The constitution of New Jersey has blended the different powers of government more than any of the preceding. The governor, who is the executive magistrate, is appointed by the legislature; is chancellor and ordinary, or surrogate of the State; is a member of the Supreme Court of Appeals, and president, with a casting vote, of one of the legislative branches. The same legislative branch acts again as executive council to the governor, and with him constitutes the Court of Appeals. The members of the judiciary department are appointed by the legislative department, and removable by one branch of it, on the impeachment of the other.

According to the constitution of Pennsylvania, the president, who is the head of the executive department, is annually elected by a vote in which the legislative department predominates. In conjunction with an executive council, he appoints the members of the judiciary department and forms a court of impeachment for trial of all officers, judiciary as well as executive. The judges of the Supreme Court and justices of the peace seem also to be removable by the legislature; and the executive power of pardoning, in certain cases, to be referred to the same department. The members of the executive council are made EX OFFICIO justices of peace throughout the State.

In Delaware, the chief executive magistrate is annually elected by the legislative department. The speakers of the two legislative branches are vice-presidents in the executive department. The executive chief, with six others appointed, three by each of the legislative branches, constitutes the Supreme Court of Appeals; he is joined with the legislative department in the appointment of the other judges. Throughout the States it appears that the members of the legislature may at the same time be justices of the peace; in this State, the members of one branch of it are EX OFFICIO justices of the peace; as are also the members of the executive council. The principal officers of the executive department are appointed by the legislative; and one branch of the latter forms a court of impeachments. All officers may be removed on address of the legislature.

Maryland has adopted the maxim in the most unqualified terms; declaring that the legislative, executive, and judicial powers of government ought to be forever separate and distinct from each other. Her constitution, notwithstanding, makes the executive magistrate appointable by the legislative department; and the members of the judiciary by the executive department.

The language of Virginia is still more pointed on this subject. Her constitution declares "that the legislative, executive, and judiciary departments shall be separate and distinct; so that neither exercises the powers properly belonging to the other; nor shall any person exercise the powers of more than one of them at the same time, except that the justices of county courts shall be eligible to either House of Assembly." Yet we find not only this express exception with respect to the members of the inferior courts, but that the chief magistrate, with his executive council, are appointable by the legislature; that two members of the latter are triennially displaced at the pleasure of the legislature; and that all the principal offices, both executive and judiciary, are filled by the same department. The executive prerogative of pardon, also, is in one case vested in the legislative department.

The constitution of North Carolina, which declares "that the legislative, executive, and supreme judicial powers of government ought to be forever separate and distinct from each other," refers, at the same time, to the legislative department, the appointment not only of the executive chief, but all the principal officers within both that and the judiciary department.

In South Carolina, the constitution makes the executive magistracy eligible by the legislative department. It gives to the latter, also, the appointment of the members of the judiciary department, including even justices of the peace and sheriffs; and the appointment of officers in the executive department, down to captains in the army and navy of the State.

In the constitution of Georgia where it is declared "that the legislative, executive, and judiciary departments shall be separate and distinct, so that neither exercise the powers properly belonging to the other," we find that the executive department is to be filled by appointments of the legislature; and the executive prerogative of pardon to be finally exercised by the same authority. Even justices of the peace are to be appointed by the legislature.

In citing these cases, in which the legislative, executive, and judiciary departments have not been kept totally separate and distinct, I wish not to be regarded as an advocate for the particular organizations of the several State governments. I am fully aware that among the many excellent principles which they exemplify they carry strong marks of the haste, and still stronger of the inexperience, under which they were framed. It is but too obvious that in some instances the fundamental principle under consideration has been violated by too great a mixture, and even an actual consolidation of the different powers; and that in no instance has a competent provision been made for maintaining in practice the separation delineated on paper. What I have wished to evince is that the charge brought against the proposed Constitution of violating the sacred maxim of free government is warranted neither by the real meaning annexed to that maxim by its author, nor by the sense in which it has hitherto been understood in America.

NUMBER 48 (JAMES MADISON)

It was shown in the last paper that the political apothegm there examined does not require that the legislative, executive, and judiciary departments should be wholly unconnected with each other. I shall undertake, in the next place, to show that unless these departments be so far connected and blended as to give to each a constitutional control over the others, the degree of separation which the maxim requires, as essential to a free government, can never in practice be duly maintained.

It is agreed on all sides that the powers properly belonging to one of the departments ought not to be directly and completely administered by either of the other departments. It is equally evident that none of them ought to possess, directly or indirectly, an overruling influence over the others in the administration of their respective powers. It will not be denied that power is of an encroaching nature, and that it ought to be effectually restrained from passing the limits assigned to it. After discriminating . . . in theory the several classes of power as they may in their nature be legislative, executive, or judiciary, the next and most difficult task is to provide some practical security for each, against the invasion of the others. What this security ought to be is the great problem to be solved.

Will it be sufficient to mark with precision the boundaries of these departments in the constitution of the government, and to trust to these parchment barriers against the encroaching spirit of power? This is the security which appears to have been principally relied on by the compilers of most of the American

constitutions. But experience assures us that the efficacy of the provision has been greatly overrated; and that some more adequate defense is indispensably necessary for the more feeble, against the more powerful, members of the government. The legislative department is everywhere extending the sphere of its activity, and drawing all power into its impetuous vortex.

The founders of our republics have so much merit for the wisdom which they have displayed that no task can be less pleasing than that of pointing out the errors into which they have fallen. A respect for truth, however, obliges us to remark that they seem never for a moment to have turned their eyes from the danger to liberty from the overgrown and all-grasping prerogative of an hereditary magistrate, supported and fortified by an hereditary branch of the legislative authority. They seem never to have recollected the danger from legislative usurpations, which, by assembling all power in the same hands, must lead to the same tyranny as is threatened by executive usurpations.

In a government where numerous and extensive prerogatives are placed in the hands of an hereditary monarch, the executive department is very justly regarded as the source of danger, and watched with all the jealousy which a zeal for liberty ought to inspire. In a democracy, where a multitude of people exercise in person the legislative functions, and are continually exposed, by their incapacity for regular deliberation and concerted measures, to the ambitious intrigues of their executive magistrates, tyranny may well be apprehended, on some favorable emergency, to start up in the same quarter. But in a representative republic, where the executive magistracy is carefully limited, both in the extent and the duration of its power; and where the legislative power is exercised by an assembly, which is inspired, by a supposed influence over the people, with an intrepid confidence in its own strength; which is sufficiently numerous to feel all the passions which actuate a multitude, yet not so numerous as to be incapable of pursuing the objects of its passions, by means which reason prescribes; it is against the enterprising ambition of this department that the people ought to indulge all their jealousy and exhaust all their precautions.

The legislative department derives a superiority in our governments from other circumstances. Its constitutional powers being at once more extensive and less susceptible of precise limits, it can with the greater facility mask under complicated and indirect measures the encroachments which it makes on the coördinate departments. It is not unfrequently a question of real nicety in legislative bodies, whether the operation of a particular measure will, or will not, extend beyond the legislative sphere. On the other side, the executive power being restrained within a narrower compass and being more simple in its nature, and the judiciary being described by landmarks still less uncertain, projects of usurpation by either of these departments would immediately betray and defeat themselves. Nor is this all; as the legislative department alone has access to the pockets of the people, and has in some constitutions full discretion, and in all a prevailing influence, over the pecuniary rewards of those who fill the other departments, a dependence is thus created in the latter, which gives still greater facility to encroachments of the former.

I have appealed to our own experience for the truth of what I advance on this subject. Were it necessary to verify this experience by particular proofs, they might be multiplied without end. I might find a witness in every citizen who has shared in, or been attentive to, the course of public administrations. I might collect vouchers in abundance from the records and archives of every State in the Union. But as a more concise, and at the same time equally satisfactory, evidence, I will refer to the example of two States, attested by two unexceptionable authorities.

The first example is that of Virginia, a State which, as we have seen, has expressly declared in its constitution that the three great departments ought not to be intermixed. The authority in support of it is Mr. Jefferson, who, besides his other advantages for remarking the operation of the government, was himself the chief magistrate of it. In order to convey fully the ideas with which his experience had impressed him on this subject, it will be necessary to quote a passage of some length from his very interesting "Notes on the State of Virginia," p. 195. "All the powers of government, legislative, executive, and judiciary, result to the legislative body. The concentrating these in the same

hands, is precisely the definition of despotic government. It will be no alleviation, that these powers will be exercised by a plurality of hands, and not by a single one. One hundred and seventy-three despots would surely be as oppressive as one.... An *elective despotism* was not the government we fought for; but one which should not only be founded on free principles, but in which the powers of government should be so divided and balanced among several bodies of magistracy, as that no one could transcend their legal limits, without being effectually checked and restrained by the others. For this reason, that convention which passed the ordinance of government, laid its foundation on this basis, that the legislative, executive, and judiciary departments should be separate and distinct, so that no person should exercise the powers of more than one of them at the same time. *But no barrier was provided between these several powers.* The judiciary and the executive members were left dependent on the legislative for their subsistence in office, and some of them for their continuance in it. If, therefore, the legislature assumes executive and judiciary powers, no opposition is likely to be made; nor, if made, can be effectual; because in that case they may put their proceedings into the form of an act of Assembly, which will render them obligatory on the other branches. They have accordingly, *in many* instances, *decided rights* which should have been left to *judiciary controversy,* and *the direction of the executive, during the whole time of their session, is becoming habitual and familiar.*"

The other State which I shall take for an example is Pennsylvania; and the other authority, the Council of Censors, which assembled in the years 1783 and 1784. A part of the duty of this body as marked out by the constitution was "to inquire whether the constitution had been preserved inviolate in every part; and whether the legislative and executive branches of government had performed their duty as guardians of the people, or assumed to themselves, or exercised, other or greater powers than they are entitled to by the constitution." . . . In the execution of this trust the council were necessarily led to a comparison of both the legislative and executive proceedings with the constitutional powers of these departments; and from the facts enumerated, and to the truth of most of which both sides in the council subscribed, it appears that the constitution had been flagrantly violated by the legislature in a variety of important instances.

A great number of laws had been passed, violating, without any apparent necessity, the rule requiring that all bills of a public nature shall be previously printed for the consideration of the people; although this is one of the precautions chiefly relied on by the constitution against improper acts of the legislature.

The constitutional trial by jury had been violated, and powers assumed which had not been delegated by the constitution.

Executive powers had been usurped.

The salaries of the judges, which the constitution expressly requires to be fixed, had been occasionally varied; and cases belonging to the judiciary department frequently drawn within legislative cognizance and determination.

Those who wish to see the several particulars falling under each of these heads may consult the journals of the council.... [T]he greater part of them may be considered as the spontaneous shoots of an ill-constituted government.

It appears, also, that the executive department had not been innocent of frequent breaches of the constitution....

The conclusion which I am warranted in drawing from these observations is, that a mere demarcation on parchment of the constitutional limits of the several departments, is not a sufficient guard against those encroachments which lead to a tyrannical concentration of all the powers of government in the same hands.

NUMBER 51 (JAMES MADISON)

To what expedient, then, shall we finally resort, for maintaining in practice the necessary partition of power among the several departments as laid down in the Constitution? The only answer that can be given is that as all these exterior provisions are found to be inadequate the defect must be supplied, by so contriving the interior structure of the government as that its several constituent parts may, by their mutual relations, be the means of keeping each other in their proper places. Without presuming to undertake a full

development of this important idea I will hazard a few general observations which may perhaps place it in a clearer light, and enable us to form a more correct judgment of the principles and structure of the government planned by the convention.

In order to lay a due foundation for that separate and distinct exercise of the different powers of government, which to a certain extent is admitted on all hands to be essential to the preservation of liberty, it is evident that each department should have a will of its own; and consequently should be so constituted that the members of each should have as little agency as possible in the appointment of the members of the others. Were this principle rigorously adhered to, it would require that all the appointments for the supreme executive, legislative, and judiciary magistracies should be drawn from the same fountain of authority, the people, through channels having no communication whatever with one another. Perhaps such a plan of constructing the several departments would be less difficult in practice than it may in contemplation appear. Some difficulties, however, and some additional expense would attend the execution of it. Some deviations, therefore, from the principle must be admitted. In the constitution of the judiciary department in particular, it might be inexpedient to insist rigorously on the principle: first, because peculiar qualifications being essential in the members, the primary consideration ought to be to select that mode of choice which best secures these qualifications; second, because the permanent tenure by which the appointments are held in that department must soon destroy all sense of dependence on the authority conferring them.

It is equally evident that the members of each department should be as little dependent as possible on those of the others for the emoluments annexed to their offices. Were the executive magistrate, or the judges, not independent of the legislature in this particular, their independence in every other would be merely nominal.

But the great security against a gradual concentration of the several powers in the same department consists in giving to those who administer each department the necessary constitutional means and personal motives to resist encroachments of the others. The provision for defense must in this, as in all other cases, be made commensurate to the danger of attack. Ambition must be made to counteract ambition. The interest of the man must be connected with the constitutional rights of the place. It may be a reflection on human nature that such devices should be necessary to control the abuses of government. But what is government itself but the greatest of all reflections on human nature? If men were angels, no government would be necessary. If angels were to govern men, neither external nor internal controls on government would be necessary. In framing a government which is to be administered by men over men, the great difficulty lies in this: you must first enable the government to control the governed; and in the next place oblige it to control itself. A dependence on the people is, no doubt, the primary control on the government; but experience has taught mankind the necessity of auxiliary precautions.

This policy of supplying, by opposite and rival interests, the defect of better motives, might be traced through the whole system of human affairs, private as well as public. We see it particularly displayed in all the subordinate distributions of power, where the constant aim is to divide and arrange the several offices in such a manner as that each may be a check on the other—that the private interest of every individual may be a sentinel over the public rights. These inventions of prudence cannot be less requisite in the distribution of the supreme powers of the State.

But it is not possible to give to each department an equal power of self-defense. In republican government, the legislative authority necessarily predominates. The remedy for this inconveniency is to divide the legislature into different branches; and to render them, by different modes of election and different principles of action, as little connected with each other as the nature of their common functions and their common dependence on the society will admit. It may even be necessary to guard against dangerous encroachments by still further precautions. As the weight of the legislative authority requires that it should be thus divided, the weakness of the executive may require, on the other hand, that it should be fortified. An absolute negative on the legislature appears, at first view, to be the natural defense with which the executive magistrate should be armed. But perhaps it would be neither altogether safe nor alone sufficient. On ordinary occa-

sions it might not be exerted with the requisite firmness, and on extraordinary occasions it might be perfidiously abused. May not this defect of an absolute negative be supplied by some qualified connection between this weaker department and the weaker branch of the stronger department, by which the latter may be led to support the constitutional rights of the former, without being too much detached from the rights of its own department?

If the principles on which these observations are founded be just, as I persuade myself they are, and they be applied as a criterion to the several State constitutions, and to the federal Constitution, it will be found that if the latter does not perfectly correspond with them, the former are infinitely less able to bear such a test.

There are, moreover, two considerations particularly applicable to the federal system of America, which place that system in a very interesting point of view.

First.   In a single republic, all the power surrendered by the people is submitted to the administration of a single government; and the usurpations are guarded against by a division of the government into distinct and separate departments. In the compound republic of America, the power surrendered by the people is first divided between two distinct governments, and then the portion allotted to each subdivided among distinct and separate departments. Hence a double security arises to the rights of the people. The different governments will control each other, at the same time that each will be controlled by itself.

Second.   It is of great importance in a republic not only to guard the society against the oppression of its rulers, but to guard one part of the society against the injustice of the other part. Different interests necessarily exist in different classes of citizens. If a majority be united by a common interest, the rights of the minority will be insecure. There are but two methods of providing against this evil: the one by creating a will in the community independent of the majority—that is, of the society itself; the other, by comprehending in the society so many separate descriptions of citizens as will render an unjust combination of a majority of the whole very improbable, if not impracticable. The first method prevails in all governments possessing an hereditary or self-appointed authority. This, at best, is but a precarious security; because a power independent of the society may as well espouse the unjust views of the major as the rightful interests of the minor party, and may possibly be turned against both parties. The second method will be exemplified in the federal republic of the United States. Whilst all authority in it will be derived from and dependent on the society, the society itself will be broken into so many parts, interests and classes of citizens, that the rights of individuals, or of the minority, will be in little danger from interested combinations of the majority. In a free government the security for civil rights must be the same as that for religious rights. It consists in the one case in the multiplicity of interests, and in the other in the multiplicity of sects. The degree of security in both cases will depend on the number of interests and sects; and this may be presumed to depend on the extent of country and number of people comprehended under the same government. This view of the subject must particularly recommend a proper federal system to all the sincere and considerate friends of republican government, since it shows that in exact proportion as the territory of the Union may be formed into more circumscribed Confederacies, or States, oppressive combinations of a majority will be facilitated; the best security, under the republican forms, for the rights of every class of citizen, will be diminished; and consequently the stability and independence of some member of the government, the only other security, must be proportionally increased. Justice is the end of government. It is the end of civil society. It ever has been and ever will be pursued until it be obtained, or until liberty be lost in the pursuit. In a society under the forms of which the stronger faction can readily unite and oppress the weaker, anarchy may as truly be said to reign as in a state of nature, where the weaker individual is not secured against the violence of the stronger; and as, in the latter state, even the stronger individuals are prompted, by the uncertainty of their condition, to submit to a government which may protect the weak as well as themselves; so, in the former state, will the more powerful factions or parties be gradually induced, by a like motive, to wish for a government which will protect all

parties, the weaker as well as the more powerful. It can be little doubted that if the State of Rhode Island was separated from the Confederacy and left to itself, the insecurity of rights under the popular form of government within such narrow limits would be displayed by such reiterated oppressions of factious majorities that some power altogether independent of the people would soon be called for by the voice of the very factions whose misrule had proved the necessity of it. In the extended republic of the United States, and among the great variety of interests, parties, and sects which it embraces, a coalition of a majority of the whole society could seldom take place on any other principles than those of justice and the general good; whilst there being thus less danger to a minor from the will of a major party, there must be less pretext, also, to provide for the security of the former, by introducing into the government a will not dependent on the latter, or, in other words, a will independent of the society itself. It is no less certain than it is important, notwithstanding the contrary opinions which have been entertained, that the larger the society, provided it lie within a practicable sphere, the more duly capable it will be of self-government. And happily for the *republican cause,* the practicable sphere may be carried to a very great extent by a judicious modification and mixture of the *federal principle.*

From "A Self-Correcting System: The Constitution of the United States." by M. Landau, 1986, *This Constitution,* no. 11, Summer, 1986, Project '87, pp. 5–10. Copyright © 1986 by the American Political Science Association. Reprinted by permission.

READING 5

A Self-Correcting System: The Constitution of the United States
Martin Landau

Berkeley political scientist Martin Landau's essay on the Constitution reads quite well as a companion piece to The Federalist Papers *as he examines the success of our constitutional system and traces it, in part, to the document's fundamental simplicity. Clearly aware of the frustrations often associated with the seeming snail's pace of American policymaking processes, Landau emphasizes that efficiency and speed were not the major goals of the Constitution's framers. Rather, they sought and valued a "self-regulating" and "high reliability" system characterized by balance, equilibrium, and stability. The article underlines the mechanistic Newtonian perspective held by the framers. Nature's way of action met by reaction and thrust by counterthrust was reflected by the dominance of checks and balances in the functioning of government. The Constitution's "flat" organization purposely includes many decision points, much duplication, and overlapping of governmental roles and responsibilities. Landau's portrait reveals a pluralist model of policymaking based on negotiation and compromise as the norm. As in* The Federalist Papers, *it may be argued that Landau does not address persuasively the concerns of those whose interests are alleged to be missing from the pluralist's marketplace. In addition, while it is clear that our constitutional system has been an enduring one, critics would contend that survival, per se, is not the fundamental goal of the "good" society and that it should not be the primary metric by which to judge the success of an approach to governance.*

That which is redundant is, to the extent that it is redundant, stable. It is therefore reliable.

W. S. McCulloch

The great English philosopher, Alfred North Whitehead, once remarked, "I know of only two occasions in history when the people in power did what needed to be done about as well as you can imagine its being possible. One was the framing of your American Constitution." (His other example was the reign of Augustus Ceasar.) The framers, Whitehead added, were able statesmen with good ideas which they incorporated "without trying to particularize too explicitly how they should be put into effect."

Years before he became president of the United States, Woodrow Wilson, in reflecting on the durabil-

ity of the Constitution, also observed its generalized character. It did little more than lay down a foundation in principle, Wilson remarked; it was not a complete system; it took none but the first steps. The Constitution, he continued, provided with all possible brevity for the establishment of a government having three distinct branches: executive, legislative and judicial. It vested executive power in the presidency, for whose election and inauguration it made careful provision, and whose powers it defined with succinct clarity; it granted specifically enumerated powers to Congress, outlined the organization of its two houses, provided for the election of its members and regulated both their numbers and the manner of their election; it established a Supreme Court with ample authority to interpret the Constitution, and it prescribed the procedures to govern appointments and tenure.

At this point, Wilson noted, the organizational work of the Constitution ended and "the fact that it [did] nothing more [was] its chief strength." Had it gone beyond such elementary provisions, it would have lost elasticity and adaptability. Its ability to endure, to survive, was directly attributable to its simplicity.

There is strong ground for such belief. State constitutions, notoriously complicated, cluttered, and rigid, have come and gone—tossed away as outmoded, inelastic, and maladaptive instruments. Since 1789, there have been some two hundred state constitutional conventions, one, it seems, for every year of our history. This should not surprise us when we observe that the average size of our state constitutions is ten times that of the national, the movement toward simplification notwithstanding. But the national Constitution, framed for a simple society marked by doubtful unity and fearsome external threat, now orders a world that would appear as science fiction to its designers. Where states have had to scrap their constitutions five, seven, even ten times, the nation's remains intact.

Despite Wilson's admiration of the simple brevity of the Constitution, he wondered about the future of a governmental system in which "nothing is direct." "Authority," he stated, "is perplexingly subdivided and distributed, and responsibility has to be hunted down in out-of-the-way corners."

In this sentence we have the crux of an unending stream of criticism which remains vigorous to this date. One frequently hears that separation of powers has resulted in continuous struggle between president and Congress, too often leading to deadlock; that the decline of Congress and the rise of an "imperial presidency" is ample testimony to the failure of checks and balances—a failure further intensified by a Supreme Court which remains beyond the reach of Congress, president, and the public. So too has federalism failed. It has fractured and fragmented the nation, nurtured the parochialism of local interests, furthered the imbalances of society, and subverted efforts to mount coordinated national programs. In the decline of the states and the ascendancy of national power, little of the original design remains. And beyond this, the staggered electoral system has prevented the majority from controlling its government or ousting one it does not want.

Whatever their logical consistency, these are frequent and familiar criticisms that derive from a variety of sources. They give rise to all sorts of remedial proposals from a fixed single term for the presidency to a parliamentary system. They abound today, and their proponents are prominent public figures who delight in telling us that no other modern government on the European continent has used the American Constitution as its model. Because of distinctive ethnic and regional problems, some have employed the principle of federalism but none has been impressed with the cumbersome and conflict-prone separation of powers. The issue, publicized in the media, is the "ungovernability" of the system: separation of power breaks down into stalemate, delay, nonfeasance, even malfeasance. What captures critics is the apparent inefficiencies of our governing institutions.

But it would do us all well to remember Justice Brandeis' injunction that the Constitution was not a design for efficiency. Nor is it by any means as simple as Wilson thought. In the brevity of the seven articles which established the government, there is contained an organizational logic that we are only now beginning to fathom. Separation of powers and federalism as we understand these concepts, do not quite cover the organizational principles involved. But they are critical elements in all "self-regulating" and "high-reliability" systems—which is what the Constitution established.

SELF-REGULATING SYSTEMS

Before turning directly to this concept, it is important to note that to the eighteenth century, the system of mechanics formulated by Isaac Newton was not simply a scientific theory. Indeed, it had become a cosmological formula so powerful as to constitute "an infallible world outlook." So it was that the English poet, Alexander Pope, could write, "Nature and nature's laws lay hid in night, God said, 'Let Newton be,' and all was light."

Whatever their political differences, those who wrote the Constitution were Newtonians. With few exceptions, they thought the governmental system they were designing was in accord with nature's way. And nature's way, so elegantly stated in Newton's Third Law, was action and reaction, thrust and counter-thrust, or what we call checks and balances. There are, John Adams had written, three branches in any government and "they have an unalterable foundation in nature": "to constitute a single body with all power, *without any counterpoise, balance, or equilibrium* is to violate the laws of nature" but "to hold powers in balance is a self-evident truth."

This was the ideal struck in Philadelphia—a government that by its natural properties minimized the risk of human error. The true principle of government, Hamilton declared, is "to give a *perfect proportion and balance to its parts,* and the power you give it will never affect your security." And to Madison, a "natural government" was such that "Its several constituent parts may, by their mutual relations, be the means of keeping each other in their proper places," of regulating and controlling each other.

So too did this image comprehend federalism. A "natural" government, after all, was a transcript of nature and nature was a machine. Look at this world, David Hume wrote—"You will find it to be nothing but one great machine, subdivided into an infinite number of lesser machines . . . adjusted to each other with an accuracy which ravishes into admiration all men who have ever contemplated them." Look at these United States, Jefferson might have written, one great government subdivided into lesser governments, adjusted to each other with an accuracy.... What he did write was:

> In time all these [states] as well as the central government, like the planets revolving around their common sun, acting and acted upon according to their respective weights and distances, will produce that beautiful equilibrium on which our Constitution is founded, and which I believe it will exhibit to the world in a degree of perfection, unexampled but in the planetary system itself.

Balance, equilibrium, stability: these were the goals the framers of the Constitution sought. Once, in exasperation, Walter Lippmann asked: "Is there in all the world a more plain-spoken attempt to contrive an automatic governor, a machine that would not need to take human nature into account?" To Lippmann, a noted political analyst, government was not a problem in mechanics, and its solutions were not to be found in a balance of forces. Such a balance, he held, leads not to stability, but to paralysis. But a ship on the high seas and a jet in the sky are stable systems. They constantly change in velocity and vector, yet they remain in equilibrium.

There are stable systems that are self-regulating. They can prevent error and they can correct error; some are able to repair themselves even as damage occurs. Generally addressed as "cybernetic," their governing principle is "feedback." By cycling back a portion of their output, they are able to avoid and suppress sharp pendulum-like swings. What is fed back regulates and stabilizes the system. This is often referred to as "feedback stabilization." That there is a striking resemblance between "checks and balances" and "feedback stabilization" was observed some years ago by the noted scientist, John R. Platt.

In a stabilization or self-regulating system, internal checks are introduced to prevent error, stress, or threat from so building that the system breaks down suddenly and dangerously. Protection is acquired, as Hamilton would phrase it, by proportioning the system so that its parts balance each other, so that they regulate each other. In modern parlance, we refer to "feedback loops" which enable parts to work against each other and even against the whole. Counter-forces of

this type prevent discontinuities, wild oscillation, and rapid fluctuation. Wholesale breakdowns, due either to extreme mutability or rigidity, are thereby avoided. This is a type of self or internal regulation which permits stable operations even as the system changes.

In the constitutional design, Platt suggested, "the idea was to set up, at every critical point.... some kind of equilibrium between opposing interests ... so as to have a steady pressure against either the excesses or defects of policy into which governments were likely to fall." Or, as James Madison put it, "to control itself," a government's "interior structure" must be so arranged that the relationship of the parts regulates the whole. This is the function of checks and balances or, in Platt's language, negative feedback.

In a self-regulating system, any number of devices are employed to maintain and insure stability of operation. Because a system constantly and inevitably faces unexpected and uncertain conditions which generate a wide variety of problems, its repertoire of response must be rather extensive. Accordingly, self-regulating systems are designed in terms of different time constants, different response levels, and brakes and accelerators—along with its multiple feedback linkages. There are problems that demand rapid action. There are others which require careful and deliberate consideration. Disturbances to a system are not all alike: they will vary in intensity, character, cost, and duration. Hence a range of time constants, of schedules and calendars, each having its own place in the system, is required.

There are also problems that directly effect the whole and must be dealt with at the systemic level. Others are, by their nature, best handled at intermediate levels. Still others, of lesser magnitude, engage only a part of the system. Decision and choice points, thus, must be located at places most appropriate to the problem. And there are times when it is necessary to slow action, or to speed action. For such circumstances, brakes and accelerators are necessary. The idea is to enable the system to act as a whole even as it distributes and differentiates authority to decide, and to produce a powerful capacity to respond to a multitude of different types of problems simultaneously.

Taken as a whole, an organization of this sort does appear to be "perplexingly subdivided and distributed" and it certainly looks messy. But a variety of time constants, differential response levels, brakes and accelerators, and multiple forms of feedback are precisely the elements that protect against dangerous fluctuations and permit a deliberate change process which insures stability.

These safeguards are all to be found in the Constitution. They were placed there by men who knew what they were doing, and explained what they were doing. One needs only to read *The Federalist Papers.* There we find explanations of the different systems of recruitment, staggered tenure, separation and division of power, concurrent authorities, varieties of decision rules, multiplicity of choice points—all arranged in such a manner as to produce networks of internal control. These failed only once; in the years of the Civil War. The repair was costly but it was effected. And since then no threat to the system was ever allowed to amplify to the point where it threatened stability. It is a plain fact that neither war, nor depression, nor natural calamity, has ever been able to shatter its self-correcting arrangements.

It is also striking to observe the number of cybernetic theorists who see analogy in the American system of checks and balances. The anthropologist Gregory Bateson and the psychiatrist Jurgen Reusch, both concerned to avoid wild swings in the interest of stable development, saw the variety of "cross-overs" in the American system as constraints and accelerators which combine to regulate "the rate or direction" of over-all change. And C. R. Dechert, in *The Development of Cybernetics* tells us:

> The founding fathers of the United States wanted the legislature sensitive to public opinion, so they introduced a House of Representatives elected biannually on the basis of population. But they did not want the decision process too sensitive to public opinion, so they introduced a Senate elected on a different basis for a different term of office whose concurrence is necessary to legislation. In order to introduce further stability into the system they decoupled the legislative from the executive branch and introduced an independent control element in the form of a Supreme Court. The inherent stability of the system has been proved over the past 175 years.

We like to tell our students that the Constitution was designed to endure, to outlast human deficien-cies: that it is a system which "by its own internal contrivances" regulates itself. There are times, to be sure, when its pace is maddeningly slow. But in the main, it has met traumatic assaults and threats without much loss of systemic stability. There are many ways to account for this but whatever the theory employed, it remains the fact, in Platt's words, that the constitutional designers understood the principles of a self-regulating system far better than our contemporary political philosophers. Nor were they oblivious to the problem of reliability.

REDUNDANCY AND RELIABILITY

Theories of organization frequently involve reference to *peaked* and *flat* systems. Peaked systems are hierarchies. There is only one central decision point, one channel of authority, one official or legitimate communication system. Each component operates in lock-step dependence, part of a single chain. Policy is determined at the top and prescribes the behavior of each subordinate unit.

The Constitution provides for a flat organization. There are many decision points, many authority centers, and many communications channels—all mandated. The entire system is constructed on the basis of duplication and overlap, and each major component—the executive, legislative, and judicial—has independent authority. Policy is determined through negotiation and constitutes an agreement by parties of equal standing.

It is the flat character of the government that Woodrow Wilson despaired of. And this is the property of the system that has been subjected to unceasing criticism. We have already rehearsed the argument: it results in conflict, deadlock, lack of accountability, and robs us of a dynamic and vital decision center capable of quick and decisive action. For the last sixty years there have been countless reorganization proposals to "peak" the system, to locate more and more decision authority in the presidency—even beyond that which naturally accrued to the office as the United States became the United State. Until the advent of the "imperial presidency" and the excesses of Watergate, there were few voices in support of the flat system designed so long ago—a design that is also remarkable in its anticipation of the theory of redundancy.

Suppose there is a structure (or process or channel) which will fail one time in a hundred. What would the probability of simultaneous failure be for two such systems—each independent of the other? What would the probability of failure be for three systems; for four, etc.? For two, the chance of failure would be 1 in 10,000; for three, 1 in 1,000,000; for four, 1 in 100,000,000. This fact, the product rule of probability, lies at the foundation of the theory of redundancy, which is a theory of system reliability. Applied properly, it lessens the risk of failure and protects against the injurious effects of major errors and malfunctions. Its cardinal element is simple repetition or duplication.

And its basic assumptions are Madisonian—that mankind is fallible—not good, not bad—just prone to error. It agrees that "if men were angels" or "if angels governed men," no special safeguards or auxiliary precautions would be necessary. The theory of redundancy simply accepts the obvious limitations of any and all systems—political, economic, social, physical, natural, and artificial—by treating their parts, no matter how perfect, as *risky actors*. The theory focuses on the whole and asks one paramount question: is it possible to construct a system that is more reliable, more perfect, less prone to failure than even the most faithful of its components? When we set this question against that time-honored maxim—a chain is no stronger than its weakest link—its full import is made clear. The theory tells us that a chain cannot only be made stronger than its weakest link, it can be made stronger than its strongest link.

It has generally escaped notice but this is the problem that much of *The Federalist Papers* dealt with. "As long as the reason of man continues fallible," as long "as enlightened statesmen will not always be at the helm," how can we devise a government that will withstand gross malfunction as it continues to serve its purposes? The answer: by so organizing it that when some parts fail *they do not and cannot automatically cause the failure of others*. The idea is to provide a system with multiple channels, independent of each other, at those points where failure can be disastrous. Where this type of redundancy is incorporated into a design, the odds against total breakdown rise by many times. The failure of one part cannot and does not irreparably damage the whole. There are alternative pathways, backups, which move the entity toward failsafe. In real machines, we have learned to insure reliability through the redundancy of simple duplication, as in a power-grid, a 747, and the dual braking system of our cars. And, intuitively, we follow the same principle when we seek a second opinion in a threatening medical situation.

The founders constructed what was, and still must be, the most redundant government in the world. They did more than introduce internal balances and controls: they "wired" the system in parallel at every crucial choice point. There is no unity of command and authority: there is no monopoly of power. The system is flat. And for each person there are, at the least, two governments—state and national, each separate and independent. There are two constitutions, two executives, two legislatures, two systems of law, two judiciaries. There are two bills of rights, two networks of checks and balances, two representation systems, and there is more. For apart from the redundancy of duplication, manifested in federalism, there is also the redundancy of checks and balances; i.e., of "overlapping jurisdictions."

In the event of damage, overlapping systems can expand their jurisdictions and "take over" when the functions of others have been lost or impaired. There are indeed limits which vary with the type of system, but an inherent protective potential is thereby established. In the case of the Constitution, our three basic branches are designed to overlap. They resist mutually exclusive jurisdictions. And they expand and contract. Scholars have for years spoken of the "cyclical" character of intragovernmental arrangements, of "pendulum" swings—frequently pointing to these as adaptive responses. The "uncertain content" (jurisdiction) of the three branches of government does not allow any one of them to sit still. If one weakens or fails, the other can affect a partial takeover. And the same holds for the national and state governments.

A system thus can sustain failure that, in the absence of overlapping jurisdictions, would destroy it. Once, on the floor of the Senate, Senator Mike Mansfield . . . warned his colleagues that their refusal to act on a critical issue would not prevail: "It is clear that when one road to this end fails, others will unfold as indeed they have. . . . If the process is ignored in legislative channels, it will not be blocked in other channels—in the executive branch and the courts." This has been the pattern of much of our history.

It is a history that confirms Whitehead's judgment. The constitutional system works as a "self-regulating" and "self-correcting" organization exhibiting a reliability, stability, and adaptability that has continually overcome its deepest strains. We like to say that ours is the oldest written Constitution in the world—yet it remains a striking novelty. Marked by a redundancy of law, of channel and code, of command and authority, the whole has been stronger than any of its parts.

FOOD FOR THOUGHT

1. In light of the readings in this chapter, was the government framed by our country's founders fundamentally radical and innovative or relatively conservative in nature? Were the founders political dreamers or primarily self-interested realists in their fashioning of a new governmental system? In your thinking, play the role of devil's advocate. What might you say to Lance Banning to counter his relatively optimistic view of the revolutionary context of the Constitution's framing? In a similar vein, what might you say to Charles Beard to argue against his more cynical portrait of the motivations of the country's founding fathers?

2. *The Federalist Papers* have been characterized by some analysts as the best documentation of the dominant political ideology or political mind-set of the American people. Based on your reading of selections from *The Federalist Papers,* how would you describe this political mind-set? Is there a distinctly "American" political ideology evident in *The Federalist* and/or in contemporary national life?

3. *The Federalist Papers* are replete with observations and generalizations about the nature of governance, political beings, and the American condition. Can you identify three themes or arguments about the nature of American government and our political processes from the sections of *The Federalist Papers* that you have read? Based on your understanding of contemporary American politics, were the authors of *The Federalist Papers* "correct" in their assessments of the American political system? Do their assertions and predictions about American politics hold true today?

4. It might be argued that one's receptiveness to Martin Landau's argument in *A Self-Correcting System: The Constitution of the United States* would depend a good deal on one's "place" in the American political system. Assess Landau's argument from the alternative perspectives of a wealthy businessperson relatively happy with the status quo, on the one hand, and a single parent on welfare struggling to make ends meet on the other.

CHAPTER 2

CONSTITUTIONAL INTERPRETATION

The act of constitutional creation, explored in Chapter One, determines in large measure the nature of the political system that emerges in a particular constitutional order. Forging a constitution, however, is just one facet of developing a working constitutional system. Equally important is the manner in which that document evolves over time and the way it is interpreted by those who give it life, meaning, and substance.

In the American system of government courts and, particularly, the Supreme Court, have asserted primacy in rendering authoritative judgments on constitutional meaning and scope. The following selections include Supreme Court decisions establishing judicial primacy in this domain, as well as adversarial readings supporting and vilifying the Court for its efforts at offering definitive meaning to arguably ambiguous and open-ended constitutional provisions. The chapter concludes with an article emphasizing that questions of who shall interpret the Constitution authoritatively and how far constitutional authority should extend are not solely of interest to academicians. Rather, debates over many constitutional interpretation issues remain spirited and complex more than two centuries after the document's framing.

In the formative years of our republic, two landmark opinions by Chief Justice John Marshall (*Marbury* v. *Madison* (1803) and *McCulloch* v. *Maryland* (1819)) served to set the tone for defining the fundamental structure of our constitutional system. Both rulings remain law today and are the starting points for analyses of the Court's unique role in rendering authoritative judgments of the Constitution's meaning, and in defining the contours of national supremacy in U.S. federalism.

In the early years of our nation's history, the Supreme Court was not the prominent, coequal branch of our national government that it is today. Indeed, it lacked prestige, rarely met, and was plagued, on the one hand, with frequent resignations of justices (at times for seemingly inferior state positions or in personal disgrace) and, on the other hand, with a dearth of prominent and qualified candidates who were willing to serve. John Marshall's long tenure as the fourth Chief Justice (1801–1835) changed the Court and the country forever. A strong Federalist, Marshall methodically utilized the Court as the preeminent nationalizing agent in a polity that had resoundingly rejected Federalist dogma at the polls in the election of Thomas Jefferson in 1800. Long after the Federalist Party disappeared from the national scene, Marshall's rulings continued to win the day for its popularly rejected nationalist doctrines and policies. *Marbury* and *McCulloch* are two primary examples of this phenomenon.

The *Marbury* case, involving a disputed commission to a minor judgeship position, was the vehicle Marshall used successfully to establish judicial review (the power of the Court to declare the acts and actions of other political authorities unconstitutional), an interpretive power the Court's critics label judicial supremacy. Marshall was a brilliant tactician in invalidating a statute that added to the Court's power rather than seeking to establish the Court's role in a case dealing with another branch's power or in one where the Court's powers had been diminished by Congress. By refusing to exercise power that Congress could not constitutionally grant, Marshall solved any potential obedience problem raised by the ruling. The Court, clearly, was not likely to disobey itself! Further, in not ordering the Jefferson administration to deliver the disputed commission to Marbury, Marshall gave the Jeffersonians the outcome that they wanted—along with the "window dressing" of judicial review.

McCulloch v. *Maryland* was a similar coup. The case, concerning federal power to charter a national bank, gave Marshall an opening to develop a classic exposition of national supremacy, formulating a theory of the union premised on a broad, expansive reading of the Constitution's "necessary and proper" and "supremacy" clauses. The notion that the union was a covenant of the American people writ large wins out over the alternative view of a union formed by a compact among sovereign states. In justifying his broad reading of federal powers Marshall declares, "We must never forget that it is a Constitution which we are expounding."

Collectively, *Marbury* and *McCulloch* offer several critical interpretive propositions. The Constitution was ordained by the people (not the states) and was intended for their benefit. It was intended to endure for ages to come and, consequently, must be adaptable. While national powers are enumerated, within the scope of those powers the federal government is supreme. Finally, the Court is the "protector" of the constitutional covenant, speaking for the people who "count," those who ordained the document, not the whims and caprices of legislative majorities of the moment. Enter the power of judicial review.

Marshall's opinions in *Marbury, McCulloch,* and numerous other cases set the parameters for future debates over constitutional interpretation, leaving ample room for differences of opinion over the issues of the Constitution's expansiveness and the role of judges in interpreting it. The contemporary writings of William Brennan and Lino Graglia illustrate the flavor of this debate.

In *The Constitution of the United States: Contemporary Ratification,* the late Supreme Court Justice William Brennan portrays an "aspirational" Constitution, treating it as a template for the pursuit of social justice and human dignity. Brennan recognizes that the Constitution is not absolutely clear but, rather, contains "majestic generalities and ennobling pronouncements" calling on the judge to offer a "public reading" speaking on behalf of the community. This reading should not attempt to simply mirror the intention of the framers, an elusive quest Brennan characterizes as "arrogance cloaked as humility" aimed at disguising the political motivations of such originalist interpreters. Rather, for Brennan, adhering to the Constitution demands that one interpret the document by applying the fundamental substantive value choices of the framers to the context of contemporary life. In effect, the framers did not want to bind American society. Rather, they sought an adaptive polity, with the Constitution's concept of human dignity the linchpin of the adaptation process. While pursuit of human dignity once meant protection of real property, society has undergone massive social, political, and economic change. Today, in a far-reaching governmental system, human dignity's pursuit requires vigilance against governmental encroachments on individual rights.

Diametrically opposed to Brennan is the originalist position espoused by conservative law professor Lino Graglia in *How the Constitution Disappeared.* Graglia contends that, after the desegregation ruling in *Brown* v. *Board of Education* (1954), the Court became, illegitimately, the nation's primary domestic policymaker under the guise of simply interpreting the Constitution. In Graglia's view, the activist decisions of the Warren Court (and many since) are patently countermajoritarian in rendering judgments against the people's will and cannot be squared with democratic governance. Note that "the people" who "matter" for Graglia are those of the here and now, often signaled by the preferences of contemporary legislative majorities. This is, of course, a vastly different perspective from that of Marshall. For Graglia, the exercise of "non-interpretive" or "non-originalist" judicial review (à la Brennan) leads to the paradox of "constitutional law without the Constitution." Taking issue with Brennan's portrait of an open-ended, rights oriented Constitution, Graglia seeks to rely less on judges and more on the constitutional amendment process and "the good sense of the American people."

The Graglia/Brennan debate and the answers to some of the questions about constitutional interpretation explored by Marshall are of more than academic interest. Concern about the appropriate role of the judiciary in interpreting the Constitution, and the substantive decisions being made about the Constitution's reach have remained subjects of considerable debate not only in academic circles but on the Court as well. And, as *New York Times* reporter Linda Greenhouse's article written in the wake of the Supreme Court's 1994–95 term suggests, the consensus about judicial precedents and the nature of American federalism that many considered to be "settled" remains in some degree of flux, with the contemporary Court "dusting off" doctrinal interpretations of an earlier and, seemingly, bygone era. Greenhouse notes that while the Court's fundamental role in defining constitutional meaning remains paramount, the meanings being drawn today are suggestive of the emergence of a considerably less expansive interpretation of federal constitutional power.

READING 6

Marbury v. *Madison* (1803)

John Marshall

The case of Marbury v. Madison *began after John Adams, a lame-duck president, had appointed John Marshall to be Chief Justice and Thomas Jefferson had ascended to the presidency. Federal Justice of the Peace positions had been created near the end of the Adams presidency, and the commissions, which were duly signed and sealed for these "midnight judgeship" positions, were to be delivered by Adams's Secretary of State (one John Marshall!). Some of the commissions were not delivered before Adams left office, and Jefferson's new Secretary of State, James Madison, refused to deliver them. William Marbury's appointment to one of these positions was not consummated, and he sought an order (a writ of mandamus) in an original action before the Supreme Court to force Madison to deliver the commission.*

In the Court's opinion, Marshall recognizes that mandamus is an appropriate remedy for Marbury; however, the Court is not empowered in an original

---

From *Marbury v. Madison* by J. Marshall, 1 Cranch 137 (1803).

action to issue mandamus under the Constitution. Thus, the Judiciary Act, which granted the Court such mandamus power, had unconstitutionally tried to alter the Court's original jurisdiction, That is, the Court's original jurisdiction was spelled out in the Constitution, and congressional power over the Court's jurisdiction only extended, according to the explicit words of the Constitution, to the Court's appellate role. Congress had overstepped its authority and Marshall and the Court declared the legislative action unconstitutional, thereby establishing precedent for the Court's power of judicial review. In the Court's refusal to grant Mr. Marbury the writ of mandamus, Jefferson and Madison had won the battle over Marbury's commission. Much more importantly, however, history demonstrates that John Marshall had won the war for judicial supremacy in interpreting the Constitution.

Mr. Chief Justice Marshall delivered the opinion of the court.

At the last term on the affidavits then read and filed with the clerk, a rule was granted in this case, requiring the secretary of state to show cause why a mandamus should not issue, directing him to deliver to William Marbury his commission as a justice of the peace for the county of Washington, in the District of Columbia.

No cause has been shown, and the present motion is for a mandamus. The peculiar delicacy of this case, the novelty of some of its circumstances, and the real difficulty attending the points which occur in it, require a complete exposition of the principles on which the opinion to be given by the court is founded....

In the order in which the court has viewed this subject, the following questions have been considered and decided.

1st. Has the applicant a right to the commission he demands?

2d. If he has a right, and that right has been violated, do the laws of his country afford him a remedy?

3d. If they do afford him a remedy, is it a mandamus issuing from this court?

The first object of inquiry is,

1st. Has the applicant a right to the commission he demands?

His right originates in an act of congress passed in February, 1801, concerning the District of Columbia.

After dividing the district into two counties, the 11th section of this law enacts, "that there shall be appointed in and for each of the said counties, such number of discreet persons to be justices of the peace as the President of the United States shall, from time to time, think expedient, to continue in office for five years."

It appears, from the affidavits, that in compliance with this law, a commission for William Marbury, as a justice of the peace for the county of Washington, was signed by John Adams, then President of the United States; after which the seal of the United States was affixed to it; but the commission has never reached the person for whom it was made out.

In order to determine whether he is entitled to this commission, it becomes necessary to inquire whether he has been appointed to the office. For if he has been appointed, the law continues him in office for five years, and he is entitled to the possession of those evidences of office, which, being completed, became his property....

This is an appointment made by the President, by and with the advice and consent of the senate, and is evidenced by no act but the commission itself. In such a case, therefore, the commission and the appointment seem inseparable....

The appointment being the sole act of the President, must be completely evidenced, when it is shown that he has done everything to be performed by him....

The last act to be done by the President is the signature of the commission. He has then acted on the advice and consent of the senate to his own nomination. The time for deliberation has then passed. He has decided. His judgment, on the advice and consent of the senate concurring with his nomination, has been made, and the officer is appointed. This appointment is evidenced by an open, unequivocal act; and being the last act required from the person making it, necessarily excludes the idea of its being, so far as respects the appointment, an inchoate and incomplete transaction.

Some point of time must be taken when the power of the executive over an officer, not removable at his will, must cease. That point of time must be when the constitutional power of appointment has been exercised. And this power has been exercised when the last act, required from the person possessing the power, has been performed. This last act is the signature of the commission....

The commission being signed, the subsequent duty of the secretary of state is prescribed by law, and not to be guided by the will of the president. He is to affix the seal of the United States to the commission, and is to record it....

It is the duty of the secretary of state to conform to the law, and in this he is an officer of the United States, bound to obey the laws.... It is a ministerial act which the law enjoins on a particular officer for a particular purpose....

The appointment is the sole act of the President; the transmission of the commission is the sole act of the officer to whom that duty is assigned, and may be accelerated or retarded by circumstances which can have no influence on the appointment. A commission is transmitted to a person already appointed; not to a person to be appointed or not, as the letter enclosing the commission should happen to get into the post office and reach him in safety, or to miscarry....

It is, therefore, decidedly the opinion of the court, that when a commission has been signed by the President, the appointment is made; and that the commission is complete when the seal of the United States has been affixed to it by the Secretary of State....

The discretion of the executive is to be exercised until the appointment has been made. But having once made the appointment, his power over the office is terminated in all cases, where by law the officer is not removable by him. The right to the office is then in the person appointed, and he has the absolute, unconditional power of accepting or rejecting it.

Mr. Marbury, then, since his commission was signed by the President, and sealed by the Secretary of State, was appointed; and as the law creating the office, gave the officer a right to hold for five years, independent of the executive, the appointment was not revocable, but vested in the officer legal rights, which are protected by the laws of his country.

To withhold his commission, therefore, is an act deemed by the court not warranted by law, but violative of a vested legal right.

This brings us to the second inquiry; which is,

2d. If he has a right, and that right has been violated, do the laws of this country afford him a remedy?

The very essence of civil liberty certainly consists in the right of every individual to claim the protection of the laws, whenever he receives an injury. One of the first duties of government is to afford that protection. In Great Britain the king himself is sued in the respectful form of a petition, and he never fails to comply with the judgment of his court. . . .

The government of the United States has been emphatically termed a government of laws, and not of men. It will certainly cease to deserve this high appellation, if the laws furnish no remedy for the violation of a vested legal right.

If this obloquy is to be cast on the jurisprudence of our country, it must arise from the peculiar character of the case.

It behooves us, then, to inquire whether there be in its composition any ingredient which shall exempt it from legal investigations, or exclude the injured party from legal redress. . . .

The power of nominating to the senate, and the power of appointing the person nominated, are political powers, to be exercised by the President according to his own discretion. When he has made an appointment, he has exercised his whole power, and his discretion has been completely applied to the case. . . . [A]s a fact which has existed cannot be made never to have existed, the appointment cannot be annihilated; and consequently, if the officer is by law not removable at the will of the President, the rights he has acquired are protected by the law, and are not resumable by the President. They can not be extinguished by executive authority, and he has the privilege of asserting them in like manner as if they had been derived from any other source.

The question whether a right has vested or not, is, in its nature, judicial and must be tried by the judicial authority. . . .

So, if [Marbury] conceives that, by virtue of his appointment, he has a legal right either to the commission which has been made out for him, or to a copy of that commission, it is equally a question examinable in a court, and the decision of the court upon it must depend on the opinion entertained of his appointment.

That question has been discussed, and the opinion is, that the latest point of time which can be taken as that at which the appointment was complete, and evidenced, was when, after the signature of the President, the seal of the United States was affixed to the commission.

It is, then, the opinion of the Court,

1st. That by signing the commission of Mr. Marbury, the President of the United States appointed him a justice of peace for the county of Washington, in the District of Columbia; and that the seal of the United States, affixed thereto by the Secretary of State, is conclusive testimony of the verity of the signature, and of the completion of the appointment, and that the appointment conferred on him a legal right to the office for the space of five years.

2d. That, having this legal title to the office, he has a consequent right to the commission; a refusal to deliver which is a plain violation of that right, for which the laws of his country afford him a remedy.

It remains to be inquired whether,

3d. He is entitled to the remedy for which he applies. This depends on,

1st. The nature of the writ applied for; and,

2d. The power of this court.

1st. The nature of the writ.

Blackstone, in the 3d volume of his Commentaries, page 110, defines a mandamus to be "a command issuing in the king's name from the court of king's bench, and directed to any person, corporation, or inferior court of judicature within the king's dominions, requiring them to do some particular thing therein specified, which appertains to their office and duty, and which the court of king's bench has previously determined, or at least supposes, to be consonant to right and justice.". . .

This writ, if awarded, would be directed to an officer of government, and its mandate to him would be, to use the words of Blackstone, "to do a particular thing therein specified, which appertains to his office and duty, and which the court has previously determined, or at least supposes, to be consonant to right and justice." Or, in the words of Lord Mansfield, the applicant, in this case, has a right to execute an office of public concern, and is kept out of possession of that right....

It has already been stated that the applicant has, to that commission, a vested legal right, of which the executive cannot deprive him. He has been appointed to an office, from which he is not removable at the will of the executive; and being so appointed, he has a right to the commission which the secretary has received from the President for his use....

This, then, is a plain case for a mandamus, either to deliver the commission, or a copy of it from the record; and it only remains to be inquired,

Whether it can issue from this court.

The act to establish the judicial courts of the United States authorizes the Supreme Court "to issue writs of mandamus in cases warranted by the principles and usages of law, to any courts appointed, or persons holding office, under the authority of the United States."

The Secretary of State, being a person holding an office under the authority of the United States, is precisely within the letter of the description, and if this court is not authorized to issue a writ of mandamus to such an officer, it must be because the law is unconstitutional, and therefore absolutely incapable of conferring the authority, and assigning the duties which its words purport to confer and assign.

The constitution vests the whole judicial power of the United States in one Supreme Court, and such inferior courts as Congress shall, from time to time, ordain and establish. This power is expressly extended to all cases arising under the laws of the United States; and, consequently, in some form, may be exercised over the present case; because the right claimed is given by a law of the United States.

In the distribution of this power it is declared that "the Supreme Court shall have original jurisdiction in all cases affecting ambassadors, other public ministers and consuls, and those in which a state shall be a party. In all other cases, the Supreme Court shall have appellate jurisdiction."

It has been insisted, at the bar, that as the original grant of jurisdiction, to the Supreme and inferior courts, is general, and the clause, assigning original jurisdiction to the Supreme Court, contains no negative or restrictive words, the power remains to the legislature, to assign original jurisdiction to that court in other cases than those specified in the article which has been recited; provided those cases belong to the judicial power of the United States.

If it had been intended to leave it in the discretion of the legislature to apportion the judicial power between the Supreme and inferior courts according to the will of that body, it would certainly have been useless to have proceeded further than to have defined the judicial power, and the tribunals in which it should be vested. The subsequent part of the section is mere surplusage, is entirely without meaning, if such is to be the construction. If congress remains at liberty to give this court appellate jurisdiction, where the constitution has declared their jurisdiction shall be original; and original jurisdiction where the constitution has declared it shall be appellate; the distribution of jurisdiction, made in the constitution, is form without substance.

Affirmative words are often, in their operation, negative of other objects than those affirmed; and in this case, a negative or exclusive sense must be given to them, or they have no operation at all.

It cannot be presumed that any clause in the constitution is intended to be without effect; and, therefore, such a construction is inadmissible, unless the words require it....

When an instrument organizing fundamentally a judicial system, divides it into one Supreme, and so many inferior courts as the legislature may ordain and establish; then enumerates its powers, and proceeds so far to distribute them, as to define the jurisdiction of the Supreme Court by declaring the cases in which it shall take original jurisdiction, and that in others it shall take appellate jurisdiction; the plain import of the words seems to be, that in one class of cases its jurisdiction is original, and not appellate; in the other it is appellate, and not original....

To enable this court, then, to issue a mandamus, it must be shown to be an exercise of appellate jurisdiction, or to be necessary to enable them to exercise appellate jurisdiction....

It is the essential criterion of appellate jurisdiction, that it revises and corrects the proceedings in a cause already instituted, and does not create that cause.... [Y]et to issue such a writ to an officer for the delivery of a paper, is in effect the same as to sustain an original action for that paper, and, therefore, seems not to belong to appellate, but to original jurisdiction....

The authority, therefore, given to the Supreme Court, by the act establishing the judicial courts of the United States, to issue writs of mandamus to public officers, appears not to be warranted by the constitution; and it becomes necessary to inquire whether a jurisdiction so conferred can be exercised.

The question, whether an act, repugnant to the constitution, can become the law of the land, is a question deeply interesting to the United States; but, happily, not of an intricacy proportioned to its interest. It seems only necessary to recognize certain principles, supposed to have been long and well established, to decide it.

That the people have an original right to establish, for their future government, such principles, as, in their opinion, shall most conduce to their own happiness is the basis on which the whole American fabric has been erected. The exercise of this original right is a very great exertion; nor can it, nor ought it, to be frequently repeated. The principles, therefore, so established, are deemed fundamental. And as the authority from which they proceed is supreme, and can seldom act, they are designed to be permanent.

This original and supreme will organizes the government, and assigns to different departments their respective powers. It may either stop here, or establish certain limits not to be transcended by those departments.

The government of the United States is of the latter description. The powers of the legislature are defined and limited; and that those limits may not be mistaken, or forgotten, the constitution is written. To what purpose are powers limited, and to what purpose is that limitation committed to writing, if these limits may, at any time, be passed by those intended to be restrained? The distinction between a government with limited and unlimited powers is abolished, if those limits do not confine the persons on whom they are imposed, and if acts prohibited and acts allowed, are of equal obligation. It is a proposition too

plain to be contested, that the constitution controls any legislative act repugnant to it; or, that the legislature may alter the constitution by an ordinary act.

Between these alternatives there is no middle ground. The constitution is either a superior paramount law, unchangeable by ordinary means, or it is on a level with ordinary legislative acts, and, like other acts, is alterable when the legislature shall please to alter it.

If the former part of the alternative be true, then a legislative act contrary to the constitution is not law: if the latter part be true, then written constitutions are absurd attempts, on the part of the people, to limit a power in its own nature illimitable.

Certainly all those who have framed written constitutions contemplate them as forming the fundamental and paramount law of the nation, and, consequently, the theory of every such government must be, that an act of the legislature, repugnant to the constitution, is void.

This theory is essentially attached to a written constitution, and, is consequently, to be considered, by this court, as one of the fundamental principles of our society. It is not therefore to be lost sight of in the further consideration of this subject.

If an act of the legislature, repugnant to the constitution, is void, does it, notwithstanding its invalidity, bind the courts, and oblige them to give it effect? Or, in other words, though it be not law, does it constitute a rule as operative as if it was a law? This would be to overthrow in fact what was established in theory; and would seem, at first view, an absurdity too gross to be insisted on....

It is emphatically the province and duty of the judicial department to say what the law is. Those who apply the rule to particular cases, must of necessity expound and interpret that rule. If two laws conflict with each other, the courts must decide on the operation of each.

So if a law be in opposition to the constitution; if both the law and the constitution apply to a particular case, so that the court must either decide that case conformably to the law, disregarding the constitution; or conformably to the constitution, disregarding the law; the court must determine which of these conflicting rules governs the case. This is of the very essence of judicial duty.

If, then, the courts are to regard the constitution, and the constitution is superior to any ordinary act of the legislature, the constitution, and not such ordinary act, must govern the case to which they both apply.

Those, then, who controvert the principle that the constitution is to be considered, in court, as a paramount law, are reduced to the necessity of maintaining that courts must close their eyes on the constitution, and see only the law.

This doctrine would subvert the very foundation of all written constitutions. It would declare that an act which, according to the principles and theory of our government, is entirely void, is yet, in practice, completely obligatory. It would declare that if the legislature shall do what is expressly forbidden, such act, notwithstanding the express prohibition, is in reality effectual. It would be given to the legislature a practical and real omnipotence, with the same breath which professes to restrict their powers within narrow limits. It is prescribing limits, and declaring that those limits may be passed at pleasure.

That it thus reduces to nothing what we have deemed the greatest improvement on political institutions, a written constitution, would of itself be sufficient, in America, where written constitutions have been viewed with so much reverence, for rejecting the construction. But the peculiar expressions of the constitution of the United States furnish additional arguments in favour of its rejection.

The judicial power of the United States is extended to all cases arising under the constitution.

Could it be the intention of those who gave this power, to say that in using it the constitution should not be looked into? That a case arising under the constitution should be decided without examining the instrument under which it arises?

This is too extravagant to be maintained.

In some cases, then, the constitution must be looked into by the judges. And if they can open it at all, what part of it are they forbidden to read or to obey?....

Why does a judge swear to discharge his duties agreeably to the constitution of the United States, if that constitution forms no rule for his government? If it is closed upon him, and cannot be inspected by him?

If such be the real state of things, this is worse than solemn mockery. To prescribe, or to take this oath, becomes equally a crime.

It is also not entirely unworthy of observation, that in declaring what shall be the supreme law of the land, the constitution itself is first mentioned; and not the laws of the United States generally, but those only which shall be made in pursuance of the constitution, have that rank.

Thus, the particular phraseology of the constitution of the United States confirms and strengthens the principle, supposed to be essential to all written constitutions, that a law repugnant to the constitution is void; and that courts, as well as other departments, are bound by that instrument.

READING 7

McCulloch v. *Maryland* (1819)

John Marshall

McCulloch v. Maryland (1819) is often considered to be Chief Justice John Marshall's greatest piece of judicial craftsmanship and his most far-reaching nationalizing decision. In offering an elaborate rationale for national supremacy, Marshall's opinion goes well beyond the substantive question at hand of whether Congress is empowered to charter a national bank.

The federal bank was opposed strongly by the anti-Federalists as an abuse of national power, and several states passed laws that severely regulated and restricted local branch operations of the federal bank. In this instance, Maryland's taxing policy would jeopardize the bank's very existence. Under federal orders McCulloch, a federal bank cashier, refused to pay the Maryland state tax. In a Maryland state court, a judgment was returned against McCulloch, and the case was appealed to the U. S. Supreme Court.

From *McCulloch* v. *Maryland* by J. Marshall, 4 Wheat 316 (1819).

Marshall's decision posits a theory of the American union centering on expansive readings of the Constitution's "necessary and proper" and "supremacy" clauses. The opinion finds that the federal government is empowered to charter the bank and, as importantly, that the bank cannot be taxed by the states.

More important than Marshall's substantive holding per se about the legitimacy of the federal bank, which was expected, was his constitutional rationale. The logic of constitutionalism dictates that the existence of the whole (the union) cannot be jeopardized by its parts (the states). The opinion portrays the Constitution's formulation as a constituent act, a covenant of the American people, and not simply an agreement among sovereign states. The Court emerges not as a neutral umpire of disputes between the federal government and the states but, rather, as a protector of national sovereignty.

Mr. Chief Justice Marshall delivered the opinion of the court.

In the case now to be determined, the defendant, a sovereign State, denies the obligation of a law enacted by the legislature of the Union, and the plaintiff, on his part, contests the validity of an act which has been passed by the legislature of that State. The constitution of our country, in its most interesting and vital parts, is to be considered; the conflicting powers of the government of the Union and of its members, as marked in that constitution, are to be discussed; and an opinion given, which may essentially influence the great operations of the government. No tribunal can approach such a question without a deep sense of its importance, and of the awful responsibility involved in its decision. . . . On the Supreme Court of the United States has the constitution of our country devolved this important duty.

The first question made in the cause is, has Congress power to incorporate a bank?

It has been truly said, that this can scarcely be considered as an open question, entirely unprejudiced by the former proceedings of the nation respecting it. The principle now contested was introduced at a very

early period of our history, has been recognized by many successive legislatures, and has been acted upon by the judicial department, in cases of peculiar delicacy, as a law of undoubted obligation. . . .

The power now contested was exercised by the first Congress elected under the present constitution. . . . The original act was permitted to expire; but a short experience of the embarrassments to which the refusal to revive it exposed the government, convinced those who were most prejudiced against the measure of its necessity, and induced the passage of the present law. It would require no ordinary share of intrepidity to assert that a measure adopted under these circumstances was a bold and plain usurpation, to which the constitution gave no countenance.

These observations belong to the cause; but they are not made under the impression that, were the question entirely new, the law would be found irreconcilable with the constitution.

In discussing this question, the counsel for the State of Maryland have deemed it of some importance, in the construction of the constitution, to consider that instrument not as emanating from the people, but as the act of sovereign and independent States. The powers of the general government, it has been said, are delegated by the States, who alone are truly sovereign; and must be exercised in subordination to the States, who alone possess supreme dominion.

It would be difficult to sustain this proposition. The Convention which framed the constitution was indeed elected by the State legislatures. But the instrument, when it came from their hands, was a mere proposal, without obligation, or pretensions to it. It was reported to the then existing Congress of the United States, with a request that it might "be submitted to a Convention of Delegates, chosen in each State by the people thereof, under the recommendation of its Legislature, for their assent and ratification." This mode of proceeding was adopted; and by the Convention, by Congress, and by the State Legislatures, the instrument was submitted to the people. They acted upon it in the only manner in which they can act safely, effectively, and wisely, on such a subject, by assembling in Convention. It is true, they assembled in their several States—and where else should they have assembled? No political dreamer was ever wild enough to think of breaking down the lines which separate the States, and of compounding the American people into one common mass. Of consequence, when they act, they act in their States. But the measures they adopt do not, on that account, cease to be the measures of the people themselves, or become the measures of the State governments.

From these Conventions the constitution derives its whole authority. The government proceeds directly from the people; is "ordained and established" in the name of the people; and is declared to be ordained, "in order to form a more perfect union, establish justice, ensure domestic tranquillity, and secure the blessings of liberty to themselves and to their posterity." The assent of the States, in their sovereign capacity, is implied in calling a Convention, and thus submitting that instrument to the people. But the people were at perfect liberty to accept or reject it; and their act was final. It required not the affirmance, and could not be negatived, by the State governments. The constitution, when thus adopted, was of complete obligation, and bound the State sovereignties....

The government of the Union, then ... is, emphatically, and truly, a government of the people. In form and in substance it emanates from them. Its powers are granted by them, and are to be exercised directly on them, and for their benefit.

This government is acknowledged by all to be one of enumerated powers. The principle, that it can exercise only the powers granted to it ... is now universally admitted. But the question respecting the extent of the powers actually granted, is perpetually arising, and will probably continue to arise, as long as our system shall exist.

In discussing these questions, the conflicting powers of the general and State governments must be brought into view, and the supremacy of their respective laws, when they are in opposition, must be settled.

If any one proposition could command the universal assent of mankind, we might expect it would be this—that the government of the Union, though limited in its powers, is supreme within its sphere of action. This would seem to result necessarily from its nature. It is the government of all; its powers are delegated by all; it represents all, and acts for all.... The nation, on those subjects on which it can act, must

necessarily bind its component parts. But this question is not left to mere reason: the people have, in express terms, decided it, by saying, "this constitution, and the laws of the United States, which shall be made in pursuance thereof," "shall be the supreme law of the land," and by requiring that the members of the State legislatures, and the officers of the executive and judicial departments of the States, shall take the oath of fidelity to it.

The government of the United States, then, though limited in its powers, is supreme; and its laws, when made in pursuance of the constitution, form the supreme law of the land, "any thing in the constitution or laws of any State to the contrary notwithstanding."

Among the enumerated powers, we do not find that of establishing a bank or creating a corporation. But there is no phrase in the instrument which, like the articles of confederation, excludes incidental or implied powers; and which requires that every thing granted shall be expressly and minutely described. Even the 10th amendment, which was framed for the purpose of quieting the excessive jealousies which had been excited, omits the word "expressly," and declares only that the powers "not delegated to the United States, nor prohibited to the States, are reserved to the States or to the people;" thus leaving the question, whether the particular power which may become the subject of contest has been delegated to the one government, or prohibited to the other, to depend on a fair construction of the whole instrument. The men who drew and adopted this amendment had experienced the embarrassments resulting from the insertion of this word in the articles of confederation, and probably omitted it to avoid those embarrassments. A constitution, to contain an accurate detail of all the subdivisions of which its great powers will admit, and of all the means by which they may be carried into execution, would partake of the prolixity of a legal code, and could scarcely be embraced by the human mind. It would probably never be understood by the public. Its nature, therefore, requires, that only its great outlines should be marked, its important objects designated, and the minor ingredients which compose those objects be deduced from the nature of the objects themselves. That this idea was entertained by the framers of the American constitution, is not only to be inferred from the nature of the instrument, but from the language.... It is also, in some degree, warranted by their having omitted to use any restrictive term which might prevent its receiving a fair and just interpretation. In considering this question, then, we must never forget, that it is a *constitution* we are expounding.

Although, among the enumerated powers of government, we do not find the word "bank" or "incorporation," we find the great powers to lay and collect taxes; to borrow money; to regulate commerce; to declare and conduct a war; and to raise and support armies and navies. The sword and the purse, all the external relations, and no inconsiderable portion of the industry of the nation, are entrusted to its government. It can never be pretended that these vast powers draw after them others of inferior importance, merely because they are inferior. Such an idea can never be advanced. But it may with great reason be contended, that a government, entrusted with such ample powers, on the due execution of which the happiness and prosperity of the nation so vitally depends, must also be entrusted with ample means for their execution. The power being given, it is the interest of the nation to facilitate its execution. It can never be their interest, and cannot be presumed to have been their intention, to clog and embarrass its execution by withholding the most appropriate means. Throughout this vast republic, from the St. Croix to the Gulph of Mexico, from the Atlantic to the Pacific, revenue is to be collected and expended, armies are to be marched and supported. The exigencies of the nation may require that the treasure raised in the north should be transported to the south, *that* raised in the east conveyed to the west, or that this order should be reversed. Is that construction of the constitution to be preferred which would render these operations difficult, hazardous, and expensive? Can we adopt that construction (unless the words imperiously require it), which would impute to the framers of that instrument, when granting these powers for the public good, the intention of impeding their exercise by withholding a choice of means? If, indeed, such be the mandate of the constitution, we have only to obey; but that instrument does not profess to enumerate the means by which the powers it confers may be executed; nor does it prohibit the creation of a

corporation, if the existence of such a being be essential to the beneficial exercise of those powers....

The government which has a right to do an act, and has imposed on it the duty of performing that act, must, according to the dictates of reason, be allowed to select the means; and those who contend that it may not select any appropriate means, that one particular mode of effecting the object is excepted, take upon themselves the burden of establishing that exception.

The creation of a corporation, It is said, appertains to sovereignty. This is admitted. But to what portion of sovereignty does it appertain? Does it belong to one more than to another? In America, the powers of sovereignty are divided between the government of the Union, and those of the States. They are each sovereign, with respect to the objects committed to it, and neither sovereign with respect to the objects committed to the other.... The power of creating a corporation, though appertaining to sovereignty, is not, like the power of making war, or levying taxes, or of regulating commerce, a great substantive and independent power, which cannot be implied as incidental to other powers, or used as a means of executing them. It is never the end for which other powers are exercised, but a means by which other objects are accomplished.... The power of creating a corporation is never used for its own sake, but for the purpose of effecting something else. No sufficient reason is, therefore, perceived, why it may not pass as incidental to those powers which are expressly given, if it be a direct mode of executing them.

But the constitution of the United States has not left the right of Congress to employ the necessary means, for the execution of the powers conferred on the government, to general reasoning. To its enumeration of powers is added that of making "all laws which shall be necessary and proper, for carrying into execution the foregoing powers, and all other powers vested by this constitution, in the government of the United States, or in any department thereof."

The counsel for the State of Maryland have urged various arguments, to prove that this clause, though in terms a grant of power, is not so in effect; but is really restrictive of the general right, which might otherwise be implied, of selecting means for executing the enumerated powers....

[T]he argument on which most reliance is placed, is drawn from the peculiar language of this clause. Congress is not empowered by it to make all laws, which may have relation to the powers conferred on the government, but such only as may be *"necessary and proper"* for carrying them into execution. The word *"necessary,"* is considered as controlling the whole sentence, and as limiting the right to pass laws for the execution of the granted powers, to such as are indispensable, and without which the power would be nugatory. That it excludes the choice of means, and leaves to Congress, in each case, that only which is most direct and simple.

Is it true, that this is the sense in which the word "necessary" is always used? Does it always import an absolute physical necessity, so strong, that one thing, to which another may be termed necessary, cannot exist without that other? We think it does not. If reference be had to its use, in the common affairs of the world, or in approved authors, we find that it frequently imports no more than that one thing is convenient, or useful, or essential to another. To employ the means necessary to an end, is generally understood as employing any means calculated to produce the end, and not as being confined to those single means, without which the end would be entirely unattainable.... This word, then, like others, is used in various senses; and, in its construction, the subject, the context, the intention of the person using them, are all to be taken into view.

Let this be done in the case under consideration. The subject is the execution of those great powers on which the welfare of a nation essentially depends. It must have been the intention of those who gave these powers, to insure, as far as human prudence could insure, their beneficial execution. This could not be done by confining the choice of means to such narrow limits as not to leave it in the power of Congress to adopt any which might be appropriate, and which were conducive to the end. This provision is made in a constitution intended to endure for ages to come, and, consequently, to be adapted to the various *crises* of human affairs. To have prescribed the means by which government should, in all future time, execute its powers, would have been to change, entirely, the character of the instrument, and give it the properties of a legal code. It would have been an unwise attempt to provide, by immutable rules, for exigencies which, if foreseen at all, must have been seen dimly, and which can be best provided for as they occur. To have declared that the best means shall not be used, but those alone without which the power given would be nugatory, would have been to deprive the legislature of the capacity to avail itself of experience, to exercise its reason, and to accommodate its legislation to circumstances. If we apply this principle of construction to any of the powers of the government, we shall find it so pernicious in its operation that we shall be compelled to discard it....

Take, for example, the power "to establish post offices and post roads." This power is executed by the single act of making the establishment. But, from this has been inferred the power and duty of carrying the mail along the post road, from one post office to another. And, from this implied power, has again been inferred the right to punish those who steal letters from the post office, or rob the mail. It may be said, with some plausibility, that the right to carry the mail, and to punish those who rob it, is not indispensably necessary to the establishment of a post office and post road. This right is indeed essential to the beneficial exercise of the power, but not indispensably necessary to its existence....

The baneful influence of this narrow construction on all the operations of the government, and the absolute impracticability of maintaining it without rendering the government incompetent to its great objects, might be illustrated by numerous examples drawn from the constitution, and from our laws....

But the argument which most conclusively demonstrates the error of the construction contended for by the counsel for the State of Maryland, is founded on the intention of the Convention, as manifested in the whole clause.... This clause, as construed by the State of Maryland, would abridge, and almost annihilate this useful and necessary right of the legislature to select its means. That this could not be intended, is, we should think, had it not been already controverted, too apparent for controversy. We think so for the following reasons:

1st. The clause is placed among the powers of Congress, not among the limitations on those powers.

2nd. Its terms purport to enlarge, not to diminish the powers vested in the government. It purports to be an additional power, not a restriction on those already granted.... Had the intention been to make this clause restrictive, it would unquestionably have been so in form as well as in effect....

We admit, as all must admit, that the powers of the government are limited, and that its limits are not to be transcended. But we think the sound construction of the constitution must allow to the national legislature that discretion, with respect to the means by which the powers it confers are to be carried into execution, which will enable that body to perform the high duties assigned to it, in the manner most beneficial to the people. Let the end be legitimate, let it be within the scope of the constitution, and all means which are appropriate, which are plainly adapted to that end, which are not prohibited, but consist with the letter and spirit of the constitution, are constitutional.

Should Congress, in the execution of its powers, adopt measures which are prohibited by the constitution; or should Congress, under the pretext of executing its powers, pass laws for the accomplishment of objects not entrusted to the government; it would become the painful duty of this tribunal, should a case requiring such a decision come before it, to say that such an act was not the law of the land. But where the law is not prohibited, and is really calculated to effect any of the objects entrusted to the government, to undertake here to inquire into the degree of its necessity, would be to pass the line which circumscribes the judicial department, and to tread on legislative ground. This Court disclaims all pretensions to such a power....

After the most deliberate consideration, it is the unanimous and decided opinion of this Court, that the act to incorporate the Bank of the United States is a law made in pursuance of the constitution, and is a part of the supreme law of the land.

The branches, proceeding from the same stock, and being conducive to the complete accomplishment of the object, are equally constitutional....

It being the opinion of the Court, that the act incorporating the bank is constitutional; and that the power of establishing a branch in the State of Maryland might be properly exercised by the bank itself, we proceed to inquire—

2. Whether the State of Maryland may, without violating the constitution, tax that branch?

That the power of taxation is one of vital importance; that it is retained by the States; that it is not abridged by the grant of a similar power to the government of the Union; that it is to be concurrently exercised by the two governments: are truths which have never been denied. But, such is the paramount character of the constitution, that its capacity to withdraw any subject from the action of even this power, is admitted.... A law, absolutely repugnant to another, as entirely repeals that other as if express terms of repeal were used.

On this ground the counsel for the bank place its claim to be exempted from the power of a State to tax its operations. There is no express provision for the case, but the claim has been sustained on a principle which so entirely pervades the constitution, is so intermixed with the materials which compose it, so interwoven with its web, so blended with its texture, as to be incapable of being separated from it, without rending it into shreds.

This great principle is, that the constitution and the laws made in pursuance thereof are supreme; that they control the constitution and laws of the respective States, and cannot be controlled by them. From this, which may be almost termed an axiom, other propositions are deduced as corollaries.... These are, 1st. that a power to create implies a power to preserve. 2nd. That a power to destroy, if wielded by a different hand, is hostile to, and incompatible with these powers to create and to preserve. 3d. That where this repugnancy exists, that authority which is supreme must control, not yield to that over which it is supreme....

The power of Congress to create, and of course to continue, the bank, was the subject of the preceding part of this opinion; and is no longer to be considered as questionable.

That the power of taxing it by the States may be exercised so as to destroy it, is too obvious to be denied. But taxation is said to be an absolute power, which acknowledges no other limits than those expressly prescribed in the constitution.... But the very terms of this argument admit that the sovereignty of the State, in the article of taxation itself, is subordinate to, and may be controlled by the constitution of the

United States.... It is of the very essence of supremacy to remove all obstacles to its action within its own
sphere, and so to modify every power vested in subordinate governments, as to exempt its own operations
from their own influence. This effect need not be
stated in terms. It is so involved in the declaration of
supremacy, so necessarily implied in it, that the expression of it could not make it more certain....

It is admitted that the power of taxing the people
and their property is essential to the very existence of
government, and may be legitimately exercised on
the objects to which it is applicable, to the utmost extent to which the government may chuse to carry
it.... In imposing a tax the legislature acts upon its
constituents. This is in general a sufficient security
against erroneous and oppressive taxation.

The people of a State, therefore, give to their
government a right of taxing themselves and their
property, and as the exigencies of government cannot
be limited, they prescribe no limits to the exercise of
this right, resting confidently on the interest of the
legislator, and on the influence of the constituents
over their representative, to guard them against its
abuse. But the means employed by the government of
the Union have no such security, nor is the right of a
State to tax them sustained by the same theory. Those
means are not given by the people of a particular
State, not given by the constituents of the legislature,
which claim the right to tax them, but by the people
of all the States. They are given by all, for the benefit
of all—and upon theory, should be subjected to that
government only which belongs to all....

The sovereignty of a State extends to every thing
which exists by its own authority, or is introduced by
its permission; but does it extend to those means
which are employed by Congress to carry into execution powers conferred on that body by the people of
the United States? We think it demonstrable that it
does not. Those powers are not given by the people of
a single State. They are given by the people of the
United States, to a government whose laws, made in
pursuance of the constitution, are declared to be supreme. Consequently, the people of a single State cannot confer a sovereignty which will extend over them.

If we measure the power of taxation residing in a
State, by the extent of sovereignty which the people of

a single State possess, and can confer on its government, we have an intelligible standard, applicable to
every case to which the power may be applied. We
have a principle which leaves the power of taxing the
people and property of a State unimpaired; which
leaves to a State the command of all its resources, and
which places beyond its reach, all those powers which
are conferred by the people of the United States on the
government of the Union, and all those means which
are given for the purpose of carrying those powers
into execution. We have a principle which is safe for
the States, and safe for the Union....

That the power to tax involves the power to destroy; that the power to destroy may defeat and render
useless the power to create; that there is a plain repug-
nance, in conferring on one government a power to
control the constitutional measures of another, which
other, with respect to those very measures, is declared
to be supreme over that which exerts the control, are
propositions not to be denied....

Would the people of any one State trust those of
another with a power to control the most insignificant
operations of their State government? We know they
would not. Why, then, should we suppose that the
people of any one State should be willing to trust
those of another with a power to control the operations of a government to which they have confided
their most important and most valuable interests? In
the legislature of the Union alone, are all represented.
The legislature of the Union alone, therefore, can be
trusted by the people with the power of controlling
measures which concern all, in the confidence that it
will not be abused....

If we apply the principle for which the State of
Maryland contends, to the constitution generally, we
shall find it capable of changing totally the character of
that instrument. We shall find it capable of arresting all
the measures of the government, and of prostrating it
at the foot of the States. The American people have declared their constitution, and the laws made in pursuance thereof, to be supreme; but this principle would
transfer the supremacy, in fact, to the States.

If the States may tax one instrument, employed
by the government in the execution of its powers,
they may tax any and every other instrument. They
may tax the mail; they may tax the mint; they may tax

patent rights; they may tax the papers of the custom-house; they may tax judicial process; they may tax all the means employed by the government, to an excess which would defeat all the ends of government. This was not intended by the American people. They did not design to make their government dependent on the States. . . .

The question is, in truth, a question of suprem-acy; and if the right of the States to tax the means em-ployed by the general government be conceded, the declaration that the constitution, and the laws made in pursuance thereof, shall be the supreme law of the land, is empty and unmeaning declamation. . . .

It has also been insisted, that, as the power of taxation in the general and State governments is ac-knowledged to be concurrent, every argument which would sustain the right of the general government to tax banks chartered by the States, will equally sustain the right of the States to tax banks chartered by the general government.

But the two cases are not on the same reason. The people of all the States have created the general gov-ernment, and have conferred upon it the general power of taxation. The people of all the States, and the States themselves, are represented in Congress, and, by their representatives, exercise this power. When they tax the chartered institutions of the States, they tax their con-stituents; and these taxes must be uniform. But, when a State taxes the operations of the government of the United States, it acts upon institutions created, not by their own constituents, but by people over whom they claim no control. It acts upon the measures of a gov-ernment created by others as well as themselves, for the benefit of others in common with themselves. The difference is that which always exists, and always must exist, between the action of the whole on a part, and the action of a part on the whole—between the laws of a government declared to be supreme, and those of a government which, when in opposition to those laws, is not supreme. . . .

The Court has bestowed on this subject its most deliberate consideration. The result is a conviction that the States have no power, by taxation or other-wise, to retard, impede, burden, or in any manner con-trol, the operations of the constitutional laws enacted by Congress to carry into execution the powers vested

in the general government. This is, we think, the un-avoidable consequence of that supremacy which the constitution has declared.

We are unanimously of opinion, that the law passed by the legislature of Maryland, imposing a tax on the Bank of the United States, is unconstitutional and void.

READING 8

The Constitution of the United States: Contemporary Ratification

William J. Brennan, Jr.

William J. Brennan, Jr., was the first Supreme Court justice born in the twentieth century and the most senior sitting justice when he retired in 1990. Brennan served on the Court for over three decades and was a prominent spokesperson for the liberal activism of the bygone Warren Court era. In 1985, while still on the Court, Brennan delivered this very controversial public lecture in which he laid bare his expansive position on the judge's role in interpreting the Constitution.

In Brennan's view, the Constitution (including the Bill of Rights and the Civil War amendments) is a document embodying the framers' aspirations for social justice and human dignity. The constitutional text is not completely clear and the interpretive responsibility of the judge is to render a "public reading" of the document, speaking on behalf of the community's quest for human dignity. This calls, of course, for more than private moral reflection on the part of the judge, and the ever present possibility exists that judicial interpretation will counteract the majority will as expressed in legislation, the "countermajoritarian difficulty" that, at times,

From "The Constitution of the United States: Contemporary Rati-fication" by W. J. Brennan, Jr., 1985, Text and Teaching Sympo-sium, Georgetown University, October 12, 1985. Reprinted by permission.

confronts judicial choice. For Brennan, however, the alternative to exercising such choice, leaving all substantive value choices to majority will, is equally problematic because our democratic system tempers majority rule with minority rights.

The most controversial facet of Brennan's constitutional striving for human dignity occurs when judicial interpretation overrides common notions of community values, for example, in his dissents against capital punishment that represents, for Brennan, the state's treating humans as something less than human. Brennan argues that, "when a Justice perceives an interpretation of the text to have departed so far from its essential meaning, the Justice is bound, by a larger constitutional duty to the community, to expose the departure and point toward a different path." In doing so, it is Brennan's hope "to embody a community striving for human dignity for all, although perhaps not yet arrived."

It will perhaps not surprise you that the text I have chosen for exploration is the amended Constitution of the United States, which, of course, entrenches the Bill of Rights and the Civil War amendments.... So fashioned, the Constitution embodies the aspiration to social justice, brotherhood, and human dignity that brought this nation into being. The Declaration of Independence, the Constitution and the Bill of Rights solemnly committed the United States to be a country where the dignity and rights of all persons were equal before all authority. In all candor we must concede that part of this egalitarianism in America has been more pretension than realized fact. But we are an aspiring people, a people with faith in progress. Our amended Constitution is the lodestar for our aspirations. Like every text worth reading, it is not crystalline. The phrasing is broad and the limitations of its provisions are not clearly marked. Its majestic generalities and ennobling pronouncements are both luminous and obscure. This ambiguity of course calls forth interpretation, the interaction of reader and text. The encounter with the Constitutional text has been, in many senses, my life's work....

[M]y encounters with the constitutional text are not purely or even primarily introspective; the Constitution cannot be for me simply a contemplative haven for private moral reflection. My relation to this great text is inescapably public. That is not to say that my reading of the text is not a personal reading, only that the personal reading perforce occurs in a public context, and is open to critical scrutiny from all quarters.

The Constitution is fundamentally a public text—the monumental charter of a government and a people—and a Justice of the Supreme Court must apply it to resolve public controversies. For, from our beginnings, a most important consequence of the constitutionally created separation of powers has been the American habit, extraordinary to other democracies, of casting social, economic, philosophical and political questions in the form of law suits, in an attempt to secure ultimate resolution by the Supreme Court. In this way, important aspects of the most fundamental issues confronting our democracy may finally arrive in the Supreme Court for judicial determination. Not infrequently, these are the issues upon which contemporary society is most deeply divided. They arouse our deepest emotions. The main burden of my twenty-nine Terms on the Supreme Court has thus been to wrestle with the Constitution in this heightened public context, to draw meaning from the text in order to resolve public controversies.

Two other aspects of my relation to this text warrant mention. First, constitutional interpretation for a federal judge is, for the most part, obligatory. When litigants approach the bar of court to adjudicate a constitutional dispute, they may justifiably demand an answer. Judges cannot avoid a definitive interpretation because they feel unable to, or would prefer not to, penetrate to the full meaning of the Constitution's provisions....

Second, consequences flow from a Justice's interpretation in a direct and immediate way. A judicial decision ... is not simply a contemplative exercise in defining the shape of a just society. It is an order—supported by the full coercive power of the State—that the present society change in a fundamental aspect.... One does not forget how much may depend on the decision. More than the litigants may be affected. The course of vital social, economic and political currents may be directed.

These three defining characteristics of my relation to the constitutional text—its public nature, obligatory character, and consequentialist aspect—cannot help but influence the way I read that text. When Justices interpret the Constitution they speak for their community, not for themselves alone. The act of interpretation must be undertaken with full consciousness that it is, in a very real sense, the community's interpretation that is sought. Justices are not platonic guardians appointed to wield authority according to their personal moral predelictions. Precisely because coercive force must attend any judicial decision to countermand the will of a contemporary majority, the Justices must render constitutional interpretations that are received as legitimate. The source of legitimacy is, of course, a well-spring of controversy in legal and political circles. At the core of the debate is what the late Yale Law School professor Alexander Bickel labeled "the counter-majoritarian difficulty." Our commitment to self-governance in a representative democracy must be reconciled with vesting in electorally unaccountable Justices the power to invalidate the expressed desires of representative bodies on the ground of inconsistency with higher law. Because judicial power resides in the authority to give meaning to the Constitution, the debate is really a debate about how to read the text, about constraints on what is legitimate interpretation.

There are those who find legitimacy in fidelity to what they call "the intentions of the Framers." In its most doctrinaire incarnation, this view demands that Justices discern exactly what the Framers thought about the question under consideration and simply follow that intention in resolving the case before them. It is a view that feigns self-effacing deference to the specific judgments of those who forged our original social compact. But in truth it is little more than arrogance cloaked as humility. It is arrogant to pretend that from our vantage we can gauge accurately the intent of the Framers on application of principle to specific, contemporary questions. All too often, sources of potential enlightenment such as records of the ratification debates provide sparse or ambiguous evidence of the original intention. Typically, all that can be gleaned is that the Framers themselves did not agree about the application or meaning of particular constitutional provisions, and hid their differences in cloaks of generality. Indeed, it is far from clear whose intention is relevant—that of the drafters, the congressional disputants, or the ratifiers in the states?—or even whether the idea of an original intention is a coherent way of thinking about a jointly drafted document drawing its authority from a general assent of the states. And apart from the problematic nature of the sources, our distance of two centuries cannot but work as a prism refracting all we perceive....

Perhaps most importantly, while proponents of this facile historicism justify it as a depoliticization of the judiciary, the political underpinnings of such a choice should not escape notice. A position that upholds constitutional claims only if they were within the specific contemplation of the Framers in effect establishes a presumption of resolving textual ambiguities against the claim of constitutional right. It is far from clear what justifies such a presumption against claims of right.... This is a choice no less political than any other; it expresses antipathy to claims of the minority to rights against the majority. Those who would restrict claims of right to the values of 1789 specifically articulated in the Constitution turn a blind eye to social progress and eschew adaptation of overarching principles to changes of social circumstance.

Another, perhaps more sophisticated, response to the potential power of judicial interpretation stresses democratic theory: because ours is a government of the people's elected representatives, substantive value choices should by and large be left to them. This view emphasizes not the transcendent historical authority of the Framers but the predominant contemporary authority of the elected branches of government. Yet it has similar consequences for the nature of proper judicial interpretation. Faith in the majoritarian process counsels restraint. Even under more expansive formulations of this approach, judicial review is appropriate only to the extent of ensuring that our democratic process functions smoothly....

The view that all matters of substantive policy should be resolved through the majoritarian process has appeal under some circumstances, but I think it ultimately will not do. Unabashed enshrinement of majority will would permit the imposition of a social caste system or wholesale confiscation of property so long as a majority of the authorized legislative body, fairly elected, approved. Our Constitution could not abide such a situation. It is the very purpose of a Constitution—and particularly of the Bill of Rights—to declare certain values transcendent, beyond the reach of temporary political majorities. The majoritarian process cannot be expected to rectify claims of minority right that arise as a response to the outcomes of that very majoritarian process. As James Madison put it:

> The prescriptions in favor of liberty ought to be levelled against that quarter where the greatest danger lies, namely, that which possesses the highest prerogative of power. But this is not found in either the Executive or Legislative departments of Government, but in the body of the people, operating by the majority against the minority.

Faith in democracy is one thing, blind faith quite another. Those who drafted our Constitution understood the difference. One cannot read the text without admitting that it embodies substantive value choices; it places certain values beyond the power of any legislature. Obvious are the separation of powers; the privilege of the Writ of Habeas Corpus; prohibition of Bills of Attainder and ex post facto laws; prohibition of cruel and unusual punishments; the requirement of just compensation for official taking of property; the prohibition of laws tending to establish religion or enjoining the free exercise of religion; and since the Civil War, the banishment of slavery and official race discrimination....

To remain faithful to the content of the Constitution, therefore, an approach to interpreting the text must account for the existence of these substantive value choices, and must accept the ambiguity inherent in the effort to apply them to modern circumstances. The Framers discerned fundamental principles through struggles against particular malefactions of the Crown; the struggle shapes the particular contours of the articulated principles. But our acceptance of the fundamental principles has not and should not bind us to those precise, at times anachronistic, contours....

Thus, if I may borrow the words of an esteemed predecessor, Justice Robert Jackson, the burden of judicial interpretation is to translate "the majestic generalities of the Bill of Rights, conceived as part of the pattern of liberal government in the eighteenth century, into concrete restraints on officials dealing with the problems of the twentieth century."

We current Justices read the Constitution in the only way that we can: as Twentieth Century Americans. We look to the history of the time of framing and to the intervening history of interpretation. But the ultimate question must be, what do the words of the text mean in our time. For the genius of the Constitution rests not in any static meaning it might have had in a world that is dead and gone, but in the adaptability of its great principles to cope with current problems and current needs. What the constitutional fundamentals meant to the wisdom of other times cannot be their measure to the vision of our time. Similarly, what those fundamentals mean for us, our descendants will learn, cannot be the measure to the vision of their time. This realization is not, I assure you, a novel one of my own creation. Permit me to quote from one of the opinions of our Court, *Weems* v. *United States,* written nearly a century ago:

> Time works changes, brings into existence new conditions and purposes. Therefore, a principle to be vital must be capable of wider application than the mischief which gave it birth. This is peculiarly true of constitutions. They are not ephemeral enactments, designed to meet passing occasions. They are, to use the words of Chief Justice John Marshall, "designed to approach immortality as nearly as human institutions can approach it." The future is their care and provision for events of good and bad tendencies of which no prophesy can be made. In the application of a constitution, therefore, our contemplation cannot be only of what has been, but of what may be.

Interpretation must account for the transformative purpose of the text. Our Constitution was not intended to preserve a preexisting society but to make a new one, to put in place new principles that the prior political community had not sufficiently recognized. Thus, for example, when we interpret the Civil War Amendments to the charter—abolishing slavery, guaranteeing blacks equality under law, and guaranteeing blacks the right to vote—we must remember that those who put them in place had no desire to enshrine the status quo. Their goal was to make over their world, to eliminate all vestige of slave caste.

Having discussed at some length how I, as a Supreme Court Justice, interact with this text, I think it time to turn to the fruits of this discourse. For the Constitution is a sublime oration on the dignity of man, a bold commitment by a people to the ideal of libertarian dignity protected through law. . . .

The Constitution on its face is, in large measure, a structuring text, a blueprint for government. And when the text is not prescribing the form of government it is limiting the powers of that government. The original document, before addition of any of the amendments, does not speak primarily of the rights of man, but of the abilities and disabilities of government. When one reflects upon the text's preoccupation with the scope of government as well as its shape, however, one comes to understand that what this text is about is the relationship of the individual and the state. The text marks the metes and bounds of official authority and individual autonomy. When one studies the boundary that the text marks out, one gets a sense of the vision of the individual embodied in the Constitution.

As augmented by the Bill of Rights and the Civil War Amendments, this text is a sparkling vision of the supremacy of the human dignity of every individual. This vision is reflected in the very choice of democratic self-governance: the supreme value of a democracy is the presumed worth of each individual. And this vision manifests itself most dramatically in the specific prohibitions of the Bill of Rights, a term which I henceforth will apply to describe not only the original first eight amendments, but the Civil War Amendments as well. It is a vision that has guided us as a people throughout our history, although the precise rules by which we have protected fundamental human dignity have been transformed over time in response to both transformations of social condition and evolution of our concepts of human dignity.

Until the end of the nineteenth century, freedom and dignity in our country found meaningful protection in the institution of real property. In a society still largely agricultural, a piece of land provided men not just with sustenance but with the means of economic independence, a necessary precondition of political independence and expression. Not surprisingly, property relationships formed the heart of litigation and of legal practice, and lawyers and judges tended to think stable property relationships the highest aim of the law.

But the days when common law property relationships dominated litigation and legal practice are past. . . . Government participation in the economic existence of individuals is pervasive and deep. . . . We turn to government and to the law for controls which would never have been expected or tolerated before this century, when a man's answer to economic oppression or difficulty was to move two hundred miles west. Now hundreds of thousands of Americans live entire lives without any real prospect of the dignity and autonomy that ownership of real property could confer. Protection of the human dignity of such citizens requires a much modified view of the proper relationship of individual and state.

In general, problems of the relationship of the citizen with government have multiplied and thus have engendered some of the most important constitutional issues of the day. As government acts ever more deeply upon those areas of our lives once marked "private," there is an even greater need to see that individual rights are not curtailed or cheapened in the interest of what may temporarily appear to be the "public good." And as government continues in its role of provider for so many of our disadvantaged citizens, there is an even greater need to ensure that government act with integrity and consistency in its dealings with these citizens. To put this another way, the possibilities for collision between government activity and individual rights will increase as the power and authority of government itself expands, and this growth, in turn, heightens the need for constant vigilance at the collision points. If our free society is to endure, those who govern must recognize human dignity and accept the enforcement of constitutional limitations on their power conceived by the Framers to be necessary to preserve that dignity and the air of freedom which is our proudest heritage. . . . Solutions of constitutional questions from that perspective have become the great challenge of the modern era. All the talk in the last half-decade about shrinking the government does not alter this reality or the challenge it imposes. The modern activist state is a concomitant of the complexity of modern society; it is inevitably with us. We must meet the challenge rather than wish it were not before us.

The challenge is essentially, of course, one to the capacity of our constitutional structure to foster and protect the freedom, the dignity, and the rights of all persons within our borders, which it is the great design of the Constitution to secure. During the time of my public service this challenge has largely taken shape within the confines of the interpretive question whether the specific guarantees of the Bill of Rights operate as restraints on the power of State government. We recognize the Bill of Rights as the primary source of express information as to what is meant by constitutional liberty.... The first eight Amendments, however, were added to the Constitution to operate solely against federal power. It was not until the Thirteenth and Fourteenth Amendments were added, in 1865 and 1868, in response to a demand for national protection against abuses of state power, that the Constitution could be interpreted to require application of the first eight Amendments to the states.

It was in particular the Fourteenth Amendment's guarantee that no person be deprived of life, liberty or property without process of law that led us to apply many of the specific guarantees of the Bill of Rights to the States. In my judgment, Justice Cardozo best captured the reasoning that brought us to such decisions when he described what the Court has done as a process by which the guarantees "have been taken over from the earlier articles of the federal bill of rights and brought within the Fourteenth Amendment by a process of absorption ... [that] has had its source in the belief that neither liberty nor justice would exist if [those guarantees] ... were sacrificed." But this process of absorption was neither swift nor steady.... As late as 1961, I could ... list the following as guarantees that had not been thought to be sufficiently fundamental to the protection of human dignity so as to be enforced against the states: the prohibition of cruel and unusual punishments, the right against self-incrimination, the right to assistance of counsel in a criminal trial, the right to confront witnesses, the right to compulsory process, the

right not to be placed in jeopardy of life or limb more than once upon accusation of a crime, the right not to have illegally obtained evidence introduced at a criminal trial, and the right to a jury of one's peers.

The history of the [last] quarter century ... need not be told in great detail. Suffice it to say that each of the guarantees listed above has been recognized as a fundamental aspect of ordered liberty. Of course, the above catalogue encompasses only the rights of the criminally accused, those caught, rightly or wrongly, in the maw of the criminal justice system. But it has been well said that there is no better test of a society than how it treats those accused of transgressing against it....

Of course the constitutional vision of human dignity has, in this past quarter century, infused far more than our decisions about the criminal process. Recognition of the principle of "one person, one vote" as a constitutional one redeems the promise of self-governance by affirming the essential dignity of every citizen in the right to equal participation in the democratic process. Recognition of so-called "new property" rights in those receiving government entitlements affirms the essential dignity of the least fortunate among us by demanding that government treat with decency, integrity and consistency those dependent on its benefits for their very survival. After all, a legislative majority initially decides to create governmental entitlements; the Constitution's Due Process Clause merely provides protection for entitlements thought necessary by society as a whole. Such due process rights prohibit government from imposing the devil's bargain of bartering away human dignity in exchange for human sustenance. Likewise, recognition of full equality for women—equal protection of the laws—ensures that gender has no bearing on claims to human dignity.

Recognition of broad and deep rights of expression and of conscience reaffirm the vision of human dignity in many ways. They too redeem the promise of self-governance by facilitating—indeed demanding—robust, uninhibited and wide-open debate on issues of public importance.... In our democracy, such discussion is a political duty; it is the essence of self-government. The constitutional vision of human dignity rejects the possibility of political orthodoxy imposed from above; it respects the right of each individual to form and to express political judgments, however far they may deviate from the mainstream and however unsettling they might be to the powerful or the elite. Recognition of these rights of expression and conscience also frees up the private space for both intellectual and spiritual development free of government dominance, either blatant or subtle. Justice Brandeis put it so well sixty years ago when he wrote: "Those who won our independence believed that the final end of the State was to make men free to develop their faculties; and that in its government the deliberative forces should prevail over the arbitrary. They valued liberty both as an end and as a means."

I do not mean to suggest that we have in the last quarter century achieved a comprehensive definition of the constitutional ideal of human dignity. We are still striving toward that goal, and doubtless it will be an eternal quest. For if the interaction of this Justice and the constitutional text over the years confirms any single proposition, it is that the demands of human dignity will never cease to evolve.

Indeed, I cannot in good conscience refrain from mention of one grave and crucial respect in which we continue, in my judgment, to fall short of the constitutional vision of human dignity. It is in our continued tolerance of State-administered execution as a form of punishment....

As I interpret the Constitution, capital punishment is under all circumstances cruel and unusual punishment prohibited by the Eighth and Fourteenth Amendments.... Much discussion of the merits of capital punishment has in recent years focused on the potential arbitrariness that attends its administration, and I have no doubt that such arbitrariness is a grave wrong. But for me, the wrong of capital punishment transcends such procedural issues. As I have said in my opinions, I view the Eighth Amendment's prohibition of cruel and unusual punishments as embodying to a unique degree moral principles that substantively restrain the punishments our civilized society may impose on those persons who transgress its laws. Foremost among the moral principles recognized in our cases and inherent in the prohibition is the primary principle that the State, even as it punishes, must treat its citizens in a manner consistent with their intrinsic worth as human beings. A punishment must not be so severe as to be utterly and irreversibly degrading to the very essence of human dignity.... The calculated killing of a human being by the State involves, by its very nature, an absolute denial of the executed person's humanity. The most vile murder does not, in my view, release the State from constitutional restraints on the destruction of human dignity. Yet an executed person has lost the very right to have rights, now or ever. For me, then, the fatal constitutional infirmity of capital punishment is that it treats members of the human race as nonhumans, as objects to be toyed with and discarded. It is, indeed, "cruel and unusual...."

This is an interpretation to which a majority of my fellow Justices—not to mention, it would seem, a majority of my fellow countrymen—does not subscribe. Perhaps you find my adherence to it, and my recurrent publication of it, simply contrary, tiresome, or quixotic. Or perhaps you see in it a refusal to abide by the judicial principle of *stare decisis,* obedience to precedent. In my judgment, however, the unique interpretive role of the Supreme Court with respect to the Constitution demands some flexibility with respect to the call of *stare decisis.* Because we are the last word on the meaning of the Constitution, our views must be subject to revision over time, or the Constitution falls captive, again, to the anachronistic views of long-gone generations. I mentioned earlier the judge's role in seeking out the community's interpretation of the constitutional text. Yet, again in my judgment, when a Justice perceives an interpretation of the text to have departed so far from its essential meaning, that Justice is bound, by a larger constitutional duty to the community, to expose the departure and point toward a different path. On this issue, the death penalty, I hope to embody a community striving for human dignity for all, although perhaps not yet arrived.

You have doubtless observed that this description of my personal encounter with the constitutional text has in large portion been a discussion of public developments in constitutional doctrine over the last quarter century. That, as I suggested at the outset, is inevitable because my interpretive career has demanded a public reading of the text. This public encounter with the text, however, has been a profound source of personal inspiration. The vision of human dignity embodied there is deeply moving. It is timeless. It has inspired Americans for two centuries and it will continue to inspire as it continues to evolve. That evolutionary process is inevitable and, indeed, it is the true interpretive genius of the text. If we are to be as a shining city upon a hill, it will be because of our ceaseless pursuit of the constitutional ideal of human dignity. For the political and legal ideals that form the foundation of much that is best in American institutions—ideals jealously preserved and guarded throughout our history—still form the vital force in creative political thought and activity within the nation today. As we adapt our institutions to the ever-changing conditions of national and international life, those ideals of human dignity—liberty and justice for all individuals—will continue to inspire and guide us because they are entrenched in our Constitution. The Constitution with its Bill of Rights thus has a bright future, as well as a glorious past, for its spirit is inherent in the aspirations of our people.

READING 9

How the Constitution Disappeared

Lino Graglia

Justice Brennan's speech responded to calls for a jurisprudence of original intention emanating from the Reagan administration during the 1980s. Lino Graglia, a conservative University of Texas law professor who reportedly was favored, considered, and ultimately blocked by his adversaries from receiving a judicial appointment during the Reagan years, issued a scathing philosophical critique best articulating the conservative position.

Graglia argues that the Court has become the nation's primary policymaker on social issues such as abortion, capital punishment, criminal procedure, obscenity, school prayer, busing, reapportionment, gender-based discrimination, libel, and other concerns. Judgments in these areas have run counter to majoritarian preferences and, Graglia argues, such judicial activism is antidemocratic.

The Brennan approach, dominating the Court for decades, is characterized as illegitimately counseling judges to go beyond the framers' intent to protect the populace from the excesses of democracy. Graglia takes issue with Brennan's open-ended, aspiring, rights oriented Constitution picturing, instead, a document concerned primarily with structuring government, establishing federalism, and protecting commercial interests. He argues further that if Brennan were correct about the obscurity or irrelevancy of the Constitution's original intent, the appropriate judicial response should not be interpretive activism but, rather, judicial self-restraint. Graglia also suggests that debates over constitutional interpretation are often smoke screens because, in his view, the issues the Court has been deciding (e.g., abortion and school busing) fall outside the realm of the Constitution's concern. Judicial decisions on such matters have frustrated the people's will and not implemented community values. The Court has rejected "political" (majoritarian or legislative) choices as the norm and substituted judicial policymaking in its place.

Whereas Brennan bases his position on the primacy of "human dignity," Graglia contends that the Court has deprived us of the most essential element of that dignity, self-governance. Obviously, Graglia's arguments are problematic for those placing greater emphasis than he does on the minority rights component of our constitutional system's establishment of limited majoritarianism.

Attorney General Edwin Meese's . . . statement in a speech to the American Bar Association that judges should interpret the Constitution to mean what it was originally intended to mean probably did not strike most people as controversial. Nevertheless it brought forth immediate denunciation by a sitting Supreme Court Justice as "doctrinaire," "arrogant," and the product of "facile historicism." "It is a view," Justice William J. Brennan, Jr. said... "that feigns self-effacing deference to the specific judgments of those who forged our original social compact," but that "in truth...is little more than arrogance cloaked as humility" because it is not possible to "gauge accurately the intent of the Framers on application of principle to specific, contemporary questions. The view is not only mistaken, but misguided, Justice Brennan continued, because it would require judges to turn a blind eye to social progress and eschew adaptation of overarching principles to changes of social circumstance.

To state that judges should interpret the Constitution as intended by those who wrote and ratified it ("the Framers") is only to state the basic premise of our political-legal system that the function of judges is to apply, not to make, the law. Indeed, it would be difficult to say what interpretation of a law means if not to determine the intent of the lawmaker. Justice Brennan's angry attack on the obvious as if it were disreputable...makes evident that much is at stake in this debate on a seemingly esoteric matter of constitutional interpretation. What is at stake is nothing less than the question of how the country should be governed in regard to basic issues of social policy: whether such issues should be decided by elected representatives of the people, largely on a state-by-state basis, or, as has been the case for the last three decades, primarily by a majority of the nine Justices of the United States Supreme Court for the nation as a whole.

The modern era of constitutional law began with the Supreme Court's 1954 decision in *Brown* v. *Board of Education,* holding compulsory school racial segregation and, it soon appeared, all racial discrimination by government, unconstitutional. The undeniable rightness of the decision as a matter of social policy...gained for the Court a status and prestige unprecedented in our history.... The result was to enable the Court to move from its historic role as a brake on social change to a very different role as the primary engine of such change.

In the years since *Brown,* nearly every fundamental change in domestic social policy has been brought about not by the decentralized democratic (or, more accurately, republican) process contemplated by the Constitution, but simply by the Court's decree. The Court has decided, on a national basis and often in opposition to the wishes of a majority of the American people, issues literally of life and death, as in its decisions invalidating virtually all restrictions on abortion and severely restricting the use of capital punishment. It has decided issues of public security and order, as in its decisions greatly expanding the protection of the criminally accused and limiting state power to control street demonstrations and vagrancy, and issues of public morality, as in the decisions disallowing most state controls of pornography, obscenity, and nudity. The Court has both prohibited the states from making provision for prayer in the schools and disallowed most forms of aid, state or federal, to religious schools. It has required that children be excluded from their neighborhood public schools and bused to more distant schools in order to increase school racial integration; ordered the reapportionment of state and federal legislatures on a "one-man-one-vote" basis; invalidated most of the law of libel and slander; and disallowed nearly all legal distinctions on the basis of sex, illegitimacy, and alienage. The list could easily be extended, but it should be clear that in terms of the issues that determine the nature and quality of life in a society, the Supreme Court has become our most important institution of government.

Since his appointment to the Court by President Eisenhower in 1956, Justice Brennan has...consistently voted in favor of Court intervention in the political process, and...he has ordinarily differed with the Court only in that he would often go even farther in disallowing political control of some issues.... [I]f the Court has been our most important institution of government for the past three decades, Justice Brennan— although his name is probably unknown to the great majority of his fellow citizens—has surely been our most important government official. To argue that the Supreme Court should confine itself or be confined to interpreting the Constitution as written is to...challenge the legitimacy of his life's work.

Constitutional law is as a practical matter the product of the exercise of the power of judicial review, the power of judges, and ultimately of Supreme Court Justices, to invalidate legislation and other acts of other officials and institutions of government as inconsistent with the Constitution. The central question presented by constitutional law—the only question the great variety of matters dealt with under that rubric have in common—is how, if at all, can such a power in the hands of national officials who are unelected and effectively hold office for life be justified in a system of government supposedly republican in form and federalist in organization? The power is not explicitly provided for in the Constitution and had no precedent in English law. . . . Alexander Hamilton argued for the power in *Federalist 78,* however, and Chief Justice John Marshall established it in *Marbury* v. *Madison* in 1803 on the ground that it is inherent in a written constitution that declares itself to be supreme law. . . .

The judges, Hamilton assured the ratifying states, would have neither "force nor will"; able to "take no active resolution whatever" in enforcing the Constitution, their power would be "next to nothing." "Judicial power," Marshall reiterated, "has no existence. Courts are mere instruments of the law, and can will nothing." . . .

Even Justice Brennan purports to recognize what, as he notes, Alexander Bickel called "the counter-majoritarian difficulty" presented by judicial review. . . . Supreme Court Justices, he acknowledges at the beginning of his speech, echoing Judge Learned Hand, "are not platonic guardians appointed to wield authority according to their personal moral predilections." At several points he even seems to offer the standard justification for judicial review, that the judges merely interpret the written Constitution. . . . These statements are consistent with the remainder of his speech, however, only if reading or interpreting a document is considered indistinguishable from composing or rewriting it. . . .

The view that the duty of judges is to read and interpret the Constitution—to attempt to determine what the Framers intended to say—is precisely the view that Justice Brennan seeks to rebut and derides as uninformed and misguided. The whole point of his speech is that judges should not be confined to that task, for so to confine them would be to give them much too limited a role in our system of government and leave us insufficiently protected from the dangers of majority rule.

Justice Brennan is far from alone today in his view of the proper role of judges in exercising judicial review and of the essential irrelevance of the Constitution to constitutional law. . . . Because it has become increasingly difficult—in fact, impossible—to justify the Court's controversial decisions as the result of constitutional interpretation, the bulk of modern constitutional-law scholarship consists of the invention and elaboration of "non-interpretivist" or "non-originalist" theories of judicial review—justifications for a judicial review that is not confined to constitutional interpretation in any sense that would effectively restrain judicial choice. Because the product of this review is nonetheless always called "constitutional law" and attributed in some way to the Constitution, the result is the paradox of non-interpretivist constitutional interpretation, constitutional law without the Constitution. . . .

Defenders of judicial activism face the dilemma that, on the one hand, judicial policy making cannot be defended as such in our system—the Justices, even Justice Brennan must concede, are not authorized to enact their personal moral predilections" into law and must therefore claim that their decisions derive somehow from the Constitution. On the other hand, it happens that the Constitution is most ill-suited as a basis for substantial judicial policy making by frequent judicial intervention in the political process in the name of protecting individual rights from majority rule. The central difficulty is that although the Constitution does create some individual rights, they are actually rather few, fairly well-defined, and rarely violated. The first task of the defender of judicial activism, therefore, is to dispose of the Constitution as unhelpful, inadequate, or irrelevant to contemporary needs. Reasons must be found why the Constitution cannot be taken to mean what it rather clearly is known to mean—especially when read, as all writings must be, in historical context—or, even better, to have any determinate meaning at all.

After disposing of the Constitution by depriving it of its historic meaning, the next task of defenders of judicial activism is to imagine a much more expansive, elevated, and abstract constitution that, having no specific meaning, can be made to mean anything and serve therefore as simply a mandate for judges to enact their versions of the public good. In response to the objection that the very thinly veiled system of government by judges thus achieved is obviously inconsistent with democracy, the argument is made that the value of democracy is easily over-rated and its dangers many. The "very purpose of a Constitution," as Justice Brennan states the standard argument, is to limit democracy by declaring "certain values transcendent, beyond the reach of temporary political majorities." In any event, no real inconsistency with democracy is involved, the argument concludes, because the judges, though unrestrained by the actual text of the Constitution, will continue to be restrained by its principles, the adaptation of which to changing circumstances is the true and indispensable function of judges....

Justice Brennan's attack on the notion of a constitution with a determinable historic meaning could hardly be more thorough.... It is almost as if the Constitution and its various provisions might have been drafted and adopted with no purpose at all....

Justice Brennan has still another, although it would seem unnecessary, nail to put in the coffin of the now demolished Constitution. Should any shred of constitutional meaning somehow survive the many obstacles he sees to finding it, he would accord it little or no value. The world of the Framers is "dead and gone," and it would not do, he believes, to hold the Constitution captive to the "anachronistic views of long-gone generations."...

Most of Justice Brennan's objections regarding the difficulties of constitutional interpretation have some basis, but they could also be made in regard to interpretation of almost any law.... In any event, from the premise of an unknowable or irrelevant Constitution, the conclusion should follow that judges have no basis or justification for declaring laws unconstitutional, not that they are therefore free to invalidate laws on some other basis and still claim to be interpreting the Constitution.

Most important, whatever the difficulties of legal interpretation, they have little or no relevance to actual constitutional decision-making by the Supreme Court because no issue of interpretation, no real dispute about the intended meaning of the Constitution, is ordinarily involved. For example, the Constitution contains no provision mentioning or apparently in any way referring to the authority of the states to regulate the practice of abortion. However one might undertake to defend the Court's abortion decisions, it does not seem possible to argue that they are the result of constitutional interpretation in any non-fanciful sense. As another example, although the Constitution does mention religion, no process that could be called interpretation permits one to go from the Constitution's protection of religious freedom from federal interference to the proposition that the states may not provide for prayer in the schools....

The constitution of Justice Brennan's vision is undoubtedly a wonderful thing, one of "great" and "overarching" principles and "majestic generalities and ennobling pronouncements [that] are both luminous and obscure." It is nothing less grand than the embodiment of "the aspiration to social justice, brotherhood, and human dignity that brought this nation into being," "a sublime oration on the dignity of man," and "a sparkling vision of the supremacy of the human dignity of every individual."...

The temptation is strong, of course, to dismiss Justice Brennan's rapturous statements as mere flights of poetic fancy or utopian ecstasy, obviously not meant as serious descriptions or explanations of the Constitution. The fact remains, however, that this view of the Constitution is the only justification offered by him, or other contemporary defenders of judicial activism, for the Court's assumption and exercise of enormous government power. Fanciful as it may seem, a constitution that is simply the embodiment of "our," or at least his, aspirations accurately describes the constitution he has been enforcing for nearly three decades to override the will of the people of this country on issue after issue. It cannot be too strongly emphasized, therefore, that the Constitution we actually have bears almost no relation to, and is often clearly irreconcilable with, the constitution of Justice Brennan's vision....

Although it may come as something of a disappointment to some, an "aspiration for social justice, brotherhood, and human dignity" happens not to have been what brought this nation, or at least the government founded on the Constitution, into being. The convention to revise the Articles of Confederation was called and the Constitution was drafted and ratified not to provide additional protections for human rights—on the contrary, the stronger national government created by the Constitution was correctly seen as a potential danger to human rights—but almost entirely for commercial purposes. The primary motivating force for the creation of a stronger national government was the felt need of a central authority to remove state-imposed obstacles to interstate trade. How little the Constitution had to do with aspirations for brotherhood or human dignity is perhaps most clearly seen in its several provisions regarding slavery.... [T]here was at the time the Constitution was adopted very little pretension to egalitarianism....

Given the original Constitution's limited and mundane purposes, it is not surprising that it provides judges with little to work with for the purpose of advancing their personal notions of social justice. The Constitution is, first of all, a very short document... and apparently quite simple and straightforward, not at all like a recondite tome in which many things may be found with sufficient study. The original Constitution is almost entirely devoted to outlining the structure of the national government.... It contains few provisions protecting individual rights from the national government—federalism, i.e., limited national power and a high degree of local autonomy, was considered the principal protection—and even fewer restrictions on the exercise of state power.... [T]he Framers, nicely illustrating their lack of egalitarian pretension, undertook to protect creditors from debtor-relief legislation by prohibiting the states from impairing contract rights.

The first eight of the first ten Amendments to the Constitution, the Bill of Rights adopted in 1791, provide additional protections of individual rights, but only against the federal government, not the states, and these, too, are fewer than seems to be generally imagined....

Additional protections of individual rights are provided by the post-Civil War Amendments.... The great bulk of constitutional litigation concerns state law and nearly all of that litigation purports to be based on a single sentence of the Fourteenth Amendment and, indeed, on one or the other of two pairs of words, "due process" and "equal protection." If the Constitution is the embodiment of our aspirations, it

must have become so very largely because of those four words. The clear historic purpose of the Fourteenth Amendment, however, was to provide federal protection against certain state discriminations on the basis of race, historically our uniquely intractable problem, but not otherwise to change fundamentally the constitutional scheme....

The Constitution's protections of individual rights are not only few but also, when read in historical context, fairly clear and definite. State and federal legislators, all of whom are American citizens living in America and generally at least as devoted as judges to American values, have, therefore, little occasion or desire to violate the Constitution. The result is that the enactment of a clearly unconstitutional law is an extremely rare occurrence.... If judicial review were actually confined to enforcing the Constitution as written, it would be a much less potent force than the judicial review argued for and practiced by Justice Brennan.

The Constitution is undoubtedly a great document, the foundation of one of the freest and most prosperous nations in history. It does not detract from that greatness to point out that it is not, however, what Justice Brennan would make of it, a compendium of majestic generalities and ennobling pronouncements luminous and obscure; indeed, its greatness and durability surely derive in large part from the fact that the Framers' aims were much more specific and limited. Far from intending to compose an oration to human dignity, the Framers would have considered that they had failed in their effort to specify and limit the power of the national government if the effect of the Constitution should be to transfer the focus of human rights concerns from the state to the national level. The Framers' solution to the problem of protecting human freedom and dignity was to preserve as much as possible, consistent with national commerce and defense requirements, a system of decentralized democratic decision-making, with the regulation of social conditions and personal relations left to the states. Justice Brennan's solution, virtually unlimited Supreme Court power to decide basic social issues for the nation as a whole, effectively disenfranchising the people of each state as to those issues, is directly contrary to the constitutional scheme.

Judicial review on the basis of a constitution divorced from historical meaning and viewed, instead, as simply "the lodestar for our aspirations" is obviously a prescription for policy-making by judges. It should therefore be defended, if at all, as such, free of obfuscating references to "interpretation" of the Constitution. The only real question it presents is, why should the American people prefer to have important social-policy issues decided for the whole nation by the Supreme Court—a committee of nine lawyers unelected to and essentially unremovable from office—rather than by the decentralized democratic process? Justice Brennan's answer to this question is, in essence, why not?...

To refuse to assume the validity of the acts of the electorally responsible officials and institutions of government is to refuse to assume the validity of representative self-government. It has, therefore, from the beginning been considered the bedrock of constitutional litigation that one who would have a court invalidate an act of the political branches must assume the burden of showing its inconsistency with the Constitution, ordinarily a most difficult task. By reversing the presumption of constitutionality, Justice Brennan would simply reject political decision-making as the norm and require elected representatives to justify their policy choices to the satisfaction of Supreme Court Justices, presumably by showing that those choices contribute to the Justices' notion of social progress.

Justice Brennan would justify the judicial supremacy he favors on the not entirely consistent grounds that, on the one hand, the Justices are the true voice of the people and, on the other, that the people are in any event not always to be trusted.... Justice Brennan does not explain why he thinks the community needs or wants unelected judges to speak for it instead or why the judges can be expected better to reflect or express the community's views.

The actual effect of most judicial rulings of unconstitutionality is, of course, not to implement, but to frustrate the community's views. For example, Justice Brennan would disallow capital punishment as constitutionally prohibited despite not only the fact that it is repeatedly provided for in the Constitution, but also the fact that it is favored by a large majority of the

American people. In some cases, however, he explains, a Justice may perceive the community's "interpretation of the text to have departed so far from its essential meaning" that he "is bound, by a larger constitutional duty to the community, to expose the departure and point toward a different path." On capital punishment, Justice Brennan hopes to "embody a community striving for human dignity for all, although perhaps not yet arrived." Interpreting an aspirational constitution apparently requires prescience as well as a high degree of self-confidence.

The foundation of all defenses of judicial activism, however, is not any fanciful notion that the judges are the true voice of the people, but on the contrary, the conviction that the people, and their elected representatives, should not be permitted to have the last word....

Legislative supremacy in policy making is derided by Justice Brennan as the "unabashed enshrinement of majority will." "Faith in democracy is one thing," he warns, but "blind faith quite another." "The view that all matters of substantive policy should be resolved through the majoritarian process has appeal," he concedes, but only "under some circumstances," and even as so qualified "it ultimately will not do." It will not do because the majority is simply not to be trusted.... How a people so bereft of good sense, toleration, and foresight as to adopt such policies could have adopted the Constitution in the first place is not explained.... It cannot be Justice Brennan's position that political wisdom died with the Framers and that we are therefore fortunate to have their policy judgments to restrain us.... Like other defenders of judicial activism, however, he seems to view the Constitution not as an actual document produced by actual people but as a metaphysical entity from an extraterrestrial source of greater authority than the mere wishes of a majority of the American people, which source, fortunately, is in effective communication with Supreme Court Justices.

The real protection against [Justice Brennan's] ... fears, however... is simply the good sense of the American people. No extraordinary degree of confidence in that good sense is necessary in order to believe that.... outrageous policies that are invariably offered as providing an unanswerable justification for judicial activism are so unlikely to be adopted as not to be a matter of serious concern. If they should be a matter of concern nonetheless. . . . the appropriate response would be the adoption of a constitutional amendment further limiting self-government in the relevant respects. To grant judges an unlimited power to rewrite the Constitution, Justice Brennan's recommended response, would be to avoid largely imaginary dangers of democratic misgovernment by creating a certainty of judicial misgovernment.

Judicial activism is not necessary to protect us from state-established churches, favored by almost no one, but it does operate to deprive the people of each state of the right to decide for themselves such real issues as whether provision should be made for prayer in the public schools. In any event, the issue presented by contemporary judicial activism is not whether majority rule is entirely trustworthy—all government power is obviously dangerous—or even whether certain specific constitutional limitations on majority rule might not be justifiable; the issue is whether freewheeling policy making by Supreme Court Justices, totally centralized and undemocratic, is more trustworthy than majority rule.

Defenders of judicial activism invariably match their skepticism about democratic policy making with a firm belief in the possibility and desirability of policy making on the basis of principle. To free judicial review from the constraint of a constitution with a determinate meaning is not to permit unrestrained judicial policy making in constitutional cases, it is argued, for the judges will continue to be constrained by the Constitution's principles, which, like the smile of the Cheshire cat, somehow survive the disappearance of the Constitution's text. According to this argument, judicial activism amounts to nothing more than the adaptation and application of these basic principles to changing circumstances, a necessary task if the Constitution is to remain a "living document" and a contributor rather than an obstacle to the national welfare. . . .

The argument that judges are constrained by constitutional principles, even though not by the constitutional text, bears no relation to reality. In the first place, it is not possible to formulate useful constitutional principles apart from or beyond the Constitu-

tion's actual provisions. . . . An even more basic fallacy is the argument's assumption that the solution of social problems lies in the discovery, adaptation, and application of preexisting principles to new situations. Difficult problems of social choice arise, however, not because of some failure to discern or adapt an applicable principle, but only because we have many principles, many interests we regard as legitimate, and they inevitably come into conflict. Some interests have to be sacrificed or compromised if other interests are to be protected . . . and there is no authoritatively established principle, rule, or generality that resolves the conflict. . . . Value judgments have to be made to solve real policy issues, and the meaning of self-government is that they are to be made in accordance with the collective judgment of those who will have to live with the results.

There is also very little basis for Justice Brennan's apparent belief that judicial review confined to the Constitution as written would somehow be incompatible with social progress—unless social progress is simply defined as the enactment of his views. . . .

Indeed, on the basis of our actual constitutional history—which includes the Supreme Court's disastrous decision that Congress could not prohibit the extension of slavery and, after the Civil War that decision helped bring on, the decision that Congress could not prohibit racial segregation in public places—it is possible to believe that social progress might go more smoothly without the Court's supposed adaptations of principles. If the Constitution can be said to have an overarching principle, the principle of federalism, of decision-making on most social-policy issues at the state level, is surely the best candidate, and that principle is not adapted or updated but violated by the Court's assertion of power to decide such issues. Far from keeping the Constitution a "living document," judicial activism threatens its demise.

Whatever merit Justice Brennan's justifications for judicial activism might have in theory, they do not seem relevant to the judicial activism actually practiced by the Supreme Court for the past three decades. It would be very difficult to justify the Court's major constitutional decisions during this period, and particularly its most controversial decisions, on any of the grounds Justice Brennan suggests. It would not seem possible to argue, for example, that the Justices spoke for the community, not for themselves, in reaching their decisions on abortion, busing, criminal procedure, and prayer in the schools. Nor does it seem that any of those decisions can be justified as providing a needed protection from a possible excess of democracy, as merely delaying effectuation of the aberrational enthusiasms of "temporary political majorities" until they could return to their senses. Judicial review may, as Chief Justice Harlan Fiske Stone put this standard rationalization, provide the people with an opportunity for a "sober second thought," but no amount of thought or experience is likely to change the view of the vast majority of the American people that, for example, their children should not be excluded from their neighborhood public schools because of their race or that no new protections of the criminally accused should be invented with the effect of preventing the conviction and punishment of the clearly guilty.

Finally, the contribution of most of the Court's constitutional decisions of recent decades to social progress . . . is at best debatable. Very few of these decisions, it seems, could be used to illustrate the adaptation of overarching constitutional principles or transcendent constitutional values to changing circumstances. They could probably more easily be used to illustrate that, rather than helping us to cope with current problems and current needs, the Court's constitutional decisions have often been the cause of those problems and needs.

Whatever the merits of the Supreme Court's constitutional decisions of the past three decades, they have as to the issues decided deprived us of perhaps the most essential element of the human dignity Justice Brennan is concerned to protect, the right of self-government, which necessarily includes the right to make what others might consider mistakes. It is not the critics of judicial activism but the activist judges who can more properly be charged with being doctrinaire and arrogant, for it is they who presume to know the answers to difficult questions of social policy and to believe that they provide a needed protection from government by the misguided or igno-

rant. An opponent of judicial activism need not claim to know the answer to so difficult a question of social policy as, say, the extent, if any, to which abortion should be restricted to know that it is shameful in a supposedly democratic country that such a question should be answered for all of us by unelected and unaccountable government officials who have no special competence to do so.

Blowing the Dust Off the Constitution That Was

Linda Greenhouse

For about half a century, debates about constitutional meaning have centered on the scope of individual rights in the context of far-reaching governmental powers, particularly at the national level. This interpretive focus was the legacy of the New Deal revolution's fostering of broad governmental authority in the domestic realm, coupled with the liberal decisions of the Warren Court of the 1950s and 1960s, which provided protections for the individual from an omnipresent government. In essence, debates about constitutional interpretation have centered on issues of rights, not powers.

Warren Burger's appointment to be Chief Justice in 1969, coupled with three other Nixon appointments, was predicted to be the catalyst for a critical turning point in constitutional interpretation, with the Warren Court's rights and liberties initiatives overturned by a solid conservative majority. Interestingly, while the Burger and even more recent Rehnquist Courts have constrained the expansive Warren Court holdings in areas such as criminal justice and the First Amendment, most major

From "Blowing the Dust Off the Constitution That Was" by L. Greenhouse, 1997. Reprinted from the *New York Times,* by permission; all rights reserved.

Warren Court rulings remain the law of the land. Further, Burger and Rehnquist Court majorities have ventured into issues largely untouched by their predecessors to expand individual protections in areas such as privacy (often implicated in abortion cases) and gender-based rights.

Throughout the Warren/Burger/Rehnquist era it has been taken for granted that fundamental questions regarding the scope of federal authority and federalism were settled. Much like a dormant volcano, however, that continues to bubble at the surface, voices for a more constrained federal government and expanded state power have been heard and, in some instances, commanded a Court majority. Such activity reached new heights in the Court's 1994–1995 term as described by New York Times *Supreme Court reporter Linda Greenhouse. Greenhouse documents a Court majority or near majority that appears to embrace an interpretive perspective rejected by Marshall's Court and obliterated by a much later Court's legitimation of the Roosevelt revolution's creation of the contemporary welfare state.*

At this writing it is, of course, impossible to predict whether these trends will blossom or be abated. Several rulings in the Court's 1996–1997 term, however, suggest that the phenomenon explored by Greenhouse is continuing. Most prominent among them was the Court's decision invalidating critical facets of the Brady Bill, the federal government's most sweeping effort at gun control, because the legislation overstepped its bounds in imposing enforcement responsibilities for the measure on the states. Further, it is equally important to recognize that underlying Greenhouse's analysis of contemporary debate rests a somewhat larger point. The U. S. Constitution is always in a state of "becoming," its definitive meaning never quite fixed and always subject to change.

The Supreme Court gift shop keeps stacks of pocket-sized Constitutions by the cash registers and sells them to tourists by the thousands each year. The little booklets are 35 pages long and are, of course, completely authentic. But when the Justices meet upstairs

to decide a case, the written Constitution is only one of several constitutions that are, in a manner of speaking, also on the table.

There is the body of precedent that defines the Constitution as currently understood.

There is the Constitution that once was, as defined by precedents that have been formally overruled or less formally placed on a shelf.

And there is, through a continual process of challenge and change dating back to the country's earliest years, another constitution struggling to be born.

GUN AND TERM LIMITS

Recent events at the Courts have moved that struggle to a new plane. Two 5-to-4 decisions...suggest that a long-discarded set of constitutional principles—a "Constitution-in-exile," to use a phrase coined by one of its advocates, Judge Douglas H. Ginsburg of the Federal appeals court here—is about to assume its place at the table as a reincarnation of the Constitution that was.

One of the decisions, United States v. Lopez, invalidated a Federal law that prohibited the possession of guns near a school. In doing so, the decision limited the scope of congressional power over interstate commerce for the first time since the New Deal.

The other decision, U.S. Term Limits v. Thornton, barely struck down state-imposed term limits for members of Congress over a startling dissent by Justice Clarence Thomas that argued not only that term limits are valid but also that the Federal Government operates in large measure at the sufferance of the states.

In an essay in...Regulation magazine, published by the Cato Institute, a libertarian think tank here, Judge Ginsburg offered an inventory of constitutional doctrines that the Court repudiated about 60 years ago when it began to endorse the exercise of national economic power at the heart of the New Deal.

Among these were the doctrine that had viewed as illegitimate the delegation of power by Congress to the administrative agencies; the demise of that doctrine was the prerequisite for the growth of the modern regulatory state. Another was the commerce clause, which the Court had viewed until the mid-1930's as a brake on the exercise of national power over the economy, rather than a charter for it. Another was the takings clause, which requires compensation when private property is "taken for public use" and which served as a limitation on Government land use regulation.

"The memory of these ancient exiles, banished for standing in opposition to unlimited government," Judge Ginsburg wrote, "is kept alive by a few scholars who labor on in the hope of a restoration, a second coming of the Constitution of liberty—even if perhaps not in their own lifetimes."

Those self referential words, written before the Lopez decision, now sound quaint. A full restoration may not be imminent, but this agenda is hardly in exile; it is, for the first time in more than a generation, in play. For example, a year ago, in Dolan v. City of Tigard, a 5-to-4 decision written by Chief Justice William H. Rehnquist took a significant step toward reinvigorating the takings clause by requiring a new degree of justification by local governments before they impose land use restrictions on property owners.

On another front, the 10th Amendment, which reserves to the states powers not given to the Federal Government by the Constitution, is in the ascendance, invoked most recently in a 1992 majority opinion by Justice Sandra Day O'Connor. In that case, New York v. United States, the Court struck down a Federal environmental law that required states either to regulate the low-level radioactive waste generated within their borders or to "take title" to the waste and assume all legal liability for it.

"States are not mere political subdivisions of the United States," Justice O'Connor said in concluding that the law infringed on state sovereignty.

Even if the Court remains unwilling to go so far as to dismantle the Federal Government as administrative state, overturn the string of precedents that extended the Bill of Rights from the Federal Government to the states, or sharply curb the scope of Federal preemption of state law—outcomes that still appear far-fetched if no longer completely inconceivable—the polarities of the debate have shifted.

The debate that has preoccupied modern constitutional law has been the question of rights: the right to privacy, to due process, to equal protection. Now the Court, for the first time in half a century, is engaging in a debate over power: where power resides in the Federal system and how the Constitution's grant of powers to the national Government is to be interpreted.

MARSHALL'S PLAN

That "the Federal Government's powers are limited and enumerated," as Justice Thomas said in his dissenting opinion last week, is almost a truism. Article 1, Section 8 gives Congress the power to impose taxes, regulate commerce, declare war, coin money, establish Federal courts below the Supreme Court level, protect copyrights, and so on.

The textual list, of course, begs the questions of interpretation. Is the list meant to be exclusive? How strictly are the enumerated powers to be read? Does Congress have implied powers, or is it limited to those expressly granted? What is the meaning of Section 8's final clause, granting Congress the right "to make all laws which shall be necessary and proper" for carrying out its powers?

These are ancient questions that Chief Justice John Marshall's opinions for the early Supreme Court had appeared to resolve in favor of a strong national government. The tone of Justice Thomas's dissent last week suggests that once again the assumptions underlying those early decisions' allocations of power are, to some members of the Court, far from self-evident truths.

One question now is how activist the current Justices are prepared to be in overturning precedent in order to bring their constitutional vision home. The Lopez decision, striking down the Federal Gun-Free School Zones Act, did not actually overturn any of the Court's commerce clause precedents. Rather, Chief Justice Rehnquist's majority opinion adopted a narrow definition of economic activity that made a more frontal assault unnecessary. But if the Lopez majority is serious, it will not be satisfied for long with what it can accomplish through indirection and redefinition.

A Federal Government whose authority was limited by the Constitution in exile could look dramatically different. If Congress could not delegate legislative authority to administrative agencies, a vast quantity of rules and regulations would wither along with the agencies that promulgated them. Land use and environmental regulation would be sharply curbed. The constitutional underpinning of Federal civil rights laws, based on the power of Congress to regulate interstate commerce, would be called into question.

The Constitution in exile is not the only vision competing with the status quo. Liberals have theirs, too, under which the Government would have affirmative obligations to guarantee housing and minimum subsistence; actions that have the effect of discrimination would be seen as violating the constitutional guarantee of equal protection even in the absence of an intent to discriminate; and constitutional norms that now apply only to government action would also apply in the private sector on the theory that there is no longer a meaningful distinction between the public and private spheres. Government would be seen as violating an individual's right to due process not only by actual misconduct but also by inaction, by a failure to protect citizens from foreseeable harm.

These principles cannot really be seen as a constitution in exile, because most have never been accepted as part of the Constitution. Rather, they make up a kind of shadow constitution that liberal scholars embrace as a natural extension of their golden age, the Supreme Court under Chief Justice Earl Warren, who retired in 1969.

Which golden age would Chief Justice Rehnquist and his allies in the Lopez majority—Justice Thomas and Justices O'Connor, Anthony M. Kennedy and Antonin Scalia—invoke if they had to select one?

Justice Kennedy, who departed from this group and deprived Justice Thomas of a majority in the term limits case, said in a concurring opinion in the Lopez case that "the wrong turn was the Court's dramatic departure in the 1930's" from the limited view of Congress's power that had lasted 150 years.

Was the golden age the Court of the 30's then? Or earlier than that, before the Civil War amendments brought the full meaning of the Constitution and the Bill of Rights home to the states? Or was it earlier still, before the Federalists won the ratification battle by which the Constitution became the law of the land? A question that would have sounded preposterous only weeks ago is now merely provocative.

FOOD FOR THOUGHT

1. Compare and contrast the views of William Brennan and Lino Graglia on the nature and meaning of the U. S. Constitution. Whose arguments do you find most compelling? Why? Based on your reading of John Marshall's opinions in *Marbury* v. *Madison* and *McCulloch* v. *Maryland,* whose view of the Constitution would he favor? Why?

2. John Marshall's ability to lead his Court and foster unanimous decisions as well as the longevity of his rulings can be traced, in part, to his use of logic and persuasiveness in making controversial and debatable questions appear to be self-evident and obvious propositions. Examine Marshall's *Marbury* and *McCulloch* opinions and identify five assertions that he presents as "fact" that, in the eyes of others, could be debatable. Does Marshall "succeed" in convincing you in each of these instances? Why or why not?

3. Users of this book have the luxury of experiencing the unfolding of events that postdate the writing of the articles that you are reading. In Linda Greenhouse's analysis of constitutional interpretation during the Court's 1994–1995 term she offers a snapshot of an emergent trend in the Court's decision making. Does that snapshot hold true today? (You may want to consult summaries of Court terms since the Greenhouse article to make your assessment. These are widely available in outlets such as the *New York Times, National Law Journal, Harvard Law Review,* weekly news magazines, and numerous other venues.) How do you account for the staying power or the changes in the trend in constitutional interpretation that Greenhouse examines. What, do you suppose, are the issues that will dominate constitutional interpretation in the foreseeable future? Why?

CHAPTER 3

CONTEMPORARY AMERICAN FEDERALISM AND THE AMERICAN POLITICAL TRADITION

Our readings on constitutional creation and constitutional interpretation have amply demonstrated that one of the core issues of debate in the American political system centers on efforts to define a working federal system, that is, an appropriate distribution of powers between the national (federal) government and the governments of the union's component states. At times the debate has been vitriolic and, at one juncture in American history, even exploded into a violent and devastating civil war. At other times, the "explosions" have been somewhat less dramatic, yet they have reflected fundamental disagreements of the highest order about the legitimate form of American democracy.

Surely one such example is the protracted constitutional crisis of the late 1930s during which the Roosevelt presidency, buoyed by a resounding electoral mandate and a compliant Congress, did battle with the Supreme Court over the legitimacy of the federal government's entry into the realm of social welfare policymaking. More recently, of course, the Gingrich-inspired conservative Congress explored ways of returning a large degree of authority, responsibility, and control over many social welfare policies, which had their genesis in the Roosevelt "New Deal," back to the states. For their part, many states have articulated great concern over the delegation of authority to them by the federal government in numerous policy domains without the granting of any resources to implement the policies, a phenomenon characterized as "unfunded mandates."

To be sure, federalism debates of today may lack the violence of the Civil War unless, of course, one wishes to view events such as the Branch Davidian conflagration, the bombing of the Federal Building in Oklahoma City, and the ongoing activities of groups, such as citizen militias and common law courts, as fundamental manifestations of opposition to the contemporary contours of American federalism. Similarly, today's federalism plotline may lack the drama of the New Deal Court battle, unless one considers the shutting down of the federal government in late 1995 following the failure of President Clinton and the Republican-controlled Congress to reach budgetary accommodation to be, to some degree, a protracted battle over the future direction of American federalism.

Throughout our focus on American federalism it is important to keep in mind that federalism is not a static construct but, rather, an ongoing system of interactive governmental processes. Clearly, there remain and likely will remain unsettled questions and areas of continued flux in the carving out of federal and state governmental relationships. The articles in this chapter serve to underscore the long-lasting bones of contention associated with contemporary American federalism, ranging from broad questions about the ideal balance between federal and state authority in the abstract to more concrete concerns regarding how government can best facilitate citizen rights and liberties, operate efficiently, foster economic growth, and pursue policy experimentation.

Most of the contributions in this chapter are argumentative in tone, with authors staking out their position on the nation–state continuum quickly and clearly. Indeed save, perhaps, for essays by Paul Peterson and Martha Derthick, the readings offered below may appear to lack analytical balance and subtlety.

For example, Henry Steele Commager argues in *Tocqueville's Mistakes* that it is the national government

73

that has been associated with the expansion of liberty and citizen rights, while threats to liberty and freedom have tended to emanate from the states. The recitation of state excesses offered here is quite on the mark, yet the article ignores the checkered federal commitment to rights and liberties evident in American history, dating back to the Alien and Sedition Acts and repeated periodically in events such as the imprisonment of American citizens of Japanese ancestry in relocation camps during World War II, the witch-hunting investigations by the House Un-American Activities Committee and Senator Joseph McCarthy during the "red scare" of the 1950s, and Richard Nixon's "enemies list" of the 1970s, to name a few prominent twentieth-century examples. In a similar vein, Michael Kinsley's *The Withering Away of the States* portrays the bureaucratic nightmares created by state governance and, in particular, disparate state laws, while tending to downplay similar problems associated with federal governmental efforts.

Pete du Pont's article, *Federalism in the Twenty-First Century: Will States Exist?* focuses on federalism's problems from the opposite perspective, yet is equally one-sided in its orientation. Indeed, it could be argued that meaningful debate is not well served by simplistic pronouncements that the design of American federalism is, in du Pont's words, "effectively dead," or by waving the banner of the 10th Amendment in support of states rights while not taking note that the Amendment's reservation of powers to the states has nothing to say about the appropriate scope of national powers. Further, du Pont's analysis offers little assurance to assuage the fears of those (such as Commager) who see an increased governmental role for the states as a threat to individual rights and liberties as well as to the continued existence of a social welfare safety net for the mass citizenry.

As hinted above, the essays by Peterson and Derthick appear to offer the most sophisticated and complex assessments of contemporary American federalism in this collection of readings. Thus, Peterson argues, in *Who Should Do What? Divided Responsibility in the Federal System,* that different levels of government perform different governmental responsibilities best—with "developmental" policies aimed at fostering economic growth appropriately lodged pri-

marily in states and localities, while "redistributive" policies seeking to move resources from society's haves to its have-nots are best pursued by the federal government. Consequently, Peterson cautions that there is grave danger inherent in today's efforts by conservatives to transfer substantial responsibilities and authority from the federal government to the states in the social welfare realm.

Derthick's analysis in *The Enduring Features of American Federalism* underscores what many analysts tend to lose sight of. That is, federalism is an interactive process in which states can and do "talk back." The important question about American federalism is not, necessarily, which level of government is "winning" or "losing" the battle over the exercise of powers but, rather, what is the nature of the bargaining and negotiation process going on between governmental levels and how does this continuing governmental dialogue serve democratic governance?

As noted above, debates about the nature of American federalism continue today as they have throughout the nation's history. It is important to recognize, however, that the contemporary language of the debate has changed somewhat in the context of the presidency of Bill Clinton, a former state governor, and a Congress led by conservative Republicans, such as Newt Gingrich, clearly bent on tipping the balance of governmental powers in the states' direction. Indeed, some would argue that, at least for today, the fundamental issue of American federalism is not whether additional governmental powers should be lodged in state governments but, rather, which powers ought they to gain.

READING 11

Tocqueville's Mistakes: A Defense of Strong Central Government

Henry Steele Commager

Henry Steele Commager is a renowned student of American political thought and the American political experience who spent most of his academic life teaching at Amherst. In this piece he focuses on Alexis de Tocqueville's classic commentary, Democracy in America, *and, in particular, the fear of centralized government expressed in that work. In Tocqueville's view, liberty was associated with local government and history demonstrated that threats to liberty tended to emanate from centralized political systems.*

Commager argues that Tocqueville's fears about centralization were largely unfounded, in part because the American federal system was and is a unique one. The states, by and large, were as big as most existing nations, rendering historical models of the way federal systems tended to operate largely irrelevant. Commager contends that American history reveals that big government is not the enemy of liberty and that the growth of central governance in this country has actually been related causally to an enlargement of personal liberty.

Among the issues and concerns that Commager alludes to in linking the federal government with the quest for liberty and the states with liberty's denial are slavery, gender equality, labor law, conservation, and equal educational opportunity. Commager's historical overview is aimed at providing a lesson for today, particularly for contemporary conservatives and neoconservatives. A recrafted federalism lessening the role of the national government is not, in Commager's view, an enlightened proposal for reform.

Alexis de Tocqueville was a statesman, a historian, a political philosopher, and the first modern sociologist. Like his mentor Montesquieu—indeed, like all judicious political philosophers, from Plato to Croce—he was first and last a moral philosopher. *Democracy in America,* the first volume of which was published 150 years ago, was far more than an interpretation of the American mind and character, or even of the institutions of democracy. It was a nineteenth-century *Spirit*

of the Laws, designed to make clear to the people of all Western nations the kind of government, society, economy, and morality they must cultivate if they wished to be saved. Ostensibly, Tocqueville visited America in 1831 to study its prisons, then the model for the Western world; but his true goal was to study the form of government and of society that he took for granted represented the wave of the future.

"In America," he would later write, "I saw more than America; I sought the image of democracy itself, with its inclinations, its character, its prejudices, and its passions." America was the laboratory—the only one on the globe at that time—that might provide some insight into the fate that awaited those nations of the Old World that would move irresistibly toward democracy. What was happening in America, Tocqueville believed, was "interesting not only to the United States, but to the whole world. It concerns not a nation, but mankind."

Democracy in America, eight years in the writing, is a comprehensive analysis of American life and character, and of American institutions. It is the most profound book that has ever been written about America or democracy, and its unique quality is its interplay of shrewdness, sagacity, and moral earnestness. It was thought through by what is now acknowledged to be the most affluent mind ever to reflect on either the American character or the character of democracy. What still excites our interest is its clairvoyance. For in his study of American democracy Tocqueville submitted questions, sounded warnings, and made prophecies that have to do with the threats to any democracy: the tyranny of the majority, the vulgarization of culture, the centralization of power, the rise of a "manufacturing aristocracy, potentially the harshest that ever existed," racial injustice, an unwieldy military, and the corruption of individualism by ambition and greed.

The so-called neoconservatives of our own time have seized upon certain of the entries in this catalogue of dangers with uncritical enthusiasm; no wonder Tocqueville is the cow from which they draw their milk. To consider all the threats that Tocqueville submitted would require a volume; I confine myself here to what is the King Charles's head of neoconservatism: the threat of centralization.

Tocqueville had an almost congenital distrust of central authority, the roots of which extended deep into the soil of Normandy. His family had suffered impoverishment and violence during the French Revolution and under Napoleon. Centralization was the theme of his masterly *The Old Regime and the French Revolution;* here, he traced its disastrous history from the days of Louis XIV through the Revolution and the Restoration.

America, and especially New England, did not so much confirm Tocqueville in his fears as in his hopes. For, with the help of the most distinguished body of teachers any young man has ever enjoyed—three past or future presidents of Harvard (Josiah Quincy, Jared Sparks, and Edward Everett); the most learned justice of the Supreme Court, Joseph Story; and Story's disciple, the philosopher-scholar Francis Lieber—he was able to appreciate to the full the virtues of town government, the local militia, jury trials, and that remarkable institution he was the first to celebrate, the voluntary association. He was able to see local government in action, and nowhere did he see centralization as either dangerous or effective. His view here was so determined by his *point* of view that he regarded Andrew Jackson as a weak executive and predicted that the American president would never pose a threat!

But what about the future of centralization: "Who shall bridle Behemoth, who shall curb Leviathan?" That, Tocqueville knew, was the oldest question in the history of government. Could democracy come up with an answer, or would democracy itself be transformed into a Behemoth and thus justify Alexander Hamilton's alleged taunt: "Your people, sir, is a great beast"?

It is against this background that we read Tocqueville's seemingly paradoxical maxim: "While liberty is the product of *Art* and can be achieved therefore only by the most scrupulous calculations, centralization is the product of *Nature,* and as such enlists the passions of all men." In the Old World, he argued, Nature had triumphed over Art. But in America, Art—by which Tocqueville meant intelligence, inventiveness, ingenuity, skill—might still contain or reverse the dictates of Nature. For America, which had come late onto the stage of history, was not the

slave of history and might even be its master. That is what Jefferson meant when he asserted that in America, history might be prospective rather than merely retrospective. "I like dreams of the future," he said, "better than the history of the past."

America was then the only place in which the elusive secret of the reconciliation of liberty and order might be discovered. A risky experiment, this. As Tocqueville wrote, "Political liberty is a difficult food to digest. It is only extremely robust constitutions that can take it."

True enough. Even in Tocqueville's day Americans had enjoyed a longer experience in the *art* of government than any other people. Could they be counted on to employ that art to enlarge liberty? They had indeed done this for almost all of America's white males; but how did it happen that a people committed to liberty had so eagerly imposed slavery on others? After all, even countries with centralized governments like France and Britain had abolished slavery by the time *Democracy* was published.

Yet, historically, Tocqueville's assumption that liberty had a closer connection with local than with centralized governments had much to be said for it. France, Prussia, Russia, Spain, and most of the Italian states confessed governments that were tyrannical. Where the central government was comparatively weak—in the Low Countries, the Swiss cantons, and, above all, England, which was Tocqueville's spiritual home—the people enjoyed a large measure of liberty. So, too, there had been a larger measure of freedom in the American colonies (in the realm of religion, for example) than in the Mother Country.

Here, however, Tocqueville's propensity for deductive rather than inductive reasoning misled him, as it has misled so many of his present-day mockingbirds. In 1789, Americans had created a "more perfect union" by giving essential authority to a central government. That historic shift toward centralization had not made for a diminution but for an enhancement of liberty. The framers of the Constitution had been mindful of John Dickinson's admonition:

> For who are a free people? Not those over whom government is reasonably and equitably exercised, but those who live under a government so constitutionally

checked and controlled that provision is made against it being otherwise exercised.

There was no perceptible threat to liberty from centralization in the America that Tocqueville observed. There was an ardent nationalist in the White House, but he had distributed a federal tax surplus to the states to spend as they pleased, vetoed a bill for an extension of the National Road, and declared war on the "Monster" Bank of the United States, thus putting an end to a promising national bank system.

What Tocqueville failed to take in as he looked over the jumble of American governmental bodies was that in a federal system like the American, where many states were larger than some nations of the Old World, the problem of the role of local and central governments had taken on a new character.

Once again it was John Dickinson who warned his colleagues at the Constitutional Convention of 1787 that "Reason may mislead us; experience must be our guide." Experience must be *our* guide, too, as we reflect on the drawbacks and advantages of centralization and on the extent to which centralization threatens or enhances liberty. It is easy enough to sound the tocsin of alarm—that is one of the noisiest of our bells—but we cannot avoid the conclusion that those who today declaim against Big Government as the enemy of liberty are ignorant of America's history. The most elementary and overshadowing fact of that history is that there has been a causal connection between the enlargement and the deepening of liberty in America and the growth of a strong national government.

What is meant by "strong national government"? Perhaps the most astonishing feature of the current attack on centralization—an attack that President Reagan...turned into a crusade—is the argument that the United States today has not a strong national government but a Big Government. This notion has been so bolstered by repetition that it is unthinkingly accepted by most Americans. Yet what is most interesting to the foreign observers who have followed in Tocqueville's tracks is how meager, outside of what is involved in "national security," are the responsibilities and activities of the American national government compared with those assumed by most other national governments. In almost every country of Eu-

rope and Asia, the national government owns and controls all forms of transportation. It owns or controls the banks, the utilities, most radio and television stations and most natural resources. All institutions of higher learning are government administered, as are opera companies and orchestras. The national government provides or finances medical services, a far broader range of social services than in our country, and much of the housing. This is not a phenomenon of communist nations; it is a matter of course in Britain, France, Holland, Denmark, Sweden, Australia, Italy, Japan, and scores of other nations. In short, Americans do not have a Big Government.

It is an interesting paradox that the passionate adversaries of centralization today are generally not ardent champions, as was Tocqueville, of the town meeting, the county court, the local militia. Most of those who are in public life appear to prefer life in Washington to life in their state capitals. Their devotion to states' rights has taken the form of devotion to white supremacy (Alabama) or to revenues from coal (Montana), oil (Texas), or tobacco (North Carolina). Many of them seem to be successors to those distinguished senators of the 1890s who were known as the senator from Standard Oil, the senator from the Sugar Trust, and the senator from the Pennsylvania Railroad. But today's "conservatives" have made some progress: popular hostility toward economic centralization has been deflected in the direction of political centralization.

Not that these "conservatives" are critical of all forms of centralization. They lend their support almost automatically to what has been the most centralizing force in American history: the military. It was the veterans of the American Revolution who were the most ardent champions of a strong national government. It was the Civil War that dramatized the need for centralization and that led to the passage of legislation nationalizing transportation, finance, and industry.

This experience, of course, was duplicated in World War I and World War II. President Eisenhower, who viewed the problem from both a military and a civilian vantage point, warned in his farewell address against the "military-industrial complex." It is almost superfluous to add that this "complex" is celebrated with unrestrained enthusiasm by precisely those whose energies are otherwise devoted to deploring centralization and celebrating states' rights and localism.

But let us turn again to the growth of liberty that has resulted from the growth of the national government. From the beginning, it has not been the states that have been the chief instruments of democracy but the central government in Washington. It was the states that maintained slavery, the national government that abolished it. It was the states that fought for slavery and tried to reinstate it, through "black codes," even after Appomatox. It was the national government that intervened with the Thirteenth, Fourteenth, and Fifteenth Amendments and a succession of civil rights acts designed to emancipate and free. It would be asking a great deal to expect blacks to look to the states or to their communities for the protection of their rights.

It would also be asking a great deal to expect women, so long denied not only their political and property rights but even access to the professions and control over their children, to look to the states for their equality. From *Muller* v. *Oregon* in 1908 to *Roe* v. *Wade* in 1973, it was the federal not the state courts that vindicated the rights of women. Suffrage, too, though first granted by the federal territory of Wyoming in 1869, required in the end a federal amendment, which was bitterly fought by those states that, half a century later, defeated the Equal Rights Amendment.

Further, it would be asking a great deal to expect labor to take its chances with state rather than national legislation. It is Congress that, over more than half a century, has enacted various charters of freedom for labor. It should be sufficient to note here the Clayton Antitrust Act of 1914, the La Follette Seamen's Act of 1915, the Civilian Conservation Corps Act of 1933, the National Labor Relations Act of 1935, the revolutionary Social Security Act of 1935, and the Fair Labor Standards Act of 1938. These laws did more to establish social justice than the whole corpus of state labor legislation since the Civil War. Nor should we forget that it was Congress and the Supreme Court that, over the vociferous opposition of state economic interests, put an end to the disgrace of child labor.

This record of the role of the national government in promoting justice and the general welfare is mirrored in federal efforts to encourage the conservation of natural resources. It was President Jefferson who launched the Lewis and Clark expedition and several others, whose mission it was to explore and chart the whole of America. And it was Jefferson who celebrated the providential blessing of "land enough for our descendants to the thousandth and thousandth generation." Alas, the people nullified that prediction, often with the connivance of the states. Theodore Roosevelt launched a conservation movement early in this century, and Franklin Roosevelt reinvigorated it. FDR did more to save and restore America's natural resources—through the Civilian Conservation Corps, the hundred-mile tree belt on the border of the Great Plains, and the Tennessee Valley Authority—than had been achieved in a hundred years. As every natural resource is continental, if not global, local governments cannot control any one of them. By neglect or exploitation, however, they can damage all of them.

In the arena of education the story is much the same. Ever since Massachusetts Bay enacted the first education laws in modern history, education has been the responsibility of local communities. But not all communities have fulfilled that responsibility. Our greatest educator, Thomas Jefferson, drafted ordinances making land grants to help support public schools and universities. That policy was expanded by the Morrill Act of 1862, which provided federal contributions to state universities throughout the nation, and by the Hatch Act of 1887, which set up scores of agricultural experiment stations. Those who now assert that education is a purely local matter are as wanting in logic as in a familiarity with history. The nation has an interest in the education of all children, each of whom, when an adult, can vote for congressmen and for president, and each of whom, therefore, can legislate for the whole of the nation, and for posterity.

Montesquieu had formulated what came to be widely accepted as a law of History. He held that the supreme principle of a monarchy was power, of an aristocracy, honor, and of a republic, virtue. Tocqueville was sagacious enough to give an American rather than a classical application to this law. "What Montesquieu meant by virtue," he wrote, "is the moral power which each individual exercises upon himself and which prevents him from violating another's right... those turbulent virtues which sometimes bring glory but more often trouble to society rank low in [American] public opinion."

Americans readily embraced this tribute while reserving judgment on its qualification. It appeared to most of them to be the common sense of the matter. The Founding Fathers themselves were all but obsessed with the idea of virtue; no public address, scarcely a private letter, failed to invoke it. A single sample must suffice, and that from the most exalted source. "There is no truth more thoroughly established," Washington said in his first inaugural address, "than that there exists in the economy and course of nature an indissoluble union between virtue and happiness, between duty and advantage, between the genuine maxims of an honest and magnanimous policy and the solid rewards of public prosperity and felicity.... The propitious smiles of Heaven can never be expected on a nation that disregards the eternal rules of order and right which Heaven itself has ordained."

Why was the ideal of virtue so essential to the American experiment? The answer to that was elementary. America was, after all, the only democratic nation in the world. It was, therefore, as Jefferson put it in his first inaugural address, "the world's best hope." Its success, its very survival, depended on the ascendance of virtue in its people. If they were not prepared to cherish and practice virtue, the audacious enterprise of democracy was foredoomed to failure.

The Founding Fathers were realists—even, with John Adams and Alexander Hamilton, somewhat cynical realists. They knew human nature and did not think highly of it. Most of them were closer to Edmund Burke than to Tom Paine. History had taught them that all men were creatures of ambition, passion, pride, envy, intemperance, greed, and inconsistency. How then could they be expected to conduct themselves collectively with prudence, dignity, honor, virtue, and magnanimity?

Tocqueville confronted that problem at its most troublesome. Only a virtuous people could make democracy work, and the American people were no more virtuous than any other people. How could America succeed where so many had failed?

Tocqueville put the question another way: What was the distinguishing characteristic of American democracy? It was, he concluded, individualism. Quite right, too, for never before had circumstances been so propitious for the exercise of (or the indulgence of) individualism by the common people, and never before had a people been so eager to indulge themselves in that exercise. To the average white American, individualism was a simple matter. It meant that he could live where he would, marry whom he would, worship as he would, have children as he wished—confident that they would not want—and associate with whom he would. He could work on a farm, follow the sea, keep a shop, or embrace a profession, and if one of these ceased to suit him, he could shift easily to another. He could sit on juries, elect his own magistrates, and himself aspire to any office in the town, the county, the state, or the nation. Where else on the face of the earth did individualism have such scope?

But was an individualism so extreme compatible with an orderly society? Tocqueville thought not. Yet he acknowledged that the system had worked for half a century: in the early years of the Republic, Americans had resisted the temptations of ambition, self-indulgence, and corruption.

Was there any reason to suppose that the good fortune that had attended America would continue? Yes, Tocqueville believed, but only if Americans could overcome the seductions of majority tyranny, the menace of militarism, the threat of an industrial oligarchy, and the dangers of centralization. Only if Americans were ready to embrace what he called "enlightened self-interest."

What might enable American democracy to escape the fate of other democracies?

First of all, a religious toleration more profound than was to be found in any other country. Then education that would promote enlightenment—an education more widespread than elsewhere on the globe. Add to these a boundless territory; resources bountiful enough to meet the needs of all and thus discourage selfish competition; a prosperity that might be expected to satisfy all ambitions, or at least to moderate them; immunity from wars; a government in which all could participate and which was encumbered with so many and intricate checks and balances that it was all but incapable of exercising tyranny. And then there is Tocqueville's homely observation that "in America it is not virtue that is great, but temptation that is small.... It is not disinterestedness that is great, it is interest that is taken for granted."

It is not only the same formidable threats that Tocqueville saw in the 1830s that now confront America, but a host of new dangers. Alas, we can no longer count on those dispensations and immunities that we enjoyed when Tocqueville contemplated our destiny. We no longer have limitless resources or immunity from attack; we are no longer confident that our democratic system works or that our system is indeed democratic. Nor, no matter how audaciously our leaders declaim it, is there any reason to believe that we are "God's chosen people."

Do we have the ingenuity to adapt to the realities of a global economy? Do we have the common sense to adjust our nationalism to a world of technology and science that is totally indifferent to national frontiers? Do we have the wisdom to realize that our fate is inextricably bound up with the fate of all the peoples of the globe? Can we practice a self-interest that is enlightened?

READING 12

The Withering Away of the States

Michael Kinsley

This analysis by liberal political commentator and journalist Michael Kinsley attests to the complexity, duplication, potential confusion, and inefficiency that are often associated with the workings of the American federal system. Kinsley offers a case study of some of the legal concerns raised in settling the estate of the late multimillionaire, Howard Hughes.

From *The Withering Away of the States* by M. Kinsley, 1981. Reprinted by permission of *The New Republic.* © 1981, The New Republic, Inc.

While recognizing that most of us do not live lives harboring such fiscal complexity, Kinsley argues, nevertheless, that "we all suffer the nuisance of living in a federal system."

Kinsley's main aim is to disarm the arguments supporting the conservative agenda of altering American federalism and returning much governmental power to the states. Contrary to the conservative positions of the Reagan administration in the 1980s and, more recently, the views of the Gingrich-led Republican congressional majority, Kinsley contends that such a reform would make American governance less productive, less democratic, more wasteful, and more bureaucratic.

Kinsley portrays a federal system in which states coexist in a continual state of political and economic competition. He views many issues as incapable of state resolution and critiques the inequities of a system in which "Federalism makes the government a much better deal for some people than for others." In Kinsley's view, the economic stresses caused by federalism have broken down the American spirit of national community. While not opting, in any sense, for the elimination of the states, Kinsley does favor their "withering away" through policy initiatives at the national level. Taking direct aim at the conservative's agenda, Kinsley concludes, "It will be no triumph for freedom to get the federal government off our backs only to have fifty state governments climb back on."

Speaking of the glories of federalism,... have you heard the one about Howard Hughes? Hughes was born and raised in Texas. He spent most of his adult life and made most of his fortune in California. Then he bought up a large chunk of Las Vegas (that's in Nevada) and moved into a hotel there. He spent his last few years flitting mysteriously around the world, and was on a plane heading back to Texas when he died in 1976.

In our glorious federal system, inheritance is one of many matters left entirely to state law and state courts. Now then. Who was to run Hughes's vast business empire while his affairs were being settled? Each of these "united" states has its own complex rules and precedents on this question. Each state also has its own rules and precedents about which state's rules and precedents to follow. Hughes's relatives persuaded a court in Delaware to appoint one of them administrator. Delaware? Almost all of Hughes's assets were in a company called Summa Corporation. Each state makes its own laws governing corporations, and Delaware turns a pretty penny making its own laws the most accommodating. So Summa, like most major U.S. corporations (General Motors, *The New Republic,* and so on), is incorporated in Delaware. But the stock certificate reflecting Hughes's ownership of Summa was in the Bank of America headquarters in Los Angeles. Los Angeles is in California. So a California official challenged Delaware's right to appoint an administrator. Litigation ensued.

Meanwhile, the famous "Mormon will" popped up. In Utah. Wills must be approved by the state where the decedent was "domiciled" and by every state where his assets are located. Where was Hughes "domiciled"? Unclear. A court in Nevada held a trial and ruled that the will was a fake. Then the issue had to be retried in California. And again in Texas. Since all three states came to the same conclusion, that the Mormon will was a fake, that particular issue was finally settled . . . after only five brisk years of litigation.

So Howard Hughes died without a will. Each state, naturally, has its own set of rules about what happens in such a case. California and Nevada have the same rules, but Texas's rules are different. The states are in miraculous agreement on the general rules about whose rules should apply, but each state has its own doctrines and precedents on specific cases, and each applies them in its own courts. Believe it or not, Hughes's relatives settled this one among themselves without litigation! There was plenty to go around.

But wait. There is the matter of inheritance taxes. The federal government has one. So do most of the states. For this reason, Texas and California both claim the late Mr. Hughes as one of their own. Delaware (remember Delaware?) also has designs. All of these taxes would add up to more than 100 percent of the estate. Nevada has no death tax; the heirs are convinced that cousin Howard always thought of Las Vegas as "home." This issue has been bouncing around the country like a billiard ball. In 1978 a Texas jury

determined in a Texas court that Hughes was a Texan. California was unpersuaded. It asked the U.S. Supreme Court to decide.

In nations not blessed with a federal system, there is a sad scarcity of courts and a straight-forward hierarchy among them. In this country there are 51 independent court systems, and the relationship among them is one of infinite complexity and beautiful subtlety of doctrine, weaved by legal artisans over 200 years. The U.S. Supreme Court decided that it did not have the power to decide the Hughes case, but several justices suggested that a federal district court could decide it. A federal district court in Texas decided that it could not decide. Then a federal appeals court decided that the district court could, too, decide. California has asked the Supreme Court to decide that the Texas district court cannot decide after all. If the district court does ultimately decide, the matter will then head up to the Supreme Court for the third time.

How many lawyers have been involved in all this? "Literally hundreds," says one of them. At what cost? Reticent pause. Millions and millions? "Oh, certainly." The conclusion is several years away.

We don't all face the problem of being heirs to Howard Hughes's fortune, but we all suffer the nuisance of living in a federal system. Now President Reagan wants to reverse the trend of 200 years and give the states a larger role in governing our lives. He hasn't yet explained why. It's clear he wants less government *in toto,* but how will shifting functions between levels of government achieve this? Some see racist intent in Reagan's revival of the term "states rights." Others argue that transferring social services "back" to the states, which never provided them in the first place, is just a sneaky way of canceling them. Reagan's people insist otherwise. But if Reagan really thinks that transferring functions and authority from Washington to the states is a sensible way to make government more efficient, more responsive, less obtrusive, and so on, he should consider how federalism really works in 1981. Anyone truly concerned about making America more productive, more democratic, less wasteful, less bureaucratic, would want to hasten the withering away of the states as quickly as possible.

Everyone knows, for example, that America fritters away far too much brainpower on legal matters while the Japanese are inventing computers that de- sign robots that build automobiles and so on. One main reason is federalism. Half of the standard three- year legal education could be wiped out if we had a single government with a single set of courts admin- istering a single set of laws. Almost that many law- yers could be wiped out, too. There are elaborate constitutional doctrines about what the states can and cannot do because they are joined in a nation, and what the central government can and cannot do be- cause we are 50 sovereign states. The gears of litiga- tion grind endlessly over what court a particular quarrel belongs in and what law that court should ap- ply. (Should a federal court sitting in Minnesota use Indiana conflict-of-law rules to decide whether an Ohio automobile guest statute should apply to a crash in Texas between a car from Alabama driven by a Louisiana woman and a truck owned by a Delaware corporation? That sort of thing.) This country also makes many important governmental decisions through the awkward and costly procedure of letting the states and the federal government sue one an- other. Unfortunately, in this litigation-crazed nation, agencies of the federal government regularly sue one another, so eliminating the states wouldn't eliminate this problem. But it would help.

On most important matters, each state makes its own laws and settles its own arguments. When a large airplane crashes, for example, lawyers may have the pleasure of debating the safety of some wing bolt or cargo hatch in dozens of courts and of researching obscure doctrines of negligence under dozens of in- dependent legal systems. Every law student learns to quote Mr. Justice Brandeis about why this is a good thing: "It is one of the happy incidents of the federal system that a single courageous state may, if its citi- zens choose, serve as a laboratory; and try novel so- cial and economic experiments without risk to the rest of the country." Its citizens seldom so choose. In- stead, there is something called the National Confer- ence of Commissioners on Uniform State Laws, which has been beavering since 1892 to bring about some kind of consistency in matters on which there is no earthly reason why the states need to disagree. Some of the commission's monuments include the Uniform Simultaneous Death Act, the Uniform Fac-

simile Signatures of Public Officials Act, the Uni- form Division of Income for Tax Purposes Act, and so on. This last one, for example, tackles the fascinat- ing question of how to apportion the income of a multistate corporation for the purpose of collecting state income taxes. The Uniform Commissioners struggled bravely and here, in part, is the formula they came up with:

> Section 9. All business income shall be apportioned to this state by multiplying the income by a fraction, the numerator of which is the property factor plus the payroll factor plus the sales factor, and the denomina- tor of which is three.
> Section 10. The property factor is a fraction, the nu- merator of which is the average value of the taxpayer's real and tangible personal property owned or rented and used in this state during the tax period and the de- nominator of which is the average value of all the tax- payer's real and tangible personal property owned or rented and used during the tax period.

Unfortunately, no state is required to accept UDITPA or the other uniform acts, and those that do generally fiddle with them first.

Mr. Reagan, with his fondness for bromides, probably believes in equal justice under the law. Fed- eralism makes this impossible in the United States. A recent survey by the *National Law Journal* found that an American will spend more time in prison for rob- bery in South Carolina than for willful homicide in half a dozen other states; that the average felony con- viction leads to 13 months of jail in South Dakota and 58 months in Massachusetts; and so on. The biggest disparity is that some states have capital punishment and others don't.

Anyone who believes that enhancing federalism is a sensible way to reduce the cost of government should look up "national" and "state" in the great po- litical science treatise, the Washington, DC, tele- phone book. The founding fathers thought that the Senate could adequately represent the interests of the states to one another and the central government. Re- agan may think that's still how it works. In fact, un- told millions are spent every year in the attempt to coordinate 50 sovereignties within a single nation.

Thirty-two state governments, at last count, have offices in Washington. Many of these are located in the "Hall of the States," an office building on Capitol Hill that also houses the National Governors Association and the National Conference of State Legislatures. But that's just the beginning. The state of California has 21 separate governmental offices in Washington. They include the state office itself, with a dozen staff members ("middle-sized," says one of them), and offices for Alameda County, Los Angeles County, San Bernadino County, San Diego County, Santa Clara County, Inglewood County, the California County Supervisors Association, Los Angeles City, six other cities and city groupings, the League of California Cities, the California university, state college, and community college systems, the California Department of Education, and the California legislature.

Besides the governors and state legislatures, there are separate National Associations (or "Assemblies" or "Conferences" or "Centers" or "Leagues") of (or "for" or "on"): Community Arts Agencies, State Art Agencies, State Units on Aging, Conservation Districts, Consumer Agency Administrators, Counties (downtown and Capitol Hill branches), Criminal Justice Planning Directors, Government Communicators, Regional Councils, State Alcohol and Drug Abuse Directors, State Aviation Officials, State Boards of Education, State Boating Law Administrators, State Budget Officers, State Credit Union Supervisors, State Departments of Agriculture, State Development Agencies, State Directors of Special Education, State Lotteries, State Mental Health Program Directors, State Mental Retardation Program Directors, State Savings and Loan Supervisors, State Universities and Land Grant Colleges, Tax Administrators, Towns and Township Officials, Urban Flood Management Agencies, City Councilmen, State Courts, and so on. And then there is the Advisory Commission on Intergovernmental Relations, a creature of the federal government itself, with a staff of 37 dedicated to grinding out fat reports on federalish topics...

Well, this is a big and complicated country, federalism or no. But these offices don't replace the coordinating function of a single central government. Most of them duplicate a whole hierarchy of federal offices on matters like historic preservation, mental health, criminal justice, and so on. These state offices generally perform two functions. One is to deal with the special problems created by federalism: 50 separate buildings codes, professional licensing procedures, criminal records systems. A more important is to lobby the federal government.

Reagan and his people seem vividly aware of how "special interest groups" thwart the functioning of democracy, clog the wheels of government, and subvert the assertion of the general will. But they seem unaware of how much federalism aggravates this problem. It turns lower levels of government from units on an established hierarchy into independent duchies, free to join with or join battle with all the other special interests. If, say, federal mental health bureaucrats want to protect or expand their turf, they must more or less go through channels, and in theory someone may even give them a fairly expeditious "no." State mental health bureaucrats may open a Washington office, hire professional lobbyists, and, if all else fails, start filing lawsuits. The people who pay state taxes are the same ones who pay federal taxes, yet the question of how much our society as a whole should spend on mental health or criminal justice or historical preservation gets made by various governmental units slugging it out as if they had nothing to do with one another. Millions of your state tax dollars are being spent every day in efforts to affect how your federal tax dollars are spent, while millions of your federal tax dollars are spent fending them off. This is efficient government?

Speaking of your taxes, federalism remakes a mess of them. Having different levels of government raising revenues independently not only makes life needlessly complicated. Taxation depends on the government having a monopoly. A rational and fair tax system is impossible when governments must compete with one another. The growth of multinational corporations has made this an insoluble problem among nations. The Balkanization of our tax system creates a perfectly needless problem in this country.

Every state has an office called something like the Industrial Development Division. The job of these offices is to entice business into the state—sometimes from abroad, but usually from other states. The main weapon is tax favors. A thick packet from the state of Michigan, for example, promises "significant tax incentives" to industries setting up in Michigan. These include exemptions from property tax for up to 12 years, a modified corporate income tax, special exemptions for things like pollution control equipment, and so on. Michigan, like most states, also offers to raise money through federal tax-exempt bonds and re-lend it to corporations that settle there. Thus ordinary, stationary taxpayers finance this competition through both their state and their federal taxes.

The March 10 *New York Times* contained a full-page ad from the New York State Department of Commerce asserting in 144-point type, "NEW YORK VOTES 'YES' FOR BUSINESS," and bragging about all the taxes that have been lowered to make New York "the best place in the world to do business." The same paper had a page-one article about how just one of these tax breaks is costing the state $100 million a year with no perceptible benefit. Certainly very little new business is generated by the nation as a whole by letting corporations play the state legislatures off against one another. In fact, the process undoubtedly makes our economy less efficient and less productive by adding artificial considerations to business investment decisions. A company that ought to be locating a new plant near its suppliers or near its markets will instead plunk it down in whatever state is temporarily ahead in the game of tax-incentive leap-frog.

State-level regulation of business creates similar absurdities. On the one hand, an entrepreneur (and we're all terribly solicitous of entrepreneurs these days) who wishes to raise money for a new product must hire a lawyer to shepherd his scheme through 51 different securities regulatory systems. Hardly good for productivity. And when you're following a truck on the interstate highway, you may observe the consequence of federalism plastered all over its rear end.

On the other hand, federalism makes sensible regulations impossible to apply and enforce. There are two reasons for this. First, we do have open state borders, for the moment, and air and water currents remain unimpressed by the doctrine of states rights. This means that matters like gun control and pollution standards simply cannot be addressed on the state level. Assertions by Reagan people that they should be are simply fatuous. Second, regulation, like taxation, must be a monopoly to work right. This may sound undemocratic, but it's actually the essence of democracy. Al-

most everybody in the country might agree that a certain regulation is desirable, but no state will be able to pass it for fear of losing business.

The catalog of bribes sent out to business prospects by the Texas Industrial Commission contains the usual promises about "one of the most favorable tax systems in the entire U.S.," industrial development loans, lack of troublesome regulations, and so on. It adds an interesting twist with a discussion of the severance tax (the tax on minerals extracted from the ground) on gas and oil wells:

> Although the number of Texas firms subject to severance tax is relatively small, the revenues provided are significant and are at least partially responsible for the favorable tax structure industry enjoys. In 1979 Texas collected $1,025,550,000 in severance taxes. While this tax accounted for more than 17% of the state's total tax revenue, it also represented 35% of all severance taxes collected in the United States.

In other words, Texas is able to entice business from other states by keeping taxes low and offering other inducements like free job-training programs because it happens to have lots of oil. Is it rational and productive, is it the best way to stimulate growth and jobs, is it one of the glories of federalism, that businesses having nothing to do with oil should be bribed away from the job-hungry northeast by the use of oil revenues?

Federalism makes the government a much better deal for some people than for others. This is not a question of letting local areas decide how much government they want. Government Balkanization lets some people get most services for less money. This can be seen most clearly in metropolitan areas, where rich suburbs are able to have lower tax rates but higher per-capita expenditures than central cities, which often must support area-wide services like museums and zoos. But there are equally dramatic disparities across the nation. For example, while the New York state and city university systems are raising tuition and cutting back on services, the University of Texas is keeping tuition low and has embarked on a lavish building program. This is not because the people of Texas have democratically decided to tax themselves more heavily to support higher education, but because late in the last century the Texas legislature assigned the universities some useless grazing land, which turned out to contain oil. As a result, the "Permanent Fund" shared by UT and Texas A&M is $1.3 billion (larger than Harvard's endowment) and growing fast.

The energy crisis has dramatized what was previously a rather academic question: who should benefit from the great mineral wealth of this country? Obviously the main beneficiaries are those lucky enough to own some of it. But often it is owned by government, and even when it isn't, the government can and does appropriate some of it through taxes for the benefit of . . . whom? Everybody in society? or just those who happen to live nearby? Right now, the system goes out of its way to keep the benefits nearby. For example, as coal production gears up in the west, various states are applying stiff severance taxes to coal mined on *federal* land. Meanwhile, the federal windfall profits tax *exempts* all oil produced on *state*-owned land. Why?

President Reagan not only is untroubled by anomalies like this, he wants to increase them. He has claimed "a very warm feeling in my heart for the 'sagebrush rebellion,'" and has endorsed that movement's principal aim, which is to transfer vast areas of federal land—much of it with valuable resources—to state ownership. This is bad policy and, worse, it is bad leadership. It feeds a dangerous growth in geographical chauvinism. Regional pride is a fine thing, but that is not what is behind the recent developments like the sagebrush rebellion, Alaska's scheme to rebate oil money based on how many years people have lived there, Texas bumper stickers that say "Let 'Em Freeze in the Dark," or proposed state laws in the industrial midwest that would forbid plants to move elsewhere. Economic stress is eroding our feeling of national community. The president should be trying to reinforce it, working to apportion the suffering and benefit equitably. Instead, Reagan is encouraging insularity and grabbiness.

Why is he doing this? Reagan claims to believe that, to the extent we must have government, state government is inherently more efficient than the federal government, and less prone to the dreaded waste, fraud, and abuse. There is no evidence to support this belief. All the growth in government employment in recent years has come on the state and local level. In 1960 there were 2.3 million people working for the federal government. In 1979 there were 2.8 million. By contrast in 1960 there were over six million state and local government employees, and today there are almost 13 million. State and local government, in other words, have more than doubled over the past two decades, while the federal bureaucracy has increased by less than 20 percent.

Anyone who reads almost any local paper will find the notion laughable that state government is better run than the national government. One of my local papers is the *Washington Post*. It covers two state governments and one jurisdiction that would like to be a state, and certainly has taken to behaving like one. In the first four days of March, the *Post* Metro section contained the following stories:

- "Study Says Most City Assessments Wrong," reporting that more than two-thirds of residential properties in the District of Columbia are assessed inaccurately.
- "Ethical Considerations in Annapolis," about a Maryland state legislator, also a tavern owner, who is sponsoring a bill to forbid teenagers from buying alcohol anywhere except in a tavern. "His case is far from isolated," says the article. "This year, as always in this part-time legislature, there are tavern owners sponsoring drinking bills, insurance agents promoting eased guidelines for their work, and lawyers and doctors whose bills would increase the business and benefits of their professions." Mention is made of a "thick new ethics law" passed last year.
- "2 Figures in Probe Get New Posts," about how the chairman and staff director of the DC Alcoholic Beverage Control Board, both being investigated by a federal grand jury for bribery and extortion, were given new city jobs with full pay.
- "City Housing Rehabilitation Unit Stripped of Funding," about a DC agency accused of "an alleged history of program foul-ups, shoddy construction, staff conflicts of interest with private contractors and improper use of city money."
- "Bill to Lower Probate Fees Opposed," about how lawyers in the Maryland legislature are preventing cheaper administration of wills.

In four whole days, there was not a single story of corruption, stupidity, waste, or other outrage by the state of Virginia! And, mind you, the Richmond legislature *was* in session. Perhaps we should turn the federal government over to Virginia.

Or perhaps we should drop it. Federalism, I mean. It was great fun, but it was just one of those things. We don't need to do anything so drastic as abolishing the states. They could remain as reservoirs of sentiment and employers of last resort for people's brothers-in-law. But billions could be saved by both the government and the private sector if we were to nationalize huge chunks of the law such as negligence, incorporation and business regulation, and professional licensing. Justice and economy would be served by unifying the court system and the punishment of crime. A single national taxing authority would put thousands of lawyers and accountants out of work. (States could still set their own tax rates, but Uncle Sam would make the rules and do the collecting for everybody.) National authority over social concerns like welfare and environmental rules would assure that society as a whole makes rational, democratic decisions about issues that affect society as a whole.

At the very least, someone should sit down with President Reagan and explain to him that he is confounding his great and universal theme of the individual versus government with the issues emerging from a particular historical oddity. It will be no triumph for freedom to get the federal government off our backs, only to have 50 state governments climb back on.

<hr>

Federalism in the Twenty-First Century: Will States Exist?

Pete du Pont

Pete du Pont's governmental service has included stints as a state legislator, a U. S. Congressman, and Governor of Delaware. In all of these capacities du Pont, a conservative Republican, has expressed great concern about and opposition to what he

perceives as federal encroachment on state prerogatives as well as open-ended expansion of federal authority. Du Pont's arguments are well summarized in this essay, which begins by asking whether states will survive into the 21st century—an uncertain prospect in the author's view.

The "culprits" in narrowing state power while expanding federal authority have been, in du Pont's view, the U. S. Congress and the federal courts, particularly the U. S. Supreme Court. These infringements, which du Pont sees as violating the "proper" conception of American federalism, are characterized as contrary to the Constitution, the Bill of Rights, and The Federalist Papers. *Arguing against the tide of developing approaches to governance throughout the world, du Pont asserts that federalism is effectively "dead" in America, with grave economic consequences for the states and a great loss of policy diversity that will hurt the citizenry. As du Pont puts it, "The beauty of federalism . . . is that one state's foolishness need not be adopted by another; Congressional foolishness, however, is universal."*

To many, du Pont's argument may seem unduly alarmist. For one, it starts from a premise about the framers' intentions that is both difficult to prove and not universally shared. Further, reliance on the 10th Amendment's reservation of those powers to the states that are not delegated to the federal government begs the questions of just what powers are delegated to the federal government and how far they extend. Finally, it is curious that du Pont relies on The Federalist Papers *for support of his position given the clear political advocacy orientation of these essays.*

<hr>

Will there be states in the Twenty-first Century? Perhaps you thought that was just a catchy title designed to attract you to this article. You were right, that was entirely its purpose. But the question is more than merely rhetorical. As is well-known . . . the power of

<hr>

state and local government has been continually narrowed over the years by both the federal courts and the federal Congress. This infringement, contrary to the spirit and letter of the Constitution, the Bill of Rights, and *The Federalist Papers,* must cease.

Sixteen years ago, in the first moments of my time as Governor of Delaware, I set forth the case for limiting the encroachment of the federal government:

> If federalism is to survive, responsibility . . . must be shared between the state and federal governments. We must promptly end the practice of writing the rules in Washington and paying the bills in our state capitols.

Unfortunately, as is usual at inaugural addresses, no one was listening—at least not in Washington. As any governor will tell you, federal mandates upon state governments continue to expand rapidly. For example, Medicare mandated services, hospital cost controls, environmental standards, welfare regulations, and wetland definitions all are enacted in Washington intentionally to limit behavior in state capitals like Dover. The sweep and reach of federal regulation seemingly knows no boundaries. As it expands, the role of state and local governments, those "laboratories of democracy," in Justice Brandeis's phrase, concurrently contracts. So the question of the role of the states in the Twenty-first Century is neither idle nor academic.

The Constitutional Convention met in Philadelphia in the summer of 1787 to revise the Articles of Confederation and increase the power of the national government. The Articles had affirmed that "each state retains its sovereignty, freedom, and independence," but they had proven too weak to sustain many of the advantages of mutual association. Separate currencies and retaliatory trade measures hobbled the nation's economy, lack of a national voice in foreign affairs caused international problems, and, most important, the national government had no effective mechanism to raise necessary revenues. So the Founders decided to seek a new system of governance.

In framing that new system, they faced a political dilemma: any national government strong enough to benefit the states and protect individual liberties is also strong enough to control the states and take those liberties away. The Founders solved this dilemma by creating a system of dual sovereignty, with some powers ceded to the national government and the others retained in the states or in the people. By 1787, federalism had already proven itself in Europe, contributing to the immense economic success of Holland in the Sixteenth and Seventeenth Centuries and of Great Britain in the Seventeenth and Eighteenth Centuries. As Barry Weingast observes, the association between federalism and economic success was "not spurious, but central to the successful economic development of each [country]." By prohibiting the national government from regulating local economies, Weingast argues, the political cost of intervention became high enough to ensure "market-preserving federalism."

Therefore, in the U.S. Constitution, the Founders sought to restrain the national government through a variety of structural devices. Among these, the most notable was the Commerce Clause, which gave Congress the limited power "to regulate commerce with foreign nations, and among the several States, and with the Indian tribes." The Bill of Rights, which soon followed the Constitution's ratification, contained further explicit restraints on the powers of the federal government; among these, the Tenth Amendment proclaimed that "[t]he powers not delegated to the United States by the Constitution, nor prohibited by it to the States, are reserved to the States respectively, or to the people." The intentions of the Framers in granting only limited powers to the national government were stated clearly by James Madison, a supporter of the new Constitution, during the ratification debates:

> The powers delegated . . . to the federal government are few and defined. . . . The powers reserved to the several States will extend to all the objects which, in the ordinary course of affairs, concern the lives, liberties, and properties of the people, and the internal order, improvement, and prosperity of the State.

But that was then, and this is now. What, in 1993, remains of the Founders' economic federalism, which they believed so crucial to the maintenance of growth and productivity? If the purpose of the written Constitution is to "define and limit" the power delegated to the national government, as Chief Justice Marshall stated in *Marbury v. Madison,* where are the limits on that national government today?

From the outset, the Commerce Clause served to prohibit the states from regulating any economic activity not completely local in character, while the national government regulated activities only truly interstate and commercial in scope. In the turmoil of the New Deal, however, the Supreme Court began to allow Congress to regulate activities within states, as long as Congress could show that the activity had some effect, whether direct or indirect, on interstate commerce. Of course, like the butterfly in Brazil whose motion influences, even if marginally, weather patterns in Texas, every economic activity, no matter how small, can be said to have some effect on interstate commerce.

Then came *United States v. Darby,* reducing the Tenth Amendment to a truism. As time passed, the Supreme Court permitted the Congress more and more latitude to regulate states' economic affairs. In a brief moment of contrition, the Court in 1976 ruled that the federal government could not regulate "traditional government functions" of the state governments themselves, but overturned even this minor limitation in 1985. In *Garcia v. San Antonio Metropolitan Transit Authority,* the Court held that because the Constitution granted the states a role in the selection of the executive and legislative branches of government, there was no need to fashion any "discrete limitations on the objects of federal authority." In short, the Court disavowed any judicial role in protecting the states from federal intrusion, leaving the states to fend for themselves and the national bull free to rampage through state china shops.

Needless to say, the national government has taken full advantage of its court-sanctioned strength. In the early 1980's, the federal government usurped the states' powers under the Twenty-first Amendment with respect to alcoholic beverages. Federal legislation mandated that states raise their minimum drinking age to 21 years or face the denial of road construction funds; the states, naturally, complied. In another example, when the people of New Jersey attempted to limit the importation of trash into their state, the federal courts forced New Jersey to accept garbage from states that did not want it within their own domain. States likewise have been prohibited from barring an influx of hazardous and radioactive waste. Whether the garbage be of the hazardous, medical, radioactive, or household variety, the Supreme Court has used the Commerce Clause to prevent states from maintaining a healthy and clean environment for their citizens.

Unfortunately, it doesn't stop there. Since the great constitutional compact which formed this nation was approved, the power over zoning and building decisions has been vested in the states and their localities. According to the federal courts, however, government housing should be located where the federal courts think is appropriate, rather than where local authorities may place it.

In my home state of Delaware, we know only too well about the overreaching of the federal government into our state and local affairs. For almost fifteen years now, the operations of our public schools have been micromanaged by the U.S. District Court through a series of busing orders. Federally defined racial balance has become the primary goal of the education system, ahead of reading skills, reasoning ability, knowledge, and the pursuit of excellence.

But perhaps the most outrageous act of the Supreme Court in recent history, clearly usurping the powers of the states, is represented by a school desegregation case from Kansas City, Missouri. In that case, the federal district court realigned the school district, finding that it was segregated, and *ordered the school district to raise local taxes to pay for the expenses caused by the court's decrees.* The Supreme Court upheld this action, finding that it was "plainly a judicial act within the power of a federal court," despite the fact that it violated the Missouri Constitution.

Liquor and garbage may seem trivial to some, but the devastation of local schools through the quotas of federal court-ordered busing and the levying of local taxes by federal courts are not. The power of state governments to deliver education to their citizens and to decide upon the breadth and depth of the taxes they will extract from their citizens go[es] to the heart of governance.

The Founders' design of federalism, then, is effectively dead. As Michael McConnell argues, "what the people ratified [in 1789] is something quite different from what they got;" the erosion of state power, however, was inevitable, for "whatever the Founders' intentions, the rules they wrote are skewed in favor of national power." And more national power we are likely to have, often at the expense of state sovereignty, for regulation is to the federal government as heroin is to the addict. More, always more, is needed to satisfy its craving. Consider two recent efforts at the national and international level affecting sensitive local issues—our families and our environment.

One proposal would federalize our child support system, an activity heretofore within the purview of the states, by turning the system over to the federal bureaucracy. A recent proposal, advanced by the unlikely duo of conservative Congressman Henry Hyde and liberal ex-Congressman Thomas Downey, would subject to federal review and modification initial state child support orders. Federal modifications could be appealed through a federal administrative process. The proposal also contains a new child support assurance program, whereby the federal government would guarantee child support payments for children whose non-custodial parents fail to pay as ordered.

Delaware Family Court Judge Battle Robinson serves on the U.S. Commission on Interstate Child Support, which recently reported to Congress that it was far from clear that the federal government could do a better job than the states in establishing and enforcing child support. Federalizing the system would end state-generated creativity and innovation. Furthermore, child support is but one aspect of family law that often arises in the context of other family issues traditionally left to states, such as divorce, custody, alimony, and property division. Federalization would also require the U.S. government to create and fund, at the federal level, a system parallel to one already existing at the state level. Although these arguments weigh against the proposal, it is not yet certain that national child support enforcement is a dead issue.

The other movement against states' power to control their own destinies will come as a surprise, for it comes from a just and good cause: the Uruguay Round of GATT. It will surely surprise most readers to learn that under GATT proposals, state consumer and environmental laws and regulations that are deemed unnecessary obstacles to international trade face revocation. Yes, GATT proposals will limit states' sovereignty by imposing internationally determined norms on state conduct. Federalization of our child support system, as unwelcome as it might be, at least leaves decisions in the hands of a federal government that is *our* government. It is something else again to turn over local power to enhance product safety and environmental quality to faceless GATTeers in placid Geneva.

Under the Sanitary and Phytosanitary Standards (for foods, foodstuffs, and beverages) sections of GATT, member nations would be required to take affirmative steps to make the laws of "subfederal" governments comply with GATT. Thus, states wishing to enact consumer or environmental protection laws would be stripped of the power to do so without first obtaining the blessing of GATT members. To enact a law requiring recycling or a carcinogen-labeling law for food products, Delaware would have to notify the U.S. government, provide foreign GATT contracting parties with an opportunity to object, have the federal government consider these foreign objections without its being required to consult Delaware, and sit back while the federal government confidentially negotiates any such objections with the objecting party (again, without Delaware's participation). California's tough new auto emissions standards could be challenged, perhaps by German luxury car exporters. Oregon's prohibition on the export of unprocessed timber could be challenged, perhaps by the Japanese, the world's largest importer of old-growth raw logs. This development could profoundly change the way states do business.

Whether one personally agrees or disagrees with the wisdom of such laws or the wisdom of prohibiting the states from enacting them is not the issue. To me, the prospect of subjecting "subfederal" legislation to veto by an unelected international bureaucracy, absent the safeguards of state and U.S. constitutions, should give us pause. In this case, however, the federal Constitution clearly gives to the Congress the power "to regulate commerce with foreign nations." Outside America's borders our nation must speak with one voice, and it is a national, not a state, voice.

Within our borders, on the other hand, the opposite rule should apply. States should have the power to experiment and innovate for the very reasons set forth in 1787: smaller units of government are better able to respond to people's interests and concerns, and they are less likely to shift economic burdens from one section of the country to another, or to impose public regulation for private gain.

Regarding economic burdens, Congress regularly plays regional favorites at the expense of the nation as a whole. Amendments to energy legislation, for example, often attempt to protect high-sulfur, "dirty" eastern coal from competition with low-sulfur, "clean" western coal. The Davis-Bacon Act, which mandates union wage scales on public construction projects, and steel and automobile import quotas are examples of public laws used for private gain. Peanut and sugar subsidies give a regional spin to the same bottle. State and local governments sometimes play these costly games too, but at least they are unable to inflict their damaging consequences on an entire nation.

The costs of the erosion of federalism are not wholly economic. A federalist form of government recognizes that there are a number of fundamental values that we all share in order to exist as a nation. Our collective dedication to constitutional democracy and a republican form of government are among the things that make us all Americans. But a federalist form of government also recognizes that, beyond our shared principles, we are free to diverge. The ability of states to diverge in manners not inconsistent with the national Constitution reflects the true wisdom of federalism: not only the freedom to set a different course, but the power to do so as well.

Of all the states that should mourn the death of federalism, my own state of Delaware should grieve the most, for its people truly enjoy the blessings of the state's power to set a different course. Most obviously, Delaware has a corporate law guarded by its nearly unique Court of Chancery. Because of these constitutional and legislative creations, Delaware is America's corporate capitol. Corporate franchise fees provide over 20 percent of its state revenues, sparing poor and working poor families the ravages of a sales tax so onerous in nearly every other state. Under a federal system, Delaware may make these choices, but under a national system it might not.

Delaware enjoys a quality of justice recognized and emulated across the nation. Delaware's constitution provides for the appointment of judges and requires a political balance on its courts. A stateless America might mandate the election of local judges,

as is the practice in California, Pennsylvania, and Texas.

In the 1980's, Delaware innovatively modernized its laws governing banking and financial services. Bell-shaped tax-rate curves and market-regulated credit cards blossomed the state's prosperity beyond its wildest dreams: welfare caseloads halved, individual income tax rates declined, and job opportunities exploded. Would this have been possible under national regulations? I don't believe so.

Consider, finally, the flow of history and the sum of our contemporary experience. From geopolitics to GM, the world has learned the perils of large, inflexible organizations and the burden they place on growth and opportunity. The USSR is gone, replaced by a confederation of fifteen governments, all more representative and more responsive to their peoples. General Motors and IBM are going, hobbled by their size and inflexibility. The monster mills of U.S. Steel could not compete; the flexible boutique mills of USX can both compete and win. Massive mainframe computers have been replaced by PC's, programmed for individual needs and networked to allow rapid exchange of locally developed information. Cafeteria employee benefit plans are replacing the one-size-fits-all plans of the past. By the early 1990's, it had become clear to most of us that market economies served by small, flexible entities capable of rapid innovation are the wave of the future.

It is both unfortunate and contradictory, therefore, that against this flow marches the Congress, set free by the federal judiciary, throttling federalism just as the world is recognizing its worth and centralizing authority just as decentralization is coming to be seen as the better option. Federalism is much more than a historical quirk: it is wisdom proven over 200 years and an organizational scheme crucial to success in the Twenty-first Century. America had best return to it, if it is to prosper in the future as it has in the past.

How, then, is the nation to rediscover the virtues of federalism? One would hope that the executive and legislative branches of national government would be the driving forces in our return to our constitutional roots. With rare exceptions, however, Presidents prefer accumulating power in the national government, and Congress's thirst for control is unlikely ever to be slaked. The Supreme Court, therefore, possesses a unique opportunity—even a duty—to lead America back to a more perfect union.

Both *Darby*'s evisceration of the Tenth Amendment and *Garcia*'s 5–4 decision that municipal mass transit systems are interstate commerce are ripe for rethinking. They are a pair of bright-line opportunities to return, in Madison's phrase, to "the sense in which the [C]onstitution was accepted and ratified by the nation" by returning to the states their Constitutional prerogative of governing local affairs. A bolder Court might disapprove federal gerrymandering of local legislative district boundaries to achieve specific racial or ethnic election outcomes, in contravention of the Constitution. In a burst of intellectual candor, the Court might even overturn *Roe v. Wade*, an exercise in denial of state authority as abundant in political support as it is lacking in Constitutional nexus.

But if all this is too unsettling, there exists one prospective opportunity for the Court that, in a single stroke, would send a powerful warning signal to the Congress and reinforce the Court's legitimacy in the eyes of the common citizen. Fifteen states have now, by large majorities, enacted at the ballot box legislative term limits. Litigation to void these voter-inspired limitations on federal power is already in progress. One cannot envisage a stronger statement to those members of Congress abusing federalism than to empower their victims, the citizens of the states comprising the nation, to limit their opportunity to do so.

So will there be states in the Twenty-first Century? Perhaps. I hope so, for as the governments closest to the people, the states and their local governments have historically represented the most responsive and dependable sources of protection and opportunity for individual Americans. Late in the Twentieth Century, we finally learned that uniformity is the enemy of opportunity and diversity its friend. Former West German Chancellor Konrad Adenauer is said to have observed that it was obvious God had placed limits on man's intelligence, but equally obvious that He had placed no such limits on man's foolishness. The beauty of federalism, of course, is that one state's foolishness need not be adopted by another; Congressional foolishness, however, is universal. We must choose carefully the path we wish to tread, for the path of centralization leads to frustration, calcification, and decline; the path of federalism, to the boundless opportunity our forebears saw in their new country and sought to bequeath to future generations of Americans.

READING 14

Who Should Do What?: Divided Responsibility in the Federal System

Paul E. Peterson

Many analysts of American federalism, as illustrated by the contributions of Commager, Kinsley, and du Pont to this volume, begin with a general premise that one level of government, be it state or federal is, broadly speaking, more "fit" to govern than another. Often, such analysts do not pay sufficient heed to the notion that there are different things that different governmental levels do "best" and that the fundamental dilemma of American federalism is, after all, finding the proper balance between state and federal authority while ensuring that each government acts within its greatest spheres of competence. This more sophisticated analytical focus is the starting point for Harvard political scientist Paul Peterson's thoughtful essay.

In Peterson's view, the development of American federalism has witnessed a shift in governmental agendas over time, with the primary responsibility for fostering economic development moving from the national level to state and local governments, which are characterized as best suited to operate in this realm. Unfortunately, Peterson argues, the current wave of conservative reformers now seeks transference of authority over a broad range of social policies to states and localities, governments that are ill-suited to perform this role.

From "Who Should Do What?: Divided Responsibility in the Federal System" by P. E. Peterson, Spring 1995, *The Brookings Review*. Copyright © 1995 by The Brookings Institution. Reprinted by permission.

In support of his position Peterson opines that the national and state governments have distinctively different domestic policy roles. He offers reasons why policies he labels as "developmental," those which manage the physical and social infrastructures necessary for the country's economic growth, are best performed by states and localities. Conversely, as Peterson argues, "redistributive" policies, those that shift resources from the haves to the have-nots, are uniquely suited to national governance.

The newly elected Republican-controlled congress arrived in Washington in January determined to turn a great deal of national policymaking over to the states. The Republicans' twin goals are to cut federal spending on state and local programs and to allow states to design public programs to fit their particular needs.

Many of their proposals—giving states more responsibility for transportation, job training, education, crime control, and other policies that affect economic development—are promising. A number are rightly winning the support of the Clinton administration. Indeed, President Clinton proposes to finance a tax cut by means of substantial reductions in federal spending on roads, housing, education, and flood control. For example, money is to be saved by combining 30 separate grants for construction and repair of mass transit systems, highways, airports, and railroads into a modest, if unified, transportation grant to states and localities.

The convergence of interest between the Republicans and President Clinton results partly, of course, from the enormous pressure exerted on federal spending by demands for tax cuts, the rising cost of senior-citizen entitlements, and the budget deficits piled up during the 1980s. But it also reflects an important trend in American federalism as it has been developing over the past two decades—a shift in economic development responsibilities from the national to the state and local level. Despite partisan infighting, it is entirely possible that some version of these proposals will be enacted and that the shift will continue.

But Republican leaders are also proposing to delegate to the states responsibility for a broad range of social policies that serve low-income citizens. Early in March, for example, the House Ways and Means Committee approved legislation eliminating Aid to Families with Dependent Children, an entitlement program, and replacing it with a fixed block grant that, unlike AFDC, would not increase or decrease depending on the number of welfare recipients. Under the proposed block grant program, states could set, within limited guidelines, their own eligibility standards and benefit levels.

Unlike the Republicans' proposals to increase the state role in economic development policymaking, transferring redistributive policy from Washington to the states would be a mistake. It would defy the logic of the existing division of responsibility between the national and state levels of government and give states responsibility for a policy role for which they are unsuited.

DIVIDING PUBLIC RESPONSIBILITIES

As relations between state and national governments have evolved over this century, the two levels of government have—for very good reasons, as I shall explain shortly—taken distinctively different domestic policy roles. Traditionally, states and localities have taken responsibility for managing the country's physical and social infrastructure—roads, education, mass transit systems, public parks, police and fire services, and sanitation systems—necessary for the country's economic growth. I shall call these kinds of policies *developmental* because without them economic progress would be retarded. The national government, by contrast, has taken responsibility for transferring economic resources from those who have gained the most from economic development to those who have gained the least—the elderly, the disabled, the unemployed, the sick, the poor, families headed by single parents, and others lacking in material resources. I shall refer to these policies as *redistributive* because they shift resources from the "haves" to the "have-nots."

Since 1962, developmental spending at the state and local level has been more than double that at the national level. In 1962, state and local spending was 9.4 percent of gross national product as compared with 4.2 percent for national spending (Figure 3.1).

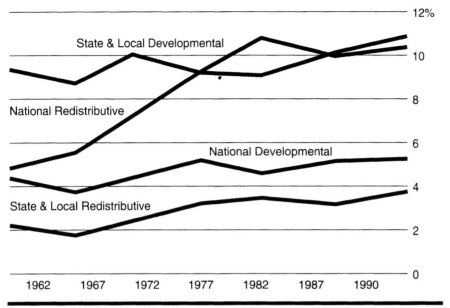

FIGURE 3.1 Redistributive and developmental expenditure of national and of state & local governments as a percentage of the gross national product, 1962–90.

Despite growth in the size of the domestic responsibilities of the national government in subsequent decades, Washington still spends less than half as much on development as the lower tiers. In 1990, the states and localities were spending 10.8 percent of GNP on the country's developmental infrastructure, while the national government was spending only 5.2 percent of GNP.

With regard to redistributive expenditure, the story is entirely different. Since 1962, the state and local share of the country's spending on the elderly, the poor, and the needy has steadily declined. While national government redistributive spending more than doubled, from 4.9 percent of GNP in 1962 to 10.3 percent in 1990, state and local redistributive spending edged up only slightly, from a very low 2.2 percent of GNP in 1962 to only a slightly higher 3.5 percent in 1990. The modest increment at the state and local levels is particularly striking, inasmuch as this was the period when the civil rights movement awakened the country to problems of poverty, the Great Society was introduced, and entitlements became an entrenched part of American social policy.

Yet the percentage of state spending devoted to redistribution increased only from 28.9 percent to 33.0 percent. And at the local level the increase was barely detectable, from 13.5 percent to 14.1 percent.

State and local reluctance to participate in the redistributive movement can hardly be attributed to the political climate. Over most of this period Democrats controlled at least part of state government in most states, and they held unified control over both houses of the state legislature as well as the gubernatorial chair in many. And despite the intent of today's congressional Republicans to transfer welfare policy to the states, there is no indication that states are becoming either more suited for or more capable of such policy.

To the contrary, the division of responsibility between national and state governments is growing more pronounced, as each level of government has learned to concentrate its spending on the things it does best. States and localities, ever more constrained by market forces, are increasingly competent at making choices affecting state and community development. But state and local capacities to care for the needs of poor and disadvantaged citizens have been diminishing.

ECONOMIC DEVELOPMENT ENGINE

Local governments are efficient mechanisms for supplying most of the physical and social infrastructure needed for economic development. In providing roads, schools, sanitation systems, and public safety to their residents, local governments must be sensitive to local businesses and residents. If they ignore them, people will vote with their feet and move to another town. Since 17 percent of the population changes its residence each year, the effects of locational choices on property values can be quickly felt. Moreover, if a locality makes a poor policy choice, its failure will soon become apparent and will be ignored by other communities. If it chooses wisely, its policy will be copied—and thus be disseminated throughout the federal system.

Not all local policies will be identical, of course. People vary in their tastes and preferences. Some towns will provide sex education in their schools; others will not. Some towns will ban smoking in stores and restaurants; others will be more permissive. Some towns will emphasize country lanes for walkers and joggers; others will concentrate on playgrounds and baseball diamonds. Part of what makes local government efficient is the variety it provides for people choosing a place to live.

Developmental policy cannot be an exclusively local prerogative, however. For example, major systems of transportation, air and water pollution control, and some forms of higher education must be coordinated across a substantial geographical area. Thus state governments, too, are significant participants in economic development.

The national government, on the whole, is the least efficient provider of economic development. Unlike states and localities, it operates under few market-like constraints. It need not fear that a series of poor economic investments will cause citizens to move to another country. But without market signals to help guide policy choices, development easily degenerates into political "pork" that does little to spur national economic growth. Proposals to create a na-

tional industrial policy have generally gone nowhere—in good part because proponents cannot convince policymakers that national bureaucracies can allocate scarce economic resources wisely.

Washington did enlarge its developmental responsibilities during the 1970s, largely through grants to state and local governments. Federal dollars were given to cities and towns to help build roads, fight crime, improve schools and redevelop deteriorating central business districts. Members of Congress delighted in taking credit for securing federal dollars that helped build bridges, dams, tunnels, and colliders. Joe McDade of Scranton, Pennsylvania, ranking Republican on the House Appropriations Committee, may have been one of the all-time winners. He secured federal monies to help build a center for the performing arts and fund a microbiology institute for cancer research at the University of Scranton (even though it has no medical school and few research scientists), restore an antique aqueduct, construct McDade Park (including a tourist-friendly museum on the history of coal mining), turn the home of second-rate author Zane Grey into a national monument, finance a flood-control project, and convert a railroad station into a fancy hotel and restaurant.

This kind of developmental pork prospered during the sixties and seventies partly because Congress was organized into subcommittees that focused member attention on narrow issues and interests. But it was also facilitated by the fact that the revenues of the national government increased automatically by means of inflation-induced bracket creep within a steeply progressive income tax. Members of Congress could enjoy increasing tax revenues without ever passing a tax increase. Indeed, it was possible to claim that taxes were being cut even when inflation was causing them to increase. (The famous Kennedy tax cut of 1963, for example, was in fact nothing other than an offset against bracket increase.)

But in 1981 income taxes were sharply reduced, brackets were indexed to inflation, and fiscal deficits mounted. In subsequent years, every new federal program had to be paid for with a new tax. Even existing programs were endangered by the squeeze created by the pressing demand for tax cuts and the rising cost of senior-citizen entitlements. Developmental pork lost its allure. The size of the intergovernmental grant program dropped precipitously, and the percentage of the remaining grants that were developmental (as distinct from redistributive) declined from a high of 59.5 in 1977 to 43.1 in 1990. Far from being a radical departure from past practice, the recent cuts in developmental spending proposed by both Republican leaders and the Clinton administration are just the latest in a decade-long series of like-minded decisions.

Not that Washington should play no role in economic development. Some policies, such as investment in scientific research, have such broad and far-reaching consequences that they must be carried out by the national government. Others, such as certain components of the communication and transportation system, must be coordinated in Washington to achieve a desired degree of national integration. Still other development aid to states and localities allows the national government to minimize the adverse effects of economic development on the environment.

Nevertheless, the national role in economic development has dwindled in recent years under the pressure of fiscal deficits, anti-tax pressures, and senior-citizen entitlements, and it will probably continue to do so.

REDISTRIBUTING THE WEALTH

For the same reason that local governments are best suited to providing economic development—the mobility of labor and capital—they are not effective at redistributing wealth. Local governments, for example, avoid progressive income taxes. No more than 3 percent of local revenues comes from this source. Any locality making a serious attempt to tax the rich and give to the poor will attract more poor citizens and drive away the rich. No amount of determination on the part of local political leaders can make redistributive efforts succeed. If no other force is able to stop their efforts, bankruptcy will.

The smaller the territorial reach of a local government, the less its capacity for redistribution. Most small suburbs in metropolitan areas have almost no capacity to meet the special needs of low-income citizens, because the effects of such actions would be immediately felt in the suburb's tax rate, property

values, and attractiveness to business. Big cities are somewhat better able to undertake redistribution because of their greater geographical reach and their control over extremely valuable land at the heart of the nation's transportation system.

The greater territorial reach of states also makes them better at redistribution than most local governments. The costs of moving across state lines is more substantial than changing residence within a metropolitan area. As against the 17 percent of the population who change residence every year, only 3 percent move across a state line. Even so, labor and capital can and do move, and states must take that possibility into account in their policymaking. Since 1970, for example, states have been in something of a race to lower welfare benefits for fear that high benefits could attract poor people to the state—thus raising social spending and perhaps triggering an exodus of taxpayers.

The bulk of the responsibility for income redistribution falls to the national government. It levies higher taxes on the well-to-do than on the poor, then carries out redistribution through pensions, welfare, health care, and other programs aimed at the needy, the old, the sick, the disabled, and the disadvantaged. The largest and most successful redistributive programs in the United States—Social Security and Medicare—are designed and administered in Washington. And again the explanation is capital and labor mobility—or rather comparative immobility. Washington is best suited to engage in redistribution because it can prevent the in-migration of labor from foreign countries and need not worry as much about the outward flow of capital. If any state or local government had attempted to mount programs like Social Security by itself, it would have gone bankrupt long before becoming a haven for the aged.

The increasing integration of the world economy has begun to erode some of the national government's redistributive capacities. Information and products can move globally at low cost. Capital also flows freely. Nevertheless, as long as the U.S. political economy remains healthy and stable, the national government will continue to have the capability of redistributing substantial amounts of the national income.

Current economic trends are having a considerably more powerful effect at state and local levels. The improvements in transportation and communication systems that have produced an increasingly integrated world economy are also at work among states and localities within the United States itself. Capital, entrepreneurial activity, and skilled labor have become ever more mobile. State and local governments now face increasingly competitive relationships with each other and must attend ever more strictly to economic development. The result is that they are growing ever more reluctant to provide for the needy within their ranks.

MAKING THE BEST OF FEDERALISM

The Republican proposals for wholesale policy shifts from Washington to the states and localities have grabbed their share of headlines, and many are likely to be signed, sealed, and delivered. Plans to transfer economic development functions to the states are not only politically feasible but also smart policy, for they place economic development in the hands of those policymakers best able to manage it.

But the Republican plans to move welfare policymaking to the nation's statehouses are more dubious, if for no other reason than that state and local officials have become increasingly reluctant to pay for the cost of social policy. It is my (perhaps reckless) prediction that any policy enacted in . . . Congress that dramatically shifts the responsibility for welfare downward to states and cities will prove unworkable and short-lived, simply because such shifts run at odds with the underlying structure of the federal system. If I am wrong and welfare policy is permanently turned over to the states, the well-being of the most marginal members of society, including large numbers of children living in poverty, will be adversely affected in serious ways.

States have demonstrated that they are increasingly incapable of sustaining welfare benefits in an ever more integrated economy. State AFDC benefits are jointly funded by the national and state governments but set at the state level. For the first 33 years after AFDC was established in 1937, states raised the real value of this benefit program steadily. The mean benefit paid to a family in the average state was $287 in 1940, $431 in 1950, $520 in 1960, and $608 in 1970 (all figures are in 1993 dollars).

But in 1970 welfare benefits began to decline, partly because states became more fearful that high benefit levels were attracting and retaining poor people within their states. In 1969 the Supreme Court decided, in *Shapiro v. Thompson,* that newcomers could not be denied access to state welfare benefits. Over the next 20 years evidence accumulated that high benefit levels acted as a (low-strength, but nonetheless detectable) welfare magnet. The debate over the welfare magnet intensified and, after 1970, welfare benefits began to fall—to $497 in 1975, $437 in 1980, $409 in 1985. In 1990 they reached $379, and in 1993 they dropped to $349, not much more than they were in 1940!

In the earliest days of this century, states often led the way to innovative social policies (Wisconsin had an unemployment compensation system before the national government did). But in recent years state proposals to reform welfare have generally taken the form of reductions in welfare assistance. In 1988 the Family Support Act explicitly gave states the opportunity to experiment with Aid to Families with Dependent Children. The first three proposals submitted to the Department of Health and Human Services all proposed new restrictions on welfare. Wisconsin and New Jersey petitioned, among other things, to withhold the increase in benefits that typically comes with the birth of an additional child. California proposed an immediate 25 percent reduction in benefits, a second further reduction for all families remaining on welfare after six months, and a restriction that limited benefit levels to new arrivals to California to the level they were receiving in their previous state of residence. What began in a few states is now spreading nationwide.

Although AFDC has been the major target of state welfare cuts, other redistributive programs have proven to be politically unpalatable as well. State general assistance programs have all but disappeared. State supplementary benefits to the long-term unemployed and to disabled persons have also been dramatically reduced, even while national benefits have kept pace with increases in the cost of living. State contributions to unemployment insurance programs have fallen far short of what is necessary to maintain their viability.

LOOKING TO THE FUTURE

Intensified state and local opposition to redistribution is understandable in an economy that has become increasingly integrated and a society that has become ever more mobile. States and localities can no longer make policy choices as if they were living in isolation from other parts of the country. The decisions they take are noticed by people elsewhere, and the impact on their economic and fiscal situation will be felt sooner rather than later. One may regret that states and localities no longer seem capable of caring for their sick and needy, but it is a price a federal system must pay in an ever more integrated society.

Because states and localities are unequipped to finance social welfare programs, their role in any welfare reform should be carefully circumscribed. The legislation approved in March by the House Ways and Means Committee to abolish AFDC gives states far too much latitude to set policy and is almost certain to worsen the "welfare magnet" problem. As some states tighten eligibility standards and reduce benefit levels, states with more generous benefits will become more powerful welfare magnets than ever before and yet will receive no commensurate increase in federal funding, as now happens, if poor people move to take advantage of the more generous benefits. And states are already making strenuous efforts to avoid losing the "race to the bottom."

The state of Wisconsin reported last summer that about 20 percent of new AFDC applicants in Milwaukee county came from new residents, many of whom were arriving from Illinois, a state with lower welfare benefits. To respond to these pressures, Wisconsin asked the national government for permission to try an experiment in which recent migrants would for six months only receive a level of benefits equal to that of the state from which they were migrating. In the past, courts have declared such discriminatory treatment of newcomers as unconstitutional, but the Supreme Court announced last fall that it would be willing to revisit this issue. If discrimination against newcomers to a state is given constitutional blessing, a new round of state welfare cuts can be anticipated.

Time has shown that the national government has a different sphere of competence than that of state and local governments. The new breeze blowing through Washington should capitalize on this increasingly well-known fact and return to states and localities most of the responsibility for maintaining the nation's physical and social infrastructure necessary to sustain economic growth. But some things, namely programs for the sick, the poor, the needy, and the elderly, remain a Washington responsibility. To turn these responsibilities over to the states is to turn the clock backward.

READING 15

The Enduring Features of American Federalism

Martha Derthick

The thrust of Virginia political scientist Martha Derthick's argument in this thoughtful essay is that, while the precise balance between state and federal power may be characterized in graphically different ways in different historical periods, there remains, nevertheless, a great deal about American federalism that is enduring and not subject to the vagaries of the times. Indeed, Derthick writes, "Our federalism is much like a piece of earth that is subject to constant redevelopment. It can be bulldozed and built up, flattened and regraded, virtually beyond recognition. Yet certain elemental properties of it, the bedrock and the composition of the soil, endure."

The enduring elements of federalism identified by Derthick are many and they are quite useful in helping us to understand the federalism dilemma. Derthick notes, for example, that the states are governments in their own right, albeit inferior ones. Congress, in dealing with the states, has discretion that can result in deference, displacement, or, most commonly, interdependence.

From "The Enduring Features of American Federalism" by M. Derthick, 1989, *The Brookings Review,* Summer 1989, pp. 34–38. Copyright © 1989 by The Brookings Review. Reprinted by permission.

One point emphasized by Derthick that is too often missed by analysts keeping score on who is "winning" the battle among governmental levels is the notion that federalism fosters bargaining among governments. States "can talk back.... They can influence the terms of cooperation." This opportunity to "talk back" is for Derthick, the prime virtue of American federalism. It allows those closest to the realities of domestic problems to have input in their solutions through a policy dialogue with federal authorities. It is critical in this dialogue, according to Derthick, that states act as governments and not as supplicants. Derthick completes her analysis by noting that the current shape of federalism is largely what the framers intended insofar as the states have, indeed, worked to aid the federal government in the task of governing.

It is a commonplace of scholarship that American federalism constantly changes.

And it is a commonplace of contemporary comment that the states are enjoying a renaissance. Their historic role as laboratories of experiment is acknowledged with praise. Their executives and legislatures are increasingly active, seizing issues, such as economic development, that the federal government has failed to come to grips with. State courts are staking out positions on individual rights in advance of those defined by the U.S. Supreme Court, while state attorneys general pursue consumer protection and antitrust cases that federal agencies have ignored. The states' share of government revenue has gained slightly on that of the federal government in the 1980s, and considerably surpasses that of local governments, contrary to a pattern that prevailed until the 1960s. The states' standing with the public and with prospective employees has improved. The governors are getting their share of good press and, what may be almost as important, of presidential nominations. As a result, state governments are perceived to have improved their position in the federal system.

Yet it is worth recalling how different the impression was but a short time ago, and how little has changed in some respects. Early in 1984 the Advisory Commission on Intergovernmental Relations pub-

lished a much-noticed report, *Regulatory Federalism,* detailing a wide range of new or expanded federal controls over state government. In 1985, in the case of *Garcia* v. *San Antonio Metropolitan Transit Authority,* the Supreme Court declined to protect the state governments from congressional regulation under the Constitution's commerce clause and then washed its hands of this crucial federalism question. In the spring of 1988 the court removed the constitutional prohibition on federal taxation of income from interest on state and local government bonds (*South Carolina* v. *Baker*).

Certain regulatory excesses of the federal government vis-à-vis the states have been modified in the past several years; rules regarding transportation of the disabled and bilingual education are two examples. Yet not even under Ronald Reagan did the federal government step back from the new constitutional frontiers mapped out in the last decade or two—frontiers such as the Clean Air Act of 1970, which addresses the states with the language of outright command ("Each state shall . . ."). The president's executive order of October 1987 on federalism may be interpreted as an attempt to draw back, with its rhetorical statement of federalism principles and its instructions to executive agencies to refrain from using their discretion to preempt state action. But to read it is to be reminded of how little unilateral power the president has. The drawing back can succeed only to the extent the national legislature and courts concur. Nor did the Reagan administration consistently adhere to its professed principles. Substantive policy goals often were in tension with devolution of power to the states; the Reagan administration could be counted on to opt for devolution only when that tactic was consistent with its pursuit of a freer market and lower federal spending.

American federalism is a very large elephant indeed, and it is hard for a lone observer to grasp the properties of the whole beast. One needs to be abreast of constitutional doctrines; of legislative, judicial. and administrative practices over the whole range of government activities, from taxation to protection of civil liberties to pollution control; of the development or disintegration of political parties (are they decaying at the grass roots? at the center? both? neither?); of the volume and locus of interest group activity; of trends in public opinion and public employment, and more. To understand the condition of federalism, one needs to comprehend the functioning of the whole polity.

Granting that the federal system is always in flux, it is harder than one might suppose even to detect the dominant tendencies. While most academic analysts probably would assert that centralization is the secular trend, such distinguished scholars as Princeton political scientist Richard P. Nathan and Brandeis historian Morton Keller have argued that centralization is not inexorable and that the evolution of American federalism follows a cyclical pattern, with the federal government and the states alternately dominating.

MAPPING THE TERRAIN

Fighting the customary temptation to concentrate on change, I want to try to identify some elemental and enduring truths of American federalism. I want to map the features of the terrain, a metaphor that may be in fact apt. Our federalism is much like a piece of earth that is subject to constant redevelopment. It can be bulldozed and built up, flattened and regraded, virtually beyond recognition. Yet certain elemental properties of it, the bedrock and the composition of the soil, endure. I will start with propositions that I take to be purely factual and then proceed to others that are more analytical and normative, hence debatable.

The states are governments in their own right. They have constitutions that derive from the people and guarantee specific rights. They have elected legislatures that make laws, elected executives that enforce laws, and courts that interpret them—and not incidentally interpret the laws of the United States as well. State governments levy taxes. Their territorial integrity is protected by the U.S. Constitution, which also guarantees them equal representation in the Senate and a republican form of government. These creatures that walk like ducks and squawk like ducks must be ducks.

Nevertheless, the states are inferior governments. In our pond, they are the weaker ducks. The stubbornly persistent mythology that govern-

ments in the American federal system are coordinate should not obscure that fact. The two levels of government are *not* coordinate and equal, nor did the winning side in 1787 intend them to be. One cannot deny the existence of the Constitution's supremacy clause and the prescription that state officers take an oath to uphold the Constitution of the United States, or the fact that the framers of the Constitution fully expected an instrumentality of the federal government, the Supreme Court, to settle jurisdictional issues in the "compound republic," as James Madison called it. See *Federalist* No. 39, in which Madison makes a feeble, unsuccessful attempt to deny that the court's having this function gives the federal government a crucial advantage.

Whether the federal government has always been superior in fact can certainly be debated. At various times and places its writ did not run very strong. Ours was a different system in the 19th century, and it is significant that the full impact on federalism of the post–Civil War Amendments on civil rights was long delayed. Only recently has the South ceased to have a deviant social system. But on the whole, the federal government has won the crucial conflicts. Surely its ascendancy is not currently in dispute. Not only are the states treated as its administrative agents; they accept such treatment as a fact of life. Not since *Brown* v. *Board of Education* (1954) and *Baker* v. *Carr* (1962) have truly strenuous protests been heard from the states against their palpably inferior status.

The states' status as governments, even though inferior ones, gives Congress a range of choice in dealing with them. It may chose deference, displacement, or interdependence. In domestic affairs Congress always has the option of doing nothing, knowing that the states can act whether or not it does. Sometimes Congress consciously defers to the states, judging that the subject properly "belongs" to them. Perhaps just as often, Congress today is not deliberately deferential but fails to act for lack of time or the ability to reach agreement. It defaults. The area of congressional inaction, be it through deference or default, is reliably quite large. It normally includes new issues, such as AIDS or comparable worth. States remain on the front lines of domestic policy, the first to deal with newly perceived problems. Congress tends to defer or default on particularly difficult issues, such as the amount of support to be given to needy single mothers with children.

Congress rarely employs its second option, complete displacement, although explicit invocations of it, using the term "preemption," are more frequent now than they used to be. The third option, interdependence, is very common, I would think predominant. Through some combination of inducements, sanctions, or contractual agreements, Congress enters into collaborative arrangements with the states in the pursuit of national ends. The most common techniques are conditional grants-in-aid, which are characteristic of programs for income support and infrastructure development, and qualified preemptions, which are typical of the "new" regulation, including environmental protection and occupational health and safety. Congress sets standards but tells states that if they meet or exceed the national standards, they may retain the function, including administration.

The vigor and competence with which state governments perform functions left to them does not protect them against congressional incursions. Here I mean to challenge one of the leading canards of American federalism. Whenever Congress takes domestic action, that action is rationalized as a response to the failures of the states. Congress has had to step in, it is said, because states were not doing the job. The only thing one can safely say about the origins of nationalizing acts is that they are responses to the power of nationalizing coalitions. When Congress acts, in other words, it is not necessarily because states have failed; it is because advocates of national action have succeeded in mustering enough political force to get their way. State inaction may constitute part of their case, but state actions that are offensive to their interests may do so as well. Pathbreaking states have often demonstrated what can be done.

Congress's usual choice, moreover, is to cooperate with the states, not to displace them, and in the relationships of mutual dependence that result, it is a nice question just whose deficiencies are being com-

pensated for. The federal government typically contributes uniform standards and maybe money. The states typically do the work of carrying out the function. The more they do and the better they do it, the more they are likely to be asked or ordered by Congress to do.

In cooperating with the states, Congress again has a choice. It can emphasize their status as governments, or It can emphasize their inferiority as such. Our ambiguous constitutional system enables Congress to view the states as equals or as agents. Congress gradually has abandoned the former view in favor of the latter. It has done so with the acquiescence of the Supreme Court, which once tried to defend "dual federalism"—that is, the notion that the states were sovereign, separate, and equal—but which has long since abandoned that doctrine. And Congress does not indulge its agents. Ask any federal bureau chief. Congress is very poor at balancing the ends and means of action. All major federal executive agencies—the Environmental Protection Agency, the Social Security Administration, the Immigration and Naturalization Service, to cite just a few—are laboring under a burden of excessive obligation.

Because states are governments, they may bargain with Congress. Bargaining is the usual mode of intergovernmental relations. State governments, even when treated by Congress as administrative agents, are agents with a difference. Unlike federal executive agencies, they are not Congress's creatures. Therefore they can talk back to it. They can influence the terms of cooperation.

This bargaining between levels of governments is good, depending on how the states use it. Here again I mean to challenge what I take to be a conventional view. Fragmentation of authority in the federal system is ordinarily portrayed, at least in academic literature, as a severe handicap to the federal government's pursuit of its goals. The federal government would be more effective, it is commonly said, if it did not have to rely so heavily on other governments. I believe, to the contrary, that the federal government needs a great deal of help, of a kind that can best be supplied—perhaps can only be supplied—by governments. It needs help with all aspects of governing, that is, with all the functions that legislatures, courts, and executives perform. Beyond that, it needs a great deal of help quite specifically in adjusting its goals to social and economic realities and to the capacities of administrative organizations.

Madison may be cited in support of this view—not the famous passage in *Federalist* No. 51 that one might anticipate, in which he argues that "the different governments will control each other, at the same time that each will be controlled by itself," but a passage less remarked, yet perhaps more prescient, in No. 62. In this essay on the Senate, Madison wrote: "A good government implies two things: first, fidelity to the object of government, which is the happiness of the people; secondly, a knowledge of the means by which that object can be best attained. Some governments are deficient in both these qualities; most governments are deficient in the first. I scruple not to assert, that in American governments too little attention has been paid to the last."

The deficiency in our attention to the means of government has never been more glaring. All institutions of the federal government—Congress, presidency, courts—have far more to do than they can do, but the executive agencies as the instruments of government action are arguably the most overburdened of all. Perhaps even more glaring today than the federal government's shortfall of institutional capacity is its shortfall of fiscal capacity. It has obligations far in excess of its willingness or ability to meet them. Whether that is a product of party politics or has other causes need not concern us here. The fact of the deficit is plain enough.

State governments help fill the federal government's performance gaps. They do much of the work of governing, as Madison anticipated. Even as an ardent nationalist, at the time of the Constitutional Convention, he held to the view that the national government would not be suited to the entire task of governing "so great an extent of country, and over so great a variety of objects." Just how right he was has never been clearer. But if the states help fill the federal government's implementation gaps, they also are very much at risk of being victimized by them. Congress will try to close the distance between what it wants and what the federal government is able to do independently by ordering the states to do it.

AN APPEAL TO TALK BACK

The states are entitled to talk back. As governments in their own right, they have an independent responsibility to set priorities and balance means against ends. Because they are closer to the practical realities of domestic problems and because they lack the power to respond to deficits by printing money, state governments are in a superior position to do that balancing.

This appeal to the states to talk back is not a call to defiance, but a call to engage federal officials in a policy dialogue—and, having done so, to address those officials with language suitable to governments. If states habitually present themselves as supplicants for assistance—supplicants like any other interest group—they will inevitably contribute to the erosion of their own status.

I believe that the states *are* increasingly using the language of governments, rather than supplicants, in their dialogue with the federal government. The enactment in 1988 of welfare reform legislation, which a working group of the National Governors Association helped to shape, is an example. The governors drew on the state governments' experience with welfare programs to fashion changes that would be both politically and administratively feasible, besides containing improved assurances of federal funding for welfare.

There are numerous explanations for the new, more authoritative voice of the states. One is that individually the states have heightened competence and self-confidence as governments, whatever the range among them (and the range between, say, Virginia and Louisiana is very great). Another is that the decline of federal aid under Presidents Carter and Reagan has compelled greater independence. A third is that self-consciousness and cohesion of the states as a class of governments have increased, as indicated by the development of organized, well-staffed mechanisms of cooperation. Their shared status as agents of Congress and objects of its influence has caused the states to cooperate with one another today to a degree unprecedented in history, even if they remain intensely competitive in some respects, such as the pursuit of economic development.

I have concentrated on relations between the states and Congress to keep the subject focused and relatively simple. But the federal judiciary rivals the legislature as a framer of federal-state relations. Federal courts, like Congress, can choose to emphasize the states' standing as governments or their inferiority as such. Like Congress, over time the courts have come to favor the latter choice, so that states today are routinely commanded to implement the detailed policy decisions of national courts as well as the national legislature.

For the states, it is one thing to talk back to Congress, quite another and much harder thing to talk back to the federal courts. Yet here as well, they have been trying to find ways to talk back more effectively. The National Association of Attorneys General and the State and Local Legal Center, both with offices in Washington, now offer advice and assistance to state and local governments involved in litigation before the Supreme Court. Such governments in the past have often suffered from a lack of expert counsel.

It is no use to portray these developments in federal-state relations as a transgression of the framers' intentions, at least if we take the *Federalist* as our authoritative guide to those intentions. Alexander Hamilton foresaw with evident satisfaction the federal-state relation that obtains today. In *Federalist* No. 27, he wrote that "the plan reported by the convention, by extending the authority of the federal head to the individual citizens of the several States, will enable the government to employ the ordinary magistracy of each, in the execution of its laws.... Thus the legislatures, courts, and magistrates, of the respective [states], will be incorporated into the operations of the national government... and will be rendered auxiliary to the enforcement of its laws." This is exactly what has happened.

What Hamilton would certainly not be satisfied with, however, is the federal government's management of its own administrative and fiscal affairs. One

therefore feels entitled to invoke Madison on the states' behalf. It is not enough today that the states help the national government with governing, the function that both Hamilton and Madison foresaw. It is important as well that they perform a modern version of the balancing function that Madison in particular foresaw. This requires that in their policy dialogue with the federal government they assert, as governments in their own right, the importance of balancing ends and means.

FOOD FOR THOUGHT

1. What are the "best" arguments that Michael Kinsley makes for the "withering away" of the states and Pete du Pont makes for their strengthening? How would each respond to the points made by the other? Should the states be made more or less powerful in the American federal system? Why?

2. Paul Peterson's argument in *Who Should Do What? Divided Responsibility in the Federal System* develops from the view that states operate best in the realm of "developmental" policy while the federal government is best suited for "redistributive" policymaking. Do you agree with Peterson's basic premise? Why or why not? Can you offer examples to support your position?

3. Can you offer an example of one policy area where contemporary American federalism is "working" and one where it is not? How can you account for federalism's performance in these two areas? Can the area in which contemporary federalism is not working be "fixed?" Why or why not? Elaborate.

4. We have seen that federalism is an ongoing process of American governance and that it is in a continually developmental state. What, in your view, are the two biggest federalism issues that will confront the United States for the remainder of the twentieth century? How should they be resolved? Can a federal system be "justified" for a polity whose problems are fundamentally national in nature?

CHAPTER 4

PUBLIC OPINION

Public opinion is a particularly important concern in a representative democracy. Representative government is based, in part, on the notion that public opinion should count. The consent of the governed is important. Does government merely reflect opinion? Does it lead opinion? Does it generate propaganda to create opinion? What is public opinion? Does it take different forms? How do various kinds of public opinion affect the political process in the United States?

V. O. Key, in a classic study of public opinion three decades ago, offers a sensible general definition of public opinion in a political system: "those opinions held by private persons which governments find it prudent to heed." These few words contain some important messages. He writes of "opinions"—not a single opinion. He does not specify how strong, how constant, how intelligent, or how well informed the opinions must be to have the potential for political salience. Nor does he indicate the objects of the opinions that matter. They do not have to be focused directly on a current public policy issue in order for the government to find them "prudent to heed."

Public opinion deals with at least three levels of political objects: policies, public officials, and the political system in general. Opinions about specific policies and specific office holders/challengers are the most observable because they are featured in polls sponsored by and reported in the mass media. Citizens' views on some substantive issues and on the competitors for various elected offices are reported frequently on television and radio and in newspapers. There is also deeper opinion about the legitimacy and relative effectiveness of the political system itself. That opinion is often probed by academics, but does not get much attention in the mass media.

A different set of questions revolves around the "quality" of public opinion on political matters. How

stable is it? How informed? How rational and coherent?

There are, both in the scholarly literature and in more popular analyses, a number of negative, even cynical, views about the capacity of the public to hold stable, sensible, meaningful opinions. The public is portrayed as largely uninformed, apathetic, fickle, and easily swayed. Attention by politicians and government officials to presumed public opinion is often portrayed as cynical manipulation for political ends. The assumptions that lead to these conclusions often seem to be that the public must be constantly interested in politics, follow and know the details about individuals and policies, and express coherent views that meet some analysts' specification of the meaning of "rationality." These assumptions are both unreasonable and unrealistic.

There are also analyses that portray quite a different situation. The first reading in this section, "Polls Portray a Considered and Stable Public Opinion" by Albert H. Cantril and Susan Davis Cantril, argues that the public has coherent, persistent views of what it wants from public policy. It also possesses a general understanding of the means it favors to achieve those ends.

How does the public inform itself about political and policy matters? Naturally, some people are more interested than others. Those who are generally interested can obtain a great deal of information from a variety of mass media: television, radio, newspapers, and magazines. Those who are consumed by politics can and do seek out additional sources of information such as newsletters or C-SPAN. Those who have little interest probably rely more on occasional conversations with friends and fellow workers and on snatches of information provided by the mass media.

The second reading in this chapter, "Media Impact on Attitudes and Behavior" by Doris Graber, addresses the political socialization of Americans by the mass media.

Various segments of the public are differentially interested in selected aspects of politics. Most probably have at least a general opinion on the legitimacy and viability of our political system at a very broad level. Opinions about the general quality of the major institutions of government—Congress, the presidency, the Supreme Court, and the bureaucracy at the federal level—are also widespread. Fewer people have opinions about specific officials, although more pay attention during election campaigns. And fewer still follow a broad range of public policy issues, although specific issues will excite subsets of the population. For example, some individuals will get very engaged in articulating strongly held opinions about abortion rights or gun control or environmental matters but may care very little about any other public issues.

As the public thinks about specific institutions the Supreme Court fares best. It is much more highly regarded than Congress. Opinion about the presidency is somewhere in between. In 1996, for example, 45 percent of the general public had "a great deal" or "quite a lot" of confidence in the Supreme Court, 39 percent felt that way about the presidency, and only 20 percent were as positive about Congress. In general, public confidence in all three institutions fluctuates in the same direction. The rank order of which institutions get the highest and lowest approval remains the same even as the specific numbers fluctuate: Supreme Court at the top, the presidency second, and Congress last.

Government in general has a two-way relationship with public opinion. In broad terms, the public tries to influence what various governmental institutions do. At the same time officials in those governmental institutions try to persuade the public that the institutions are doing what the public wants. Public opinion constrains what the government can do; government agencies set some limits to and directions for public opinion.

Each of the principal governing institutions has somewhat different relationships with its publics. Both Congress and the president are particularly visible to the public, which has opinions about both. The courts are less visible.

In the case of Congress, several general statements capture the essence of the general public's view. First, Congress as an institution is not very highly regarded. In recent years only between one in five and one in three Americans have expressed general approval of the way Congress is doing its job. In the abstract, the general public expresses support for the notion that members of the House and Senate should have limits on how long they can serve.

At the same time, however, the electorate has returned a very high proportion of incumbents running for reelection to office. Even in the election of 1994, which saw the Republicans capture a majority in the House of Representatives for the first time since the election of 1952, and regain a majority in the Senate for the first time since the election of 1984, over 90 percent of the incumbents running for reelection in both houses won. In 1996, 95 percent of incumbents in both houses seeking reelection won. In the 24 congressional elections between 1950 and 1996 only 5 times did the percentage of incumbents who were successful in seeking reelection fall below 90 percent. And in those five cases, between 87 percent and 89 percent were successful.

Turnover in Senate membership is greater than in the House because of the longer term for members (six years), the advanced age of many incumbents, and the fact that high visibility challengers such as governors often contest Senate seats. But even so, in the 24 elections from 1950 through 1996 almost 80 percent of the incumbents running for reelection won.

In recent years the public, when asked, has stated its preference for having the presidency and Congress controlled by different political parties. Presumably they don't trust either party a great deal and/or like the additional visible "check and balance" presumably created by a situation of "divided government." They reaffirmed this preference in the 1996 election by re-electing both a Democratic president and Republican majorities in the House and Senate.

The president, of course, is the object of much attention and much polling. Pollsters repeatedly ask the public how they think the president is doing throughout his time in office. At election time (which, as defined by the media and the necessities of campaign fundraising, begins several years before the election) the candidates are the focus of attention and, in the last few months before the election, are the object of literally continuous polling. The president and his advisors are certainly well aware of how he is viewed at all times.

Can aggressive presidents also move public opinion? The broad answer is affirmative. More popular presidents have a greater chance of moving opinion than less popular presidents. And presidents have a greater chance of molding public opinion than other federal officials because they are so constantly in the public view and have so many outlets for airing their opinions. However, even popular presidents can move public opinion only a short distance. The American people are unlikely to be swayed suddenly to change their opinions dramatically and fundamentally just because a popular president tries to create that kind of movement. In fact, most modern presidents calculate fairly carefully how far they might move public opinion on a few selected issues of most importance to them.

Public opinion also has an impact on the Supreme Court, although it is more indirect than in the case of impact on elected officials in the White House and Congress. Over time, persistent and strongly held public opinion will show up in Court decisions because that same opinion will help influence who is elected to the presidency—the source of nominations for open seats on the Court—and to the U. S. Senate, which is responsible for confirming or rejecting presidential nominations. Justices are also aware of the public's view of the Court's legitimacy, an awareness that exercises a subtle influence over Court opinions. But in the short run, justices have a great deal of freedom to act without much regard to current swings in public opinion on the issues they must decide. The Court does little to create or change public opinion. Ultimately, it is constrained by the same forces and political context—including public opinion—that limit all governing institutions in the United States.

The third reading, "Public Opinion and the Rehnquist Court" by Thomas R. Marshall, explores this relationship from the mid-1980s to the mid-1990s.

What impact does public opinion on policy questions have on government decision making? Again, the idea of constraints is helpful. Public opinion at the general level can posit general goals and can at least rule out certain means of achieving those goals. More attentive publics will have more explicit ideas about desirable means. At this point, public opinion be-

comes transmitted in part by interest groups, which often compete over both goals and means.

The fourth reading, "Can Inattentive Citizens Control Their Elected Representatives" by R. Douglas Arnold, explores the dynamics of public policy preferences and the degree of control exercised over legislators. He argues that elections, in fact, provide a reasonably good means of general control.

Public opinion at the aggregate level is a familiar item to anyone who watches television news, listens to radio news, or reads newspapers or newsmagazines. It is familiar because of the frequency of public opinion polls. Some of the polls are well done and meaningful. Others are less well done and less helpful. But they are a fact of American public and political life and will remain so. The final reading in this section, "Advice to Poll Consumers" by Herbert Asher, carefully analyzes some of the aspects of polls and gives readers some hints on how to evaluate them. Officials read polls carefully—and commission a number of them as well. Citizens interested in public affairs also need to know how to read polls intelligently. The polls may be imperfect, but, when read correctly, good polls can tell us a great deal about our collective preferences and mood.

READING 16

Polls Portray a Considered and Stable Public Opinion

Albert H. Cantril and Susan Davis Cantril

This article serves two major purposes. First, it summarizes empirically supported conclusions about the nature of American public or mass opinion. In doing so it draws on five decades of social science research on public opinion. Second, the article indicates that some cynical views of the capacity of

From "Polls Portray a Considered and Stable Public Opinion" by A. H. Cantril and S. D. Cantril, 1996, *The Public Perspective,* June/July 1996, pp. 23–26. © *The Public Perspective,* a publication of the Roper Center for Public Opinion Research, University of Connecticut, Storrs. Reprinted by permission.

the American people to accumulate and process information on public matters are based on polls—or at least reports of poll results—that do not probe deeply enough for the underlying structure of thought that contains links that make seemingly shallow, unconnected, changing opinions much more coherent, rational, and stable. The authors examine conventional wisdom about the inadequacies of the American public and find that conventional wisdom wanting.

Albert and Susan Cantril, consultants on survey and opinion research based in Washington, D. C., argue that, properly conducted and understood, polls reveal a public that knows what it wants from public policy, has a good sense of the best means of achieving its goals, and holds stable underlying opinions. At the same time, the wording of, frequency of, and publicity given opinion polls often makes the public seem whimsical, inattentive, and unstable. The authors blame the pollsters and, by inference, the media for giving this impression.

The seven general statements about the nature of U. S. public opinion they use to summarize the evidence in a vast literature are all worth extended discussion. One of the most important is the first: "While most people are only marginally attentive to political matters, they pay attention to those that are important to them." Sometimes, students of politics and public affairs fall into the trap of thinking that unless the general public pays as much attention to such matters as they do that the public is, therefore, composed of defective citizens. That is not the case. Politics does not need to be an all-consuming passion on the part of all citizens all of the time to have a functioning democracy.

Differing assessments of the capabilities of the American public have animated debate about its appropriate role in our political process since the beginning of the republic.

Evidence of the general public's uneven knowledge and attention to issues is the usual take-off point when the issue comes up. But, since there has been no marked decline in public awareness in recent years, today's concern must have a different origin.

We suspect notice now given the matter arises largely because of difficulties our political institutions are having in playing their traditional role mediating between the public's concerns and governmental action.

We share Robert Dahl's sense that the scale and complexity of issues facing the country make it more difficult to find common ground in efforts to solve the nation's problems. This is reflected in a lack of comity between ends of Pennsylvania Avenue, diffused power of the political parties, and the proliferation of interest groups protecting ever narrower pockets of public policy.

At the same time, our diversity as a nation becomes a more prominent feature of public discourse as windows keep opening for the "direct" expression of opinion: talk radio, electronic town meetings, and "grassroots" lobbying (often aided by new technologies and fed by special interest money). To Dahl all of this means more of what we don't need (fragmentation) and less of what we do need (integration).

We would add that the shifting institutional arrangements have changed the environment in which polls are conducted and consumed. More than ever, pollsters have become brokers between the public and the tangled trade-offs inherent in most policy issues.

This, in turn, has reinforced the "referendum paradigm" in polling. Incentives are for an up/down rendition of public opinion on the hot topic of the day rather than a fuller portrait of the public's thinking. News organizations that sponsor polls want the "bottom line" of whether the public is for or against an issue. Polls sponsored by private interests often want to show a solid public consensus behind some agenda.

All of this troubles many in polling who are uneasy with the simplified characterizations of public opinion that so often drive political debate. But, more generally, thoughtful people wonder whether poll percentages portray a public opinion that is considered and stable enough to play so prominent a role in our politics.

POLLSTERS AND THEIR ASSUMPTIONS

Early polling was driven by the populist premise that an innate wisdom resided in the people and that the polls uniquely could express that opinion as a counterbalance to the moneyed special interests. Challenges to these assumptions were at first philosophical. But with time the pollsters were challenged to advocate less for their profession and use their tools to check out their assumptions.

An early empirical challenge came in 1964 with publication of Philip Converse's analysis of data from the National Election Studies of the late 1950s. It called into question the pollsters' confidence that their polls were tapping "true" opinions and that there was coherence in public thinking.

In looking at responses given by respondents who were interviewed three times from 1956 to 1960, Converse was alarmed by four findings: some people gave different answers to the same question when interviewed at different times; what seemed minor changes in question wording had a major effect on responses; people's views on issues did not hang together in substantively compatible patterns; and few people invoked abstract political concepts when describing their thinking about issues.

This led Converse to conclude that poll interviews were less a window on the "belief systems" of respondents than they were accounts of random answers people gave off the tops of their heads and that most people did not have "meaningful beliefs" on most issues. His analysis set off vigorous debate in academic circles which, in time, dealt with the issues he had raised.

Meanwhile, political science, sociology, and psychology all had public opinion in their scope. But they came at it from differing perspectives. Political science and sociology tended to look at public opinion in the aggregate whereas psychology focused on the individual as the holder of an opinion. As a consequence political science and sociology often glossed over individual differences and psychology was less concerned with generalizing from findings at the individual level to the public as a whole. Neither approach was "right" or "wrong." Instead the two were focusing on different parts of the problem.

In the last 30 years, the field of opinion research has come a long way, due in large part to what the different disciplines have brought to their common topic. Political scientists are more alert to factors explaining *individual* behavior, psychologists are more attentive to

how their insights may be reflected in *collective* opinion, and "political psychology" has come into its own.

THE BURDEN OF THE EVIDENCE

There is much to draw on when looking at what has been learned *empirically* about the savvy the public brings to its responsibilities in our democracy.

Our best sense of where the burden of evidence now lies can be summarized in seven conclusions:

1. While most people are only marginally attentive to political matters, they pay attention to those that are important to them.

Different studies have used different criteria to judge whether the public is on top of current issues and knowledgeable about the basics of our system of government. Russell Neuman has reviewed extensive survey data on the matter. He identifies "three publics:" about 5% who are highly active and attentive to politics, 20% who are mostly passive and inattentive, and the remaining 75% who are minimally attentive.

But while most Americans fall in the "minimally attentive" public identified by Neuman, they do track issues that are of particular concern to them. For example, people most supportive of choice in reproductive matters are also most likely to learn about court decisions on the issue.

2. The political beliefs of Americans are not organized on a left-right continuum.

Many people may identify themselves as "liberals" or "conservatives" but it does not follow that they see the distinction as one between polar positions on issues. For one thing, self-identified "liberals" and "conservatives" use fundamentally different concepts to describe their ideology rather than voice opposing views on common concepts. For another, identity with one ideological position or the other is as much a matter of liking or disliking an ideological label as the mix of one's positions on issues.

It has also been shown that as many as five ideological dimensions may be needed to account for the public's views on specific issues. Thus, while views on specific issues can frequently be anticipated by knowing a person's views on a more general issue, a left-right conception is inadequate in accounting for the way most people think about politics.

3. Values cannot be left out of the picture.

Values, as used here, are the explicit and implicit standards people use to gauge the desirability of both ends and means of action. The importance of values to opinion research is that people are usually quite clear about their values. Case studies have shown values to be key to understanding the "inner coherence" among the political opinions people have. Quantitative research has also shown that respondents' views on specific issues are usually linked one way or another to some underlying value.

Further evidence of the stability values contribute to opinion is that answers respondents give to questions about seemingly disparate issues tend to hold together if they evoke some common value. This is why careful analysis of poll data can pinpoint themes that underlie views on issues that may not at first appear related to one another.

4.   Public opinion tends to be quite stable on most issues and, when it changes, tends to do so in sensible ways and for good reasons.

Benjamin Page and Robert Shapiro examined shifts in opinion over fifty years as measured by more than 1,000 questions that were repeated word-for-word at different times. Fewer than half (42%) of these soundings picked up a change from an earlier measure that was larger than might be explained by chance in the sampling process. When statistically significant changes did emerge, they were modest (almost half of them amounting to less than ten percentage points).

Three additional findings from their analysis of opinion change should be noted. First, changes almost always followed some event or could be accounted for by the effect of some social or economic trend on people's lives. Second, when opinion changed, it usually did not swing back to its earlier position. Third, when opinion changed, it tended to do so in roughly the same degree for all subgroups in the population.

5. Polls are able to pick up much of the social surroundings within which an individual expresses an opinion.

Some contend it is gilding the numbers to characterize poll percentages as "public opinion" since they represent nothing more than a tally of replies from individuals living in completely separate worlds. The argument is that "mass opinion" is being measured, because there is no sense in which "the public" has participated as a collectivity in arriving at the opinion. Unlike public opinion, it is argued, mass opinion is not more than the sum of its parts.

There is much evidence that this distinction between "public" and "mass" opinion is blurred in the real world. Respondents in polls are not atomized and totally insulated from the experience of others. They take their cues on most issues from a variety of sources including public figures they esteem, everyday encounters, and more generally those who share similar goals, assumptions, and frustrations. By definition these influences bring the individual's opinions into contact with others, the intersection where, in the words of Bill Kovach, "personal opinion must contest with public responsibility."

6. Attitude consistency is in the eye of the opinion-holder.

It is not uncommon when analyzing the results of a poll to find people expressing opinions that appear to be in conflict. The way questions have been worded may account for some of these apparent contradictions. But something else is usually occurring.

Most often the explanation is found by uncovering some additional dimension of opinion that underlies the two views that seem inconsistent. Consider the respondent who wants the US to be stronger militarily while at the same time advocating a reduction in defense spending. The tension between these views will disappear if one learns the respondent also thinks we can get more military bang for the buck.

A related process can be at work, but at a more basic level, when an issue brings two or more values into conflict. We found, for example, that many respondents who expressed moral concern about homosexuality *also* affirmed the privacy of such a relationship between consenting adults.

Among other factors that have been identified as accounting for an individual's seemingly inconsistent views are cultural norms, past experience, an individual's ability to tolerate inconsistency, and how much the respondent's sense of self is invested in an opinion.

7. People differ in the ways they think about politics.

We are aware today of the many different ways people take in information and how this can affect the way they view issues. But much early research regarding public opinion and political behavior slighted this consideration by taking one of two tacks.

One approach used what Brewster Smith has called the "sociological proxy for individual level information." It is seen in the analysis of voting research of the 1940s which concluded voters' preferences resulted from cross-pressures from conflicting loyalties (such as to social class, ethnic group, religion, or labor union). This conclusion was based on the presumption that people with a given mix of social and demographic characteristics would have similar views. From the psychologist's vantage point, this assumption was open to serious question since opinions can derive from factors not captured by sociodemographic characteristics.

A second approach was to spell out a sequence of steps or pattern of reasoning people might take when making a choice between, say, two candidates. The study design would then be to see how well the sequence held up statistically among all respondents. But even if some such sequence was supported by the data, the psychologist would be uneasy because the study design had presumed that all people made decisions in the same way.

The lesson from these approaches is that use of a socio-demographic or one-size-fits-all conception of how opinions come together precluded the possibility of seeing whether there were differences among people. No amount of statistical manipulation of the data can compensate adequately for measures of individual differences that have not been included in the first place.

Case studies have proven to be a gold mine when it comes to understanding the relationship of individual opinions to facets of personality including such things as traits, predisposition, and temperament. The challenge has always been to extend these insights to the population as a whole. It is a daunting task to adapt measures that work at the individual level (which often involve elaborate batteries of items) to questions suitable for a regular public opinion poll, especially when measures of other important variables compete for limited questionnaire space.

It has been shown, for example, that matters such as an individual's ability to tolerate ambiguity or willingness to buck conventional ideas explain as much or more about opinions on civil liberties issues as any demographic characteristics or even a person's values. Effective measurement of such individual differences can be crucial in understanding *why* people hold the opinions they do.

CONCLUDING WORD

Where does this leave us regarding the capabilities of the public in our democratic system? The picture that emerges out of this brief review is of a public whose attention to politics is uneven but whose opinions have coherence, tend to be stable, and reflect solid common sense. It is a public able to size up the broad goals of public policy and, over time, determine whether the means adopted are in fact serving those goals.

True, opinions elicited by polls at times may be composed on the spot. But this does not mean they are not "considered." The process of responding to specific poll questions is creative—not haphazard. When people answer questions many elements are brought to bear at once: their basic values, experience, loyalties, personal style, and level of information.

For this public opinion to be given voice through the polls, it falls to the pollster to ask enough questions to capture the many dimensions of opinion. This is hard work. But, especially at a time when the polls seem to be playing a mediating role in our political process, to do less is to let the public down.

READING 17

Media Impact on Attitudes and Behavior

Doris A. Graber

In this selection Doris Graber, a political scientist at the University of Illinois at Chicago, explores aspects of how political knowledge is transmitted to the

From *Mass Media and American Politics,* Fifth Edition by D. A. Graber, 1997, Congressional Quarterly Press, pp. 189–197. Copyright © 1997 by CQ Press. Reprinted by permission.

American public by the mass media. Such knowledge is important because it helps citizens orient themselves to the political system in general as well as providing them with information that informs their opinion about parties, policies, politicians, and voting choices.

First, she deals with the question of whether the print media and the broadcast media have consistently differential effects on people. There are differences in what the various media convey best substantively. But, in effect, those differences do not seem to be so consistent that different rates of exposure result in predictably different impacts on attitudes and behavior. Moreover, people often self-select what they watch, listen to, or read. So, for example, more educated people who are more well off are more likely to get more of their information from newspapers than are other people. Yet such individuals are more likely to seek factual information on politics and policies than other people. Therefore, the fact that newspaper readers are better factually informed cannot be attributed to an independent effect of the newspapers. Rather, the reader seeks the information.

Second, Graber examines the role of the media in politically socializing both children and adults. She defines political socialization as "the learning about structures and environmental factors and internalizing of customs and rules governing political life." She summarizes what we know about media effects at different stages in the life cycle.

Finally, she addresses the question of whether various population groups defined by race, socioeconomic class, region, and other factors function in "different communication environments." The underlying question is whether the mass media unite or divide the American people. The answer is that they do a bit of both, but probably unite more than divide. Divisions may be reinforced by self-selection in media usage.

DIFFERENTIAL EFFECTS OF PRINT AND BROADCAST NEWS

Most Americans are exposed to combinations of all the media either directly or indirectly through contacts with people who have been exposed. We may know that American troops have been dispatched to Bosnia. We may feel pride or anxiety about the venture and consider it a good or bad foreign policy. But which of these thoughts and feelings come from television, or newspapers, or conversations, or from a combination of media? It is nearly impossible to disentangle such strands of information.

Each medium, however, does make unique contributions to learning. For example, television, because of its visuals, is especially powerful in transmitting realism and emotional appeal. It does less well conveying abstract ideas. In one fairly typical study researchers asked viewers about the main points of specific stories; viewers failed to identify 72 percent of them. Miscomprehension rates for individual stories ranged from 16 percent to 93 percent.

Print media excel in conveying factual details. Because most tests of learning from the media focus on factual learning and rote memory, print media are generally credited with conveying more knowledge than audiovisual media do. In fact, media scholar Neil Postman warns that massive use of television will turn America into a nation of dilettantes who avoid serious thinking because television trivializes the problems of the world. It gives people the illusion of being knowledgeable when, in fact, they are distracted from probing issues in depth.

The claim that the nature of the medium accounts for differences in knowledge gain is not clear-cut, however. Demographic differences may be part of the explanation. Heavy newspaper users tend to be better informed than persons who do not read the paper, but they also generally enjoy higher socioeconomic status and better formal education. Their status in life, therefore, provides above-average incentives for the factual learning that is usually measured. Attitudes toward the media matter as well. Print media are viewed by most people as sources of information, whereas electronic media are viewed as sources of entertainment. These additional differences, rather than the nature of each medium, may explain some of the differences in effects. Television becomes the most instructive medium if one tests for information that is best conveyed audiovisually, such as impressions of people and the inferences they engender or comprehension and long-term memory for highly dramatic events.

Television's greatest political impact, compared with that of other media, is derived from its ability to reach millions of people simultaneously with the same images. Major broadcasts enter nearly every home in the nation instantaneously and simultaneously. Televised events become shared experiences. Millions of Americans were present vicariously when the *Challenger* spacecraft exploded, when a lone student defied armed might at China's Tiananmen Square, and when O.J. Simpson's white Bronco sped along Los Angeles freeways after he had been accused of his ex-wife's murder. America's print media have never attained such a reach and the power that flows from it. Moreover, 23 million American adults are functionally illiterate and therefore are almost entirely beyond the reach of print media. What the poorly educated now learn about politics from television may be fragmentary and hazy, but it represents a quantum leap over their previous exposure and learning.

In short, the research on the differential effects of various types of media reveals that different types present stimuli that vary substantially in nature and content. It would be surprising, therefore, if their impact were identical, even when they deal with the same subjects. However, [as W. Russell Neuman writes] "there is no evidence of *consistent* significant differences in the ability of different media to persuade, inform, or even to instill an emotional response in audience members. Because current research does not provide adequate answers about the precise effects of these stimulus variations and about the processes by which individuals mesh a variety of media stimuli, we will focus on the end product—the combined impact of all print and electronic media stimuli.

THE ROLE OF MEDIA IN POLITICAL SOCIALIZATION

Political socialization—the learning about structures and environmental factors and internalizing of customs and rules governing political life—affects the quality of interactions between citizens and their government. Political systems do not operate smoothly without the support of most of their citizens, who must be willing to abide by the laws and to support government through performing duties such as voting, paying taxes, or serving in the military. Support is most readily obtained if citizens are convinced of the legitimacy and capability of their government and if they feel strong emotional ties to it. If political socialization fails to instill such attitudes, policies and laws that depend on public support, such as energy conservation or traffic regulations, may become unenforceable. If political socialization fails to provide citizens with sufficient knowledge, elections may become a sham at best; at worst, they may become a mockery in which clever politicians manipulate an ignorant electorate. Likewise, surveillance of government activities is impossible if people lack a grasp of the nature of government and public policies.

Childhood Socialization

Political socialization starts in childhood. Children usually learn basic attitudes toward authority, property, decision making, and veneration for political symbols from their families, and in recent decades from television. When they enter the more formal school setting, teaching about political values becomes quite systematic. At school, children also learn new factual information about their political and social world, much of it based on mass media information.

Children's direct contacts with the media are equally abundant. Millions of babies watch television. In the winter, young children in the United States spend an average of thirty-one hours a week in front of the television set—more time than in school. Between the ages of twelve and seventeen, this drops to twenty-four hours. Eighty percent of the programs children see are intended for adults and therefore differ substantially from the child's limited personal experiences. Children watch military combat, funerals, rocket launchings, courtships, seductions, and childbirth. If they can understand the message, the impact is likely to be great, because, lacking experience, they are apt to take such presentations at face value.

When asked for the sources of information on which they base their attitudes about the economy or race problems, or war and patriotism, high school students mention the mass media far more often than they mention their families, friends, teachers, or personal experiences. Youngsters who are frequent media users gain substantial information from the media. Compared to infrequent users, they show greater understanding and support for basic American values, such as the importance of free speech and the right to equal and fair treatment.

The finding that mass media strongly influence socialization runs counter to earlier socialization studies that showed parents and teachers as the chief socializers. Several reasons account for the change. The first is the increasing pervasiveness of television, which makes it easy for even the youngest children to be exposed to mass media images. The second reason involves deficiencies in measurement. Much of the early research discounted all media influence unless it came through direct contact outside the classroom between the child and the media. That excluded indirect media influence, such as contacts with parents and teachers who convey media information to the child. These exclusions sharply reduced findings of media effects. Finally, research designs have become more sophisticated. In the early studies children were asked to make their own general appraisal of learning sources. A typical question might be, "From whom do you learn the most: your parents, your school, or newspapers and television?" The questions used in recent studies have been more specific, inquiring first what children know about particular subjects, such as immigration or nuclear energy, and then asking about the sources of their information. In nearly every case the mass media were named as the chief sources of information and evaluations.

What children learn from the mass media and how they evaluate it depends heavily on their stage of mental development. Child psychologist Jean Piaget contended that children between two and seven years of age do not independently perceive the connections among various phenomena or draw general conclusions from specific instances. Many of the lessons presumably taught by media stories therefore elude young children. Complex reasoning skills develop fully only at the teenage level. Children's interests in certain types of stories also change sharply with age, as do their attention and information-retention spans. Most children strongly support the political system during their early years but often become quite disillusioned about authority figures during their teenage years. This skepticism diminishes as education is completed and the young adult enters the work force.

What role the media play in this transformation is unclear. Knowledge is also slim about children's and adolescents' imitation of behavior depicted by media stories, the duration of memories, and the persistence of media effects on learning, behavior, and social relationships.

Adult Socialization

The pattern of heavy media exposure continues into adulthood. The average American adult spends more than four hours a day watching television, well over two hours listening to radio, often while working or traveling by car, eighteen to forty-five minutes reading newspapers, and six to thirty minutes reading a magazine. Time spent with the mass media has jumped 40 percent since the advent of television, mostly at the expense of other leisure activities. Television alone now takes up nearly half of the leisure time of most Americans. On an average day, 80 percent of all Americans are exposed to television and newspapers. On a typical evening, the television audience is close to 100 million people. This can double for extraordinary events when more than 90 percent of the population may gather in front of the nation's television screens.

This massive exposure contributes to the lifelong process of political socialization and learning. The mass media form

> the mainstream of the common symbolic environment that cultivates the most widely shared conceptions of reality. We live in terms of the stories we tell, stories about what things exist, stories about how things work, and stories about what to do. . . . Increasingly, media-cultivated facts and values become standards by which we judge.

Once basic attitudes toward the political system have been formed, they usually stabilize, and later learning largely supplements and refines earlier notions. The need to cope with information about new events and shifting cultural orientations force the average person into continuous learning and gradual readjustments, although the basic value structure generally remains intact, even when attitudes are modified. However, major personal or societal upheavals may lead to more or less complete resocialization and revised political ideas.

People learn about political norms, rules, values, events, and behaviors largely from the mass media, including fictional as well as factual stories. Personal experiences are severely limited compared with the range of experiences offered to us directly or indirectly by the media about the social order and political activities. An accident report, for example, besides telling what happened, may suggest that police and fire forces respond too slowly and that emergency facilities in the local hospital are inadequate. When societal problems such as poverty or pollution are framed as discrete events, such as one family's starvation or a particular oil spill, attention is likely to be focused on individual solutions, obscuring the larger societal problems. Soap operas on radio and television may persuade audiences that most politicians are corruptible—after all, the majority of those shown on television are. In fact, fictional stories are the most widely used sources for political information. Surveys show that only one half to two thirds of the adult public regularly exposes itself to explicit political news.

People's opinions, feelings, and evaluations about the political system may spring from their own thinking about facts supplied by the media; from attitudes, opinions, and feelings explicitly expressed in news or entertainment programming; or from a combination of the two. Many people who use the media for information, and as a point of departure for formulating their own appraisals, reject or ignore attitudes and evaluations that are supplied explicitly or implicitly by media stories. For example, the fact that independent presidential candidate Ross Perot financed his own campaign in 1992 was condemned by most media as an attempt to "buy" the presidency. Nonetheless, many Americans viewed it as a praiseworthy effort to attain the office without entangling financial supporters.

People are prone to accept newspeople's views about national and international issues whenever they lack personal experience or guidance from social contacts. Even when people think that they are forming their own opinions about familiar issues, they often depend on the media more than they realize. Exten-

sive television exposure has been shown to lead to "mainstreaming," turning people into bland middle-roaders with a basically uniform outlook on political life that is "congruent with television's portrayal of life and society."

When audiences have direct or vicarious experiences to guide them, and particularly when they have already formed opinions grounded firmly in their personal values, they are far less likely to be swayed by the media. In practice, this means that the least informed and least interested are most likely to reflect the viewpoints expressed in the media, particularly television. Parroting of viewpoints espoused by political commentators explains why people uninterested in politics often spout seemingly sophisticated opinions if they have been extensively exposed to news stories.

Media's persuasiveness does not mean that exposure is tantamount to learning and mind changing. Far from it! In fact, two thirds of the people generally do not know their newspaper's preferred position on specific economic, social, and foreign policy issues. Most media stories are promptly forgotten. Stories that become part of an individual's fund of knowledge tend to reinforce existing beliefs and feelings. Acquisition of new knowledge or changes in attitude are the exception rather than the rule. Still, they occur often enough to be highly significant.

PATTERNS IN SOCIALIZATION

Media exposure patterns may be a partial explanation for knowledge and attitude differences among racial and ethnic groups. For example, African Americans rely less on general mass media for political information than do whites. Accordingly, in a study done in the 1970s, whites in a low-income Los Angeles neighborhood relied on print and electronic political information almost twice as much as their African American neighbors. Hispanics found print and electronic media even less useful for keeping themselves politically informed than did African Americans. Such alienation from major sources of political information, which is persisting, may hamper the political effectiveness of Hispanics and African Americans in dealing with the majority culture.

African Americans and whites extract different information even when they use the same media. African Americans are more apt than whites to believe that factual as well as fictional stories presented by the media are true to life. Therefore, the images that many African Americans form about lifestyles or societal patterns are more likely to mirror the distortions found in media presentations. A study of the diffusion of information about six assassinations showed that each racial group dwelled heavily on news that dealt with its own race. Although all African Americans and whites had heard about the deaths of Martin Luther King, Jr., and President John Kennedy and his brother Robert, many more African Americans than whites (10 percent to 24 percent more) knew about the assassinations of Medgar Evers and Malcolm X. In the same way, many more whites than African Americans knew about the death of white Nazi leader George Lincoln Rockwell.

There are many possible explanations for demographic variations in media use and socialization patterns. Despite the successes of the civil rights movement, most African Americans still belong to different social groups than whites, and they lead lives quite unlike those of the white middle-class to whose tastes most media cater. More African Americans than whites fall into youthful age brackets where readership is generally lower. Fewer African Americans than whites drive to work; hence fewer listen to radio news. For the many African Americans whose schooling has been poor, deficient reading skills make newspaper reading unattractive. Television is an appealing alternative. Accordingly, African Americans on an average watch about 15 percent more television than do whites, albeit different programs.

Some researchers doubt the media and socialization differences between African Americans and whites are based on race-linked cultural differences. Instead they attribute divergences to the fact that the African American population is more frequently poor and educationally deprived and contend that within the subculture of poverty, African Americans and whites use the media in similar ways. Other scholars argue that race and its cultural consequences are indeed important factors in media exposure and impact. Leo Bogart, for example, found racial differences in media use patterns regardless of socioeconomic status. The unresolved issues thus revolve around the causes of subcultural differences rather than their existence. If differences spring from race-linked cultural differences, they may be resistant to change. If they are linked to socioeconomic status, they may change readily with rising incomes, better education, and improved occupational status.

Gender, age, income, education, region, and city size also generate differences in newspaper reading, radio listening, and television viewing. For instance, men and women differ sharply in daytime television viewing; age has a bearing on newspaper reading; southerners listen to much less radio than do northerners. Program preferences vary as well. Women aged fifty and older are the heaviest viewers of television news, followed by men fifty and older. Twelve- to seventeen-year-olds are the lightest news watchers. Men far exceed women in following sports coverage, whereas women spend more time watching television drama.

Differences in media-use patterns are particularly pronounced between income levels. High-income families, who usually are better educated than poor families, use print media more and television less than the rest of the population. Upper income people also use a greater variety of media: 57 percent are multimedia users compared with 27 percent in the lower economic groups. Thus the well-to-do potentially have much more information and a greater variety of information available to them. This helps them to maintain and increase their influence and power in American society. In part, the poor pay less attention to print media because these media cater to upper income groups rather than the needs and concerns of the poor. Low income audiences prefer television and radio programs, which are easy to grasp and carry a great deal of light entertainment.

The notion of vastly different communications environments for various population groups should not be carried too far, however. The bulk of media entertainment and information is similar throughout the country and is shared by all types of media audiences. The same network television and cable programs are broadcast on the East Coast and the West Coast, in big cities and small towns. Differences among individual media enterprises are slight. Hence television comes close to being a single, nationwide source of news and commentary. Radio is more diverse, but even many radio news programs are little more than national wire service reports. Insofar as newspaper stories are based on wire service information, they, too, are fairly uniform everywhere.

. . . [N]ews media cover basically the same categories of stories in the same proportions. Specific stories vary, of course, depending on regional and local interests. Newspapers on the West Coast are more likely to devote their foreign affairs coverage to Asian affairs than are newspapers on the East Coast, which concentrate on Europe and the Middle East. Tabloids put more stress on sensational crime and sex stories than elite papers such as the staid *New York Times*. Nevertheless, news sources everywhere provide a large common core of information and interpretation that imbues their audiences with a shared structure of basic values and information.

READING 18

Public Opinion and the Rehnquist Court

Thomas R. Marshall

University of Texas at Arlington political scientist Thomas Marshall examines the relationship between public opinion and the Supreme Court of the United States in this original essay. He looks at three dimensions: 1) the congruence of major court decisions with public opinion on the issues dealt with in those decisions; 2) public attitudes toward the Rehnquist Court; and 3) the influence of the Court in shaping public opinion.

The relationship between the Supreme Court and public opinion is complex. Members of the Court, whether now or in the past, are neither unaware of nor impervious to strongly held public opinion. However, the evidence is that the Rehnquist Court, like its predecessors, is in agreement with

public opinion on some issues and in disagreement on others. It is a more conservative Court than its predecessors, but this conservatism is not driven directly by public opinion. Instead, the election of Republican presidents and a Republican Senate, coupled with the timing of openings for Court seats, has produced the increasing conservatism of the Court.

The institutional standing of the Court with the general public has fallen, along with the standing of virtually every other American institution. It is still more highly regarded than the presidency or Congress, but one can speculate that the Court has somewhat tarnished its public image by making unpopular decisions.

The evidence is convincing both for the Rehnquist Court as well as for earlier Courts that the Court plays little role in shaping public opinion. Legal decisions are complicated by nature, which inevitably blunts some of the Court's impact. And, of course, the justices—unlike the president or members of the House and Senate—do not openly set out to shape public opinion. The justices are concerned with the law and with making persuasive arguments for other judges and lawyers.

A broader issue is whether the Court can be profoundly out of touch with majority sentiment for a fairly long period of time and still retain its high standing with the public. The answer to that question is almost surely no. But the Rehnquist Court is not running that risk.

As the Rehnquist Court concludes its first decade, judicial scholars have closely examined its impact on American politics. Since 1986 several older, more liberal justices (such as William Brennan or Thurgood Marshall) retired, and were replaced by younger, more conservative justices (such as David Souter or Clarence Thomas). Not surprisingly, the Rehnquist Court took an increasingly more conservative direction in many areas, such as criminal rights or racial cases. Even the addition of two Clinton appointees, Ruth Bader Ginsburg and Stephen Breyer, has not yet clearly reversed the Rehnquist Court's conservative tilt.

But how closely does the Rehnquist Court reflect American public opinion? Can the Rehnquist Court actually influence American public opinion through its rulings?

This article reexamines the Rehnquist Court's first decade by comparing specific rulings with national public opinion polls. Since the mid-1930s, public opinion pollsters have often written questions to tap public attitudes toward controversial Supreme Court cases. By now, some 185 Supreme Court rulings can be "matched" or compared with comparable poll questions from a scientific, random sampling nationwide poll. Thirty of these 185 poll-to-ruling matches date from the Rehnquist Court's first decade. These 30 poll-to-ruling matches allow us to see how often Supreme Court rulings agree with American attitudes.

To be sure, these 30 poll-to-ruling matches are not a purely random sample of the Rehnquist Court's rulings. Pollsters usually write poll questions only for the Court's best-known and most controversial rulings. On the average, three or four Supreme Court decisions a year can be matched, or compared, with an available poll question.

Available polls on the Rehnquist Court also go well beyond simply comparing individual Court rulings to public opinion poll questions. Pollsters have also measured public approval toward the Supreme Court. Other polls measure public awareness of Supreme Court rulings. Less frequently, pollsters have asked an identically worded question, both before and after a Court ruling, or else several times after a ruling. These repeat questions permit attitude changes to be tracked over time to see if Supreme Court rulings themselves appear to influence public opinion. A few authors have even carried out local surveys to determine if Supreme Court rulings affect attitudes in the local communities from which court cases originally arose.

REPRESENTING PUBLIC OPINION

Consider, for example, the Supreme Court's ruling in one dispute from *Planned Parenthood of Southeastern Pennsylvania v. Casey* (1992), upholding a state law that required women seeking abortions to wait 24 hours before having the abortion. This part of the *Ca-*

sey ruling agreed with a 73 to 23 percent majority in a 1992 Gallup Poll, and was classified as "*consistent*" with public opinion. The "poll margin" on this ruling would be a +50 (73 percent in support of the Court's ruling, minus 23 percent opposed to the Court's ruling).

Now consider *U.S. Term Limits v. Thornton* (1995). In this ruling, a 5 to 4 Supreme Court majority struck down an Arkansas term limits restriction on U. S. senators and representatives. The Court's 5 to 4 decision disagreed with a 61 percent to 37 percent Gallup Poll majority in 1994, as well as with large majorities in several other nationwide polls. The *Term Limits* ruling was classified as "*inconsistent*" with public opinion. The "poll margin" on this ruling would be a –24 (37 percent minus 61 percent).

Figure 4.1 lists the Rehnquist Court's five most consistent and five least consistent rulings, and how well or poorly each ruling reflected American public opinion.

The ten Rehnquist Court's rulings depicted in Figure 4.1 include both the most consistent and least consistent rulings. For example, among the most popular Rehnquist Court rulings was its decision to uphold a mandatory drug testing requirement for public safety workers, in *Skinner v. Railway Labor Executives' Association* (1989). Also very popular with public opinion was the Court's decision to uphold Pennsylvania's "informed consent" requirement for abortion, in *Planned Parenthood of Southeastern Pennsylvania v. Casey* (1992), or to uphold Minnesota's two-parent notification requirement for a minor's abortion, in *Hodgson v. Minnesota* (1989). Also included are *Board of Education v. Mergens* (1990), allowing religious groups to use public schools for after-school meetings, and, as described above, another part of the *Casey* (1992) ruling, upholding a state-imposed 24-hour waiting period for abortions.

At the other extreme, several Rehnquist Court rulings rank among the Supreme Court's most unpopular rulings historically—such as the "Baby Jessica" decision in *DeBoer v. Schmidt* (1993), in which the Court declined to hear an appeal by the adoptive parents of a young child to retain custody. Also quite unpopular was *Cruzan v. Director, Missouri Department of Health* (1990), refusing to allow parents of a comatose, brain-dead victim of an automobile accident to decide whether to continue treatment, or *Sable v. FCC* (1989), allowing sexually explicit telephone pay calls for adults. Also included are *Penry v. Lynaugh* (1989), permitting the death penalty for mentally retarded convicted murderers, and a provision of the *Casey* (1992) ruling, striking down a state-imposed husband notification requirement for women seeking abortions.

Overall, 57 percent (or 17 of 30) of the Rehnquist Court's rulings were consistent with American public opinion. The remaining 43 percent (or 13 rulings) were inconsistent with American public opinion. The 57 percent consistent figure for the Rehnquist Court is slightly lower than the 63 percent consistent figure for the earlier 1934 through 1985 Court terms, or than the 62 percent consistent figure for the Burger Court.

The Supreme Court reflects American public opinion in its decision making about as often as do elected officeholders. One study reported that 55 percent of a much larger sample of public policy decisions were consistent with American public opinion during the 1980–1991 period. By comparison, 56 percent of Supreme Court decisions were consistent with public opinion during the same 1980–1991 period.

The examples in Figure 4.1 show that the Supreme Court can sometimes hand down strikingly un-

popular rulings. What happens when the Supreme Court hands down a strikingly unpopular ruling? These rulings are the most likely to be challenged, and sometimes overturned by Congress, constitutional amendment, executive action, or later Supreme Court rulings.

Several Rehnquist Court rulings have already been challenged, at least twice successfully. Following *Bray v. Alexandria Women's Health Clinic* (1993), Congress passed new legislation to ban abortion clinic blockades. The Court then upheld most (although not all) of the new law's provisions, 6 to 3, in *Madsen v. Women's Health Center, Inc.* (1994). The Court's *Rust v. Sullivan* (1991) ruling, upholding a Bush Administration guideline banning federally funded clinics from counseling pregnant women about abortion methods, was bypassed when the Clinton Administration ended enforcement of the so-called gag order during Clinton's second full day in office. Like most Court rulings later overturned, both the *Bray* and *Rust* rulings had been inconsistent with a poll majority.

In at least two other instances, Court rulings were seriously, although (as yet) not successfully challenged. In both instances, the Court's ruling was inconsistent with a public opinion majority. After the 5 to 4 *Texas v. Johnson* (1989) ruling to allow flag burning as a political protest, Congress passed fed-

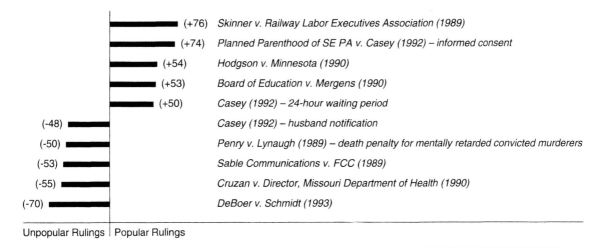

(+76)	*Skinner v. Railway Labor Executives Association (1989)*
(+74)	*Planned Parenthood of SE PA v. Casey (1992) – informed consent*
(+54)	*Hodgson v. Minnesota (1990)*
(+53)	*Board of Education v. Mergens (1990)*
(+50)	*Casey (1992) – 24-hour waiting period*
(-48)	*Casey (1992) – husband notification*
(-50)	*Penry v. Lynaugh (1989) – death penalty for mentally retarded convicted murderers*
(-53)	*Sable Communications v. FCC (1989)*
(-55)	*Cruzan v. Director, Missouri Department of Health (1990)*
(-70)	*DeBoer v. Schmidt (1993)*

Unpopular Rulings | Popular Rulings

FIGURE 4.1 The ten most consistent and ten least consistent Rehnquist Court rulings, compared with public opinion polls.

eral level legislation to ban flag burning. In that instance, the Court also struck down the Congressional act on a similar 5 to 4 vote in *U.S. v. Eichman* (1990). In *U.S. Term Limits v. Thornton* (1995), the Court struck down a state-imposed term limits measure. By a 227 to 204 majority, the U. S. House then voted for a term limits constitutional amendment. The amendment failed, however, because it did not win the required two-thirds majority.

Historically, over a third (37 percent) of those Supreme Court rulings that were initially inconsistent with majority public opinion have been overturned by Congress, by constitutional amendment, by later Court rulings, or by other actions. By comparison, only 10 percent of Supreme Court rulings consistent with majority public opinion were later overturned.

Some of the Rehnquist Court's justices have been much more consistent with American public opinion than others. Of the justices who cast votes in at least ten of the thirty decisions examined here, Chief Justice Rehnquist and Justice White most often voted consistently with public opinion majorities—doing so in 75 percent and 73 percent of their votes, respectively. Interestingly, since the 1930s the Supreme Court's chief justices have usually been more consistent with American public opinion than other justices. At the other extreme, of justices voting in at least ten decisions, Justices Brennan and Marshall least often voted consistently with nationwide polls—doing so in only 28 percent and 40 percent of their votes, respectively.

Because several justices have yet cast only a few votes that can be matched with available public opinion polls, it may be more meaningful to compare the Rehnquist Court's conservative and liberal blocs. Justices Rehnquist, Kennedy, White, Scalia, O'Connor, Souter, and Thomas all voted "conservative" in at least two-thirds of their votes, thereby forming the Rehnquist Court's "conservative bloc." Justices Brennan, Marshall, Stevens, Blackmun, Powell, Ginsburg, and Breyer all voted "liberal" in at least two-thirds or more of their votes, thereby forming the Rehnquist Court's "liberal bloc."

Overall, the Rehnquist Court's conservative bloc was more often consistent with nationwide polls than the liberal bloc. As Table 4.1 shows, the Court's con-

servative bloc agreed with public opinion majorities (or pluralities) almost two-thirds of the time. The Court's liberal bloc agreed with the polls less than half the time.

One reason why the Rehnquist Court's conservative bloc more often reflected American public opinion is that nationwide opinion on these 30 decisions was itself much more often conservative than liberal. American public opinion was ideologically conservative in 20 rulings (or 67 percent of the time), and liberal only 8 times (or 27 percent of the time). Two rulings could not clearly be classified as either liberal or conservative.

The Supreme Court reflects American public opinion much more often in highly publicized cases or when public opinion is very one-sided on an issue. For example, since the mid-1930s, the Court has been consistent with public opinion 76 percent of the time when a dispute was a top national concern. The Rehnquist Court also agreed with American public opinion much more often when the polls were very one-sided. For example, when two-thirds (or more) of Americans agreed on an issue, the Rehnquist Court was consistent with public opinion 63 percent of the time. On issues where the polls were more closely divided, the Rehnquist Court was consistent with the polls in only 33 percent of its rulings. The Rehnquist Court was also most likely to be consistent on the abortion issue, where 8 of its 11 rulings were consistent with available polls.

TABLE 4.1 Conservative and liberal blocs' agreement with the polls

	CONSERVATIVE BLOC	LIBERAL BLOC
Percent Consistent with Nationwide Polls	67%	42%
Percent Inconsistent with Nationwide Polls	33%	58%
Total	100%	100%
Total Votes	153	96

Note: A chi-square would be significant at .05.

In disputes in which public opinion is clearly one-sided, or in which public and media attention is highly focused on an issue, the justices may more clearly perceive public pressure. To be sure, justices have less reason to follow public opinion than do elected officeholders. Once confirmed, the justices have life tenure "with good behavior." Even so, several justices, including Chief Justice Rehnquist, have written that they are sometimes influenced by public opinion shifts.

> No judge worthy of his salt would ever cast his vote in a particular case simply because he thought the majority of the public wanted him to vote that way, but that is quite a different thing from saying that no judge is ever influenced by the great tides of public opinion that run in a country such as ours. Judges are influenced by them...

PUBLIC OPINION TOWARD THE REHNQUIST COURT

Available polls also provide evidence as to public attitudes toward the Rehnquist Court. For example, the Gallup Poll reports that the Rehnquist Court dropped 10 percent in its approval ratings—from 54 percent of Americans who reported "a great deal" or "quite a lot" of confidence in the Court in July 1986 to only 44 percent who gave similar ratings in April 1995.

The National Opinion Research Center (NORC) uses a different question wording, but reports similar results. According to the 1994 NORC poll, 30 percent of Americans said they had "a great deal" of confidence in the Supreme Court. Fifty percent of Americans had "only some" confidence, while 16 percent had "hardly any" confidence, and the remaining 3 percent had no opinion.

The Court's drop in approval ratings is the second largest drop among nine public and private institutions continually measured by Gallup Poll over that time period. Only Congress suffered a greater drop in public approval—falling 20 percent from 41 percent to 21 percent. Most institutions suffered smaller drops in their approval ratings—including public schools (9 percent), newspapers and big business (7 percent), banks (6 percent), and organized labor (3 percent). Only organized religion and the military did not suffer dropping approval ratings (with no change and a 1 percent improvement, respectively).

Even so, as of 1995, the Supreme Court still enjoyed above-average approval, with 44 percent of Americans recording a "great deal" or "quite a lot" of confidence in the Court. Only the military (at 64 percent), the police (at 58 percent), organized religion (57 percent), and the presidency (45 percent) recorded higher approval ratings. Most other American institutions ranked lower in public approval—including banks (at 43 percent), the medical system (41 percent), public schools (40 percent), television news (33 percent), newspapers (30 percent), organized labor (26 percent), Congress and big business (both at 21 percent), and the criminal justice system (20 percent).

What accounts for the Rehnquist Court's drop in approval ratings? In part, the drop in public esteem for the Supreme Court reflects a broader decline in public trust and confidence over the last decade. In part, the Supreme Court's approval ratings also decline when its rulings are ideologically out of line with prevailing public opinion, or when the Court strikes down federal laws.

PERSUADING THE PUBLIC

Political scientists have long debated whether Supreme Court decisions influence (or "manipulate") public opinion. At one time many political scientists believed that the Supreme Court's prestige could favorably influence American public opinion to support its rulings.

More recent studies, however, cast doubt on that idea. Several experimental studies suggest that Court rulings have only a slight effect on public attitudes toward specific issues. The Court's rulings may affect public approval toward the Court itself, or polarize public opinion on highly publicized rulings (such as abortion). Yet public opinion does not usually "follow" Court rulings on specific decisions, either when polls are available before, versus after a Court ruling, or when several polls are available following a Court ruling. Polling results from local communities where a local issue reached the Supreme Court also offer mixed evidence as to whether Court rulings affect local public opinion. Court rulings on civil liberties issues may influence public opinion somewhat more than rulings on economic issues.

Consider, for example, the *Rotary International v. Duarte* (1987) ruling, which held that private clubs did not have a right to exclude potential members on the basis of sex. In June 1987, shortly after *Duarte,* some 63 percent of Americans agreed with the Court's ruling. A year later, in July 1988, the percentage agreeing with the Court's decision declined to 56 percent. The 7 percent poll shift was away from the Court's ruling.

Still other polling evidence also suggests that Supreme Court decisions do not greatly affect American public opinion, even when the Court hands down a string of decisions. Consider, for example, the Court's abortion rulings during the Rehnquist Court period. Beginning in *Webster v. Reproductive Health Systems* (1989) through *Planned Parenthood of Southeastern Pennsylvania v. Casey* (1992), the Court allowed a number of specific state restrictions on a woman's right to obtain an abortion. The Court upheld a ban on abortions in public hospitals, a requirement for fetal viability tests at the fifth month of pregnancy, a one-parent or a two-parent notification requirement (with a judicial alternative), an "informed consent" requirement, a 24-hour waiting period, and a one-parent consent requirement (with a judicial alternative).

Yet public opinion polls showed no movement at all toward the Court's new position. In April 1989 (pre-*Webster*), 50 percent of Americans said abortions should be legal "only under certain circumstances." Another 27 percent said abortion should be legal "under any circumstances," and the remaining 18 percent said abortion should be "illegal in all circumstances."

By February 1995, American public opinion had not shifted toward the Court's rulings. Just as before the Court's shift, an identical 50 percent of Americans preferred the Court's new policy of allowing abortions "only under certain circumstances." The percentage of Americans approving abortion "under any circumstances" actually rose from 27 to 33 percent, a poll shift exactly opposite to the Court's shift in direction. The percentage stating abortion should be "illegal in all circumstances" dropped slightly, from 18 percent to 15 percent.

These results suggest that the Supreme Court does not greatly influence American public opinion on specific issues, even when the Court is consistent in its rulings and when those rulings are well publicized. On the average, Supreme Court rulings have led to public opinion poll shifts toward the Court's rulings of less than one percent, when pre- and post-decision polls are available. On the average, liberal, activist rulings lead to the largest (favorable) poll shifts on specific issues, but (the flag burning and term limits rulings notwithstanding) these are the very rulings that the generally conservative Rehnquist Court seldom hands down. Poll shifts following a Supreme Court ruling are also much smaller than those that typically occur during presidential news conferences, or when scientific experts, popular presidents, or news commentators announce a policy position on nightly newscasts.

One reason the Supreme Court may have little impact on American public opinion is that few Court rulings are well understood by the public. For example, on the widely discussed and highly controversial *Texas v. Johnson* (1989) and *U.S. v. Eichman* (1990) flag-burning rulings, one poll asked "(d)o you happen to know . . . did the Supreme Court rule that laws banning flag-burning are constitutional, or did they rule that such laws are unconstitutional?" Only 52 percent (correctly) responded that flag-burning laws were now unconstitutional, while 31 percent (incorrectly) responded constitutional, and 17 percent did not know.

As discussed above, the Supreme Court may not be able to influence public opinion favorably toward its rulings because of its limited popularity with the public. Somewhat fewer than half of Americans (44 percent) say they have "a great deal" or "quite a lot" of confidence in the Court, and even more report having "some" (39 percent) or "very little" (14 percent) confidence in the Court, according to an April 1995 Gallup Poll. In the 1994 NORC poll, only a third (30 percent) gave the Court a clearly favorable opinion. True, the Supreme Court may be more popular than several other American public institutions. Yet its popularity may not be enough to influence public opinion on specific rulings.

CONCLUSION

The Rehnquist Court has been an increasingly conservative Supreme Court. By the mid-1990s the Rehnquist Court had cut back on liberal precedents in death penalty cases, affirmative action cases, abortion cases, and other areas.

Ironically, however, the Rehnquist Court appears to be no more (and perhaps, slightly less) consistent with American public opinion than was the Supreme Court in earlier years. Like earlier Courts, its rulings have run the full gamut from widely popular rulings to equally unpopular rulings. On issues that were sufficiently high profile to lead to a public opinion poll question, the Rehnquist Court agreed with American public opinion just over half the time.

Students of the modern Supreme Court should carefully distinguish between the different meanings of the word *majoritarian* as it applies to the Court. One meaning of that term is that the Court defers to the judgment of elected federal, state, or local policymakers. Yet in many instances challenged federal, state, or local laws and policies do not themselves reflect American public opinion. In the decisions here, for example, 29 percent of federal level policies, and 37 percent of state or local policies, did not agree with American public opinion nationwide.

To be sure, the Rehnquist Court does defer more often to elected policymakers than did the earlier Warren Court, or even the Burger Court. However, this deference does not inevitably mean that the Court is "majoritarian" in the sense of reflecting public opinion poll majorities. In fact, the Rehnquist Court no more often agrees with majority public opinion than earlier Courts did. Ironically, although the Rehnquist Court defers to elected policymakers more than earlier Courts did, its public approval ratings have continued to sag.

Finally, these results also suggest that the Supreme Court can seldom "manipulate" or influence American public opinion on specific issues. Over time, Supreme Court rulings may influence how favorably Americans view the Court. Yet little evidence exists to suggest that specific Court rulings normally greatly influence American public opinion.

READING 19

Can Inattentive Citizens Control Their Elected Representatives?

R. Douglas Arnold

R. Douglas Arnold, a political scientist at Princeton University, addresses the broad question of whether the public, only sporadically attentive to public affairs, can control their elected representatives in legislatures. He develops and explains two models for how such control might be exercised. The first model, which he views as the dominant one in the current literature, inevitably leads to the pessimistic conclusion that because public preferences are so ill-formed, after the fact, that sporadic little control is exercised. He argues, however, that the assumptions on which this "standard control model" is based create an unreasonable definition of control. Only legislatures populated by "instructed delegates" in a very pure sense would be controlled by the citizenry.

Arnold instead proposes a revised model that he thinks is both reasonable theoretically and observably accurate empirically. This is a model that produces what he calls "controlled agents" in the legislature. Citizens, in his view, audit the behavior of legislators from time to time in line with their policy preferences, some of which are held before the legislature acts and some of which emerge after action has been taken. These political audits—as with financial audits, such as those of tax returns conducted by the Internal Revenue Service—are selective, after the fact, and involve only a sample of what has happened. He argues that this form of control is genuine. Legislators, in his view, have latitude in their actions but are also accountable to the public. They recognize this accountability and conduct themselves accordingly for the most part.

From "Can Inattentive Citizens Control Their Elected Representatives?" by R. D. Arnold, 1993, in *Congress Reconsidered,* Fifth Edition, pp. 401–414, ed. L. C. Dodd and B. I. Oppenheimer. Copyright © 1993 by Congressional Quarterly Press. Reprinted by permission.

As with the Cantril and Cantril article on the nature of public opinion, this piece by Arnold contradicts the excessively cynical and negative view of the American public's capacity both to hold coherent views and to inject them meaningfully into public decision making, in this case through the mechanism of elections.

How much are ordinary citizens—people who pay only occasional attention to politics and public affairs—able to control the behavior of their elected representatives? In principle, it might seem relatively straightforward for citizens to control legislators. If legislators wish to be reelected and if citizens reward and punish them for their actions in office, one should expect legislators to do whatever citizens desire. In practice, the issue of control is more problematic. How can citizens control legislators when most citizens pay scant attention to public affairs? Why should legislators worry about citizens' preferences when they know most citizens are not really watching them? How, in fact, can even the most conscientious legislators follow their constituents' preferences when so many of those preferences are unformed, unclear, and unstable?

Popular beliefs about citizens' control appear to follow the more pessimistic line. Many believe that legislators give greater weight to special interests and to their personal interest than to constituents' interests....

Scholars' beliefs about the extent of citizens' control are more complicated, but the general theme is still pessimistic. In their classic article "Constituency Influence in Congress," Warren Miller and Donald Stokes found some evidence that local constituencies controlled the actions of their representatives, but their influence seemed restricted to the domain of civil rights and did not embrace the equally important domains of social welfare and foreign policy. A more recent book by Robert Bernstein, subtitled "The Myth of Constituency Control," finds even less supportive evidence and declares that "elections do not serve as a mechanism through which citizens control their government." Although some scholars have found greater evidence of democratic control than these findings suggest, it is fair to say that the scholarly literature supports more than it refutes the notion that ordinary citizens have little control over their elected representatives.

This essay explores the mechanisms by which citizens can control elected representatives. My quarrel with previous research on the subject is that most scholars have focused on a single mechanism for control. Failing to find evidence that citizens use that method, they conclude that citizens lack any meaningful control. The mistake is to assume that a single mechanism is necessary for effective control. Although I am prepared to believe that a single mechanism is a sufficient condition for citizens to control their representatives, I am not convinced that such a mechanism must also be a necessary condition for control. As long as there are other ways in which citizens could control legislators, scholars are in no position to conclude that examination of a single method says anything definitive about either the existence or the extent of democratic control of government....

LEGISLATORS AS INSTRUCTED DELEGATES: THE STANDARD CONTROL MODEL

The standard control model presumes that citizens are active controllers. Citizens are conceived to be much like automobile drivers. They know where they want to go, they can select the best routes (policies) to get there, and they are capable of steering their vehicles (legislators) to reach their chosen destinations. The proper test for how well motorists control their vehicles is their success in navigating unfamiliar routes, bypassing various obstacles, and arriving at their destinations in time for their appointments. The proper test for how well citizens control legislators is their success in getting legislators to support and enact their most preferred policies.

The most basic assumption of the standard model is that citizens have both outcome preferences and policy preferences. Outcome preferences are attitudes about the desirability of specific ends, such as safe communities, clean air, protection from foreign attack, and the maintenance of a sound economy. Policy preferences are attitudes about the proper means toward those ends. Examples are preferences about instituting a seven day waiting period before handguns can be purchased, requiring mechanical scrubbers on coal powered plants, increasing the number of aircraft carriers in the Navy, or cutting federal expenditures across the board to bring the budget into balance.

The second assumption is that on the important issues of the day citizens evaluate legislative candidates by focusing on both their positions and their actions. For challengers, the focus is on the policies they promise to support and those they promise to oppose. For incumbents, the focus is on both their promises and their past actions. Citizens are presumed to be especially attentive to legislators' roll call votes. The logic of the model is that citizens reward and punish legislators based on how compatible legislators' roll call positions are with citizens' own policy preferences.

The third assumption is that legislators are strongly interested in being reelected to Congress. Most legislators are career-minded politicians who seek to retain their current positions—at least until a more promising political position becomes available. With citizens choosing among candidates by focusing on their positions and their actions in office, it follows that legislators will work diligently to reflect their constituents' current policy preferences. It also allows that challengers will work to position themselves even more closely to citizens' current policy preferences.

These three assumptions are all that is required for citizens to control legislators in office. Legislators act as instructed delegates, working to discern their constituents' policy preferences and doing their best to follow the majority's preferences. When individual legislators fail to act as good delegates, either by intentionally following the preferences of a minority or by failing to discern the majority's preferences, citizens replace them with those who promise to be better delegates. . . .

LEGISLATORS AS CONTROLLED AGENTS: THE ALTERNATIVE MODEL

The alternative control model presumes that citizens are somewhat more passive than the citizens of the standard control model. Citizens are regarded more like tax auditors, who notice when things are seriously out of line, than like drill sergeants, who direct troops to march left and right in precise formations. Passivity, however, should not be confused with a lack of influence. Auditing can be an efficient and effective means of controlling legislators' behavior.

The alternative control model rests on four basic assumptions, one of them identical to an assumption in the standard control model, two of them modifications of the original assumptions, and one completely new. The identical assumption is that legislators are strongly interested in reelection. This simple motivational assumption is basic to any model of representation in which legislators respond to citizens' preferences. In settings where legislators are not strongly interested in reelection, legislators lack the basic incentive to discover and follow citizens' wishes.

The second assumption in the alternative control method is that citizens have outcome preferences and can easily acquire preferences after the legislature acts, even though they may not have had policy preferences in advance of legislative action. This is a modification of the assumption in the standard control model in which citizens are presumed to have both outcome and policy preferences in advance of legislative action. The modified assumption is considerably more realistic than its predecessor. It allows citizens to develop policy preferences as a response to debates among policy experts and politicians rather than in advance of such debates. Citizens may acquire policy preferences as a direct consequence of legislative debate or when they first notice a change in governmental policy or in the middle of a subsequent electoral campaign, when a challenger questions the wisdom of an incumbent's actions in office.

The third assumption is that citizens are capable of evaluating incumbent legislators by focusing on their policy positions and then actions in office. This is a modification of the assumption in the standard control model in which citizens actually evaluate legislative candidates according to their positions and actions. The revised assumption simply states that citizens are capable of such evaluations once they become aware of what their representatives have done in office.

The new assumption is that the system contains activists who have incentives to monitor what legislators are doing in office and to inform citizens when legislators fail in their duties. Challengers to incumbent legislators have perhaps the strongest incentives for monitoring legislators' behavior and mobilizing voters. Few challengers fail to sift through incumbents' voting records in search of issues that can be used against incumbent legislators. In addition, groups that bear major costs under a particular policy may help publicize what incumbent legislators have done to contribute to their plight. Whereas challengers seek to replace incumbents, these groups may seek to persuade incumbents to avoid electoral repercussions by altering their positions and working for the groups' benefit.

These four assumptions recognize a division of labor between citizens and professional politicians. Legislators, challengers, and activists do most of the real work. Citizens act more like spectators who register their approval or disapproval at the end of a performance. This division of labor reflects the incentives that drive each type of actor.

In the political world described by these four assumptions, legislators have strong incentives to anticipate citizens' future preferences. Even when citizens seem unaware of an issue or indifferent toward it, legislators do not assume that they are free to vote as they please. Instead, legislators consider the possibility that someone might work to inform their constituents about their policy position before the next election and that their constituents might not be pleased by their positions and might be inspired to oppose their reelection. To forestall such a reaction, legislators choose their policy positions very carefully. Although it is true that most issues do not present legislators with life or death choices in which a single wrong decision can lead to electoral defeat, legislators create acceptable voting records one issue at a time. They vote carefully on every issue because that is the safest way to guarantee that their voting records cannot be used against them in future elections.

Challengers have equally strong incentives to uncover potentially unpopular positions that incumbents have taken on past roll call votes. Ordinarily, incumbents are better known than challengers, and most incumbents have spent their years in office showering their districts with newsletters, baby books, press re-leases, services, and an unending stream of favorable publicity. Challengers need to find ways to generate negative publicity about incumbents and favorable publicity about themselves. Scandal aside, challengers have discovered that unpopular roll call votes provide them with the best way to jump start their campaigns, attract media attention, generate campaign funds, and get voters to notice them.

The leaders of interest groups also have incentives to inform their members (and perhaps more generally) about legislators' actions in office. Interest group leaders are themselves politicians who need to maintain the support of their members and attract the support of new members. By focusing citizens' attention on the errors of government and the actions of specific legislators, interest group leaders attempt to mobilize their members to support continued group action. Single-issue groups may publicize legislators' votes on specific issues, whereas broader based groups often compile and publish ratings of all legislators to show how friendly or unfriendly individual legislators have been to their group's interests.

Individual citizens have fewer incentives to become actively involved in monitoring legislators' performance in office. A single citizen can do so little to reward or punish an individual legislator, that it hardly makes sense for that citizen to invest a lot of time and energy in acquiring information about legislators' actions in office. Even passive citizens, however, can acquire a great deal of politically relevant information when interest group leaders and challengers slip messages about legislators' performances in office into the daily diet of news stories, advertisements, and direct mail. Citizens are capable of learning a great deal when they are presented with information indirectly; they simply have little incentive to acquire it directly.

The alternative model conceives of legislators as controlled agents rather than as instructed delegates. Legislators do not simply follow the preferences of those few citizens who already have policy preferences. Instead, legislators anticipate what policy preferences might exist at the time of the next election—including preferences that citizens already hold and preferences that might be generated by challengers and interest groups working to tarnish their reputations. According to this model of representation, legislators must pay attention to both the preferences of attentive publics and the potential preferences of inattentive citizens.

Uncertainty abounds in a system like this. Legislators cannot possibly know for sure what policy effects will follow from specific governmental actions, how challengers or interest group leaders might use governmental actions or inactions to stir up citizens, or whether citizens might blame or absolve legislators for their connections with specific actions. What is certain is that legislators will do their best to anticipate citizens' preferences, to avoid the most dangerous mine fields, and to chart as safe a course as possible through the treacherous territory before them.

Legislators are most fearful of electoral retribution when they consider proposals that would impose large and direct costs on their constituents. Few legislators are willing to consider doubling the gasoline tax, cutting Social Security benefits, eliminating the tax deduction for mortgage interest, closing military bases in their district, or eliminating food stamps because they know that their roll call votes on these issues can be used against them in future elections. The costs are so great and the connections to their own actions are so obvious that legislators feel certain that journalists, challengers, and interest group leaders will inform citizens of their votes and that some citizens will come to believe that their representatives are not serving their interests.

Legislators have much less fear of electoral retribution when they consider proposals that would impose only small costs on individual citizens or when the issues are sufficiently narrow or technical that it would be difficult for citizens to understand exactly what was at stake. Issues relating to the depreciation of capital assets in the defense industry, the formula for calculating dairy price supports, or the sale of licenses for radio stations are examples. Although these three issues are readily understandable to defense contractors, dairy farmers, and broadcasters—and as a consequence legislators need to weigh carefully the preferences of these three groups—the issues are so obscure to most citizens that it is difficult to imagine challengers making them into campaign issues.

The vast majority of policy questions lie between these two extremes, where electoral retribution is neither certain nor highly unlikely. A vote on a technical issue relating to air pollution might appear harmless, but it could become politically dangerous if a powerful environmental group used it as a litmus test for whether legislators were friendly or hostile to the environment. A vote on the details of a formula for distributing grants for urban redevelopment might appear benign, but it could become politically dangerous if a challenger showed that an incumbent voted for a formula that cost her district millions of dollars. To guarantee that a seemingly easy issue today does not come back to haunt them in a subsequent campaign, legislators need to think about every issue that comes their way.

Exactly how legislators estimate the electoral consequences of their decisions in office is a complicated matter—one that goes well beyond the scope of this essay. It helps that legislators handle many of the same issues year after year. It also helps that legislators are not alone. They learn from interest groups, committee hearings, staff members, and other legislators about the policy consequences and the political consequences of specific decisions.

When legislators adjust their voting decisions to avoid generating preferences among inattentive citizens, is it fair to suggest that legislators are controlled by those inattentive citizens? It is indeed. I have already argued that citizens are considered influential (or in control) to the extent that legislators' decisions reflect citizens' preferences about policy issues. It makes little difference whether legislators are responding to citizens' existing policy preferences or to the preferences they believe would arise if they voted carelessly. The essence of citizens' control is for legislators to satisfy citizens' wants and interests. If legislators can manage to satisfy citizens' wants before they become transformed into detailed policy preferences, more power to them.

Notice how similar this kind of political control is to the economic control exercised by consumers in the marketplace. Movie producers do not survey movie audiences to discover their exact preferences about scripts, locales, and special effects; nevertheless, producers attempt to anticipate and satisfy the public's preferences so that their films will make money. When we say "the consumer is king," we do not mean that the consumer directs the design and production of movies, automobiles, or town houses. We mean that movie makers, auto makers, and real estate developers attempt to anticipate and satisfy consumers' preferences. Those who fail to satisfy consumers' tastes are eventually driven out of business, just as legislators who fail to anticipate citizens' policy preferences are eventually driven out of office.

This conception of legislators as controlled agents is very similar to the way agents in other areas are controlled. Corporate stockholders are largely unaware of what corporate managers are doing day-by-day, but managers still attempt to serve stockholders' interests in order to forestall negative evaluations by stock analysts and declines in stock prices, both of which stockholders would notice. Legislators are equally unaware of what bureaucratic officials are doing day-by-day, but bureaucrats still attempt to serve legislators' political interests in order to keep interest groups and citizens from complaining to legislators.

The comparison of citizens' oversight of legislators' decisions with that of stockholders over managers (or legislators over bureaucrats) is a useful reminder that these control relationships are imperfect. Although corporate managers may be controlled agents, they also have ample freedom to serve their own interests. The current uproar over executive salaries, in which compensation seems to increase as corporate profits decline, is a good example. Similarly, legislators have ample discretion in some policy areas; they know that their constituents will never notice the decisions they have made since the decisions will have only tiny effects on individual citizens.

The power of occasional audits to induce people to keep their behavior within the bounds of what those in control find acceptable is most compelling if we consider how the Internal Revenue Service monitors and controls 110 million taxpayers. Essentially, the IRS allows taxpayers to write their own tax bills and pay what they believe they owe the government. The IRS then audits about 1 percent of the tax returns, looking for income that taxpayers failed to report or deductions that they invented or exaggerated. Despite the infrequency of audits, the American system has an enviable record of collecting taxes. The best available research suggests that 96 percent of all households

with tax liability file tax returns. Individual taxpayers report between 91 and 95 percent of their true taxable incomes, and the overreporting of itemized deductions, personal exemptions, and business expenses is only about 2 percent of total personal income.

Most taxpayers report most of their income most of the time because the IRS has other sources of information and because it can impose heavy fines and criminal sanctions on those who cheat the government of its lawful share of income. The other sources of information include reports of wages and salaries from employers, reports of interest and dividends from financial institutions and corporations, reports of real estate transactions from closing agents, and reports of stock transactions from stockbrokers. The results of extensive compliance audits by the IRS demonstrate that taxpayers are most accurate in reporting items for which the IRS has good alternative sources (for example, wages, salaries, interest, and dividends) and least accurate in reporting items for which the IRS has no good alternative sources (for example, capital gains or income from small businesses). The government also encourages taxpayers to be relatively honest by imposing heavy fines on those it finds cheating and by prosecuting for criminal fraud those who seriously flout the law. A single visible prosecution, such as the conviction of Leona Helmsley for tax fraud, can help to deter many others from practicing similar deceits.

This account of how the Internal Revenue Service monitors and controls American taxpayers helps to reveal how citizens can monitor and control elected legislators without knowing much about what legislators are doing day-by-day. First, it shows the importance of auditable records. Although legislators may feel free to vote as they please on voice votes, they must be far more cautious when they face roll call votes because these actions are permanently and publicly recorded. Second, it shows the efficiency of having others collect and process raw information. Challengers and interest group leaders monitor what legislators have been doing and then inform citizens of legislators' misdeeds, much as employers, banks, and brokers monitor taxpayers' behavior and send summary accounts to the IRS. Third, it shows the deterrent power of heavy sanctions. Legislators anticipate and respond to citizens' preferences and potential preferences because they fear electoral defeat, much as taxpayers anticipate and respond to the rulings of the IRS because they do not wish to risk fines, public humiliation, or imprisonment.

One virtue of the alternative control model is that it avoids the four basic mistakes in identifying control relationships that were outlined in the previous section. It does not confuse the frequency with which citizens monitor legislators' behavior with the extent of their control over legislators' actions, for it allows other people to do most of the day-to-day monitoring. It does not assume that if citizens are to be influenced they must have well-established policy preferences in advance of legislative action, for such preferences are required only before the next election (and only then if legislators have failed to anticipate what preferences citizens would form at that time). It does not confuse the frequency of electoral defeat with the extent of control, for such defeats are evidence of the breakdown of control. Finally, it does not assume that legislators play the electoral game only once and therefore are willing to take small risks on any given issue; instead, it assumes that legislators' aspirations for long political careers give them incentives to anticipate citizens' future preferences on every issue put before them for fear that small risks will cumulate over time and threaten their continuance in office.

READING 20

Advice to Poll Consumers

Herbert Asher

Virtually all public officials, as well as large portions of the general public, including those most interested in public affairs, pay attention to public opinion polls. They are an integral part of modern American political life. Citizens, therefore, need to know how to understand and interpret them.

In the first part of this reading, Herbert Asher, a political scientist at Ohio State University, presents practical advice for consumers of polls. He notes that polls vary in quality and are often not neutral. He gives some hints to general consumers of polls on the matters they should assess as they interpret polls for themselves: the measurement of nonattitudes, the impact of how questions are worded, the impact of the order in which questions are presented, the nature of the sample, the effect of interviewing itself, the nature of the sponsorship of a poll, and the reasonableness and persuasiveness of the interpretation of a poll that is offered. He adds that polls are never reported to the general public in such a way that an interested consumer has all of the necessary information to make the above judgments.

The measurements of opinion reported by polls play various roles in the political life of the nation and, in some instances, help shape public decisions. In the second part of this reading, Asher explores the question of whether polls help increase public influence in the political and policy processes. The answer is mixed. Polls can be misused by elites to give the impression of public support that does not really exist. Some have argued that polls limit the range of political debate and limit the flexibility of the public in raising new issues, because the issues are, to some extent, determined by those who conduct the polls.

On the plus side, however, some subjects may be injected more forcefully into public debate as a result of being the object of a poll. And, fortunately, there are enough polls of high quality that we do have a good continuing picture of the broad shape of American public opinion.

From "Advice to Poll Consumers" by H. Asher, 1995. *Polling and the Public: What Every Citizen Should Know,* pp. 163–175. Copyright © by the Congressional Quarterly Press. Reprinted by permission.

To death and taxes should be added public opinion polls, an integral and unavoidable part of American society today. Public opinion polling is a contemporary manifestation of classical democratic theory; it attests to the ability of the rational and wise citizen to make informed judgments on the major issues of the day. Polling makes it possible for political organizations to demonstrate that public opinion is on their side as they promote their ends. Polling is also enamored by news organizations, in part because polls seem to elevate the citizen (and thus the media audience) into a more prominent political role; in effect, the polls transform the amorphous citizenry into a unified actor in the political process. Poll results that are not supportive of government actions provide the media with stories of conflict between the government and the people, just as points of contention between the president and the Congress or between the House and the Senate become a media focus.

As the technology of polling has been continually refined, upgraded, and made more available, many institutions, organizations, and private groups have gained the ability to sponsor and conduct polls. These organizations can readily hire pollsters for surveys that will promote their aims, or, if they want to be absolutely sure that the poll results will be favorable, they can conduct their own surveys. Such self-serving polls are replete with loaded questions, skewed samples, and faulty interpretations....

Adding to the proliferation of surveys, the major news organizations have heavily invested in their own in-house polling operations. The resulting increase in the number of polls they conduct justifies their investment and enables them to keep up with the competition. That is, for certain news stories, such as presidential debates, a news organization that fails to conduct and report a poll on who wins is open to the criticism of incomplete news coverage. The unseemly contest among the media to be the first to "call" the outcome of particular elections illustrates how the pressures of competition and ratings promote the widespread use of polls. The media operate under the assumption that the public reactions to major news events are meaningful and that public opinion polls enhance the news value of a story.

HOW TO EVALUATE POLLS: A SUMMARY

Polls are a significant way for citizens to participate in society and to become informed about the relationship between the decisions of government and the opinions of the citizenry. As more organizations conduct polls and disseminate their results, whether to inform or to sway public opinion, citizens should become wary consumers, sensitive to the factors that can affect poll results. Gaining this sensitivity does not require familiarity with statistics or survey research experience. Consumers need only treat polls with a healthy skepticism and keep in mind the following questions as tools to evaluate poll results.

One basic question poll consumers should ask is whether a public opinion survey is measuring genuine opinions or nonattitudes. Are respondents likely to be informed and have genuine opinions about the topic? Or is the focus so esoteric that their responses reflect the social pressures of the interview situation, pressures that cause respondents to provide answers even when they have no real views on the subject at hand?...

Another question to consider when evaluating polls concerns screening. Have the researchers made any effort to screen out respondents who lack genuine attitudes on the topic? Unfortunately, reports frequently omit information about prior screening questions and their effects. Often one cannot tell what proportion of the total sample has answered a particular item and what proportion has been screened out. To do a better job of reporting this information, news organizations should, at minimum, provide the number of respondents who answered a particular question. When this number is substantially smaller than the total sample size, they should explain the discrepancy.

When screening information is not presented, citizens are forced to form impressionistic judgments about whether the measurement of nonattitudes has been a problem in the survey. Of course, some issues of public policy that have been hotly debated and contested by political elites, even issues such as tax reform, may not be of much interest to many Americans and thus may be highly susceptible to the measurement of nonattitudes

Citizens are in a better position to evaluate the potential effects of question wording than the presence of nonattitudes. Because the media usually provide the actual wording of questions, citizens can judge whether any words or phrases in the questions are blatantly loaded, whether the alternatives are presented in a fair and balanced fashion, and whether a question accurately reflects the topic under study. If a report of a survey omits question wording, particularly on items dealing with controversial issues, the consumer should be wary and ask why.

Question wording is just one reason a complete questionnaire should be made available with a survey report. A complete questionnaire is also helpful when a survey contains many questions on a topic but reports the results for only one or two items. Without the complete questionnaire, a poll consumer is unable to assess whether the selective release of results has created any misleading impressions.

Another reason to examine the entire questionnaire is to assess the potential effects of question order. This is seldom possible, since press releases (other than those issued by news organizations) and news stories rarely include the complete survey form. However, it is important for citizens to be aware that the way earlier questions are asked can affect responses to subsequent queries. This is a subtle phenomenon for which most citizens have little intuitive feel, yet the strategic placement of questions is one of the most effective ways to "doctor" a survey. While each individual question may be balanced and fair, the overall order of the questions may stimulate specific responses preferred by the sponsor of the survey. One clue that this problem exists is the refusal of an organization, such as a political campaign team, to release the entire poll results.

The next question consumers should address is sampling. Although it is the most mysterious part of polling for most poll consumers, sampling is probably the least important for them to understand in detail. Sampling error is *not* where polls typically go astray. Reputable pollsters pick samples and typically report sampling error and confidence level so that citizens can form independent judgments about the significance of results. To make sure that a sample properly reflects the aims of a poll, a poll consumer should pay close attention to how a sample is defined. And certainly the consumer should confirm that a sample is a scientifically selected probability sample rather than a purposive sample that an investigator selected for reasons of convenience.

One aspect of sampling that citizens should not overlook is the proportion of the total sample to which a particular finding applies. For a variety of reasons,

such as the use of screening questions or the need to study analytically interesting subsets of the original sample, the proportion of respondents on which a result is based may be substantially smaller than the overall sample. Thus, one should know not only the sampling error of the total sample, but also the sampling error of the subsets.

As consumers evaluate polls, they also need to be aware that interviewers and interviewing are aspects of polling that can influence outcomes, but they are aspects that are not easily questioned. It is almost impossible for citizens to evaluate the effects of interviewing on poll results because reports usually provide too little information about the interviewing process beyond the method of interviewing (for example, telephone or personal) and the dates of the interviews. The poll consumer must normally assume that an interview was performed competently, undoubtedly a safe assumption with reputable polling firms. But consumers should note that an interviewer with the intention of generating biased responses has many opportunities to achieve that end while asking questions. The best way for the poll consumer to gain some sense of potential interviewer effects is to be a poll respondent who carefully observes the performance of the interviewer—an opportunity that may or may not come one's way.

The final questions to ask when evaluating a poll relate to the end products, analyses and interpretation. Most citizens do not have access to raw poll data; instead they must rely upon the analyses and interpretations provided by the media and other sources. Therefore, poll consumers need to ask whether a source is likely to have a vested interest in a particular poll outcome. If so, they should scrutinize poll results even more carefully. For example, a poll sponsored by the insurance industry purporting to demonstrate that the liability insurance crisis is due to the rapacious behavior of trial lawyers should be viewed with greater skepticism than a similar poll sponsored by an organization with a less direct interest in the outcome. Likewise, election poll results released by a candidate should be viewed more cautiously than those released by a respected news organization.

After evaluating the source of a poll, the consumer then faces the more difficult task of ascertaining whether the pollster's conclusions follow from the data. This task is problematical because often, as noted previously, only a portion of the relevant evidence is presented in a news story or press release. Or a poll may have included many items on a particular topic, yet the report may present only a subset of those items. Without knowledge of the total questionnaire, one can only hope that the analyst has reported a representative set of results, or speculate on how different items on the same topic might have yielded different results. Likewise, reports might include results from the entire sample, but not important variations in the responses of subsets of the sample. Lacking direct access to the data, the citizen is left to ponder how the overall results might differ within subsets of respondents.

The interpretation of a poll is not an automatic, objective enterprise; different analysts examining the same polling data may come to different conclusions. Although this may occur for a variety of reasons, an obvious one is that analysts bring different values and perspectives to the interpretation of polls. Often there are no objective standards on what constitutes a high or low level of support on an issue; it may indeed be partly cloudy or partly sunny depending upon one's perspective. Hence, poll consumers should ask themselves a fundamental question—whether they would necessarily come to the same conclusions on the basis of the data that have been presented. Just because the poll is sponsored by a prestigious organization and conducted by a reputable firm does not mean that one has to defer automatically to the substantive conclusions of the sponsors. And if a poll is conducted by an organization with an obvious vested interest in the results, then the poll consumer is certainly warranted in making an independent judgment.

POLLS AND THEIR EFFECT ON THE POLITICAL SYSTEM

Do polls promote or hinder citizens' influence in their society? Is the overall effect of the polls on the political system positive or negative? These questions continue to be vigorously debated. Writing in 1940, Cherington argued that polls enhanced the public's influence since they provided a way for the voices of a representative cross section of Americans to be heard; no longer would the views of a tiny segment of the population be the only ones to gain prominence. Meyer further argued that the polls provided political decision makers with accurate information about the preferences of the citizenry, thereby enabling political leaders to resist the pressures of narrow groups pushing their own special agenda in the name of the broader public.

The preceding arguments are still true today, yet the limitations inherent in polls as a mode of citizen influence must be recognized. First of all, the United States is a representative democracy that includes, in addition to elected representatives, a wide variety of organized groups trying to promote their own interests. Any assumption that the results of public opinion polls can be translated directly into public policy is naive. Moreover, it might not be desirable if public opinion polls were routinely translated into public policy. After all, polls at times may tap only the most ephemeral and transitory of opinions. Little deliberation and thought may have gone into the responses offered by the public. And certainly the rich complexities of issues can never be captured in a public opinion poll as well as they can be in a legislative debate or a committee hearing.

Second, even if the public's views as reflected in the polls were well formed, the implementation of those views might be objectionable. Polling often demonstrates that there is no majority view on an issue; opinion may be split in many different ways. The problem then becomes one of determining which subset of public opinion merits adoption. But automatically opting for the majority or plurality position would call into question such cherished values as the protection of minority rights. One can envisage situations in which the unqualified use of public opinion polls might threaten rather than enhance representative democracy and related values.

Third, a focus on poll results ignores the processes by which the public's opinions are formed and modified. For example, one factor that shapes popular opinion is the behavior of political elites. Thus, when the White House orchestrates a massive public relations campaign laden with a nationally televised presidential address, subsequent highly publicized presidential travels, and the submission of a legislative package to Congress, it is not surprising to see public opinion shift in the direction intended by the While House. Public opinion is not always an independent expression of the public's views; it can be an opinion that has been formed, at least in part, from manipulation by elites.

Sometimes the behavior of political elites initiates a shift in opinion, and sometimes the behavior is the result of a shift. For example, the president may take the lead on an unpopular issue, as typically occurs during an international crisis. After the president delivers a major address to the nation, public opinion polls usually indicate an upsurge of support for the president's actions emerging from feelings of patriotism and a desire for national unity in times of crisis. Such was the case with the Persian Gulf crisis that arose in 1990.

In reverse, the president may scramble to catch up with and then shape public opinion. This happened in the summer and fall of 1986 in response to Americans' heightened concern about the drug abuse problem. With the tragic deaths of famous athletes and increased media coverage of the drug crisis, a CBS News/*New York Times* poll conducted in August 1986 showed that a plurality of Americans cited drugs as the nation's most important problem. Congress, particularly House Democrats, trying to get out in front on this issue, proposed a major antidrug offensive. The White House responded by taking the initiative from Congress: President Reagan offered his own proposals, and he and the first lady gave an unprecedented joint address on national television. Major new legislation was passed to address the drug problem. Then, in 1989 President Bush declared a war on drugs and named a drug czar to coordinate federal initiatives. The president announced many antidrug proposals, which, according to the polls, were supported overwhelmingly by Americans even though they felt strongly that Bush's plan did not go far enough.

What do the preceding examples have to say about citizen influence? Certainly, the drug example suggests the potency of popular opinion on issues that arouse the public. But even here the salience of the issue was very much a function of the behavior of media and political elites who brought it to the fore; the public responded to the issue, but did not create it. The

adoption of antidrug measures into law suggests that public opinion, once aroused, spurs government policy initiatives. But when the media and political leaders stop talking about drugs, the issue becomes less salient and recedes from popular consciousness, and citizens may have a misguided feeling that somehow the problem has been resolved. Certainly the prominence of the crime issue in the 1994 elections was due in part to the skillful exploitation of the issue by the candidates and the heavy media emphasis on the topic.

The Persian Gulf example raises a different problem—namely, elites' misinterpretation (deliberate or unintentional) of what the polls are actually saying. Unfortunately, political leaders sometimes fail to recognize the limitations and circumstances of poll responses and automatically construe supportive poll results as ringing endorsements of a broad policy agenda. The tendency of Americans to rally around the leadership of the president during an international crisis should not be blindly interpreted as a popular mandate for particular policies, even though in the case of the Persian Gulf crisis, citizen support for the president's policies at each stage of the crisis was genuine.

Ginsberg has argued that polling weakens the influence of public opinion in a democratic society. He asserts that there are many ways besides participating in a poll for citizens to express their opinions, such as demonstrations and protests, letter-writing campaigns, and interest group activities. But because polling is deemed to be scientific and representative of the broad public, it has dominated these other types of expression.

Ginsberg identifies four basic changes in the nature of public opinion that are attributable to the increased frequency of polling. First, responding to a public opinion survey is an easier form of expression than writing a letter or participating in a protest—activities usually performed by citizens who are intensely committed to their positions. Anyone can respond to a poll question, whether or not the feelings about an issue are strong. Hence, in a public opinion poll the intense opinions of a small minority can be submerged by the indifferent views of the sizable majority. Indeed, government leaders may try to dismiss the views of dissidents by citing polls that indicate that most Americans do not support their position.

Second, polling changes public opinion from a *behavior,* such as letter writing or demonstrating, to an *attitude,* as revealed in a verbal response to a poll question. Ginsberg argues that public opinion expressed through polls is less threatening to political elites than are opinions expressed through behavioral mechanisms. Moreover, polls can inform leaders about dissidents' attitudes before they become behaviors. The information on attitudes gives government a form of early warning as well as an opportunity to change attitudes either by seeking remedies to problems or by relying on public relations techniques to manipulate opinions.

Third, polls convert public opinion from a characteristic of groups to an attribute of individuals. This enables public officials to ignore group leaders and instead to attend directly to the opinions of citizens. Unfortunately, this attention may effectively weaken individuals' political power because organized activity, not individual activity, is the key to citizen influence in the United States. If government leaders are able to use the polls as an excuse to ignore group preferences, then citizen influence will be lessened

Finally, polling reduces citizens' opportunities to set the political agenda. The topics of public opinion polls are those selected by the polls' sponsors rather than by the citizenry. Therefore, citizens lose control over the agenda of issues, and the agenda as revealed through the polls may differ in major ways from the issues that really matter to people.

Ginsberg's fundamental conclusion is that polling makes public opinion safer and less threatening for government. Opinions expressed through the polls place fewer demands and constraints on decision makers and provide political leaders with an enhanced ability "to anticipate, regulate, and manipulate popular attitudes." In short, Ginsberg's thesis is that the advent and growth of public opinion polling have been detrimental to citizen influence.

Ginsberg has raised some important issues about potential dangers inherent in the increased amount of public opinion polling, even if one does not agree with all of his conclusions. Clearly, we must be on guard against allowing public opinion to become synonymous with the results of public opinion polls. Public opinion manifests itself in many ways, including those

Ginsberg mentioned—protests, letter-writing campaigns, direct personal contact with decision makers, and many others. Political elites recognize the potential costs of ignoring these alternative forms of political expression, but it is critical that the media also recognize that polls are not the only legitimate expression of public opinion. We too must avoid allowing a passive activity such as responding to a poll to replace more active modes of political participation.

Although there is evidence that direct electoral participation has declined in the United States, other group-based activities are on the rise. And if groups have the resources, they can use polls to promote their agenda when it differs from that of the political elites. And, contrary to Ginsberg's assertion, polls need not make public opinion a property of individuals rather than groups. Polls can identify clusters of citizens (often defined by demographic characteristics) who do not share the prevailing views of the citizenry at large. Whether Ginsberg's concerns are overstated or not, the polls are playing an increasing role in American political life, in campaigns, in governance, and in popular discourse.

Observers have been concerned about the effect of polls not only on citizens' political clout but also on the performance of elected officeholders. More than forty years ago Bernays warned that the polls would dominate the political leadership, and that decision makers would slavishly follow the polls in order to please the people and maintain their popularity. The polls might even paralyze political leaders, preventing them from taking unpopular positions and from trying to educate the public on controversial issues. Political observers like Bernays still contemptuously deride politicians who run around with polls in their pockets, lacking the courage to act on their own convictions no matter what the polls say.

Some officeholders do blindly follow the polls, but today the greater concern is over those who use, abuse, manipulate, and misinterpret them. In particular, presidents have increasingly tried to manage and manipulate public opinion. For example Altschuler describes how President Johnson tried to take the offensive when his poll ratings began to decline. To convince key elites that he was still strong, Johnson attacked the public polls, selectively leaked private polls, and tried to influence poll results and poll reporting by cultivating the acquaintance of the pollsters.

The Reagan presidency developed one of the most skillful public relations efforts; in-house polling was a central part of the enterprise. Writing about the Reagan administration, Beal and Hinckley argued that polls became more important after the presidential election than before it, that polls were a much more important tool of governing than was commonly recognized. Likewise, polling is central to the operation of the Clinton White House. Certainly, no one would deny the president and other elected officials their pollsters. But the measure of an incumbent's performance should not simply be the degree of success achieved in shaping public opinion in particular ways.

One final effect of polls on the political system merits consideration—namely, the contribution of polls to political discourse. Whether as topics of conversation or more structured exchange, the polls contribute to political debate. And because they often are cited as evidence in support of particular positions, they become a central part of political discussion. But polls have more subtle effects; in particular, Americans' awareness of the attitudes of their fellow citizens as learned through the polls may alter their opinions and subsequent behaviors. This phenomenon has been explained in terms of the theories of the spiral of silence and pluralistic ignorance.

The spiral of silence thesis, developed by Noelle-Neuman, argues that individuals desire to be respected and popular. To accomplish this, they become sensitive to prevailing opinions and how they are changing. If individuals observe that their opinions seem to be in the minority and are losing support, they are less likely to express them publicly. Consequently, such opinions will seem to the individuals to be weaker than they actually are. On the other hand, if people perceive that their views are popular and on the ascendance, they are more likely to discuss them openly. Such opinions then gain more adherents and seem stronger than they actually are. Thus, one opinion becomes established as dominant, while the other recedes to the background. Pluralistic ignorance refers to people's misconception of what other individuals and groups believe. This, in turn, affects their own views and their willingness to express them. Lang and Lang link the notions of pluralistic ignorance and the spiral of silence in a discussion of American racial attitudes:

> Typical of pluralistic ignorance has been the unwillingness of many whites to acknowledge their own antiblack prejudice, which they believe to contradict an accepted cultural ideal. As a way of justifying their own behavior, these whites often attribute such prejudice to other whites by saying "I wouldn't mind having a black neighbor except that my neighbors wouldn't stand for it."
>
> But what if such fears about their neighbors' reactions proved unjustified? What if polls showed an expressed readiness for a range of desegregation measures that these whites do not believe others are prepared to accept? Such a finding contrary to prevailing belief would be controversial. Where the real opinion lies may be less important than the change in perception of the climate of opinion. A definitive poll finding can destroy the premise that underlies the justification for behavior clearly at variance with professed ideals. In these circumstances a spiral of silence about the real opinion fosters a climate inhospitable to segregationist sentiment and drives it underground.

As this example illustrates, public opinion polls provide us with a mechanism for knowing what our fellow citizens think and believe. If the polls can accurately measure the underlying beliefs and values of the citizenry, then we no longer have to be at the mercy of unrepresentative views that mistakenly are thought of as the majority voice. The polls can tell us a lot about ourselves as part of American society, and this self-knowledge may foster a healthier and more open political debate.

FOOD FOR THOUGHT

1. Do you agree with Cantril and Cantril's assessment that polls often do not probe deeply enough for individuals' underlying structures of thought? If so, how should public opinion be assessed to include additional factors, such as cultural norms and personal experience? What would be the advantages and disadvantages of conducting in-depth interviews instead of polls? According to Cantril and Cantril, how might polls be improved?

2. In the reading "Advice to Poll Consumers," Herbert Asher notes several problems with public opinion polling, including the nature of the sample, the measurement of nonattitudes, and the impact of how questions are worded and the order in which they are asked. Should the press make greater efforts to provide such information to the public when reporting poll results? What might be some topics on which the public is unlikely to be informed? In your view, do polls increase public influence in the political and policy processes?

3. A recurring theme throughout this section on public opinion has been the extent of public awareness of and participation in politics. How does Asher's description of the measurement of nonattitudes influence your view of the necessity of an informed public in a democracy? According to Graber, are certain groups or types of citizens more informed than others? If so, what does this difference mean for the representation of their interests?

Graber notes that most children strongly support the political system, become disillusioned during their teens, and grow less skeptical as they complete their education and enter the workforce. How does this finding compare with your own experience?

4. Like Asher, Arnold addresses the necessity of an informed public in the selection "Can Inattentive Citizens Control Their Elected Representatives?" While other scholars contend that citizens can control legislators in office only when they possess both outcome and policy preferences and actively evaluate legislators' records in office, Arnold argues that the public can control their representatives once they are made aware of legislators' voting records and that the public's preferences in regard to legislative outcomes are sufficient. According to Arnold, how is the public made aware of their representatives' actions in office? Why does Arnold believe that the public's preference for outcomes is sufficient? What is the role of campaigns and elections in Arnold's revised model?

5. In the selection "Public Opinion and the Rehnquist Court," Marshall explores how closely Supreme Court rulings reflect American public opinion and whether these rulings affect the public's attitudes. Based on your reading of Marshall's work, how much does the public know about the Supreme Court and how aware are citizens of its rulings? According to Marshall, what are the implications of unpopular Supreme Court rulings? The Court's approval ratings would decline if the Supreme Court frequently made unpopular rulings, but would such rulings affect the Court's power or legitimacy? Compare the Supreme Court in this regard to the presidency or Congress.

CHAPTER 5

THE MEDIA

Analysts of the role of the media in American politics often take as their starting point the conventional political science wisdom that the media don't tell us what to think but, rather, they tell us what to think about. While, strictly speaking, empirical research on media effects generally supports this "agenda setting" characterization, the surface simplicity of the observation is belied by the complex of implications and consequences for the American political system that derive from media coverage of political processes and governmental institutions. Quite clearly, for example, the outcomes of political campaigns, important presidential decisions, the successful passage of controversial legislation, and public understanding of complex, emotionally laden Supreme Court decisions will be affected by media coverage.

In this chapter we have selected a group of readings that explore the multiple facets of the linkages to their government that the media provide to the American citizenry. Collectively, the articles will demonstrate the difficulty of making broad generalizations about the media's implications and importance for, as we shall see, there are critical differences among various forms of media as well as among the political and governmental venues that they cover. Consequently, for example, local newspaper coverage of a presidential campaign may have little to offer the analyst studying network television coverage of that same campaign, and even less to say to the student of how network newscasts cover the Supreme Court.

In recognition of this complexity, this chapter offers a diverse set of readings that will go far towards dispelling any simplistic, reductionist characterization of the multifaceted role of the media in American politics. Starting at the broadest level, Berkman and Kitch's provocative essay explores the relationship between the media and democracy, offering a sober-ing account of the role that the media, particularly television, have played in supporting democratic processes. Far from more equitably spreading information to the citizenry, a beneficial consequence from the perspective of democratic theory, Berkman and Kitch assert that the contemporary media have had an opposite effect, contributing to further stratification in the American polity. Indeed, Berkman and Kitch attest to the "banality of politics" in a media age that is dominated by the "politics of confusion," themes that are not too distant from those developed by James Fallows in the selection that concludes this chapter.

Three of the readings reprinted here (selections by Schmertz, Cook, and Greenhouse) focus explicitly on the manner in which the press covers the three distinct branches of American national government, executive, legislative, and judicial. We offer these selections not solely for symmetry in our anthology's coverage but to demonstrate graphically that both the nature of media attention and the implications and consequences of the media's role in American politics differ significantly across these three institutional settings. Interestingly, several of the selections in the chapter focus on contemporary changes in political journalism, commonly attributed to the diffusion of television. Importantly, whether marked by change or consistency in media practices, the simple fact of media coverage has critical implications for the manner in which our political processes (such as campaigns and elections) and our governmental institutions function, save, perhaps, for the uniquely isolated and insulated Supreme Court.

For example, Herbert Schmertz asserts that the extraordinary attention the media places on the presidency creates a context in which appearances and not accomplishments count, and presidential style dominates over presidential substance. The president, in effect, has become a master of ceremonies presiding over the public will, too preoccupied with maintaining presidential popularity to truly govern. The consequences of such a change in the nature of presidential leadership are portrayed as having enormous implications from the standpoint of democratic theory. In effect, presidents can no longer be representatives of the people in the Burkean sense, that is, as agents who exercise leadership and judgment on the people's behalf. Instead, they become the people's surrogates and lead through sampling public opinion.

Timothy Cook's examination of media coverage of Congress moves the reader to a setting in which substantial journalistic attention is both more recently arrived (largely as a consequence of allowing cameras into the coverage of legislative processes), and members of Congress must vie with each other for the media's attention. Cook's thesis underscores that the publicity gained by congressional members through media coverage does not, of necessity, hinder congressional lawmaking ability, nor is such media attention irrelevant to legislating. Rather, Cook argues, a Congressman or Congresswoman's ability to make laws is integrally related to his or her ability and success in making news.

Finally, when Linda Greenhouse turns our attention to the Supreme Court, we are met by a relatively invisible governmental institution about which the public knows very little. Further, what the public does know comes largely from relatively meager journalistic coverage. Perhaps ironically, the Court appears to care little about its linkage to the mass public. Supreme Court norms and processes, such as its scheduling of decision announcements and the continued refusal to allow television cameras in the courtroom, coupled with journalistic constraints and practices that make the Court a relatively unattractive news source, result in media coverage of the third branch that is quite problematic in terms of both its breadth and its depth.

Rounding out the chapter, James Fallows offers an assessment of political journalism that levels a summary indictment of the journalistic profession itself. Why, Fallows asks, should the public view political journalists seriously and treat them as credible analysts when the profession itself has failed, on many levels, to warrant such public respect?

It will be difficult for the reader to leave this collection of readings without some degree of frustration about the citizenry's predicament. While many of us are disinterested in and/or cynical about the world of politics, one might question the degree to which our assessments reflect the actual functioning of our political institutions and officeholders or, alternatively, whether our views are driven by the manner in which the media portray the political world. At the same time, one might ask whether the very things that make us cynical and distrustful about politics reflect efforts by politicians and officeholders to be responsive to media demands rather than to publicly articulated interests and needs.

READING 21

Media and Democracy
Ronald Berkman and Laura Kitch

In this selection, political scientist Ronald Berkman and sociologist Laura Kitch examine the role that the media, particularly television, have played in American democratic processes. Historically, they note, information was derived at the local level. As society grew more complex newspapers and, subsequently, television became the citizenry's major informational sources. The early dominance of newspapers contributed to inequality in public access to information, because newspapers were not available universally and illiteracy was widespread. Consequently, information tended to trickle down through American society, with considerable reliance on interpretive elites. Arguably, the widespread accessibility of television would bring about a more equitable source of public information but, Berkman and Kitch assert, this has not occurred.

The authors picture a reality in which media conglomerates dominate the marketplace of ideas, public access to the media is quite limited, and people serve primarily as receivers of the media's message. The passive television medium requires little of its viewers who, for the most part, treat information as background noise. The media public is characterized as bored, apathetic, and unlikely to evaluate critically the content of media messages. Cynicism and confusion reign in a manipulable citizenry. While television can manipulate, it is also manipulable as well, responding largely to those forces favoring the status quo.

Berkman and Kitch argue that the political impact of the media can be seen in many ways, most broadly in fostering changes in campaigns and elections that have trivialized political dialogue while reducing the role of political parties as viable linkages between the citizenry and politics. With parties no longer capable of building policy consensus, the media often become the means through which government governs. The consequences of this include weakened public links to democratic processes (evidenced in low voting turnout) and fragmented interest-group politics. Policy development occurs in a media environment favoring the advantaged and the authors conclude ominously that the media serve as censors in American politics with respect to the ideas, groups, and policies receiving public attention.

POLITICAL INFORMATION AND DEMOCRACY

Information is the fuel of democracy. In a society in which citizens are expected to participate in political decision making, it is essential. Without the availability of reliable, objective, and politically diverse information, citizens are without the raw material needed to exercise their political franchise intelligently. While good information will not, in and of itself, guarantee a healthy democracy, it represents an important step in that direction.

The difficulty of providing citizens with the information necessary to promote effective participation was never squarely faced by the early democrats.

Jefferson, for example, put great faith in local institutions as a means for fostering dialogue and participation. In part, this faith was justified because America was largely an agrarian society, composed of thousands of small hamlets and villages, each with a local government.... But as America grew more industrialized and urban, many fewer citizens directly participated in local political activities. If they wanted to acquire political information, they had to find alternative sources.

In the past, the most widely available source for political information was newspapers. Even while town hall democracy flourished, newspapers were regarded as the means for citizens to learn about national and international issues, which were unlikely to be debated at town meetings. Early democrats regarded newspapers as a panacea for the defects of democracy. This faith is reflected in Jefferson's very strong stance in favor of press freedom and in the constitutional protections afforded the press. But newspapers were not available in many parts of the country, and many citizens were simply not able to read. While newspapers provided a direct source of information for the educated classes, the majority of the population had to depend on a "trickle down" effect for their information and news. At the time, politics was much more of a local grassroots activity than it is today, and there were a variety of opinion leaders who acted as conduits for political information. Consequently, there was a means for the citizen who could not read to acquire information. Despite this flow of information, the direct access and control of information enjoyed by the governing classes became an important tool for maintaining political power.

With the growth of the newspaper industry and the birth of the mass circulation newspaper, information became more widely available, but the innovations which held the promise of eliminating the inequality of access were radio and television. Soon after its invention, radio became an affordable commodity, and millions of Americans purchased radio sets. With the invention and subsequent mass production of television, the means to close the information gap, to democratize the dissemination of information, seemed available.

The early democrats' faith in the ability of newspapers, was matched by the faith of those who heralded the electronic media as a means to revitalize the democratic process. At first, while newspapers, radio, and television were essentially local enterprises, there seemed reason for optimism. Decentralized ownership provided opportunities for greater and more diverse participation. However, local ownership and control of both electronic and print media had a rather short life span. Radio and television were quickly consolidated into the hands of a few giant corporations. Newspaper chains extended their empires. Media conglomerates, involved in all aspects of the production and dissemination of printed and electronic entertainment and news, became the growth industries of the sixties and the seventies. Today, the ownership of virtually all mass media is vested in fifty giant corporations.

The political consequences of this centralized control are far-reaching. Several giant news organizations influence the portraits of reality that appear in all the national media. Another result of this consolidation has been a substantial change in the ratio of givers of opinions to receivers of opinions.... The opportunities for access to the mass media are limited, and the costs are prohibitively high. The mass media have become the center of political action, but only a select number of groups and individuals are able to participate. The remainder of the population is confined to the role of receivers of information. It is impossible to have a political dialogue with television, radio, or newspapers.

THE POLITICS OF CONFUSION

It is not that there is any lack of political information being sent through the mass media. Although television began as an entertainment medium, it has, over the years, become increasingly political. In the last five years, the amount of programming devoted to news has vastly increased. On the average, an affiliate television station will air 100 minutes of national news (minus commercials) and somewhere between 165 and 240 minutes of local news. This increase is not the result of any hunger for news in the general population. In fact, the majority of Americans seem to have a limited interest in politics. There is more news on television because news has turned out to be a profitable enterprise, more profitable than a lot of entertainment programs.

If the sheer quantity of news produced greater competency in the citizenry, we would have a society of political masters. Yet, just the opposite is occurring. There has certainly been no significant increase in voting since television began delivering increasing quantities of news into American households. There is little evidence to support the claim that Americans are better informed politically than they were immediately before the advent of television news. In fact, the evidence seems to point in the other direction; political knowledge and interest seem to be continually declining. Of course, all the blame for limited participation cannot be laid at the door of the media. Television news may have actually created greater participation among some segments of the population. Black political participation may have been heightened by the attention given to the Civil Rights Movement during the sixties and seventies. And there is an increasing body of evidence which shows that television has had a significant impact on citizens' knowledge of, and attitudes toward, politics.

Television may not have created a better-informed public, but it has certainly created certain political effects in the viewing public.... Television is essentially a passive medium. It requires less involvement than reading a newspaper. Because there is less effort involved in receiving and processing the message—a message which is dominated by visual symbols—there is less of a sustained reaction to the message being transmitted.

> Unless news is directly perceived as signaling a potential or actual personal threat, most people accept such information in the same manner as they accept the sounds of music they like. News is sensed rather than appreciated or analyzed. News has become so much background stuff.

The continual use of a set of standard stereotypes further limits the involvement of the viewer. Many viewers eventually become bored and apathetic. Few take the time to evaluate critically the content of the messages. The very low level of involvement in the messages transmitted through television creates a large class of viewers who become increasingly more susceptible to subtle and not-so-subtle forms of manipulation. As Jarol Manheim explains, there is a direct relationship between one's involvement and one's susceptibility to change: "... the less an individual cares about, is interested in, and/or views as central to his personal well-being the holding of a particular attitude, the more easily he may be persuaded to change that attitude...."

Some observers, such as Michael Robinson, strongly believe that individuals who watch television become more confused and cynical in their attitudes concerning politics. The effects of a diet of television news are no longer a matter of speculation. Research on the effects of television found that those "... who rely upon television in following politics are more confused and cynical than those who do not. And those who rely totally on television are the most confused of all." This cynicism and confusion are the result of a generally negative portrait of the political world painted on television news, according to Robinson....

There is every reason to believe that the individual who depends on television to understand the political world stands a good chance of becoming confused and cynical. The recurring use of stereotypes and the fascination with dramatic and divisive issues create the image of a political world without an internal logic. When individuals try to relate what they see on the television news to concerns that permeate their everyday existence, the confusion is likely to multiply.

Despite the evidence indicating that regular watchers of television news are more cynical about politics, there is no reason to assume that television news will continually transmit the same values or have the same impact on the viewers. During periods when power brokers are able to exercise strong control over the agenda, they are better able to transmit their values through the media—values that generally reinforce the legitimacy of the basic powersharing arrangements. Television is not simply a medium that manipulates; it is also easily manipulated. Even in periods when there are dissension and doubt, the media tend to give the basic political and economic arrangements a high de-

gree of legitimacy. If we depend on television to educate the generations coming of age, there will not be enough people with political education and/or interest [to] meet the demands placed on them as democratic citizens. Without knowledge of the political world, the democratic citizen is no longer an actor in the political system. Citizens devoid of information and wedded to a series of stereotypes are the potential victims of those who desire to bend reality to serve some personal, commercial, or political self-interest. No one saw these possibilities more clearly than Walter Lippmann...years ago:

> ...men who have lost their grip upon the relevant facts of their environment are the inevitable victims of agitation and propaganda. The quack, the charlatan, the jingoist, and the terrorists can flourish only where the audience is deprived of independent access to information. But where all news comes at second-hand, where all the testimony is uncertain, men cease to respond to truths, and respond simply to opinions. The environment in which they act is not realities themselves, but the pseudo-environment of reports, rumors, and guesses. The whole reference of thought comes to be what somebody asserts, and not what actually is.

Further, there is no reason to believe that such new technologies as cable television, which have eroded the networks' share of prime-time audience, will upgrade the level of political discourse and overcome "the pseudo-environment of reports, rumors, and guesses." Most people who turn to cable television have changed for the movies and the sports, not for the news shows.... Cable is likely to produce some additional access for political groups. However, these increased opportunities will probably be absorbed by the better-funded and organized single interest groups, who will use cable to mobilize the "believers."... Finally, now that the FCC has permitted the networks to enter the cable market and intends to remove nearly all restrictions on ownership..., it seems likely that small operators and minority groups will be driven out.

SOCIAL CLASS AND INFORMATION

The effects of using the mass media to acquire political information are not evenly spread throughout the population. The attitude of the viewer plays a strong role in determining effects, as does the dependence of the individual on the media as a source of information. In addition, there are structural factors which determine the potential impact of political messages. One's socioeconomic status or class position conditions what information will be accessible and how it will be digested and used.

Information pumped into a stratified society will be received and used in different ways by different segments of the population. Information is a commodity which must, like other commodities, be purchased. Sometimes the costs are tangible, such as the purchase price of books, magazines, or specialized media. Often the cost is the time which must be invested to consume the information. In general, one's class position, determined by education, income, and occupation, will decide the "costs" one must pay to acquire information. Education, for example, has been found to be an important determinant of both costs and benefits.

> ... several studies have supported the hypothesis that as the flow of information into a social system increases, groups with higher levels of education often tend to acquire this information at a faster rate than those with lower levels of education.

As the mass media make more information about particular issues available, the gap between the initial understanding of different groups does not narrow, as one might expect, but actually widens:

> As a result of the differential rates of acquisition, gaps in knowledge between segments with different levels of education tend to increase rather than decrease. Knowledge of space research is an example; after several years of heavy media attention to space rocketry and satellites, the gap in knowledge about that research across educational levels was greater than it had been before the space research program began.

Income is an important factor in determining the "cost" of information. Of course, those with larger incomes are likely to have more education and reap the benefits of that differential. Income also determines whether an individual can purchase books, travel, and invest the time to become politically informed. The access to free information channels definitely rises with income. High-income individuals are not totally dependent on the mass media for political information. They have the time, the inclination, and the contacts to acquire specialized and diverse sources of information. But the factory worker, who has just completed another eight-hour day, does not have the energy, the time, or the resources to purchase this type of information. Because the average individual cannot afford to get information, he must depend, in most cases, on the mass media.

The political consequences are dramatic. Not only do high-income individuals better understand their political interests (an understanding which is partly derived from their ability to purchase information at lower costs), they also know how to recognize and use information consistent with those interests. The low-income individual must, according to Anthony Downs, a political scientist who has written a fascinating treatise on this subject, depend on the high-income individual, whose interests are often not the same as his own, to supply him with information.

> ... since the mass media of communications in many democracies are owned or dominated more by high-income interests than low-income ones, low-income citizens are more likely to receive data selected by principles conflicting with their own than are upper-income groups.

Without the time and resources to make independent judgments about their interests, individuals are forced to rely on the mass media or to factor out interests as a basis for making political choices.

The dependence of much of the population on the mass media as a source of political information deepens the inequality of political resources by widening the information gap between certain classes. Certain groups are able to obtain the information necessary for them to understand their interests and make political choices based on those interests, while other groups are left to sort out the political world on their own. When these groups turn to the mass media for guidance in understanding the political world, they are left even more confused, and the information gap grows wider. Without a means to understand their interests and the impact of certain policies on those interests, much of the population makes political choices based on the lure of certain symbols or personality traits. The increasing use of images, symbols, and psychological appeals, a political tableau necessitated by the increased reliance on television, further confuses those without independent sources of information and further erodes the place of group interests in the political process. The information gap is a prime means by which the ruling class is able to win the allegiance of groups with antithetical interests. It may be foolish to believe that the news media can be much more perfect than the society in which they function. But the news media not only reflect some of the problems of American democracy (the inequality of opportunities, for example) but often magnify and intensify some of those problems as well.

THE MEDIA AGE CAMPAIGN

Mass media have not only changed public attitudes toward politics but also have fundamentally restructured the way politics is practiced and the way power is distributed. These political changes occasioned by the burgeoning power of the mass media have, in turn, had a further impact on public attitudes about politics, the democratic system, and their role within the system. Elections are a prime example of a political transformation occasioned by the media. Theoretically, citizens in a democratic society are supposed to exercise considerable influence in the electoral process. Traditionally, elections were supposed to provide an opportunity and a focus for political debate and give various interests in the society an opportunity to have some impact on policy and election outcomes. Elections were to be an opportunity for citizens to become givers of opinion and, thereby, more directly participate in the formation of public opinion. They were to be a civic exercise that helped maintain the balance in the ratio of givers of opinion to receivers of opinion, which C. Wright Mills saw as essential to the maintenance of a healthy democracy.

Political parties were supposed to provide the vehicle for individual and group participation in the electoral process. Parties would have a central role in the electoral process, collecting campaign money and using the many volunteers to stimulate interest in the election. Historically, party bosses gained the leverage to exercise considerable influence over the candidates chosen to carry the party's banner. Even more important than their role in selecting candidates, organizing participation, and raising money was the contribution they made in sorting out and making the political world intelligible.

> By inspiring "party identification" in most people they provided the main cognitive sorting devices that enable ordinary people to make sense out of politics and furnish them with a meaningful basis for voting on a wide variety of issues and in frequent elections.

Parties provided the political glue which held together the very fragile and fragmented political and social systems. These parties not only gave people some reason to have political beliefs, they also gave them something to believe in.

Political parties were profoundly affected when the media, particularly television, became the arena for electoral contests. Certain politicians used television to overcome the power of the party to control the nomination of candidates and to shape the issues in the campaign. When television took over as the arena and arbiter of electoral contests, it was not only the party bosses that lost their traditionally powerful role but also the millions of party workers who brought the campaigns to the neighborhoods. It seemed to make little sense to cultivate and train volunteers to make telephone calls, knock on doors, discuss the campaign, or pass out leaflets at shopping centers when a 30-second television or radio commercial could reach far more people. The deemphasis on traditional grassroots campaigning fractured one of the few natural links between the political world and the public. Using television as the premier campaign tool not only dried up opportunities for participation and involvement by party regulars, volunteers, and members of various interest groups but also changed the nature of campaigning in ways that left citizens more confused about politics and about their obligation to participate.

When political campaigning moved from the streets and factories to the television studios, it was not merely a change of scene but also a change of characters and scripts. Media consultants took the lead in shaping the candidates' image and the themes for the campaign. They quickly disabused candidates of the notion that they could simply transplant the traditional political methods to television. If candidates were to use television effectively to get votes, they had to use the techniques which had a proven record of attracting interest. Candidates had to sell themselves. That's what people do in television commercials—they sell things—and they sell them by using provocative images, not by using appeals to principles and beliefs. An astute and sensitive political man like Adlai Stevenson, who ran as the Democratic candidate for President in 1952 and 1956, when television was first being used in presidential campaigns, could not help but observe that candidates selling themselves on television as a promoter sells a box of cereal would assuredly have a detrimental effect on the democratic process.

If television commercials have not fully undermined traditional campaign dialogue, they certainly have trivialized the discussion. Incrementally, television transformed the language of politics and the logic of democracy. In order to use the medium of television to its fullest, politicians have, to a very large degree, abandoned the traditional discourse of politics. Political advertising does not contain political messages; it is simply a commercial message about something political. What was often special and significant about politics—the effort to confront and solve human problems and build a better, more just society, a notion that informed political dialogue since Plato and Aristotle—has been lost.

The drop in participation and party identification, not solely but importantly the result of television campaigning, has loosened democracy from its moorings.... A political system built on mass participation must expect, and even encourage, change. It is the changing sands of democracy which allow it to evolve and remain vital. In order to weather these changes and provide a basis for political transitions, there must be some institutions that promote a degree of stability. Political parties have been an important source of that political stability.

Without parties to provide political focus or forge alliances among the multiple, overlapping, and conflicting interests that characterize the American political scene, the electorate has been fragmented into little pockets of single-interest groups. These small, narrowly-focused, single-interest groups promote a politics of selfishness, intolerance, and zealotry. This kind of politics reopens old wounds, separates rather than unites, and poses a mighty threat to the principles of democracy. Meg Greenfield, a writer familiar with the Washington political world, vividly describes the impact of these changes:

> I can't remember a time in Washington when interest group issues and politics so dominated events. And every day the units of protest and concern seem to be subdividing into even smaller and more specialized groupings.... By now, there can hardly be a cultural, racial, regional, economic or professional group for whom the lawmakers in Washington have not fashioned some special statutory blessing—a prerogative, a grant, an exemption, a reimbursement, something. It puts a premium on identifying yourself with the special subgroup and helps to thin, if not destroy, whatever feelings of larger national loyalty various citizens might have.

If further confirmation of this political fragmentation is needed, there are ample illustrations in recent voting trends. Half the registered Democrats who cast their votes for Gary Hart in the primaries said they would vote for Ronald Reagan in the general election. Organized labor was not able to deliver its ranks to the Democratic party, despite a strong organizational effort. Candidates increasingly tailored their campaigns to cash in on this political fragmentation. The mayor of New York City ran on both the Democratic and the Republican lines. Candidates have commonly disassociated themselves from their political traditions and have run campaigns based on appeals to narrow interests or campaigns focused on seductive symbols of leadership, patriotism, and power. Party affiliations, or the support of traditional alliances based on political interests, are no longer a measure of a candidate's electoral chances. Candidates with the right formula and the means to project it are able to succeed in an electoral world that has been transformed by television. It is a world in which many voters make political choices using virtually the same criteria they use to make commercial choices.

If the existence of this large number of single-interest groups gives the impression that more people are involved in political activity, the impression is false. There are more groups, but there are fewer people politically participating. The number of citizens who choose even to vote, the easiest form of participation, declines with each election. The United States now has the lowest rate of voter turnout in the world.... It is the political world's marriage with television that is one of the prime factors in this decline in voting. In much the same way that people are lulled into boredom and apathy by trying to disentangle and understand the political world presented in the news, they are tranquilized by the media's obsession with the vicissitudes of election campaigns and the drumbeats of politicians trying to sell themselves over the tube. It is not simply the quantity of information—although there certainly is an abundance of campaign news—that sends all but the political addicts scurrying for relief but also the quality of that information, which deepens the apathy that is already far too pervasive.

There are some theorists who are not particularly concerned about political apathy or its effects on the democratic process. They regard the decline in voting as the result of a "sorting out process." Those with the most interests in the results of an election are the ones who participate, which, according to these observers, is the way it should be.... There is no reason to take comfort from the assertion, even if it were true, that those who vote, have a high interest in the outcome. All this reveals is that fewer and fewer people feel as if they have a stake in the political system. And when fewer people feel as if they have a stake in the society in which they live and more people surrender their rights and ignore their obligations, there are political and social dues that must be paid.

Of course, not all Americans can devote large blocks of time to civic and political activities. For many, the difficulties in simply earning enough to satisfy basic needs and carving out a little time for leisure occupies most of their energy. Yet there are fundamental obligations and responsibilities that must be met if democracy is to be more than a word roundly celebrated but widely ignored or misunderstood. No matter what justifications some social scientists and propagandists give for the astonishing levels of political apathy, it means that the system is in a state of decay.

Yet there have been instances in which the population has shown surprising interest in political events. These flashes of interest confound some theorists. Observers wonder why 60 million people voluntarily watched the Carter/Reagan debate. They wonder why the speeches of Governor Mario Cuomo and the Reverend Jesse Jackson at the Democratic Convention stirred such political interest and emotion throughout the country. The answer is fairly simple. People tuned in on the debate because they expected to see a more authentic and spontaneous discussion of political issues, which they did not get, and they were moved by the speeches of Jackson and Cuomo because they were truly different from the normal political babble. There is a latent political interest in the country which is smothered by the banality of politics in the media age.

GOVERNING THROUGH THE MEDIA

Television and other mass media are no longer solely used for the purpose of winning elections. Presidents and other political actors use the mass media to govern. In part, the realization that the mass media could be used for this purpose has required only a small extension of logic. However, the need to use the media to govern was created when candidates invested their political fortunes in television. Politicians' reliance on the mass media in elections withered the organic roots of power and so fragmented the electorate that it was much more difficult to get the consensus necessary to govern. Parties could not provide any real support. There were no enduring alliances and little cooperation among interest groups. With each new issue, it was necessary again to build a consensus. Politicians sought to enlist the vaunted powers of television to build this consensus. Using the mass media for one political purpose created additional needs and further incentives to use the media for other purposes. In a very real sense, it has created a dependence which will not be easily undone.

The mass media's coverage of the political world further contributes to the dependence of politicians on the technologies of mass communication. In the process of creating the stereotypes for news, the "good guys" and "bad guys," the winners and the losers, the rising and failing stars, the news media exert a pressure for immediate results. Through their exposure to the news, people come to believe that democracy should operate with the speed and efficiency of a network news broadcast.

> Television seldom covers the long, often dull meetings where democratic decisions are worked out. As a result, many viewers come to believe that great problems can be quickly resolved. T.V. has helped to produce a "turned on" generation that wants immediate experience and gratification at the flick of a switch.

Entertainment programing, including the many political dramas and docudramas, has further reinforced this conception of the way problems get resolved:

> . . . entertainment television is full of dramas and "docudramas" in which a problem of some sort, often social and political, is set forth, fought through, and resolved in an hour or two, minus commercials. One result is surely a spreading of the general assumption that life's problems can be understood and resolved quickly, with no messy strings left dangling, if only people with vision and courage deal with them.

In order to keep pace with the expectations created by television, politicians feel compelled to use television. There is, in their minds, no faster way to affect public perceptions. Since the success or failure of particular policies is a matter of interpretation, mass media provide a means for the power holders to provide their interpretation—to create an image of success or, if the need arises, to put the best face on failure.

This cycle has transformed and commercialized the policy-making process. At first, presidents and other political actors would determine policy and use the media to explain the policy and build support. These were largely separate processes. They are no longer quite so separate. The wisdom and advisability of particular policies are now considered in light of the potential for the policy to be successfully sold to the news media. The probability that the policy will produce some quick results, or can be portrayed as producing results, becomes a major concern. Whether a policy is good or bad, or whether a policy is necessary, is no longer the paramount concern. Leaders do not lead, they follow the changing tastes of the public

opinion market. They listen to their pollsters and media and political consultants, who provide up-to-the-minute readings of the latest ideological fashion. Everything is calibrated and calculated. Since the news media are quick to define policies as strategies, the public is aware of the politicians' subservience to public tastes. Politicians who opportunistically change to benefit from some present ideological fashion cause people further to doubt the integrity and seriousness of political officials and the pronouncements of policy that they utter.

OTHER POLITICAL ACTORS

It is not only the world of the president, the senator, the congressperson, the governor, and other political officials that has been transformed by "media politics"; corporations, interest groups, reform movements, and revolutionary movements, as well as others seeking to gain power, change the balance of power, or influence policy have been equally affected by the transformation in the political world.

For the corporation, these developments have proven to be something of an unexpected windfall. Politicians have legitimized using commercials and commercial devices to sell public policy. This has opened the door for the corporations to use precisely the same devices to sell their point of view on political issues to the public. Of course, the corporations have been using precisely these methods for years and are generally more sophisticated, better able to produce sustained information campaigns, and to pay the costs of enormously expensive advertising campaigns. . . .

The freedom to use the airwaves and newspapers to persuade the public of the corporations' point of view provides the corporations with an incredibly strong political weapon. Because of their skill and resources for using the mass media effectively for persuasion, political advertising will undoubtedly become one of the strongest weapons in the corporations' political arsenal. One thing that American democracy does not need is an enormously wealthy corporate sector with even more power to determine the direction of the political agenda.

While the mass media will help to enhance corporate power, it may have the opposite effect on protest movements. Since most reform organizations do not have the resources to carry out advertising campaigns to inform the public of their ideas and positions, they are dependent on the mass media for an identity and a gateway to the public opinion arena. If a movement is able to gain the attention of the media, as the Civil Rights and anti-war movements were able to do, the media can be an enormous asset in focusing attention on the problems that the movement is seeking to redress and on the movement itself. Yet, without an independent means of conveying information about the activities and goals of a movement, even the most powerful movements are subject to definition by the mass media. "Mass media define the public significance of movement events," writes Todd Gitlin, who has extensively researched the media coverage of the organization called Students for Democratic Society. By ignoring certain events, or characterizing certain activities negatively, the media "... actively deprive them of larger significance." In this way, the media help shape the direction of protest movements, which are forced to choose between accommodation to the values of the media or political obscurity. The choices made about which movements are given legitimacy are not random but reflect the ideological outlook of the media and the political establishment:

> The more closely the concerns and values of social movements coincide with the concerns and values of elites in politics and in media, the more likely they are to become incorporated in the prevailing news frames. Since the sixties, for example, consumer organizations have been elevated to the status of regular newsmakers; they and their concerns are reported with sympathy, sufficiently so as to inspire corporate complaints and counter-propaganda in the form of paid, issue-centered advertising.

While certain reform organizations can eventually get standing in the media, organizations that fundamentally threaten elite interests can, according to Gitlin, achieve standing only as deviants. Americans are systematically deprived of access to more radical ideas for social change....

Within this spectrum of competing interests in American society, some interests are simply "more equal" than others. The media wield an enormous amount of influence in determining which interests will be heard and in creating the context within which they will be evaluated. The media respond to economic realities by selling space or air time only to those who can afford them. On the other hand, the media may respond with a genuine interest in reform movements like the Civil Rights Movement, consumerism, and environmentalism. However, the media also have the power to ignore, and often do ignore, those who cannot afford to buy space or time, those who represent a radical alternative, or those who are effectively disenfranchised through poverty, lack of education, and lack of the appropriate media skills.

The media have come to act as censors in determining which groups, ideas, and policies will be given public attention. As the media regulate the flow of political communication, they deprive the public of the right to learn and to determine independently the viability and merits of various groups' ideas. With the media acting as mediators, it becomes increasingly difficult for those seeking change to generate the necessary sparks and cultivate support for their interests. There are, of course, limitations on the number of groups and organizations that the media can cover. Yet there is a pressing need to broaden and deepen political discussion to include those who now stand outside the media's frame of reference.

READING 22

The Media and the Presidency

Herbert Schmertz

In "The Media and the Presidency," corporate executive Herbert Schmertz contends that the publicity focused on the contemporary president

---

From "The Media and the Presidency" by H. Schmertz, 1986, *Presidential Studies Quarterly,* vol. XVI, no. 1, Winter 1986, pp. 11–21.

exceeds the wildest imaginings of those who came before him, and that the office cannot be considered apart from the media's influence on it. In Schmertz's scathing critique, the presidency appears to exist for the media's convenience rather than for the performance of critical governmental functions, and endless media pursuit of the president feeds an ever-expanding adversarial relationship between the public and our chief executive.

The fundamental problem in the media–presidency relationship stems from differential approaches to political issues. While the president's primary tasks include resolving conflict, media success necessitates feeding on and, perhaps, exacerbating such conflict. The media's conflict orientation can divert the president from his policy priorities, and "non-news news events" are created to fill an insatiable media appetite. Important presidential decisions are hastily arrived at to meet media desires for immediacy and deadlines, and are articulated in the most simplistic fashion. Ultimately, even the president may view the world in the media's simplistic terms with attendant negative policy consequences.

Schmertz's prescription for media reform centers on lessened access to the presidency, an added premium placed on presidential privacy, and greater journalistic professionalism. It appears, however, that Schmertz casts too much blame and responsibility on the media and not enough on the presidency for the problems he describes. Certainly, Schmertz underestimates the president's own weapons in his efforts to govern through the media. One might also take issue with the author's predominantly benign characterization of the presidency as a policy oriented office attuned to democratic values. While Schmertz writes that, "Americans need to rediscover something we all know about the Presidency—that it works very well indeed when no one is standing there watching everything it does," there are those who would contend that events such as executive behavior in the Vietnam war era, the Watergate scandal, the Iran–Contra affair, and more recent campaign finance transactions all counsel greater, not diminished, media scrutiny of the president and the presidential office.

In his great *Oxford History of the American People,* the historian Samuel Eliot Morison says of our first President that: "Everything that the Washingtons said was repeated; everything they did was watched. No other subsequent President of the United States has lived in such a glare of publicity." That Morison could write this in 1964, after the death of President John F. Kennedy—called "the first television President"—is puzzling and even peculiar. In Washington's day, political ideas and political news took a long time to travel.... But in our own day, political news has become virtually instantaneous, and I would say—*contra* Morison—that the glare of publicity is now so merciless as to have been unimaginable in Washington's day....

So pervasive has the influence of the media on the President now become that it is virtually impossible to consider that office apart from the media and their influence upon it as a political institution. It is a cynosure—almost a stage setting surrounded by lights, microphones, photographers, and watchers who never sleep. The White House is no longer a home or retreat: it is never quiet, never still; it can never relax, The press—and by way of the press, the world—is an eternal and vigilant presence within the walls.

But in truth, the media are far more than just a presence and must be seen by those occupying the Oval Office as critics and adversaries on most of the issues confronting the Presidency. The attitude of the U.S. political leadership toward the media is perhaps best summed up in a sentence from Geraldine Ferraro's ... book about her ... campaign for the Vice Presidential spot on the Democratic ticket. In the opening of her book, Mrs. Ferraro says: "But nothing is worse than looking as if you don't know where you are going." One might amend this and say that nothing is worse *to the media* than looking as if you don't know where you are going. Among the electorate, I am sure, there would most certainly be a far different perception; namely, that "Nothing is worse than *looking as if you know where you are going when you don't.*"

There has been no period of American history, of course, when the Presidency was free of media influence. We can recall that there were newspapers in Washington's day who felt that his driving about

New York in a coach and six was merely the overture to his installation as King.... Whether the muckraking journalists of the Progressive Era used Theodore Roosevelt, or whether Teddy was using them, is still open to debate—but certainly they seem to have worked in harness to advance both political and Presidential goals. Out of President Theodore Roosevelt's recognition that he was able to manipulate the media to advance his cause with the public came: the first permanent White House quarters for the press; the first daily interviews with reporters; the first Press Secretary; the first management of White House news to take advantage of deadlines and of the best days on which news might be made....

Woodrow Wilson was the first to schedule Presidential press conferences as a regular matter, holding them usually twice a week and opening them to all accredited reporters. Presidential interest in conducting these press conferences has thereafter waxed and waned.... Franklin Delano Roosevelt...held over 900 press conferences during the 13 years he held the Presidency. There was, however, in Roosevelt's day, no question about who was managing whom. He refused to be quoted directly and would lecture reporters who gave him stupid questions....

Roosevelt, too, was an early advocate of the advantages to be gained by use of the new broadcast medium. His "Fireside Chats' were a pioneering and effective use of the airwaves by the Presidency to advance the Presidential goals. Likewise Eisenhower, who had the much respected James C. Hagerty as his Press Secretary throughout both terms, pioneered with television to gain support for his programs. But it was Kennedy, whose four televised debates with Nixon were crucial in his election, who made the electronic media an art.

Consider, however, how the White House has been invaded by the media in our own day and age. We read of the President and his wife attempting to find some recreation at a remote hilltop ranch in California while the press watches continually from a nearby mountain top through huge telescopes.... No presentation from the White House seems complete to us without the horde of reporters and photographers and their tons of lumbering ancillary equipment as they scurry about like schools of fish seeking the best vantage points from which to view and record everything the President says and does,

Yet their attitude is hardly that of docile fish, but is as if they themselves owned the place. All of us have seen their badgering of the President, the shouts to him from reporters after he has tried to conclude his press conference or while he is attempting merely to go about his business in a simple and direct way. Someone is always bellowing something like: "What about Nicaragua?" It is as if the President and the White House exist for the entertainment and convenience of the media rather than to get a difficult job done for us, for the electorate.

As the public continually observes the media in hot and heated pursuit of the President, the public's perception of the office changes. We see a man pursued by a herd of irritable and irritating inquirers, barking at him like dogs after a bear, demanding answers to their questions, and soon—on a subliminal plane—we begin to see him as perhaps our own opponent, our legitimate quarry, and perhaps even our foe.

This subliminal suspicion is further advanced by endless hair-splitting indulged in by the media concerning every Presidential word, gesture, bump, and at present, as ridiculous as it seems, the pimples upon his nose. This is very obviously not the behavior of people attempting to get something done *together*. It is rather a mark of those enveloped in a fog of mutual suspicion that is arising from what seems to be a fundamental hostility.

We have become—under the media's prodding—a people who do not trust *anything* that comes out of the White House. The President's medical condition is not just of natural interest, but is transformed into a matter for inquisition and investigation. Medical reports are not to be trusted; doctors are not to be believed, but are instead interrogated as if they were on trial when they attempt to report to the public on the President's condition. Legitimate curiosity about a President's health has passed over into morbid fascination with every detail....

We are treated to a Jules Feiffer cartoon that begins with a drawing of a man in some dark tunnel and a voice is saying "This is Dan Rather from inside the President's colon, which is to be removed today." Instead of being outraged we grin ruefully and realize that this is the situation into which the media—and perhaps the White House—have led us.

Part of the problem arises from the different approaches to political issues that must be taken by the President and the media. The Presidency by its very nature is a place in which conflicts must be confronted and resolved. As Truman expressed it, "the buck stops" *there,* and the major intractable conflicts of the day and the age inevitably end up on the desk in the Oval Office. The President must continually seek ways in which to reconcile violent differences between various factions and people and even nations. To reporters, on the other hand, conflict is the stuff of which headlines and careers are made. It is therefore in their interest to *emphasize* the divisiveness and conflict that abound in a center of power such as the White House. The thirst for conflict lends fuel to the endless blather of speculation about what the President is up to. Will he be as tough as Gorbachev, as resolute as Thatcher, as wily as the Chinese, as clever as the Japanese, as audacious as the Israelis? No day ever passes without a comparison being drawn between the behavior of the American President and that of other statesmen—here and abroad—facing the same or similar problems.

Presidents are elected because they have promised to achieve certain national goals; they would undoubtedly prefer to concentrate on those promises. Reporters and the media, however, now have the power to set a *new* national agenda by their stories, their questions, by what they choose to emphasize or investigate. It is therefore entirely possible today for the press to divert the President and the White House from the national agenda and to have these public servants focus their attention entirely upon a *different* agenda—one that has been set by the press rather than by the President or the electorate.

A small army of reporters, photographers, and sound technicians—generally about 200 people—represents the media at the White House. For all the reporters this is a choice assignment; for all their employers, a rather expensive one. There is a natural tendency to demand news in return, and this exigency fosters the propensity of *both* the White House press corps and the presidential press secretaries to *manufacture* news—or at least *stories*—even when no

news exists. People in desperate search of material will tend to manufacture material if none is readily at hand. The White House therefore gives birth to a lot of so-called "news" only because the reporters are there and there is an urgent need to have a story....

It is out of this compulsion for news that the media created the non-news news event; namely, someone standing in front of the White House fence or the White House fountain and reporting ponderously that the President has gone off in the helicopter to view the mountains at Camp David. Often these reports involve something that is not news in any generally-accepted sense. A President going off for a weekend is hardly a news story, and someone *telling* us the President has gone off for a weekend is hardly a news story, but the public may eventually begin to suspect that someone standing in front of the White House fountain with a microphone in his hand and telling us where the President has gone for the weekend is a news event. When this happens, we are corrupting not merely the reporter, but the public's view of what makes news. We are creating a national misperception about what is a legitimate interest in Presidential activities.

Once we have seen a few hundred of these vapid and empty television reports, it becomes obvious that the purpose of much television news is not to report what is happening, but to fill up the space. Someone has bought and paid for these minutes; therefore, something must be put into them that appears to be news. Therefore, we shall have reporters stand in front of the White House fence and tell us that the President has gone away to Camp David for the weekend.

News would be far more entertaining—and in my view have far higher ratings and generate far higher advertising revenue—if television were willing to restrict its reporting to real events: to seek out the real stories of the day and not give us floods of vapid posturing in front of White House bushes and fences.

The result of this inordinate media focus on the White House is that Presidential personality has become more important than Presidential achievement. A President who charms and fascinates and entertains us becomes more precious than one who advances the nation's goals. If you doubt this, note the erosion of policies and issues as factors in Presidential campaigns, and their replacement by campaigns that focus on personality and leadership characteristics. It is difficult to investigate the issues—which are usually complex and often mysterious. It is far easier to do a sort of vulgar psychoanalysis of Presidential habits, to report gossip about Presidential personality, to speculate about Presidential likes and dislikes. Candidates find it hard to resist this media pressure, and the result is their focus upon personal issues rather than political issues; the result is to see them declare—as Mrs. Ferraro does—that "Nothing is worse than looking as if you don't know where you are going."

It is from this mutually-indulged fascination with the Presidential image that we see the Presidency gradually being turned from an executive position to a sort of a sacerdotal or shamanistic position—one in which the President, rather than execute the laws of the nation and perform the public will, becomes instead a figure who presides over the nation's public ceremony, and one who attends to and consecrates the popular will rather than executes the nation's and his own.

As we view recent Presidential campaigns, one cannot evade a suspicion that the media have decided their business is to entertain us rather than educate us. The stories they love are the "horse race" stories, not the issue stories. The pieces they write are the personality stories, not the historical perspective stories. The issues they raise are rarely philosophical but meretriciously personal: who will get the biggest office; who will have the maximum Presidential influence; who sat next to the President at lunch or rode in the car with him; who was forbidden to ride in the car with him and why; who went to the zoo with the First Lady instead of going to the speech with the President? To which we might all heartily respond: Who cares?

The public reads these stories, I suppose, because they are easy to take, diverting, entertaining, and go down so much more pleasantly than the difficult political analysis that would be required if there were less gossip to fill up the broadcasts and columns.

Television is particularly tempted, in my view, to make every Presidential story a personality story. It is easy to put people on television and simplicity itself to portray their disagreement. It is, in sorry contrast, extremely difficult to examine complex political issues on television—because the reporters themselves would have to understand the issues and find visual symbols that would bring out the philosophical disagreements and illustrate the nature of the argument. One cannot do this without arduous study and analysis. Generally the time constraints and profit constraints in television are such that no one ever bothers to do it. It is cheaper and more fun to do the personality piece, the human interest story, the piece about a conflict rather than attempt a piece of complex analysis.

Another terrible pressure on the Presidency wrought by the media results from the small capacity for patience among reporters who have daily deadlines to meet in both broadcast and print media. A manager such as the President must often rely upon extraordinary patience as he attempts to sift through and reconcile the conflicting aspects of some large political or military issue. The pressure from the media for immediate solutions has often produced immediate solutions in cases where delay, and deeper thought and analysis, would have been the preferable mode of behavior.

A President may have to consult a dozen advisors and half-a-dozen other nations before coming up with a solution to some grave political crisis. Reporters do not have time for this: they must have the answer now—for tonight's front page, for the seven o'clock news.

Because they are so anxious to do personality pieces, the media are continually contrasting the behavior of this President with that of his predecessors or of other world leaders. We are told that Jimmy Carter would not have been so insensitive about South Africa; that Lyndon Baines Johnson would not have been so relaxed about letting Congress go its own way; that Eisenhower would have been quicker to let the Russians know where he stood on Angola. In the media's eye it is never enough for a President to be himself—he also must outshine all those who have gone before him.

Another popular diversion for the media is to pit one branch of government against the other. The Senate is continually pitted against the House, and the Congress against the Presidency. The judiciary is dragged in regularly and set in battle array against both the Congress and the Presidency. The harm, as I see it, is not so much that this is done in print or on television discussion shows, but that the parties themselves—the organs of law and government—are continually approached and pitted. The White House is asked whether it approves of what Senator Dole has just said. Senator Dole is asked whether he is going to put up with White House inaction on one of his pet projects. The general thrust of this agitation is to foster action where action may be inadvisable or hasty, and to speed the occurrence of events or battles that might better be delayed.

The effect of all this tumult and turmoil is to inundate the public every day in almost every medium of communications—newspapers, magazines, radio, and television—with news about the Presidency. We know how the President dresses, how his wife dresses, how he handles his meetings, and who sits where, and where he goes and when he goes there and what he does when he gets there, and who dines with him in the public spaces of the White House and who in private.

This is not occurring because the public has some sort of insatiable interest in all the trivia connected with the White House and the Presidency. It is occurring because all of these hordes of people are hanging around the White House with cameras and tape recorders and microphones and nothing else to do in their careers except make news emerge from the White House. They are not leading a public hunger; this is a relatively recent phenomenon in American history, this daily inundation of news from 1600 Pennsylvania Avenue.... People heretofore got along very well without this, and this flood the media are creating is doing actual damage to the Presidency.

Given their pernicious influence on the institution of the Presidency, it is worthwhile to consider, briefly, the nature of the values brought by the media to that institution *versus* those the President must have and those that the public have enshrined in that office.

The media's values are not those attuned to the democratic values enshrined in the White House, but rather to far more mundane concerns such as headlines, career advancement, selling newspapers, filling up television and radio time, and entertainment. The President himself is in the White House because he wants to lead. The values he brings to the job are those inherent in any leadership assignment or challenge. So the media bring values to the White House that are not just different from those of the President, but that actually *impede* the successful execution of the President's own objectives and values....

Among the media there is also a natural tendency to seek the largest audience for a given story or a given feature, to make it as *embracing* as possible. This inclination runs against the basic diversity and pluralism of the electorate. We are a large and varied country with large, diverse, and varied interests, but one would never know this from looking at the coverage of the Presidency. Everything is simplified, boiled down to the least-common denominator, purged of the complex and obdurate realities involved in pluralism and the conflict of interests. Since it is so hard to cover the White House properly, we are usually treated to coverage that is childishly simple.

The danger in this coverage is that even the White House may start to lose its capacity to deal with ambiguity and complexity. It may tend to answer questions and choose political initiatives in a way that is easy for the press to understand (and explain and sell to the rest of us) but may not be designed to solve the problem in the most democratic and ethical way. Any President must be hard put to keep a valid perspective on his place in the tide of events and history and in his ability to influence world affairs when confronted by a horde of reporters that besiege him as though he could roll back the tides and turn lead to gold. One result is that the White House itself begins to get a perverted view of its importance and power in politics and world events. If every Presidential pimple is of universal significance, then indeed the President is not like unto the rest of us. He is not merely someone we have chosen to execute our will, but rather someone of different substance entirely and perhaps *entitled* to powers and influence the rest of us do not possess. This incredible focus by the media on the *personality* of the White House and its incumbent tends to pervert the democratic values inherent in the institution as *conceived by the Constitutional Framers.*

There is an analogous debilitating effect upon Presidential decision-making, since reporters like everything to be simple and clear cut, and a President—

if he wants to please them—must try to deliver everything in that style and cut. Matters that should require great deliberation and painstaking analysis—such as the approach to summit conferences between the American President and the leader of the USSR—become instead a propaganda chess game in which the Russians advance a propaganda initiative (a la "Star Peace") and the Americans counter that and then advance one of their own; then the Russians counter and everyone breathlessly awaits the next American move. There is little time in this process for deliberation and the sort of reclusive silence out of which great decisions are born.

Media pressure tends to drive the Presidency in directions the public would not favor. Americans do not elect their President to govern by sampling or on the basis of public-opinion polls. They select the candidate who seems to possess the wisdom and judgment that will enable him to choose wisely among the difficult alternatives that come across his desk. In the public sense, the President is elected to make those decisions *on his own* for a term of four years, but now the media are trying to turn the Presidency into a popular referendum that goes on seven days a week and where sudden disaster may befall any incumbent of the White House who ignores the raging currents of public opinion. The public may begin to believe this is proper, and this may change the Presidency from what the Constitutional Framers had in mind into a jovial Master of Ceremonies for popular opinion.

Another real danger created by the media pressures on the White House is that the President may tend to conduct his business not in the right way, but in the "public relations" way—in ways the media approve, in ways so that they write commendatory stories and ladle out large dollops of applause. Once that starts to happen, painful choices will *never* be made, arduous initiatives will *never* be undertaken, and arduous challenges will be ignored in favor of the simpler pleasures of public applause and commendation. The country, in my view, would be far better off if every President were to make his decisions with far less attention paid to the *impression* they will have not just upon the media and the organs of communication but even upon the public itself.

In a recent discussion on this very topic, *Newsweek* magazine asserted that the Presidency is "the office that belongs to all Americans." But this isn't so. Why the Presidency more than the Congress or the Supreme Court or the local council? These offices do *not* belong to all Americans, but rather to those we have chosen to fill them and to fulfill the promise inherent in them. We send a President to Washington, or a judge to the bench, or a Member to Congress *in order to act in our stead* in considering the problems of the day and to make the wisest choice among the alternatives that confront them in their work. They are not our surrogates but our *agents,* and even as agents, not actually to do *our* will but rather the best they can when confronted with situations unheard of at the time elections and appointments take place. There is much more freedom to be had in *that* conception than in the one we seem to be moving toward, in which everything is done under the pressure of public opinion and the pitiless glare of the media.

One solution might be to evict reporters from the White House. Let them cover that institution as they do so many other things—from their offices, on foot, and by telephone. Removing them from the White House would help make it more difficult for a President to use the media as an instrument of his policy and will. Tom Wicker of *The New York Times* has called the Presidential press conference "more an instrument of Presidential power than a useful tool of the press," and there is a large measure of truth in that observation. Both the press and the Presidency would be better off if reporters covered the White House as outsiders rather than members of the family. So would *we the people.*

I believe it would also be advisable to provide a better understanding of the Presidency in courses and in schools of journalism. Whatever the function of the Presidency, he is not elected to be "the great communicator" and should never be measured on his communication skills. That skill has to do with elections but it is not inherent in our concept of good government. Reporters seem to have but little appreciation of the *other* main branches of our government—the legislative, the judiciary, and (a factor virtually ignored by the press) the role of the *states* in our system of federalism. If journalists held a better knowledge of the Presidency, we would get a better perspective on the news, and surely a lessening of the floods of publicity now emanating from 1600 Pennsylvania Avenue.

I believe, too, that a national reexamination of how much privacy the President is entitled to is now in order. Do we want this horde of reporters following him everywhere he goes? Do we want telescopes on nearby mountain tops to pry into the privacy of his vacation? Do we want everyone who has anything to do with him to be under continual siege from the press about his business with, or his relationship to, the President? If Americans want wisdom from the White House—and there is no question but that we do—should not the President be permitted the solitude and time for reflection that are the absolute prerequisites for wise choices?

Americans need to re-discover something we all know about the Presidency—that it works very well indeed when no one is standing there watching everything it does. We need to act on our knowledge that in some political problems, the glare of the media operates to pervert and distort decisions, to foment courses of action chosen for their impact rather than their justice or wisdom.

If there were less media attention on the White House, perhaps Americans could discover that indeed many things can happen (including their own lives) *without* being shown on television or discussed in the newspapers. We could learn that problems confront the White House that simply cannot be displayed in a 30-second news script but that instead require deep and painful thought, and perhaps extremely painful action, for their resolution.

I would hope as well that less media attention focused on the White House would help Americans to rediscover another truth about our democracy: that it is not the President who is sovereign in this system of government, but rather the people, and that the future of the country and democracy does not depend on what the President does, or what the media tell him to do, but on what we the people do. This is a fact that *both* White House reporters and White House staffs tend to forget. We the people get no coverage on television and little attention from the media—but the obdurate reality is that we, and not the incumbent of

the House on Pennsylvania Avenue, are the United States of America.

READING 23

Making Laws and Making News
Timothy E. Cook

Timothy Cook is a political scientist who teaches at Williams College and is an astute analyst of political communication. This article, drawn from the book of the same title, examines the changes brought about in legislative policymaking processes, particularly those in the House of Representatives, by the introduction of television cameras, including those of C-SPAN, to congressional coverage. At bottom, according to Cook, what had been an institution that did its work in relative obscurity through behind-the-scenes negotiations became, over time, one that was more media conscious, utilizing television as part of the arsenal of resources through which legislative proposals were pursued.

Cook's article documents the many changes that television's presence has brought to Congress and its members, ranging from the ascendancy of media specialists on congressional staffs and the decline of the apprenticeship norm in the House, through fundamental changes in the nature of congressional campaigns. The primary thrust of the analysis, however, centers on the degree to which a more media-oriented Congress has brought about significant changes in the House's pursuit of its lawmaking function.

Cook eschews the alternative conventional wisdoms that suggest, on the one hand, that members' efforts to attract media publicity have diminished the House's legislative role, as well as the alternative perspective that such publicity seeking is irrelevant to legislation. He arrives at a different conclusion. That is, "newsmaking is neither incompatible with nor superfluous to the legislative process. Instead, perhaps making news has become a viable component of making laws."

Based on his research, which included a good deal of elite interviewing and personal observation, valuable tools for political scientists, Cook analyzes the multifaceted relationship between members of congress and reporters. He demonstrates clearly the degree to which each has become reliant on the other for successful performance of his or her job, a prototypical example of what political scientists call an "exchange relationship."

March 19, 1979, was like many other work days in the U.S. House of Representatives. Speaker Thomas P. (Tip) O'Neill, Jr., called the House to order at noon. After the chaplain's prayer and a smattering of one-minute speeches, a relatively minor bill, the Strategic and Critical Materials Stockpiling Act, was sent to the floor and introduced by Charles Bennett of Florida. The act passed with a minimum of debate and a voice vote. Several communications were reported to the Speaker, followed by debates on the international shipment of lottery materials and on establishing a new Select Committee on Committees. After three one-minute speeches and three short special orders, the House adjourned at 2:21 p.m. All in all, a quiet day.

In one important respect, however, the legislative day was unlike any previous one: for the first time, floor proceedings were televised and broadcast across the country through C-SPAN, the Cable Satellite Public Affairs Network, to 350 affiliated cable systems. A transformation begun in the early 1970s had finally been completed; in less than a decade the House had changed from an institution that virtually prevented television from covering any part of the legislative process to one that almost welcomed its presence.

The House of the late 1960s was what one scholar termed "a large impersonal . . . machine for processing bills." Its unspoken norms and folkways favored behind-the-scenes specialization and legislative labor, and the rules discouraging reporters' access to crucial behind-closed-doors decisions supported those norms. But by the end of the 1970s, at any of its legislative stages the House could bar scrutiny from reporters only with difficulty, and both print and electronic journalism were paying closer attention to it. The legislative process since then has occurred not so much in the light of sunshine laws but under the media's spotlight. Switching on the television cameras on March 19, however, may have been a landmark not in what it did but what it symbolized, the advent of a media-conscious institution.

That consciousness was very much a product of the mid-1970s, which remain a watershed in recent American history for all political institutions. After the Watergate scandal, the forced resignation of President Nixon in the summer of 1974, and the Democratic landslide in that fall's elections, reform-minded politicians came to Washington to clean it up. In the process they may have created arrangements that made the policy process, never known for its coherence or completeness, even more dispersed and fluid. As more groups took advantage of the new permeability of the political process and entered the fray, coalition building moved away from assured management toward artful construction, issue by issue. The process of governance became more cumbersome, volatile, and unpredictable. All these changes should have encouraged, or at least facilitated, a more media-conscious membership, and indeed, changes within the House itself increased the importance of the media.

- The personal staffs of members expanded tremendously, and most legislators now employ full-time press secretaries, a post that was a rarity in 1970.
- The so-called Subcommittee Bill of Rights in 1973 mandated that committees set up subcommittees according to established jurisdictions, and the House Democratic Caucus in 1975 prevented members from chairing more than one subcommittee, effectively providing more bases for hearings and other events designed to win publicity.
- Junior members were no longer expected to serve an apprenticeship in which they might be seen but not heard. By the end of the decade virtually any member was expected to have a chance to sit on a

desirable committee and to address his or her concerns.

- Sunshine reforms opened up committee and subcommittee hearings and deliberations to outside scrutiny. Closing committee meetings to keep out the press became the exception to the rule.
- The number of reporters credentialed to cover Congress grew dramatically, providing legislators more potential points of access to print and electronic media.
- Television began to dominate many congressional campaigns. By the end of the 1970s, over half of House campaign budgets went for media and advertising. A new generation was elected that was, of necessity, comfortable with the new technology.
- Members of the House and reporters for national news outlets had begun to discover each other, especially because the extraordinarily positive coverage of the House Judiciary Committee hearings in 1974 on the impeachment of President Nixon showed representatives what could be done with media attention and showed reporters that the House could be newsworthy.

As a result of all this, one would expect changes in the House and how it deals with publicity—as Michael Robinson phrased his "First Law of Videopolitics": "Television alters the behavior of institutions in direct proportion to the amount of coverage provided or allowed; the greater the coverage, the more conspicuous the changes." But has the ubiquity of the media really changed the most essential functions of the House? Has the new importance of making news transformed the process or the outcomes of making laws?

Many would reply that it has. Senators charged that the House's new visibility was enhancing the legislative power of the "other chamber" to their detriment. At least, that was the argument successfully advanced by senators who wished to follow the House's lead in televising floor proceedings. In 1985 Robert Byrd, then Senate minority leader, complained, "The Senate is fast becoming the invisible half of Congress. We cannot hold our own with the White House and the House of Representatives when it comes to news coverage of the important issues of the day." Others alleged that the chamber had become a group of unruly individuals more concerned with self-publicizing than with legislative labor.

This interpretation was not only widely held but plausible, and it continues to have proponents. Nevertheless, I consider it mistaken. But neither do I find the counterargument—that the media's impact on legislating in the House has been vastly exonerated because the news reflects rather than creates internal influence—fully satisfying. Newsmaking is neither incompatible with nor superfluous to the legislative process. Instead, perhaps making news has become a valuable component of making laws.

OBSERVATION: PUBLICITY DRIVES OUT LEGISLATING

The news media are accustomed to being blamed for (or credited with) many political developments. Television, especially, has been accused of contributing to the drop in the public's confidence in political institutions, the decline of political partisanship, the rise of image-oriented and candidate-centered campaigns, the drift toward a government more dominated by the president, and the general fragmentation of the American political system. Critics have also contended that the media aided the dispersion of power within the House and made congressional leadership and collective decisionmaking even more awkward and difficult than it already was. Making laws and making news, they have argued, are not compatible tasks.

Claims of such a dichotomy are nothing new. They hearken back to the oft-cited distinction between industrious work horses and self-promoting show horses, the two hypothesized types of members of Congress. There was renewed concern, however, that show horses were becoming dominant. In an influential 1984 article in *Atlantic Monthly,* Gregg Easterbrook declared, "The yearning for a Washington badge of recognition and the additional perquisites that would make Capitol Hill life what [the new legislators] imagined it to be can set in almost immediately.... Fame may be an elusive goal, but publicity is not." Publicity was said to undermine the coherence of the legislative process. Hedrick Smith argued, "Television helped break up the policy monopolies of established committees and throw open the power game. Overshadowing the grinding inside spadework of bill drafting in committee, television offered shortcuts and a showcase ... a marketplace for all 435 members of the House and one hundred senators to become policy entrepreneurs. That is one major reason why Congress seems so unruly today." Or in the words of a political scientist who wrote on the nationalization of American politics, "The corrosive influence of television does not end when the elections are over. The Senate is now notorious for being less a legislative body than a publicity mill for many members, and the same trends are spreading, inexorably, to the House."

The most sophisticated version of this observation has contended that the fragmentation of power within Congress is directly connected with the growth of the Washington media, the ascendancy of television as a major news source, and its gradual incursion into the workings of the institution. The media have supposedly helped create an "open Congress," in which members need not play by inside rules to advance the issues that concern them or to advance their careers. Mavericks are no longer tacitly disciplined and team players are no longer quietly rewarded; mavericks receive welcome attention, while the others are lost in the shadows. Members who seek publicity also have available to them increased staff and technological support, and legislative coalition building has taken a back seat to public relations. The media have, it is said, contributed another centrifugal force, dispersing power and hindering leadership and collective decisionmaking.

There is certainly evidence favoring this point of view. Many members have achieved publicity without leadership or committee positions. Members have devoted more resources to publicizing themselves and have become more sophisticated in pursuit of the now-willing Washington reporters. Yet, while credible, this conventional wisdom from the early 1980s has not gone unchallenged.

RESPONSE: PUBLICITY IS IRRELEVANT TO LEGISLATING

In *The Ultimate Insiders* Stephen Hess began by attacking the Achilles' heel of the argument, showing that most members of Congress are invisible to the national press. Those covered most heavily are "the *Ultimate Insiders,* the ones who call the committee meetings or direct the floor action, or would do so if their party were in the majority." Zealously seeking publicity pays little dividend if the publicity-seeker is not in a category that reporters find newsworthy— presidential candidate, party leader, committee chair, sponsor of a key proposal, and so forth. The show horse–work horse dichotomy makes no sense as long as those receiving most of the attention are also those contributing most to legislative labors. The power of the media has been exaggerated, Hess concluded; instead of determining power on Capitol Hill, the press reflects it. Making news is then superfluous, even irrelevant, to making laws.

This perspective has also had proponents beyond the ranks of political scientists. A 1987 article on power in Congress argued, "Reporters will want to talk to [a committee chair or party leader] regardless of how articulate he is or how well he looks before a camera. What he has to say is important because of who he is, not how he says it." An op-ed piece in the *New York Times* during the 1988 campaign also considered that reporters reflect power, but interpreted the situation as being less benign: "[Journalists] have frequently ended up pulling their punches for fear of appearing biased.... Too often, the press has functioned as merely a stenographer to power."

But the response was not without its own problems. Though a handful of senators are accorded the lion's share of national media attention, such dominance cannot suggest that other members have not altered their behavior. Hess granted this point, though he argued that it would be irrational for senators to pursue national publicity, given the media's lack of interest. Yet legislators could be more inclined to seek publicity diligently without succeeding every time. In fact, if backbench legislators are actively pursuing publicity, leaders might be maintaining their place in the spotlight only by aggressively wooing reporters, in which case the primacy of leaders in the news is even more to be expected.

More important, Hess argued that the Capitol Hill press corps is "almost totally reactive." Yet in a collegial institution in which the chain of command is attenuated, knowing who or what to react to is far from obvious. Because current journalistic practice requires stories featuring individual authorities, covering Congress has been called "the search for the ultimate spokesman." Elsewhere in Washington, such a search is more straight-forward. Throughout the executive branch, press officers are designated to speak for the agency, the department, or the president. Reporters' tasks are simplified: they need only turn to the appropriate spokesperson when a given topic becomes newsworthy. With Congress, the solution is less simple. After all, neither chamber has anyone who can speak on behalf of all or even most of its members.

The national media do disproportionately favor leaders, committee chairs, and senior members as being in a position to know. But holding such a position is no guarantee of news coverage. After all, even if much of legislators' visibility can be explained by institutional power, there remains at least as much that is unexplained. Either additional reasons have yet to be discovered, or much of the coverage of members of Congress remains unpatterned and unpredictable. Reporters, even when conscientiously attempting to depict congressional power accurately, inevitably exercise choice in deciding whom to cover in Congress. Merely reflecting congressional power without contributing to it may be the goal of reporters, but it is a well-nigh impossible task.

A THIRD POSSIBILITY: MAKING NEWS LEADS TO MAKING LAWS

To comprehend the relationship of making news to making laws, one must understand that reporters and politicians are constantly negotiating and renegotiating the process by which news is made. Instead of a Congress that plays by reporters' rules or reporters that defer to Congress's decisions about what is important, the interactions between legislators and reporters are shifting and flexible. Making news can become a constructive component of the legislative process. By anticipating what a reporter will find newsworthy, House members can use the media to address an issue, move a proposal along, and enhance their career ambitions. Indeed, given the contemporary confusion in American politics, a media strategy may be a necessary part

of many legislative strategies. Such a process is most accessible to those who wield the most power; but backbenchers, too, can become an authoritative source on a particular issue and thereby court publicity and accomplish legislative goals.

To understand how this process works, one must recognize that newsworthiness is inherently an elusive quality. If reporters are asked for the difference between news and non-news, they are likely to provide anecdotes or examples, not a hard-and-fast dividing line. Yet the demand for fresh news is incessant. To standardize an inherently unpredictable process, reporters routinely turn to people in positions of authority within an institution, thus not only ensuring a steady flow of copy but also helping guard against charges of bias or incompleteness by covering politicians whom peers, superiors, and audiences generally agree upon as newsworthy.

Such connections work to officials' advantage. Their involvement makes something newsworthy enough to get in the paper or on the air and creates events that can serve as occasions to write stories. Because reporters must worry about alienating their main sources, they come to report the world in ways fundamentally similar to the perspectives of those they are covering: they become "unwilling adjuncts to City Hall."

Yet the reporters do not merely reflect a reality constructed by others. News inevitably constructs and reconstructs a public reality from privately experienced events. And Journalists' selections and emphases do diverge from those that their authoritative sources would make. American journalism is based on the tenet that news must be both important and interesting. Reporters' judgments on what is important and interesting must anticipate not merely the political sources but the judgment of the news organization for which they work. Collusion is unlikely because reporters and politicians do not share identical definitions of what news is and how it should be covered. The media thus act as powerful gatekeepers to the political arena.

Instead of determining or reflecting power on Capitol Hill, reporters and sources *negotiate* power, constantly bargaining with each other over the rules of their interactions and the shape of the final product.

Each tries to manage the other—the sources to place the most favorable light on their activity and the journalists to extract the information they seek with minimal difficulty. Sometimes the relationship may be adversarial. More typically, however, politicians need publicity and journalists need copy, and the two sides can and do perform valuable services for each other.

Despite some disagreements with journalists, House members may, through effective media strategies, be able to manage the news from Capitol Hill. Journalists may go along to ensure the routine production of news. Frequent interaction leads to an unspoken set of ground rules. The forces encouraging collaboration instead of conflict tend to be greatest in dealing with those legislators who are important and hence regular, prized newsmakers. The adversarial model does not work most strongly at the highest levels of the political hierarchy, then; it may actually be most applicable toward those who *least* frequently make the news.

At the same time, there is enough flexibility in covering a collegial body that observations cannot stop there. As more members are perceived to be important newsmakers, they may be able to use media strategies to raise issues to prominence and advance their careers. Moreover, the ones reporters consider more interesting may be able to win coverage if leaders cannot provide news that conforms to the media's demands.

So concerns that backbenchers can grab headlines are not unfounded.... [T]he media in general and the national media in particular have become more important for members of the House as the dispersion of power has made legislating more difficult. Legislators can use the media in various ways in addition to pursuing the publicity necessary for getting reelected. But this is not to say that the House is overrun by a new breed of legislators interested in publicity for its own sake. Making laws and making news are not contradictory. Nor are they synonymous. Instead, they are different but complementary parts of the same process.

The outside strategy allowed by media publicity offers the potential to manage an increasingly unmanageable work load in a balkanized and [bulky] political system. In the lingo of Washington the retail method of persuasion has been supplemented if not supplanted by the wholesale style. After all, the number of interest groups has dramatically increased, the legislative agenda is crowded, and the dispersion of power to more individuals makes one-on-one lobbying increasingly difficult. As presidents and interest groups find persuasion through media more useful to get things done in Washington, the same should be expected on Capitol Hill. After all, the media provide an important means to help set the Washington agenda, winnow down the alternative courses of action, keep pressure on politicians, and thus get something done in Congress.

MEDIA POWER AND CONGRESSIONAL POWER

The House of Representatives has long witnessed the chaotic comings and goings of its 435 members—from offices to committee rooms to the floor and back again while lobbyists and constituents try to get in a word or two on the run. But increasingly relations with the news media seem to take up legislators' time and effort. Dressed in telegenic blue shirts and red neckties, they stand before television cameras in the swamp, the section of the Capitol lawn set aside for interviews. Inside the Capitol, too, floor debates are often aimed at the discreetly placed cameras that broadcast the proceedings to members' offices, the press galleries, and homes across the country. Staffers and interns dash from one gallery to the next with stacks of press releases to be distributed. Reporters crowd outside hearing rooms to receive a committee report or corner a witness. In short, much of the hubbub of Capitol Hill today is contributed by the press and their would-be subjects. Making laws is far from the only business of the House. It has been supplemented by making news.

Making news was not always so important. Reporters have been present on Capitol Hill for nearly two centuries, but rarely before has seeking publicity been such a significant part of every House member's job. For most of the twentieth century the way to get things done and to advance a career in Washington was to play an inside game, building relationships with colleagues, deferring to senior members, and bargaining, while slowly building up the legislative longevity necessary to achieve a position of power.

Legislators paid little attention to reporters except those from the press back home, and they severely restricted the access of radio and television to the House. The House was governed by party leaders and committee chairs who preferred to stay out of the spotlight whenever possible.

Now all that has changed. The media are useful to members for publicity to help them get reelected, of course, but increasingly also in policymaking, wielding influence in Congress and in Washington, and pursuing their personal ambitions. Making news has frequently become integral to the legislative process. Reporters for all kinds of news outlets can now be present at any stage of the legislative process and can be instrumental in shaping the results. Sophisticated House press operations try to create national constituencies for issues on which members can serve as authoritative sources and build reputations. At the very least, legislators who wish to be considered influential experts have to ensure that their media image fits their chosen self-portrait, so few of them, inside or outside leadership circles, can pass up opportunities to be newsworthy. Making news, in short, has become a crucial component of making laws.

... The conditions that made it not only possible but necessary to use the media to get legislative business accomplished ... show few signs of abating. The expansion of congressional staffs in the 1970s will not be reversed: and each new Congress will see members naming more full-time press secretaries. Likewise, the number of Washington reporters should continue to grow steadily. News organizations may be tightening their belts, but the rise of newspaper chains, the abundance of stringers, and the creation of groups such as Conus that contract out television news services mean that virtually any news outlet can have a relatively inexpensive link to Washington. Such easy hookups allow members to add their comments to stories that are bouncing among various newsbeats in the capital. Above all, the news media help House members set the legislative agenda, define the alternatives, influence public moods, and affect outcomes at a time when the political process is confused and unpredictable.

Yet if legislators need reporters, reporters also need legislators to create the events or provide the observations that can become the basis of a story. Even though the needs of the two are rarely identical, they can work in a symbiosis. House members, even at high levels of power, cannot automatically make news. Instead, they must ensure that their information and stories meet journalistic standards of timeliness, pertinence, and interest. Reporters' dependence on authoritative sources to suggest news means that journalism tends to reflect the perspectives of the more powerful. But such power is not absolute, because while politicians control definitions of importance, journalists still decide what is interesting. So House members and reporters negotiate and renegotiate newsworthiness. The question should not then be what the news media have done *to* the House, or what the House has done *to* the news media, but what these two institutions have done *with* one another. What is the effect of this negotiation on policymaking and on representative democracy? The answers must be speculative, but they are well worth contemplating.

POLICYMAKING PROCESS AND THE MEDIA

The power of the press often buttresses established power and procedures in the House. Hill traditions of pursuing expertise and influence dovetail with reporters' search for sources who are in a position to know. Reporters accord a reassuring coherence to the legislative process by focusing on "particularly and peculiarly congressional actions," stressing the gradual, orderly nature of the way bills are passed rather than the chaos or stasis that characterizes much of congressional life.

But the priorities of journalists and politicians are not always so synchronized. Reporters have less leeway in whom to report about or when to report it than in the issues that will receive coverage. Some of the coverage of Congress is a by-product of the coverage of issues. Issues most likely to make news are easily described, have clearly characterized sides, affect a large part of the audience, and come with straightforward reform remedies. Journalists tend to pass up matters that are complex, unfamiliar, specialized, or not apparently easily addressed.

If members want news coverage, they must choose clear-cut issues or try to present the complex as simple. But such choices invite distortion or omission of complicating factors. The alternative ways to achieve tax reform in the Ninety-ninth Congress, for instance, were displaced by an either-or question: "Are you for tax reform or against it?" Likewise, the inadequacies of the patchwork system of unemployment compensation went unreported when journalists converged on the single problem of hundreds of thousands of unemployed in danger of being precipitously dropped from the rolls when the Federal Supplemental Compensation program expired.

Setting the agenda is only the first step in the journey of legislation; press attention affects later stages, too. Bargaining among members, once the hallmark of a legislative institution, becomes more difficult when reporters are watching—not so much because members act differently in public than in private but because reporters' dislike for noncommittal stances tends to discourage the fluidity and maneuverability necessary to resolve differences on the fine points and to enact legislation.

Legislators who wish to get something done must be both outside and inside players. Press coverage can enhance their reputations and direct colleagues' attention toward them as people to listen to. Inside strategies can lead to the influential post that can be used to gain the media's attention. Using them [inside and outside strategies] together can be synergistic, accomplishing more than using either one on its own. But…changing from one approach to another is not always easy to handle.

To the extent that the press spotlights problems and helps set the legislative agenda, an additional complication arises: the clock of Congress will resemble that of the news. The media have a limited attention span. They discover problems suddenly, but their interest rapidly wanes, whether or not the problems have been solved. As entrepreneurial politicians take advantage of the brief window of opportunity to get something done, agenda items can rise and fall in importance with dizzying rapidity. In such a fast-forwarded context legislators feel pressured to respond and may grab the first alternative presented to them, often in spite of the details, while hoping that the other chamber will take care of the problem. Cooling-off periods in committee or in conference may be necessary, as with the anti-drug abuse bill in

the One-hundredth Congress, when the legislative process overheats.

Yet for all these drawbacks, the conjunction of media strategies and legislative strategies can aid policymaking, particularly in surmounting entrenched interests and facilitating large-scale legislative initiatives. The news suggests problems or alternatives that Congress has bypassed. It helps inform and mobilize public opinion. At the very least it forces legislators to look beyond the interests of organized groups with the most immediate stakes and perhaps toward the larger public interest. When members would prefer to do nothing, publicity can increase the risks of inaction. In short, members in the spotlight are pressured to deal with problems in a way that corresponds to their readings of public opinion.

| READING 24 |

Telling the Court's Story: Justice and Journalism at the Supreme Court

Linda Greenhouse

The Supreme Court is the most invisible branch of American government and the branch about which the public is most ill-informed. In such a setting, especially when an institution (such as the Court) has no direct links with the public, the informational role of the media looms particularly large. In this selection veteran New York Times *Supreme Court reporter Linda Greenhouse examines the journalist/ Court interface, illuminating many problems for the public that, at least in part, the limitations of Supreme Court coverage bring about.*

Greenhouse's thesis is straightforward. She asserts that, "there exist conventions and habits both within the press and within the Supreme Court itself

From "Telling the Court's Story: Justice and Journalism at the Supreme Court" by L. Greenhouse. Reprinted by permission of The Yale Law Journal Company and Fred B. Rothman & Company from *The Yale Law Journal*, Vol. 105, pp. 1537–1561.

that create obstacles to producing the best possible journalism about the Court." While documenting these "conventions and habits," Greenhouse recognizes that many will never change and that some, indeed, shouldn't. Nevertheless, she does feel that the Court itself has a critical need for better press coverage, a reality that the institution and its members do not appear to recognize.

Greenhouse's fascinating portrayal of the job of the Supreme Court reporter demonstrates the many ways in which covering the beat differs from other political journalism venues. Her analysis and criticism of Supreme Court reporting pulls few punches, placing responsibility for inadequate coverage jointly at the doorstep of the Court itself and the journalistic profession. The solutions to the problems she details can only come from a joint commitment to meaningful change. Indeed, Greenhouse concludes, "I am naive enough, and out of step enough with the prevailing journalistic culture, to think of these two institutions as, to some degree, partners in a mutual democratic enterprise to which both must acknowledge responsibility. The responsibility of the press is to commit resources necessary to give the public the most accurate and contextual reporting possible about the Court.... The Court's responsibility is to remove unnecessary obstacles to accomplishing that task."

The relationship between the fairness and accuracy of political journalism and the health of electoral politics in the United States has been the subject of frequent study and comment. Both scholars and journalists have expressed alarm at the corrosive effect that cynical, adversarial, or sensationalistic reporting has had on the process of running for office and governing the country.

But the relationship between the quality of legal journalism and the vitality of our judicial institutions has received much less attention, with perhaps the sole exception of the continuing debate over permitting live television coverage of proceedings such as the O. J. Simpson murder trial.

This Essay starts from the premise that press coverage of the courts is a subject at least as worthy of public concern and scholarly attention as press coverage of politics, perhaps even more so. Political candidates who believe that their messages are not being conveyed accurately or fairly by the press have a range of options available for disseminating those messages. They can buy more advertising, speak directly to the public from a talk-show studio or a press-conference podium, or line up endorsements from credible public figures. But judges, for the most part, speak only through their opinions, which are difficult for the ordinary citizen to obtain or to understand. Especially in an era when the political system has ceded to the courts many of society's most difficult questions, it is sobering to acknowledge the extent to which the courts and the country depend on the press for the public understanding that is necessary for the health and, ultimately, the legitimacy of any institution in a democratic society.

My focus in this Essay is journalism about the Supreme Court of the United States, which I have covered since 1978 as a correspondent in the Washington Bureau of the *New York Times.* Fortunately, the environment at the Court, both for its life-tenured occupants and for the several dozen reporters who chronicle its work, remains considerably more civil than that of the campaign trail. But neither the Court nor its press corps exists in a bubble, immune to the broader political culture that in recent years has included Supreme Court confirmation battles of intense and lasting bitterness as well as a general skepticism about the perquisites of high office and, indeed, about the exercise of government power generally.

Furthermore, every generalization that can be made about the barriers to public understanding of the judicial system is particularly true of the Court: To the public at large, the Supreme Court is a remote and mysterious oracle that makes occasional pronouncements on major issues of the day and then disappears from view for months at a time. The nine individuals who exercise power in its name are unaccountable and essentially faceless.... It may be helpful to note...that while fifty-nine percent of the public in a sample of 1200 randomly selected adults, could name the Three Stooges, fifty-five percent could not name a single Supreme Court Justice. Given such widespread ignorance, and in light of the Court's role as an important participant in the ongoing dialogue among American citizens and the various branches and levels of government, journalistic miscues about what the Court is saying and where it is going can have a distorting effect on the entire enterprise....

My thesis is that there exist conventions and habits both within the press *and* within the Supreme Court itself that create obstacles to producing the best possible journalism about the Court, journalism that would provide the timely, sophisticated, and contextual information necessary for public understanding of the Court. Some of the habits and traditions I identify as obstacles are unlikely ever to change, and I do not necessarily think that they should; I do not expect to see Justices holding news conferences to explain and elaborate on their written opinions, however appealing or even titillating that prospect might be to journalists. Nor do I expect newspapers to call up reserve troops and open up page after page of shrinking news holes to accommodate the flood of late-June opinions. I also recognize that the interests of these two vital and powerful institutions, the Court and the press, can never be entirely congruent; the press is always going to want more information than the Court is ever going to want to share. But I hope that the process of identifying where the obstacles lie may nonetheless foster some fruitful discussion—within the press, within the Court, and, radical as the thought may be, even between the two—of those problems that can be solved and of those mutual concerns that can be addressed without threatening the identity or integrity of either institution.

GETTING THE STORY

Covering the Supreme Court is such an unusual form of journalism that it may help to describe the process itself. Sources, leaks, casual contact with newsmakers—none of these hallmarks of Washington journalism exists on the Court beat, leaving even experienced reporters baffled and disoriented, as I was when I began my job there.

Before I began covering the Court, I was a member and eventually chief of the *New York Times* bureau in Albany that was responsible for covering the New York State government. The mid-1970s in Albany

was a chaotic and cacophonous period of fiscal crisis and public policy innovation. The press room in the state capitol was located on the third floor, fittingly between the Assembly and Senate chambers. The two houses of the State legislature were controlled by different parties, and, in the process of shuttling back and forth in search of the latest developments, reporters inevitably became messengers between the leadership of the two houses and between the legislature and the office of the Governor on the floor below. The press, in other words, was very much part of the process in Albany, as witnessed by the location of the press seats in the well of the two legislative chambers, in direct view of the members. Once, as I tried to keep myself awake during a midnight session of the State Assembly by eating a candy bar, an assemblyman walked across the chamber to my seat, told me to stop eating junk food, and handed me an apple.

Occasionally, my job required me to cover decisions of the New York Court of Appeals, the state's highest court, which is down the hill from the capitol. The judges of that court, who in those days ran for election, made a point of getting to know the reporters, and some would stop by the press room when business brought them to the capitol.

When I arrived in Washington, D.C., to take up my new assignment at the Supreme Court, I was met by silence. The contrast with my past life could scarcely have been greater. The press room at the Court is far from the action, in a ground-floor location that is actually a kind of half-basement, with small windows high up on a few walls. The Court's newsmakers, the Justices, are rarely seen on that floor, except for the few who eat an occasional meal in the public cafeteria down the hall. The Justices are visible, of course, on the bench whenever the Court is in session, but opportunities for casual or unscheduled contact are almost nonexistent. The journalist's job is almost entirely paper-dependent, defined by the endless flow of conference lists, order lists, petitions for certiorari, and opinions. While most politicians will cheerfully or angrily critique any story in which their name has appeared, Justices rarely respond to public comment, or even to rank error.

The press corps at the Court is a small one, with about three dozen accredited correspondents representing organizations ranging from the *Wall Street Journal* to the Cable News Network to *USA Today.* Many additional reporters show up and receive one-day press passes to the courtroom on the days of major arguments and toward the end of the Term, when important decisions are expected. But on a typical day during the Term, when the Court is not on the bench and when the business at hand consists of reading certiorari petitions and briefs on the merits in granted cases, the numbers are much smaller. It would be unusual to find more than a half-dozen reporters at work at their desks on such a day, fewer now than when I began reporting on the Court.

The reason is that the commitment of the media to full-time coverage of the Court is shrinking, and most of the reporters assigned to the Court are also responsible for covering the Department of Justice, other courts, perhaps the Judiciary Committees in Congress, or, often, legal developments in the country at large. The television networks have cut back sharply on the attention they pay to the Court, a very unfortunate development considering the number of people who rely on television as their primary news source. One of the country's biggest newspaper chains, the Scripps-Howard chain, last year reassigned its experienced and respected Supreme Court reporter to another beat and left the job unfilled.

Developments like these represent a major failure of journalistic responsibility and pose a significant obstacle to achieving excellence in writing about the Court. Major decisions will be covered, one way or another. What is lost to the reader or viewer is the texture and flavor of the Court's day-to-day work, particularly its performance in its case-selection function—the circuit conflicts left unresolved, the open questions left unanswered for another Term. Reporters who do not have the luxury of making the Court beat their full-time job cannot possibly pay attention to the thousands of certiorari petitions that are denied or to the decisions in cases that may not qualify for page-one status.

TELLING THE STORY: WHAT HAPPENED?

So what's the story at the Supreme Court? That's what my editors and colleagues want to know when I get back to the office after a busy morning at the Court. My job is to answer that question. What did the Court do?

"The Supreme Court ruled today..."

The question is relatively straightforward, but the answer is not. It sometimes appears to be almost completely discretionary, even random. At the very least, the answer is deeply invested with editorial judgment—value judgment, to use a more loaded term; news judgment, to use a less loaded one. Which, if any, of fifty or more denials of certiorari are worth reporting in a limited space—perhaps 1200 words for a round-up Court story in the *New York Times,* significantly less for most of my colleagues on the Court beat. Which of several decisions should be the focus of the story? Is a second, or even a third story warranted? What about the oral arguments that morning? More than in many other beats, the reporters tend to make these calls because editors have no independent means for evaluating the importance of the dozens of discrete events that may constitute the Supreme Court's activities on a given day. While this circumstance offers an unusual amount of freedom to the reporter, it also means there is unlikely to be much informed discussion with colleagues and editors back at the office.

The most consequential judgment call of all is probably that of evaluating the meaning and importance of a Supreme Court decision on the merits. A few examples from the 1994 Term may suffice to illustrate what may be involved in completing the sentence: "The Supreme Court ruled today that. . . ." I offer these examples to illustrate the process, not because I am sure that I was right; the articles that resulted simply represented my best judgment by deadline time.

First, was affirmative action dead in the wake of *Adarand Constructors v. Pena?* It was obvious both to me and to my editors that this was the question I needed to answer. On the face of the decision, it appeared so, because the Court for the first time held that federal affirmative action programs must be narrowly tailored to achieve a compelling state interest— in the equal protection context, the constitutional standard of strict scrutiny, which sets a hurdle nearly impossible to overcome. But what did it mean when the author of the *Adarand* opinion, Justice Sandra Day O'Connor, wrote for the five-to-four majority that "we wish to dispel the notion that strict scrutiny is 'strict in theory, but fatal in fact'"? What kind of strict scrutiny was this?

So my lead the next day did not decleare federal affirmative action to be dead: If the Court blinked at the last minute, so did I. The first paragraph of my story, which led the paper under a three-column headline, read as follows: "In a decision likely to fuel rather than resolve the debate over affirmative action, the Supreme Court today cast doubt on the constitutionality of Federal programs that award benefits on the basis of race."

That was an easy call compared to the decision two weeks later in *Miller v. Johnson,* striking down a majority-black Georgia congressional district as a racial gerrymander. What was the story there? Were dozens of majority-black legislative districts around the country now presumptively unconstitutional? Had the Court dropped the other shoe it had been holding over the new majority-black districts since its decision in *Shaw v. Reno* two years earlier? It looked that way to me, and I was in the middle of crafting just such a lead in mid-afternoon on the final day of the Court's Term when I got a call informing me that the Court had just announced that it would hear two new redistricting cases in the coming Term. This announcement, which was completely unexpected—ordinarily, the Court would have remanded those cases back to the lower courts for disposition in light of the newly announced standard in the Georgia case—suddenly made sense of the unusual and cryptic comment that Justice Ruth Bader Ginsburg, one of the dissenters in the Georgia case, had made from the bench that morning to the effect that the Court had not yet spoken its "final word" on the role of race in redistricting. Suddenly, things did not appear to be quite so conclusively decided. I pushed the delete button on my computer and erased the sweeping implications I was in the process of drawing, substituting instead a more conditional verb tense and tone. My lead paragraph read: "In a bitterly contested decision that *could* erase *some* of the recent electoral

gains made by blacks in Congress and state legislatures, the Supreme Court ruled today that the use of race as a 'predominant factor' in drawing district lines should be presumed to be unconstitutional."

So what's the story? These examples demonstrate a singular feature of journalism about the Court: the impossibility of using one obvious journalistic technique for fathoming the Court's actions, that of interviewing the newsmakers to ask them what they meant. I would have given a great deal last April to have been able to call Justice John Paul Stevens when, in *McIntyre v. Ohio Elections Commission,* he wrote a majority opinion holding that there is a First Amendment right to distribute anonymous campaign literature. This holding would appear to call into question various core provisions of federal election law, which require certain kinds of disclosure of the identities of those who give money to and speak on behalf of candidates. The Stevens opinion contained some rather sweeping language with potentially broad application, as Justice Antonin Scalia pointed out in his dissent, as well as some other language that appeared to qualify the holding. How far did the author of this majority opinion mean to take the Court, and how far would other Justices follow him? It would have been unthinkable simply to call him up and ask him. So all I could say in my story was that "the ruling appears likely to prompt a new round of challenges to the disclosure requirements contained in Federal and numerous state election laws."

As Justice Ginsburg pointed out in a recent talk at Georgetown Law School on how the Court communicates, not only does the Court speak to the public solely through its opinions, but the case law process itself precludes the Court from including, even if Justices were so inclined, a "'practical effects' section in which [the Justices] spell out the real world impact of the opinion" because a Supreme Court decision is usually only one segment of a continuing public dialogue with or among "other branches of government, the States, or the private sector."

We are all so accustomed to these journalistic facts of life that we rarely think about them. Yet they underscore the importance of the role of the press in conveying the meaning of the Court's work. Other courts, of course, are similarly reticent about speaking directly to the public, but judges of lower federal courts and state courts are at times willing to help reporters understand opinions. Informal arrangements under which these judges make themselves available, on background, for this purpose are not uncommon. I recall one decision by the New York Court of Appeals that I covered during my tenure in Albany. The court rejected a constitutional challenge to a piece of the solution to New York City's fiscal crisis, and the judges were highly aware of the importance to the financial markets of accurate reporting about the ruling. The court invited reporters to participate in a "lock-up," an arrangement under which those willing to take part could come to the court early in the morning, perhaps an hour before the decision was to be publicly announced, to read the opinion at leisure. Once in the room, no one was permitted to leave until the time of announcement. One of the judges then made himself available by telephone for the rest of the day as a resource, not to be quoted, that reporters could contact to verify their understanding of the decision and its implications. I availed myself of this offer. To my knowledge, none of the reporters who took part in this episode broke the rules or betrayed the court's confidence. If it did nothing else, the exercise underscored, for each reporter who took part, the need for care and accuracy, forcefully reminding us that we were doing the *public's* business. Although I was intimately familiar with the fiscal crisis as a legislative issue, I had had no legal training at that point, and little experience with judicial opinions. The experience was sobering.

It is obvious from the earlier examples that a useful story about a Supreme Court decision, in my view, is necessarily interpretive. It entails more than an accurate statement of the holding, even when the holding is indisputably clear. Readers also need to know the context of the decision, what the decision means, how the case got to the Court in the first place, what arguments were put to the Justices, what the decision tells us about the Court, and what happens next. Not all of these elements are necessary in each story, and not all of the questions can be answered in every case. There are ways—conditional verb tenses or outright confessions of ignorance—of telling the reader "I don't know" or "I don't know yet," and thus of preventing the story from pretend-

ing to be more definitive than it could possibly be under the circumstances.

What Did Not Happen

In telling the story, I think it is also important to respect the reader's intelligence, on the one hand, and to acknowledge, on the other, the limits of the reader's knowledge of Supreme Court procedure. The story sometimes lies in what the Court, or a particular Justice, did not do, and that has its own journalistic perils. Exaggerating the meaning of a denial of certiorari is a common journalistic error. While denials of certiorari can certainly be important and newsworthy in their own right, the reader should be reminded in each such story that the denial does not represent a judgment by the Court on the merits of the case. The Court's recent denial of certiorari in a case challenging the constitutionality of the new federal law to protect abortion clinics against violent protest was widely reported as an "upholding" of that law or, somewhat more subtly but no less incorrectly, as a survival of the law in a major Supreme Court test. Much of the public is now substantially misinformed about the legal status of the law, which continues to be challenged on a variety of constitutional grounds and which may yet be reviewed on the merits by the Supreme Court, where the outcome is by no means preordained.

Every time I think I have seen it all when it comes to denials of certiorari, I find a new example. Early in the current Term, the Court denied a petition for certiorari challenging a ruling by the Supreme Court of Wisconsin. The state court had remanded a custody dispute between two lesbians who had shared the raising of a child before an acrimonious breakup, interpreting the state law on visitation not to preclude the woman who was not the child's biological mother from establishing a legal right to visit the child. The biological mother's appeal from a nonfinal judgment on a question of state law hardly presented the Court with a certiorari-worthy case, and, predictably, certiorari was denied without comment. But if the Court did not comment, *USA Today* certainly did. Its story the next day began as follows: "The U.S. Supreme Court on Monday helped reshape the definition of the American family in a case on gay parents' rights."

Any time I err on the side of self-righteousness on this subject, I am likely to be betrayed by my own copy desk. It happened most recently as this Essay was being edited, in connection with an appeal by Christian Scientists from a state court judgment of liability for the death of a child who was treated by prayer instead of medicine. A story of mine about the denial of certiorari in the appeal appeared on page one of the *New York Times* under this headline: "Christian Scientists Rebuffed in Ruling By Supreme Court." Since the lead paragraph said that the petitioners "failed today to persuade the Supreme Court to hear their appeal," I knew that I was not responsible for the headline's error, but I was abashed nonetheless. In a brief article revisiting the case the next week, I tried again to make myself clear: "The nonruling set no legal precedent, but perhaps it set an example." I also discussed the issue with two editors, who were appropriately dismayed, but I know that, under deadline pressure and the need to make headlines fit in tight spaces, a similar mistake will happen again someday.

Justice John Paul Stevens has adopted the commendable practice—I can only assume in reaction to incidents such as this—of occasionally writing opinions "respecting the denial of certiorari" that serve as explicit reminders that "an order denying a petition for certiorari expresses no opinion on the merits of the case." Most recently, he wrote such a memorandum when the Court denied certiorari in a highly visible California death penalty case. He explained that, while the case raised "a novel and important constitutional question," it arguably did not present a final judgment for the Court to review.

If it is important not to exaggerate the meaning of a Court action, it is also important to resist oversimplifying. When a decision turns on a concept like state action or standing or some other threshold jurisdictional issue, this can be explained to the reader quite explicitly, so that the disposition makes sense, and not simply swept under the label of "for technical reasons."

Court coverage should also not overlook the minutiae that offer some insight into the life of the institution. If I can figure out, from whatever clues might be available, that a Justice has changed his or her vote during the course of deliberations on a case, I will in-

clude that information in the story of the decision. It is interesting gossip, of course, but, more than that, it sheds some useful light on a process in which Justices really do struggle with the cases in the course of reaching a decision. Last June, for example, it appeared obvious to me that Justice Stephen Breyer had changed his vote during the Court's five-month course of deliberations over the First Amendment issue presented in the Florida Bar lawyer-solicitation case, *Florida Bar v. Went For It, Inc.* This five-to-four decision was the last to be handed down of the eleven cases the Court had heard during its January sitting. It was Justice O'Connor's third opinion from the January sitting, leaving Justice Anthony M. Kennedy with none—a strong indication that he had lost the opinion. Justice Kennedy's dissent took a wry dig at Justice Breyer, a member of the majority, by means of an otherwise gratuitous discussion of the Federal Sentencing Guidelines, of which Justice Breyer is an author. Based on the public views of the other members of the majority on lawyer advertising, Justice Breyer was the only one likely to have switched sides. In my story, I explained this chain of reasoning as the basis for concluding that there was "strong evidence" that the Court had initially voted to strike down the thirty-day moratorium on solicitation that was at issue in the case, but that an original member of the majority, probably Justice Breyer, had changed sides.

Some might object that this kind of speculative reporting conveys little information of value and results in diminishing respect for the Court. I actually think the reverse is true. The decisional process is such a black box that the public rarely has a chance to see the Justices working through the difficult problems posed by close cases. Yet it hardly diminishes the Court to suppose that this process is often neither tidy nor the result of a set of unexamined premises and foregone conclusions. The occasional vote switch is a window, albeit a very partial and hardly satisfying one, on how the Court works.

Choices and Values

Some of the guidelines I have given here beg the deeper question of how a reporter decides what is important. I have argued for an approach to writing about the Court that is inherently analytical, or at least not limited to reducing the holding to jargon-free English prose. Is this not an inherently value-laden process?

What journalism is not value-laden, after all? As Jon Katz, media critic for *Wired* magazine, recently wrote: "[A]nyone who writes (or reads) knows that all stories aren't covered, all questions aren't asked, all answers aren't included. Journalists present facts not laterally but in sequence of importance. This is in itself a subjective process." That is a useful perspective for any discussion of journalistic "objectivity"— a goal that should command respect without inviting paralysis.

Those who cover the Court, to be sure, have views and find themselves more sympathetic to some results and to some Justices than to others. The question is, how germane are those views to the work we do? I have found that years of reading conflicting lower court opinions and hearing arguments on both sides of every question have made me much less certain of the right answers than I was in the simple days when I covered real politics. I am not trying to say, as Justice Clarence Thomas did during his confirmation hearing, that I have shed all ideological baggage and "'stripped down like a runner,'" but rather that the nuances and complexities of the issues before the Court are my constant companions when I sit down to write. What I want from the Court on a day-to-day basis, as I sit down to face my deadline, is clarity, coherence, and reliability. And compared with covering politics, although it would certainly be rewarding to have behind-the-scenes discussions with the Justices about the Court's work, there is a certain liberation in not having the kind of personal, mutually beneficial relationships that many political journalists have with the people they cover. I don't have to worry about losing access.

Of course, deciding what is important among the thousands of individual Court actions, which will be reported, and what pattern will be discerned from them can never be value-free. Those who make these judgments are the products of what they care about and also what they know. I am still chagrined that it took me until the late 1980s to understand and write about the revolution in habeas corpus jurisprudence that had been taking place in the Court right under my

nose. I simply had not understood either the subject or its importance. I failed a few years ago to appreciate the import of a Tenth Amendment decision that anticipated the regrouping and rebirth of a majority on the Court concerned with state sovereignty in the federal system. In retrospect, I think I was so mesmerized by the school prayer and abortion decisions that came down during the same Term that I was unable to take account of a major opinion that looked, at least to some degree, in an opposite or at least nonconforming direction. I have missed the significance of other important cases as well, from *Pennsylvania v. Union Gas Co.,* a major Eleventh Amendment decision (which the Court appears likely to overrule someday soon, so perhaps it is just as well that I spared my readers the burden of learning about it) to *Chevron U.S.A. Inc. v. Natural Resources Defense Council, Inc.,* an administrative law landmark that tilted the playing field toward the executive branch and had substantial political consequences during the Reagan and Bush years of divided government.

Inattentiveness or lack of sophistication on the part of those who cover the Court, myself included, is surely an obstacle to good journalism about the Court. In her speech at Georgetown, Justice Ginsburg recounted the classic story that when the Court handed down *Erie Railroad v. Tompkins,* the 1938 landmark decision that created a revolution in federal jurisdiction by ruling that there is no universal common law and that federal courts must apply state law in diversity cases, every newspaper in New York failed not only to understand but even to report the case. Not until Justice Stone complained a week later to Arthur Krock, the chief of the *New York Times* Washington Bureau, and prodded him to write about what Krock was finally persuaded to call a "transcendentally significant opinion," did the lay public know anything about this development. It should not surprise us that in the absence of anything resembling a real press corps covering the Court in 1938, a decision about something so remote and obscure as federal jurisdiction was overlooked. I would not offer any guarantees, unfortunately, that it would not be overlooked today.

A variety of journalistic needs and practices also pose obstacles to good journalism about the Court. Newsprint is expensive, and space is tight in newspapers and getting tighter all the time. On a busy decision day in June, when the Court issues four, five, or six major decisions, the news hole does not expand correspondingly. Nor do presses start later. Deadlines remain deadlines, no matter how much news there is to process. On the final day of the 1988 Term, the Court not only decided an important abortion case, *Webster v. Reproductive Health Services,* but also granted certiorari in *Cruzan v. Director, Missouri Department of Health,* portending a major ruling on the right to die. Although I had prepared the *Cruzan* case on the basis of the certiorari petition, which the Court had held for some months pending the disposition in *Webster,* I ran out of time and the paper ran out of space. The *Times* used a wire-service story for the grant in *Cruzan.*

I am always a little uncomfortable with the convention that calls for wrapping up the Term with a sweeping analysis that discerns and proclaims a theme, a movement from some point to another. Is this really accurate? Suppose the Justices just think they are deciding cases, one at a time. What's the story, after all? In an interesting recent essay entitled *Spin Doctoring Darwin,* Stephen Jay Gould offered a wry comment on the human need to see evolution not as a random process but as a glorious story that led inevitably onward and upward to producing homo sapiens. When I read that essay, I had just finished wrapping up the Court's last Term in a 4000-word piece with the following headline (which, I hasten to add, I did not write): "Farewell to the Old Order in the Court: The Right Goes Activist and the Center Is a Void." What, I wondered, would Darwin, Stephen Jay Gould, and the Justices think about that?

Stuart Taylor, Jr., of the *Legal Times* recently made the observation that the Supreme Court press corps has been writing for years about the Court's imminent shift to the Right, a pattern he views as just so much crying wolf when the Court remains near the center or even slightly left of the center of public opinion on many major issues. He wrote: "There is, of course, one perspective from which this Court looks unambiguously—and alarmingly—'conservative': the personal views of the (predominantly liberal) journalists who so characterize the Court, and of the other journalists, law professors, and big-city practitioners

whom they talk to." Taking his point, at least to some degree, I'm still not quite bold enough to flout the basic journalistic convention that requires me to find something thematic to say at the end of every Term, something other than "Court decides many important cases and recesses for the summer."

TELLING THE STORY: WHO WON?

In addition to whatever oversimplification is involved in adhering to the journalistic convention of finding a yearly theme of the Court's calendar cycle, the convention also inherently requires the designation of a winner. The conservatives "won" last Term. While I wrote that and believe it to be true, I am often uneasy about the binary won-lost approach to reporting on the Court. To what extent do stories like these, even the most nuanced and sophisticated, mislead readers and risk overly politicizing discourse about the Court and its work?

Wrapping It Up

One point the sweeping end-of-Term wrap-up usually overlooks is that every Term is more a work-in-progress than a finished story. And while it may be dramatically inviting to portray the Court as the venue for an ongoing Manichean battle, the reality is, of course, quite different. Of the eighty-two signed opinions last Term, thirty-five, or forty-three percent, resolved cases by nine-to-zero votes. Yet, because the Term's most consequential decisions tended to be the closely divided ones, the overwhelming impression that journalism about the Court—including my own—probably conveyed to the casual reader was of an institution locked in mortal combat, where sheer numbers rather than force of argument or legal reasoning determined the result. This is not an argument for not reporting conflict at the Court, but simply a note of concern about the consequences to public understanding about the Court of an unrelenting diet of conflict when the reality is often otherwise....

The week before the current Term opened, I was a guest on a National Public Radio talk show. One caller asked for comment on the numerous five-to-four decisions from the Supreme Court. He said it was distressing that such important issues were decided by such narrow margins. I answered that question as I usually do, by saying that I find it neither surprising nor particularly distressing that issues that have divided the country, and in most cases have also split the lower courts, should prove divisive on the Supreme Court. The next caller found this answer inadequate. Why don't we just cut out the pretense that these people are anything more than politicians, he said, placed on the Court by other politicians to carry out a political agenda? According to this caller, it was simply naive to talk about the Court in any other way.

Even if I believed that to be the case, and I do not, I would find that view disquieting for the long-term health of our democracy. In fact, I told my caller that I disagreed with him. While the Justices naturally draw on their own values and perspectives in approaching cases, most of them, most of the time, act not as politicians but as judges, working within the constraints of precedent and of the judicial enterprise to give judicial answers to the problems that people bring to the Court.

The answer is not, of course, quite that easy. While I do not think that "low" politics plays a major role at the Court, "high" politics certainly does. I do not believe that partisan advantage or the fate of Newt Gingrich's *Contract With America* was a factor in the Court's invalidation last Term, with one five-to-four stroke, of the state-imposed congressional term limits of twenty-three states. But in what turned out to be a fascinating debate about state sovereignty and the sources of the federal government's authority, the Court surely exercised "high" political power. And there is no denying that fault lines exist on the Court these days over the most profound questions about the structure of our political system and the relationship of the individual to the state. Nearly forty years ago, during another tumultuous time in the Court's relationship with the political system, political scientist Robert Dahl wrote that "Americans are not quite willing to accept the fact that [the Court] is a political institution and not quite capable of denying it; so that frequently we take both positions at once." Our cognitive dissonance, in other words, is hard-wired into our system.

Furthermore, with gridlock elsewhere in the political system, the Court happens to be the battleground on which some of the major political wars of our time are being fought. I remember the day in 1992 when the Court decided *Planned Parenthood v. Casey,* the Pennsylvania abortion case that trimmed the margins but reaffirmed the essentials of *Roe v. Wade.* By the time I got back to my office, there were two huge stacks of faxes on the floor by my desk, one pile generated by the right-to-life side and the other by the pro-choice side. Both sides were claiming defeat, surely an interesting variant on the usual Washington spin control. The right-to-life reaction was understandable on the face of the decision. The pro-choice reaction had more to do with institutional politics: The pro-choice groups, anticipating a loss of *Roe v. Wade* in its entirety, had planned a major political campaign on that premise and were simply unable to switch gears as quickly as the Court had appeared to. I remember one of the lawyers on that side calling me with her statement. I became exasperated. "You're telling me you lost this case, and I'm telling you that you won it and I'm going to tell my readers that you won it," I remember saying to the startled lawyer. That was an unusual day and an unusual case, but efforts to influence public perceptions of important cases are quite common, and at times like these I have found that there are relatively few honest brokers. That is understandable. For political purposes, at least in the short term but often longer— witness the continued misunderstanding about the Court's school prayer decisions of the 1960s—what the Court is perceived to have done is often as important as what the Court actually did.

The Struggle for History's Verdict

Because the Court is so important and is being asked to carry so much weight, a fierce battle is being fought across the political spectrum over the Court's story— over which ideas will prevail and how history will judge this period. It is a battle of public perception as well as reality, and journalism about the Court matters a great deal to the combatants. "A [s]truggle for the [s]oul of the Court," Robert H. Bork called it in an acerbic op-ed article that appeared in the *New York Times* the week after the *Casey* decision. Aiming his sarcasm at the three authors of the plurality opinion,

Justices Kennedy, O'Connor, and Souter, he said that the opinion was "intensely popular with just about everybody Justices care about: The New York Times, The Washington Post, the three network news programs, law school faculties and at least 90 percent of the people Justices may meet at Washington dinner parties."

I do not have the luxury of ignoring this struggle, because I am aware that my own coverage of the Court is subject to minute scrutiny from both the left and the right. A few years back, I wrote that the expected conservative counterrevolution at the Court was stalling because of the moderating influence of Justices O'Connor, Kennedy, and Souter. I then was criticized by liberals for failing to convey the full extent of the conservative dominance at the Court and by conservatives for trying, through what some of these commentators have dubbed the Greenhouse effect, to confer on these Justices the blessings of the liberal establishment and hence to inspire them to stray even further from the true path.

When this started happening, I was nonplussed to find myself part of the Court's story. My previous assignment in Albany, as the *Times* bureau chief in the midst of the fiscal crisis, had placed me in a somewhat visible position. But never did I attract the kind of personal attention that I find myself getting these days. Just to cite a few recent examples, I read this summer in a publication by the National Legal Center for the Public Interest, a group on the conservative side of the spectrum, that I displayed "hysterical anguish" at how close the Court came to upholding congressional term limits. This was apparently a reference to an article, labeled "news analysis," in which I wrote that it is only a slight exaggeration to say that the Court, in the term limits case, had come within a single vote of reinstalling the Articles of Confederation. I knew when I wrote that line that it was a provocative image, and my purpose was to give my readers a handle on the dimensions of the debate that had engaged the Court. I was even more surprised to read in an op-ed column in the *Dallas Morning News* that I was unhappy with the whole Term but "particularly distraught" over the decision in *United States v. Lopez,* which invalidated a federal gun law on Commerce Clause grounds. This observation was apparently based on another news

analysis in which I had said that the Court seemed ready to reassume a role as an "activist policeman of the Federal-state boundary." In contrast to my deliberately provocative analysis of the term limits decision, in the *Lopez* piece I thought that I was simply stating the obvious.

I was fascinated by both of these decisions, but hardly upset or distraught over either one. Quite the opposite, I thought it was exciting to be writing about such interesting debates over such important ideas. I asked my colleagues whether I had seemed particularly unhinged, and they all said that they remembered me as quite cheerful during that period. But that is obviously beside the point. I have learned how much it matters to the Court's various interested publics what the *New York Times* has to say about what the Court does because, in contrast to a legislature or some other public institution, there are so few significant paths of information from the Court to the public. In some respects, it is part of the continuing battle over the Bork nomination and the legacy of Judge Bork's rejection by the Senate. More fundamentally, it is a battle over the judgment of history.

For the past decade, conservatives rather than liberals have expressed the most concern about journalistic judgments about the Court, a fact that I interpret as reflecting frustration with the fitful nature of the vaunted conservative revolution at the Court and a search for an explanation as to why it has not proceeded more smoothly. Judge Bork's 1992 op-ed article, cited above, is one example. David Bryden of the University of Minnesota Law School offered an explanation in a 1992 article, asserting that "the liberal positions on cultural-social issues...are the positions of the most powerful elites in the media, academe, and the practicing bar." Consequently, he said, "[t]he reputations of the Justices, the warmth of their welcome on their frequent visits to law schools, and their places in history, depend chiefly on the evaluations of their work by liberal journalists and scholars.... [T]hey would not be human if it did not occasionally affect some of them."

Any discussion of factors bearing on the judgment of history and on public perceptions of the Court's legitimacy cannot ignore recent confirmation battles like the struggle over Judge Bork's nomination.

There is a direct trajectory between my cynical caller on the public radio program and some of the political battles over nominations to the Court. While keeping my journalistic distance, I think it is safe to say that a President who nominates an individual who is not supported by the existing political consensus risks labeling his nominee a political tool, regardless of whether the nominee is ultimately successful.

This perception was reflected in a recent discussion at my newspaper over whether to require identification, in all articles that name federal judges in the course of describing court decisions, of the President who appointed those judges. For a time last year, such a rule was, in fact, in force. Several of my colleagues and I objected that the rule placed the *Times* in the position of insinuating that all federal judges are simply carrying out the agendas of their political sponsors; in other words, that they are acting as politicians and not as judges. After further consideration, the rule was dropped. Federal judges will be identified by the Presidents who named them only if such identification makes sense as a news judgment in the context of the specific story. The fact that the rule existed even for a short time at the *Times* tells us something disquieting about the legacy of the confirmation battles of the Reagan and Bush years. I do not mean to single out the *Times.* I have a pile of commentary on the Court from a range of publications, much of it making the unstated or explicit assumption that some of the Justices are just politicians in robes. Anyone who has evidence that such is the case should of course document it and write it. But to incorporate the untested assumption into journalism about the Court disserves the goal of increasing public understanding.

TELLING THE STORY:
DOES THE ORACLE SPEAK?

There is also the question of the Court's own responsibility for telling its story. The Court's habits present substantial obstacles to conveying the work of the Court accurately to the public. To cite one example, on June 29, 1995, the final day of the Court's last Term, the Court handed down opinions in two voting rights cases, two important religious speech cases, and a major statutory case construing the Endangered Species

Act. Together, these decisions take up nearly eighty pages in the tiny type of *United States Law Week.* Even for a paper like the *Times,* with a commitment to opening up some extra space and giving me help on excerpting text, and even with a colleague on the environmental beat to whom I could farm out the Endangered Species Act case, this was pressing the limits of the possible. The Court had issued no opinions at all on the preceding two days, a Tuesday and Wednesday. Perhaps none of these decisions was ready for release until Thursday morning. Perhaps, as I suspect, there was a lack of desire on the Justices' part to interrupt their mornings earlier in the week by going on the bench to announce those opinions that were ready.

That closing day was relatively easy compared with some others. The last day of the 1987–1988 Term was a journalistic nightmare that has attained the status of legend. The Court issued nine decisions that filled 446 pages in the *United States Reports,* including a number of important cases and one, the decision that upheld the independent counsel statute, of landmark significance.

I once mentioned this problem to Chief Justice Rehnquist, suggesting the Court make a greater effort to spread out the decision announcements in the last weeks of the Term. He received my suggestion cordially and made a counterproposal of his own. "Just because we announce them all on one day doesn't mean you have to write about them all on one day," he said. "Why don't you save some for the next day?" On one level, this was harmless, and cost-free, banter. On another, it offered a dramatic illustration of the gulf between us. It appeared to me that the Chief Justice understood my comment to be a form of journalist's special interest pleading. My point, rather, was that the decisions would all be reported on the day they were released in any event, and that a slight change in the Court's management of its calendar could substantially increase the odds that the decisions would be reported well, or at least better—an improvement the Court might see as serving its own interest as well as the interest of the press.

A recent episode offered another illustration of the Court's unwillingness to bend, even a bit, in the direction of facilitating better journalism. Alderson Reporting Company, the outside contractor that transcribes the Court's argument sessions, recently informed the Court that current technology would enable it to provide same-day transcripts, eliminating the two-week delay that makes the transcripts all but useless as an aid to accurate renditions of the debate during oral arguments. A group of reporters wrote to the Chief Justice, explaining the benefit of having same-day transcripts and asking the Court to take Alderson up on its offer. After some weeks of consideration, the proposal was rejected without explanation. Those of us who had made a proposal we thought was sensible and hardly radical were taken aback by the response, which guarantees that quotations in argument stories will not be as accurate as they could be.

CONCLUSION

One recent book about Supreme Court journalism, one of the few scholarly studies on this subject, concluded that the Court has developed an elaborate apparatus to keep itself mysterious and remote, thus maintaining "public deference and compliance." In the view of the author, political scientist Richard Davis, "the press is a public relations tool for the Court specifically for the task of reinforcing deference toward its decisions." That is not the Court and not the press corps I have observed for these last eighteen years. Rather, I see a Court that is quite blithely oblivious to the needs of those who convey its work to the outside world, and a press corps that is often groping along in the dark, trying to make sense out of the shadows on the cave wall. The public enlightenment that this process does provide is a testament to the essential strength of our institutions, but we must guard against complacency on the part of the press, the Court, and those of us who care about both.

Is there a model for press-Court interaction that would serve the needs of both and, ultimately, lead to greater public understanding of the Court? A story from long ago offers a starting point for looking ahead. In 1932, following his retirement, Justice Oliver Wendell Holmes received a letter of congratulations and gratitude from a journalist to whom, sixteen years earlier, he had extended a hand in an hour of great journalistic need. As the letter writer, George Garner of the *Manufacturers Record* in Baltimore,

recounted the incident to Justice Holmes, Mr. Garner had been a young Washington reporter for the *Louisville Courier-Journal* when he found himself suddenly assigned to report on an opinion by the Justice. Not knowing where else to turn, he presented himself late in the afternoon at the Justice's home. Mr. Garner's letter (referring to both himself and his addressee in the third person) described their meeting:

> Called to the door, Justice Holmes explained to the correspondent that he was entertaining guests at tea and might not very well desert them; but, if the scribe would drop around later, he would be glad to help. Then, spontaneously: "No; come upstairs with me now, and we'll go over it." For an hour, this Justice of the Supreme Court of the United States patiently and clearly spelled out the story to the scribe, literally dictating much of the article in newspaper language. It ran, as one recalls, a couple of columns in the Courier-Journal and was esteemed as a clear and intelligible newspaper story. Never has the correspondent forgotten that great kindness and courtesy by Justice Holmes. Often he has related it to friends.

I obviously could not offer this charming and quaint episode as a model for today; for one thing, Mr. Garner's need for emergency assistance reflected an ignorance of the Court's docket and a lack of preparation that I certainly do not advocate on the part of the Supreme Court press corps. Nor should busy Justices be expected to interrupt tea parties or other endeavors to give a helping hand to what would soon become an endless stream of deadline panicked journalists.

But neither is this incident completely irrelevant. It reflects, on the part of Justice Holmes, an openness and a willingness to step out of the institutional role that would be quite unthinkable under similar circumstances today. There is a loss there, surely.

It is clear that the interests of the press and the Court can never be consonant. To cite just one example, it would greatly simplify my life if, in addition to receiving the weekly conference list of new petitions for certiorari that are ready for the Justices' action, I could also see the "discuss list" of those cases, culled from the larger list, that are the only actual candidates for a grant of cert. Yet I cannot imagine the Court permitting press access to the discuss list, for the reason that all of the cases not on the discuss list would

be publicly identified, in advance, as "cert.
' in all but name.

t despite our divergent interests—the press
interest in accessibility and information, the
in protecting the integrity of its decisional
—I am naive enough, and out of step enough
ie prevailing journalistic culture, to think of
..... wo institutions as, to some degree, partners in
a mutual democratic enterprise to which both must
acknowledge responsibility. The responsibility of the
press is to commit the resources necessary to give the
public the most accurate and contextual reporting
possible about the Court, its work, its members, and
its relationship with other branches of government.
The Court's responsibility is to remove unnecessary
obstacles to accomplishing that task.

I recognize that the word "unnecessary" assumes
shared premises that may simply not exist. Nevertheless, it should be easy to define some practices, such
as lack of timely argument transcripts or the refusal to
space opinions during a given week, as unnecessary.
Begin there and who knows? Might clearer, more
straightforward opinions follow? I do not expect the
impossible. I simply propose a mutual journey of self-
examination from which the press, the Court, and, ultimately, the public can only benefit.

| READING 25 |

Why Americans Hate the Media

James Fallows

*James Fallows, a well-known journalist and media
critic, is currently the editor of* U. S. News and
World Report. *This article, published in and while
Fallows was an editor at* The Atlantic Monthly,
*served to foreshadow his scathing book critiquing
political journalism,* Breaking the News.

From "Why Americans Hate the Media" by J. Fallows, 1996, *The
Atlantic Monthly,* February. Copyright © 1996 by The Atlantic
Monthly Company. Reprinted by permission.

*Fallows's critical eye takes a shotgun approach
in this selection, synthesizing many of the themes
raised throughout this chapter. At the broadest level,
political journalism is faulted for focusing on the
game of politics instead of its substance. Fallows
masses substantial evidence for his argument by
drawing together numerous contemporary examples
of political reporting that will be familiar to most
readers. At bottom, he argues, the journalistic focus
on political maneuvering instead of substantive
issues is not what the public wants from the news,
underscoring the title of the piece.*

*Among the conventions of contemporary
political journalism that draw Fallows's greatest ire
are the tendency for reporters to treat all public
issues as, fundamentally, political in nature, the
overemphasis journalists place on "pointless
prediction," the propensity for journalists to be
passive recipients of administration-fed news, the
reticence of prominent journalists to disclose and be
forthcoming about their own political and financial
interests, and the pronounced tendency for journalists
to be out of touch with the public. All of these
concerns foster losses in journalistic credibility as the
journalistic calling is transformed into a sideshow. As
Fallows notes, "The message is: We don't respect
what we're doing. Why should anyone else?"*

*The points Fallows makes are quite well taken.
Cynics, however, would contend that he is wrong in
suggesting that what we get in political reporting is
something other than what we want. That is, perhaps
Fallows's dictates for substantively oriented
journalism that is analytically focused on policy
issues would not find the necessary audience to
sustain itself in commercially driven media settings.
While this may be an empirical question, Fallows's
retort, as a* professional *journalist, would be a simple
one.*

A generation ago political talk programs were sleepy
Sunday-morning affairs. The Secretary of State or
the Senate majority leader would show up to answer
questions from Lawrence Spivak or Bob Clark, and
after thirty minutes another stately episode of *Meet
the Press* or *Issues and Answers* would be history.

Everything in public life is "brighter" and more "interesting" now. Constant competition from the weekday trash-talk shows has forced anything involving political life to liven up. Under pressure from the Saturday political-talk shows—*The McLaughlin Group* and its many disorderly descendants—even the Sunday-morning shows have put on rouge and push-up bras.

Meet the Press, moderated by Tim Russert, is probably the meatiest of these programs. High-powered guests discuss serious topics with Russert, who worked for years in politics, and with veteran reporters. Yet the pressure to keep things lively means that squabbling replaces dialogue.

The discussion shows that are supposed to enhance public understanding may actually reduce it, by hammering home the message that issues don't matter except as items for politicians to fight over. Some politicians in Washington may indeed view all issues as mere tools to use against their opponents. But far from offsetting this view of public life, the national press often encourages it. As Washington-based talk shows have become more popular in the past decade, they have had a trickle-down effect in cities across the country. In Seattle, in Los Angeles, in Boston, in Atlanta, journalists gain notice and influence by appearing regularly on talk shows—and during those appearances they mainly talk about the game of politics.

NOT ISSUES BUT THE GAME OF POLITICS

In the 1992 presidential campaign candidates spent more time answering questions from "ordinary people"—citizens in town-hall forums, callers on radio and TV talk shows—than they had in previous years. The citizens asked overwhelmingly about the *what* of politics: What are you going to do about the health-care system? What can you do to reduce the cost of welfare? The reporters asked almost exclusively about the *how:* How are you going to try to take away Perot's constituency? How do you answer charges that you have flip-flopped?

After the 1992 campaign the contrast between questions from citizens and those from reporters was widely discussed in journalism reviews and postmortems on campaign coverage. Reporters acknowledged that they should try harder to ask questions about things their readers and viewers seemed to care about—that is, questions about the differences that political choices would make in people's lives.

In January of last year there was a chance to see how well the lesson had sunk in. In the days just before and after Bill Clinton delivered his State of the Union address to the new Republican-controlled Congress, he answered questions in a wide variety of forums in order to explain his plans.

On January 31, a week after the speech, the President flew to Boston and took questions from a group of teenagers. Their questions concerned the effects of legislation or government programs on their communities or schools. These were the questions (paraphrased in some cases):

- "We need stronger laws to punish those people who are caught selling guns to our youth. Basically, what can you do about that?"
- "I notice that often it's the media that is responsible for the negative portrayal of young people in our society." What can political leaders do to persuade the media that there is good news about youth?
- Apprenticeship programs and other ways to provide job training have been valuable for students not going to college. Can the Administration promote more of these programs?
- Programs designed to keep teenagers away from drugs and gangs often emphasize sports and seem geared mainly to boys. How can such programs be made more attractive to teenage girls?
- What is it like at Oxford? (This was from a student who was completing a new alternative-school curriculum in the Boston public schools, and who had been accepted at Oxford.)
- "We need more police officers who are trained to deal with all the other different cultures in our cities." What can the government do about that?
- "In Boston, Northeastern University has created a model of scholarships and other supports to help inner-city kids get to and stay in college.... As President, can you urge colleges across the country to do what Northeastern has done?"

Earlier in the month the President's performance had been assessed by the three network-news anchors: Peter Jennings, of ABC; Dan Rather, of CBS; and Tom Brokaw, of NBC. There was no overlap whatsoever between the questions the students asked and those raised by the anchors. None of the questions from these news professionals concerned the impact of legislation or politics on people's lives. Nearly all concerned the struggle for individual advancement among candidates.

Peter Jennings, who met with Clinton as the Gingrich-Dole Congress was getting under way, asked whether Clinton had been eclipsed as a political leader by the Republicans. Dan Rather did interviews through January with prominent politicians—Senators Edward Kennedy, Phil Gramm, and Bob Dole—building up to a profile of Clinton two days after the State of the Union address. Every question he asked was about popularity or political tactics. He asked Phil Gramm to guess whether Newt Gingrich would enter the race (no) and whether Bill Clinton would be renominated by his party (yes). He asked Bob Dole what kind of mood the President seemed to be in, and whether Dole and Gingrich were, in effect, the new bosses of Washington. When Edward Kennedy began giving his views about the balanced-budget amendment, Rather steered him back on course: "Senator, you know I'd talk about these things the rest of the afternoon, but let's move quickly to politics. Do you expect Bill Clinton to be the Democratic nominee for reelection in 1996?"

The *CBS Evening News* profile of Clinton, which was narrated by Rather and was presented as part of the series *Eye on America,* contained no mention of Clinton's economic policy, his tax or budget plans, his failed attempt to pass a health-care proposal, his successful attempt to ratify NAFTA, his efforts to "reinvent government," or any substantive aspect of his proposals or plans in office. Its subject was exclusively Clinton's handling of his office—his "difficulty making decisions," his "waffling" at crucial moments. If Rather or his colleagues had any interest in the content of Clinton's speech as opposed to its political effect, neither the questions they asked nor the reports they aired revealed such a concern.

Tom Brokaw's questions were more substantive, but even he concentrated mainly on politics of the moment. How did the President feel about a poll showing that 61 percent of the public felt that he had no "strong convictions" and could be "easily swayed"? What did Bill Clinton think about Newt Gingrich? "Do you think he plays fair?" How did he like it that people kept shooting at the White House?

When ordinary citizens have a chance to pose questions to political leaders, they rarely ask about the game of politics. They want to know how the reality of politics will affect them—through taxes, programs, scholarship funds, wars. Journalists justify their intrusiveness and excesses by claiming that they are the public's representatives, asking the questions their fellow citizens would ask if they had the privilege of meeting with Presidents and senators. In fact they ask questions that only their fellow political professionals care about. And they often do so—as at the typical White House news conference—with a discourtesy and rancor that represent the public's views much less than they reflect the modern journalist's belief that being independent boils down to acting hostile.

REDUCTIO AD ELECTIONEM: THE ONE-TRACK MIND

The limited curiosity that elite reporters display in their questions is also evident in the stories they write once they have received answers. They are interested mainly in pure politics and can be coerced into examining the substance of an issue only as a last resort. The subtle but sure result is a stream of daily messages that the real meaning of public life is the struggle of Bob Dole against Newt Gingrich against Bill Clinton, rather than our collective efforts to solve collective problems.

The natural instinct of newspapers and TV is to present every public issue as if its "real" meaning were political in the meanest and narrowest sense of that term—the attempt by parties and candidates to gain an advantage over their rivals. Reporters do, of course, write stories about political life in the broader sense and about the substance of issues—the pluses and minuses of diplomatic recognition for Vietnam, the difficulties of holding down the Medicare budget, whether immigrants help or hurt the nation's economic base. But when there is a chance to use these issues as props or raw material for a story about political tactics, most reporters leap at it. It is more fun—and easier—to write about Bill Clinton's "positioning" on the Vietnam issue, or how Newt Gingrich is "handling" the need to cut Medicare, than it is to look into the issues themselves.

Examples of this preference occur so often that they're difficult to notice. But every morning's newspaper, along with every evening's newscast, reveals this pattern of thought.

• Last February, when the Democratic President and the Republican Congress were fighting over how much federal money would go to local law-enforcement agencies, one network-news broadcast showed a clip of Gingrich denouncing Clinton and another of Clinton standing in front of a sea of uniformed police officers while making a tough-on-crime speech. The correspondent's sign-off line was "The White House thinks 'cops on the beat' has a simple but appealing ring to it." That is, the President was pushing the plan because it would sound good in his campaign ads. Whether or not that was Clinton's real motive, nothing in the broadcast gave the slightest hint of where the extra policemen would go, how much they might cost, whether there was reason to think they'd do any good. Everything in the story suggested that the crime bill mattered only as a chapter in the real saga, which was the struggle between Bill and Newt.

• Last April, after the explosion at the federal building in Oklahoma City, discussion changed quickly from the event itself to politicians' "handling" of the event. On the Sunday after the blast President Clinton announced a series of new anti-terrorism measures. The next morning, on National Public Radio's *Morning Edition,* Cokie Roberts was asked about the prospects of the proposals' taking effect. "In some ways it's not even the point," she replied. What mattered was that Clinton "looked good" taking the tough side of the issue. No one expects Cokie Roberts or other political correspondents to be experts on controlling terrorism, negotiating with the Syrians, or the other

specific measures on which Presidents make stands. But all issues are shoehorned into the area of expertise the most-prominent correspondents do have: the struggle for one-upmanship among a handful of political leaders.

• When health-care reform was the focus of big political battles between Republicans and Democrats, it was on the front page and the evening newscast every day. When the Clinton Administration declared defeat in 1994 and there were no more battles to be fought, health-care news coverage virtually stopped too— even though the medical system still represented one seventh of the economy, even though HMOs and corporations and hospitals and pharmaceutical companies were rapidly changing policies in the face of ever-rising costs. Health care was no longer political news, and therefore it was no longer interesting news.

• After California's voters approved Proposition 187 in the 1994 elections, drastically limiting the benefits available to illegal immigrants, the national press ran a trickle of stories on what this would mean for California's economy, its school and legal systems, even its relations with Mexico. A flood of stories examined the political impact of the immigration issue—how the Republicans might exploit it, how the Democrats might be divided by it, whether it might propel Pete Wilson to the White House.

• On August 16 last year Bill Bradley announced that after representing New Jersey in the Senate for three terms he would not run for a fourth term. In interviews and at the news conferences he conducted afterward Bradley did his best to talk about the deep problems of public life and economic adjustment that had left him frustrated with the political process. Each of the parties had locked itself into rigid positions that kept it from dealing with the realistic concerns of ordinary people, he said. American corporations were doing what they had to do for survival in international competition: they were downsizing and making themselves radically more efficient and productive. But the result was to leave "decent, hardworking Americans" more vulnerable to layoffs and the loss of their careers, medical coverage, pension rights, and social standing than they had been in decades. Somehow, Bradley said, we had to move past the focus on short-term political maneuvering and determine how to deal with the forces that were leaving Americans frustrated and insecure.

That, at least, was what Bill Bradley said. What turned up in the press was almost exclusively speculation about what the move meant for this year's presidential race and the party lineup on Capitol Hill. Might Bradley challenge Bill Clinton in the Democratic primaries? If not, was he preparing for an independent run? Could the Democrats come up with any other candidate capable of holding on to Bradley's seat? Wasn't this a slap in the face for Bill Clinton and the party he purported to lead? In the aftermath of Bradley's announcement prominent TV and newspaper reporters competed to come up with the shrewdest analysis of the political impact of the move. None of the country's major papers or networks used Bradley's announcement as a news peg for an analysis of the real issues he had raised.

The day after his announcement Bradley was interviewed by Judy Woodruff on the CNN program *Inside Politics*. Woodruff is a widely respected and knowledgeable reporter, but her interaction with Bradley was like the meeting of two beings from different universes. Every answer Bradley gave was about the substance of national problems that concerned him. Every one of Woodruff's responses or questions was about short-term political tactics. Woodruff asked about the political implications of his move for Bill Clinton and Newt Gingrich. Bradley replied that it was more important to concentrate on the difficulties both parties had in dealing with real national problems.

Midway through the interview Bradley gave a long answer to the effect that everyone involved in politics had to get out of the rut of converting every subject or comment into a political "issue," used for partisan advantage. Let's stop talking, Bradley said, about who will win what race and start responding to one another's ideas.

As soon as he finished, Woodruff asked her next question: "Do you want to be President?" It was as if she had not heard a word he had been saying—or *couldn't* hear it, because the media's language of political analysis is utterly separate from the terms in which people describe real problems in their lives.

The effect is as if the discussion of every new advance in medicine boiled down to speculation about whether its creator would win the Nobel Prize that year. Regardless of the tone of coverage, medical research will go on. But a relentless emphasis on the cynical game of politics threatens public life itself, by implying day after day that the political sphere is nothing more than an arena in which ambitious politicians struggle for dominance, rather than a structure in which citizens can deal with worrisome collective problems.

POINTLESS PREDICTIONS: THE POLITICAL EXPERTS

On Sunday, November 6, 1994, two days before the congressional elections that swept the Republicans to power, *The Washington Post* published the results of its "Crystal Ball" poll. Fourteen prominent journalists, pollsters, and all-around analysts made their predictions about how many seats each party would win in the House and Senate and how many governorships each would take.

One week later many of these same experts would be saying on their talk shows that the Republican landslide was "inevitable" and "a long time coming" and "a sign of deep discontent in the heartland." But before the returns were in, how many of the fourteen experts predicted that the Republicans would win both houses of Congress and that Newt Gingrich would be speaker? Exactly three.

What is interesting about this event is not just that so many experts could be so wrong. Immediately after the election even Newt Gingrich seemed dazed by the idea that the forty-year reign of the Democrats in the House had actually come to an end. Rather, the episode said something about the futility of political prediction itself—a task to which the big-time press devotes enormous effort and time. *Two days* before the election many of the country's most admired analysts had no idea what was about to happen. Yet within a matter of weeks these same people, unfazed, would be writing articles and giving speeches and being quoted about who was "ahead" and "behind" in the emerging race for the White House in 1996.

As with medieval doctors who applied leeches and trepanned skulls, the practitioners cannot be blamed for the limits of their profession. But we can ask why reporters spend so much time directing our attention toward what is not much more than guesswork on their part. It builds the impression that journalism is about what's entertaining—guessing what might or might not happen next month—rather than what's useful, such as extracting lessons of success and failure from events that have already occurred. Competing predictions add almost nothing to our ability to solve public problems or to make sensible choices among complex alternatives. Yet such useless distractions have become a specialty of the political press. They are easy to produce, they allow reporters to act as if they possessed special inside knowledge, and there are no consequences for being wrong.

SPOON-FEEDING:
THE WHITE HOUSE PRESS CORPS

In the early spring of last year, when Newt Gingrich was dominating the news from Washington and the O. J. Simpson trial was dominating the news as a whole, *The Washington Post* ran an article about the pathos of the White House press room. Nobody wanted to hear what the President was doing, so the people who cover the President could not get on the air. Howard Kurtz, the *Post*'s media writer, described the human cost of this political change:

> Brit Hume is in his closet-size White House cubicle, watching Kato Kaelin testify on CNN. Bill Plante, in the adjoining cubicle, has his feet up and is buried in the *New York Times*. Brian Williams is in the corridor, idling away the time with Jim Miklaszewski.
>
> An announcement is made for a bill-signing ceremony. Some of America's highest-paid television correspondents begin ambling toward the pressroom door.
> "Are you coming with us?" Williams asks.
> "I guess so," says Hume, looking forlorn.

The White House spokesman, Mike McCurry, told Kurtz that there was some benefit to the enforced silence: "Brit Hume has now got his crossword puzzle capacity down to record time. And some of the reporters have been out on the lecture circuit."

The deadpan restraint with which Kurtz told this story is admirable. But the question many readers would want to scream at the idle correspondents is *Why don't you go out and do some work?*

Why not go out and interview someone, even if you're not going to get any airtime that night? Why not escape the monotonous tyranny of the White House press room, which reporters are always complaining about? The knowledge that O. J. will keep you off the air yet again should liberate you to look into those stories you never "had time" to deal with before. Why not *read a book*—about welfare reform, about Russia or China, about race relations, about anything? Why not imagine, just for a moment, that your journalistic duty might involve something more varied and constructive than doing standups from the White House lawn and sounding skeptical about whatever announcement the President's spokesman put out that day?

What might these well-paid, well-trained correspondents have done while waiting for the O. J. trial to become boring enough that they could get back on the air? They might have tried to learn something that would be of use to their viewers when the story of the moment went away. Without leaving Washington, without going farther than ten minutes by taxi from the White House (so that they could be on hand if a sudden press conference was called), they could have prepared themselves to discuss the substance of issues that affect the public.

For example, two years earlier Vice President Al Gore had announced an ambitious plan to "reinvent" the federal government. Had it made any difference, either in improving the performance of government or in reducing its cost, or was it all for show? Republicans and Democrats were sure to spend the next few months fighting about cuts in the capital-gains tax. Capital-gains tax rates were higher in some countries and lower in others. What did the experience of these countries show about whether cutting the rates helped an economy to grow? The rate of immigration was rising again, and in California and Florida it was becoming an important political issue. What was the latest evidence on the economic and social effects of immigration? Should Americans feel confident or threatened that so many foreigners were trying to make their way in? Soon both political parties would be advancing plans to reform the welfare system. Within a two-mile radius of the White House lived plenty of families on welfare. Why not go and see how the system had affected them, and what they would do if it changed? The federal government had gone further than most private industries in trying to open opportunities to racial minorities and women. The Pentagon had gone furthest of all. What did people involved in this process—men and women, blacks and whites—think about its successes and failures? What light did their experience shed on the impending affirmative-action debate?

The list could go on for pages. With a few minutes' effort—about as long as it takes to do a crossword puzzle—the correspondents could have drawn up lists of other subjects they had never before "had time" to investigate. They had the time now. What they lacked was a sense that their responsibility involved something more than standing up to rehash the day's announcements when there was room for them on the news.

GLASS HOUSES:
JOURNALISTS AND FINANCIAL DISCLOSURE

Half a century ago reporters knew but didn't say that Franklin D. Roosevelt was in a wheelchair. A generation ago many reporters knew but didn't write about John F. Kennedy's insatiable appetite for women. For several months in the early Clinton era reporters knew about but didn't disclose Paula Jones's allegation that, as governor of Arkansas, Bill Clinton had exposed himself to her. Eventually this claim found its way into all the major newspapers, proving that there is no longer any such thing as an accusation too embarrassing to be printed if it seems to bear on a politician's "character."

It is not just the President who has given up his privacy in the name of the public's right to know. Over the past two decades officials whose power is tiny compared with the President's have had to reveal embarrassing details about what most Americans consider very private matters: their income and wealth. Each of the more than 3,000 people appointed by the President to executive-branch jobs

must reveal previous sources of income and summarize his or her financial holdings. Congressmen have changed their rules to forbid themselves to accept honoraria for speaking to interest groups or lobbyists. The money that politicians do raise from individuals and groups must be disclosed to the Federal Election Commission. The information they disclose is available to the public and appears often in publications, most prominently *The Washington Post.*

No one contends that every contribution makes every politician corrupt. But financial disclosure has become commonplace on the "Better safe than sorry" principle. If politicians and officials are not corrupt, the reasoning goes, they have nothing to fear from letting their finances be publicized. And if they are corrupt, public disclosure is a way to stop them before they do too much harm. The process may be embarrassing, but this is the cost of public life.

How different the "Better safe than sorry" calculation seems when journalists are involved! Reporters and pundits hold no elected office, but they are obviously public figures. The most prominent TV-talk-show personalities are better known than all but a handful of congressmen. When politicians and pundits sit alongside one another on Washington talk shows and trade opinions, they underscore the essential similarity of their political roles. The pundits have no vote in Congress, but the overall political impact of a word from George Will, Ted Koppel, William Safire, or any of their colleagues who run the major editorial pages dwarfs anything a third-term congressman could do. If an interest group had the choice of buying the favor of one prominent media figure or of two junior congressmen, it wouldn't even have to think about the decision. The pundit is obviously more valuable.

If a reporter is sued for libel by a prominent but unelected personality, such as David Letterman or Donald Trump, he or she says that the offended party is a "public figure"—about whom nearly anything can be written in the press. Public figures, according to the rulings that shape today's libel law, can win a libel suit only if they can prove that a reporter knew that what he or she was writing was false, or had "reckless disregard" for its truth, and went ahead and published it anyway. Public figures, according to the law, pay a price for being well known. And who are these people? The category is not limited to those who hold public office but includes all who "thrust themselves into the public eye." Most journalists would eloquently argue the logic of this broad definition of public figures—until the same standard was applied to them.

In 1993 Sam Donaldson, of ABC, described himself in an interview as being in touch with the concerns of the average American. "I'm trying to get a little ranching business started in New Mexico," he said. "I've got five people on the payroll. I'm making out those government forms." Thus he understood the travails of the small businessman and the annoyances of government regulation. Donaldson, whose base pay from ABC is reported to be some $2 million a year, did not point out that his several ranches in New Mexico together covered some 20,000 acres. When doing a segment attacking farm subsidies on *Prime Time Live* in 1993 he did not point out that "those government forms" allowed him to claim nearly $97,000 in sheep and mohair subsidies over two years. William Neuman, a reporter for the *New York Post,* said that when his photographer tried to take pictures of Donaldson's ranch house, Donaldson had him thrown off his property. ("In the West trespassing is a serious offense," Donaldson explained.)

Had Donaldson as a journalist been pursuing a politician or even a corporate executive, he would have felt justified in using the most aggressive reportorial techniques. When these techniques were turned on him, he complained that the reporters were going too far. The analysts who are so clear-eyed about the conflict of interest in Newt Gingrich's book deal claim that they see no reason, none at all, why their own finances might be of public interest.

Last May one of Donaldson's colleagues on *This Week With David Brinkley,* George Will, wrote a column and delivered on-air comments ridiculing the Clinton Administration's plan to impose tariffs on Japanese luxury cars, notably the Lexus. On the Brinkley show Will said that the tariffs would be "illegal" and would merely amount to "a subsidy for Mercedes dealerships."

Neither in his column nor on the show did Will disclose that his wife, Mari Maseng Will, ran a firm that had been paid some $200,000 as a registered foreign agent for the Japan Automobile Manufacturers Association, and that one of the duties for which she was hired was to get American commentators to criticize the tariff plan. When Will was asked why he had never mentioned this, he replied that it was "just too silly" to think that his views might have been affected by his wife's contract.

Will had, in fact, espoused such views for years, since long before his wife worked for the JAMA and even before he had married her. Few of his readers would leap to the conclusion that Will was serving as a mouthpiece for his wife's employers. But surely most would have preferred to learn that information from Will himself.

A third member of the regular Brinkley panel, Cokie Roberts, is, along with Will and Donaldson, a frequent and highly paid speaker before corporate audiences. She has made a point of not disclosing which interest groups she speaks to or how much money she is paid. She has criticized the Clinton Administration for its secretive handling of the controversy surrounding Hillary Clinton's lucrative cattle-future trades and of the Whitewater affair, yet like the other pundits, she refuses to acknowledge that secrecy about financial interests undermines journalism's credibility too.

OUT OF TOUCH WITH AMERICA

In the week leading up to a State of the Union address White House aides always leak word to reporters that this year the speech will be "different." No more laundry list of all the government's activities, no more boring survey of every potential trouble spot in the world. This time, for a change, the speech is going to be short, punchy, and thematic. When the actual speech occurs, it is never short, punchy, or thematic. It is long and detailed, like all its predecessors, because as the deadline nears, every part of the government scrambles desperately to have a mention of its activities crammed into the speech somewhere.

In the days before Bill Clinton's address a year ago aides said that no matter what had happened to all those other Presidents, this time the speech really would be short, punchy, and thematic. The President understood the situation, he recognized his altered role, and he saw this as an opportunity to set a new theme for his third and fourth years in office.

That evening the promises once again proved false. Bill Clinton gave a speech that was enormously long even by the standards of previous State of the Union addresses. The speech had three or four apparent endings, it had ad-libbed inserts, and it covered both the details of policy and the President's theories about what had gone wrong with America. An hour and twenty-one minutes after he took the podium, the President stepped down.

Less than a minute later the mockery from commentators began. For instant analysis NBC went to Peggy Noonan, who had been a speechwriter for Presidents Ronald Reagan and George Bush. She grimaced and barely tried to conceal her disdain for such an ungainly, sprawling speech. Other commentators soon mentioned that congressmen had been slipping out of the Capitol building before the end of the speech, that Clinton had once more failed to stick to an agenda, that the speech probably would not give the President the new start he sought. The comments were virtually all about the tactics of the speech, and they were almost all thumbs down.

A day and a half later the first newspaper columns showed up. They were even more critical. On January 26 *The Washington Post*'s op-ed page consisted mainly of stories about the speech, all of which were withering. "ALL MUSH AND NO MESSAGE" was the headline on a column by Richard Cohen. "AN OPPORTUNITY MISSED" was the more statesmanlike judgment from David Broder. Cohen wrote: "Pardon me if I thought of an awful metaphor: Clinton at a buffet table, eating everything in sight."

What a big fat jerk that Clinton was! How little he understood the obligations of leadership! Yet the news section of the same day's *Post* had a long article based on discussions with a focus group of ordinary citizens in Chicago who had watched the President's speech. "For these voters, the State of the Union speech was an antidote to weeks of unrelenting criticism of Clinton's presidency," the article said.

"Tonight reminded us of what has been accomplished," said Maureen Prince, who works as the office manager in her husband's business and has raised five children. "We are so busy hearing the negatives all the time, from the time you wake up on your clock radio in the morning...."

The group's immediate impressions mirrored the results of several polls conducted immediately after the president's speech.

ABC News found that eight out of 10 approved of the president's speech. CBS News said that 74 percent of those surveyed said they had a "clear idea" of what Clinton stands for, compared with just 41 percent before the speech. A Gallup Poll for *USA Today* and Cable News Network found that eight in 10 said Clinton is leading the country in the right direction.

Nielsen ratings reported in the same day's paper showed that the longer the speech went on, the larger the number of people who tuned in to watch.

The point is not that the pundits are necessarily wrong and the public necessarily right. The point is the gulf between the two groups' reactions. The very aspects of the speech that had seemed so ridiculous to the professional commentators—its detail, its inclusiveness, the hyperearnestness of Clinton's conclusion about the "common good"—seemed attractive and worthwhile to most viewers.

"I'm wondering what so much of the public heard that our highly trained expert analysts completely missed," Carol Cantor, a software consultant from California, wrote in a discussion on the WELL, a popular online forum, three days after the speech. What they heard was, in fact, the speech, which allowed them to draw their own conclusions rather than being forced to accept an expert "analysis" of how the President "handled" the speech. In most cases the analysis goes unchallenged, because the public has no chance to see whatever event the pundits are describing. In this instance viewers had exactly the same evidence about Clinton's performance that the "experts" did, and from it they drew radically different conclusions.

In 1992 political professionals had laughed at Ross Perot's "boring" and "complex" charts about the federal budget deficit—until it became obvious that viewers loved them. And for a week or two after this State of the Union speech there were little jokes on the weekend talk shows about how out of step the pundit reaction had been with opinion "out there." But after a polite chuckle the talk shifted to how the President and the speaker and Senator Dole were handling their jobs.

TERM LIMITS

As soon as the Democrats were routed in the 1994 elections, commentators and TV analysts said it was obvious that the American people were tired of seeing the same old faces in Washington. The argument went that those who lived inside the Beltway had forgotten what it was like in the rest of the country. They didn't get it. They were out of touch. The only way to jerk the congressional system back to reality was to bring in new blood.

A few days after the new Congress was sworn in, CNN began running an updated series of promotional ads for its program *Crossfire*. (Previous ads had featured shots of locomotives colliding head-on and rams locking horns, to symbolize the meeting of minds on the show.) Everything has been shaken up in the capital, one of the ads began. New faces. New names. New people in charge of all the committees.

"In fact," the announcer said, in a tone meant to indicate whimsy, "only one committee hasn't changed. The *welcoming* committee."

The camera pulled back to reveal the three hosts of *Crossfire*—Pat Buchanan, John Sununu, and Michael Kinsley—standing with arms crossed on the steps of the Capitol building, blocking the path of the new arrivals trying to make their way in. "Watch your step," one of the hosts said.

Talk about not getting it! The people who put together this ad must have imagined that the popular irritation with inside-the-Beltway culture was confined to members of Congress—and didn't extend to members of the punditocracy, many of whom had held their positions much longer than the typical congressman had. The difference between the "welcoming committee" and the congressional committees headed by fallen Democratic titans like Tom Foley and Jack Brooks was that the congressmen can be booted out.

"Polls show that both Republicans *and* Democrats felt better about the Congress just after the 1994 elections," a Clinton Administration official said last

year. "They had made the monkey jump—they were able to discipline an institution they didn't like. They could register the fact that they were unhappy. There doesn't seem to be any way to do that with the press, except to stop watching and reading, which more and more people have done."

LOST CREDIBILITY

Here is an astonishing gulf between the way journalist—especially the most prominent ones—think about their impact and the way the public does. In movies of the 1930s reporters were gritty characters who instinctively sided with the common man. In the 1970s Robert Redford and Dustin Hoffman, starring as Bob Woodward and Carl Bernstein in *All the President's Men,* were better-paid but still gritty reporters unafraid to challenge big power. Even the local-TV-news crew featured on *The Mary Tyler Moore Show* had a certain down-to-earth pluck. Ted Knight, as the pea-brained news anchor Ted Baxter, was a ridiculously pompous figure but not an arrogant one.

Since the early 1980s the journalists who have shown up in movies have often been portrayed as more loathsome than the lawyers, politicians, and business moguls who are the traditional bad guys in films about the white-collar world. In *Absence of Malice,* made in 1981, an ambitious newspaper reporter (Sally Field) ruins the reputation of a businessman (Paul Newman) by rashly publishing articles accusing him of murder. In *Broadcast News,* released in 1987, the anchorman (William Hurt) is still an airhead, like Ted Baxter, but unlike Ted, he works in a business that is systematically hostile to anything except profit and bland good looks. The only sympathetic characters in the movie, an overeducated reporter (Albert Brooks) and a hyperactive and hyperidealistic producer (Holly Hunter), would have triumphed as heroes in a newspaper movie of the 1930s. In this one they are ground down by the philistines at their network.

In the *Die Hard* series, which started in 1988, a TV journalist (William Atherton) is an unctuous creep who will lie and push helpless people around in order to get on the air. In *The Bonfire of the Vanities* (1990) the tabloid writer Peter Fallow (Bruce Willis) is a disheveled British sot who will do anything for a free drink. In *Rising Sun* (1993) a newspaper reporter known as "Weasel" (Steve Buscemi) is an out-and-out criminal, accepting bribes to influence his coverage. As Antonia Zerbisias pointed out in the *Toronto Star* in 1993, movies and TV shows offer almost no illustrations of journalists who are not full of themselves, shallow, and indifferent to the harm they do. During Operation Desert Storm, *Saturday Night Live* ridiculed American reporters who asked military spokesmen questions like "Can you tell us exactly when and where you are going to launch your attack?" "The journalists were portrayed as ignorant, arrogant and pointlessly adversarial," Jay Rosen, of New York University, wrote about the episode. "By gently rebuffing their ludicrous questions, the Pentagon briefer [on *SNL*] came off as a model of sanity."

Even real-life members of the Washington pundit corps have made their way into movies—Eleanor Clift, Morton Kondracke, hosts from *Crossfire*—in 1990s releases such as *Dave* and *Rising Sun*. Significantly, their role in the narrative is as buffoons. The joke in these movies is how rapidly the pundits leap to conclusions, how predictable their reactions are, how automatically they polarize the debate without any clear idea of what has really occurred. That real-life journalists are willing to keep appearing in such movies, knowing how they will be cast, says something about the source of self-respect in today's media: celebrity, on whatever basis, matters more than being taken seriously.

Movies do not necessarily capture reality, but they suggest a public mood—in this case, a contrast between the apparent self-satisfaction of the media celebrities and the contempt in which they are held by the public. "The news media has a generally positive view of itself in the watchdog role," wrote the authors of an exhaustive survey of public attitudes and the attitudes of journalists themselves toward the press. (The survey was conducted by the Times Mirror Center for the People and the Press, and was released last May.) But "the outside world strongly faults the news media for its negativism.... The public goes so far as to say that the press gets in the way of society solving its problems...." According to the survey, "two out of three members of the public had nothing or nothing good to say about the media."

The media establishment is beginning to get at least an inkling of this message. Through the past decade discussions among newspaper editors and publishers have been a litany of woes: fewer readers; lower "penetration" rates, as a decreasing share of the public pays attention to news; a more and more desperate search for ways to attract the public's interest. In the short run these challenges to credibility are a problem for journalists and journalism. In the longer run they are a problem for democracy.

TURNING A CALLING INTO A SIDESHOW

Even if practiced perfectly, journalism will leave some resentment and bruised feelings in its wake. The justification that journalists can offer for the harm they inevitably inflict is to show, through their actions, their understanding that what they do matters and that it should be done with care.

This is why the most depressing aspect of the new talking-pundit industry may be the argument made by many practitioners: the whole thing is just a game, which no one should take too seriously. Michael Kinsley, a highly respected and indisputably talented policy journalist, has written that his paid speaking engagements are usually mock debates, in which he takes the liberal side.

> Since the audiences are generally composed of affluent businessmen, my role is like that of the team that gets to lose to the Harlem Globetrotters. But I do it because it pays well, because it's fun to fly around the country and stay in hotels, and because even a politically unsympathetic audience can provide a cheap ego boost.

Last year Morton Kondracke, of *The McLaughlin Group,* told Mark Jurkowitz, of *The Boston Globe,* "This is not writing, this is not thought." He was describing the talk-show activity to which he has devoted a major part of his time for fifteen years. "You should not take it a hundred percent seriously. Anybody who does is a fool." Fred Barnes wrote that he was happy to appear in a mock *McLaughlin* segment on *Murphy Brown,* because "the line between news and fun barely exists anymore."

The McLaughlin Group often takes its act on the road, gimmicks and all, for fees reported to be about

$20,000 per appearance. *Crossfire* goes for paid jaunts on the road. So do panelists from *The Capital Gang.* Contracts for such appearances contain a routine clause specifying that the performance may not be taped or broadcast. This provision allows speakers to recycle their material, especially those who stitch together anecdotes about "the mood in Washington today." It also reassures the speakers that the sessions aren't really serious. They won't be held to account for what they say, so the normal standards don't apply.

Yet the fact that no one takes the shows seriously is precisely what's wrong with them, because they jeopardize the credibility of everything that journalists do. "I think one of the really destructive developments in Washington in the last fifteen years has been the rise in these reporter talk shows," Tom Brokaw has said. "Reporters used to cover policy—not spend all of their time yelling at each other and making philistine judgments about what happened the week before. It's not enlightening. It makes me cringe."

When talk shows go on the road for performances in which hostility and disagreement are staged for entertainment value; when reporters pick up thousands of dollars appearing before interest groups and sharing tidbits of what they have heard; when all the participants then dash off for the next plane, caring about none of it except the money—when these things happen, they send a message. The message is: We don't respect what we're doing. Why should anyone else?

FOOD FOR THOUGHT

1. In *Media and Democracy* Berkman and Kitch highlight the negative consequences of the media for American democracy. Can a credible argument be made about the benefits to democracy and American democratic processes brought about by contemporary political journalism? Whether or not you agree with Berkman and Kitch, play the role of devil's advocate and make the strongest possible case against their position.

2. All of the authors represented in this chapter, to some degree or another, offer well-developed critiques of media coverage of American politics and, in particular, American political institutions. We have suggested, however, that not all of the blame for the state of political journalism lies with members of the press and the journalistic profession. Choose one branch of American government and demonstrate why and how it may be responsible, at least in part, for some of the coverage that it receives. In what ways could the branch of government that you are examining try to insure that it receives "better" coverage?

3. Which branch of American government receives the best media coverage and which, in your view, receives the worst? How so? Elaborate. Is this state of affairs inevitable or does it only reflect journalistic practices of the moment?

4. Some analysts argue that the press trivializes American politics by focusing on personalities and political gamesmanship instead of on the real issues of public policy that politicians must decide. Others claim that American politicians and political institutions manipulate the press and use it to facilitate their efforts at governing effectively. Which of these statements is more accurate? Are they necessarily mutually exclusive characterizations of the relationship between the press and politics? Why or why not? Elaborate.

CHAPTER 6

POLITICAL PARTIES

In some ways American political parties are like Rodney Dangerfield—they get no respect. Some observers proclaim that they have become irrelevant parts of the American political scene or are at least well on their way to irrelevancy. Some suggest that the era of the political parties is ended altogether. Others suggest that at least one of the two present major parties will be replaced by a new party. Some are upset that they do not look like European parties and assume, often without saying so, that the European model defines the only "real" political party system.

In fact, American political parties are a very real and continuing part of our political landscape. The two major parties exist primarily to win elected office. Minor parties come and go and exist largely to push specific issues onto the political agenda. American citizens are less attached to the two major parties now than in previous years, but they are not necessarily terribly dissatisfied with them.

Political parties can be thought of as existing at three levels: in the electorate, in government, and as organizations competing for office. In the electorate they exist as objects with which large numbers of voters identify. At this level there is a partially ghostly quality to the parties. No one is quite sure what the concept of membership means. Primarily, a party member is created when an individual calls himself or herself a member of a specific party. Shifts in this self-identification are extremely important in determining election results.

Initial identification with a party tends to persist over time. For example, new voters entering the electorate during the Depression of the 1930s had many reasons to identify predominantly as Democrats. They did so then and that preference tended to continue. New voters entering during the Reagan years of the 1980s had more reasons to identify predominantly as Republicans. They did so and that tendency has persisted. Thus the electorate as a whole is made up, in a sense, of different age cohorts with differing partisan leanings. The secular trend over the last several decades has been for Republicans to gain at the expense of Democrats, but there is now less identification with either party than there was in the 1940s and 1950s.

The percentage of self-identified independents—those citizens not identifying themselves as either Republicans or Democrats—has gone up fairly steadily for the last four decades.

Parties also exist inside government. Politicians seeking the White House or seats in Congress almost all run either as Republicans or Democrats. Once in government, successful candidates for Congress create party organizations in the House and Senate. These legislative parties choose officials such as the Speaker of the House, majority leaders, minority leaders, whips, and chairs of caucuses and various party committees. Legislative party organizations are vital in conducting the business of the chambers.

The president also serves as head of his party and makes a number of his decisions based, at least in part, on partisan considerations.

The third level at which American political parties exist is organizational. Parties are formal organizations that have physical locations (with phones, faxes, street addresses, and e-mail addresses), officers, and employees. They hold meetings. These organizations raise enormous amounts of money to support campaigns for public office.

Political parties exist at virtually every level of American society. There are national party organizations, state party organizations, and county party organizations. The Republicans and Democrats are in evidence everywhere. A few other parties have some organizations, but the degree of organization is minimal.

Despite the appearance of a hierarchical arrangement—national parties as the most comprehensive, state parties as more limited, and city–county parties even more limited—there is no hierarchical arrangement. The national party organizations do not tell state parties what to do or how to behave. State parties do not control county parties. None of these bodies controls legislative parties. Parties also vary enormously in terms of organizational sophistication and strength.

Until very recently it could accurately be claimed that the weakest party organizations were those at the national level. State and local party organizations were much more important. That is no longer the case. Ironically, increasing numbers of candidates have for several decades been conducting election campaigns that downplay their party affiliation. The "Democrat" or "Republican" on campaign signs is sometimes simply absent or, at minimum, in very small type. All kinds of analysts proclaim that the era of "candidate-centered campaigns" has replaced the era of "party-centered campaigns." That is true in many senses; yet the insatiable demand for campaign money has made party organizations—including those at the national level—more important.

The first reading in this chapter, "The Revitalization of National Party Organizations" by Paul Herrnson, explores the importance of national party organizations for campaign fund-raising and dispersion of those funds. He also explores the importance of these party organizations in providing campaign expertise and information useful for successful campaigning.

Interest groups have a particularly complicated relationship with political parties. Both parties and interest groups are major mediators between broad, unfocused public opinion and government. But they engage in different activities. Political parties at various territorial levels are in existence primarily to nominate candidates, help finance and otherwise aid campaigns, and win elections. Interest groups have, by definition, specific interests to pursue—both through elections and through the daily working of governmental agencies and institutions, executive, legislative, bureaucratic, and even judicial.

Interest groups also try to influence parties to nominate candidates most favorable to their interests, fund those with the greatest chance of winning, and urge the candidates to feature the interest groups' favored issues in appealing to the electorate.

At the same time, the political parties try to co-opt various interest groups. The parties want financial support from interest groups and interest group Political Action Committees for campaigns. They want the votes of the interest group activists.

In broad terms, political parties as organizations are coalitions of other formal groups and clusters of individuals who perceive they have common interests. Parties constantly woo groups and clusters to add them to the coalition.

In a large and diverse nation parties need to patch together a winning electoral coalition. They and their pollsters will target groups in the electorate—the famed "angry white males" in the 1994 congressional elections or the "soccer moms" in the 1996 presidential election serve as good examples—for special attention. This is a different form of coalition-building that is focused on elections. We will discuss it in the next chapter, which is about elections.

Marjorie Randon Hershey, in "Citizens' Groups and Political Parties in the United States," the second reading in this chapter, explores several aspects of the relationship between political parties and interest groups.

Neither major American political party is monolithic in its beliefs, let alone organization. Each of the two parties is constantly redefining itself. Between presidential elections there is no particular pressure to come up with any kind of coherent definition of positions on issues. The localism of American politics and the ideological diversity of individuals bearing the same nominal party label do not bother the voters.

The third reading, "The Making of the New Democrats" by Jon Hale, explores how forces within the Democratic Party moved it from being a reliably liberal party toward the center of the political spectrum in the years before Clinton's nomination in 1992.

In the fourth reading, Stephen Nichols, in "Independent Presidential Candidates in the Candidate-Centered Age: A Window of Opportunity," argues that the changing importance of the two dominant parties opens new possibilities for independent presidential candidates. The fifth reading in the chapter is

"An End to Politics as Usual" by Everett Carll Ladd. He puts the growing attractiveness of independent presidential candidates in a broader context. He argues that it is only one symptom of many that, in his view, shows increasing alienation of the American public from American political parties.

| READING 26 |

The Revitalization of National Party Organizations

Paul S. Herrnson

For much of the 20th century the national parties barely existed in any meaningful fashion. The party organizations that mattered were in some states and large cities. But the national party organizations have become increasingly important in the last several decades.

The Democratic National Committee was formed in 1848. The Republicans created their national committee in 1856. Both parties established separate campaign committees for the House of Representatives just after the Civil War. Both parties created Senate campaign committees in 1916 after a constitutional amendment made Senate seats popularly elected. During much of their existence these committees had relatively little power and were often overshadowed by state and local party organizations. Over the last several decades party-centered campaigns began to be replaced by candidate-centered campaigns, a development that seemed to militate against important central party committees.

In this reading, political scientist Paul Herrnson describes how the needs of candidates—still running

From "The Revitalization of National Party Organizations" by P. S. Herrnson. Approximately 15 pages from *The Parties Respond: Changes in American Parties and Campaigns, Second Ed.,* ed. by L. S. Maisel. Copyright © 1994 by Westview Press. Reprinted by permission of Westview Press.

with a party label although not in a group as a party slate—helped the central party bodies revive and become more important. As he puts it: "The increased needs of candidates for greater access to expertise, political information, and money created an opportunity for national and some state party organizations to become the repositories of these electoral resources."

He concludes with the observation that "American political parties are principally electoral institutions." And he notes that they have recaptured considerable importance in the new era of candidate-centered elections. In the election of 1996 both parties raised huge amounts of money at the center. Some of the fund-raising—for example, from foreign interests—was subject to serious question. Near the end of the campaign both major party presidential candidates somewhat lamely supported campaign finance reform—a topic about which they had done little in their positions of power before the campaign.

Once characterized as poor, unstable, and powerless, national party organizations in the United States are now financially secure, institutionally stable, and highly influential in election campaigns and in their relations with state and local party committees. The national party organizations—the Democratic and Republican national, congressional, and senatorial campaign committees—have adapted to the candidate-centered, money-driven, "high-tech" style of modern campaign politics....

Although the party decline was a gradual process that took its greatest toll on party organizations at the local level, party renewal occurred over a relatively short period and was focused primarily in Washington, D.C. The dynamics of recent national party organizational development bear parallels to changes that occurred in earlier periods. The content of recent national party organizational renewal was shaped by the changing needs of candidates. The new-style campaigning that became prevalent during the 1960s placed a premium on campaign activities requiring technical expertise and in-depth research. Some candidates were able to run a viable campaign using their own funds or talent. Others turned to political consultants, PACs, and special interests for help. However, many candidates found it difficult to assemble the money and expertise needed to compete in a modern election. The increased needs of candidates for greater access to technical expertise, political information, and money created an opportunity for national and some state party organizations to become the repositories of these electoral resources.

Nevertheless, national party organizations did not respond to changes in the political environment until electoral crises forced party leaders to recognize the institutional and electoral weaknesses of the national party organizations. As was the case during earlier eras of party transformation, crises that heightened office holders' electoral anxieties furnished party leaders with the opportunities and incentives to augment the parties' organizational apparatuses. Entrepreneurial party leaders recognized that they might receive payoffs for restructuring the national party organizations so that they could better assist candidates and state and local party committees with their election efforts....

INSTITUTIONALIZED NATIONAL PARTIES

The institutionalization of the national party organizations refers to their becoming fiscally solvent, organizationally stable, and larger and more diversified in their staffing and to their adopting professional-bureaucratic decisionmaking procedures. These changes were nec-

essary for the national parties to develop election-related and party-building functions.

Finances

National party fund raising improved greatly in the late 1970s and 1980s. During this period the national parties raised more money from more sources and using more varied approaches than ever before. The information presented in Table 6.1 indicates that the Republican committees raised more money than did their Democratic rivals in all seven election cycles (but also that, following the 1980 election, the Democrats began to narrow the gap in fund raising)....

Most national party money is raised in the form of direct-mail contributions of under $100. Telephone solicitations also are used to raise both small and large contributions. Traditional fund-raising dinners, parties, and other events experienced a revival as important vehicles for collecting large contributions from individual donors during the 1988 election....

Infrastructure

Success in fund raising has enabled the national parties to invest in the development of their organizational infrastructures. Prior to their institutionalization, the national party organizations had no permanent headquarters. For a while, the four Hill committees were

TABLE 6.1 National Party Receipts 1976–1992 (in million $)

PARTY	1976	1978	1980	1982	1984	1986	1988	1990	1992
Democrats									
DNC	13.1	11.3	15.4	16.5	46.6	17.2	52.3	14.5	65.8
DCCC	.9	2.8	2.9	6.5	10.4	12.3	12.5	9.1	12.8
DSCC	1.0	.3	1.7	5.6	8.9	13.4	16.3	17.5	25.5
Total	15.0	14.4	20.0	28.6	65.9	42.9	81.1	41.1	104.1
Republicans									
RNC	29.1	34.2	77.8	84.1	105.9	83.8	91.0	68.7	85.4
NRCC	12.1	14.1	20.3	58.0	58.3	39.8	34.5	33.8	34.4
NRSC	1.8	10.9	22.3	48.9	81.7	84.1	65.9	65.1	72.3
Total	43.1	59.2	120.4	191.0	245.9	209.7	191.4	167.6	192.1

Source: Federal Election Commission.

quartered in small offices in congressional office buildings. Upon leaving congressional office space they became transient, following the national committees' example of moving at the end of each election cycle in search of cheap office space. The national parties' lack of permanent office space created security problems, made it difficult for them to conduct routine business, and did little to bolster their standing in Washington.

All six national party organizations are now housed in party-owned headquarters buildings located only a few blocks from the Capitol. The headquarters buildings furnish the committees with convenient locations for carrying out fund-raising events and holding meetings with candidates, PACs, journalists, and campaign consultants. They also provide a secure environment for the committees' computers, records, and radio and television studios. The multimillion-dollar studios, each of which is owned by one of the congressional campaign committees, allow the parties to produce professional-quality campaign commercials for their candidates.

Staff

Each national party organization has a two-tiered structure consisting of members and professional staff. The members of the Republican and Democratic national committees are selected by their state parties, and the members of the Hill committees are selected by their colleagues in Congress. The national parties' staffs have grown tremendously in recent years. Republican committee staff development accelerated following the party's Watergate scandal, whereas the Democratic party experienced most of its staff growth after the 1980 election. In 1992 the DNC, DCCC, and DSCC employed 270, 64, and 35 full-time staff, respectively, whereas their Republican counterparts had 300, 89, and 135 full-time employees. Committee staffs are divided along functional lines; different divisions are responsible for administration, fund raising, research, communications, and campaign activities. The staffs have a great deal of autonomy in running the committees and are extremely influential in formulating their campaign strategies. In the case of the NRCC, for example, committee members have adopted a

"hands-off" attitude toward committee operations similar to that of a board of directors.

Party Building

The institutionalization of the national party organizations has provided them with the resources to develop a variety of party-building programs. The vast majority of these are conducted by the two national committees. Many current RNC party-building efforts were initiated in 1976 under the leadership of Chairman Brock. Brock's program for revitalizing state party committees consisted of (1) appointing regional political directors to assist state party leaders in strengthening their organizations and utilizing RNC services; (2) hiring organizational directors to help rebuild state party organizations; (3) appointing regional finance directors to assist state parties with developing fund-raising programs; (4) making computer services available to state parties for accounting, fund raising, and analyzing survey data; and (5) organizing a task force to assist parties with developing realistic election goals and strategies. Brock also established a Local Elections Campaign Division to assist state parties with creating district profiles and recruiting candidates, to provide candidate training and campaign management seminars, and to furnish candidates for state or local office with onsite campaign assistance.

Frank Fahrenkopf, RNC chair from 1981 to 1988, expanded many of Brock's party-building programs and introduced some new ones.... The DNC's party-building activities lagged behind those of its Republican counterpart and did not become significant until the 1986 election. During that election Chairman Paul Kirk created a task force of thirty-two professional consultants who were sent to sixteen states to assist Democratic state committees with fund raising, computerizing voter lists, and other organizational activities. In 1988, the task force went to another sixteen states to help organize and strengthen their Democratic state committees. The task forces are credited with improving Democratic state party fund raising, computer capacities, and voter-mobilization programs and with helping Democratic state and local committees reach the stage of organizational development achieved by their Republican rivals in earlier years.

National committee party-building programs have succeeded in strengthening, modernizing, and professionalizing many state and local party organizations. Agency agreements between the Hill committees and state party organizations further contribute to these efforts by encouraging state parties to spend their money on organizational development, state and local elections, and generic party campaigning rather than on House and Senate elections. These programs have altered the balance of power within the parties' organizational apparatuses. The national parties' ability to distribute or withhold party-building or campaign assistance gives them influence over the operations of state and local party committees. The DNC's influence is enhanced by its rule-making and enforcement authority. As a result of these developments, the traditional flow of power upward from state and local party organizations to the national committees has been complemented by a new flow of power downward from the national parties to state and local parties. The institutionalization of the national party organizations has enabled them to become more influential in party politics and has led to a greater federalization of the American party system.

NATIONAL PARTY CAMPAIGNING

The institutionalization of the national parties has provided them the wherewithal to play a larger role in elections, and national party campaign activity has increased tremendously since the 1970s. Yet the electoral activities of the national parties, and of party organizations in general, remain constricted by the electoral law, established custom, and the level of resources in the parties' possession.

Candidate Recruitment and Nominations

Most candidates for elective office in the United States are self-recruited and conduct their own nominating campaigns. The DNC and the RNC have a hand in establishing the basic guidelines under which presidential nominations are contested, but their role is defined by the national conventions and their rec-

ommendations are subject to convention approval. The rules governing Democratic presidential nominations are more extensive than are those governing GOP contests, but state committees of both parties have substantial leeway in supplying the details of their delegate-selection processes.

Neither the DNC nor the RNC expresses a preference for candidates during its party's presidential nomination. Such activity would be disastrous should a candidate who was backed by a national committee be defeated, because the successful, unsupported candidate would become the head of the party's ticket and its titular leader. As a result, candidates for the nomination assemble their own campaign staffs and compete independently of the party apparatus in state-run primaries and caucuses. Successful candidates arrive at the national conventions with seasoned campaign organizations composed of experienced political operatives.

The national party organizations, however, may get involved in selected nominating contests for House, Senate, and state-level offices. . . .

The General Election

Presidential Elections.   Party activity in presidential elections is restricted by the public-funding provisions of the FECA. Major party candidates who accept public funding are prohibited from accepting contributions from any other sources, including the political parties. The amount that the national parties can spend directly on behalf of their presidential candidates is also limited. In 1992, George Bush and Bill Clinton each received $55.2 million in general election subsidies, and the national committees were each allowed to spend approximately $10.3 million directly on behalf of their candidates.

The legal environment reinforces the candidate-centeredness of presidential elections in other ways. Rules requiring candidates for the nomination to compete in primaries and caucuses guarantee that successful candidates will enter the general election with their own sources of technical expertise, in-depth research, and connections with journalists and other Washington elites. These reforms combine with the FECA to create a regulatory framework that limits national party activity and influence in presidential elections.

Nevertheless, the national parties do play an important role in presidential elections. The national committees furnish presidential campaigns with legal and strategic advice and public relations assistance. National committee opposition research and archives serve as important sources of political information. The money that the national committees spend directly on behalf of their candidates can boost the total resources under the candidates' control by more than 15 percent. The national committees also assist their candidates' campaigns by distributing "soft money" to state parties so they can finance voter-mobilization drives and party-building activities....

Congressional Elections.   The national party organizations play a larger role in congressional elections than in presidential campaigns. The national parties contribute money and campaign services directly to congressional candidates. The parties provide candidates with transactional assistance that helps them obtain campaign resources from political consultants and PACs. Most national party assistance is distributed by the Hill committees to candidates competing in close elections, especially those who are nonincumbents. This arrangement reflects the committees' goal of maximizing the number of congressional seats under their control....

Even though individuals and PACs still furnish candidates with most of their campaign funds, political parties are currently the largest single source of campaign money for most candidates. Party money comes from one, or at most a few, organizations that are concerned with one goal—the election of their candidates. Individual and PAC contributions, however, come from a multitude of sources that are motivated by a variety of concerns. In addition, it is important to recognize that, dollar for dollar, national party money has greater value than the contributions of other groups. National party contributions are often given early and function as "seed money" that candidates use to generate more funds. National party contributions and coordinated expenditures often take the form of in-kind campaign services that are worth many times more than their reported value. Moreover,

national party money and transactional assistance help candidates attract additional money from PACs.

The national parties also furnish many congressional candidates with campaign services ranging from legal advice to assistance with campaign advertising. The national parties distribute most of their services to competitive contestants, especially those who are nonincumbents. National party help is more likely to have an impact on the outcomes of these candidates' elections than on those incumbents holding safe seats or of nonincumbents challenging them....

CONCLUSION

American political parties are principally electoral institutions. They focus more on elections and less on initiating policy change than do parties in other Western democracies. American national party organizations were created to perform electoral functions. They developed in response to changes in their environment and the changing needs of their candidates. National party organizational change occurs sporadically. Electoral instability and political unrest have occasionally given party leaders opportunities to restructure the national parties. The most recent waves of party organizational development followed the turbulent 1968 Democratic convention, the Republicans' post-Watergate landslide losses, and the Democrats' traumatic defeat in 1980. These crises provided both opportunities and incentives for party entrepreneurs to restructure the roles and missions of the national, congressional, and senatorial campaign committees.

The result of this restructuring is that the national parties are now stronger, more stable, and more influential in their relations with state and local party committees and candidates than ever before. National party programs have led to the modernization of many state and local party committees. The national parties also play an important role in contemporary elections. They assist presidential candidates with their campaigns. They give congressional candidates campaign contributions, make coordinated expenditures on their behalf, and provide services in areas of campaigning that require technical expertise, in-depth research, or connections with political consultants, PACs, or other organizations possessing the resources needed to conduct a modern campaign. The national parties provide similar types of assistance to candidates for state and local offices. Although most national party activity is concentrated in competitive districts, candidates of varying degrees of competitiveness benefit from party mass media advertisements and voter-mobilization drives. The 1980s witnessed the reemergence of national party organizations as important players in party politics and elections.

<hr>

READING 27

Citizens' Groups and Political Parties in the United States

Marjorie Randon Hershey

A frequently heard argument is that American political parties are becoming weaker in part because interest groups have become stronger and more independent of parties. This argument assumes that parties and interest groups (called "citizens' groups" in this article) are involved in a zero sum game for the loyalties and energies of citizens—that is, a citizen will choose one or the other if he or she seeks to be involved in a mediating institution.

Marjorie Hershey, a political science professor, explores the complex relationship between interest groups and political parties in a more sophisticated way. She acknowledges that there are elements of competition between parties and interest groups for the loyalty and energy of citizens. But she also discusses how parties and interest groups often work together for a common end. And she discusses a third kind of relationship—one in which groups seek to take over a party organization from within.

The view that groups and parties are natural enemies is partially inaccurate. Sometimes groups and parties reinforce each other and seek the same

general end. Sometimes interest groups do make life difficult for parties.

The 1996 Republican campaign for the presidency displayed a cluster of groups centered around the Christian Coalition both capturing the party and yet at odds with it. The very conservative Christian groups won virtually all the battles over specific provisions in the Republican platform. However, the Republican nominee, Bob Dole, paid little attention to the platform and did not run on the issues important to the conservative Christians.

The 1996 Democratic campaign presents a mirror image. The labor unions had little impact on the Democratic platform. And the renomination of President Bill Clinton was never in doubt. The unions worked for Clinton's election because the alternative was worse. They worked especially diligently for the election of more Democrats to the House and Senate because this is where they thought more supporters would be critical.

<hr>

Exercising popular control over government is not among most people's favorite daily activities. Instead, we rely on intermediary institutions such as political parties, interest groups, and the media of mass communication to gather and spread information about candidates, track the progress of public issues, monitor the ethics of leaders, and simplify the choices that the public is asked to make. Without these intermediaries, it is difficult to imagine how a democracy could function in a nation of 250 million people.

Political scientists' research on the workings of intermediaries has heavily emphasized parties and interest groups, with a strong normative presumption in favor of the former. As Jack Walker put it, when most political scientists are asked to judge whether parties or interest groups are preferable as a means of mobilizing citizens, "the parties win, hands down." Parties are typically regarded as the only intermediaries capable of aggregating broad sets of interests and providing coherent leadership in the American setting. Citizens' and other interest groups, in contrast, are thought to polarize legislators and citizens, speak primarily for narrow interests, and prevent the parties from performing their vital organizing role.

From "Citizens' Groups and Political Parties in the United States" by M. R. Hershey, *Annals of the American Academy of Political and Social Science* (528), pp. 142–156. Copyright © 1993 by Sage Publications. Reprinted by permission of Sage Publications, Inc.

These two types of intermediaries, then, are usually described as competitors: when one gains strength, it causes the other to weaken. And when it is the parties that weaken, democracy suffers. But is that necessarily so? Are citizens' groups an antiparty development, or can they be integrated into existing patterns of partisan politics? This article will examine the links between citizens' groups and the political parties: the ways in which these groups compete with parties, work with or use the parties, or circumvent party organizations. . . .

CITIZENS' GROUPS AND THE POLITICAL PARTIES

There is a complex relationship between parties and citizens' groups, described by Sorauf as one of "mixed competition and cooperation." Both parties and groups recruit leaders and mediate interests. Both want power; they help elect their allies to office by giving money and training campaigners. Both also want to affect public policy, through developing programs and influencing policymakers and the public. They differ, in part, in terms of their emphasis. The traditional view is that citizens' and other interest groups focus on issues and policies, whereas parties are primarily concerned with winning power. . . .

Are the American Parties in Decline?

Political parties in the United States have always faced an ambivalent climate of opinion. The early leaders of the republic, including George Washington, expressed intense hostility toward parties and other "factions"—even though many of these same leaders were instrumental in the development of a party system within the next decade. This ambivalence has affected the strength and coherence of the parties they created and those that followed, which have tended to be less unified, disciplined, and ideological than their counterparts in other nations.

Party organizations reached their pinnacle in the patronage-rich era of the late 1800s. But they soon fell under successful attack by the Progressive movement of the early 1900s. As the Progressive-sponsored direct primary was adopted by states, for instance, parties lost much of their power over nominations. The party machines were also weakened by pressures for professionalization in the delivery of services and by the post-World War II expansion of the middle class and the movement into the suburbs, where people were out of the reach of, and had less need of, the urban party's services.

So the recent increase in citizens' groups could not have caused the phenomenon of party decline in general, because several aspects of party functioning had been weak or in decline long before these groups appeared; indeed, the climate had been hostile to parties well before the Progressive movement. Further, other aspects of party functioning either held their own or gained strength while citizens' groups have been on the rise. Party cohesion in Congress, normally limited, reached an all-time low in the late 1960s but then increased through the 1980s. Party organizations showed no evidence of weakening in the 1960s and 1970s. In fact, the parties' national organizations—especially that of the Republicans—are now better funded and more active in the provision of services than ever before.

But there was substantial further erosion of one important party function during the 1960s and 1970s: citizens' attachment to parties. It could be seen in declines in the proportion of strong partisans, positive evaluations of the parties, and straight-ticket voting. The erosion halted later; with the first Reagan administration came an increase in the proportion of party-identified individuals. But the parties' current relationships with voters have not yet recovered to pre-1960 levels.

One reason was the increasing educational level of voters. The party label can be an important cue to citizens who must make large numbers of choices in an election without much information. As educational levels and literacy increased, however, voters could process more complex cues than "Democrat" and "Republican." Indeed, in the large number of cities with nonpartisan elections—also a Progressive reform—party cues were of little help.

Alternative sources of political information were also proliferating at this time. In addition to radio and newspapers, television was becoming a more important source of information about candidates and issues, and after the mid-1960s, direct mail provided still more cues. The mass media were coming to rival the parties as intermediaries between government and citizens—and access to the media did not depend on party loyalty. Parties became less important to voters, cognitively and emotionally, than they had been in the 1950s.

Another cause of this erosion was the change in issues that catalyzed public attention beginning in the 1960s. Questions arose concerning women's rights, environmental issues, abortion, [and] nuclear energy, constituting what Russell J. Dalton has called "the agenda of advanced industrial societies." According to Dalton, this agenda "often appears unsuited for mass political parties.... [The parties] are reluctant to take clear positions on these issues because of the uncertain electoral benefits." The issues are too narrow to bring in major new party support, and in many cases they have the potential to split the established parties. While increasingly sophisticated citizens paid more attention to these new and complex issues, the major parties remained wedded to the old New Deal issues, "the Old Politics cleavage of class and religion." Their group ties showed the same pattern, with the Democrats remaining close to organized labor and the Republicans to business. But by clinging to the old alignments, the parties have not been able to escape the pull of the new issues; New Left activists have rent the Democratic Party, as have New Right elements in the Republican Party.

These declines in voter attachment to the major parties during the 1960s and 1970s occurred just at the time that the number of citizens' groups, and citizens' attachment to them, were increasing (see Figure 6.1). As is discussed elsewhere in this volume, large proportions of citizens' groups were founded in these two decades, resulting in "an explosion in the number of groups representing the interests of broad publics and the disadvantaged."

These new groups were motivated by the very issues that proved so damaging to citizens' relationships with the major parties. Thus they were quickly expected to challenge the parties' role as primary political intermediaries. In addition, as citizens' groups worked to promote their views, they came increasingly to see partisan politics as a relevant terrain and

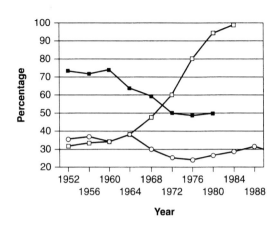

- ■ — Percentage expressing a positive evaluation of at least one of the two major parties.
- ○ — Percentage claiming to be strong Democrats or strong Republicans.
- □ — Cumulative proportion of citizens' groups by the year of their founding. Note that this data line starts at 32 percent because 32 percent of all citizens' groups existing in 1983 had been founded prior to 1952.

FIGURE 6.1 Indicators of decline in voters' party attachments and in expansion of citizens' groups.

thus to place new demands on the parties. The threat to party cohesion soon became apparent. For example, pro-life groups' efforts to get the Republican Party to work for a ban on all abortions were successful beginning in 1980, but at the cost of ongoing conflicts not only with pro-choice Republicans but with party activists who feel that hot-button issues distract from the traditional Republican agenda....

IN WHAT WAYS DO CITIZENS' GROUPS WEAKEN THE PARTIES?

How might citizens' groups cause or encourage party decline? One possibility is that groups and parties compete for the same resources—citizens' emotional attachments and their time and money—so that when citizens' groups get more, the parties get less. In the 1950s, someone fascinated by the arms race might have felt that the best way to make a difference in that area was to become a party activist; there were not many alternative means. With the decline in partisan loyalties, he or she might seek another organizational avenue of influence, joining groups such as Americans for Peace, SANE, or Nuclear Freeze, many of which did not exist in the 1950s. To Berry, these groups channel people away from party work. "The essence of the public interest philosophy is that party politics cannot be trusted. Parties are impure; they stand for compromise rather than hard-fought principles."

The antiparty message may not take, of course. The vivid, dramatic, and often negative appeals that citizens' groups must make in order to attract media coverage, and thus public support, have a short half-life; their impact decays rapidly, according to Salisbury, on both public opinion and policymakers. There is little evidence that people who join such groups consequently withdraw their support from a political party; in fact, research shows that most politically active people who take part in party politics are also associated with one or more interest groups. Nevertheless, the simple existence of larger numbers of citizens' groups offers individuals an avenue outside the parties through which to become involved in campaigns and issues—an avenue that has greatly expanded in the last two decades.

Citizens' groups expand the options for candidates as well. The more group money that comes into campaigns, the less candidates need to rely on other sources of funds, including their party's. In the late 1960s and early 1970s, new campaign techniques such as increased use of television and polling left candidates in critical need of cash. The parties of that time were not well designed to fill the need. Political action committees (PACs), some formed by citizens' groups, moved into the void. These new PACs also put interest groups in more direct competition with parties, by giving groups a more secure role in the campaigning process, which is the parties' primary focus.

The parties might have tried to ally with citizens' groups at that time, to help guide the competition. But that proved difficult to do. Structural differences worked against cooperation; because many citizens' groups were not highly structured, cohesive organizations with a stable membership that could reliably deliver votes, the parties had less incentive to seek them as allies. Nor were many groups eager to choose sides in partisan politics; that would limit their access to legislators of the other party.

The protest and unconventional political tactics used by citizens' groups can also compete with the parties' ability to gain media attention and set the public agenda. The outside strategy that citizens' groups follow, seeking media coverage in order to gain members and do grass-roots lobbying, may, especially during campaigns, compete with the parties' grass-roots activities.

CAN CITIZENS' GROUPS AND PARTIES COMPLEMENT ONE ANOTHER?

In more recent years, however, the increasing involvement of citizens' groups in elections has probably brought about a closer relationship with the parties. As Walker argues, the Reagan administration's ideological and partisan tone, expressed particularly in its effort to "defund the [interest group] left," was the cause. During the Reagan years, ideological compatibility with the administration's goals seemed to be a prerequisite for groups seeking cooperation from the administration, to a greater extent than before. Because Reagan was attempting to make basic changes in the nature of public policy, large numbers of liberal groups found their favorite programs in jeopardy. It became clear that the results of presidential elections would affect their ability to achieve their policy goals. As the ideological polarization continued, in Walker's view, citizens' groups and other interest groups were pushed into contending conservative and liberal camps. Political parties, becoming more ideologically distinct themselves, were in a good position to lead these coalitions. These groups therefore found themselves "being drawn into alliances with one of the two major political parties in order to protect their futures, whether they like[d] it or not."

This is not unprecedented, of course; consider the lengthy, close relationship between the Democratic Party and the American Federation of Labor and Congress of Industrial Organizations. This relationship has taken on a new dimension, however, with the increase in PACs, including those of citizens' groups. In recent years, the fastest-growing category of PACs has been the "non-connected" category, most of which are ideological organizations. Both parties—and especially the Republicans—have begun working with PACs to fund campaigns. PAC liaisons have been appointed to share information about candidates and legislation of mutual interest. The parties select close races where interest group money could make a difference and then guide groups to targeted candidates with compatible stands. This clearly benefits the parties, whose contributions to targeted candidates are augmented by citizens' groups' money. It also helps the more partisan and ideological PACs, because it provides information—about the election chances and policy stands of candidates—that would otherwise be more costly.

Since the early 1980s, a few citizens' groups' PACs have begun to follow the lead of labor PACs in taking on partylike functions, such as registering voters. Most citizens' groups, however, have not taken these further steps into the electoral arena. Their PACs' efforts consist mainly of soliciting and making campaign contributions, rather than offering expertise and services to candidates. The parent groups' efforts are centered around the articulation of new issues, many of which the major parties are not prepared to champion. "Seen in this light, the two forms of political organization are complementary and together constitute a much more responsive and adaptive system than either would be if they somehow operated on their own."

In short, although the relationship between citizens' groups and parties is potentially conflict filled, there has been recent movement in the direction of greater complementarity....

When Citizens' Groups Work from Within

The picture changes, however, when we examine the activities of citizens' groups within the parties, with respect to presidential nominations. Citizens' groups may become involved in the internal dynamics of the major parties for several reasons. For one, the American party system is not nearly as hospitable to the workings of third parties as are many European party systems. If citizens' groups are to be involved in partisan politics, then, they must expect to deal with the two existing parties.

Second, groups were virtually invited to become involved by the Democratic Party reforms of the 1970s. The reforms encouraged a shift from a party-based to a candidate-based system of presidential nominations. Reformers had assumed that once the party bosses were out of the way, their place in the process would be taken by a more representative set of grass-roots activists. Candidates, however, still needed an organizational base for winning delegates. A variety of citizens' and other interest groups provided a ready alternative, in the form of an organized base of supporters, funds, and endorsements.

The groups that gained the most from this change were those capable of affecting the results of the reform-produced primaries and caucuses: groups that could turn out small armies of members in a large number of states, especially those with early or otherwise important delegate-selection events. Groups most able to turn out large numbers were those whose members were highly dedicated to a cause—in short, citizens' groups. The groups benefited as well. Prior to the reforms, citizens' and other groups had to work through the party organizations in order to affect presidential campaigns, but that diluted their influence. After the reforms, they could gain more direct access.

The change left a giant imprint on the national party conventions. The organized interests that had long held sway—labor unions in the Democratic Party and business associations in the Republican—now had to fight to be heard. The ideological motivation of citizens' groups meant that rhetoric and demands within the convention became less moderate, and, to some, more radicalized, than when party leaders were clearly in control of the process and could serve as effective brokers. Presidential nominations and campaigns became less predictable. A reaction quickly set in, led by an effort to bring back the "peer review" that party leaders serving as convention delegates could provide. But that only highlighted the irony, as Shafer notes, that the official party had been transformed into yet another organized interest.

The increasing role of citizens' groups has been felt more in Democratic Party functions than in Republican. It was the Democratic Party in which the participatory reforms began and where they reached full flower. Further, the grass-roots character—or perhaps the ideological slant—of many citizens' groups may be tolerated better by the Democratic nominating process, given its greater emphasis on participation. To Jo Freeman, the bigger role of citizens' groups within the Democratic Party is explained by its coalitional nature. Because power in the party flows upward from its various constituency groups, the Democrats are more permeable to organized pressure, whereas in the Republican Party, which is more unitary, the greater deference to the leadership tends to discourage competing group loyalties.

The prominence of feminist groups in the Democratic nominating process shows the extent to which citizens' groups have penetrated the post-reform party. Feminist groups were virtual outsiders when they first made demands on the party at the 1972 Democratic convention. But by the 1980s, once the party had come to perceive them as a prospective source of group support at a time when other such sources were diminishing, feminist organizations had become an important force within the nominating process. At the 1980 Democratic convention, more than one in five delegates were members of the National Women's Political Caucus or the National Organization for Women (NOW). Organized groups of feminist delegates successfully lobbied the convention to adopt a platform plank calling for government funding of abortions for poor women. Feminist strength was even more evident in 1984, when a vice president of NOW served on the platform committee, where she was "given the leading role on matters of concern to NOW." Women's groups' preferences were also heard in the choice of the vice presidential nominee, Representative Geraldine Ferraro. The visible influence of feminist groups in that convention led to concern by some Democrats that the party was perceived as the captive of special interests. Yet in 1988, feminist groups' issues were again negotiated into the platform, over the initial objections of Democratic National Chair Paul Kirk. Several sets of citizens' groups, including women and gays, won formal recognition as "official caucuses" of the Democratic National Committee in the early 1980s....

IMPLICATIONS FOR AMERICAN POLITICS

...[T]he impact of citizens' groups on the American parties is complex. These groups are not necessarily party wreckers. For instance, the competition posed by citizens' groups seems to have prompted the national party organizations to respond by becoming more institutionalized and more active in fundraising and service delivery. To a great extent, these party and group changes are part of the same broader social changes: rising educational levels, making comprehension of new issues possible; increased access to mass media, expanding the options for intermediation; a more affluent public, permitting more groups to survive on public contributions; and a government of broader scope, touching more aspects of people's lives, thus provoking more groups to form.

But the discussion of these shared influences should not obscure some very real dangers to the parties. Unquestionably, citizens' groups have benefited from the (at least temporary) weakening of voters' psychological attachments to the major parties and may help to further undermine them. In addition, the expanded participation of these groups in the parties' nominating processes can, in some cases, bring party organizations to the brink of internal warfare. Do these changes strengthen or weaken democracy?

It is frequently alleged that because some aspects of parties have been weakened, there has been undesirable change in the policy process, which has become more fragmented, less stable, and less predictable. In theory, at least, strong parties can provide broad and coherent alternatives for citizens, counter the fragmenting influence of interest groups, and give less advantaged people a chance to be heard....

It is accurate to state that the policy process has become less stable during this time. The stable system of subgovernments that had formerly been described as dominating some policy areas has often given way to a more volatile system of issue networks with an expanded set of players. But is that undesirable?...

With respect to the representativeness of the system, researchers differ as to whether the rise of citizens' groups is beneficial or worrisome. In general, interest politics tend to amplify the voices of narrow, well-organized groups, which are disproportionately well educated and upper income. The interests of broad publics and disadvantaged groups can probably be more effectively represented through the parties and the electoral system.

On the other hand, parties do not always excel at aggregating diverse interests. They do not always work hard to mobilize the public or to facilitate coordination between branches of government. Nor are citizens' groups necessarily the narrow, selfish factions that interest groups are thought to be. Citizens' groups often represent segments of American society that have not made their voices heard in the past, and thus can help to reduce inequalities between interests. With their assertive use of the mass media, citizens' groups may force concerns onto the public agenda that might otherwise be overlooked....

These changes in the parties may not, then, pose a danger to representation in one sense. But they may well enhance another sort of threat to representation, by expanding the maneuvering room available to political leaders. The destabilization of the policy process and the increase in citizens' group participation mean that officials probably have more discretion to select policy alternatives; almost any alternative will have some group support....

The greatest danger, then, would be a weakening of the processes of deliberation and mediation, which interest groups and parties can provide, in favor of an increasing dominance of elected leaders—especially presidents—with a direct, unmediated, personality-based relationship with their constituents. Whether citizens' groups continue to splinter the parties, complement them, or form new ones, their relationships with the party system will help shape the responsiveness and policy capability of American politics.

READING 28

The Making of the New Democrats

Jon F. Hale

American political parties do not maintain a fixed set of policy commitments over a long period of time. They change positions in the quest for electoral victory. Our two major national parties have been

---

From "The Making of the New Democrats" by J. F. Hale. Reprinted with permission from *Political Science Quarterly*, vol. 110, no. 2 (1995), pp. 207–232.

continuously in existence and nationally competitive for a long time: the Democrats since the 1820s and the Republicans since the late 1850s. But where they stand on issues and in relation to each other is in continuous flux.

The article from which this reading is drawn is by Jon Hale, a political science professor at the University of Oklahoma. Most of the original article describes in detail how the Democratic Leadership Council, a group of moderate elected Democrats created in 1985, helped reshape the public image of the party so that it was viewed as centrist enough to elect a Democratic president, Bill Clinton, in 1992. The beginning and the conclusion of the article are presented here because they deal with the broader lessons of the 1985–1992 experience.

Movement of the Democratic Party away from many left-liberal positions meant that Bill Clinton could try to win without being saddled with positions that had helped the Democrats lose five of the six presidential elections between 1968 and 1988. After winning in 1992, Clinton, in the first two years of his first term, abandoned much of the "new Democrat" image, was severely chastened by the congressional election in 1994 that produced Republican majorities in both houses, reinvented himself as a centrist once again, and won reelection—along with a Republican-controlled House and Senate—in 1996.

This reading underscores the fact that the major American parties are not static ideologically. The party not in control of the White House has a special stake in pondering the necessity of redefining some of its policy positions.

Each of the major parties contains a number of active factions that are trying to define the party along lines they each desire. A great deal of policy competition in the United States takes place within the two major parties, not just between them. American political parties are, by definition, coalitions of factions and interests that often disagree with each other on specifics. This fact helps guarantee policy change. The emergence of candidate-centered politics has not altered the core fact that internal competition shapes the ultimate policy positions taken by the parties.

In 1992, a "new" Democratic party was presented to Americans as Bill Clinton captured the party's nomination and won the presidency. Clinton's oft-made assertion that he was "a different kind of Democrat" was meant to suggest to voters a centrist candidate more attuned than his immediate predecessors to the concerns and values of the white, middle-class voters who had deserted the party in its losing presidential campaigns in the 1980s. The prominent use of the phrases "New Democrat" and "a different kind of Democrat" by the Clinton campaign gave clear indication of its perception that the preexisting identity of the national Democratic party was a handicap that needed to be overcome for Bill Clinton to be elected president. Clinton did not want to be regarded as a Democrat in the line of Michael Dukakis, Walter Mondale, Jimmy Carter, and George McGovern. The New Democrat rhetoric, however, was not simply campaign rhetoric concocted by Clinton's coterie of talented campaign strategists. It stood for a substantively new Democratic approach to active government that had been developing since the early years of the Reagan administration.

The story of the New Democrats is, in large part, the story of the Democratic Leadership Council (DLC), an unofficial party organization of elected Democrats put together by a political entrepreneur in 1985. The DLC's objective was to move the national Democratic party, in both perception and substance, toward the center of the political spectrum in order to break the Republican hold on the White House. Over time, the DLC gained the institutional capacity to draw prominent Democratic politicians into its sphere and to develop a centrist alternative for the party. Had it not been for the institutional success of the DLC, the New Democratic message would not have been articulated and Bill Clinton would have been a considerably less appealing and probably less successful candidate for president.

The purpose of this article is to explain the rise of the New Democrats in Democratic party politics from 1980–1992. In so doing, it promises to shed light on several topics of interest to scholars of American parties: out-party policy development, the role of unofficial party organizations, party factionalism, and in general the role of parties in candidate-centered politics.

The party that does not hold the White House faces the need to generate ideas and policy responses that can form the basis of a message and agenda in the next election. Unofficial party groups tend to emerge to fulfill functions, such as policy development, that official party organizations are neglecting. Unofficial groups often represent factions vying for control of the party message, agenda, and, most important, presidential nomination. The influence of unofficial groups ultimately depends on having an affiliated candidate fare well in the party's presidential nominating process. Unofficial groups that focus on party policy serve the needs of the party's elected officials by providing them with much-needed policy ideas and analysis that individual politicians lack the means to generate for themselves. This holds true for presidential candidates too, as they are "both consumers and interpreters of the policy ideas generated within the party." Presidential candidates and, ultimately, administrations need intellectual fuel on which to campaign and to govern....

NEW DEMOCRATS AND PARTY THEORY

Out-Party Policy Development and Unofficial Party Organizations

As the present case suggests, out-party policy development can and does occur at various locations within the party network, and not necessarily within official party organizations. The national committee seems especially ill suited for policy development because of pressures to include representatives from all facets of the party. When this does not occur, an effort within the national committee to develop policy is seen as captive of a party faction. When it does occur, the output tends to be a general statement of common ground among party members rather than a settling of differences between different factions in the party. This would appear to be a more acute dilemma for the ideologically diverse Democrats than for the more homogenous Republicans. Yet the conservative themes that have dominated the Republican party since the late-1970s were fashioned in conservative groups outside of the official party. Republican National Committee policy development efforts during that period are more accurately characterized as policy *publicity* efforts, promoting the new conservative agenda. Additionally, the party-building and supplemental campaign activities of the national committees are so extensive that they have little time or resources to devote to policy development.

Alternative party organizations arise when the official party fails to address important party functions. In the case of the New Democrats, the DLC emerged to develop party message and policy after efforts inside the official party failed to do so. The DLC demonstrates that unofficial organizations can play an important role for parties. In this case, it helped the party find its voice.

Party Factionalism

Yet the question remains, where were party liberals? Why do they lack an organization like the DLC? Unofficial party organizations also arise from the perception that the official party structure is not adequately representing a particular subgroup within the party. Arthur Stevens et al., using the founding of the Democratic Study Group (DSG) in the House of Representatives as an example, explain the emergence of alternative organizations as arising from the perception of bias in institutional structures designed for collective decision making. Just as the DSG was organized to counteract the perception that institutional arrangements in the House were biased in favor of conservatives, the DLC organized to counteract the perception that institutional arrangements in the national Democratic party were biased in favor of activist liberal elements in the party and against moderate elected officials.

This helps explain why party liberals lacked an organization like the DLC, but does not address why they failed to produce a new liberal message for the party, particularly as a response to the New Democrats, regardless of the location in the party network of such an effort. A general answer lies in the nature of the liberal wing of the party itself. Liberal Democrats since 1968 have been more a collection of groups representing some salient characteristic (labor, education, African Americans, Hispanics, women, homosexuals) or issue concern (antiwar, welfare rights, environmen-

tal, consumer, gun control, antinuclear, nuclear freeze, abortion rights) than a self-conscious ideological faction. This group-based politics did not produce a broader group identity out of which might grow a coherent liberal message and agenda for the party.

A more specific answer lies in an area that is oft neglected in political science: political leadership, particularly entrepreneurial leadership. In the case of the New Democrats, it took the initial vision of Gillis Long and eventually that of a career staffer, Al From, to bring the New Democrats into existence. The DLC, its organizational structure, and its output are all the result of From's entrepreneurial abilities. In the final analysis, party liberals did not have this kind of leadership.

The Role of Parties in Candidate-Centered Politics

In electoral politics, parties have adapted to the needs of the new style politician, who puts together a capital-intensive candidate-centered enterprise to run for office. As recent scholarship on American parties amply attests, parties have taken on the role of supplementary campaign organizations, providing money and technical expertise to candidates. In contrast, the official party organizations have been less effective at serving the contemporary elected officials' policy needs. Today's politicians, in large part, are descendants of James Q. Wilson's amateurs insofar as they are more interested in the politics of ideas and policy making than the old-style professionals; yet they are, quite literally, too busy to engage in detailed efforts at idea and policy development. Hence, today's politician turns to entities such as congressional caucuses, think tanks, and interest groups for help. The DLC demonstrates that unofficial party groups should be added to the list and that party groups have the potential to adapt to the policy needs of contemporary politicians.

The DLC also demonstrates how parties can get elected officials more involved in party affairs. In the candidate-centered era, elected officials must see involvement in national party affairs as furthering their primary career goals of reelection, policy making, and influence. To get elected officials involved, incentives must be offered that will help them achieve their career goals. The DLC was structured around that basic premise. The DLC enhanced members' re-election goals by providing a "moderate" party organization with which they could identify while continuing to distance themselves from the "liberal" party, and by moderating the overarching ideological landscape in the party. It enhanced members' policy-making goals by providing ideas, policy information, and forums for discussion. The DLC enhanced members' influence generally by serving as an organizational vehicle for moderate Democrats to pursue interests in Washington and, for those who wished to avail themselves of it, the DLC provided an alternative leadership structure to enhance personal influence and leadership skills. The success of the DLC is tied to this incentive structure. Without it, the DLC would not have drawn the membership and leadership necessary to develop the New Democrat message. The DLC, in other words, is an adaptation to the needs of the contemporary politician.

READING 29

Independent Presidential Candidates in the Candidate-Centered Age: A Window of Opportunity

Stephen M. Nichols

In U.S. history, third parties have not been terribly successful at replacing one of the two major parties. The last time it happened was in the mid-1850s as the Whigs shattered over the issue of slavery and the Republicans emerged from the wreckage and brought along some anti-slavery Democrats with them. The election of Abraham Lincoln as a Republican president in 1860 and the ensuing Civil War, with its victory for the Union, made the new party permanent. Talk about new major parties since then has always turned out to be just talk.

However, independent candidates for president, although never victorious, have had discernable impact both in terms of helping determine which of

the two major party candidates won (for example, a third party candidacy by Theodore Roosevelt in 1912 probably threw that election to the Democrat Woodrow Wilson) and in terms of highlighting some issues that later receive serious attention by the president and Congress (for example, if campaign finance reform is addressed seriously after the 1996 election the independent candidate, Ross Perot, can surely claim some credit).

In a piece written expressly for this reader, Stephen Nichols, a political science professor at California State University, San Marcos, explores the potential for third-party or, more accurately, independent presidential candidates. He argues that changed conditions now make it "conceivable for an independent nominee actually to capture the White House."

His thesis remains to be tested. Ross Perot, who attracted 19 percent of the popular vote in 1992 as an independent presidential candidate, got only 9 percent of the popular vote in 1996 when he ran again. No other independent candidate made any kind of dent. But even if an independent never wins the presidency—which is surely the safest bet—the enhanced ability of an independent to get a sizeable portion of the vote could add some unexpected twists to U.S. politics in the coming years.

Running viable campaigns for the United States presidency as an independent, rather than from within the ranks of one of the major parties, seems almost commonplace of late. In 1992 the usual cohort of third-party and independent hopefuls that appear on virtually every presidential ballot was joined by H. Ross Perot, Jr. The Texas billionaire surprised most analysts by winning nearly one of every five votes, more than any nonmajor party hopeful since 1912.

Perot captured less than half that number of votes in 1996, and yet by some measures 1996 engendered even greater interest in independent or third-party presidential possibilities. Perot had to fend off a challenge from former Colorado governor Richard Lamm for the Reform Party's top spot, and another nationally known figure, consumer advocate Ralph Nader, headed the Green Party ticket. Major party nominees

Clinton and Dole breathed a sigh of relief when the widely popular Colin Powell opted not to run, and the list of political heavyweights said to have pondered an independent candidacy in 1996 included Jesse Jackson, Lowell Weicker, Pat Buchanan, and Bill Bradley.

Perhaps so many luminaries are playing to the audience of self-identified independents because the audience is of considerable size. A 1995 Times Mirror survey found that more than one-fourth of Americans would support a then-unnamed independent candidate in a hypothetical three-way race with Bill Clinton and the eventual Republican nominee. Likewise, a poll of California registered voters identified two-thirds of that state's electorate as potential third-party supporters. In short, there is clear evidence that a substantial bloc of voters are willing to stray from the major parties.

In fact, recent developments on a number of fronts in American politics may have opened a window of opportunity for candidates from outside the dominant parties. A review of third-party and independent presidential efforts in the two-party U. S. political system and the obstacles confronting such candidates will serve as a prelude to an analysis of the current situation. The central thesis advanced here is that there are fewer hurdles facing independent candidates, to the point that it is conceivable for an independent nominee actually to capture the White House.

THIRD-PARTY FUTILITY
IN TWO-PARTY AMERICA

Elections in the United States have long been two-party affairs; for the last 140 years, in fact, the *same* two parties have dominated the fight for the nation's highest office. Two-party dominance makes the recent spate of independent presidential possibilities all the more intriguing. Sometimes conducted under the guise of a third-party "front" (e.g., George Wallace's American Independent party was a party in name only; in reality it was Wallace's personal campaign organization) but frequently without any party label, independent bids for the White House are not only more common of late, they have also enjoyed greater success. The epitome of their good fortune, of course, is Perot's strong showing in the 1992 elec-

tion. Perot's share of the popular vote, at just under 19 percent, stands as the highest ever amassed by an independent nominee.

"Success," though, is a relative term: even Perot's remarkable popular vote tally failed to garner a single electoral college vote. Other nonmajor party efforts have fared better in the electoral college: George Wallace won 46 electors in 1968; Strom Thurmond's Dixiecrat party claimed 39 electoral college votes; and both those totals are eclipsed by Theodore Roosevelt's "Bull Moose" effort of 1912, which captured 88 electoral college votes. Nonetheless, even these strongest of nonmajor party bids fell short of winning the presidency. The more prevalent pattern of third-party and independent efforts is one of utter failure. Only seven times in U. S. history has a third-party effort carried even a single state in a presidential election; the combined vote share of all independent and third-party candidates is commonly less than one percent of the popular vote total. In short, this record of futility suggests that the term *third party* (an appellation sometimes inaccurately applied to independent campaigns) designates an effort generally consigned to "third place"—and, in the two-party United States, third place is tantamount to last place.

It is no accident that third-party and independent presidential challenges have never succeeded, for such efforts must surmount formidable obstacles blocking their path to the White House. These obstacles are primarily of two sorts, and may be thought of as hurdles operating against nonmajor party hopefuls at two levels. At one level, a number of institutional and legal barriers confront candidates from without the major parties. In addition, various attitudinal obstacles, some of them interacting with the structural barriers, work against independents and third parties.

First, nonmajor party hopefuls face cumbersome requirements for merely getting on the general election ballot. This task is greatly complicated by the fact that ballot access stipulations are different in every state, thus forcing candidates to mount 51 separate, expensive efforts to place their names on the ballots of all states plus the District of Columbia. Nonmajor party candidates typically must collect a specified number of petition signatures in order to appear on a state's ballot, but the number of signatures required, the period during which they may be gathered, rules regarding the eligibility of signers, and other aspects of this requirement vary tremendously from state to state. One noted scholar refers to ballot access restrictions as the foundation of the "institutionalized electoral duopoly."

A second structural hurdle, and a contributor to the ballot qualification problem, involves government financial assistance for presidential campaigns. Under the 1974 Federal Elections Campaign Act (FECA), the federal government awards campaign money to candidates, but only after they have received at least five percent of the popular vote in an election and have qualified for at least ten state ballots. Minor party contenders are thus victims of a vicious circle: With the money, they may be able to generate the requisite level of support, but they cannot get the money until they show the support. Independent and third-party bids, then, are typically financially strapped, with most of the resources they do have going toward ballot access. Both the campaign finance and ballot access laws, of course, were created by representatives from the major parties, and are clearly designed to preserve the majority status of the dominant parties by lessening the probability of a successful third-party challenge. Some have labeled FECA a "major party protection act."

Thus the institutional and legal disadvantages of independents and third parties are considerable. In addition to these structural hurdles, however, nonmajor party hopefuls must also contend with a variety of attitudinal constraints operating at the level of the individual voter. The first of these attitudinal impediments stems from pessimistic assessments of the victory prospects of an independent or third-party effort, and such assessments hinge, in turn, on the nature of electoral constituencies in American presidential politics. This obstacle, then, is part structural and part attitudinal in nature.

The U.S. presidential elections are not determined by a national tally of the popular vote. Rather, a presidential contest is comprised of plurality elections in state electoral college constituencies, a collection of winner-take-all contests in 51 "single-member districts" (the 50 states plus the District of Columbia). This combination—plurality elections in which the winner receives all of a state's electoral college votes—offers little incentive for voters to support a candidate lacking any real chance of winning outright. Consequently, many voters who prefer an independent candidate nonetheless defect to a major party camp, because the voter rightly perceives that the independent has little chance of winning, and that such a vote is therefore wasted. This perception is self-fulfilling, of course: Any chance the independent might have had evaporates as would-be supporters cast ballots for their second choice. Known by some analysts as "sophisticated" or "strategic" voting, this phenomenon has plagued all minor party efforts in U. S. presidential contests.

Another attitudinal force operating against the electoral fortunes of nonmajor party efforts concerns the fleeting issue appeal of third-party and independent hopefuls. There is little doubt that, on occasion, major party neglect of an important issue can tempt voters to seek alternatives to the offerings of the dominant parties. This temptation is often short-lived, though, because the major parties are quick to recognize the gains made by their minor party competitors, and quick to avert further losses by co-opting the issue for themselves. If one or both of the major parties adopt some of the minor party's issue stance, the latter is robbed of its distinctiveness. Moveover, voters may then find their issue preferences satisfied by a party with a greater probability of actually winning the presidency; in that event, why should the voter remain loyal to the independent or minor party cause?

Yet another attitudinal constraint on the success of nonmajor party presidential efforts is the powerful psychological bond that ties most voters to a specific political party. The vast majority of these ties, of course, are to a major party: Fewer than one in a thousand Americans identifies with a minor party. Partisanship has long been the most reliable predictor of U. S. electoral behavior, and the partisan continuum in America is anchored by only two parties. To the extent that party loyalties shape presidential election outcomes, third-party efforts are disadvantaged.

With these imposing structural and attitudinal hurdles in mind, one readily understands the long record of futility of third-party and independent movements of the past. Few are able to surmount even the ballot access and campaign finance obstacles, and, thus, never run a credible national campaign. Of those who have done so, none has ever overcome the attitudinal obstacles and won. How, then, are we to explain Perot's relatively excellent showing in 1992 and 1996, along with the long list of political luminaries who pondered an independent presidential run in 1996?

THE DECLINE OF ATTITUDINAL BARRIERS TO INDEPENDENT SUCCESS

Part of the recent success of independent presidential aspirants may be attributed to a slight easing of the structural impediments described above. Past independents have brought legal challenges against egregious ballot access constraints: George Wallace, Eugene McCarthy, and John Anderson, for example, all waged successful court battles against burdensome ballot qualification rules in Ohio, Maryland, New Mexico, Maine, and Kentucky, thereby paving the way for subsequent independent efforts. More recently, a federal judge in New York struck down as unconstitutional a state law requiring all petition signers to provide their precinct and legislative district numbers (i.e., bits of information few of us know) next to their signatures. In the same month the State Supreme Court of Colorado allowed the inclusion of an independent legislative candidate on the ballot, despite the fact that she had not been registered as an independent for a full year prior to submitting her petition signatures, as required by state law.

These are but small victories in a much larger war, however, and the smaller parties have also suffered their share of judicial setbacks, including a recent Supreme Court ruling that states may ban the practice of *fusion* (the simultaneous nomination of an individual by two or more political parties; minor parties support this practice because it allows their candidates to run under multiple party banners and thereby maximizes their vote potential). Clearly, contenders from outside the major parties must still go to great lengths to qualify for state ballots and to run viable national campaigns. The legal and institutional barriers remain insurmountable for all but the most resourceful of the lot, and prove daunting even for well-funded independents like Perot.

The real credit for the relative success of recent independents, then, must be given to a substantial decline in the attitudinal obstacles confronting nonmajor party efforts. In short, a number of relatively recent changes in the attitudes of American citizens seem to have combined to create a window of opportunity for a successful independent presidential bid.

First, there is evidence of an emerging political issue—a tandem of issue preferences, actually—on which an independent's appeal may rest, safe from worries of major party co-optation. Specifically, a growing number of Americans seem to be fiscal conservatives (preferring, for example, less governmental involvement in economic affairs), but hold moderate to liberal views on social matters (they are, e.g., pro-choice on abortion). Such persons, of course, prefer the Republican party's fiscal views, but side with the Democrats on social policy. The difficulty the major parties face is that neither can wholly satisfy this sizable bloc of voters, because the issue tandem cuts across the traditional liberal–conservative cleavage that separates the parties. In the words of former Senator Paul Tsongas, in 1994:

> both major parties have allowed a vacuum to be created that neither seems capable of filling. . . . The vacuum is still there, a phenomenon created by the unease people have about the social views of the Republicans and the fiscal views of the Democrats. And the reality is that neither major party seems poised to rethink their basic message.

Tsongas hints at why this particular issue tandem is resistant to major party co-optation: the combination is at least partly inconsistent with the basic ideological foundation of both parties, and therefore adopting it would require either major party to fundamentally restructure itself. Republicans have difficulty selling themselves as social moderates, and Democrats have similar problems with respect to fiscal conservatism.

Not surprisingly, each of the most prominent independent presidential possibilities of 1996—Powell, Bradley, Richard Lamm, and Perot—espoused this tandem of fiscal conservatism and social tolerance: All have called for greater fiscal discipline, and all hold moderate-to-liberal views on social issues.

Second, citizen loyalties to the major parties, and to the two-party arrangement itself, have waned considerably over the last several decades. The first piece of evidence along these lines is the decline of individual partisan ties in the American electorate. Indications of the decline first surfaced in the mid-1960s and have continued to the present. Many scholars have concluded that, while partisanship remains an important determinant of the vote, party loyalties are considerably weaker today than in the past.

Additionally, there seems to have been a more general distancing of the electorate from the parties, even among those who still claim to be party loyalists. Considerable evidence suggests that what underlies this detachment is not only negativity toward the parties, but also neutrality toward them: Many have come to view the parties as largely irrelevant to the electoral process. This perception is not surprising in light of the reduced presence of political parties in what scholars have dubbed the "age of candidate-centered politics." Parties have receded into the background of the contemporary political scene: They can no longer select their own nominees (voters do so in primaries), for example, and their presence is more difficult to portray via television, the medium by which most citizens get their campaign information. In short, parties are less visible in modern American elections. It is candidates, not parties, who occupy the center of the political stage today.

One consequence of the perceived irrelevance of the major parties is that independent presidential candidates now compete with one less electoral liability. In a party-centered political environment, those without the backing of a major party were at a considerable disadvantage; such is not the case in the contemporary era of candidate-centered politics. To those who perceive the parties as irrelevant, an independent is merely another candidate in the race, and the absence of a party label is little cause for concern. Incidentally, this may also explain why the most impressive nonmajor party bids of recent years (e.g., John Anderson's 1980 campaign, and Perot's efforts in 1992 and 1996) have all been of the independent, rather than third-party, variety: Why go to the considerable additional effort of creating an entire new party if a large portion of the electorate does not think in partisan terms to begin with?

Extending the logic of this argument, we see that contemporary independents are also less likely to fall prey to sophisticated voting defections. Given that such defections are prompted by the belief that a candidate lacking a major party label cannot win, sophisticated voting defections should be less problematic for an independent competing in the candidate-centered era. The lack of a major party's blessing will be less relevant to voters, because the parties themselves are less relevant. The belief that independents are automatically consigned to third—last—place, then, is less applicable in an electoral setting defined by individual candidates rather than by parties.

This is not to suggest that the workings of the Electoral College will no longer winnow the number of realistic voter choices to only two. This does mean, though, that the extent of strategic defections should decline in an electoral setting wherein independents compete on a more level playing field, and are thus more viable candidates. Additionally, one should not automatically assume that the independent will be the "odd man out" when voters desert a likely loser in favor of a second choice with better victory prospects. It is entirely possible, in a candidate-driven electoral setting, for one of the major party nominees to be perceived as the weakest of the lot, and to thus become the victim of sophisticated voting. Indeed, some analysts believe George Bush narrowly avoided this fate in 1992.

CONCLUSION

The attitudinal forces that once so effectively thwarted the efforts of independent presidential aspirants now seem to have ebbed considerably. Modern independents have an issue that is resistant to major party co-optation; the weakening party loyalties of many voters have created a political world wherein candidates loom largest, allowing independent candidates to compete on more equal footing with party nominees. As a result, the forces that prompted citizens to jump off an independents' bandwagon in favor of a more probable winner likewise seem to have declined.

None of this, however, should be taken to mean that an independent presidential victory is imminent. The fact remains that legal and institutional obstacles are sufficient to block all but the most determined and wealthy of their kind. Nonetheless, it also seems clear that neither major party will soon adopt the tandem of issue preferences that has fueled recent independent hopes. Likewise, the forces behind the rise of the candidate-centered political world, which in turn contributed to the lessening of some of the psychological constraints that once worked so powerfully against independent voting, will not soon be undone. Thus, while the structural impediments remain formidable, the decline of the once pervasive attitudinal barriers to independent success has opened a window of opportunity for such candidates unlike any before in American electoral history. Not surprisingly, a host of contenders stand at the window, poised to take advantage of the opening.

READING 30

An End to Politics as Usual

Everett Carll Ladd

Everett Carll Ladd, a professor of political science and director of the Roper Center for Public Opinion Research at the University of Connecticut, explores the growing alienation of the American population from many of the major features of the American political system, such as the unquestioned dominance of the two major parties in competing for elected office, unlimited terms for elected legislators, identification with either party as opposed to self-identification as an independent.

The prominence of dissatisfaction with aspects of campaign finance late in the 1996 presidential race stems from the same skepticism about the

From "An End to Politics as Usual" by E. C. Ladd, 1995, *The Chronicle of Higher Education*, 24 November. Copyright © 1995 by E. C. Ladd. Reprinted by permission of E. C. Ladd.

American political system on the part of many people.

Ladd, like Nichols in the previous reading, sees growing importance in "third-party and independent challenges." He does stop short, however, of claiming that a candidate from other than the Democratic or Republican parties could actually win the presidency.

In 1996 dissatisfaction with the political system can be glimpsed through yet another decline in turnout—the percentage of eligible voters who actually voted. It stood at about 49 percent for president—the lowest since 1924.

At the same time that cynicism and apathy characterize considerable parts of the public reaction to the political system, it is also worth noting that 1996 brought a much more accepting stance on the part of voters toward incumbents. Not only was President Clinton reelected, but so were 95 percent of incumbent members running for re-election in both the House and Senate.

Perhaps the message is that those citizens who participate in politics are more willing to put the system's flaws in the context of a system that, to them, seems to work fairly well. Those citizens who do not participate—and that is an increasing proportion—perhaps see the flaws as predominant.

For 130 years, the Democratic and Republican Parties have ruled America electorally. No one has come to the Presidency since these two parties began competing in the 1850s who was not nominated by one of them. Today, only one member of Congress (Rep. Bernard Sanders of Vermont) was elected as an Independent, rather than as a Democrat or a Republican.

But now some political scientists and public-opinion pollsters see signs that this two-party dominance may be coming to an end. On three occasions this year, the Gallup Organization has asked survey respondents whether they would favor or oppose "the formation of a third political party that would run candidates for President, Congress, and state offices against the Republican and Democratic candidates." Each time, large majorities—62 per cent of the respondents in the most recent survey, conducted in August—said they favored formation of a new party.

After Ross Perot, the Texas billionaire who drew significant support in his independent run for the Presidency in the 1992 election, announced in September that he was trying to get a new "Independence" party on the ballot for the 1996 Presidential election, 46 per cent of those polled by Gallup said they approved of the effort, and only 29 per cent were opposed; 25 percent had no opinion.

Surely something big is happening in American politics, but I do not think the findings I've just cited are a precise indicator of what it is. Several factors make me question whether backing for a new party is as strong as the polls suggest. Third-party efforts are not uncommon, but none to date has overturned Democratic and Republican dominance. As the political scientist Clinton Rossiter observed in *Parties and Politics in America,* only one third party, the Populists, ever mounted a serious challenge to the two current parties.

Political traditions do not die easily in the United States. It is one thing for people to be receptive to the general idea of a third party, but it's something quite different for them actually to vote for it. Although 46 per cent of the respondents told Gallup they favored Mr. Perot's efforts to establish a third party, only 26 per cent of the respondents said they could see themselves joining it. (And, among that 26 per cent, only one in four respondents said he or she was "very likely" to do so.)

Another reason to be cautious about opinion surveys that seem to show strong support for a new party is that throughout our history, a great many Americans have seen themselves as independent-minded, willing to "vote for the best person" regardless of party. Political scientists long have called attention to this phenomenon and frequently have lamented the degree of independence and the party weakness it has produced.

Yet although the odds remain great that the next President will be a Democrat or a Republican, as will the vast majority of members of Congress and state and local officials, it is likely that third-party and independent challenges will be more common and will command more serious attention in the years ahead.

One reason is the increasing importance of television. It is now possible for a candidate without the endorsement of a major party to attract voters' attention quickly, if he or she has enough money to buy time on television—as Mr. Perot clearly demonstrated in 1992. Candidates can enter voters' living rooms night after night without leaving a comfortable television studio. Electronic campaigning may not work as well in local politics, but Mr. Perot showed that it can get results in a national contest.

Further, the proportion of Americans who think of themselves as independents is greater now than it was three or four decades ago. I have charted these data over the years, most recently for the October/November issue of *Public Perspective,* published by the Roper Center for Public Opinion Research at the University of Connecticut. Although polling experts differ on how much the ranks of independent voters have grown over the years, it is clear that many more Americans now are splitting their tickets—a sign of independence from the major political parties—than did in earlier eras.

Voters today clearly are considerably more dissatisfied with the way the great game of politics is played than voters were from the 1930s through the 1960s. Many surveys have asked respondents to indicate their level of satisfaction with government performance or their confidence in the workings of the political process. Most such measures show dissatisfaction climbing from the late 1960s through the 1970s, moderating in the first half of the 1980s, and then rising to extremely high—often all-time high—levels from the late 1980s to the present. Those data have been summarized well by Fred Steeper and Christopher Blunt in "The Discontent and Cynicism of the American Public," a report released in October by Market Strategies, a national survey company.

This unease with politics as usual encourages more than attempts to form new parties and an increased number of split tickets. It is also behind Americans' strong support for term limits for legislators. Since 1990, 22 states have enacted some form of term-limits legislation, and every time opinion surveys have asked about term limits, respondents have backed them overwhelmingly.

In a poll taken by Princeton Survey Research Associates for *Newsweek* in January, 75 per cent of the respondents said they favored "term limits on how long members of Congress can stay in office," while only 21 per cent were opposed. Voters see term limits as a way of reining in the politicians. Similarly, Americans consistently have expressed strong support for a constitutional amendment requiring a balanced federal budget, as another way to discipline officeholders seen as practicing politics as usual.

The current high levels of dissatisfaction with the political process, and the resulting support for reforms, stand in striking contrast to the experience of the electoral era that preceded our own. During the New Deal and its immediate aftermath, voters focused on big economic and foreign-policy problems—the Great Depression, World War II, and the Cold War—rather than on the political process. But the recent situation isn't unique when viewed from a longer perspective. The way government is working has prompted lively public concern throughout U.S. history. As a nation, we never have seriously considered changing the structure laid out in our Constitution, but we have periodically protested against the way politicians run our institutions.

The Progressive era, at the beginning of this century, is full of parallels to our own era. As I explained in a recent article, the Progressives gained enormous political influence in much of the country, and their *raison d'être* was reform of the political process. Many of their achievements—allowing citizens to place referenda and political initiatives on the ballot, providing for the nomination of political candidates through direct primaries rather than by party committees or conventions, and curbing patronage—remain embedded in our political system. The Progressives were troubled by what they saw as "unresponsive government." They argued that too many institutions—including state legislatures and cities' governing boards—had come under the thumb of "the interests," especially economic interests profiting at the public's expense. Public life was seen as riddled with graft.

Today, graft as such isn't a big factor, but once again it's "the people *versus* the interests." Government now touches much more of national life, and the roster of special interests seeking benefits from it extends far beyond the business interests that most worried the Progressives. The focus of concern has shifted from the states and localities to the federal government, which many people feel is being run according to the priorities and interests of those "inside the Beltway."

The strongest message that Americans are sending today, then, is not so much that we crave a new political party as that we want meaningful change in the way politics works. We want less insider politics; we want to see the concerns of individual citizens elevated and those of interest groups diminished. We want real responsiveness—which is not to be confused with pandering to pressure groups. These desires, and the frustrations that underlie them, cannot be addressed quickly. They require changes in performance by government over time, regardless of who runs for and wins the Presidency. Whether voters see such changes as forthcoming will do much to determine the future strength of third-party challenges.

FOOD FOR THOUGHT

1. In his essay, "The Revitalization of National Party Organizations," Paul S. Herrnson describes the important role that the national parties fulfill in electing candidates to Congress and how the national political parties have adapted to the era of modern campaign politics. Are there other organizations in American politics that might fulfill these functions? What effect might restrictions on soft money have in presidential campaigns? What might be the consequences of further restricting PAC contributions to congressional campaigns? Would you agree with the argument that, because the chairs of the national parties as well as the congressional and senate campaign committees are often legislators, the party in government is actually the most powerful or influential of the three branches of political parties?

2. Marjorie Randon Hershey, in her essay "Citizens' Groups and Political Parties in the United States," argues that both competition and cooperation are present in the relationships between political parties and interest groups. For example, the Christian Coalition clashed with factions of the Republican party during the party's 1996 convention and threatened that it would not allow the selection of a pro-choice running mate on the party's ticket. Similarly, she notes that liberal interest groups cooperated with the Democratic party when the conservatism of Reagan era politics necessitated it. What do Hershey's argument and these examples lead you to conclude about the conditions under which cooperation or competition between political parties and interest groups might occur?

3. After reading Jon Hale's essay on the Democratic Leadership Council as an example of out-party policy development and the role of unofficial party organizations, can you speculate why President Clinton failed to behave as a "new Democrat" in office or change the face of the Democratic party? To what extent is it possible that the long-established affinity groups of the Democratic party hindered Clinton's progress in being a Democratic moderate? Would the Democratic Leadership Council be more successful with mass support? Does the public view the Democratic party itself as liberal and simply perceive Clinton as a moderate candidate?

4. Stephen Nichols argues that the electoral prospects of independent or third-party candidates have improved because there are now fewer institutional

barriers to their success and voters are more accepting. Is his argument persuasive? Do you think that an independent candidate will soon sit in the White House or do legal and institutional barriers remain too great? Is the recent trend of high-profile independent presidential candidates limited to a few wealthy individuals with strong political ambitions?

5. In his essay "An End to Politics as Usual," Everett Carll Ladd speculates on the dissatisfaction of voters with the American political system. Support for term limits and the formation of a third political party, as well as an increase in split-ticket voting all suggest the public's discontent with politics as usual. Do you believe that such dissatisfaction will lead to a reform era in American politics? Why or why not? Ladd notes that, because American political traditions do not die easily, a third party is unlikely. Are there any additional reasons that a third political party is unlikely to be successful in electoral politics? How many of these reasons are institutional in nature?

CHAPTER 7

ELECTIONS

Free elections are essential in any functioning democracy. They produce the individuals who are supposed to represent the entire population and who are responsible for governing. Voters express their opinions about candidates directly and about policies indirectly.

The United States has a history of generally free and fair elections since its creation. Indeed, many of the colonies had already established that tradition prior to independence. The size and nature of the electorate has, of course, changed. The most advanced democratic colonies before independence or the most advanced democratic states in the early years of the Republic only allowed white males to vote, but did so without property qualifications. All property qualifications were pretty well gone within a few decades into the 19th century. Nominally, African Americans, newly freed from slavery, were given the vote shortly after the Civil War. Genuinely open access to the ballot box in all parts of the country did not really become universal until late in the 20th century. Women were extended the suffrage on a national basis only with the passage of the 19th amendment to the Constitution in 1920.

Elections are, of course, a vast topic. This introduction contains a few general propositions about American elections as we near the 21st century.

First, although elections are both interesting and entertaining in their own right, it needs to be underscored that they are important because they produce the officials who, in office, make public policy. To some extent, voters vote because they have policy preferences. That, of course, is not the only reason they vote. They also vote because of their overall feelings toward specific candidates. Or they may vote out of habit or out of party loyalty. (So much has been made out of the decline in party loyalty that is is worth reminding you that millions of people still vote, in large

part, for that reason.) In short, voters do not directly choose policies. They choose the people who make policies and hope that they guess correctly about what policies will emerge if the candidates they favor win.

When candidates become officeholders they face institutional pressures in addition to the electoral pressures they internalize from the past election and that they clearly will face in the next election. The institutional pressures tend to push for slow policy change. Paul Herrnson, in the first reading in this chapter, "Congressional Elections and Governance," discusses the links between congressional elections and the institutional necessities of functioning in Congress and also with constituents. He helps us understand how elections produce both representation and, ultimately, governance.

Second, basic party realignment—that is, the emergence of new loyalties and voting patterns to replace old ones—typically occurs gradually over the period of several elections. Incremental change is constant. More sudden, dramatic realignments in so-called key elections occur only rarely. The second reading in the chapter, "The Republican Tidal Wave of 1994," by Alfred Tuchfarber and his colleagues, explores the results of the 1994 congressional elections for signs of long-range change.

Third, overall realignment is usually made up of many different movements all at once. The movement is different for different groups of people classified by gender, race, education, income, and other characteristics. The chapter's third reading, "Has Godot Finally Arrived?: Religion and Realignment," by Lyman Kellstedt and his colleagues, analyzes recent shifting party loyalties and voting habits on the part of specific religious groups. Such movement might best be thought of as micro-realignments. If enough micro-realignments shift in the same direction at the same time, then the potential for a broad realignment is present. Much of the time, of course, micro-realignments will be moving in different directions and offsetting each other, at least in part.

A great deal of the change in voting habits comes from new cohorts entering the electorate rather than from dramatic departures of previous cohorts from their habits. When the direction of the two changes—new cohorts with beliefs and loyalties that differ significantly from those of previous cohorts *and* incremental change on the part of cohorts already in the electorate—coincide, then more dramatic electoral changes can and do occur. As the electorate became more Republican and more conservative in the 1980s and 1990s, both types of change were occurring.

Fourth, in the 20th century long-term stability between realignments is typical of American elections. The fourth reading in the chapter, "The Status-Quo Election," by Everett C. Ladd, argues that the 1996 presidential and congressional elections represent a stabilization process at work.

Fifth, the growing independence of voters—or, put another way, the shrinking loyalty to one of the two major parties—may well be the main force behind diminishing turnout at the polls. Turnout for the presidential election in 1996 was the lowest percentage since 1924. Not only is turnout for elections at a low point, but cynicism about government, officials, and politics is at a high point, as is alienation from the political system. "Independence" sounds good in that it could signify a thoughtful electorate willing to suspend judgment until it had heard the arguments and joined in the debate. In fact, "independence" may be firmly tied to increasing lack of interest or faith in politics as a way of addressing public problems. There is also good evidence that "independents" who do vote really behave as if they identified themselves as Republicans or Democrats. They do not differ in any major way.

Sixth, television has become a dominant force in American elections. Campaigns, conventions, and other political events are planned primarily to cater to the needs of the television industry and to maximize impact on voters who get most of their information from television. Sound bites, choosing candidates who look good on television, timing events to catch the evening news, and brief attack ads have all become features of American politics.

It should be noted that the United States is not alone in having elections dominated by television. The rest of the world, particularly the democratic developed world, looks similar. We may have intensified the impact of television, however, because we have no laws limiting the length of campaigns and because our limits on the amount of money that can be spent on television are either nonexistent or, in effect, toothless.

Seventh, the state of campaign finance is, like Mark Twain's comment on the weather, a topic about which everyone talks but about which no one does anything. Loopholes in the law are more potent than limits. The First Amendment, as interpreted by the courts, prevents some limits from being acceptable constitutionally. Lack of political will prevents some limits that would be constitutionally valid. The reason for the lack of will is obvious: politicians, both incumbents and aspirants, have a stake in keeping access to money relatively easy. If meaningful, constitutional limits were put on campaign finance, everyone would be subject to those limits. But few who might stand to lose in the short run are willing to take the lead in designing and enacting such limits.

Jonathan Salant and David Cloud, in the fifth reading in this chapter, address one specific aspect of campaign finance: the proclivity of Political Action Committees, regardless of ideological preferences, to favor incumbents in Congress with greater contributions than they give to challengers. They calculate that incumbents will remember who helped them most when policies are being decided.

READING 31

Congressional Elections and Governance
Paul S. Herrnson

Politicians run for the House and Senate. Some win; some lose. Virtually all of those who succeed never

From *Congressional Elections: Campaigning at Home and in Washington* by P. S. Herrnson, 1995, pp. 225–240. Copyright © 1995 by Congressional Quarterly Press. Reprinted by permission.

stop running for reelection. But running for reelection is quite different from running for the first time. Now a member must also function within an institution—either the House or Senate—and, presumably, build a record there that he or she can proudly take to constituents.

This reading by Paul S. Herrnson, a political science professor at the University of Maryland, explores the differences between elections to Congress and governance within Congress. He also explores the links between the two basic jobs of the member of the House or Senate: running for reelection on the one hand and participating as a member of the body on the other hand. Members calculate how their behavior inside the House or Senate will play in their constituencies. They campaign directly for reelection when they return home, as most do with great frequency. They also campaign for reelection in part through the record they seek to make as legislators. Senators and representatives try to build a record in Washington that is satisfying in terms of their policy preferences, but they also want to take that record home and show it to constituents with the belief that it will help their bid for reelection.

Herrnson's central point, a quite accurate one, is that Congress is inherently decentralized. This means that policy changes occur in fairly small increments. Only when there is a "widespread consensus for change among the American people" is power centralized, usually in partnership between the president and Congress. And only then is major policy change likely to occur. This happens only rarely, 1913–1914, 1933–1934, 1965, and, perhaps, 1981 may be the only instances in the 20th century. Herrnson helps explain why that is the case.

"The election is over, and now the fun begins." Those were the words of one new House member shortly after being elected to the 103rd Congress. Others had more measured, if not more realistic, visions of what lay ahead. While getting elected to Congress is difficult, especially for those who have to topple an incumbent, staying there also requires great effort. The high reelection rates enjoyed by members of Congress are not a guarantee of reelection; they are the result of hard work and the strategic deployment of the resources that Congress makes available to its members....

THE PERMANENT CAMPAIGN

As locally elected officials who make national policy, members of Congress almost lead double lives. The main focus of their Washington existence is framing and enacting legislation, overseeing the executive branch, and carrying out other activities of national importance. Attending local functions, ascertaining the needs and preferences of constituents, and explaining their Washington activities are what legislators do at home. Home is where members of Congress acquire their legitimacy to participate in the legislative process and individual mandates to act. The central elements of legislators' lives in both locations are representing the voters who elected them, winning federally funded projects for their state or district, and resolving difficulties that constituents encounter when dealing with the federal government. The two aspects of a member's existence are unified by the fact that much of what representatives do in Washington is concerned with getting reelected, and a good deal of what they do at home has a direct impact on the kinds of policies and interests they seek to advance in the legislature. In a great many respects, the job of legislator resembles a permanent reelection campaign.

Members of Congress develop home styles that help them to maintain or expand their bases of electoral support. One element of these home styles concerns the presentation of self. Members build bonds of trust between themselves and voters by demonstrating that they are capable of handling the job, have many things in common with constituents, and care about them. Legislators try to give voters the impression that they are whom they claim to be and are living up to their campaign promises.

A second component of home style is concerned with discussing the Washington side of the job. Members describe, interpret, and justify what they do in the nation's capital to convey the message that they are working relentlessly in their constituents' behalf. Many respond to the low opinion that people have of Congress by trying to separate themselves from the institution in the minds of voters. Members frequently portray themselves as protectors of the national interest locked in combat with powerful lobbyists and feckless colleagues.

Legislators and their staffs spend tremendous amounts of time, energy, and resources advertising the legislator's name among constituents, claiming credit for favorable governmental actions, and taking strong but often symbolic issue positions to please constituents. Their offices provide them with abundant resources for these purposes....

A DECENTRALIZED CONGRESS

Reelection Constituencies

The candidate-centered nature of congressional elections provides the foundation for a highly individualized, fragmented style of legislative politics. Members are largely self-recruited, are nominated and elected principally as a result of their own efforts, and know they bear the principal responsibility for ensuring they get reelected. Local party organizations, Washington-based party committees, PACs, and other groups and individuals may have helped them raise money and win votes, but politicians arrive in Congress with the belief that they owe their tenure to their own efforts.

Legislators owe their first loyalties to their constituents, and most organize their work in Washington to strengthen this relationship. Most staff their offices, decide which committee assignments to pursue, and choose areas of policy expertise with an eye to maintaining constituent support.

Campaign supporters, including those who live in a legislator's district or state and those who live outside of it, form another important constituency. Local elites and Washington-based PACs that provide campaign contributions, volunteer labor, or political advice routinely receive access to members of Congress, further encouraging legislators to respond to forces outside of the institution rather than within. Other personal goals, including advancing specific policies, accruing more power in the legislature, or positioning themselves to run for higher office, also have a decentralizing effect on the legislative process. Much of the work done to advance these goals—issue research, bill drafting, attending committee meetings, bureaucratic oversight,

and meeting with constituents, campaign contributors, and lobbyists—is borne by staffers who owe their jobs and their loyalties to individual legislators more than to the institution. This, in turn, makes their bosses less dependent on congressional leaders and encourages members to march to their own drums.

Congressional Committees

The dispersal of legislative authority among 22 standing committees and more than 120 subcommittees in the House, 17 standing committees and 86 subcommittees in the Senate, 4 joint committees, and a small number of select committees in each chamber adds to the centrifugal tendencies that originate from candidate-centered elections. Each committee and subcommittee is authorized to act within a defined jurisdiction. Each is headed by a chair and ranking member who are among the majority and minority parties' senior policy experts. Each also has its own professional staff, office, and budget to help it carry out its business. By giving expression to the differing views of representatives, senators, and their constituents, the committee system decentralizes Congress....

Congressional Caucuses

Congressional caucuses—informal groups of members who share legislative interests—have a similar but less powerful decentralizing impact on Congress. They create competing policy leaders and alternative sources of information and they are additional sources of legislative decision-making cues. Groups such as the Congressional Black Caucus and the Pro-Life Caucus are recognized as advocates for specific segments of the population or points of view. The Democratic Study Group and the Republicans' Wednesday Group are among the caucuses that are recognized for their research capacities. The Sunbelt Caucus, the Western States Senate Coalition, and other geographically based groups seek to increase the clout of legislators from particular regions.

Although they do not hold any formal legislative powers, most caucuses have staff, office space, elected officers, and by-laws. Many receive financial and staff support from private organizations. Congressional caucuses work to influence the legislative process by researching and publicizing issues, organizing meetings, planning strategies, and providing a framework for networking among legislators who have common interests. Virtually every member serving in the House or Senate during the early 1990s belonged to at least one of the 130 or so congressional caucuses. Caucuses further add to the decentralization and fragmentation of Congress.

Interest Groups

Privately funded interest groups, which form an important part of the political environment with which Congress interacts, also have decentralizing effects on the legislative process. Like caucuses, interest groups are sources of influence that compete with congressional leaders for the loyalty of legislators on certain issues. Roughly 80,000 people work for trade associations, legal firms, and consulting agencies in the Washington area. Not all of these people are lobbyists, but in one way or another they work to advance the political interests of some group, and Congress is their number one target.

Interest groups work to influence the legislative process in a number of ways, and their collective effect is to fragment Congress. Some groups advertise on television, on radio, in newspapers, or through the mails to influence the political agenda or stimulate grass-roots support for or opposition to specific pieces of legislation. Their efforts often resemble election campaigns. The advertisements purchased by the health-care and insurance industries in opposition to President Clinton's health-care reform package in 1994 exemplify these, as do the advertising campaigns waged by unions and other groups in support of or opposition to the North American Free Trade Agreement (NAFTA) in 1993.

Most interest groups also advocate their positions in less visible ways that are designed to play to the legislative and electoral needs or individual members of Congress. Representatives of interest groups are frequently given the opportunity to testify at committee hearings. Group representatives contact legislators at their offices and often make informal contacts over dinners and lunches. Lobbyists use these and other forums to provide members and their staffs with technical information, impact statements of how congressional activity (or inactivity) can affect their constituents, and insights into where other legislators stand on the issue. Sometimes they go so far as to draft a bill or help design a strategy to promote its enactment.

Many groups supplement these "insider" techniques with approaches that focus directly on the electoral connection. Trade and business groups ask local association members to contact their legislators. Unions, churches, and other large membership groups frequently organize telephone and letter-writing campaigns. The objective of these communications is to make the point that legislative decisions can have electoral consequences. They show members of Congress that important blocs of voters and their advocates are watching how the members vote on specific pieces of legislation.

Interest groups, congressional subcommittee members, and executive-branch officials form collegial decision-making groups that are frequently referred to as "iron triangles," "issue networks," or "policy subgovernments." These issue experts often focus on the minutiae of arcane, highly specialized areas of public policy. Because they form small governments within a government, they further contribute to the decentralization of Congress.

POLITICAL PARTIES: CENTRALIZING AGENTS

Unlike these other structural, organizational, and political factors which work to decentralize Congress, political parties act as a glue (albeit a weak one) to bond members together. They socialize new members, distribute committee assignments, set the legislative agenda, coordinate congressional activities, disseminate information, and carry out other tasks that are essential to Congress's law-making, oversight, and representative functions. Although they are not the central actors in elections, parties do help legislators with their campaigns and carry out communications designed to whip up public support for their candidates' positions or undermine support for the opposition. Parties also work to rally their members to vote for legislation that is at the core of their partisan agenda.

The leadership organizations of America's congressional parties are structured similarly to those of legislative parties in other countries. The Democrats and Republicans are each headed by one leader in each chamber—the Speaker and minority leader in the House and the majority and minority leaders in the Senate. Each party has several other officers and an extensive whip system to facilitate communications between congressional party leaders and rank-and-file legislators. Legislative parties convene caucuses and task forces to help formulate policy positions and legislative strategy. Congressional party leaders' ability to provide campaign assistance, give out committee assignments and other perks, set the congressional agenda, structure debate, and persuade legislators that specific bills are in the best interests of their constituents and the nation are important tools for building coalitions.

Nevertheless, party leaders have less control over the policy-making process than do their counterparts in other democracies. The persuasive powers of party leaders are usually insufficient to sway members' votes when party policy positions clash with those of legislators' constituents and campaign supporters. Recognizing the primacy of the electoral connection, party leaders generally tell legislators to respond to constituents rather than "toe the party line" when the latter could endanger their chances of reelection. The efforts of congressional party leaders are probably less of a factor in explaining how party members cast their roll-call votes than are commonalities in political outlook or similarities among legislators' constituents. Party leaders are most able to overcome the forces that work to fragment Congress when they seek to enact policies that possess widespread bipartisan support or when the majority party possesses many more seats than the opposition and proposes popular legislation that advances its core principles....

Congress can overcome its normal state of decentralization when there is a widespread consensus for change among the American people. Widespread consensus enables congressional leaders to centralize power. Using the committee system, whip structures, and other institutions, they are able to pass legislation that initiates fundamental change. Once public support for sweeping change erodes, however, the centrif-

ugal forces that normally dominate Congress reassert themselves, and the legislature returns to its normal, incremental mode of policy making. The parochialism of members of Congress, bicameralism, the internal decentralization of the House and the Senate, and other centrifugal forces promote political cycles marked by long periods of incremental policy making followed by short periods of major policy change.

The Republican Tidal Wave of 1994

Alfred J. Tuchfarber, Stephen E. Bennett, Andrew E. Smith, and Eric W. Rademacher

In 1994 Republican congressional campaigns resulted in a spectacular triumph for the party. The Republican candidates for the House of Representatives ran a coordinated national campaign centered around their adherence to a ten-point "Contract with America." This is extremely rare in modern congressional elections; most races are local events and appear national only in retrospect. The acknowledged leader of the effort, Newt Gingrich, a Republican from Georgia, served as the focal point of the campaign and made clear he wanted to be Speaker if the Republicans won a majority. They Republicans did win and Gingrich, in fact, became Speaker. Their win was stunning, both because of the size of the turnover involved and because Republicans had last won a majority of House seats in the election of 1952.

Republican senators had not been closed out of majority status for as long, because they had punctuated the post-1954 period of minority status

From "The Republican Tidal Wave of 1994: Testing Hypotheses about Realignment, Restructuring, and Rebellion" by A. J. Tuchfarber, et al., 1995, *PS* December 1995, pp. 689–696. Copyright © 1995 by the American Political Science Association. Reprinted by permission.

with six years in the majority (1981–87). Republicans also did very well in state and local elections.

In this reading four political scientists from the University of Cincinnati examine the meaning of the Republican victories in the 1994 elections. They finally take a cautious position that it is premature to speak of realignment because of this election and argue that the 1996 and 1998 elections, when examined together with the 1994 election, will allow us to conclude just how much realignment is occurring.

Focusing on a single election as realigning is only rarely useful. Two elections, 1860 and 1932, were dramatic in the changes they brought. But even they are part of longer, multi-election changes. The Republican ascendancy signaled by the 1860 election of Abraham Lincoln to the presidency was presaged by the 1856 and 1858 elections and solidified by the wartime elections of 1862 and 1864. The Democratic ascendancy signaled by the 1932 election of Franklin Roosevelt to the presidency was a logical product of changes in the electorate evident in analysis of the 1928 and 1932 elections. The Democratic era was solidified in the subsequent elections of 1934 and 1936. Changes wrought in a single election have to last in order to qualify as realignment.

The 1994 elections produced an historic shift of power from Democrats to Republicans at all levels of government. Using data from several sources, including the National Election Studies, an Ohio Poll panel survey of likely and actual voters, Gallup polls, New York Times/CBS News polls, and polls conducted for the *Times Mirror* Center for The People & The Press, we test hypotheses that politicians, pundits, and professors have offered to account for what happened on November 8, 1994. We also explain why voters handed control of the Congress and many state and local governments to the GOP.

The GOP's victory raises four key questions about the significance of the 1994 elections:

1. Did the outcome primarily turn on the failure to vote by key blocs of the Democratic party's constituency?

2. Do the elections reflect *only* a short-term rebellion against the Democratic party in general and Bill Clinton in particular?

3. Were the results due to *enduring* structural shifts in the parties' electoral coalitions?

4. Was 1994 a "critical election" indicating that a *realignment* has occurred?

DIFFERENTIAL TURNOUT?

Several analysts claim that the Democrats' debacle in November 1994 was the result of abstention by key elements of the party's core constituency: African Americans, women, and the poor, while voting surged among "angry white men."...

David Bositis contradicts the notion that low turnout among African Americans was a significant factor in 1994. He points out that African Americans' turnout rose 207% between 1990 and 1994, and that African Americans made up 10% of the 1994 electorate, compared to only 5% four years earlier.

The differential turnout hypothesis also founders on the shoals of survey data showing no substantial shift in the ratio of core components of the Democratic coalition's reported turnout relative to groups alleged to vote disproportionately for GOP candidates. NES polling shows African Americans' reported turnout rose from 35% in 1990 to 48% four years later. Because reported voting among whites also rose, from 43% to 60%, African Americans' turnout ratio relative to whites remained constant at about .8 to 1.

National Election Studies also show no change in the ratio of women's reported turnout to that among men. Forty percent of women told the NES that they voted in 1990, as did 43% of men, for a women-to-men ratio of .94. Fifty-seven percent of women claimed to have cast ballots in 1994, compared to 61% of men, or a ratio of .94.

NES data on family income also cast a pall on the turnout hypothesis. Twenty-seven percent of the lowest income quintile said they voted in 1990, compared to 52% for those in the highest quintile. Hence, the turnout ratio of the poorest citizens relative to the well-heeled was .52 in 1990. Thirty-nine percent of the lowest income quintile reported voting in 1994, as did 73% of the highest quintile. That gives a turnout ratio of .53 for the poorest voters relative to the richest in 1994. The ratios of the second, third, and fourth quintiles relative to the highest were nearly the same in 1990 and 1994.

Thus, differential turnout does not explain the dramatic differences in the 1990 and 1994 election results. More importantly, the characterization of the 1994 elections fiasco for the Democrats as an "angry white male" phenomenon is also *inaccurate.* Although white men did move toward the Republicans in large numbers, so too did white women...

VOTER REBELLION?

American voters have been in a surly mood during the last three national elections—1990, 1992, and 1994. Even though few congressional incumbents who sought reelection in 1990 were actually turned out, the reduced margins by which many won convinced some that "business-as-usual" inside Washington's Beltway might be inadvisable. In many states, term limit measures were victorious, putting politicians on notice that the voters' patience had worn thin. George Bush was given the "royal order of the boot" in 1992, largely because a large slice of the electorate concluded he represented the status quo and was insufficiently attentive to the difficult economic circumstances many Americans thought they were facing.

The 1994 elections were different from 1990 in one important sense: in 1994 voters connected their distrust of government in general, and disapproval of Congress in particular, to their voting. The 1994 NES shows that the more people distrusted the federal establishment the more likely they were to vote Republican in House races. In 1990, on the other hand, the relationship between trust in government and voting in House elections was not statistically significant. In addition, the more people said they disapproved of the job being done by Congress, the more likely they were to vote for GOP candidates in 1994.

At the *very least,* the 1994 elections represent a rebellion against the Democratic party and Bill Clinton.... Lydia Saad, looking at the Gallup Organization's polls, found: (1) voters dissatisfied with Clinton showed up in larger numbers than did those dissatisfied with previous sitting presidents in 1988,

1990, and 1992: and (2) "[t]he Republican Party's gains in last week's congressional elections reflect both a national shift toward the GOP and a Republican electorate that is at once more partisan and more mobilized." Voter reactions to "liberals/liberalism" and "conservatives/conservatism" also hurt Democratic candidates (see below).

"Change" has been a common theme in the last two national elections. Bush was viewed as the proponent of an unacceptable *status quo* in 1992. In 1994, the Democrats in Congress, also seen as representing an unacceptable *status quo,* were dismissed in large numbers. Having staked out a position on many issues that voters are likely to believe represents the *status quo,* Bill Clinton will be very vulnerable if he goes into November 1996 with that image.

RESTRUCTURING?

Many analysts still debate whether a realignment has occurred. Few, however, would argue that several regions of the country have moved from Democratic control to Republican control. While the Northeast remained solidly Democratic, and the Plains and Mountain states remained solidly Republican, both the Midwest and the South switched to Republican control in the 1994 elections.

The GOP's showing in the South was such that some observers asked whether the vote in the South symbolized the final step in a decades-long, "rolling" regional realignment that began with the 1948 presidential election and accelerated on the presidential level after 1964.

Given the racial makeup of voting in the United States and especially in the South, one has to look at whites separately to determine how much to believe assertions that realignment has now come to that region....

One thing that stands out is the lingering importance of tradition. White southerners may have liked Reagan, and dallied with Bush in 1988, but, with the possible exception of those under age 30 in 1982, white southerners returned to their Democratic heritage in House races. The effect is particularly pronounced between 1982 and 1990. Although small numbers require we hedge our conclusions, the data indicate that, as recently as 1990, large slices of the white southern electorate "returned home" to the Democratic party when it came to races for the House of Representatives.

In 1992 we see a dramatically different pattern. Even though George Bush could not attract a majority of southern whites, a majority of those under age 45 backed GOP candidates for the House. Two-party voting was almost evenly split among white southerners aged 45–64, and those 65 and older continued to back Democrats by roughly two-to-one. Things were different in 1994, when majorities of white southerners backed Republican candidates in the House almost regardless of age. Indeed, among those segments of the population known for the highest rates of turnout (30–64), the GOP drew over three-fifths of whites' ballots.

The 1992 and 1994 House vote data also indicate another problem for the Democratic party in the South; its House candidates drew best among those over 65, those voters most likely to be gone in the future. If the normal tendency for voters' party loyalty to congeal as they age continues among white southerners, the Republican party's fortunes in that region are bright indeed.

Although they did not shift to the same degree as southerners, midwesterners have also tilted more toward the Republicans in 1994. . . .

REALIGNMENT?

The restructuring of the electorate in the South and the 1994 elections' outcome have revised interest in critical realignment theory, first proposed by V. O. Key, Jr. in 1955 and modified and improved by Key and then by many authors, such as Walter Dean Burnham and James Sundquist. Realignment theory posits that major political shifts in the United States can be defined and identified by rather dramatic changes in the electorate and in partisan control of federal, state, and local governments.

Critical Election?

One feature of realignment theory is its cyclical nature, with a critical election and a new party system oc-

curring every 30 years or so. It is now 60 years since the 1930s realignment, however, and scholars have not been able to agree whether or not a new party system has developed. The Republican party's ability, first under Nixon and then Reagan/Bush, to capture the White House indicates that the party system arising out of the 1930s has changed. At the same time, however, the Democratic party has been able to maintain control of both houses of Congress (with minor interruptions) as well as most state legislatures and governorships. Political analysts recognized that things had changed, but were unable to declare that a critical election had occurred. This led other scholars to doubt that, in the modern era of televised campaigns and weakened party structures, the concept of "realignment" still applies. We will not try to resolve the debate over whether a realignment occurred before the 1990s. Instead, we focus on the contemporary situation and the 1994 elections.

Shift in Electoral Control

Obviously there was a dramatic shift in electoral control at the national level. Republicans now also control 60% of state governorships, 22 lower houses of state government, and 24 state senates. Republicans control both houses of the legislatures as well as the governorship in 15 states. The GOP was the dominant party in 1994 in terms of its ability to win elections, although it has not yet shown that it will be able to dominate elections in the future. As someone has surely said, "a landslide does not a realignment make."

Partisanship and Ideology

The evidence for a shift in the public's partisan makeup is less clear. The Gallup Poll has been asking about party identification since 1937, thereby providing the longest running indicator of the partisan composition of the U.S. public. The most recent Gallup data show little change in the percentage of Americans who consider themselves Democrats, Republicans, or Independents. In short, Gallup polls *do not* show a shift in the electorate to a Republican majority. However, they do show a narrowing of the gap between Republicans and Democrats in recent times, and have found Republicans to have a plurality lead in a number of polls conducted in 1995.

Polls conducted for the *Times Mirror* Center for The People & The Press, however, do reveal growing affiliation with the GOP....

Data on party identification, then, do not clearly confirm a shift to a Republican majority in the electorate, although there has probably been some movement toward the Republicans. It is important to note here, however, that partisanship as measured by the classic Gallup and Michigan questions is very volatile. Several times during the 1937–1993 years of Democratic dominance, polling by Gallup showed Republicans were the plurality party or very close to the Democratic party in partisan support (note especially the period between 1939 and early 1947). More importantly, demographic trends indicate that the current rough parity between the Democrats and Republicans is likely to shift towards the Republicans in coming years. Cohort replacement in the electorate over the past several years is replacing older Democrats—politically socialized during the New Deal—with young voters who were politically socialized under Reagan....

Shift in Ideology

While the electorate has become only marginally more Republican, it has become more likely to identify itself as conservative and much less likely to identify itself as liberal. In May 1972, 32% of Americans responding to a Gallup Poll described their point of view on political and governmental matters as "moderately liberal" or "very liberal," 33% identified themselves as "middle of the road," and 27% identified themselves as "moderately conservative" or "very conservative." A comparable question, asked in an August 1995 Gallup Poll, found that just 17% of Americans described their political views as "liberal" or "very liberal." 44% identified themselves as "moderate," and 33% identified themselves as "conservative" or "very conservative."

This shift in ideological identification would not be crucial to understanding the 1994 elections if both parties were becoming more conservative over time. However, Fred Steeper's analysis of the 1994 elections indicates that the parties and voting behavior are becoming more polarized. He argues that short-

term election factors usually push all ideological and demographic groups in the same partisan direction. For example, in the 1992 presidential election, liberals, moderates, and conservatives all voted more Democratic than they had in the 1988 election. Other demographic groups behaved similarly. By contrast, when demographic subgroups move in different directions, this is evidence of an electoral realignment.

Ideological groups did *not* all move in the same direction in 1994. Voters who identified themselves as conservatives were far more likely than "normal" to have voted for the Republican party, and voters who identified themselves as liberals were more likely to have voted for the Democratic party....

Catalysts for Realignment

The 1994 elections were probably phase one of a "critical election" period. What was the catalyst for 1994? *We believe the current realignment stems from widespread economic fear generated by rapid restructuring of the U.S. and international economies and, surprisingly, America's victory in the Cold War.* Although economic statistics suggest that the U.S. economy is relatively sound, polls show that many Americans worry about stagnant wages and losing their jobs. Although unemployment is low (<6%), many, if not most blue collar and white collar employees live in constant fear that they will be "restructured" or "downsized" or "right-sized" out of a job.

Realignments in the 1890s and 1930s also turned on economic issues, when substantial segments of the public looked to government to solve economic woes. Today, however, polls reveal increasing dissatisfaction with the "solutions" government has offered during the last 60 years. The Republican party is the chief beneficiary of growing anti-big government sentiment.

The other reason for the current realignment is less obvious. Both parties lost a portion of their *raison d'etre* when the Soviet Union collapsed. The GOP forfeited much of its ability to tout the importance of strong national security policies, one consequence of which was, ironically, a powerful centralized state. The Democrats lost something even more vital: the statist prop for their domestic programs. No longer could Democrats rely on a seemingly successful, fearfully strong Soviet socialist state to justify domestic policies emphasizing the role of a large central government. Losing the intellectual basis for a strong government was crucial for, save in time of war, domestic affairs drive far more votes than does foreign policy.

The effect of the parties' losses was a large net gain for the Republican party. . . .

Most Americans appear convinced that big government is not the answer to their problems. As Everett Carll Ladd put it, "While not turning against government, Americans have become more skeptical about its efficacy, less inclined to agree when a politician approaches them saying, in effect, 'We have a terrific problem, and this new program is what's needed.'" The fate of the Clinton administration's health care reform proposals illustrates Ladd's point. Popular when first proposed, when the plan's intrusiveness and cost became evident, most Americans jumped ship. Americans do not totally trust the unfettered "free market" as a solution to all their problems, but they are even more skeptical of statist solutions.

If fears about the economy, statism, and the Democratic party were the catalyzing issues in the 1994 elections, can they really be strong enough issues to lead to an electoral realignment? We believe so, but we must all wait and see. Nineteen ninety-six and 1998 will tell the tale.

| READING 33 |

Has Godot Finally Arrived?: Religion and Realignment

Lyman A. Kellstedt, John C. Green, James L. Guth, and Corwin E. Smidt

Individuals who analyze the changing voting habits of the American voter use many specific categories in trying to figure out what broad changes are occurring. Students of elections are busy

From "Has Godot Finally Arrived? Religion and Realignment" by L. A. Kellstedt, et al., 1995, *The Public Perspective,* June/July, pp. 18–22. © *The Public Perspective,* a publication of the Roper Center for Public Opinion Research, University of Connecticut, Storrs. Reprinted by permission.

proliferating various categories for classifying voters. They want to determine if voters' longer-term loyalties are changing or staying the same. If loyalties are changing, they want to know how fast and in what direction.

Categories for classifying voters include gender, age, self-identification with a party or as an independent, race, income, education, region, place of residence (e.g., urban, suburban, rural), religion, union membership, and political philosophy, among others. And, of course, all of these single categories can be used together so that, for example, urban Catholic white union members who did not go beyond high school and earn less than $40,000 annually can be singled out to contrast with suburban Catholic white nonunion members who had at least some college and make more than $40,000 annually. The possibilities are endless.

The following reading, by political scientists at Wheaton College, the University of Akron, Furman University, and Calvin College, explores the religious dimension in relation to changing voting habits. Naturally, no single dimension explains overall major shifts in the electorate. However, these authors analyze the data and make clear that one factor in the disintegration of the New Deal coalition and the swing of the electorate in a more Republican direction is the fact that white evangelical protestants and Roman Catholics have, over time, abandoned their former Democratic loyalties in large numbers and are now solidly Republican.

Everett Ladd has noted that talk of party realignment is akin to "Waiting for Godot." Does the stunning Republican victory in 1994 mean the wait is finally over? While GOP gains may prove ephemeral, exit poll data reveal that one kind of realignment is indeed underway: a religious one. Members of the nation's two largest religious groups, white Evangelical Protestants and Roman Catholics show every sign of a fundamental reordering of political preferences. In 1994, Evangelicals entrenched themselves as the senior partner in the Republican coalition, while Catholics departed once again from their traditional Democratic moorings, after a brief visit home in 1992. Interestingly, the key GOP supporters in both groups were regular church attendees, the easiest to mobilize through such channels.

THE RELIGIOUS VOTE IN 1994

How did major American religious groups vote in 1994? Table 7.1 reports the GOP House vote for the three largest traditions among whites (Evangelical and Mainline Protestant and Roman Catholic), for those who claim no religious identification (seculars), and several smaller groups of whites (such as Jews and Mormons). For purposes of comparison, the voting of nonwhite ethnic groups is also included.

The 1994 vote had significant religious underpinnings. The strongest Republican vote came from Mormons, with 78% backing House GOP candidates. Evangelicals were a close second at 75%. The size of the GOP House vote may not be a record for Mormons, a small group concentrated in the West, but is probably a historic high for the more numerous Evangelicals who not only dominate the South but are a major presence elsewhere.

In contrast, Mainline Protestants, long the backbone of the GOP, gave Republicans just over half their votes, only modestly more than Roman Catholics, once the strongest pillar of the Democratic ethnoreligious establishment. Note that among both Evangelicals and Catholics, regular church attendees were more Republican, a tendency long evident among Mainline Protestants, but which, ironically, almost disappeared among them in 1994. The remaining religious and ethnic groups were much less Republican, ranging from 44% of seculars to only 10% among black Americans.

The second two columns in Table 7.1 summarize the religious composition of party electorates. Evangelicals provided almost three out of ten GOP voters; weekly attendees alone supplied more than one fifth, Mainline Protestants contributed slightly more than one quarter, Catholics, slightly less. Note that regularly attending Catholics actually outnumbered their Mainline counterparts among GOP voters. Taken together, all weekly church attendees constituted just over half the Republican electorate, highlighting both the salience of social issue conservatism and the great tensions it provokes among Republicans.

What about the Democrats? As one might expect, their coalition is more diverse. Mainline Protestants provided about a quarter of the total, while Catholics accounted for just over one-fifth, slightly more than did non-whites. Seculars and Evangelicals each contributed slightly more than one-tenth, as did combined Jews, Hispanics, and whites of other religions. In contrast to the GOP, religiously observant whites provided less than a third of the Democratic coalition, helping to explain both the dominance of social issue liberalism and less attention towards religion within the party.

HISTORICAL BACKDROP

The magnitude of change within religious traditions is more impressive when put into historical context. Surveys from the 1950s reveal Evangelicals and Catholics as fixtures of the Democratic House electorate, supplemented by small numbers of seculars and religious minorities, while Mainline Protestants were the core of the GOP. In the 1960s, Evangelicals moved away from the Democratic Party, first in presidential contests, then in down-ticket races, a process now well advanced but not yet complete.

Catholics drifted from their historic Democratic moorings as well, but the first defectors were often those with minimal religious attachments. By the late 1980s and 1990s, however, defectors were often the more religiously observant, especially among younger Catholics, replicating the Evangelical pattern. During the same period, Mainline Protestants were headed in the opposite direction. Many, but particularly the least religiously involved, were abandoning the GOP. Also, the steady growth in the number of secular voters since the 1950s provided an additional source of Democratic votes in House races.

ANATOMY OF THE 1994 RELIGIOUS VOTE

Thus, the 1994 vote had a significant religious component, reflecting a long term realignment of important groups. What factors help explain these findings?

A good place to begin is with issues. Exit poll respondents were asked: "Which two issues mattered most in deciding how you voted for U.S. House?" Not surprisingly, responses differ significantly by religious

TABLE 7.1 Religious Groups, Voting and Partisanship in the 1994 Elections

	GOP Vote	PARTY COALITIONS (BY 1994 VOTE)		PARTY IDENTIFICATION		PARTY COALITIONS (BY PARTY ID)	
		Rep.	Dem.	Rep.	Dem.	Rep.	Dem.
White Mormons	78%	4%	1%	56%	12%	5%	1%
White Evangelicals:	75	29	11	52	21	30	12
Regular Church Attenders	78	(22)	(7)	56	17	(24)	(7)
Not Regular Church Attenders	68	(7)	(4)	42	30	(7)	(5)
White Mainline Protestants:	56	27	24	38	31	27	21
Regular Church Attenders	56	(9)	(8)	40	28	(10)	(7)
Not Regular Church Attenders	55	(18)	(16)	36	31	(17)	(14)
White Catholics:	53	22	22	33	38	21	23
Regular Church Attenders	57	(13)	(12)	35	37	(13)	(13)
Not Regular Church Attenders	49	(9)	(10)	29	38	(8)	(10)
White Seculars	44	9	12	27	40	9	11
White Other Religions	39	2	4	20	33	2	3
Hispanics	35	2	3	29	60	2	4
White Jews	25	1	4	12	62	1	5
Blacks	10	2	17	6	77	2	19

Source: 1994 Mitofsky International exit poll.

group and church attendance. Regular church attendees among Evangelicals were much more likely to name family values (47%) or abortion (29%) as most important, while nonattenders cited crime (31%), family values (28%), plus taxes and economic issues (both 25%). Among Mainline Protestants, church attendees and nonattenders were quite similar with crime the top priority (36% mentions for both), economic concerns (25% and 32%, respectively), and taxes (24% and 29%). Catholics in both groups resembled their Mainline Protestant counterparts in priorities, with the exception that regular attendees were considerably more likely to name family values (22%) or abortion (17%) as important vote determinants. Seculars put little emphasis on abortion or family values, stressing instead crime, economics and taxes as the most important issues, while giving education a higher rating than did voters in the major traditions. Mormon choices paralleled those of Evangelicals, while Jews and blacks responded like seculars.

What impact did issue priorities have on the vote? Table 7.2 shows the Republican House vote for those making each issue a priority. Three important patterns stand out. First, regardless of issue focus, Evangelicals were the most Republican and seculars the least, with Mainline Protestants and Catholics falling in between. Second, with few exceptions, regular attendees were more Republican than their less observant counterparts, regardless of tradition or issue focus. Third, there are some strong partisan/issue patterns. Republicans gained from concern with family values, and taxes in all religious groups and attendance levels. In contrast, they gained markedly less from voters' worries on education, health care, or crime. Abortion was clearly the most divisive issue. Over 90% of regularly attending Evangelicals choosing it voted Republican, but only 20% of seculars for whom the issue was salient opted for the GOP. Mainline Protestants and Catholics were also sharply divided by abortion. For both groups, weekly attendees

TABLE 7.2   Percentage Voting Republican: House Elections 1994
[Whites by: religious traditions, church attendance, issue salience, and selected demographic characteristics.]

	EVANGELICALS		MAINLINE PROT.		CATHOLICS		SECULARS
	RegCh	*NotReg*	*RegCh*	*NotReg*	*RegCh*	*NotReg*	
Respondents listing the issue as key for them:							
Abortion	90%	83%	56%	24%	65%	38%	20%
Family Values	88	74	70	69	73	67	60
Taxes	85	83	69	61	71	66	77
Crime	72	72	55	60	52	52	48
Education	67	58	48	44	49	28	31
Economy/Jobs	60	70	54	55	54	47	45
Health Care	59	49	44	42	36	36	24
Respondent's Education:							
High School	66	59	51	52	46	46	52
Some College	82	70	59	60	57	49	51
College Grad	87	80	66	62	61	58	37
Post Grad	78	81	47	46	65	42	36
Respondent's Income:							
Less than $30K	73	59	45	53	44	42	40
$30K–$75K	79	74	60	58	60	49	43
Over $75K	87	93	60	55	66	62	49
Respondent's Gender:							
Male	78	74	61	61	64	52	47
Female	78	65	52	51	52	48	38
Group's 1994 GOP Vote	78	68	56	55	57	49	44

Note: RegCh = Regular Church Attendance. NotReg = Less than Regular Church Attendance. The n's are small for some groups of "post graduate" education and high [$75 Thousand +] income.

Source: 1994 Mitofsky International exit poll.

choosing the issue voted Republican while the less observant voted Democratic. Finally, emphasis on the economy and jobs had mixed effects: nonregular attendees among Evangelicals selecting this option were the most Republican, while seculars were the most Democratic.

The data also revealed some important interactions between religious tradition and demography in producing partisan choices. A staple of the New Deal Democratic coalition was support from working class voters. This classic alliance was undermined in 1994, at least among Evangelicals. As Table 7.2

shows, large majorities of lower income Evangelicals went Republican, especially among churchgoers, voting their beliefs, not their pocketbooks. Among both Mainliners and Catholics, those in the low-income and low-education groups also voted Republican in substantial numbers.

Similar exceptions to the classic New Deal pattern work in the other direction, such as the relatively strong support given the GOP by the least educated secular voters and the Democratic preferences of voters with post graduate education among Mainline Protestants, nonobservant Catholics, and seculars. Perhaps this latter group constitutes a highly educated, politically liberal "New Class" of professionals which spans several religious traditions. Yet, the classic effect of education still holds among regularly attending Catholics, who become more Republican with every step up the educational and income ladders. In some cases, status and religion reinforce each other, as among high income Evangelicals, who were the most Republican of any demographic voting group in Table 7.2.

One more demographic factor in Table 7.2 is worth considering, gender. Many pundits noted the large gender gap in 1994, reporting a massive male "backlash" against the Democrats. Indeed, men gave the GOP more votes than women in almost every religious group except for two. Among churchgoing Evangelicals, males and females voted Republican at exactly the same rate, and among faithful Mormons the gender gap was actually reversed. Clearly, Republican gains involved strong support from conservative, religious women, not just disaffected men.

Considering these results, it is not surprising that statistical controls for various demographics have no impact on religious voting patterns, confirming the findings of other analysts that religion was more powerful than economics in 1994.

LONG TERM EFFECTS?

Do these findings signal realignment? If realignment is conceived as a process involving changes in the partisan alignments of major groups, then Godot may well have arrived for white Evangelicals and Catholics.

We examined the impact of church attendance and age on the Republican House vote in 1994. GOP support was very high among churchgoing, younger Evangelicals (85%), so high in fact that its long term persistence seems assured. Older church attending Evangelicals were strongly GOP as well (67%), but less than their younger co-parishioners. And younger non-attending Evangelicals voted just as Republican (68%) as older church attendees, but much more so than older non-attenders (53%).

Among Mainline Protestants, age had little impact on voting, with young and old voting Republican in roughly equal measure. Among Catholics, however, age mattered a great deal, with younger Catho-

lics more likely to vote Republican. Among regular attendees, 58% of those under the age of 40 voted for the GOP, while 52% of those over 60 did the same. Among nonobservant Catholics the difference is even greater, with 53% of those under 40 voting Republican, while only 35% of those over 60 did the same.

Finally, what about party self-identification? Table 7.1 presents data on this much-watched indicator (Independents are excluded for purposes of presentation.) Mormons (56%) and Evangelicals (52%) are by far the most Republican, while Mainliners (38%) and Catholics (33%) exhibit deep partisan divisions, with the Mainliners marginally more Republican and Catholics slightly more Democratic. These figures alone suggest a fundamental change in party coalitions. Seculars are two fifths Democratic, and the Democratic bias tends to increase for the remaining groups. Hispanics and Jews are more than three fifths Democratic and blacks nearly four fifths. Note that in the three largest traditions, church attendees are more Republican, although by varying margins.

The end result of these long term changes in the parties' core constituencies can be noted in the two right hand columns in Table 7.1. Among 1994 voters, Evangelicals were the largest Republican constituency, easily outnumbering Mainliners. Catholics constituted one fifth of the GOP identifiers and all the remaining groups combined for one fifth. Thus, Mainline Protestants are no longer the GOP's religious backbone. Catholics are still the largest Democratic religious constituency (23%), but barely edge out Mainline Protestants for top honors. Blacks are slightly less numerous, but when combined with other racial and ethnic minorities, account for more than one quarter of the Democratic total. The remaining one quarter is similarly diverse, with equal proportions of Evangelicals and seculars, plus Jews and other smaller groups.

EMERGING ETHNO-RELIGIOUS COALITIONS

The importance of these changes can hardly be overstated. The core groups of the New Deal coalition, namely white Evangelicals and white Catholics, have, to varying extents, deserted the Democratic Party. Evangelicals are now at the center of the Republican coalition, and Catholics are up for grabs.

Thus, after years of gradual disintegration, the New Deal religious coalition is now in shambles, and with it the Democratic lock on congressional and state government. Although the GOP has gained substantially from partisan shifts within religious traditions, it has suffered some losses as well. Mainline Protestants have left the GOP in large numbers, and like Catholics, are now an electoral swing group. Democrats also have gained or maintained support with less observant members of the major traditions, among the growing number of seculars, and various ethnic minorities.

New forms of ethno-religious politics are emerging, with the GOP drawing the more religiously observant voters, at least among whites, and the Democrats attracting the least observant in the major traditions, seculars, and various minority groups. While it is unclear exactly how these trends will play out, the Grand Old Party has at least one short run advantage: as recent elections demonstrate, grassroots religious institutions can mobilize the Republican religious constituencies. There is at present a comparable set of institutions mobilizing less-religious Democratic voters. This Republican advantage can be erased, however, if religious mobilization goes too far, driving dissident groups to the Democrats, the traditional "party of diversity." Thus, religious realignment poses serious challenges for both parties as 1996 approaches.

READING 34

The Status-Quo Election

Everett C. Ladd

In the following selection, Evertt Carll Ladd, Director of the Roper Center for Public Opinion Research, summarizes the meaning of the 1996 election.

From "The Status-Quo Election: Introduction" by E. C. Ladd, 1997, *The Public Perspective,* December/January, pp. 4–5. © *The Public Perspective,* a publication of the Roper Center for Public Opinion Research, University of Connecticut, Storrs. Reprinted by permission.

The 1996 election produced a "status quo" result in a very obvious way: Incumbents prevailed. The sitting Democratic president, Bill Clinton, was reelected despite significant popular concern about perceived character flaws. At the same time the Republicans, who had gained control of both the House and Senate in 1994, retained their majorities. Not every incumbent, Republican or Democrat, who ran won. But a very high proportion did—95 percent of the incumbents running in the general election. And only marginal changes in the size of the majority occurred: The Republicans saw their total number of seats in the House shrink from 236 to 227 (out of 435), but Senate Republicans saw their seats increase by two, from 53 to 55.

Ladd argues that 1996 was also a status-quo election in the sense that the conservative mood among voters was solidifying and was accurately represented in the election results. Public opinion data show that the generally conservative, anti-activist government stance of the electorate continues to consolidate. The majority of the electorate prefers smaller government, fewer services, and more latitude for the private sector. The continued drop in turnout of eligible voters also suggests that they view government as less important than in the past and/or they view politicians with greater distaste than in the past.

This general pattern of preferences and behavior suggests that candidates from both parties, for both president and Congress, will continue to drift to the right: the Republicans to a fairly hard-right position and the Democrats to a center to center-right position. President Clinton in his second term already occupies a center to center-right position. For the immediate future what remains of the liberal left in the federal government will be represented in Washington primarily by a small number of Democratic House members who come from very liberal, unquestionably Democratic districts, primarily in large cities in the Northeast and in California.

Since the balloting we have often been told that it was a "status-quo election." For once, the conventional wisdom is correct. But the extent to which there was continuity goes well beyond what is commonly understood.

It was obviously a status-quo election in that it left control of the government essentially unchanged. The Republicans retained their majorities in both the House and Senate—the first time they managed to do so for consecutive terms since 1928. They picked up two seats in the Senate, bringing their majority to 55–45, but lost House seats, leaving their margin in the lower chamber at 22 (with two Texas run-offs not concluded when we went to press). While this was happening, Mr. Clinton won re-election and did so by a margin similar to the one he gained four years earlier.

The election's status-quo character was reaffirmed more profoundly as the country stayed on course ideologically. Over the last two decades, the US has undergone a profound philosophical realignment, which centers around changing views of government. Over this span, Americans became more skeptical about government's efficacy, less inclined to agree when a politician approaches them saying, in effect, "We have a terrible problem, and this new federal program is what's needed." It's certainly true that many people continue to want government to do many things. This acknowledged, more government is a vastly harder sell now than it was from the Depression through the Great Society. The health care debate of 1993–94 evinced important elements of this shift. It began centering on one question: Do we have major problems, especially involving escalating costs and coverage? The emphatic answer was (and still is) yes. In the later stages, though, the debate focused on a different question: Do you favor extended governmental management of the health care system? And to this, the answer was no. The Democrats won the debate when it focused on the first question and lost when it shifted to the second.

There hasn't been, since 1994, any movement back toward a "more government" stance. I've examined a wide range of questions charting the public's assessment of government performance, and its preferences as to how much government it wants, asked in late 1994 and early 1995, and then again in 1996. And, I've been unable to find an instance where sentiment shifted significantly. For example, asked "Would you

say you favor smaller government with fewer services, or larger government with many services?," 63 percent of respondents chose the smaller government option in a *Los Angeles Times* poll taken in January 1995, and the exact same proportion chose it in an ABC News/*Washington Post* poll of August 1996.

The surveys taken November 5 of voters leaving polling stations around the country showed them remaining in a generally conservative mood. Asked by Voter News Service (VNS) which was closer to their views, that government "should do more to solve problems," or that it is "doing too many things better left to businesses and individuals," respondents chose the latter by a 52–41 percent margin. Just 18 percent of those participating in the VNS exit poll said they thought the new federal welfare law cuts spending too deeply, while 39 percent said it doesn't cut deeply enough, and 37 percent thought it about right. President Clinton wound up signing the legislation, of course, but it's still striking that only 25 percent of those voting for him told VNS that the legislation cuts too much, while 27 percent of them said it doesn't trim enough.

Finally, the status-quo character of the November 5 balloting is evident in voters' judgments about Bill Clinton. They first elected him four years ago unenthusiastically, indeed with great doubts, and then re-elected him this year with much the same concerns and uncertainty. Asked in the VNS exit poll whether they considered Mr. Clinton "honest and trustworthy," respondents replied by a 54–41 percent margin that they did *not*. Twenty percent of those voting to re-elect him said they didn't consider him honest and trustworthy. By a margin of 60 to 33 percent, the exit poll respondents said they believed Mr. Clinton hadn't told the truth "in explaining Whitewater and other matters under investigation." The poll finding that most strikingly reflects the reluctance with which Americans re-elected the President is that 48 percent of all voters, and 23 percent of those giving Mr. Clinton their ballots, said they would have voted for Colin Powell had he been the Republican nominee; just 36 percent indicated they would have voted for Clinton had Powell been the Republican choice.

Many analysts have described the 1996 presidential vote as evidence of the economy, or issues, trumping character. Now it is true that 58 percent of

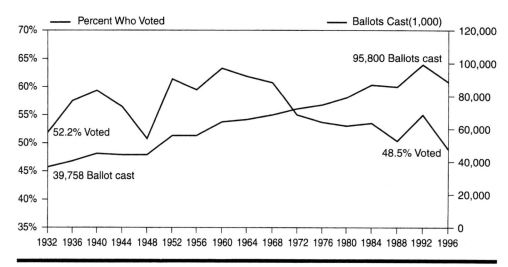

FIGURE 7.1 Voter turnout 1932–1996.

those polled by VNS said that the candidates' "position on the issues" was the more important factor in their presidential decision, while just 38 percent indicated that "personal character and values" loomed larger. But one can't conclude from numbers like these that character mattered little.

Having decided to vote for him, Mr. Clinton's backers more or less had to say that issues were more important than character in determining their vote—and they did say this by a margin of 82 to 14 percent. But many Clinton voters gave him only tepid support—because of their concerns about his character. And many others who might have voted to re-elect him—at a time when the economy was booming, and given the Republican nominee was unable to inspire—either voted reluctantly for Mr. Dole or stayed home. The end result—re-electing the President by a modest margin, while expressing grave reservations about him, and constraining him with a Republican majority in both houses of the Congress—may seem peculiar. But it makes considerable sense given the alternatives voters were presented.

One area where the 1996 story was *not* one of continuity is voter turnout. The number voting was *down* by an extraordinary 9 million—even though the number of people eligible to vote had increased substantially. It's likely that the 1996 turnout rate was the lowest since mass popular balloting was introduced in the 1830s. The 1924 election is technically the one with the lowest turnout, but it was the first contest following the introduction of women's suffrage—which doubled the voting age population. It took many women a little while to assume their new right—making the 1924 turnout an abberation. The magnitude of the 1996 drop-off (see Figure 7.1) is in fact unprecedented.

READING 35

To the '94 Election Victors Go the Fundraising Spoils

Jonathan D. Salant and David S. Cloud

Campaign finance is one of the ever-present and never-solved problems of American politics. In fact, despite a very large amount of rhetoric surrounding

From "To the '94 Election Victors Go the Fundraising Spoils" by J. D. Salant and D. S. Cloud, 1995, *Congressional Quarterly Weekly Report* (53)15: 1055–1059. Copyright © 1995 by Congressional Quarterly Press. Reprinted by permission.

the issue, often the problem is not addressed concretely.

Running for an office of any importance in the United States is very costly. In 1996, for example, presidential primary and general election campaigns collectively spent over $400 million. All campaigns for the Senate, both winning and losing, cost almost $300 million. All campaigns for the House, both winning and losing, cost almost $500 million.

The most expensive winning Senate campaign was that of incumbent Senator John Kerrey [D-MA] and cost almost $11 million. The most expensive losing Senate campaign was that of a Democratic challenger in Virginia and cost close to $12 million. In House campaigns the costliest win was that of House Speaker Newt Gingrich (R-GA), who spent over $5.5 million. His Democratic challenger spent $3.3 million in the losing effort, the most expensive losing campaign for a House seat.

Even little noticed state races cost a lot. For example, one hotly contested race for one of the 33 seats in the Ohio state Senate in 1996 cost the incumbent over $200,000 in a winning effort. Naturally, big state governorships cost an enormous amount. In 1994 in California, for example, the two major candidates spent over $38 million between them.

There are many aspects of campaign finance to consider. The following reading by two staff members of Congressional Quarterly Weekly Report *looks in some detail at one of them. It considers the financial contributions to congressional campaigns from Political Action Committees (PACs). Their central point is that PACs are typically more driven by incumbency than by ideological preference. Many PACs that ideologically were more in tune with Republican candidates nevertheless gave a good deal to Democratic candidates when the Democrats seemed to have a lock on majority status in Congress. Above all, PACs wanted favorable legislative treatment. They get this from whomever holds office, not from ideological soul mates who may lose. But when the Republicans gained a majority in Congress, then conservative PACs could give to incumbents and to aspiring Republicans and simultaneously act in accord with their ideological preferences.*

On Dec. 9, 1994, Rep.-elect Jon Christensen was named to the House Ways and Means Committee, with its jurisdiction over health care and the taxation of life insurance policies. The same day, the freshman Nebraska Republican received a $5,000 contribution from the Mutual of Omaha insurance company's political action committee.

During the campaign, the Mutual of Omaha PAC had contributed $5,335 to Christensen's opponent, Democratic incumbent Peter Hoagland, who was, until his defeat, also a member of Ways and Means.

"If you help the other guy and the other guy is no longer there, it [giving to the winner] is all part of the process," Christensen said. "It may be common sense."

Christensen's experience isn't unique. Since the GOP election landslide Nov. 8, business-related PACs have dramatically shifted their giving from the Democrats who used to run Congress to the Republicans who do now.

What makes this shift so significant is that the groups representing corporations, cooperatives and trade organizations make up 63 percent of the 4,618 PACs registered with the Federal Election Commission. They rang up 68 percent of the $189.4 million spent by PACs during the 1993–94 election cycle.

The 10 business-related PACs most active immediately after Election Day gave $581,949 to congressional candidates from Nov. 9 to Dec. 31, 1994. Republicans received $518,900—89 percent of the total. Before the election, those same PACs spent $10 million, dividing their contributions equally between candidates from the two major parties.

Labor-affiliated PACs, on the other hand, remained firmly in the Democratic camp both before and after the election.

Though it is early, the pattern of increased giving to Republicans was discerned both in the contributions doled out by PACs immediately following the election, and in the first months of 1995, which is the opening of the 1995–96 election cycle.

In some cases, business PACs are scrambling to make up for the support they gave to a winner's opponent in the 1994 election—backing incumbent Democrat Hoagland over Republican challenger Christensen in Nebraska's 2nd District, for example. Others are feverishly using dollars to forge relationships with the new GOP masters of Capitol Hill, whom they may have slighted before.

"There are those without Republican ties who are heavily engaged in panic buying," observed John R. Vogt, a lobbyist for the Public Securities Association, which has a PAC.

But most business PACs are feeling liberated by the GOP takeover. For years, they have maneuvered warily between the Democrats who were in charge of committees and regularly threatened retribution unless business PACs gave generously to Democratic candidates, and the Republicans, who claimed to better represent the interests of business PACs and were outraged at their support of Democrats.

Now pragmatism and ideology happily coincide.

"PACs are, in a sense, going back to their roots," said Paul A. Equale, an official with the Independent Insurance Agents of America PAC. "With Republicans, you have the affinity of ideology, the affinity of business, plus the fact that they are in the majority."

The surge in post-election giving to Republicans is not surprising, but the early returns leave several unanswered questions: Can the Republican Party continue to raise money at the accelerated pace it has set this year? And will business PACs continue to give in such disproportionate levels to one party?

Republican leaders do not hesitate to remind business PACs that they are watching contributions closely and that they expect to be supported for moving an agenda that is business-friendly. The clear threat is that PACs that play both sides of the fence can expect less cooperation from the GOP leadership.

"Our members have felt they were carrying the legislative water for many of these groups who then gave their money to the other side," said Rep. Bill Paxon of New York, chairman of the National Republican Congressional Committee (NRCC).

"It's very difficult for me to argue that people should open their arms to those who are embracing their opponents. I certainly am not going to embrace someone who's constantly stabbing me in the back. We're making sure that the members know who's wielding the knife," Paxon said.

His counterpart, Rep. Martin Frost, D-Texas, chairman of the Democratic Congressional Campaign Committee, acknowledged the obvious. "Now that the Republicans are in the majority, you'd expect that the PACs would give to the majority party," Frost said. "It is natural that they would have an easier time raising money than they had in the past."

SHIFT IN DIRECTION

The signs of the shift toward the GOP are many:

• Before Nov. 8, United Parcel Service's PAC—the most generous in the country—gave $1.4 million to Democrats and $1.1 million to Republicans. From Nov. 9 through Dec. 31, the PAC gave only $1,625 to Democrats. Republicans, on the other hand, received $66,000.

• Democrats took in 55 percent of the contributions made by the National Association of Life Underwriters PAC before the election, garnering $645,640 to the Republicans' $529,250. From Nov. 9 to the end of 1994, the PAC gave $76,500 to congressional candidates. All went to Republicans.

• AT&T's PAC gave Democrats 64 percent of its contributions before the the election, or $744,453. The GOP received $425,496. After the election, however, Republicans received 80 percent of the contributions, or $63,695. The Democrats received $16,050.

The pattern of substantially increased giving to Republicans was evident both in the final months of 1994 and the first months of 1995, which is the start of the 1995–96 election cycle.

During January and February of 1993, when the Democrats were in control of Congress, the American Bankers Association divided its PAC contributions almost evenly: 51 percent to the Republicans, 49 percent to the Democrats. During the same period this year, the bankers' PAC gave 87 percent of its contributions to the GOP.

"We have always tried to work with people who were supportive of bank issues," said Floyd E. Stoner, director of legislative operations for the bankers' group. "If they were defeated, we looked at those who won."

Not everyone waited until after the results were known to bet on the Republicans. A Congressional Quarterly computer analysis of data from the National Library on Money and Politics found some PACs shifting loyalties a month before the election.

In October 1992, for example, the American Medical Association PAC gave 53 percent of its contributions to Republican candidates. In October 1994, it gave Republicans 64 percent. The Credit Union National Association's PAC gave Republicans 27 percent of its contributions in October 1992 and 57 percent in October 1994. AT&T's PAC gave 30 percent of its October contributions to Republicans in 1992, but 51 percent in 1994.

THE INCUMBENT ADVANTAGE

No matter the ideology of business PACs, most of their money traditionally has gone to incumbents, which until now meant Democrats.

Although Republican calls for less regulation and lower taxes mirrored the corporate agenda, business PACs for years supported Democratic incumbents rather than aiding long-shot GOP challengers.

"The majority controls the legislation on the floor," said veteran Democratic fundraiser Terrence McAuliffe. "They want to deal with the party in control. It's as simple as that."

Federal Election Commission records tell the story of business PACs' relationship with the Democrats. During the 1979–80 election cycle, business PACs gave $3 to Republicans for every $2 they gave to Democrats. But during the 1980s, that ratio gradually shifted; during the 1991–92 election cycle, Democratic candidates took in $10 million more than Republicans did from business PACs.

Michael J. Malbin, a professor of political science and director of the Center for Legislative Studies at the State University of New York's Rockefeller Institute of Government, explained that until 1994 Democratic incumbents were able to deliver a simple message to business PACs: "We control the levers; we control the agenda. . . . You can choose to take the long shot and hope to get people in office who you like a lot better, but . . . the odds are 9 out of 10 that you're going to be dealing with the people you're looking at."

In the just-concluded election cycle, business PACs contributed $66.8 million to the Democrats and $62.5 million to the Republicans. The Democratic edge, however, came from the amount of money its incumbents received, according to statistics compiled by Malbin.

Looking solely at PACs representing corporations, Malbin found that House GOP challengers received an average of $11,944, almost 10 times the $1,289 that Democratic challengers averaged. Democratic incumbents averaged $96,780 to Republican incumbents' $90,673.

Malbin found, however, that corporate PACs were more GOP-oriented in their Senate giving. Republican incumbents averaged $531,539 in contributions, compared with $378,473 for Democratic incumbents. GOP challengers received an average of $103,040, which was 15 times more than the $6,639 given to Democratic challengers.

A STAKE IN THE GOP AGENDA

Many of the largest contributors since the election have issues on the GOP agenda.

The House Republicans' "Contract With America" contains proposals near and dear to the business community, including cutting taxes, rolling back government regulation and making it more difficult to collect damages from companies that are found to produce faulty products.

During the 1993–94 election cycle, the American Society of Anesthesiologists PAC ranked 75th in the amount of money given to congressional candidates. Since the election, it has ranked 16th.

Before the election, Democrats received $274,000, or 60 percent, of the anesthesiologists PAC's contributions. Republicans received $180,000, or 40 percent. After the election, the PAC gave 92 percent of its contributions to the GOP, or $23,000. The PAC gave only $2,000 to Democrats.

The anesthesiologists society is one of the groups pushing for a $250,000 cap on awards for pain and suffering in liability cases, including medical malpractice. The cap was part of a civil liability bill (HR 956) that passed the House March 10 and is pending in the Senate.

Three of the top 10 givers since the election have a stake in telecommunications deregulation: AT&T,

Ameritech and BellSouth. All three groups gave a majority of their PAC contributions before the election to Democrats; after the election, they switched to Republicans.

The Progress and Freedom Foundation, headed by close political allies of Speaker Newt Gingrich, R-Ga., is a strong advocate of deregulation. AT&T and BellSouth are among the foundation's contributors.

Other groups have issues they plan to bring to the forefront when Congress returns from its recess.

From Nov. 9 to Dec. 31, the National Rifle Association was the most prolific giver to congressional candidates. Of the $84,892 the NRA handed out during that period, 96 percent went to the GOP. Both Gingrich and Senate Majority Leader Bob Dole, R-Kan., have agreed to take up the issue of repealing last year's ban on certain assault weapons.

IDEOLOGICALLY IN TUNE

Republicans have not been shy about delivering the message that those PACs who have ridden for years with the Democrats should get on board the Republican train before it leaves the station without them. The NRCC compiled a list of the top 400 PACs and the amount they gave to each party. "It was always a mystery to me why so many major corporations financed Democrats," said freshman Rep. Helen Chenoweth, R-Idaho, who received $27,250 in PAC contributions from Nov. 9 to Dec. 31. "Philosophically, the Republicans were more in tune with them. We're beginning to talk about that very openly now. Major corporations need to come home to their philosophy."

Many GOP lawmakers—especially freshmen trying to pay off campaign debts from this past fall—have been busily raising money since Election Day. The NRCC has hired staff to help them raise money.

"Every political consultant will tell you about the need to start fundraising right away," said Joe Scarborough, R-Fla.

Capitalizing on their status as deliverers of the GOP majority, many freshman Republicans have increased the going price of attending their fundraisers to $1,000, PAC officials said. Previously, only chair-

men and other influential members could command such sums.

In some cases, as soon as a freshman received a committee assignment, the industries under that panel's jurisdiction marked the occasion with a donation. Rep. Fred Heineman, R-N.C., was named to the Banking and Financial Services Committee on Dec. 9. From then to the end of the year, he received $8,500 in PAC contributions, with 41 percent coming from banking and insurance interests.

Since becoming the only freshman on the Senate Environment and Public Works Committee on Jan. 4, James M. Inhofe, R-Okla., has taken in at least $69,065 in PAC contributions. Transportation-related PACs accounted for $30,500—44 percent of the total.

Meanwhile, the fundraising is continuing. Several GOP freshmen said they planned to spend part of the April recess raising money back home. Paxon said he believed they would have no trouble finding financial support. "Their potential is rather unlimited now," he said.

A PRICE TO PAY

In a sense, Democrats are paying a price for not limiting PAC contributions when they controlled Congress, said Candice Nelson, an assistant professor of political science at American University and director of the school's Campaign Management Institute.

Democrats have long advocated a system of partial public financing coupled with spending limits as the best way to overhaul the campaign finance system. That proposal was anathema to many Republicans, but it was never fully embraced by House Democrats, either. It took until late last year for Democrats to devise a compromise to reduce PAC giving, and by then the bill was vulnerable to a Republican filibuster in the Senate. It died in late September.

"What's ironic is the Democrats weren't willing to compromise on PACs last time," Nelson said. "It was shortsighted of them. Now they're going to lose all that PAC money. It's going to go to Republicans. They're ideologically and philosophically more aligned with business PACs anyway. Now politics and philosophy work together."

FOOD FOR THOUGHT

1. In their analysis, Tuchfarber and his colleagues note that the 1994 elections represented a rebellion against the Democratic party and Bill Clinton, yet less than one year later, Bill Clinton was reelected to another term. Why do you think that might have occurred? Did Bill Clinton change his position on issues that represent the status quo, which the authors of this article suggested might be his electoral vulnerability? If Clinton's positions did not change greatly, what accounts for his reelection? How important do you consider the character issue to be in the decision to vote? After reading Ladd's article, are you convinced that there has been a shift in the public's ideology? Discuss whether the public's fears about the economy, big government, and the Democratic party are sufficient to lead to an electoral realignment.

2. What is your assessment of the role of religion in voting and partisanship? Why do you think white Evangelicals and white Catholics have "deserted the Democratic Party"? Statistics show that religion was more powerful than economics in the 1994 election, but why do you think that this was the case? To what extent can the importance of religion in voting be attributed to the mobilization of regular churchgoers by political action committees such as the Christian Coalition? How do these developments square with observations that Americans are more secular now than ever?

Observers have created a cottage industry of writing about the "angry white male" voters of 1994 and the "soccer moms" of 1996. Are you convinced of the existence of a gender gap in American politics? If so, what is its cause or impetus?

3. Many congressional scholars take the perspective that the behavior of legislators is goal-driven. That is, whether members of Congress want to remain in office, gain power in Washington, or make good public policy, these goals shape their behavior in office. For example, members might be viewed as undertaking casework in order to make themselves known to constituents and thereby improve their reelection chances. Discuss Herrnson's work using this perspective. Is there any aspect of congressional behavior that the "member goals" view cannot explain? The goal-driven view of congressional behavior is a controversial one; how persuasive do you find it to be?

4. Salant and Cloud's reporting offers convincing evidence of both the pervasiveness of PAC money and the shift of PAC giving to Republicans. Do you think that members of Congress should act to limit PAC contributions? Why does the goal-driven view of member behavior suggest that such limits will not be popular among incumbents? Do you find it troubling that many of the largest PAC contributors have a stake in issues on the congressional agenda?

CHAPTER 8

INTEREST GROUPS

Interest groups are a prominent feature of American politics at national, state, and local levels. They engage in particularly visible activity in seeking specific results from Congress, state legislatures, and local legislative bodies such as city councils. They also seek specific results from chief executives, such as the president, state governors, and mayors. Interest groups play a more subdued, but often important, role with courts.

Most Americans have one or more groups claiming to represent them. Even those who rail against group influence are, almost surely, "represented" whether they are aware of it or not. David Segal, in the first reading in this chapter, "A Nation of Lobbyists," makes the point. He does not, however, raise the question of how legitimate the claims of the groups are or how much attention public officials need to pay to the claims.

Some observers are aghast at the number and presumed power of interest groups. Others claim that their functioning is an important, inevitable, and generally desirable part of a democratic society. Some commentators argue that interest groups have grown more important as public attachment to political parties has weakened. Some, including us, take a middle view: There are abuses by some groups on some occasions, but the competition of groups pursuing different interests is, on balance, inevitable and can be healthy. Groups, like parties, help mediate between the public and officials. However, claims that all interests are represented equally are not empirically supportable. Some interests are better represented than others.

The membership basis for various groups differs. Some have individuals directly enrolled as members. Some have only other organizations as members. Some have a combination of individual and institutional members.

The size and permanence of groups also varies. Some last only a few years and have a staff member or two in a rented office with the basic communication necessities of phone, fax, and e-mail. Others are permanent fixtures, with their own building, a staff of hundreds, and elaborate graphics and film capacities as well as the more rudimentary communications devices.

The number and range of interests represented is remarkably large and continues to grow. Kay Schlozman and John Tierney, in the second reading in this chapter, "More of the Same: Washington Pressure Group Activity in a Decade of Change," report on the basic structure and activities of Washington-based groups. Their data are from the 1970s and early 1980s but the picture they paint of activity is also accurate for the 1990s. The major change is that the number of groups has continued to grow.

The structure of groups in the United States is biased toward the more well-off interests in society. Business interests are particularly advantaged. This has been true throughout our national history. Kay Schlozman examines the contemporary situation in the third reading in the chapter, "What Accent the Heavenly Chorus? Political Equality and the American Pressure System." Saying that the system is biased or weighted in a specific direction is, however, not the same thing as saying that all decisions get made only in the direction of the bias. There are contending interests that also prevail on some issues. And it is important to remember that public officials are not simply the pawns of interest groups.

Interest groups are pervasive in approaching all of the governing institutions in one way or another and at all territorial levels. At the federal level, the members of the House and Senate are the most visible and most frequent targets of lobbying by interest groups. But members of the executive branch, both presidential appointees and career civil servants, are the object of lobbying. The president himself receives concentrated attention from interest groups.

In a more restrained and indirect way, interest groups also lobby federal judges and Supreme Court justices. The fourth reading in the chapter, "Winning in the Courts: Interest Groups and Constitutional Change" by Frank Sorauf, examines the impact of interest groups on constitutional matters.

Interest groups have a rich array of techniques to use as they pursue their goal of influencing public policy. Schlozman and Tierney summarize a number of these techniques in the second reading. A number of interest groups have also gotten heavily involved in direct marketing to segments of the population in order to help build public support for their interests. They then count on this public support to be applied to officials making policy. Groups seek to magnify their impact through demonstrating that some segment of the population holds the views being advocated by the group. The groups, of course, try to impress on members of Congress and the president that the concerned individuals are voters.

Among all of the techniques available to interest groups, the one that generates the most journalistic interest—and a great deal of interest on the part of political scientists, too—is raising and contributing money to political candidates, campaigns, and parties. The purpose of such giving is, of course, to influence policy. But that does not mean that all giving "buys" policy in any direct sense. Frank Sorauf, in "Inside Campaign Finance: The Purchase of Legislatures," the final reading in this chapter, explores the impact of Political Action Committee giving.

Some observers make the claim, in one form or another, that interest groups representing social and economic elites somehow interact and dictate a broad web of national policy favoring their interests. A recent careful study (Heinz, Laumann, Nelson, and Salisbury, *The Hollow Core*, Harvard University Press, 1993) concludes, as the title suggests, that there is no empirical evidence that such an interlocking network of elite groups exists.

It also needs to be stressed that public officials are not passive beings simply waiting to be pressured by various, and sometimes contending, groups. Public of-

ficials are also activists and seek to co-opt groups to help them further their own ends. A legitimate question often arises of who is pressuring whom in the relationship between any specific official or cluster of officials and one or more groups. Politicians build coalitions to get what they want out of the policy process. They will often seek—and do so with considerable success—to add groups to those coalitions.

It is often helpful to see aspects of American politics in comparative perspective. Lest we become fixated on American uniqueness it is worth remembering that all open democratic societies feature interest groups and lobbying as permanent parts of the landscape. Regulation of the groups, of lobbying, and of campaign giving vary from society to society. But the generic phenomena are universal.

A recent thoughtful comparative overview of how American groups compare to those in other developed democracies is instructive (Graham K. Wilson, "American Interest Groups in Comparative Perspective," in *The Politics of Interests,* ed. by Mark P. Petracca, Westview Press, 1992). Wilson distinguishes between "economic interest groups" (for example, those stemming from occupations such as lawyer, doctor, farmer; businesses; or labor unions) and "representational groups" (those that encompass all interests that are not centrally economic).

After reviewing the evidence from a number of developed democracies he concludes:

> the American interest group system presents a remarkable contrast in comparative perspective. The economic interest groups seem fragmented and often weak compared to foreign equivalents, the noneconomic interest groups strong. Economic interest groups...frequently make a useful contribution to the tasks of governance. Noneconomic groups are less equipped to do so. In its interest group system, the United States reflects a balance that might be said to be true of its political system more broadly: Emphasis is placed more on representation and less on effective governance. No interest group system exceeds the capacity of the American one to represent effectively a wide diversity of views. Of course, many sectors of society (such as the poor) are badly represented, but diffuse interests (such as the protection of the environment or the rights of women) are represented better in the American interest group system than in most

others. In contrast, the opportunities for producing better governance or improved growth through the sort of partnership between government and economic interests found in Japan or Sweden are absent in the United States.

READING 36

A Nation of Lobbyists

David Segal

In this reading David Segal, a reporter for the Washington Post, *makes the point that virtually everyone in the country is, often unknowingly, represented by one—and probably more—lobbies. He uses many specific examples that demonstrate his point.*

His article raises a number of interesting questions. Can people's interests be genuinely "represented" if they are not aware that a group is claiming to represent them and if they have no input on the positions taken by the group? By the same token, should government officials really attribute much legitimacy to the claims of groups about the number of people they "represent"? Those claims are almost surely going to be inflated and will often include individuals in a class claimed as clients by the group but not really members.

An even more interesting question is whether even those individuals who are formally members of a group have much input into the policy positions taken by the organization itself. In most cases the professional staff members of the organization decide what they want to do and assume that the membership is behind them. Professional staff will, of course, claim the full weight of their membership is behind them when they lobby members of Congress or the executive branch. They are likely to imply that

From "A Nation of Lobbyists" by D. Segal, 1995, *The Washington Post National Weekly Edition* 12(37):11. © 1995 The Washington Post. Reprinted with permission.

they speak for an even larger number of citizens, even though a sizable portion of them are not formal members of the group. Sometimes these claims have some validity, but public officials surely should at least be skeptical about such claims.

For most Americans the words "Washington lobbyist" have roughly the same cachet as, say, "deadbeat dad." But if you think of lobbyists only as expensively dressed backslappers who promote corporations and other special interests, you may be surprised to learn the dirty little secret of Washington lobbying: They also are working for us.

The hired guns that have long plied their trade on Capitol Hill have been joined by representatives from scores of Main Street groups boasting millions of members, and new trade and new professional groups have been flocking to Capitol Hill for years. There are 7,400 national associations with headquarters in Washington D.C., according to the National Trade and Professional Associations of the United States.

The upshot is that if you are employed, active in community groups or just a functioning member of society, then you probably have at least a handful of lobbyists toiling on your behalf.

Take John Cloyne, for instance. Cloyne, a salesman who lives with his wife and three children in the capital's Virginia suburbs, considers Washington lobbyists "wheeler-dealers," but because of his affiliations it turns out that quite a number of them are wheeling and dealing for him.

Cloyne is a member of the American Automobile Association, a group that lobbies Congress on behalf of its 34 million members to spend more money on roads. He and his family attend nearby St. Mark's Church, which is part of the United Catholic Conference, a group with four full-time lobbyists. And he earns his living as a sales representative for Datatec, a company that belongs to the National Retail Federation, the International Mass Retail Association and the Food Marketing Institute, all of which employ lobbyists.

Cloyne typifies one of the more noticeable paradoxes in the American body politic.

"People are constantly saying that we should get rid of lobbyists, but they have memberships that support lobbying," says Wendy Mann, a spokeswoman for the Greater Washington Society of Association Executives. "The average person doesn't make the connection between the benefits they receive from associations and the fact that it took someone working on Capitol Hill to get those benefits."

That doesn't mean that the influence of highly paid representatives for big special interests, such as foreign governments and major U.S. corporations, has waned. There still are plenty of those lobbyists roaming the halls of the Capitol, but they're not alone.

How did we become a nation of lobbyists? To begin with, just about any group—from nudists to bowling alley owners—that could come to Washington and ask for some benefit has arrived. The Encyclopedia of Associations has been adding organizations at a rate of 10 a week since 1970.

Membership in these groups has been booming. A 1990 Hudson Institute study found that 7 of 10 Americans belong to at least one association, the vast majority of which engage in lobbying. Comparable figures from decades past aren't available, but one can get a sense of how many people are joining these organizations by looking at the American Association of Retired Persons, one of the most powerful groups in the country. In 1967, the group had fewer than 1 million members; today, it has 33 million members.

Henry Ernsthal, former head of George Washington University's association management program, says the growth parallels the growth of government's role in our lives—the more government does, the more Americans want a say in how it does it. And in 1990 the Internal Revenue Service, following Congress's lead, issued regulations that made it easier to spend money on grass-roots lobbying, a move that has all but encouraged people to start their own groups and make the rounds on Capitol Hill.

Nonetheless, few of us include ourselves when we denounce lobbyists. Last year a Harris poll found that 79 percent of those surveyed believed that Washington lobbyists wield too much power.

"It's fairly typical for Americans," Ernsthal says. "People love their doctor, but don't like doctors;

they love their member of Congress, but don't like politicians; the groups that represent our interest aren't special interest, it's the other guy."

Then again, many of us became lobbyists unwittingly. For years we've been giving money to organizations that few would think of as pressure groups.

If you receive Consumer Reports magazine, for example, you are contributing money to Consumer's Union, which lobbies on banking, insurance and product safety laws.

Is your child farming with the National 4H Council? The council lobbies Congress and the Agriculture Department for additional dollars.

Do you have a daughter in the Girl Scouts, or have you bought any Girl Scout cookies lately? If so, you're subsidizing a group that has been fighting against taxing charitable contributions for years. The Boy Scouts, meanwhile, have hired a Washington law firm to handle their lobbying.

If you are one of 6.7 million members of the Parent Teacher Association, 75 cents of your annual dues goes to the national office to help the group weigh in on issues that range from dropout prevention to drug labeling.

The YMCA has a lobbying group in Washington for its 14 million members as well. "We call it advocating," says Jan McCormick, the group's director of association development.

Joining the National Guard makes you a member of one of the most effective lobbying forces in the country, a group that years ago won an extraordinary deal from Congress. Guard members are paid at the same daily rate as full-time soldiers, but anyone working for one day in the Guard gets paid for two days.

Foundations such as the Ford Foundation and Carnegie Foundation lobby on Capitol Hill. Then there are groups like the American Heart Association, the American Cancer Society and the American Lung Association that seek government funding to fight various diseases.

"When people think of lobbyists, they think of the back room cigar-chomper of 30 years ago," says Bob Smucker, vice president of Independent Sector, an umbrella group for public-interest groups. "The typical person giving to the American Cancer Society doesn't think he's giving to a lobbying group. But that's lobbying too."

These public-minded organizations differ little from other lobbying groups in their overall strategies. Most are simply scrapping for a bigger slice of the federal pie, and nearly all of them are ardent foes of lobbying reform. Last year a coalition of nonprofit groups organized by Independent Sector joined a group that helped to snuff out a lobbying reform bill, which would have added a number of disclosure requirements. Members of the coalition included the American Foundation of the Blind and the Child Welfare League of America.

"The fact is that you'll have a hard time getting your calls answered on Capitol Hill if you call up and say 'I'm Jane Doe and I want to bring this to your attention,'" says Nan Aron, head of the Alliance for Justice, an association for public interest advocacy groups, which fought last year's lobbying reform bill. "And more nonprofits are realizing that they can't afford to sit on the sidelines while Congress acts on, or doesn't act on, issues that affect them."

For those who have avoided associations, consider this: You don't have to join these groups to receive benefits. If you fit their member profile, associations fight for you whether you've paid your dues or not. If you run a truck stop, for example, the National Association of Truck Stop Operators is in your corner, even if you don't pony up the $700 annual membership fee. The same is true for home-appliance manufacturers, advanced life underwriters, federal veterinarians and gifted children. A group is doing their bidding, even for non-members.

"Associations face a classic freeloader problem," says Ron Shaiko, a government professor at American University. "You can do nothing and get all the benefits. Which is why so many associations offer tote bags and discounts on hotel rooms and things like that. It's not always economically rational to spend the money for membership."

It is increasingly hard to imagine a person who isn't somehow either represented by, or subsidizing, a Washington lobbyist. Such a person would have to have no career, avoid certain magazines, social clubs, civic groups and cookies. But if there are enough people with a similar demographic profile, rest assured, someone will start an association on their behalf.

More of the Same: Washington Pressure Group Activity

Kay Lehman Schlozman and John T. Tierney

In this reading, Kay Schlozman and John Tierney, political scientists at Boston College, report on the type and level of pressure group activity in the 1970s and early 1980s. Their account remains valid for the present, even though some of the specific groups have changed. Their observations are based in part on the result of interviews with people working for 175 Washington-based lobbying institutions.

The authors record a great deal of activity. They also put it in historical perspective. The phenomena they analyze are not new. Interest groups have been important in American politics from the beginning. This reading confirms that they remain very important and have proliferated. It also confirms that interest groups avail themselves of a large number of techniques as they seek to influence the agencies of government. Finally, they make it clear that although interest groups use new, electronic technologies, they also continue to use a variety of "old-fashioned" techniques that focus on personal persuasion.

Scholzman and Tierney report increases in the number and activity of Washington-based interest groups. Increased activity and a larger number of groups do not necessarily equate with increased influence on the part of groups, however. The authors suggest that structural changes in government, particularly Congress, may mean that more activity

From "More of the Same: Washington Pressure Group Activity in a Decade of Change" by K. L. Schlozman, and J. T. Tierney, 1983, *Journal of Politics,* vol. 45, May 1983, pp. 351–377. Copyright © 1983 by the University of Texas Press. Reprinted by permission of the authors and the University of Texas Press.

and more groups are needed simply to retain the same level of influence. Journalists often make the mistaken assumption that activity automatically becomes influence. That is not necessarily the case. To be sure, citizens should be concerned about the degree of influence wielded by interest groups, but they should not become hysterical without analyzing what is actually happening.

TECHNIQUES OF INFLUENCE

Let us look...directly at the level of group activity. In an effort to piece together a comprehensive picture of exactly what techniques groups use in their efforts to influence, either directly or indirectly, what goes on

in government, we devised an encompassing list of 27 such techniques. We presented our respondents with this list and asked them to tell us, with respect to each one, whether or not the group uses it. We show the results of that inquiry in Table 8.1 in which we list in descending order the proportion of groups using each of the 27 methods....

MORE ACTIVITY?

Of course, "a lot" of activity is not necessarily more activity. However, our data provide ample evidence not only of the large volume of group activity but also of recent expansion in that activity. Among the first questions we asked our respondents was an open-ended one inquiring about the changes over the past decade in the

TABLE 8.1   Percentage of groups using each of techniques of exercising influence

1. Testifying at hearings	99%
2. Contacting government officials directly to present your point of view	98
3. Engaging in informal contacts with officials—at conventions, over lunch, etc.	95
4. Presenting research results or technical information	92
5. Sending letters to members of your organization to inform them about your activities	92
6. Entering into coalitions with other organizations	90
7. Attempting to shape the implementation of policies	89
8. Talking with people from the press and the media	86
9. Consulting with government officials to plan legislative strategy	85
10. Helping to draft legislation	85
11. Inspiring letter-writing or telegram campaigns	84
12. Shaping the government's agenda by raising new issues and calling attention to previously ignored problems	84
13. Mounting grassroots lobbying efforts	80
14. Having influential constituents contact their congressman's office	80
15. Helping to draft regulations, rules, or guidelines	78
16. Serving on advisory commissions and boards	76
17. Alerting congressmen to the effects of a bill on their districts	75
18. Filing suit or otherwise engaging in litigation	72
19. Making financial contributions to electoral campaigns	58
20. Doing favors for officials who need assistance	56
21. Attempting to influence appointments to public office	53
22. Publicizing candidates' voting records	44
23. Engaging in direct-mail fund raising for your organization	44
24. Running advertisements in the media about your position on issues	31
25. Contributing work or personnel to electoral campaigns	24
26. Making public endorsements of candidates for office	22
27. Engaging in protests or demonstrations	20

way their groups went about trying to influence what goes on in Washington. The question, not surprisingly, netted dozens of answers going off in many directions. However, the single most frequent reply—articulated by 32 percent of the respondents—was some variation on the simple theme of "We are more active than we used to be."...

Our open-ended question was followed immediately by a closed-ended item asking about changes in the group's level of activity over the past decade. A remarkable 88 percent of the respondents indicated that their groups had become more active in recent years. Nine percent said that their activity level was largely unchanged, and a mere three percent said that their activity had diminished....

MORE OF EVERYTHING?

On this basis we feel secure in concluding that the apparent explosion in group activity is not merely illusory, a by-product of the realization by a few groups that the media will cover whatever is noisy and interesting. In our introductory discussion, we posited that certain changes in the environment in which pressure groups operate—most importantly the revolution in electronic technologies and the strengthening of the connection between representative and constituency—would have the effect of not merely escalating group activity but transforming it. More specifically, we expected especially rapid rates of growth for certain techniques: those engaging the use of the media (for example, talking to people from the press and electronic media or running ads to publicize group positions); those facilitated by the use of computers (for example, direct-mail fund-raising, communicating with organization members, and inspiring letter-writing campaigns); and those exploiting the links between legislator and constituency (for example, mounting grassroots lobbying efforts, alerting representatives to the effects of legislation on their districts, and arranging communications from influential constituents about policy matters)....

To make some sense of these observations, we attempted to contrive some summary figures. We scanned the list of 27 methods and designated six that seemed most clearly linked to electronic technology

and five that seemed most clearly linked to a strong representative constituent bond. (As anticipated by our earlier discussion, two techniques—mounting grassroots lobbying efforts and inspiring letter-writing campaigns—fell into both of these categories.) Then we specified five other techniques that seemed to conform to the classical stereotype of lobbying in Washington as it has been conducted for over a century. Finally, for each of these three broad categories, we found the average proportion of groups indicating increased use of the individual techniques in that category, with the following results:

Mean percentage of groups using techniques more often

Electronically relevant techniques:	50%
Constituency-based techniques	53%
Classic direct lobbying techniques	53%

What we have found...is substantiation of our earlier observation about the nature of the growth in pressure group activity—a variant of the theme "more of everything." We are not saying that there has been a uniform expansion across each of the many techniques groups employ. However, our expectation that the advent of television and computers or the importance of advocacy representation would transform pressure group activity is not borne out. We did not find selective increases in either electronically related or constituency-based modes of interest group activity. Use of these forms of interest representation, of course, has skyrocketed, but so too has the use of the time-honored direct methods of contact and consultation. Thus, the massive increase in group activity is built upon expanded use of all kinds of techniques.

MORE OF THE SAME?

Our respondents—and the journalists who chronicle their doings—might read the foregoing and point out with a sigh that our statistical summaries reveal little of the texture of political life, that we have overlooked the many subtle changes in kind as well as degree of activity. We can use our respondents' answers to an open-ended question about changes in how their groups go about influencing what goes on in Washington to suggest some areas in which to investigate subtle alterations. As we have mentioned, the largest proportion of our respondents (32 percent) reported simply that their group was more active. However, shedding additional light on the significant ways in which group activity may have changed, roughly 20 percent of our respondents spoke of changes in the nature of grassroots lobbying and another 20 percent pointed to what they regard as the enhanced professionalism of Washington lobbying, particularly as evidenced by a greater reliance on technical information.

To discern whether the changes identified by our respondents are in fact real, we needed a fuller understanding of the nature of group activity before the dawn of the new era. Accordingly, we consulted historical accounts of the Washington lobbying scene. We discovered that the absence of a systematic approach in the scholarly and journalistic works of previous eras would make it difficult to use these works to establish any kind of historical benchmark. We have no way of knowing whether the examples cited by these observers are typical or merely striking. Still, as we delved into this historical literature we were surprised to find precedents for techniques often considered unique to our modern era. Thus, we began to realize that we had found in our survey not only "more" but "more of the same."...

WHY MORE ACTIVITY?

Useful as our data are in demonstrating an increase in interest group activity, they are less helpful in clarifying just why this expansion has taken place. However, we at least can draw some suggestions by looking at the remarks made by our respondents: in addition to the third of them who reported more activity over the past decade, many others pointed to some specific change in the Washington scene that had spurred them to increased efforts. These responses are useful for providing clues as to some of the sources of the recent escalation in pressure group activity.

We looked to see, for example, if our respondents mentioned that they are more active in recent years as a reaction to increased activity by groups they consider antagonistic to their interests. This explanation is posited often by group theorists who assume that groups will inevitably coalesce and act in defense of their own interests—especially in the face of organized threats. Given the importance of this stimulus-response concept in group theory, we were surprised to find that only 5 percent of our respondents volunteered that they are more active today because their antagonists—whether business or public interest groups—are more active. Groups in fact may escalate their efforts in response to what their opponents do, but our results indicate that group representatives do not perceive this to be a cause for their actions.

Governmental Activity as a Spur?

A theme that arose more often—discussed by 14 percent of those replying to our open-ended question—is that because the government has grown so much and become so much more intrusive, their organizations have become more politically involved. Commenting on the expanded scope of federal involvement, a lobbyist for a major corporation observed:

> More and more groups and companies have recognized the increasing size of government and have therefore stepped up their involvement. Economically, the government is much more important these days than it was ten years ago. Great Society legislation and the environmental and consumer laws have all combined to make companies feel they need to be more active in Washington.

The current administration, however, is trying aggressively to diminish the size of the federal government. In view of the connection some of our respondents drew between federal expansion and interest group activity, what can we expect to happen to pressure group activity as the government shrinks? Insofar as the retreat means withdrawal of support for their favored programs, we can expect even louder clamor from interest groups....

It is not surprising that government reductions would engender pressure activity as groups rise to defend subsidy programs from which they have benefited. But what about deregulation? Can we expect corporate political activity to constrict as the government lifts the regulatory crown of thorns that has (at least in the eyes of businessmen) rested so oppressively on the corporate brow? Before we leap prematurely to the conclusion that, if the government gets out of the business of economic regulation, corporations will get out of the business of political influence, let us consider what we learned in our interviews with four corporations in a recently deregulated industry, the airlines.

Although our respondents from all four airlines indicated that deregulation makes life easier for their companies, they all remain very active politically, utilizing an average of 20 out of our 27 techniques of political influence. (For all corporations in the sample the average was 18.) Not only are they very active, these companies are *more* politically active now. All four said that their activity had risen in recent years. Furthermore, on average they have increased their usage of 16 of the 27 techniques. (Across the sample, the corporate average was 13.) This is not to say, however, that nothing has changed. The issues have changed—from routes and fares to airports and airways. The principal target has changed—from the Civil Aeronautics Board to the Federal Aviation Administration. But our discussions with airline executives make clear that their corporations remain highly active politically. Thus, if the experience of the airlines is any indication, substantial deregulation may not result in a wholesale contraction in corporate attempts to influence government—at least not in the short run.

Changes in Congress

We were not surprised to be told that increased pressure group activity is fostered by new threats either from organizational opponents or from the government. After all, the literature on interest groups has long since raised these points. We were struck, however, when twice as many of our respondents—28 percent—attributed their increased activity to the reforms of congressional organization and procedure since 1974. The many changes on Capitol Hill over the past decade—the proliferation of subcommittees, the diminished importance of congressional staff, the greater number of policy entrepreneurs, the requirements for open meetings, the rapid turnover in congressional membership—have altered the environment of legislative lobbying and have left pressure groups bent on influencing officials with little choice but to escalate the range and volume of their activi-

ties. These changes in Congress have evoked more pressure activity primarily by multiplying the number of access points and expanding the variety of opportunities interested parties have to exert their political will. Because the patterns evidenced are somewhat intricate, we wish to elaborate.

In the aftermath of procedural reforms in Congress that diminished the powers of committee chairmen and multiplied the number of subcommittees, it is no longer possible for a group to make its case effectively by contacting only a few powerful legislators. Lobbyists must cultivate a broader range of contacts not only because there are more subcommittees whose jurisdictions touch each group's interests, but also because single committees and subcommittees no longer exercise as complete control over legislation as they once did. With the growing tendency to refer bills to multiple committees, and with the general relaxation of the norms inhibiting floor challenges to committees, threats to a group's legislative interests may come from anywhere in the chamber and at many more points over a bill's progression through the legislative labyrinth.

By increasing the number of people with whom groups need to establish contacts, the expansion and professionalization of congressional staff also have led to more work for interest groups. Because staff members can provide valued access to the legislators and increasingly act as a policy-making force in their own right, groups find it desirable to cultivate good working relationships with them.

Sunshine rules, which open once-secret meetings to public scrutiny, were mentioned—although substantially less frequently—by our respondents as having similar effects: creating new opportunities for influence and thereby escalating the work load. According to the legislative counsel for one of the major hospital associations:

> It's great for the lobbyists, but the members of Congress hate it. There in the back of the hearing room are all these lobbyists watching a markup session and giving a thumbs-up or a thumbs-down to specific wordings or provisions. It's a fishbowl for them.

A final development in congressional politics that has meant more work for many groups is the accelerated turnover in congressional membership. In

1971 the ratio of newcomers to veterans was 1.2 to 1. By 1981 that ratio had risen to more than 3 to 1. The rate of turnover by 1981 had led to a decidedly junior Congress. By 1981 a majority of House members had served six terms or less, and 54 percent of the senators were in their first term. Many of our respondents commented that the absence of institutional memory that follows from such a rapid turnover has forced them to intensify their educational efforts as they patiently inform, programmatically, ignorant legislators and their staff members about the purposes, operation, and benefits of cherished programs. The director of a feisty social welfare action group described the Sisyphean task this way:

> One problem is that half the Congress has served fewer than six years. Much of the case made for food programs in the late 1960s was made to people who are no longer on the Hill. Current members of Congress only see the success of those earlier efforts; they look around now and, finding less malnutrition, don't see there's *still* a problem. Consequently, our lobbying task is being willing to tell the same story time after time to one legislator after another—making them see that hunger and malnutrition are reduced now *because* those programs [food stamps, school lunches, etc.] are in place, and that we can't afford to eliminate them. You have to have stamina to tell the story over and over—to persuade people who don't understand.

Thus, in yet another way the impact of changes on Capitol Hill is to demand that a conscientious group augment its efforts.

We consider it worth noting that although the architects of the congressional reforms of the 1970s had many purposes in mind, inducing more vigorous pressure from groups was not among them. Had the reformers paid attention to the lessons of history, they would have realized that this unintended consequence has precedent. Writing in 1929, in terms foreshadowing today's literature, Herring pointed to changes in Congress that invigorated group activity and altered the scope and methods of lobbying. In particular, he cited the reform of rules of procedure in the House of Representatives in 1911 that broke up the power center and distributed control more generally in the House; he also pointed to the adoption, at about the same time, of open congressional committee hearings as being a spur to group activity.

What we have learned about the impact of changes in Congress upon interest group activity helps us to solve an earlier puzzle. To review briefly, we originally expected to find selective escalation in the use of certain group techniques—those facilitated by electronic technologies and those capitalizing upon the close relationship between representative and district. We did, indeed, uncover increased employment of those methods of influence. However, we also found enhanced use of old-fashioned methods of direct lobbying.

The foregoing analysis of the implications for pressure groups of congressional reforms helps to explain why. These changes, taken collectively, spell both more opportunities for influence and more work for interest groups: more policymakers with whom one must consult and to whom one must present a case; more freshmen and issue amateurs requiring education; more meetings to attend; more hearings at which to testify and present technical information; more campaigns demanding contributions. These developments imply an increase in virtually all of the techniques relevant to legislative influence. In particular, however, they imply an increase in the use of those techniques we associate with old-fashioned lobbying. Thus, we now understand why the employment of these traditional methods has risen as quickly as the use of the clusters of electronically related or constituency-based methods. . . .

READING 38

What Accent the Heavenly Chorus? Political Equality and the American Pressure System

Kay Lehman Schlozman

In this selection Professor Schlozman continues her examination of the modern "pressure system." Here she investigates the status of an aphorism from

From "What Accent the Heavenly Chorus?: Political Equality and the American Pressure System" by K. L. Schlozman, 1984, *Journal of Politics*, vol. 46, November 1984, pp. 1006–1032. Copyright © 1984 by the University of Texas Press. Reprinted by permission of the author and the University of Texas Press.

Professor E. E. Schattschneider in a 1960 book that "the flaw in the pluralist heaven is that the heavenly chorus sings with an upper-class accent." He was reacting to the claims of some analysts that everyone could be represented equally in the open American pressure system.

Schlozman does not have the data she would like to have in an ideal world, but she is, nevertheless, confident that she has enough evidence to support the claim that business dominance grew in the two decades after Schattschneider wrote. Business groups have become major institutions on the Washington scene. Once established they almost never vanish. These two characteristics— institutional status and persistence—differentiate them from many other types of groups, which are, in the aggregate, more dependent on membership to sustain themselves and more likely to exist for a while and then vanish.

This pro-business bias remains intact in the American political system. In addition to the general map presented by Schlozman it should also be noted that business political action committees have more money to spend on political campaigns and parties than do other political action committees.

It needs to be underscored, however, that this bias does not mean that all public policy is made solely to respond to business interests. Nor does it mean that countervailing groups do not have some influence. Nor does it mean that business groups take a position on every issue. Nor does it mean that all business groups agree on every issue. In fact, they sometimes disagree vigorously. But the fact of the pro-business bias is a fact of American political life that needs to be taken into account when analyzing the content of American public policy.

In recent years academic analysts of American politics have given admirable attention to the electoral process as a linkage mechanism; they have, however, tended to neglect questions of representation pertaining to the more direct contacts between political leaders and groups of jointly interested citizens. This inattention to the representative function of interest group politics is perhaps ironic, for political scientists of an earlier era once placed pressure groups at the heart of the Ameri-

can political process and emphasized not only the ubiquity of interest group activity but also the inevitability of the organizational representation of joint interests in politics. Moreover, the question of how permeable organized pressure politics is to newly emergent issues and groups was one of the most fundamental issues dividing the group theorists from their critics. Antipluralists disputed the notion that the pressure system is universal, arguing that group theorists had both underestimated the height of the barriers to entry into the marketplace of political competition and overestimated the inclusiveness of the interests represented. Among the dissenters was E. E. Schattschneider, who observed that the representation of latent interests is not at all automatic and that two particular kinds of interests— the interests of the poor and the interests of broad publics—are likely to remain unorganized.

If Schattschneider's description is accurate for the 1950s—and we really do not know if it is since his supporting evidence is illustrative rather than systematic—there is reason to believe that important changes have occurred since he wrote. With the mobilization of new interests over the past two decades, the nature of the pressure system has undoubtedly been altered. Since the 1960s, we have witnessed the mobilization of many groups and the emergence of many new organizations—ranging from Common Cause and the Wilderness Society to the National Urban Coalition and the Native American Rights Fund—representing the very sorts of interests that he observed to be underrepresented in the pressure system. This development has received considerable attention from both journalists and scholars....

Do these developments mean that, at just the time when pluralist analysis was being subjected to heavy criticism, its promise was being fulfilled?... Because questions of equal representation of interests are so fundamental to democracy, this paper adduces systematic data to investigate the overall shape of the set of organized private interests in Washington....

THE CONTOURS OF THE PRESSURE SYSTEM

Let us begin by inquiring into the contours of the pressure system today in order to learn what kinds of interests are represented in Washington politics. Table 8.2 presents the results of a tally of the organizations listed in *Washington Representatives*. The left-hand column shows the distribution for the 2,810 organizations (43 percent of the total) that have their own Washington offices. The right-hand column shows the distribution for the 6,601 organizations that either maintain an office in the capital to handle political matters or hire Washington-based counsel or consultants. There is one obvious difference between the distributions in the two columns. Corporations constitute 45.7 percent of all organizations having a Washington presence but only 20.6 percent of those having Washington offices.

This discrepancy should not blind us to the overall message of both columns in Table 8.2. Whether one considers all the organizations having a Washington presence or just those having their own Washington offices, it is clear that the generalizations Schattschneider made about the shape of the pressure system in the late 1950s are apt today. Taken as a whole the pressure system is heavily weighted in favor of business organizations. . . .

Bias in the Pressure System: A Further Probe

The pressure system, of course, includes groups organized around a vast array of dimensions—from oc-cupation, race, age, and gender to hobbies. We can get a better idea of the degree of bias within the pressure system by considering the groups active on a single fault line of political cleavage. In Figure 8.1 we present data about what is probably the most important axis of political conflict in American politics: economic roles. The left-hand bar presents data, based on the 1980 Census, about the proportion of American adults in various economic roles: most adults (59 percent) are working in various occupations; others are unemployed and looking for work, in school, at home, unable to work, or retired. The right-hand bar, based on our catalogue of those organizations having offices in Washington, shows the distribution of groups organized around these roles.

The correspondence between the economic roles in the left-hand bar and the economic groups in the right-hand one is far from perfect. We have already noted the problem of ascertaining who is represented by an organization that has no members in the ordinary sense, and there are other difficulties as well. Not all professionals, for example, are represented by professional associations. Some, such as elementary and high school teachers, are represented by unions. Many of those included in the manager/administrator category—college deans, hospital administrators, and the like—are not employed by businesses and are

TABLE 8.2   The Washington pressure system

	GROUPS HAVING THEIR OWN WASHINGTON OFFICES (%)	ALL GROUPS HAVING WASHINGTON REPRESENTATIONS (%)
Corporations	20.6%	45.7%
Trade Associations and Other Business	30.6	17.9
Foreign Commerce and Corporations	.5	6.5
Professional Associations	14.8	6.9
Unions	3.3	1.7
Public Interest Groups	8.7	4.1
Civil Rights Groups/Minority Organizations	1.7	1.3
Social Welfare and the Poor	1.3	.6
New Entrants (Elderly, Gays, Women, Handicapped)	2.5	1.1
Governmental Units—U.S.	1.4	4.2
Other Foreign	1.2	2.0
Other/Unknown	13.2	8.2
	99.8%	100.2%
	(N = 2810)	(N = 6601)

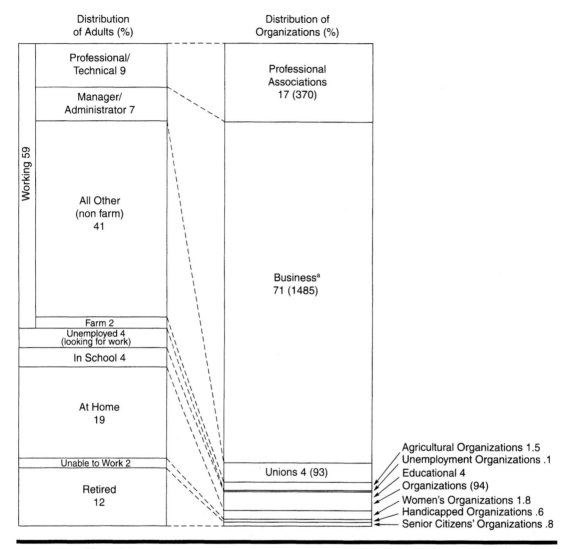

FIGURE 8.1 The public and the pressure system: Economic roles of adults and economic associations having Washington offices.

Sources: Information about public based on U.S. Bureau of the Census, *Statistical Abstract of the United States,* 102d ed. (Washington, D.C.: U.S. Government Printing Office, 1981), 379, 401-4. Information about organizations based on Close (1981) and Akey (1981).

[a]Corporations, trade associations, other business associations, associations of business professionals.

represented, if at all, by professional associations. Of the ninety-two educational organizations in the right-hand column, only one, the American Student Association, is devoted to promoting the interests of students. And none of the thirty-nine women's organizations is expressly organized to act on behalf of the interests of homemakers. These points lead us to treat the data in

Figure 8.1 with circumspection, and they indicate that, in the absence of more finely grained categories, we are undoubtedly overstating the number of *people* in the business and professional categories and the number of *groups* representing homemakers and students. If anything, then, the set of economic interest groups is even more skewed than Figure 8.1 would suggest.

Bearing in mind all of these qualifications, the broad outlines of the message contained in Figure 8.1 are quite clear. When we consider the substantial portion of the pressure system consisting of groups organized about economic roles, the class bias of the Washington pressure system is unambiguous. The professionals and managers who might be considered haves constitute at most 16 percent of American adults; they are represented by 88 percent of the economic organizations. Business organizations alone constitute 71 percent of the total. What is more, these data are only for the distribution of organizations having their own offices in Washington. Had we used figures for all economic organizations involved in Washington politics—those that hire counsel or consultants as well as those that have their own offices—the data would have been even more skewed. Fully 93 percent of the economic organizations having a Washington presence represent business or professionals, and 86 percent represent business alone....

Bias in the Pressure System: A Qualification

The set of organized private interests arrayed along an economic dimension is clearly biased in favor of the well-off. However, the opposite is true when the sets of groups constellated around other axes of cleavage are examined. There are, for example, nearly forty organizations on the Washington scene explicitly devoted to promoting the interests of women; there are none representing the interests of men. While there are over a dozen senior citizens groups with offices in Washington, there are none representing the interests of the middle-aged. In addition, while organizations like the Italian American Forum, the Japanese American Citizens League, and the Ukrainian National Information Service promote the interests of Americans of foreign ancestry and defend their cultural distinctiveness, there is no association performing a similar function for the culturally dominant white Anglo-Saxon Protestants. There are organizations dedicated to promoting the interests of whites; however, unlike the NAACP and the National Urban League, the Ku Klux Klan and the American Nazi Party operate almost entirely outside the ordinary pressure system and lack political legitimacy. It might be argued that members of the dominant age, gender, and racial group—middle-aged, white

men—receive ample representation in the pressure system through their dominant role in the unions, business, and professional associations that form the preponderance of organizations active in Washington. Still, this fundamental difference exists among the distributions of groups organized along economic and noneconomic axes of cleavage. While the class bias in the distribution of economic organizations is unmistakable, it is the have-nots among age, gender, and ethnic groups who command the preponderance of what organized political representation there is....

Movement In and Out of the Pressure System

How can the data about the birth of new groups representing the previously underrepresented be reconciled with evidence indicating the increasing overrepresentation of business? The term "pressure system" may lend a misleading aura of immutability to the set of groups active in national politics. In fact, the pressure system is quite fluid. Changes in the composition of the pressure system from one time to another represent not only the entry into politics of fledgling organizations but also the mobilization for politics of previously apolitical organizations and the exit of both organizations that leave politics, either temporarily or permanently, but continue to function as organizations and organizations that go out of business altogether. Quite simply, organizations vary in terms of the constancy of their political activity. Some, especially those having offices in Washington, are on the scene year in and year out. Others participate more sporadically, galvanized for politics only on those occasions when a specific issue impinges upon their vital interests. Some groups are self-consciously temporary, formed to deal with a particular policy matter.

We can get a better feel for the movement of organizations in and out of the pressure system by considering the data presented in Table 8.3. Using various sources, we were able to amass information about the subsequent histories of three-fourths of the organizations listed in the index to the *Congressional Quarterly Almanac* of 1960. As Table 8.3 indicates, there is a remarkable amount of continuity. Sixty percent of all the organizations listed in 1960—or 79 percent of those for which we could find information—

TABLE 8.3   1980 status of organizations active in Washington politics in 1960 (%)

	STILL ACTIVE—STILL IN POLITICS	STILL ACTIVE—NOT IN POLITICS	INACTIVE/OUT OF BUSINESS	NO INFORMATION	TOTAL	N
Corporations	63%	8	0	29	100%	(84)
Trade and Other Business Associations	61	6	10	24	101	(216)
Professional Associations	79	7	0	14	100	(28)
Unions	77	7	4	12	100	(56)
Public Interest Groups	33	13	27	27	100	(46)
Civil Rights/Social Welfare/Poor	50	12	0	38	100	(8)
Women/Elderly/Handicapped	78	11	0	11	100	(9)
Other/Unknown	46	18	3	33	100	(76)
All Organizations	60	9	7	24	100	(523)

were part of the pressure system two decades later (having been listed in the *Washington Representatives—1981* directory). Another 9 percent—or 12 percent of those we could trace—were still active as organizations but were not involved in Washington politics (not having been included in the directory). We further confirmed that an additional 7 percent—or 9 percent of those we could locate—had become inactive as organizations or had gone out of business entirely. Some of these defunct organizations—for example, the National Committee to Liberalize the Tariff Laws on Art and the Committee for the Return of Confiscated German and Japanese Property—have names that suggest they were self-consciously founded to deal with a specific issue. Thus, it is not surprising that they passed from the scene along with the issues on which they were intended to do battle. Others, such as the Clothespin Manufacturers of America and the Mobile Homes Dealers National Association, sound more like the kind of traditional organizations we expect to persist from year to year. The received social science wisdom about the adaptive capacities of organizations to the contrary, it is clear that some organizations do go out of business.

Public interest groups are an exception to the general pattern that emerges from Table 8.3. Only 33 percent of the public interest groups listed in 1960 were still active in politics two decades later. Fully 27 percent (a substantially higher figure than for any

other type of organization) were not around at all. Considering only those organizations for which we have information, 80 percent or more of the corporations, trade and other business associations, professional associations, unions, organizations of women, the elderly, and the handicapped, and civil rights and social welfare organizations—but only 45 percent of the public interest groups—that were active in Washington in 1960 were listed twenty years later....

Although some of the specific issues have changed—from loyalty oaths and temperance to handguns and abortion—the relative weight of single-issue groups has remained unchanged....

The Changing Pressure System: A Summary

We are now in a position to draw together the various lines of argument and indicate how the net result of all these processes of change could be a pressure system whose contours have been altered relatively little. To summarize, a very large share of the civil rights and social welfare organizations and of the groups representing women, the elderly, and the handicapped are new, having been established since 1960. Although their numbers have grown substantially, there are, however still so few of them compared with other kinds of organizations that they do not form a more significant component in the pressure system.

Many new public interest groups have also been born over this period. Like the organizations just mentioned, there are still too few of them to figure significantly in the pressure system. What is more, the public interest organizations that were a part of the pressure system as of 1960 seem to be characterized by unusually high rates of attrition. This factor has had the effect of reducing public interest representation in the pressure system.

Union representation has, on the other hand, remained remarkably stable over the last two decades; the number of unions has not grown significantly. Furthermore, a large proportion of the unions active in 1980 were part of the pressure system in 1960. This stability, in a period during which many new organizations have come on the scene and many old ones have been politically mobilized, yields a situation in which the union share of the pressure system has diminished substantially. A similar, though less exaggerated, pattern is characteristic of trade associations as well. The birth rate for trade associations has been somewhat lower than for other kinds of organizations. In addition, because so many trade associations were already active in politics in 1960, the process of political activation has been less pronounced than for corporations. The net result is that trade associations, while still a crucial component of the pressure system, have lost their former unambiguous predominance. At one time the trade association was deemed the pressure group par excellence. It would be an overstatement to make such a claim today.

The pattern for corporations—and, to a lesser extent, for professional associations—is different again. The birth rate for these organizations, especially for corporations, is relatively low. However, the massive mobilization of organizations formerly outside the pressure system more than compensates for the low rate of entry of newborn organizations. Thus, in spite of their low birth rates, both professional associations and corporations have increased their share within the pressure system. Corporations alone account for 52 percent of the organizations that either maintain offices in the capital or hire counsel or consultants to represent their interests. This massive influx of corporations into the pressure system means that, in spite of the relative eclipse of trade as-

sociations, the overall business share of the pressure system has been enhanced....

READING 39

Winning in the Courts: Interest Groups and Constitutional Change
Frank J. Sorauf

In this selection, Frank Sorauf, a political scientist at the University of Minnesota, reminds us that interest groups do not just deal with legislators, legislative staff members, and members of the executive branch, although they do spend the bulk of their time with such individuals. They also seek to influence decisions by courts. The role of interest groups in influencing judicial decisions is often ignored by analysts of American politics. Such influence is, however, present and sometimes it is important in shaping how judges and justices interpret the Constitution.

The techniques used by interest groups in approaching the judiciary, especially the federal judiciary, are different from those used in approaching the legislative or executive branches. The principal technique open to interest groups in "lobbying" the federal judiciary is their sponsorship of cases by providing the legal talent needed for litigation. In cases in which relevant groups are not formally parties they can file information ("briefs") as "friends of the court." In this way they can express their interest in the outcome and present their arguments for favored constitutional interpretations. "Lobbying" in the sense of buttonholing judges and arguing a case outside of court is, of course, improper.

Sorauf notes particularly important constitutional cases in the past that have been

From "Winning in the Courts: Interest Groups and Constitutional Change" by F. J. Sorauf, 1984, *This Constitution*, no. 4, Fall 1984, Project '87, pp. 4–10. Copyright 1984 by the American Political Science Association. Reprinted by permission.

"sponsored" by one or more interest groups. The most notable is the 1954 case, Brown v. Board of Education, *in which the Supreme Court ruled that racial segregation in public schools is unconstitutional.*

Naturally, groups sponsor cases in which their views do not prevail. But by simply getting cases to high-level courts the groups help create the policy agenda for constitutional decisions by judges. Because our judiciary only deals with real cases rather than offering advisory opinions, this agenda-setting function is very important.

In 1924 the Congress proposed and sent to the states a constitutional amendment that would have authorized it to regulate, even outlaw, goods in interstate commerce made by child labor. By 1930 only five states had ratified it. Even with the impetus of the depression and Franklin Roosevelt's victories in 1932 and 1936, only 28 of the 48 states, eight short of the necessary 36, had ratified it by the late 1930s. A powerful coalition of liberals, organized labor, women's groups, and urban reformers could not break through the social, religious, and economic conservatism that resisted the amendment in much of the country.

The child labor amendment had been born in frustration. Congress twice passed legislation to abolish the movement of child-made goods in interstate commerce, and twice the Supreme Court had struck down the statutes, once as an unlawful use of Congress's commerce power and once as an improper use of its power to tax (*Hammer* v. *Dagenhart,* 1918; *Bailey* v. *Drexel,* 1922). The second of those decisions, in fact, came only two years before the proposing of the amendment. But the movement that was strong enough twice to pass legislation and then see a constitutional amendment through a less than reformist Congress could not muster the national strength and the extraordinary majorities necessary to amend the Constitution.

In the end, though, it made little difference. The Supreme Court taketh away, but the Supreme Court giveth back. As a part of the Fair Labor Standards Act of 1938, the Congress once again outlawed the movement of goods made by children. Three years later the

Court upheld, the entire statute, conferring on the Congress the very powers that a national movement of impressive strength and persistence could not (*U.S.* v. *Darby,* 1941). Included in the opinion of the majority in *Darby* was, moreover, a renunciation of the very decision that had led to the amendment in the first place:

> The conclusion is inescapable that *Hammer* v. *Dagenhart* was a departure from the principles which have prevailed in the interpretation of the Commerce Clause both before and since the decision and that such vitality as a precedent, as it then had, has long since been exhausted. It should be and now is overruled.

Observers of constitutional politics could draw only some very familiar conclusions. Given the difficulty of the process of formal amendment, constitutional change falls largely to the Supreme Court. Moreover, in the Court one doesn't need mass movements or extraordinary majorities, but merely a suitable case, sympathetic justices, and a bit of strategic skill or luck.

Such lessons have not been lost on American interest groups. They have pursued the goals of constitutional change in the courts with increasing vigor and effectiveness in the last forty years. The trend has been especially marked among groups fighting for individual rights or equality of treatment. The National Association for the Advancement of Colored People [NAACP] and the American Civil Liberties Union [ACLU] have indeed come to symbolize the rise of group litigation for constitutional goals.

FINDING THE RIGHT QUESTION FOR THE ANSWER

Two key words—*cases* and *controversies*—dot the convoluted phrases in Article Three of the Constitution.

> The judicial power shall extend to all cases, in law and equity, arising under this Constitution, the laws of the United States, and treaties made, or which shall be made, under their authority; to all cases affecting ambassadors, other public ministers and consuls; ... to controversies to which the United States shall be a party; to controversies between two or more states. . . .

The Supreme Court has always interpreted them to mean that it and the other federal courts would decide only genuinely adversarial cases in which the parties had real and opposing interests. In other words, there must be, as the titles of cases suggest, someone against someone else—thus, no opinions about "possible" legality or constitutionality, no hypothetical questions, no answers to "let's suppose" questions. The federal courts, therefore, decide constitutional issues only when they are embedded in conflicts which the combatants bring to them.

If there is no legitimate "case," of course, an issue never comes to the Supreme Court. The Court never settled the constitutionality of the Alien and Sedition Acts because the Jeffersonians repealed them before a conviction under them could reach the Supreme Court. Other issues have come tardily to the Court. The Supreme Court had no occasion to rule on the constitutionality of the 1940 Smith Act—which made it a crime to urge, advocate, or teach the overthrow of the United States—until leaders of the American Communist party were convicted under the statute and appealed their conviction to the Court in 1951.

So, while the Supreme Court provides the constitutional answers, it is the litigants who ask the questions. In a real sense they control the Court's agenda, for while the justices can pick among the cases they are asked to decide, they cannot reach beyond them. For this reason the Court is often described as a passive body, the prisoner of both the issues and the factual settings others bring to it.

In setting the judicial agenda, litigating groups have two tasks: to convince the Court to take the case, and then to convince it to decide it "favorably." The first of the tasks is often more difficult, for the Supreme Court, in exercising its enormous discretion to pick and choose its cases, takes fewer than one in ten of those cases pressed upon it. Some of those cases—those on "appeal"—must be heard and decided, but in its much larger "certiorari" jurisdiction, federal statutes permit the Court to take what cases it wishes. (It is, therefore, very often pure bluster for disappointed litigants to threaten to "take this case all the way to the Supreme Court.")

The "case" then is the vehicle of litigating groups, and their relationship to it differs widely. At the maximum, a group may have organized all aspects of a case from the beginning—picking plain-

tiffs, providing lawyers, setting strategies, and paying costs. The NAACP, for example, sponsored all five desegregation cases that reached the Supreme Court in 1952 as *Brown* v. *Board of Education of Topeka.* But at the other extreme, a group may do no more than enter an existing case with a brief as a friend of the court, an "amicus curiae." (In Allan Bakke's celebrated challenge to the constitutionality of affirmative action programs, a record total of 116 organizations filed 58 amicus briefs; *University of California* v. *Bakke,* 1978.) In between those two extremes lies an almost infinite variety of litigating roles. A group may "adopt" an existing case for its appeal to the Supreme Court in order to assure the best possible legal argument, for example, or it may advise the lawyers and plaintiffs in a case without assuming full responsibility for it.

While entry into a case as an amicus curiae permits the group only a written legal argument, the more extensive roles allow it to set the higher strategies of litigation. Full and early sponsorship of a case often permits the group to choose between federal and state courts, to select the plaintiffs in the case, to frame the facts and recruit expert testimony, to decide on the direction of the legal argument, and to provide the legal and organizational talent to carry the enterprise forward. In short, the greater the role in the case, the greater the opportunity for strategic play and interaction with the courts.

Consider the NAACP and the Supreme Court as they approached the deciding of the desegregation cases between 1952 and 1955. The Court had already signaled its impatience with segregation by construing the prevailing "separate but equal" doctrine very literally. Texas had created a separate law school for blacks, but the Court found, not surprisingly, that it lacked the reputation, quality of faculty, and influential alumni (!) of the established law school at the University of Texas (*Sweatt* v. *Painter,* 1950). So, if the separate schools were not equal, integration was the alternative. Yet the "separate but equal" doctrine (*Plessy* v. *Ferguson,* 1896) still stood, and it was that nineteenth-century doctrine itself that was anathema to the NAACP.

It was easy for the NAACP to seize the moment. It had brought that Texas case to the Court, just as it had brought a similar test of Oklahoma's segregated graduate study. Its New York legal staff, headed by Thurgood Marshall, and its network of cooperating attorneys in the states were in touch with local NAACP chapters and local controversies over black elementary and secondary education. Its desegregation cases in Kansas, Delaware, Virginia, South Carolina, and the District of Columbia were simply the next leg of a journey well under way. Those five cases, moreover, bore the unmistakable marks of NAACP sponsorship. The arguments of the lawyers in charge of each case had been sharpened in the usual NAACP rehearsals at the Howard Law School. All cases also used the same expert testimony to show the effects of segregation on the self-esteem of black children. (The experts, though, did differ from case to case; the best known of them, Kenneth Clark, testified in only two of the five cases.)

At the same time, however, the NAACP was able to present the Supreme Court with a useful diversity of findings and arguments. Three of the cases depicted distinctly inferior black schools, but the trial judge in the Kansas case found the separate school systems substantially equal. In the D.C. case the black plaintiffs had not even bothered to allege any disparities, preferring the more aggressive argument that segregation per se was unconstitutional. In these latter two cases, in other words, relief for the black plaintiffs was possible only if the Supreme Court were to overturn the "separate but equal" doctrine, which it did.

THE GROUP ROLE: HOW STRONG THE TREND?

One set of cases, no matter how celebrated, does not make a trend or movement. Just how common is group participation in constitutional litigation, and when indeed did it begin? Certainly it began well before the American public became aware of it. Clement Vose, for example, has described the work of the National Consumers' League in defending wage and hour legislation in American courts as early as 1907. (The group strategy then was the reverse of today's; legislatures were willing to pass maximum hour and minimum wage laws, but such legislation needed the most persuasive defense to survive challenges in more conservative courts.) It was, in fact, Florence

Kelley and Josephine Goldmark of the League who recruited the Boston attorney Louis Brandeis (Miss Goldmark's brother-in-law) to argue the cause of the state legislation. With him they fashioned the detailed, factual brief that came to bear his name. After Brandeis's appointment to the Supreme Court, the resourceful Kelley and Goldmark found a young Felix Frankfurter to take up some of his work.

Whatever the past of group litigation, there is every reason to think it has increased over the last generation or two. Examining all noncommercial cases that came to the Supreme Court from 1928 to 1980, Karen O'Connor and Lee Epstein find that the percentage of cases with amicus curiae briefs has risen sharply from less than two percent of the cases between 1928 and 1940 to more than 53 percent from 1970 to 1980. That latter percentage, however, masks variations in the rates of amici in specific kinds of noncommercial cases. They are at two-thirds or above for cases of race or sex discrimination, for example, but only 37 percent in criminal cases.

As useful as those data are, they leave some questions unanswered. They don't specify the rate of amicus participation in commercial cases; by the accounts of all observers, it is far lower. They also don't separate constitutional litigation from the total load of the Court; observers, though, would expect amici to be more common in cases hinging on the Constitution. Finally, these data on amici record the growth of only the least important of group roles.

For a fuller picture of group involvement one focuses on a single area of constitutional litigation, the establishment of religion clause, for example. Between 1951 and 1971, a total of sixty-seven cases raising constitutional issues of the separation of church and state reached the U.S. Supreme Court, the federal courts of appeal, or the highest courts of the states. Twelve of them involved publicly supported bus rides for pupils of religious schools, and ten resulted from prayer or Bible-reading in the public schools. Others grew out of a wide variety of disputes—tax exemptions for religious property, public support for religious schools and hospitals, and a cross in a public park among them.

As that total of sixty-seven cases suggests, the fifties and sixties were the period in which the meaning of the "no establishment" clause was first developed systematically. By the most generous count, the Supreme Court had decided only four church–state cases in the 160 years before 1950. In just the next two decades, it decided ten.

Stationed in the middle of this swirl of constitutional litigation were three national groups: the American Civil Liberties Union [ACLU], the American Jewish Congress [AJC], and Americans United for Separation of Church and State [AU]. The first came to separationism from secular humanism, the second from reform Judaism, and the third from conservative Protestantism. Individually or in alliance they participated in fifty-one of the sixty-seven cases (76 percent), and at least one had a role in all ten cases that the Supreme Court decided.

Despite the different sources of their separationism, the three groups divided only once in these sixty-seven cases—a case on tax exemptions for property owned by religious groups. The ACLU opposed all such exemptions, but AU favored them if the property was used for religious purposes; the AJC was divided internally and therefore silent. Both AU and the AJC drew membership support from religious congregations; the ACLU did not. In truth, differences over the meaning of separation did surface in another issue: the hiring of Roman Catholic nuns as teachers in public schools. AU opposed it per se; the other two groups opposed it only if the nuns engaged in religious teaching or proselyting. Their differences were at least one reason why the issue was never brought to the Supreme Court.

Cooperation among the three groups was much more seriously impeded by their conflicting goals for constitutional litigation. For the AJC they were scrupulously legal: favorable judicial precedents and thus influence over the direction of constitutional development. The national organization of the ACLU agreed; its litigation guide explained:

> The ACLU cannot take every case where there is a civil liberties question being raised. Rather, it should direct its efforts to cases which have some reasonable promise of having broad impact on other cases. Thus, it is always appropriate to take a case which offers the possibility of establishing new civil liberties precedents which will control other cases.

But local ACLU affiliates and the local chapters of AU frequently wanted to press litigation for sheer vindication of their separationist position. Moreover, litigation often offered organization-building possibilities. Local publicity and fundraising benefited from participation in a deeply-felt crusade in the courts. The result was litigation and appeals of litigation that the AJC considered reckless and even irresponsible.

Despite different goals and philosophies, the three separationist groups worked cooperatively in many cases and shared a collective wisdom about strategies in them. They certainly agreed on the wisdom of entering a case as soon as possible. In these sixty-seven cases, one or more of the groups were sponsors— "present at the creation," as it were—in twenty and something more than amici in another twenty-one. They preferred plaintiffs who came to their separationist position from religious conviction, who were stable members of the community, and who preferred anonymity to publicity. Increasingly they came to prefer bringing their cases in federal courts, because they usually provided a speedier and less costly route to the Supreme Court than state courts and because their judges were more sympathetic to separationist arguments and more willing to let the plaintiffs build a full factual record.

The most challenging moments for these three groups—for all litigating groups—involved the grander strategies. Ought an issue to be taken to the Supreme Court in the first place? To risk losing a case is to risk a greater loss: an unfavorable precedent that decides other cases. What ought a group to do about an unfavorable precedent, such as the Court's decision from the 1940s permitting public funding for transportation to religious schools? Attack it or work around it? Despite some reservation from AU, the groups chose the latter course, attacking bus rides instead in those states—Wisconsin, Oregon, and Hawaii, for instance—where the state constitutions erected higher walls of separation.

Such strategy touches also the pacing, timing, and sequencing of issues. In the words of a short-lived agreement among the ACLU, AU, and AJC:

> It would be desirable if the next case to come to the Supreme Court dealing with aid to sectarian schools

showed a substantially higher degree of aid than busses down the road to full aid. Our best chance of turning it away from that road is to pose an issue requiring a large step or none.

The most skillful litigation groups, in other words, play something of a constitutional chess game, trying always to limit the options or force the moves of the Court.

However, not even three purposeful, national groups can control an entire universe of constitutional litigation. Some cases emerge and are decided too rapidly for group intervention. The challenge of the Louisiana Teachers Association to the state's aid to parochial schools in 1970 was filed on September 8 in a local court, removed to the state supreme court, and then argued before that court on September 25. More often, local groups or individuals begin ill-conceived litigation and cannot be talked out of it. The litigation of Madalyn Murray O'Hair is a series of cases in point. Her earthy and combative style, her desire not to have co-plaintiffs, her ties to organized atheism, and her insistence on dominating her cases all made her an unacceptable collaborator. (She also considered the ACLU, AU, and AJC unacceptable allies.) Moreover, the quality of the legal work and the records of fact in her cases were at best unpredictable.

There is, of course, another side to all this church–state litigation: the groups that seek some form of government support for religion (the "accommodationists"). Since the Roman Catholic church operated the vast majority of religious schools in the country, the chief organization on the "other" side was the arm of the Catholic bishops, the U.S. Catholic Conference. However, the structure of church–state litigation inevitably cast some hapless school board, legislature, or other public authority in the role of defendant, rather than the Catholic Conference or another "accommodationist" group. The Catholic Conference had to create a place for itself in the cases as a codefendant, an intervening defendant, or an informal partner or advisor to the defendants. It is rarely easy, in other words, to translate adversarial group conflict into adversarial litigation.

THE INGREDIENTS OF GROUP SUCCESS

How is it that group litigation of constitutional issues has flourished? In part because the Supreme Court has blessed it. As the NAACP worked for enforcement of the desegregation decision in the South, a number of states retaliated. Virginia charged the organization's lawyers under old laws making barratry (the exciting or encouraging of litigation) a crime. In the final resolution of the case, the U.S. Supreme Court ruled that the activities of the NAACP were forms of political activity, protected by the First Amendment and thus not subject to Virginia's law (*NAACP* v. *Button*, 1963). Wrote Justice Brennan:

> In the context of NAACP objectives, litigation is not a technique of resolving private differences; it is a means for achieving the lawful objectives of equal treatment by all government, federal, state, and local, for the members of the Negro community in this country. It is thus a form of political expression. Groups which find themselves unable to achieve their objectives through the ballot frequently turn to the courts. Although the 1963 decision came well after the growth of litigating groups, it protected their gains.

Group litigation flourishes also because the groups are good at it. Not many plaintiffs command the legal expertise and experience that Thurgood Marshall and Leo Pfeffer exemplify. Pfeffer, of the American Jewish Congress, was not only the most experienced advocate in church–state law, but a major scholar in the field as well. Interest groups as well have the persistence, the memory, and the long-range view that enable them to see beyond the immediate case or incident. They also have the resources for litigation. It is not that they are wealthy. They are not, but their resources are at the disposal of constitutional litigation, and those of most wealthy Americans are not. To take a major case to the Supreme Court may require a cash outlay well into six figures. The central question is not whether a litigant is able to pay, but whether he, she, or it is willing to pay.

Perhaps the greatest asset of the litigating group is the trust of the courts, born both of respect and of need. Since groups develop better records of fact and make better legal arguments than do individual plaintiffs, the courts depend greatly on them, especially in constitutional cases. That fact probably accounts to a great extent for the success of litigating groups in getting their cases into the Supreme Court. Courts also know that groups will pay attention to the cues they give. When some justices of the Supreme Court became convinced that they had erred in permitting local school districts to force young Jehovah's Witnesses to salute the flag and indicated so in a footnote in a later case (*Jones* v. *Opelika,* 1942) they must surely have been confident that lawyers for the Witnesses would read the footnote and act on it.

GROUP LITIGATION IN THE EIGHTIES

The group role in constitutional litigation continues to expand. In part, its growth reflects the increasing mobilization of interests, the explosion of group politics, in American political life. In part, too, it reflects the expanding agenda of American politics. Issues such as those of the environment, equality for women, abortion, and freedom of sexual preference have only lately become dominant, and each has brought new groups into litigation. As a consequence, group activity enjoys a support and respectability it never did in earlier decades. The Ford Foundation, for instance, has made substantial grants to several groups litigating cases on women's rights.

Explanations for the growth of the group role, however, cannot ignore the increasing willingness of the courts themselves to be agents of constitutional change. That willingness, even eagerness, to seize and decide controversial issues, to use the judicial power actively, inevitably encourages constitutional litigation. Judicial "activism" means easier access to the courts and a greater likelihood that judges will address the policy concerns of litigants. Innovating judges thus attract innovating litigants.

Group litigation is expanding in another significant way. It combines the more conventional litigating of constitutional questions with litigation based on legislation. The 1970s especially saw the growth of rights and statuses in congressional legislation. So, while women's groups continue to [litigate] under the "equal protection" clause of the Fourteenth Amendment, they also litigate under the sections of the Civil Rights Act forbidding discrimination because of sex. Groups such as the environmentalists, moreover, have virtually no constitutional bases for their claims; of necessity they are largely limited to litigating statutory issues.

In their pursuit of constitutional goals, some groups succeed and some do not. Their litigation, however, does have an important and inevitable consequence beyond their individual goals: it alters the very judicial process it seeks to influence. Litigating groups have helped create public expectations that courts should and will be active, unabashed agents of constitutional change. They fuel the very judicial activism they reflect. Their skill in litigating also increases the pace of litigation, bringing one difficult question after another to the courts, especially to the U.S. Supreme Court. By bringing the courts more often into policy disputes, they leave them more and more vulnerable to the displeasure of losers in the disputes. In short, now that the struggle and competition among groups over public policy has come to the courts, neither the groups nor the courts will ever be the same again. Nor will the Constitution.

> **READING 40**

Inside Campaign Finance: The Purchase of Legislatures

Frank J. Sorauf

In this selection, Frank Sorauf, a political scientist at the University of Minnesota, returns to the question of campaign finance, previously addressed in the Salant and Cloud reading in the chapter on elections. Sorauf presents a sophisticated review of recent major empirical research by political scientists on the effect of Political Action Committee campaign contributions on substantive outcomes in Congress.

In a prelude to the material included here, Sorauf cites several examples—both by journalists and by scholars—in which uniform condemnation is made of campaign giving. The assumption in such statements is that all giving is bribery and results directly in the the desired outcome. Sorauf's analysis in this reading is a careful attempt to demonstrate why that view is incorrect empirically. He carefully

From *Inside Campaign Finance: Myths and Realities* by F. J. Sorauf, 1993, pp. 193–174. Copyright © 1993 by Yale University Press. Reprinted by permission.

examines the data, and does not apologize for excesses or abuses in the system. But his careful scholarship provides an antidote to simple-minded, ill-informed generalizations and condemnations.

There is no doubt that PACs choose their campaigns and candidates to further their legislative causes. They give to campaigns in order to influence decisions, not because they are public-spirited citizens who just want to make sure candidates can get their messages to the electorate.

But systematic analysis presents a subtle appreciation of what this money buys. It is given, for the most part, to individuals already inclined to be supportive of legislation favored by the donor. It does help increase participation of those individuals. And, ultimately, it probably helps produce favorable results on less visible, fairly narrow issues. Naturally, if there are competing PACs, as there often are, not all of them can win.

Neither our comments nor Sorauf's piece are meant to suggest that there are not legitimate public issues to address in pondering how best to finance campaigns. But we join Sorauf in stressing that blanket condemnations of all giving—especially from PACs whose purposes may not appeal to the commentator—are not helpful in understanding the real issues.

THE PURCHASE OF LEGISLATURES

The question of motive haunts every campaign finance system relying on voluntary contributions. *Why* do they give? When a disclosure system discloses as much as the American one does about a visible set of organized givers representing society's major interests, the question rises to a salience that campaign finance rarely achieves. The answer to it is beyond dispute; they give to influence governmental decisions. The hard questions come next: the nature of the influence the contributors seek, the ways they go about seeking it, and the extent to which they achieve it.

The debate over the purchase of legislatures is not about generic contributors. It is about PAC contributors, whether they appear explicitly or are merely implied in such phrases as "the best Congress money

can buy." Their splendid visibility as the organizations of the "special interests" links them and their contributions to the ongoing, century-long debates over the three-way alliance of money, organization, and interest in American politics. Now that PACs increasingly give to secure legislative access, a strategy in which their ties both to incumbents and to lobbyists are closer, they underscore all of the old concerns. We no longer talk of PAC attempts to penetrate electoral politics but of their part in the traditional struggle of interests in American legislatures. Almost imperceptibly, but fundamentally, the debate has shifted from influence in election outcomes to influence over legislative outcomes.

Thanks to the reporting and publicity the FECA forced on candidates, PACs, and parties, the FEC oversees the largest data archive on any system of campaign finance anywhere in the world. Its data are easily accessible, and the "law of available data" has led to a flowering of research on them, both by the scholarly community and by journalists and public-interest organizations. Their industriousness has produced works of many genres, but one of the most common—a veritable industry in itself—is the exploration of the PAC-Congress nexus. The variants on the theme, too, are recognizable: the largest PAC contributors to congressional candidates over a cycle or a decade, the major recipients of PAC money in the Congress, the contributions from PACs of one industry to the members of one committee or to supporters of a particular bill or cause, the mounting flow of PAC money from one sector of the economy as its interests are threatened or challenged. Often the investigations have a current stimulus; they are the campaign finance angle on the broader story, say, of the savings-and-loan crisis, the rewriting of the federal tax code, or the attempt to pass the Brady bill's restrictions on the sale of handguns.

Such reports share one limiting defect: they establish correlation, not cause. Yes, PACs do largely give money to candidates who will vote the way they want them to; it would be surprising if that were not the case. Contributors contribute to like-minded candidates, just as voters vote for like-minded candidates. That relationship is easy to document, but the harder question remains: do PACs contribute to candidates because they know how they will vote, or do legislators conform to the wishes of PACs that gave money to their campaigns? Does the money follow the votes, or do the votes follow the money? It is a problem in simultaneous cause, cause that seems to move both ways between one act and another. Any analysis or campaign finance is repeatedly bedeviled by such problems.

If that were not enough, the journalistic evidence suffers because it is anecdotal, focusing on the limited, often dramatic event. Furthermore, the event and the evidence are often chosen to show a relationship, not because they are representative of the full universe of PAC-incumbent exchanges. So, the anecdotes are almost invariably of PAC successes in the legislative process. But what of PACs representing interests on "the losing side"? PACs and their parent organizations suffer frequent, even monumental losses. Many of the savings-and-loan victories were won over the opposition of the banking industry, and the real estate interests absorbed big losses (for instance, the limiting of real estate investments as tax shelters) in the 1986 revision of the income tax laws, sometimes even at the hands of legislators who had received contributions from the Realtors PAC.

Beyond these failures of design and method are problems of explanatory assumption. Many of the PAC-Congress studies use money and the whole apparatus of campaign finance to the exclusion of other explanations of legislative behavior. If the PACS do "buy" the Congress, if we are to conclude they are major shapers of legislative decisions, what then of the ability of the parties, the president, the voters, the lobbyists, and Washington representatives to shape those same outcomes? And what of the impact of the personal beliefs and attitudes of the members themselves? The PAC of the National Rifle Association, called the Victory Fund, disburses about $4 million each cycle ($4.2 million in 1988) to candidates for the Congress; the NRA budget for Washington lobbying probably exceeds that figure. The NRA also commands the loyal support of 2.8 million members, who focus intently, even solely, on NRA issues in their voting and grass-roots lobbying. Some Western members of the House believe that the NRA vote in their districts can shift vote totals by close to 5 percent. One does not easily separate out the effects of the NRA

in these various systems of influence, but it should at least be evident that its PAC contributions have not made its other political activities superfluous.

Academic scholars, for their part, attack the same questions in more systematic ways. They cannot, however, escape the need to establish correlations and to infer cause from them, nor can they escape the problem of simultaneity in doing so. Using larger bodies of data—large numbers of roll-call votes, for instance—and more sophisticated measures of correlation, they generally find little if any relationship between the money and the votes. In research typifying the best of academic analysis, Janet Grenzke studied the contributions of 10 of the largest PACS to 172 long-term members of the House in the 1970s and early 1980s. The PACS were involved in a wide range of policy issues, and all had specified earlier a list of House votes they were interested in during the period. Using a two-stage least-squares regression to control for the effect of factors other than the contributions—the political composition of the member's district, for example—she specified the hypothesized direction of cause in the simultaneous correlation: from money to votes. In the subsequent analysis Grenzke found little support for the hypothesis that PAC contributions influence the roll-call votes of House members.

How does one explain the gap between popular knowledge and academic conclusion? In part it results from the usual popular overestimation of PAC will and capacity. PACs themselves are more realistic about their bargaining position with incumbents than is the general public. They say over and over that they want to support like-minded men and women in public office and that they seek only "access" to legislators, an opportunity to persuade or make a case. Organizationally they are not adapted to greater political ambitions than that, and they have come slowly to realize it. As John Wright concluded in his study of the contributions of five of the country's most affluent PACs, "The ability of PACs to use their campaign contributions to influence congressional voting is severely constrained by the organizational arrangements through which money is raised.... Because money must be raised at a local grassroots level, local PAC officials, not Washington lobbyists, are primarily responsible for making allocation decisions. Consequently, congressmen who desire contributions must cultivate favorable relationships with local officials, and this arrangement tends to undercut the value of contributions as a bargaining tool for professional lobbyists." Behind that conclusion lies Wright's finding that contributions from the five PACS increased only marginally the probability that the recipient House members would vote the position of the contributing PAC—would shift, that is, from an expected vote as measured by the liberal-conservative scale of the Americans for Democratic Action (ADA). Ultimately, Wright comes to the conclusion of many other political scientists: "Of the numerous variables that influence the voting behavior of congressmen, the campaign contributions of PACS appear to take effect only infrequently. Only when other cues, such as party, are weak can PAC contributions be expected to be important." In short, what PACS do is a reflection of what they are able to do. The ability, in turn, stems from their own nature and the bargaining position of incumbents in the exchange.

Such conclusions run counter to the conventional wisdom, and like most academic writing on campaign finance, they fail to disturb or dislodge it. The supporters of the conventional wisdom are tireless, and they have a platform. They also have telling testimony from members of Congress that PACS do indeed change votes—always the votes of other members—with their contributions. To be sure, the testimony is notoriously unspecific; most (but not all) of it comes from liberal Democrats, some of it is ex parte or self-justifying, and some of it is little more than sophisticated scapegoating. Still, congressional observations are not easy to dismiss out of hand. Insiders of any kind are at their strongest in arguments on the nature of influence in the legislative process.

The common sense of the word *access* also makes the case for the conventional wisdom. If access is indeed the goal of PAC contributions, will PACS settle merely for the "opportunity to persuade"? Won't they expect success in a certain number of instances? Will they be satisfied with an invitation to the gaming table if they lose every spin of the wheel? Moreover, the nature of influence in a legislative body involves much more than final roll-call votes. PACS exert influence at other points in the legislative process—in initiatives not taken, in committee

amendments, or in special rules affecting floor consideration. Some academic political scientists, one should add, have long shared reservations about an exclusive reliance on roll calls.

A side-by-side illustration of studies of the PAC-committee connection, one by a public interest group and one by two political scientists, makes many of those points. In 1991 Congress Watch, the "legislative advocacy arm" of Ralph Nader's Public Citizen, studied votes in a subcommittee of the House Banking Committee on proposals and amendments to proposals that would "substantially deregulate the nation's banks." In its summary, Congress Watch reports, "On five key votes, the top five recipients of banking PAC money averaged $190,378 in receipts and voted against banking interests only 24 percent of the time. Conversely, the five lawmakers who received the least bank PAC money averaged $35,521 in receipts and voted with consumers and against the banking industry 76 percent of the time. The data suggest that the bank PACS are clearly mixing their contribution strategies, and that by and large they give much more money to committee members sympathetic to them. One has no hint, however, of how to unravel the problem of simultaneous cause. Is there anything more here than decisions by a number of bank PACS to contribute to House members who had proven themselves sympathetic to the banks' interests and policy positions?

Political scientists Richard Hall and Frank Wayman begin the report of their research on PAC money and House committees by reconstructing the logic of what PACS seek with their contributions. "First, we suggest that in looking for the effects of money in Congress, one must look more to the politics of committee decision making than those of the floor.... Second, and more importantly, our account of the member-donor exchange leads us to focus on the *participation* of particular members, not on the votes.... If money does not necessarily buy votes or change minds, in other words, it can buy members' time. The intended effect is to mobilize bias in congressional committee decision making." Hall and Wayman focus, therefore, on three House committees and three different issues before them—and on the effects of PAC contributions to members of the committees. Instead of using votes in committee as the dependent variable, Hall and Wayman construct a measure of various kinds of participation in the business of committees (such as speaking in committee or offering amendments during markup). In each of the three cases they found that PAC contributions had a moderate but significant degree of influence, explaining more than 55 percent of the variance in participation by individual members. PAC money, therefore, mobilized already like-thinking members to more active support of the PACS' interests in committee. Their conclusion about one of the cases applies to all three: "The more money a supporter received from the dairy PACS and the stronger the member's support, the more likely he or she was to allocate time and effort on the industry's behalf (e.g., work behind the scenes, speak on the group's behalf, attach amendments to the committee vehicle, as well as show up and vote at committee markups). Alternatively, money may have diminished the intensity of the opposition." Regardless of why the PACS give, they seem to get heightened activity and support from their congressional sympathizers. We are left, however, to speculate about the ultimate results of such support and activity on congressional decisions.

A consensus about PAC influence is emerging among scholars of campaign finance. It is founded on two central conclusions. First, the influence of PAC contributions tends to be strongest on the narrower, less visible issues before the Congress. Members have long called them "free votes," free in that they are liberated from the usually dominant influences of party, district, leadership, and mass opinion. These are the votes available for less influential constituencies (such as contributors) or even for classic legislative log-rolling or horse-trading. Second, the influence of contributions can be directed at all the points of access and influence in the legislative process in the Congress. The kinds of policy refinements and strategic maneuvers crafted in committee may be important for specific interests even though they do not involve great issues of policy. The same can be said of many appointments to the courts and to executive agencies. Contributors do not necessarily seek, or even expect, to score impressive policy victories measured by final roll-call votes. In the world of reduced expectations in

which PACS are forced to live, the smaller accomplishments have to suffice.

The Hall and Wayman findings narrow the gulf between the academy and conventional wisdom, but the gulf remains. In part it results from major disagreements about evidence and authority, about the credibility of participants and observers in the Congress versus the data-based analyses of scholars, and about fundamental questions of what evidence it takes to come to conclusions. In essence, the gulf reflects different wills to believe. Some scholarship, to be sure, but even more journalistic analysis, begins with deeply set convictions, rooted in the Progressive worldview, about the impact of money on public officials. The line between dispositions to believe and foregone conclusions is very thin.

Most durable are the differences across the gulf on analytical issues. One concerns the credibility of the testimony of participants, and even the weight their words carry vis-à-vis the detailed data of the scholars. Consider Charles Keating as an authority on the question of the influence of the contributor. Keating, a political pariah now, is nonetheless widely quoted as evidence of the effect of money. When asked by a Senate committee whether his contributions influenced senators to take up his causes, Keating replied, "I want to say in the most forceful way I can: I certainly hope so." The conferral of authority here may reflect only the news media's fondness for campaign finance machismo, but it may reflect, too, a disposition to give great weight to the words of participants. The danger of granting authority status to participants—contributors or recipients—is that authority is conferred even on clearly self-serving conclusions merely because the authority's message is useful or congenial.

Beneath the controversies over the conventional wisdoms, there are also great differences over who carries the burden of proof. Scholars will not readily consent to demands that they accept responsibility for proving or disproving an assertion they do not make: the one about PACS' buying influence over the making of policy. Nor will they concede that any assertion is valid until it is disproven. Ultimately, however, the debate comes down to the kinds and weight of evidence that will establish the tie between money and votes or other activity in the Congress. One of the greatest strengths of any conventional wisdom is that by definition it is validated by the sheer number of people who subscribe to it. Such validation does not yield easily to the desiccated numbers and equations of empirical social science.

The conventional wisdom is vulnerable also for its assumption that PACS dominate the exchange between contributor and candidate—an analytical predisposition that comes out of the late 1970s. But we now have abundant evidence that the exchange is bilateral rather than unilateral, that candidates have leverage in it, and that the incumbents among them increased that leverage in the 1980s as their reelection rates soared. As PACS have shifted more and more to the support of incumbents, and to the search for access to them, their freedom of action has diminished. Whereas incumbents have organized with increasing effectiveness, PACS have not. Nor have they maintained their ability to enforce expectations. PAC sanctions depend on the value of withdrawn contributions, and since PACS have continued to disperse their contributions widely, the average PAC contribution amounts to well less than one-half of 1 percent of the average House incumbent's receipts in an electoral cycle. Even a major contribution of $5,000 or more accounts for only a few percent of the average candidate's receipts. Consequently, the PAC position in the 1990s is not what it was in the 1970s.

Finally, the countervailing controls of American pluralism constrain even the most determined PACS. Organizations of interests have greatly proliferated since the 1970s. The larger the number of groups (that is, PACS), the greater the offsetting and limiting effect on the political claims of any one of them. The greater the number of PACS making contributions to a specific member of Congress, the greater the likelihood that the claims of one on his or her loyalties will be opposed by the claims of another. In the words of Rep. Barney Frank, a Democrat from Massachusetts, "Business PACS invest in incumbents. It's the banks against the thrifts, the insurance companies against the banks, the Wall Street investment banks against the money center commercial banks. There's money any way you vote."

A caveat to that conclusion is, however, in order. The mechanism of offsetting, countervailing group activity probably best fits policy disputes over the larger issues that are part of broader ideological positions over issues such as medicaid funding or hazardous waste disposal. The model works less well when the dispute is single-sided, where the activity of one set of interests does not jolt another set of interests, perhaps those of consumers, into action. The nonresponding interests may be too general, too invisible, or of too low a priority to warrant political action. So, the hypothesis of countervailing interests meshes well with the conclusion that PACS have their greatest impact on the less visible politics of narrow and particularistic interests in which the conflicts, and thus the controls, of pluralism are not joined.

Critics of Tony Coelho and the DCCC raise an issue with a new twist on the money-votes relationship. If it is in fact true that the money, especially the PAC money, follows the voting records of incumbents, why can't incumbents change the record to lure the money? That, they charge, is exactly what the House Democrats did under Coehlo's leadership in the early 1980s. It is true that Democrats began to attract more business money then and that Coehlo unabashedly urged the party to do so. It is also true that PACS closely scrutinize the voting records, or "scores," of incumbents. The argument suffers, however, from the monism that haunts the subject: the belief that money explains all. Why the assumption that the Democrats are politically so free to move to the center—that the influence of money rather than the mood of voters governs their political calculus? What, too, about the countervailing influence of other contributors, especially those of organized labor, that fight for a move *away* from the center? Logic and assumptions aside, however, the central factual premise of the argument does hold up. The ratings of the roll-call positions of House members by the AFL-CIO, the U.S. Chamber of Commerce, the Americans for Democratic Action, and the American Conservative Union all give House Democrats collectively a more liberal score in 1990 than they had in 1980.

That an increasingly national "contributor constituency" has entered American electoral politics seems beyond contest. Electoral politics remain local because the constituencies are geographically defined with only one representative and two senators per constituency and because the American political parties have been decentralized and local. Now PACS and other representatives of national interests find a small but measurable additional edge in electoral politics. They increasingly ally themselves with the lobbying of the interests they share, and it becomes increasingly difficult to say whether their victories come through contributing or lobbying. It is far easier to say simply that contributions have become one more limited means among many in the pursuit of policy goals—and one more piece of evidence that the localism of American electoral politics is increasingly anomalous. Campaign finance serves as a shaper of national politics as well as one of its consequences.

FOOD FOR THOUGHT

1. Kay Lehman Schlozman and John T. Tierney, in their 1983 essay "More of the Same: Washington Pressure Group Activity in a Decade of Change," find more Washington-based interest groups and increased interest group activity, but suggest that institutional change makes more interest groups necessary to maintain influence. In the decade since Schlozman and Tierney's research was conducted, critics have accused members of Congress, such as Tom DeLay, of allowing lobbyists to write legislation and participate in its markup. Does it follow that there are now too many interest groups or is it more the case that the influence of PAC money is pervasive? Schlozman and Tierney also contend that the professionalization of congressional staff decreases group influence, while turnover in Congress increases it. What might the effects of term limits be on interest group influence in Congress?

2. In "A Nation of Lobbyists," David Segal writes that the "special interests" are actually us; everyone can be said to be a potential member of one interest group or another. Speculate on the questions raised in the headnote to this reading: Can people's interests be genuinely "represented" if they aren't aware that a group is claiming to represent them and if they have no input to the position taken by the group? Should government officials really attribute legitimacy to group claims about the number of its "members?"

3. In "What Accent the Heavenly Chorus? Political Equality and the American Pressure System," Kay Lehman Schlozman investigates whether the "better off" are better off in terms of political representation, and concludes that there is a class bias to the Washington pressure system. She finds that among age, gender, and ethnic groups the have-nots make up the bulk of formally organized interests, however. Should underrepresented groups be given assistance in organizing? Should limits be placed on the organizational efforts of wealthy interests or are their activities a form of speech or expression and therefore not subject to regulation?

4. Frank J. Sorauf, in his essay "Winning in the Courts: Interest Groups and Constitutional Change," describes how interest groups seek to influence policy and judicial agenda-setting through the sponsorship of test cases or the filing of amicus briefs. Other scholars have found that interest groups' briefs actually serve as a cue to the Supreme Court that a case should be heard. What are some other, less formal ways in which the judiciary is susceptible to public opinion and interest group pressure?

5. In "Inside Campaign Finance: The Purchase of Legislatures," Sorauf suggests that campaign contributions do not buy influence in legislatures and that the evidence as to its consequences is mixed. What evidence do you find most convincing? Are these distinctions between influence, access, and activity consequential?

CHAPTER 9

CONGRESS

Congress is a fascinating institution. It is the most independently powerful elected legislature in the world. It has played a vital role in dealing with every major public policy area in which the federal government has had a role since it first met in 1789. Despite constant change, the 105th Congress in 1997–1998 has features that were recognizably present in the 1st Congress in 1789–1790. There is a great deal of continuity in Congress even though some observers—many journalists and even some political scientists—from time to time proclaim "new eras" on the basis of short-term change. Like any long-lived political institution in the modern world, Congress is in constant flux, but within the context of some important stable features.

The quality of the members of the House and Senate have ranged from statesmen and stateswomen of the highest order to scoundrels and felons. In general, the members are serious public servants. They are, to be sure, concerned with Washington politics, reelection, and their own career advancement. But they are also concerned with helping create what they consider to be good public policy.

The electorate has its most constant and immediate access to determining who makes policy through elections every two years. And because the entire House of Representatives is up for election every two years, the electorate has an opportunity to make major changes in the membership, even though it often sticks mostly with the incumbents. Changes in Senate personnel are less dramatic because only one-third of the seats are up for election at any one time. But changes also occur there.

In recent decades the public has collectively taken a dim view of the quality of how Congress functions as an institution. The public grouses about corruption, slowness, and politics in decision making as negative features of Congress. Despite these nega-

tive views of the collective enterprise, the public also expresses no doubt that we should have a national legislature of two equally powerful chambers. That fact is simply assumed as a legitimate part of the system by which we govern ourselves.

To further complicate an understanding of how the public reacts to Congress, it should also be noted that most individuals are quite positive about their own member of Congress. An oft-repeated phrase asserts that voters "hate Congress, but love their congressman." This "love" is expressed in the high rate of reelection of incumbent members.

Is the generally negative image of Congress as a functioning collectivity a product of coverage by the media? Careful research, summarized by University of Nebraska political scientists John Hibbing and Elizabeth Theiss–Morse in the first reading in this chapter, "The Media's Role in Fomenting Public Disgust with Congress," suggests that media coverage of Congress is superficial and largely negative *but* that the coverage does not cause the negative opinion.

Congress is central in the American governing process. The details of how it exercises that centrality vary. But the centrality itself has been a constant in our national history.

The analysis of the mix of congressional change and stability at any specific point in time is set within that central fact of American political life in the second reading in the chapter, "The Republican Takeover: Change and Continuity," by Roger Davidson. He wrote the chapter from which this reading is taken shortly after the stunning congressional election of 1994, which produced the first Republican majority in the House of Representatives since the election of 1952 and also produced a Republican majority in the Senate for only the fourth two-year period since the election of 1952. He acknowledges that the 1994 election did, in fact, produce real change but also analyzes those changes in the context of important continuities.

Roger Davidson also wrote the third reading in this chapter, "The Emergence of the Postreform Congress." He offers a picture of congressional development in the last six decades occurring in three major periods: "The Conservative Coalition Era" (1937–1964), "The Reform Era" (1965–1978), and "The Postreform Era" (1979–present). Once again he skillfully demonstrates that change and continuity coexist as Congress evolves.

Congress is, of course, a creature of the electorate in that the voters populate the House and Senate with their members. In the chapter on elections several of the readings dealt with aspects of congressional elections.

Once the members are in Washington, collectively they constantly deal with a wide variety of other political actors as they make public policy. These other actors include, centrally, the president and institutional presidency, various bureaucratic units and individual officials in them, and interest groups. Readings in the chapters focusing on the president, the bureaucracy, and interest groups deal with some aspects of these relationships.

Does it matter whether the president and the majority of both houses of Congress are controlled by the same political party? Scholars disagree on how much and what kind of differences are present in two basic situations: "unified government"—in which the presidency, Senate, and House are all controlled by a single party—and "divided government"—in which at least one house of Congress is controlled by a party other than the president's.

The question of whether there are predictable differences between unified government and divided government is not merely theoretical or abstract. The American electorate has produced a situation of divided government more often than not since World War II. In the 52 years between early 1947 and early 1999 the electorate produced divided government for 32 years (62 percent of the time) and unified government for only 20 years (38 percent of the time). The divided government involved a Republican president with a Democratic Congress (usually both houses, always the House) half of the time (26 years) and a

Democratic president with a Republican Congress for six more years. A Democratic president had a Democratic Congress for 18 years and a Republican president had a Republican Congress for only 2 years.

A number of scholars and journalists have long argued that divided government does not work very well because legislative stalemate of one sort or another tends to occur under such conditions. Same party control of the presidency and both houses of Congress does not guarantee legislative productivity in the view of these individuals, but it is only under a condition of same party control that there is much likelihood that a coherent legislative program will pass that will address at least some of the major problems faced by the nation.

Others scholars disagree. They argue that the costs of divided government are modest and stress that important laws are passed during years of divided government.

To the extent that divided government exacerbates bickering between president and Congress, the size of the deficit, the length of time it takes to pass legislation, or the nonprogrammatic nature of the legislation passed, however, this situation, when created by the voters, may also create public alienation from the political system. Divided government certainly makes clear accountability more difficult for the voters to ascertain, another fact that may increase their dislike of the political system.

Journalists also disagree on the costs and benefits of divided government. Some blame "gridlock" on divided government. Others defend divided government as producing compromises, not "gridlock."

The fourth reading in the chapter, "The Politics of Divided Government" by Gary Cox and Samuel Kernell, considers how the political stakes change in a situation of divided government.

Congress does not rely solely on its elected members to conduct its business. It has also staffed itself well to deal with the complexities of modern government. In 1993, for example, Congress had a total of about 11,500 personal staff and over 3,100 committee staff. It also maintains three major staff organizations: the Congressional Budget Office, the Congressional Research Service, and the General Accounting Office. In 1993 these three organizations employed about 6,000 more people. The fifth reading in the chapter, "U.S. Congressman as Enterprise" by Robert Salisbury and Kenneth Shepsle, analyzes the interactions of staff and elected members in getting the work of Congress done.

The Media's Role in Fomenting Public Disgust with Congress

John R. Hibbing and Elizabeth Theiss–Morse

Congress as an institution is not well thought of by the general population. However, when individual members face the voters on election day they fare much better. In most congressional elections since World War II, over 90 percent of all incumbents seeking reelection have won.

Many explanations have been offered for the dim view taken of Congress by the general public. The most compelling has to do with the long time Congress takes to arrive at decisions, the lack of immediate positive impact that can be attributed to most of those decisions, and an impatience with politics inside the government, both within Congress and between Congress and other important players, especially the president.

Some have also advanced the notion that the shallow, often negative, often sensationalist coverage given Congress in the mass media, both print and electronic, produces the public's negative view. In the following reading, University of Nebraska political science professors John Hibbing and Elizabeth Theiss–Morse examine that hypothesis carefully. Their work is based on careful analysis of a large amount of data, even though this article

From "The Media's Role in Fomenting Public Disgust with Congress" by J. R. Hibbing and E. Theiss–Morse, Reprinted by permission from *Extensions*, Fall 1996, a copyrighted publication of the Carl Albert Congressional Research and Studies Center, University of Oklahoma.

simply reports the findings and summarizes the data analysis in very broad terms.

Their bottom line is that the public image of Congress is not uniformly negative, that negative views of many aspects have been around as long as Congress has, and that there is no evidence that media coverage, even though it is far from informative and thorough most of the time, causes negative views. Such coverage may, however, reinforce preexisting negative views.

The compromises that are necessary to get anything done in any free legislature may never sit well with the majority of the American people. We tend to demand immediate solutions and immediate results. Congress, by definition, is not likely to produce such results. Neither, for that matter, is our political system in general with its foundations in checks and balances that make compromise—and the time it takes to reach compromise—major enduring features of the system.

Media coverage of serious political matters has declined in quantity and quality in recent decades—and coverage of Congress is no exception to this general statement. Likewise, the public's image of Congress is extremely negative, with disapprobation reaching an all-time high in 1996. Many observers have put these two situations together and concluded that the media, through negative and shallow stories, have caused the decline in popular approval of Congress. While we are not in total disagreement with this line of thinking, it is, at the same time, only partially accurate. Drawing on recent research we have done concerning public attitudes toward Congress, we present a more complete and objective assessment of the role of the media in public evaluations of Congress. In the process, we hope to clarify the real relationship between media coverage of and public attitudes toward Congress.

To examine the relationship between increased media negativity and increased public disapproval of Congress, we must first determine if the media have indeed become more negative in recent years. While media coverage of the modern Congress is undeniably hostile, this does not necessarily mean that coverage long ago was different. In the nineteenth century, Mark Twain was far from the only journalist to heap scorn upon the nation's legislature. Congress could expect a barrage of uncharitable stories from the press associates of whichever political party did not control a majority in Congress. The twentieth century saw a continuation of press negativity. In 1906, William Randolph Hearst acquired *Cosmopolitan* and commissioned a series of articles by journalist David Graham Phillips entitled "The Treason of the Senate." These articles were vintage muckraking and were disavowed by virtually all members of the responsible press. Still, they doubled *Cosmopolitan*'s circulation and were widely discussed and reprinted. Coming as they did, hard upon well-publicized congressional scandals involving John Mitchell of Oregon and Joseph Burton of Kansas, the articles fanned the flames that would eventually produce direct elections of U.S. Senators and other populist reforms. Public suspicions about the absence of integrity in Congress seemed to be confirmed by the articles. While negativity may have diminished during the two world wars, on the whole Mark Rozell must certainly be correct when he concludes after extensive content analysis of the print media that "although the tone in recent years has become more severe, more disturbing, negative and superficial congressional coverage is nothing new."

Though the Congress of 100 years ago may have had to contend with the likes of Twain and Hearst, it did not have to deal with electronic media—and modern electronic coverage of Congress is decidedly unfavorable. Content analyses of television news stories reveal, to the surprise of few, that "television networks have paid less and less attention to Congress, and their coverage has become progressively less policy oriented and more heavily focused on scandals and unethical behavior." Radio is no better and probably worse. A recent survey revealed radio talk-show hosts to be more hostile to Congress than any other group working in mass media.

Negative electronic coverage of Congress is especially dangerous because most citizens receive news from electronic sources, specifically television. In our random national survey of 1400 adults conducted in 1992, we found that nearly 60 percent of respondents claimed to "usually obtain their news" from television; about 30 percent usually received their news from newspapers; and 10 percent relied primarily on radio. By more than a 2 to 1 ratio, people receive their news primarily from electronic sources; and, since we know there is a tendency for people to claim to read the newspaper when they do not actually do so, the real ratio is probably closer to 3 to 1. Thus, the "gotcha" journalism popular in television newsmagazine[s], the preference of nightly news broadcasts for scandals rather than issues, and the inflammatory rhetoric that has become de rigueur on radio talk shows all leave their mark. While we should not lose sight of the fact that coverage of Congress has almost always been unfavorable, evidence exists that, more than before, the image of Congress conveyed to most Americans by the media today typically is an institution that is "lobby-ridden, incompetent, and slow."

The second part of the media-disapproval relationship points to the recent decline in the public's approval of Congress. Yet current descriptions of public disapproval often downplay the extent to which Congress has been unpopular for most of the country's history. It is hard to make confident historical statements for the time predating modern survey research techniques, but it appears there is little evidence that Congress was ever popular with a sizable majority of the American public for an extended period of time. Blips of popularity appear in the 1950s and the mid-1960s, and the last twenty-five years reveal a slight downward trend in approval, but Congress has never had the chance to get used to being popular. It has consistently been the least approved political institution, and levels in 1996 are only a few points lower than in 1971.

Like media coverage of Congress, public approval of Congress has inched down from a low level, not, as we are sometimes led to believe, fallen off the table of issue-steeped, balanced, charitable coverage and cheery, approving people. Still, the key question is whether media coverage has played a role in fostering the negative public attitude toward Congress. Here again, the popular answer is yes, but a more empirically based response encourages caution.

Through standard statistical techniques, we controlled for other factors such as respondents' partisanship, education, ideology, age, gender, and so on. Once this was done, we found that the source of a respondent's news (television, newspapers, or radio) and the number of times in a week that respondents were exposed to news had little to do with their approval or disapproval of Congress. Interestingly, however, the source and amount of news were both strongly related to whether or not respondents had negative emotional reactions to Congress. In other words, a typical American is not led by the media to be more or less approving of Congress but is led by the media to have negative emotional reactions to Congress. The media do not seem to affect what we *think* of Congress but they do affect how we *feel* about Congress. People who rely on television or radio for news and who absorb a substantial amount of news are much more likely to be angry, disappointed, and disgusted with Congress than are people who rely on print media. But people who rely on television or radio and who obtain much news are not more likely to be disapproving of the job members of Congress are doing.

This combination of findings may seem confusing at first but upon reflection makes perfect sense. Television, especially, is renowned for its ability to inspire emotional reactions, and this can be seen in the case of Congress. Media coverage of Congress is not responsible for the low approval ratings but must apparently shoulder an important share of the responsibility for stirring up the poisoned mood, the emotional caldron of bad feelings swirling in so many people these days. And, we would argue, it is these negative feelings toward Congress that are at the core of the modern public mood. Disapproval of Congress is much less novel than the wild-eyed anger and palpable hostility citizens direct at Congress so frequently these days.

These negative emotional reactions as well as the low approval ratings are generally confined to the members of Congress. If people can be made to think of Congress as an institution rather than a collection of 535 squabbling, fallible humans, approval soars. Eighty-eight percent of all respondents approve of Congress as an institution whereas only 24 percent approve of Congress as a collection of members. People make a distinction between Congress as a set of buildings and historical traditions on the one hand and Congress as a cadre of politicians on the other. Today we hear too much loose talk about public negativity toward Congress when the truth is that people like parts of Congress (their own member; the institution) and dislike others (congressional leaders; members generally).

We have attempted in this brief article to clear up some of the confusion surrounding the extent to which the media have caused the negative public attitude toward Congress about which we hear so much these days. Our analyses demonstrate that the media are partially responsible for negative emotional reactions to members of Congress. But we also find that:

(1) the public is favorable toward aspects of Congress;
(2) the public has never been particularly favorable toward Congress; and
(3) evidence of the media *causing* disapproval is lacking.

This situation leads us to conclude with a plea to be more discriminating in associating the media with negative public attitudes toward Congress. Members of Congress and close observers alike are fond of giving the impression that if Congress could just get a better public relations agent, everything would be right with the world. We have argued elsewhere that the problem is deeper than this. We wish the media would treat Congress in a more responsible fashion, but at the same time we believe the root explanation for public negativity is that people have not been taught to appreciate the messiness of democracy. If they were, people could better put the media's coverage of Congress into perspective.

It is undeniable that the media play up scandals and play down issues, and this hurts Congress. But setting this aside, the public reacts negatively to the way members of Congress do their job as well. This is not the fault of the media; it is the fault of the people. It is the people who ignore the fact that they disagree with each other on almost every major policy issue. Survey results from reputable polling agencies during early 1996 indicate that on many key issues the public could hardly be more divided. On the issue of flag burning, 51 percent supported a constitutional amendment and 48 percent said no; on the issue of balancing the budget, 45 percent supported Clinton's plan and 42 percent supported the Republican plan; on the related issue of cutting social programs, 45 percent feared the country would go too far in cutting while an identical 45 percent felt the danger was that we would not cut far enough. The list could be extended to other issues but there is no need. Americans disagree deeply with each other.

Yet Americans expect elected officials to represent this divided public opinion by never disagreeing with other elected officials. Every time politicians lock horns, the public cries out about the evils of gridlock and about the pointless bickering of partisan politicians. Every time politicians attempt to compromise to manufacture some solution from diverse popular sentiments, the public becomes apoplectic about deal-making and selling out on principles. The people somehow believe that real leaders do not debate and real leaders do not compromise. This belief, of course, could not be further from the truth. Real leadership in a democracy is nothing without reasoned debate and sensible compromise. Without these things, we know from Arrow's Theorem and common sense that solutions in a divided polity are unlikely to be in the offing.

Given that the people are split down the middle and that politicians are supposed to reflect the beliefs of the people, how can they be expected to reach an agreement without debate and compromise? The people have unrealistic expectations about democratic procedures, and politicians and the educational curriculum are primarily to blame. To remove Congress from the unhealthy swamp of public negativity, members of Congress must quit promising that they can achieve substantial changes without compromising, and students must be taught that when they see Congress debating and compromising, this is not evil; this is democracy. As tempting as it might be to hold up the media as the sole source of public negativity toward Congress, it is also quite wrong. At the same time, it would certainly be welcome if the media would assist in the process of reeducating citizens about the nature of democratic procedures in a divided society. We disagree with traditional media critics in the following regard: the usual complaint is that the media need to emphasize issues more and

"horse races" less; our complaint is that the media do not do enough to show people that disagreements in a democracy such as ours are a natural course of events and that the difficult, ugly process of working through these disagreements is not a sign that something has gone wrong with the system but rather is a sign that something has gone right.

R E A D I N G   4 2

The Republican Takeover: Change and Continuity

Roger H. Davidson

This selection by Roger Davidson, a political science professor at the University of Maryland, is the last chapter in a book of original essays on change and stability in Congress in the 1990s. The book appeared after the Republican capture of both the House and Senate in the 1994 elections, so that "earthquake," although Davidson is somewhat skeptical that this description is accurate, was taken into account.

He addresses several major questions about how Congress functions and demonstrates that the results of any single election do not turn the institution upside down. He also provides some of the details of what was happening internally in Congress in the last decades of the 20th century. This summary underscores the truth of what he tells us about the general functioning of Congress.

First, he makes it clear that in the midst of change there is also a great deal of stability. Congress is not an institution that is completely moribund and stagnant. It does change. But even during periods of accelerated internal change it still

From "Wielding the New Broom: What It Swept Away, What It Left in Place" by R. H. Davidson, in *Remaking Congress: Change and Stability in the 1990s,* eds. J. A. Thurber and R. H. Davidson. Copyright © 1995 by the Congressional Quarterly Press. Reprinted by permission.

retains major portions of continuity with its past—procedures, attitudes, and some positions on policies affecting the institution. Despite relatively low public appreciation of the institution, at least as revealed in public opinion surveys, a key to its endurance has, no doubt, been this ability to provide both stability and change at the same time. The mix varies at any specific point in time, but the mix is always present.

Second, he indicates that major change does not occur overnight, but develops over time. The "earthquake" of 1994—both electorally and in terms of the internal functioning of the institution—had foreshocks for several decades before it occurred.

Third, not everything changes at once. For example, he argues that fundamental campaign finance reform and reform of regulations on lobbying are as unlikely as ever.

Already the 1994 elections are regarded as a turning point in American politics. Commentators quickly employed such terms as "earthquake" and "revolution" to dramatize what had happened. Scholars, no less intrigued but slower to pass judgment, debate whether a partisan realignment has occurred or is in progress.

That we are passing a major political milestone cannot be denied.... The party fortunes of nearly two generations were upended; the public policy agenda has been transformed, and along with it the institution of Congress. Issues that had been kept hidden or subordinated suddenly came tumbling from the closet: downsizing the federal establishment, devolution of power to states and localities, welfare reform, budget stringency, and a regulatory ceasefire. Facing a struggling presidency, the resurgent Republicans on Capitol Hill confidently took command over policy initiation, media attention, and public expectations. Inside Congress, party leaders flexed their muscles, activity levels soared, and innovative procedures were explored and tested. Most notably, a House Speakership stronger than any seen in nearly a century captured the imagination and attention of the pundits and public alike.

What shall we conclude about the events we have witnessed: the popular unrest of the 1990s and the partisan turnover of 1994? This is no simple task. It is far easier to assess past events than to understand developments that are still unfolding. As the distinguished journalist Walter Lippman once remarked about the Russian Revolution, "The hardest thing to report is chaos, even if it is evolving chaos." Still, the evidence brought together in this volume suggests several important conclusions about the so-called earthquake of 1994.

Despite the publicity surrounding the 1994 vote itself, we are unquestionably faced with something that spans more than a single election.... Congress has undergone a period of upheaval that intensified throughout the 1980s and reached crisis stage by the early 1990s. The ways in which this crisis revealed itself on Capitol Hill...[include] variable leadership, dysfunctional committees, partisan strife, interchamber tensions, increasingly redundant procedures, and scandals both large and small—all played out against a melancholy backdrop of public distrust and scorn. Historically, this era rivals other such periods of political upheaval and change: the Progressive uprisings around 1910, the post-World War II turnover and reorganization of the mid-1940s, and the liberal reformism associated with the 1974 "Watergate" elections but spanning a much wider time frame.

Institutional attributes and trends demonstrate impressive continuity, even during periods of outward upheaval. The 1994 "earthquake," if it can be called that, was no isolated event but part of an extended period of tremors and aftershocks. The reinvigorated House Speakership owed much to the personality and cohesive cohorts of Georgia Republican Newt Gingrich, but...today's strong Speakership actually dates from the 1970s, when Democratic reformers fought to counteract the conservative "old bulls" who controlled many of the committees. Nor were the Republican plans for reforming Congress concocted overnight; they were incubated mainly within the House Republican Conference during a decade-long partisan struggle against an entrenched, sometimes overbearing Democratic majority. Even the celebrated "Contract with America" was a platform culled from the conservatives' accumulated wish-list, much of which had been bottled up in committees under Democratic rule. And although the duration of this present reform era cannot be known, it does not seem to have run its course....

The stability of our governmental institutions is a function of constitutional design and historical precedent. Separated branches of government, including the bicameral legislature, rarely experience change at precisely the same moment or at exactly the same rate. Diverse constituencies, staggered elections, and overlapping terms of office generate inertia as well as responsiveness. So do long-standing internal arrangements, which on Capitol Hill include partisan leadership hierarchies, division of labor through the committee system, and norms of reciprocity among individuals and between chambers. Such attributes cannot halt change, but at the very least they absorb and cushion it.

Continuity pervades even when an institution changes in significant ways. Although the pace of change accelerated in the early 1990s, Congress—like all living institutions—shifts and adapts all the time. The 1993 Joint Committee on the Organization of Congress, only the third such joint effort (the others convened in 1945 and 1965), built upon a rich post-World War II history of congressional self-examination and structural and procedural adjustment, most of it incremental and hardly noticed by outsiders. Much of the territory traversed by the 1993 panel...had already been mapped out by 1970s reformers, especially in the House and Senate committee realignment efforts (of 1973–1974 and 1976–1977, respectively). Although initially judged a failure because few of its recommendations were acted upon, the 1993 Joint Committee left two invaluable legacies. First, its hearings and reports provided a detailed historical record of Congress's operational characteristics and defects. Second, it served as a forum for drafting, debating, and revising a series of reform proposals that could be achieved once the votes became available to pass them. Accordingly, the House Republicans who had served on the joint Committee drafted the relevant portions of the "Contract with America" and subsequently provided specific language to be inserted into Republican Conference or House rules.

Congressional committees, examined by reform panels in the 1970s and becoming increasingly dysfunctional in the 1980s, were naturally targeted by reformers of the 1990s. Committee reform was a core theme of the Joint Committee's hearings, studies, and reports; members and staff alike named it the Hill's most urgent issue. As a result both chambers, espe-

cially the House of Representatives, overhauled their committee systems. Although the 103rd Congress rejected most reorganization proposals, including those from the Joint Committee, several nontrivial innovations were adopted by the House: it reduced subcommittees and members' assignments, axed four nonlegislative select committees, and permitted the public naming of discharge petition signers. The new House majority continued the reform process in the 104th Congress, eliminating three committees, dropping more subcommittees and members' assignments, and altering certain procedures. (For instance, proxy voting and "rolling quorums" were forbidden wholesale.) But because of the same forces that had long stymied reform under Democratic rule, these Republicans shrank from more thorough-going revision, such as realignment of committee jurisdictions. Over on the opposite side of the Capitol, senators took steps to trim committee spending and limit subcommittees but resisted major structural reforms or staff reductions.

House and Senate floor procedures likewise exhibit few major departures but numerous incremental adjustments. The two chambers had settled into distinctive but divergent patterns in the postreform era. Always a haven for minority views, the Senate is characterized by extremely lax floor rules that seem virtually impossible to overturn. In contrast, majority party rule dominates House floor proceedings so completely as to stifle legitimate albeit time-consuming debate and amending activity—not only by the minority party, but by minority factions within the ruling party. Although the 104th Congress brought many changes, these left untouched the divergent biases underlying the two chambers' procedures. The Republicans, in fact, strengthened the House's majoritarian character (perhaps to excess); the Senate continued its individualistic (and seemingly irreversible) ways.

What changed was the identity of those favored or disadvantaged by the rules of the respective chambers. In the Senate it had been majority Leader George J. Mitchell, D-Maine, who in 1993 proposed modest restrictions on filibusters, whereas under GOP rule complaints came most often from the more militant supporters of the majority party's agenda—especially younger conservatives who had "graduated" from the more partisan House. Over on the House side the triumphant Republicans forgot most (though not all) of their bitterest grievances against majority rules, whereas the Democrats, unused to minority status, loudly protested what they now considered heavy-handed exploitation of those rules.

Congress's modern-day obsession with budgetary issues has spawned a veritable museum of novel structures and procedures. Yet ever since the new era began with the Congressional Budget and Impoundment Control Act of 1974, budgetary politics has involved a recurrent quest for procedural solutions to substantive policy problems. These procedural solutions—from the 1974 act through Gramm-Rudman-Hollings I and II (1985 and 1987), the Budget Enforcement Act of 1990, and the Omnibus Budget Reconciliation Act of 1993—have had only limited success. All have aided members in avoiding individual blame for budget decisions; all have encouraged accounting tricks to magnify reported savings and hide real costs. Three long-term trends have continued: (1) toward a zero-sum game that pits budgetary commitments against one another and tends to favor existing programs over new ones; (2) toward centralized, top-down controls designed to limit deliberations and discourage interventions; and (3) toward greater complexity—a system now accessible mainly to budget-making specialists.

Continuity also marks two seemingly urgent issues of political ethics: campaign finance and lobby reform. As for campaign funding, no issue better exemplifies the venerable maxim that "where you stand depends on where you sit." Whether Republican or Democrat, whether a senator or representative, one's stance on these questions can be predicted from one's sources of funding. The 1994 elections...may actually diminish the likelihood of new campaign finance legislation in the short run. Traditionally successful in overall partisan fund raising, the now-majority Republicans will be in no hurry to rein in political action committees: they are set for a bonanza from PACs, which in the past favored incumbent Democrats. In any case Republicans would prefer to postpone campaign reform to win a better deal from a hoped-for GOP president. Meanwhile, Bill Clinton's veto pen protects Democrats from any punitive measures concocted by congressional Republicans. Nor will such

an impasse necessarily be unpopular. Nelson suggests that, contrary to the assumptions of many politicians and analysts, the public really cares very little about the issue. So the long-term stalemate surrounding campaign funding shows little sign of ending.

Even more than campaign finance, the issue of lobbying regulation is insulated against fundamental change. Here the major constraint is no mundane matter of political interests, but nothing less than the cherished First Amendment guarantees of free speech, assembly, and petition. Two growing trends in contemporary lobbying...exacerbate the problems of regulating lobbying activities. One is the rise of grassroots lobbying, in which interest groups supplement their face-to-face contacts with lawmakers by mobilizing their constituencies through internal communications and the mass media—processes explicitly protected by the First Amendment. Even such seemingly innocent proposals as disclosure of grassroots lobbyists can ignite fierce opposition, as reformers discovered. The second trend is the practice of building complex coalitions of groups on particular issues. How can all the constituent groups be identified, and their contributions tallied? The common element of both trends is the intermingling of lobbyists, group members, and sympathetic citizens. Lobbying, in other words, is a matter of "us," not just "we versus they." Under such circumstances, lobbying "reform" is an elusive goal indeed.

READING 43

The Emergence of the Postreform Congress

Roger H. Davidson

In this selection, Professor Roger Davidson, a political scientist at the University of Maryland,

---

explores the work of Congress since 1937 in terms of its basic policy stance and how that was related both to the internal distribution of power within the body and to external developments in the nation, especially in the economic realm. He divides the years from 1937 to the early 1990s (the chapter from which this reading is drawn appeared in 1992) into three eras: the Conservative Coalition Era (1937–1964), the Reform Era (1965–1978), and the Postreform Era (1979–present). His characterizations of each era are clear, as are the contrasts between the eras.

His linkage between changing economic reality in the country and the emergence of the postreform Congress is particularly interesting. He draws a picture of an institution adapting to external reality both in terms of the kinds of legislation it passed and in terms of its internal organizational arrangements. He persuasively argues that Congress made conscious choices in these adaptations but also that external changes made those choices highly likely. The ideological predilections of congressional leaders and of presidents Carter, Reagan, and Bush made some difference. But one clear message is that ideology did not drive all changes. Rather, organizational adaptation to reality helped drive change.

What of the period since Davidson wrote? One interpretation of President Bill Clinton's predilection for not sticking with any specific position for very long is that he, too, is trying to adapt to external realities. His rejection of traditional (that is, New Deal) Democratic party values and policies can be interpreted that way. Naturally, he was also spurred in the direction of the political center—and perhaps more waffling—by the 1994 congressional election results, which brought a very conservative Republican House majority into office, along with a more moderate Republican Senate majority. The 1996 election confirmed for President Clinton the necessity and desirability of staying in the right/ right-center part of the political spectrum in terms of policy positions.

Davidson poses the question concretely: How free are our politicians to choose what institutions do? How constrained are they by external events?

Innovation in Congress's structures, procedures, and practices is a persistent theme in writing and commentary about the institution. Scholars, journalists, reformers, and ordinary citizens have publicly complained about how badly Congress works since even before the Progressive Era at the turn of the twentieth century. Manifestos, issued periodically, declare that various changes must be adopted to cure legislative ills (most recently, campaign finance reform). These worries have spawned an enormous literature on *congressional innovation,* typically reflecting a reformist viewpoint.

Other analysts have investigated what can be called the *mechanics of legislative innovation.* They are less interested in reforming the institution than in describing and understanding whatever changes take place within it. In the earliest days of political science as an organized discipline, scholars trained in public law naturally concentrated on formal structures: rules, precedents, and procedures. It was this legalistic and formalistic tradition that the young Woodrow Wilson sought to replace with the study of politics' "rough practice," in order to discover "the real depositories and the essential machinery of power." Following Wilson's lead, succeeding generations of investigators exposed the "rough practice" of Capitol Hill politics with ingenuity, skill, and a wide range of theoretical assumptions and methodological tools.

The most recent generation of congressional scholarship has zealously explored what Hedrick Smith calls the "power earthquake" of the 1960s and 1970s: a multifaceted onslaught of changes, or reforms, that shattered the older seniority leaders' power, opened up the decision-making game to wider circles of players, and dramatically recast House and Senate rules and procedures....

Increasingly, however, it is evident that Congress has embarked on a postreform period of adjustment and development. To be sure, most of the reform-era innovations remain formally in place and continue to shape the assumptions and expectations of both observers and members about how the system operates. Nonetheless, the evidence of continued change and adaptation is undeniable. In ways both subtle and profound, Congress has changed markedly since the reform era of the 1960s and 1970s; it is, among other things, more routinized, more partisan, and even more hierarchical. While explicit tinkering with rules and procedures is not as pronounced as in the prior era, the postreform Congress has acted to minimize or reverse some of the central reformist trends. In the House of Representatives, this has meant stronger leadership and stricter management of floor business. The Senate has undergone more subtle but still noticeable shifts in its operations....

THE CONSERVATIVE COALITION ERA (1937–1964)

From Franklin Roosevelt's second administration through the mid-1960s, Congress was dominated by an oligarchy of senior leaders—sometimes called "the barons" or "the old bulls." Whichever party was in power, congressional leaders overrepresented safe, one-party regions (the Democratic rural South, the Republican rural Northeast and Midwest) and reflected the narrow legislative agenda of the bipartisan conservative coalition that controlled so much domestic policy-making. This created a hostile environment for activist presidents and their legislative allies. "Deadlock on the Potomac" was how James MacGregor Burns described the situation in Roosevelt's second term....

Harry Truman's clashes with Capitol Hill began early and lasted throughout his presidency. "Except for the modified Employment Act of 1946," relates Donovan, "the [Democratic] Seventy-ninth Congress had squelched practically every piece of social and economic legislation Truman had requested." Truman's other Congresses were equally frustrating, though in different ways. The Republican Eightieth Congress "gave [Truman] his most enduring image. Facing an opposition-controlled legislative body almost certain to reject any domestic program he proposed, he adopted the role of an oppositionist." Truman campaigned successfully in 1948 by excoriating the "awful, do-nothing Eightieth Congress." Yet the Democratic Eighty-first Congress rejected virtually all of Truman's major Fair Deal initiatives; his final congress, the Eighty-second, marked by depleted Democratic majorities and the Korean War stalemate, was even more hostile to new legislative initiatives.

The 1950s were years of outward quiescence accompanied by underlying, yet accelerating, demands for action and innovation. Dwight Eisenhower, whose legislative goals were far more modest than Truman's, was increasingly placed in the position of offering scaled-down alternatives to proposals floated on Capitol Hill by coalitions of activist Democrats and liberal Republicans. The legislative work load through this period was relatively stable and manageable from year to year. A large proportion of the bills and resolutions were routine—immigration, land claims, and private legislation, categories of questions not yet delegated to the executive branch for resolution. Demands were building, however, for new legislation to address civil rights and other urban suburban concerns.

Internally, the key committees of the 1950s (the taxing and spending panels plus House Rules) tended to be cohesive groups...boasting firm leadership and rigorous internal norms of behavior. These committees kept a tight lid on new legislation, especially in fiscal affairs. The appropriations panels, in particular, served as guardians of the U.S. Treasury, holding in check the more rapacious inclinations of the program-oriented authorizing panels.

Journalists and political scientists closely studied the postwar Congress, constructing a detailed picture of its operations.... The leading intellectual framework saw the institution as an interlocking pattern of personal relationships in which structure and function worked in rough equilibrium. Ironically, by the time observers got around to completing this coherent portrait of a tight, closed, internally coherent congressional world, that world was already being turned upside down. Pressures for change and reform mounted, heralding a remarkable period of reformist politics.

THE REFORM ERA (1965–1978)

The cozy domains of the barons were eventually pulled apart by nothing less than a "power earthquake," as journalist Hedrick Smith calls it. The earthquake touched virtually every corner of the political landscape: the presidency, courts, parties, interest groups, and media, not to mention citizens themselves.

The boundaries of this reform era, as of other eras, are somewhat imprecise. The course of change began in earnest after the 1958 elections, which enlarged the Democrats' ranks by sixteen senators and fifty-one representatives, many of them programmatic liberals. The elections had an immediate impact on both chambers. Senate Majority Leader Lyndon Johnson's autocratic rule softened perceptibly; two years later, Johnson relinquished his leadership post to the mild-mannered liberal Mike Mansfield (D-Mont.). In the House a small band of liberal activists formally launched the Democratic Study Group, which subsequently spearheaded efforts for procedural reforms. Speaker Sam Rayburn (D-Tex.) resolved in 1961 to break the conservatives' hold on the powerful House Rules committee. The reform era reached its climax in the mid-1970s with successive waves of changes in committee and floor procedures and, in 1975, the ouster of three of the barons from their committee chair positions.

One underlying cause of the upheaval was a series of unmet policy demands pushed by urban and suburban voting blocs as well as minority groups, and adopted by activist presidents. The spirit of the era was reflected in the popular movements that came to prominence: civil rights, environmentalism, consumerism, and opposition to the Vietnam War. Longer-range causes included reapportionment and redistricting, widened citizen participation, social upheaval, and technological innovations in transportation and communications.

Internally, the resulting changes pointed Congress in the direction of a more open, participatory legislative process: greater leverage for individual lawmakers, and dispersion of influence among and within the committees. More leaders existed than ever before, and more influence was exerted by non-leaders. More staff aides were on hand to extend the legislative reach of even the most junior members.

Individual senators and representatives, while enjoying their enhanced legislative involvement, were obliged at the same time to devote greater attention to their constituents back home. No longer was frantic constituency outreach confined to a few large-state senators and representatives from swing districts; now it was practiced by all members (or their staffs) to purchase electoral security in an age of dwindling party support. In their home styles, members tended to exchange the workhorse role for that of the show horse.

The reforms were propelled by, and in turn helped to facilitate, an ambitious and expansionary congressional work load. It was the era of such presidential themes as the New Frontier and the Great Society, witnessing a host of landmark enactments in civil rights, education, medical insurance, employment and training, science and space, consumer protection, the environment—and five new cabinet departments and four constitutional amendments. Legislative activity soared in those years by whatever measure one chooses to apply—bills introduced, hearings, reports, hours in session, floor amendments, recorded floor votes, and measures passed. The processing of freestanding bills and resolutions became the centerpiece of committee and subcommittee work.

The decentralization of the 1960s and 1970s was accompanied by a weakening of the appropriations committees' grip over spending, at the same time building up the authorizing committees' power. The ascendant authorizing panels engineered a revolution in federal spending practices through ingenious use of "backdoor spending" provisions in much of this new legislation—such as contract authority, budget authority, direct Treasury borrowing, and especially entitlements—thus stripping the appropriations panels of much of their formal fiscal guardianship role. One analyst calculates that three-quarters of the domestic spending growth between 1970 and 1983 occurred in budget accounts lying outside annual appropriations; that is, beyond the appropriations committees' reach.

Like the earlier period, the reform era of the 1960s and 1970s was well documented by journalists and scholars. Symptomatic of the decentralization and fragmentation of the reform era was its most popular scholarly paradigm, drawn from economics. Lawmakers were now seen not as role players in a complex system of interactions in equilibrium, but as individual entrepreneurs in a vast, open marketplace that rewarded self-interested competitiveness with little or no regard for the welfare of the whole.

THE POSTREFORM ERA (1979–)

By the 1980s Congress again faced an environment that diverged in significant ways from what had gone before. Although the shift is popularly associated with the Reagan administration, it was under way by 1979 or 1980 (the Ninety-sixth Congress).

The advent of the so-called *zero-sum society* no doubt lay at the root of the changed political atmosphere. The economy no longer seemed to support the federal government's array of services, many of them enacted during the reform period. The core problem was productivity—the engine that over the long haul enables a nation to raise its standard of living and underwrite an expanding array of public services. After 1973 the nation's productivity stagnated in comparison with both its economic rivals and its previous record. The 1970s and 1980s were the poorest productivity decades of the twentieth century.

Lagging productivity affected not only government tax receipts but also citizens' attitudes toward their economic well-being. In the late 1970s the economy was buffeted by *stagflation,* a double whammy of high inflation and high unemployment. A serious recession occurred in the early 1980s and again a decade later. Meanwhile, the government's costly and relatively impervious system of entitlements and, after 1981, tax cuts and program reallocations turned the fiscal dividends of the postwar era into structural deficits.

Intellectual fashion and political realities repudiated the notion that government intervention could solve all manner of economic and social ills. Disenchantment with the results of government programs, many of which had been shamelessly oversold to glean support for their enactment, led to widespread demands for a statutory cease-fire: disinvestment, deregulation, and privatization. At the same time, spurred by "bracket creep"—which raised the marginal and real tax rates of millions of U.S. citizens—a series of tax revolts swept through the states to the nation's capital. The "no new taxes" cry of Presidents Reagan and Bush, however unrealistic and misleading, was politically a long-running hit with politicians and voters.

The advent of zero-sum politics is popularly associated with the Reagan administration, which took office in 1980 with the pledge of cutting taxes, domestic aid, and welfare programs. Reagan's election was, to be sure, interpreted at the time as a major change in American politics; certainly, Reagan's policies—

especially the 1981 revenue cuts and the repeated threats to veto new taxes and domestic spending—hastened the trend toward constricting the legislative agenda. However, deteriorating economic conditions and shifting attitudes had already propelled former President Jimmy Carter in some (though not all) of these policy directions; by the Ninety-sixth Congress (that is, by 1979–80), the altered environment had already produced a decline in legislative work load. Had Carter been reelected in 1980, it is probable that he, and Congress, would have traveled further along the road toward zero-sum politics.

The president and Congress were preoccupied in the postreform period with resolving fiscal and revenue issues, rather than designing new programs or establishing new agencies. In the domestic realm, the emphasis was on reviewing, adjusting, refining, or cutting back on existing programs. "There's not a whole lot of money for any kind of new programs," remarked Mississippi GOP Senator Thad Cochran, "so, we're holding oversight hearings on old programs...which may not be all that bad an idea." Accordingly, individual members were less tempted to put forward their ideas as freestanding bills or resolutions. Such new ideas as were saleable were more apt to be conveyed in amendments to large-scale legislative vehicles: reauthorizations, continuing appropriations, debt limit, or reconcilication bills.

The environment of the 1980s reversed the previous era's liberal activism. Few new programs were launched and few domestic programs were given added funding. Although the public continued to expect Congress to take action to solve problems, there was equal sentiment for cutting back "big government" and reducing public-sector deficits. Faith in government activism plummeted in the wake of criticisms of waste and ineffectiveness in government programs.

The economic predicament and its attendant intellectual shift severely curtailed legislative productivity. "Rarely in peacetime has a single issue dominated politics here the way the budget deficit is doing now," observed a *New York Times* correspondent. "The most important legislative measures of the year [1989]—tax cuts, expansion of child-care benefits, changes in Medicare and Medicaid and many others—are paralyzed." In some cases zero-sum politics was practiced literally, as members bartered such items as congressional mailing costs with the war on drugs. Senate Majority Leader George J. Mitchell characterized the budget dilemma as "the whale in the bathtub that leaves no room for anything else."

ELEMENTS OF THE POSTREFORM CONGRESS

The results of what some observers call *cutback politics* are predictable; (1) fewer bills are sponsored by individual legislators; (2) key policy decisions are packaged into huge "mega-bills," permitting lawmakers to escape adverse reactions to individual provisions: (3) techniques of blame avoidance are employed to protect lawmakers from the adverse effects of cutback politics; (4) noncontroversial, commemorative resolutions are passed into law—nearly half of all laws produced by recent Congresses; (5) driven by budgetary concerns, party-line voting is at a modern-day high on Capitol Hill; and (6) leadership in the House and Senate is markedly stronger now than at any time since 1910. Today's leaders not only benefit from powers conferred by reform-era innovations of the 1960s and 1970s, they also respond to widespread expectations that they are the only people who can, and should, untangle the legislative schedule....

CONCLUSION

The premise of this analysis is that Congress is motivated by the need to respond—through structural or procedural changes, legislation, or other activities—to demands emanating from the larger economic, social, political, and government environment. The largely uncoordinated and unexpected evolution of what we call postreform Congress provides a compelling illustration of this premise.

The postreform Congress betokens not a concerted reform effort but a gradual adaptation to radically altered political and legislative agendas. Confronted by a lagging economy, divided government, and divisions over the efficacy of government programs, Congress markedly changed the way it approached its legislative work load, in the process retreating from the decentralized system established by the reforms of the 1960s and 1970s.

One message conveyed by this story is the institution's resiliency in adapting to the demands made upon it. Confronted with stresses brought on by changes in its external environment, an organization normally does not willingly choose to emasculate its missions or radically transform its work. Rather, the typical organization pursues one or more adaptive strategies. It may seek to adopt structural or operational changes that will adjust its output capability upward or downward, as the case may be. Or it may seek to reshape its effective domain by contracting or expanding it—sloughing off categories of work load in the former, appropriating new tasks in the latter. Both strategies are designed to achieve an equilibrium between the expectations and demands and the institution's work-load capacities.

READING 44

The Politics of Divided Government

Gary W. Cox and Samuel Kernell

Gary Cox and Samuel Kernell, political science professors at the University of California–San Diego, examine the causes and consequences of "divided government": the situation in which the White House and at least one house of Congress are controlled by different parties. As the chapter introduction indicates, this is a very common situation since World War II. "Divided government" is much more common than "unified government."

The Cox and Kernell reading is taken from the last chapter of a 1991 book with chapters written by a number of different authors. In this last chapter of the book Cox and Kernell edited, they summarize key findings from throughout the text and refer to the authors of other chapters by last name. They tie the causes of divided government to the American party system. In effect, without using the phrase they support the notion that the "candidate-centered" nature of modern politics increases the chances of divided government. Some of their explanation of causes needs to be reconsidered a bit since they were analyzing a situation that seemed to make a Republican president and a Democratic Congress the natural split. Since 1994, as well as in 1947–1948, the division has involved a Democratic president and a Republican Congress.

In the section on the consequences of divided government, the authors focus on the bargaining options open to the parties. In a very real sense, the same necessity for bargaining and the same options are open to the president and Congress in a situation of "unified government." But the fact that two different parties control the branches adds additional complications and challenges to the effort to bargain in such a way that compromises emerge, rather than "gridlock."

Leroy Reiselbach, a senior congressional scholar at Indiana University, has recently reminded us that divided government is only one possible cause of "gridlock," when it occurs. He argues (in his chapter in Peter F. Galderisi, ed., Divided Government, *Rowan and Littlefield, 1996) that "electorally-induced localism, congressional decentralization, and presidential leadership failure" also "may contribute to policy immobilism," along with divided government.*

One of the first things that the beginning student learns about U. S. political parties is that they serve various important "functions" in the larger political system. Prominent among these functions is that of providing "a force for unification in the divided American political system." In addition to connecting state and federal politics, U. S. political parties are looked to as vehicles to link the constitutionally separated powers exercised by the president, House, and Senate—harnessing them all to an overall national purpose. In this way, the governmental paralysis that might ensue if the branches could not agree or the working at cross-purposes that might result if they pursued different aims can be avoided.

Although modern textbooks still mention the need to unify what the constitution has put asunder, they are apt nowadays to note that political parties have not always been up to the task in recent decades. Governmental paralysis, such as that evidenced in the 1990 budget standoff, has been a frequent complaint. And U. S. foreign policy has been decidedly at cross-purposes on occasion: While the Reagan administration pursued a hard-line policy toward the Sandinista regime in Nicaragua—elements of which had been specifically forbidden by Congress and were thus carried on in secret—Speaker James Wright and the Democrats in the House of Representatives pursued their own quite different policy, independently of White House control.

Stalemate and conflicting actions, rather than vigor and complementary actions, are to be expected given that no single party has controlled all branches of government in recent years. A party can unify government if it wins control of both the executive and the legislative branches; but if no party wins such a broad electoral mandate, then to the institutional separation of power contrived by the Founding Fathers must be added a partisan separation of purpose.

The question—whether parties act out their textbook role, promoting vigorous government by unifying constitutionally separate powers or, in contrast, exacerbate the divisions in U. S. government by entrenching themselves in distinctive institutional bastions—then becomes one of frequency. If the electoral system is structured in a way that promotes party sweeps of all branches of government or if mass behavior by itself produces sweeps, then parties can perhaps perform their unifying function and overcome the institutional separation of powers. But if the electoral system regularly produces divided control, then partisan differences will magnify, rather than diminish, the importance of the institutional separation of powers.

Moreover, the direction of causality may be the opposite of that suggested in the textbooks. Rather than clean party sweeps in the electoral system unifying separate institutions, the institutional separation of powers may actually disunify electoral competition. The notion that parties are characterized by electoral *nuclei,* with each nucleus specializing in the task of winning control of a particular office or institution, is a well-known one in the literature on party organization. What we may have been seeing since about the mid-1950s is an increase in the degree to which the party nuclei clustering around the Senate, House, and presidency are separate organizations with separate electoral imperatives....

THE CAUSES OF DIVIDED GOVERNMENT

The first theme appears most prominently in the essays by Jacobson and Petrocik. Both emphasize that different issues matter in presidential and congressional elections and that the parties (or their appropriate nuclei) seem to have established advantages on different sets of issues (the Republicans on "presidential" issues, the Democrats on "congressional" issues). Thus, for example, Jacobson uses survey data to demonstrate both a Republican advantage on such "national" issues as the budget deficit, foreign affairs, and defense policy and a Democratic advantage on the more district-specific issues entailed in domestic policy.

There is even an explanation for why different parties might acquire advantage in different institutionally defined issue areas. To put it more baldly than its many proponents would, this explanation is that voters want aggressive benefit-seekers (that is, Democrats) for their own districts, coupled with tightfisted (that is, Republican) presidents to keep overall spending and taxes to a reasonable level. As long as voters act as if they think this way, there will be a tendency toward divided control; whichever party gains the advantage as the "provider of benefits" automatically loses a step as the "controller of spending and taxes."

Petrocik complements this institutionally focused explanation with one that looks more to the nature of the electoral coalitions to which the two parties cater. Executive elections tend to be difficult for the party with the larger and more heterogeneous coalition—the Democrats. Their very success in adapting to all the varied electoral niches in the legislative arena is a handicap when it comes to waging a unified campaign for the presidency.

Wattenberg adds another dimension to the argument by noting the structural advantages that the Republicans have acquired in the presidential nomination process. The Democrats have unintentionally developed a nomination process that exacerbates intraparty squabbling, with consequent damage to their general election prospects. Both of these explanations for the prevalence of divided government at the federal level—one focusing on the parties' differential successes at establishing credible and attractive positions on different sets of issues, the other on the parties' different nomination procedures—are brought into question by the high incidence of divided partisan control in the states. Fiorina and Petrocik, too, suggest that the forces producing divided government may be at work throughout the federal structure. If so, previous explanations based exclusively on national politics may be too "level specific."

Fiorina argues that our current electoral system makes change in partisan control of a legislative body unlikely, relative to change in partisan control of an executive office. This leads to a recurrent pattern wherein the electorate punishes the dominant party by electing a governor (or president) of the opposite party. In some ways, this line of thought stands the old notion of a referendum vote on its head. Instead of the legislative vote being a referendum on the executive, the executive vote is a referendum on the party controlling the legislature; whenever things are going badly, the verdict is negative, and divided government results.

THE CONSEQUENCES OF DIVIDED GOVERNMENT

The extent to which different party nuclei now face different electoral contexts (different issues, different rules of the game, or different electoral exposures) is the primary explanation given here for the recent frequency of divided government. The consequences of this division in control at the federal level are dealt with in the essays by Kernell, Cox and McCubbins, McCubbins, and Stewart.

One important consequence of divided government, with which the essays by Kernell and Stewart deal, is institutional conflict. Even after more than two hundred years of accumulated practice and precedent, there remains considerable ambiguity in the

Constitution's prescriptions. As a result, both parties aggressively—and strategically—assert the prerogatives and powers of whatever branches of government they happen to control.

Another important consequence of divided government, taken more or less as a given in all these essays, is that all major policy decisions are now the result of an institutionally structured bargaining process, with each party possessing a veto. Knowing little more than this about U. S. politics, coupled with a bit of bargaining theory, one can account for some of the prominent features of our recent governmental experience.

Note first that the parties have three broad bargaining options. They can bargain "within the beltway," accepting the cards that the electoral and constitutional systems have dealt them. They can attempt to expand the context within which bargaining occurs by appealing beyond the beltway to public opinion. Or they can seek to prosecute policy without the assent of the other party. Let us consider each of these options in reverse order.

The last option is largely a decision not to bargain and instead to pursue policy goals with the resources available to whatever branches of government one controls. One of the most dramatic examples is the pursuit of separate foreign policies by the Reagan administration and the Wright speakership regarding Nicaragua. Such attempts by one or the other branch to "go it alone" must eventually come into conflict with the regular policymaking process, as Colonel Oliver North and Admiral John Poindexter found out. As long as each branch is willing to defend its constitutionally mandated role, in other words, unilateral pursuit of policy can only be a temporary strategy—a postponement of bargaining, rather than a total avoidance of it. Nonetheless, the ability to pursue a policy unilaterally can present the other branch with a fait accompli that it is difficult or impolitic to overturn. The president's use of his warmaking powers under the War Powers Act—illustrated by President Bush's handling of the 1991 Gulf war—is a case in point.

In addition to the "go it alone" option, there is also the option of "going public." The most prominent is a bridge-burning tactic: making public commitments to particular positions in order to raise the costs of reneging and thereby strengthen one's bargaining position. This was exemplified by George Bush's "read my lips" pronouncement, before he changed it to "read my hips."

The third option is bargaining within the beltway, on the terms established by electoral outcomes and constitutional prescriptions. Such bargaining is typically characterized by delay and brinksmanship, careful attention to reversion points, and the selling out of junior partners. We shall say a few words about each of these by way of illustration.

Delay is one of the primary techniques in *any* bargaining game in which the assent of all parties is necessary to an agreement; moreover, it is virtually the only credible "within the beltway" method that the parties have to demonstrate toughness and determination. Thus, when the parties are far from agreement yet some agreement must be reached (as has notoriously been true in budget politics of the Reagan and Bush administrations), one finds that the early stages of negotiation seem to go nowhere. Agreements are reached only at the eleventh hour or after, as the pressures of budgetary chaos mount and extort compromises from the opposing sides.

The game that the parties play is something like the game of chicken: The worst outcome for both is no agreement, but neither wants to be the one to back down first. As the fiscal year deadline nears, the risk of the "no-agreement" outcome increases, and the side that fears this outcome more backs down. Willingness to delay—and thereby increase the risk of the "no-agreement" outcome—is the primary mechanism for demonstrating toughness (and for bluffing).

There seems to be some doubt about this line of analysis in the journalistic world. For example, an analysis of the 1990 budget crisis referred to divided government as the "snap" explanation for the recurring budgetary paralysis, of which 1990 was the latest and greatest example. The analysis went on to argue that "it is not clear whether the government would act more decisively if the same party controlled Capitol Hill and the White House. Democrat Jimmy Carter's rocky relations with a Democratic-controlled Congress provide a sobering counterexample." Yet, if one looks at the record, one finds that the delay in appropriations bills during Reagan's first six years was, at least when measured by how much of the federal government was financed in omnibus continuing resolutions, significantly greater than the delay under Carter. In Carter's four years (FY 1978 to FY 1981), an average of $55 billion in appropriations was effected through omnibus continuing resolutions. The corresponding figure for Reagan's first six years (FY 1982 to FY 1987), when the Republicans also held the Senate, was over five times as large.

A second important feature of the bargaining context, not so obvious as budgetary brinksmanship, is that vetoes mean different things in different policy areas. The key consideration is the "reversion point"—the policy that will stand in force if no agreement is reached. In some policy arenas, such as taxation, failure to reach an agreement means that the status quo is perpetuated. In others, such as appropriations, failure to reach an agreement means that substantial cuts in spending will ensue. Which kind of reversion point a given policy arena has affects the bargaining outcome in sometimes nonobvious ways, as is illustrated amply in the essays by Kernell, Cox and McCubbins, McCubbins, and Stewart.

Finally, in politics one generally bargains with those who can deliver the votes. This simple maxim means that Republican presidents ultimately have to deal with the Democrats, who control Congress, rather than with their Republican colleagues, who do not. The consequence has been frequent strains in the relationship between congressional Republicans and their presidents—as we saw in the dramatic disagreement over the 1990 budget.

A strong indication of the frequency of these interinstitutional strains within the Republican party is the lowered party cohesion among House Republicans when their party controls the White House. A straightforward regression analysis of Republican unity on roll call votes from the 73rd to 100th congresses shows two things: First, party cohesion among House Republicans has steadily eroded over this time period; second, House Republicans have been significantly less cohesive when their man is in the White House.

A similar regression analysis of Democratic unity on roll calls shows that the House Democrats have not suffered nearly as much of a decline in party cohesion over the same period and—more important

for present purposes—that they do not experience a significant decline in cohesion when there is a Democratic president. This latter finding makes some sense when one recognizes that Democratic presidents since Woodrow Wilson (except Harry Truman during the 80th Congress) have always bargained directly with the legislative leaders of their *own* party. Just like Republican presidents, they often seek the bulk of votes needed to pass legislation from the majority party. This, together with the natural desire of legislative leaders to maintain the majority status of their party and hence to please the party's constituencies, leads to legislation that the Democratic party can support. It is instructive to recall that during the 80th Congress (the one instance in which a Democratic president faced a Republican Congress), Democratic legislators complained about the president's lack of consultation with them. For example, when Truman introduced his tax proposals in that Congress, the ranking member of the Ways and Means Committee complained: "We Democrats were not called into consultation when the bill was being prepared."

A CASE IN POINT: THE BUDGET CRISIS OF 1990

The general points just made about the consequences of divided government for bargaining within the beltway are all nicely illustrated in the budget crisis of 1990. Long before there was a crisis, it was recognized that both the Republican president and the Democratic Congress would have to agree to the major outlines of the budget—after all, both had a veto. In light of this fact, the two sides set up a working group composed of a large number of key congressional and White House players, charged with developing a workable compromise. Many months later, this working group had produced nothing but an occasional headline about whose intransigence was preventing progress.

This might have been anticipated. Delay meant an increased chance that no budget would pass and hence that either the government would be forced to close, the automatic cuts of the Gramm-Rudman Act would be invoked, or both. Willingness to incur these fearsome reversionary outcomes was the primary method by which each negotiator could demonstrate the depth of his or her commitment to whatever point was at issue. Thus, the interminable wrangling that characterized the initial attempts at making a budget, though far from inevitable, was not surprising.

In the next stage of the negotiations, the group assigned to come up with a proposal was pared down to just the majority and minority party leadership of the House and Senate and the top White House negotiators. Brinksmanship continued, but finally, at the last moment, a deal was cut.

The fatal flaw in this deal can be diagnosed as a premature selling out of the junior partners. The congressional Democrats had insisted that any budget compromise receive not only a public endorsement from the president but also the votes of a majority of House and Senate Republicans. In this way, the Democrats insured themselves against being blamed in the upcoming election for any new taxes or other unpopular features of the package. But by the same token, the Democrats' insistence on Republican support in Congress empowered a group that was rarely so empowered: If a majority of Republicans chose to vote against the budget, they could kill it.

Partly for this reason, the initial large group of negotiators and the final smaller group had both included Republicans. And it is likely that their input was taken more seriously than in other White House congressional negotiations in which the Democrats had not insisted on Republican support in Congress. But neither the leaders nor the followers in the House Republican party were united in their view of their president or the budget package to which he agreed. Indeed, many of them were utterly dismayed by Bush's renunciation of his "no new taxes" pledge—this very pledge formed an important part of both their personal ideology and their campaign strategy. But from the president's perspective, it was the price he had to pay to get the Democrats to agree on a budget. What did he get in return? Primarily, it seemed to have been avoidance of the reversionary outcome—implementation of the Gramm-Rudman Act's across-the-board budget cuts—and avoidance of the blame for this outcome.

The outcome itself was terrible for both sides: the Democrats particularly feared the damage to their domestic programs, and Bush especially loathed the cuts in defense spending. In the game of budgetary chicken, Bush's position was perhaps less strong—given his engagement in the Middle East with Saddam Hussein—and he blinked first (by renouncing his pledge on taxes). But Bush may also have recognized that the final stage of the game before implementation of the Gramm-Rudman cuts was a final, take-it-or-leave-it offer from the Democrats in Congress. Such an offer was unlikely to be much better than a compromise arrived at earlier, and, if the president vetoed it, the Democrats were in a good position to lay most of the blame for the resulting broad cuts at the door of the White House.

The important thing to note about what the president apparently got out of his recantation on taxes is that it benefited him, not congressional Republicans. Many congressional Republicans, especially in the House, would have preferred a hard-line maintenance of the "no new taxes" pledge. But Bush, given a choice between what looked best for the next presidential election and what some firebrands in the House thought best for the impending midterm elections, chose predictably.

In other words, to deal with the party that controlled Congress, the president followed the path of many of his predecessors and sold out his junior partners in Congress. Given the rare opportunity to retaliate effectively, these junior partners—led by Minority Whip Newt Gingrich—did so. Despite the fact that the president had made a nationally televised appeal for passage of the budget compromise, it became obvious well before the end of the vote in the House that the Republicans would not come up with their required majority. This freed a great many Democrats who had been holding back from a hard decision, and the bill went down to a resounding defeat.

One might wonder about the strategic reasoning of the Republicans who voted against the budget compromise. After all, in the next round of negotiations between the White House and Congress, their interests were even less well represented because both sides knew that it would have to be mostly Democratic votes that passed any agreement. And the budget that passed was clearly worse from the perspective of those Republicans who voted against the initial proposal. As *The Economist* put it in a brief budget postmortem: "The five-year package eventually passed stuck closely to the budget-summit deal rejected by the House in early October.... The main changes were a smaller rise in petrol taxes, an increase in the top income-tax rate from 28% to 31% and a smaller bite out of Medicare." If one asks who benefited from these changes, the answer seems to be oil-state Democrats (via smaller petrol taxes) and liberal Democrats (via an increased top income tax rate and a smaller bite out of Medicare).

But it was probably more an electoral than a policy calculation that led these Republicans to vote in the way that they did, and they may have held out some hope that Bush would once again hang tough on taxes—all the way to the election. In any event, the kind of divisions among House Republicans that the vote on the initial budget proposal revealed were not unusual or unprecedented, as indicated by the regression results on Republican voting cohesion presented earlier.

READING 45

U.S. Congressman as Enterprise

Robert H. Salisbury and Kenneth A. Shepsle

Understandably, when citizens, students, journalists, and scholars examine Congress they tend to focus on the behavior of the elected members of the two houses. However, it is important to remember that Congress has also provided itself with a large professional staff. Individual members have staffs in Washington and in their districts or states. Committees and subcommittees have both majority and minority staffs. The entire body has three major organizations that staff Congress collectively: the Congressional Budget Office, the Congressional

Research Service, and the General Accounting Office.

Observers of Congress usually comment on the meaning of increased staffing in regard to Congress's overall ability to process information and handle an enormous workload, its capacity to interact and/or compete with the executive branch, and its performance in serving constituents and reacting to their requests, especially in ways that redound to the electoral advantage of incumbent members. In this reading, Robert Salisbury, a political scientist at Washington University, and Kenneth Shepsle, a political scientist at Harvard University, explore yet another dimension of the impact of increased staffing. They focus on the interaction of that staff and the structural character of Congress. They examine the impact of having individual members of Congress serving as entrepreneurs heading "enterprises."

They certainly understand that the institutional aspects of Congress do not function apart from the personal styles (or even the "personalities") of the members who happen to populate Congress at any specific point in time. However, they also analyze patterns of behavior that transcend any particular set of personalities. Thus, even though they wrote the article from which this reading is taken in 1981, their analytical points still apply. In fact, the size of congressional staff in 1981 was almost exactly what it is today. The great growth occurred in the period just before they wrote and involved, for example, a doubling of congressional staff between 1967 and 1979.

[W]e argue that as a consequence of staff expansion each member of Congress has come to operate as the head of an enterprise—an organization consisting of anywhere from eight or ten to well over one hundred subordinates.

From "U. S. Congressman as Enterprise" by R. H. Salisbury and K. A. Shepsle, 1981, *Legislative Studies Quarterly,* vol. 6, November 1981, pp. 559–576. Copyright © 1981 by the Comparative Legislative Research Center. Reprinted by permission.

STRUCTURAL COMPONENTS OF MEMBER-CENTERED ENTERPRISES

The core of any congressional enterprise is the personal staff of the member. This is so in part because the personal staff is unequivocally and entirely dependent on the member for hiring and promotion. Its explicit responsibility is to serve the member's needs and interests, and its primary normative commitment is loyalty to the member. There is considerable variety in the ways that members organize their staffs. Some place a large fraction of the casework personnel in the state or district, for instance, retaining principally the legislative aides in the Washington office. Some sharply differentiate among staff functions so that the responsibilities of the press aide and of the administrative or legislative assistants seldom overlap. In other offices, on the other hand, "everybody does everything as needed—we hope." Some offices are organized along strict hierarchical lines with authority concentrated in the hands of a single senior aide, while other members prefer less clearly delineated lines of authority and responsibility.

There is not much evidence to suggest that organizational form as such affects the substance of what members do. It may affect the efficiency with which things are done, especially in processing casework. In addition, the choice of organizational style may often reflect the member's own conception of his or her role and the functional priorities associated with it. Thus a member who puts most of the staff in the district is seen thereby to be stressing casework and constituency service and *ceteris paribus* may reasonably be regarded as placing a high value on reelection as against legislative achievement.

It is dangerous, however, to stress the pattern of personal staff arrangements, precisely because a large proportion of the members have additional staff components within their total enterprise. Most committee and subcommittee staff are appointed by, or think of themselves as primarily subordinate to, a particular member. Prior to the "democratization" movement of the early 1970s, the primary appointing member was generally the committee chairman. The recent wave of reforms, however, has vested de facto and generally de jure authority in subcommittee chairs, minority members, and, in some cases, every member of a particular committee. As a consequence, all members of the Senate and most members of the House have at least some voice in the selection of committee or subcommittee staff members. This means that a given member is able to draw not only upon the skills and talents of his or her personal staff but on certain committee or subcommittee personnel as well. A committee chairmanship thereby adds a sizable cadre of assistants to a member's enterprise. A subcommittee chairmanship likewise yields significant assistance. A Democratic senator in 1980 might reasonably expect to head one full committee and/or one or more subcommittees; the resultant staff increments available therefrom might range from a low of about twenty to a high of over one hundred. Individual House members do not profit so richly from the available staff resources; indeed, not every House member, even of the majority, is able to profit at all. Those House members who do gain committee or subcommittee staff assistance may thereby gain a relatively larger advantage vis-a-vis their lower-ranking colleagues. Still, in the House as in the Senate, committee staff are distributed among a large number of members. Decentralization of power is thereby enhanced. And for a large number of members, the problem is posed as to how to manage this organization, this collection of personnel differentiated by political function and legal status, but nevertheless subordinate to the specific member.

Other Personnel Resources

Before we pursue this question, let us look briefly at four other types of personnel resources that may contribute to the strength of particular members. One derives from the auxiliary agencies, such as the Congressional Research Service (CRS), the Office of Technology Assessment (OTA), the Congressional Budget Office (CBO), [and] the General Accounting Office (GAO), where some members may have particularly effective access. For example, it was widely alleged that Senator Kennedy (D.-Mass.) had used OTA as a source of quasi-patronage such that some of its staff would be especially attentive to the Senator's needs. Kennedy's influence over OTA staff was derived from his position as chairman of the committee overseeing the operation.

A second kind of extended staff dependency may result from proliferation of "alumni networks," composed of people who once worked for a member and now work elsewhere on the Hill, but continue to carry the more or less clearly acknowledged blessing of their erstwhile principal. . . .

A third variety of "once-removed" enterprise member is the former staffer now comfortably ensconced in a trade association, labor union, or law firm located in the downtown Washington "K Street Corridor." . . .

Finally, there are the executive-branch alumni of the enterprises of particular legislators." . . .

Given the variegated character of the personnel system of a senator or congressman, to regard him as an isolated individual or even as a personality buffered against and buffeted by contending outside forces is inappropriate. To do so is to err, in the same way that it is mistaken to treat the actions of a corporate executive primarily in terms of his (or, rarely, her) personality rather than as constrained by the context of forces well beyond his or her individual uniqueness.

In this discussion, we will not discuss the relationships members develop with particular groups of other members, including special interest caucuses, ideological coalitions, state delegations, and so on. These interactions, insofar as they are effective, certainly complicate the structure of congressional action, but as they contribute no additional staff resources as such (indeed, they often require member contributions of staff), they do not alter the enterprises themselves. Collusion among a particular set of firms does not as such alter the character of the firms, and so it is with congressmen.

THE CONSEQUENCES OF AN ENTERPRISE PERSPECTIVE

. . .The literature on the modern Congress recognizes fully that the institution has been transformed and generally points accurately to the reasons behind the transformation. We do not seek here to contribute so much to the explanation of this change as to articulate a useful way to characterize it. By considering congressmen as organizations, we are led to investigate some critical questions of organizational behavior that we might not think of if the members were regarded solely as individuals. . . .

Promotion Activities

Every member-enterprise engages in member-promotion activities on a continuous basis. Media-related efforts, casework, newsletter production, trips to the district, and the wide range of credit-taking ploys of which the modern member is a master generate attention and, hopefully, support that ultimately will be revealed in the next election. Not every member feels the same need for promotional efforts, of course. Some, on the other hand, seem interested in little else. Senators may accentuate promotional work in the period prior to a reelection campaign and slack off a bit at other times, but increasingly the style seems to be to routinize much of the promotional work and at a high volume. Even the member who has already announced the intention to retire generally continues the publicity mill at an undiminished pace.

Much of the member-promotion is done by the personal staff, of course, and as every member has such a staff regardless of seniority, committee assignment, or leadership responsibility, it may fairly be regarded as the core of the member-enterprise, the sine qua non of the other functions. But, as Fenno has shown, committee work often has its promotional aspects, too, and it is obviously a mistake to assume that policy-centered efforts, from bill sponsorship to floor management, have no implications or are not exploited for the advancement of the member's career. A subcommittee staff counsel is often as attentive to the constituency needs of the subcommittee chairperson as the latter's press aide or campaign manager.

The relationship of the member-enterprise to the reelection campaign itself is often tricky legally and ambiguous organizationally. No congressional funds may be used to pay people who are working on a campaign staff or to purchase campaign materials. Nevertheless, it is common for individual staffers to move from a personal or, less often, committee payroll to the campaign payroll for all or part of the campaign and then return to a Hill position, either the old one or another within the member's enterprise. This movement of individuals among formal organizational units need not affect very much what they actually do. A speech writer or a press aide may carry on in much the same manner whether employed by the member-representative or the member-candidate. The point is that in either capacity the staffer is part of the member's enterprise, the latter having been enlarged and somewhat modified in function for the duration of the campaign proper, and the niceties of legal restrictions on who may be paid by whom for what only marginally affect the behavioral realities of member-staff interactions.

Policy Formation

Every member-enterprise engages in public policy formation. At minimum, the member votes on the floor and in committee. We do not suggest that members vote against their preferences or the interests of their constituents. Despite occasional conspiracy theories to the contrary, it rarely occurs that the enterprise—that is, the staffers tied to the specific member—will decisively alter this direction of member voting. Nevertheless, the sheer scope and complexity of the legislative agenda make it impossible for even the most indefatigable member to master the substance of every issue sufficiently well to reach in isolation a judgment about how to vote. While the Administration, congressional party leaders, and other cue-givers provide important guidelines for member behavior, one consequence of the growth of member enterprises is that substantial guidance can come from within the enterprise, i,e., from the staff.

Beyond the "simple" acts of voting, member-enterprises are engaged in bill and amendment drafting and sponsorship, participation in floor debate, and involvement during committee and subcommittee sessions including hearings, investigations, markups, and report preparation. That the individual member may not always personally perform each and every function does not diminish the impact of the work, or the member's ultimate responsibility for what is done in his or her name. Sometimes, as in voting, the member cannot delegate, and generally the extent to which member-enterprises are dependent on the visible performance by the principal is far greater than in most small business enterprises where even the most charismatic of proprietors may occasionally leave subordinates in charge. Nevertheless,

staffers do enormously expand the scope and range of each member's policy-relevant activity. Much of it may have promotional effects, of course—a bill designed for election purposes with no real intention of pushing it through to enactment, an amendment intended to benefit a district interest, or a floor speech to be distributed under the frank throughout the state.

It may often be that committee staffers give less explicit attention to the promotional implication of an action than would a member's personal staff. Some policy specialists within a given member's enterprise—foreign policy advisers, for example—may be instructed not to worry about the back-home implications of an issue. In general, however, we may expect the distinction between policy-oriented and promotional activity not to be sharply drawn. A very large proportion of what any member-enterprise does affects both promotional and policy goals and any attempt rigidly to compartmentalize the two would force the enterprise into a thoroughly artificial and generally misconceived situation.

Building Influence

Fenno's third motivation affecting congressmen in committees is achieving influence within the House. We may adapt this for our purposes by suggesting that many, though perhaps not all, member-enterprises seek to build influence, not only within the House or Senate but in some meaningful political arena(s). It might be a committee or even a subcommittee. It might be a "cozy triangle," a policy subsystem involving member-enterprises, executive agencies, and interest groups. It might be a state delegation, a party caucus, an ideological grouping, or some combination of all of these. The influence in question might remain quite diffuse, taking the form of a general reputation as someone to be reckoned with. Or it might be very specific, having as its objective the protection of an agency's jurisdiction or even election as Speaker. Since motivation is so intertwined with opportunity, the prudent member will seldom delimit the objects of ambition unnecessarily. You never can tell what might develop.

The point is that in seeking power within the institution, the modern member utilizes not only his or

her personal skills and opportunities but those afforded by the whole enterprise the member heads. It
follows that, by and large, the bigger and more well-
placed that enterprise in its various elements may be,
the better the chances for additional power to be secured. Hence a committee chair confers power, not
simply anymore by the sheer authority of the position
but through the increment of staff to the member-
centered enterprise. Each subcommittee assignment
carries staff resources for the member, sometimes
small and sometimes very substantial. Seniority of
service is likely to be accompanied by a growing
corps of "alumni." The wider distribution of staff resources resulting from such developments as the
Subcommittee Bill of Rights, S. Res. 60, H. Res. 5,
and so on, however, has decentralized power and rendered member-enterprises somewhat more equal.

Survival and Success

In a fundamental sense, the "bottom line" is measured by enterprise survival in the relevant electoral
arena and by success in the arenas of policymaking
and institutional power. Within a given member-
enterprise, however, these imperatives will often be
too imprecise to animate and guide the diverse individuals who comprise the "organization." It is, therefore, a consequence of this perspective that we must
pay attention to the structure of signals and incentives that operates within member-enterprises to constrain and shape behavior.

Our perspective may seem to subordinate the
elected senator or representative by placing him or her
in an organizational context, but it must be remembered that it is the member who hires and fires, fixes
salaries and sets responsibilities, and generally establishes the framework of expectations, substantive and
procedural, that will define the enterprise and constrain its members. It is the member individually who
must be reelected and whose policy priorities must
nearly always have first claim on staff effort. Yet in
many specific situations, these acknowledged obligations constitute no more than a general guide to action. "The boss wants to do something for consumers.
Fine—but what?" The staff must develop a legislative
proposal. More commonly, "The boss needs to look

like he's been effective up here. He needs to be able to
take credit for doing something." The staff must devise the "something."

Some members give close guidance to staff,
monitoring the choices of substance and strategy and
supervising every stage of the enterprise. Other members delegate some areas—casework, for example—
while retaining certain substantive policy areas for
personal input. Still others are content to front for the
organization and let staffers do nearly all the day-to-
day detail work. Different enterprises play it in different ways. It may be that senior Southern Democrats
and a few other "old style" members tend to delegate
less and control more directly and tightly the work of
their enterprises than do the newer members who are
more accustomed to extensive staff support. Apart
from this very tentative observation, we have not been
able to discern systematic differences in the closeness
of articulation or, alternatively, organizational slack or
flaccidity. Our main concern is to suggest that among
the members heading these congressional enterprises,
there are important variations in style that follow very
different lines from those observed in the past by students of individual-level congressional behavior.

ABOVE THE BOTTOM LINE:
STAFF STYLES AND AMBITIONS

Staffers, too, have diverse styles and ambitions, of
course, and we must note how these affect the functioning of congressional enterprises. Price…has distinguished between "professionals" and "policy
entrepreneurs" in assessing staff motivations. A "professional" is a staff member whose primary commitment is to a particular role and its attendant norms,
such as that of parliamentarian, appropriations clerk,
or tax lawyer concerned with the technical niceties of
the Internal Revenue Code. A "policy entrepreneur"
is seeking to use his or her staff role to advance a particular policy objective. Both these types of staff may
readily work in many different member-enterprises,
though the policy entrepreneurs are presumably constrained by ideological limits and would comfortably
fit only in "right-thinking" companies. One might
wish to add to Price's pair a third type of staffer, the
"politico," whose overarching concern is to serve

neither role nor policy but rather the career of the member who heads the enterprise. Politicos may move among several distinct roles and pursue multiple policy objectives, but these are always subordinate to the needs of the member.

In general, it is our strong impression that during the past two decades both professional and entrepreneurial staff types have become fewer in number, while member-serving loyalty at all levels of staff performance has become more and more pervasive. Insistent policy entrepreneurs often seek (or are encouraged) to move outside the realm of the congressional enterprise, to executive branch, think tank, or interest group settings where essentially similar policy objectives may be pursued apart from the constraints of the member-enterprise (though, of course, constrained by other forces). Certain types of professionals can also find opportunities outside the congressional milieu, though others have specialties for which Congress provides the only institutional market. Sometimes politicos can transfer from one enterprise to another; sometimes, the personal component of the enterprise—"We're a real family in this office"—is too salient to stand the move.

There are many combinations of motives and ambitions, rewards and alternatives, giving shape and direction to staff behavior. When these are linked with diverse types of leadership provided by members, the resulting patterns of member-enterprise operation, organizational efficiency, and substantive purpose are so numerous that generalization at this stage of our understanding is hazardous. We believe that systematic empirical work couched in terms of the member-as-enterprise conception of Congress will in due course yield illuminating results. . . .

CONCLUSION

When we consider Congress as an organization, we tend to focus on the formal structural units of committees, leadership posts, and the like. Individual members are characterized in terms of their respective memberships in these units, and their behavior is described in terms of moving back and forth from one structurally-determined set of activities to another; now working on subcommittee business, now

serving constituents, now participating in the party caucus or helping develop leadership strategy. We do not recommend abandoning this formulation of reality. Rather, we would integrate it with another perspective which emphasizes that, in every one of these so-called roles, the member is working with and through associated staff personnel who share an identity and a set of goals not because of the payroll they are on, the office they work in, or the tasks they perform, but because of their loyalty and commitment to that particular member.

FOOD FOR THOUGHT

1. In their article, "The Media's Role in Fomenting Public Disgust with Congress," Hibbing and Theiss–Morse begin to explain the truism that the public "hates Congress, but loves their congressman." Do you agree with data that suggest that people make distinctions between Congress as an institution and as a collection of 535 politicians? How do you react to Hibbing and Theiss–Morse's suggestion that the public should be reminded that democracy is messy and requires debate, negotiation, and compromise? Do you agree that, because the public is divided on many issues, it is little wonder that their elected representatives are divided as well, and that policy is muddled as a result? Finally, what might the media do to improve this situation?

2. Davidson's essay, "The Republican Takeover: Change and Continuity," places the 1994 congressional elections within a larger context of institutional change and continuity, but can the factors he discusses be classified as internal or external to the institution? Do you find one set of factors to be more decisive in determining institutional change than the other?

3. In his essay, "The Emergence of the Postreform Congress," Davidson reviews institutional reform and responses to contextual change in the modern Congress. Recount the consequences of the dispersion of influence among individual members and committees. What were the advantages of such changes? The disadvantages? What are the factors that Davidson identifies as leading to a retreat from congressional decentralization? Would you argue that institutional change in Congress is better characterized as driven by the goals of individual members or as part of an inevitable movement toward a more active, more "professionalized" legislature?

4. Cox and Kernell review several different causes of divided government, ranging from the issues that voters associate with each political party to an institutional structure that favors the Republican party in presidential elections. Do you believe that voters consciously attempt to create divided government when voting or that they find the notion of divided government attractive due to their distrust of the parties? Can you identify any additional causes of divided government? Would these apply to divided government at the state level as well?

In regard to the consequences of divided government, Cox and Kernell describe how the bargaining context between Congress and the president changes when each branch is held by a different political party, but what are the consequences of such a situation? There seem to be two camps on this question. One group claims that stalemate, gridlock, weak pol-

icy, and a lack of public accountability are the result of divided government, while others argue that the effects of divided government are few. A major difference between these two groups is that the former considers normative values and the latter, for the most part, does not. With which group would you side? Do you consider divided government to be problematic for the legislative process or the American political system?

5. In subsequent research on congressional staffs, scholars conclude that congressional staffers rarely act independently or deviate from the policy preferences of the member who is their employer. If such research is correct, what does Salisbury and Shepsle's proposal to recognize when studying Congress that members work with staff personnel ultimately contribute? This volume's readings on elections and term limits suggest that when members are limited in the number of terms they can serve in Congress, staffers assume greater power or responsibility in the institution. Do you agree with such an argument?

_____CHAPTER 10_____

THE PRESIDENCY

The American presidency is, without doubt, at the focal point of politics and government in the United States, and the American president plays a multifaceted leadership role in both the domestic and international realms. The centrality of the presidency in American governance is difficult to overestimate and is hinted at by the Table of Contents in this volume. Thus, while we are only now moving to a consideration of articles that explicitly focus on the presidency, virtually every chapter in this anthology contains readings that analyze the presidency in some external context such as, for example, in its relationships with Congress, the courts, the bureaucracy, public opinion, and the media. The conclusion is inescapable that, at least to the public eye, ours is a presidentially centered system.

At the same time, however, the question may legitimately be raised of whether American presidents have the necessary tools to effectively exercise all of the powers and roles our governmental system affords them. Certainly, in the most recent presidential administration we have experienced, we have witnessed the frustrations of Bill Clinton in his pursuit of policy initiatives, his efforts to lead public opinion, his ability to sway Congress, and his potential for altering the direction of world affairs.

We have brought together in this chapter a collection of readings that include classic expositions as well as some more contemporary assessments of the presidential condition focusing on the stewardship of Bill Clinton. It is our hope and expectation that, in the wake of reading all of these pieces, readers will emerge with a more realistic assessment than they currently have of the presidential potential for governing, as well as a clearer understanding of the constraints and limits under which presidential administrations labor.

We begin by juxtaposing two pieces written by William Howard Taft and Theodore Roosevelt, two men who occupied the nation's highest office. The

selections, which are of far more than historical interest, present the reader with alternative conceptions of the legitimate scope of presidential authority (Taft's "constitutional" view and Roosevelt's more expansive conception), a subject that has never been far removed from center stage in discussions of the American presidency. The debate over presidential powers tends to reach its highest pitch when expansive presidential actions are taken in times of perceived crisis or armed conflict.

One can point to many such instances in American history when questions have been raised about the legitimacy of presidential actions such as, for example, controversies over Abraham Lincoln's partial suspension of civil liberties during the Civil War and presidential initiatives taken a century later by Lyndon Johnson and Richard Nixon in Vietnam. Post-Vietnam international scenarios have also resulted in controversial actions by our past five chief executives (Gerald Ford, Jimmy Carter, Ronald Reagan, George Bush, and Bill Clinton), such as efforts to rescue the Mayaguez, a captured American vessel, attempts to rescue American hostages in Iran, the invasion of Grenada, the trading of arms with Iranians in exchange for hostages while covertly supporting the Contra forces in Nicaragua, invading Panama, sending troops to Somalia, and enforcing a no-fly zone in Iraq. While all of the examples mentioned, save for Lincoln's, occurred after the writings of Taft and Roosevelt, the themes that they explore remain at center stage in contemporary discussions of presidential power.

While Taft and Roosevelt write about the scope of presidential authority, Richard Neustadt's classic analysis, *Presidential Power,* is much more concerned with how a president can most effectively exercise the power that he does have. Neustadt's book remains one of the most cited works on the presidential condition several decades after its initial publication. "The

Power to Persuade," perhaps the most frequently reprinted chapter from the book, remains as interesting and important today (perhaps more so) than when it was written. Ironically, it has been suggested that Neustadt wrote the book for an audience of one. Just as Machiavelli attempted to counsel his prince, it has been suggested that Neustadt was attempting to advise John F. Kennedy on how to best control the reins of presidential governance.

Concerns about power and its exercise, which abound in the contributions of Taft, Roosevelt, and Neustadt, can also be seen in Thomas Cronin's fascinating unfolding of *The Paradoxes of the Presidency.* Indeed, taking the broad view, analyses of the modern presidency have, in somewhat sequential fashion, meandered through a number of extreme ideal characterizations of the office. These range from portraits of an all-powerful benevolent institution (the "textbook" presidency of the 1950s), through a similarly powerful yet less benign institution (the "imperial" presidency of the Vietnam era), to a weakened post-Watergate "imperiled" presidency. Some would add to the chronology the "beleaguered" presidency, a characterization that might capture some of the facets of the Clinton years.

None of these characterizations of the office truly tapped the realities of the presidential condition when they were written, and such simplistic characterizations are no more accurate today. In essence, as Cronin describes it here, the presidency is a somewhat "schizophrenic" office with numerous conflicting expectations thrust on it. In such a setting, disapproval of specific presidential actions and more general declines in presidential popularity over time (which even touched the "teflon presidency" of Ronald Reagan) appear virtually inevitable. In effect, the paradoxes of the presidency, explored by Cronin, can be an invitation to presidential failure.

The two selections with which we close this chapter, written by Charles O. Jones and Jeffrey Lantis, respectively, focus on the presidency of Bill Clinton and the specific context in which it is governing. While, in this sense, these pieces are case studies, the concerns that they address clearly extend beyond the confines of the Clinton years.

Jones's analysis emphasizes that ours is a "separated" system of government (as, indeed, Martin

Landau's essay on our "self-correcting" system of government, reprinted in Chapter 1, suggests in somewhat different and more general terms) in which presidents must be cautious regarding what they promise to deliver. In Clinton's case, he promised a good deal at the beginning of his administration, which was particularly problematic because presidents "are held responsible for that over which they have limited control." The "risks" for the Clinton presidency in a separated system grew even larger midway through the president's first term when the separated system was joined with divided government, a context in which the president confronts a congress controlled by the opposition party.

Context also plays an important role in Jeffrey Lantis's essay, which argues that President Clinton has managed to gain short-term successes in the foreign policy arena without the existence of an overarching foreign policy strategy. In the absence of strategy, "political events and timing" often worked to the president's advantage as he attempted to try to satisfy, simultaneously, domestic and international constituencies.

Viewed collectively, the selections in this chapter underscore the precariousness of the presidential condition. While none of the analyses take issue with the continued centrality of the presidency in American governance, they are clearly suggestive of an institution on which unrealistic demands and expectations are often placed, whose occupants must remain acutely sensitive to the inherent strengths and liabilities of their position if they are to make the most out of their opportunity to govern.

READING 46

Two Perspectives on Presidential Power

William Howard Taft and Theodore Roosevelt

From *Our Chief Magistrate and His Powers* by H. Taft, 1925. Columbia University Press, pp. 125–157, and from *The Autobiography of Theodore Roosevelt* by T. Roosevelt, 1958, Charles Scribner's Sons, pp. 197–201.

William Howard Taft was a president whose views of the office are, perhaps, best understood from the recognition that he viewed his later attainment of the position he most coveted, the Chief Justiceship of the United States, as the crowning achievement of his career. In the first perspective offered below, Taft develops what may be termed a "constitutional" view of presidential power, carefully linking presidential authority to constitutional or statutory mandates. Such a perspective may not, necessarily, presuppose a weak president but, rather, one who is concerned about the justification for the authority that he wields.

In contrasting Abraham Lincoln to his own political nemesis, Theodore Roosevelt (whose views are also reprinted below), Taft contends (and other analysts might differ here) that Lincoln, unlike Roosevelt, was always careful to attempt to forge a linkage between the broad powers he asserted during the Civil War and appropriate authority for the power's exercise. Roosevelt (who, ironically, had handpicked Taft to succeed him in the White House), in contrast to and in criticism of Taft, felt that executive authority did not have to be based on any specific authorization but, rather, was only limitable by explicit constitutional or congressional prohibitions.

In Roosevelt's view, the executive was to serve as a steward for the people, and stewardship did not allow a president "to content himself with the negative merit of keeping his talents undamaged in a napkin." For Roosevelt, the people were the ultimate source of support for a president who acted expansively, as he did. In contrast, Taft sees the gravest danger in a situation in which presidents act beyond the appropriate scope of their authority and the people are behind them.

Clearly, the presidential landscape is not as black and white as the dichotomy between the Taft and Roosevelt conceptions of the office might suggest. Just as clearly, controversy continues to exist over the issue of whether or not there are inherent presidential powers that are not lodged in the Constitution, per se, or traceable to an act of Congress.

Primary responsibility for resolving constitutional matters, as we have seen, lies with the Supreme Court. Here, as elsewhere, the Court's answers have had their ambiguities. Clearly, presidents have been given substantial latitude in the areas of foreign affairs and war-making, particularly when evidence can be found of congressional acquiescence in presidential actions. When Congress has acted to constrain the president, however, the Court has been more apt to decide against the assertion of executive authority.

Further, in the critical case of U.S. v. Nixon *(1974), which is reprinted in Chapter 13, the Court decided the fate of the secret White House tapes that held a key to discovering the president's complicity in the Watergate affair. Here, the Court unanimously rejected Nixon's claim for executive privilege, which amounted to a claim for presidential immunity from the compulsory processes of a court. While the Court's resolution of the issue, as in many cases dealing with presidential power, left much unresolved, it was, nevertheless, a proximate cause of Nixon's subsequent resignation from office.*

The Limitations of the President's Powers

William Howard Taft

[I]n theory, the Executive power and the Legislative power are independent and separate, but it is not always easy to draw the line and to say where Legislative control and direction to the Executive must cease, and where his independent discretion begins. In theory, all the Executive officers appointed by the President directly or indirectly are his subordinates, and yet Congress can undoubtedly pass laws definitely limiting their discretion and commanding a certain course by them which it is not within the power of the Executive to vary. Fixing the method in which Executive power shall be exercised is perhaps one of the chief functions of Congress. Indeed, by its legislation, it often creates a duty in the Executive which did not before exist. Then in prescribing how that duty is to be carried out, it imposes restrictions that the Executive is bound to observe.

Congress may repose discretion in appointees of the President, which the President may not himself control....

So, too, as between a court directing the action of a marshal and a contrary order of the President, the marshal is bound by law to follow the court's direction.... If the marshal is obstructed in the performance of his duty, however, and he or the court calls upon the President to send the army to overcome the obstruction, the President cannot be compelled to act.

Two principles, limiting Congressional interference with the Executive powers, are clear. *First,* Congress may not exercise any of the powers vested in the President, and *second,* it may not prevent or obstruct the use of means given him by the Constitution for the exercise of those powers.

In the matter of appointments, Presidents have been quick to resent encroachments by Congress. The power of appointment is not in Congress....

While Congress may not exercise the power of appointment, it may certainly impose rules of eligibility within which appointees are to be selected.... No court and no other authority, however, can compel the President to make a nomination, and the only method of preventing his appointing someone other than the one specified by law is for the Senate to refuse to confirm him, or for Congress to withhold an appropriation of his salary, or for the Comptroller of the Treasury to decline to draw a warrant for his salary on the ground of his ineligibility under the law....

The President is made Commander-in-Chief of the army and navy by the Constitution evidently for the purpose of enabling him to defend the country against invasion, to suppress insurrection and to take care that the laws be faithfully executed. If Congress were to attempt to prevent his use of the army for any of these purposes, the action would be void.... [I]n the carrying on of war as Commander-in-Chief, it is he who is to determine the movements of the army and of the navy. Congress could not take away from him that discretion and place it beyond his control in

any of his subordinates, nor could they themselves, as the people of Athens attempted to, carry on campaigns by votes in the market-place.

The President is required by the Constitution from time to time to give to Congress information on the state of the Union, and to recommend for its consideration such measures as he shall judge necessary and expedient, but this does not enable Congress or either House of Congress to elicit from him confidential information which he has acquired for the purpose of enabling him to discharge his constitutional duties, if he does not deem the disclosure of such information prudent or in the public interest...

Executive power is sometimes created by custom, and so strong is the influence of custom that it seems almost to amend the Constitution....

In a very recent case, in which President Roosevelt had exercised the power to withdraw lands, which were open for settlement under an act of Congress, from the operation of the act, and in which course I had followed him with very considerable doubt as to my power, the validity of our action was brought before the Supreme Court and sustained, on the ground that the practice of the Executive for a great many years, with the acquiescence of Congress in such withdrawals, justified the exercise of the power and made it legal as if there had been an express act of Congress authorizing it.

One of the great questions that the Executive has had to meet in the past has been how far he might properly differ from the Supreme Court in the construction of the Constitution in the discharge of his duties. Jefferson, in a letter to Mrs. John Adams, laid it down with emphasis with reference to the Sedition Law, in which he said:

> The Judges, believing the law constitutional, had a right to pass a sentence of fine and imprisonment, because the power was placed in their hands by the Constitution. But the executive, believing the law to be unconstitutional, might remit the execution of it, because that power has been confided to them by the Constitution. That instrument meant that its coordinate branches should be checks on each other. But the opinion which gives to the Judges the right to decide what laws are constitutional, and what not, not only

for themselves in their own sphere of action, but for the legislature and executive also, in their spheres, would make the judiciary a despotic branch.

And so Jackson in his message vetoing the renewal of the charter to the bank of the United States in respect to the opinion of the Supreme Court confirming the constitutionality of the previous charter, said:

> ...The Congress, the Executive and the Court must each for itself be guided by its own opinion of the Constitution. Each public officer who takes an oath to support the Constitution swears that he will support it as he understands it, and not as it is understood by others. It is as much the duty of the House of Representatives, of the Senate, and of the President to decide upon the Constitutionality of any bill or resolution which may be presented to them for passage or approval as it is of the Supreme judges when it may be brought before them for judicial decision. The opinion of the judges has no more authority over Congress than the opinion of Congress has over the judges, and on that point the President is independent of both. The authority of the Supreme Court must not, therefore, be permitted to control the Congress or the Executive when acting in their legislative capacities, but to have only such influence as the force of their reasoning may deserve.

Mr. Lincoln in his reference to the Dred Scott case said:

> I do not forget the position assumed by some that constitutional questions are to be decided by the Supreme Court, nor do I deny that such decisions must be binding in any case upon the parties to a suit as to the object of that suit, while they are also entitled to very high respect and consideration in all parallel cases by all other departments of the Government.... At the same time, the candid citizen must confess that if the policy of the Government upon vital questions affecting the whole people is to be irrevocably fixed by decisions of the Supreme Court, the instant they are made in ordinary litigation between parties in personal actions the people will have ceased to be their own rulers, having to that extent practically resigned their government into hands of that eminent tribunal....

I do not intend to dispute the attitude of these distinguished men. Nor is it necessary to do so. It is sufficient to say that the Court is a permanent body, respecting precedent and seeking consistency in its decisions, and that therefore its view of the Constitution, whether binding on the Executive and the legislature or not, is likely ultimately to prevail as accepted law.

While it is important to mark out the exclusive field of jurisdiction of each branch of the government, Legislative, Executive and Judicial, it should be said that in the proper working of the government there must be cooperation of all branches, and without a willingness of each branch to perform its function, there will follow a hopeless obstruction to the progress of the whole government. Neither branch can compel the other to affirmative action, and each branch can greatly hinder the other in the attainment of the object of its activities and the exercise of its discretion.... The life of the government, therefore, depends on the sense of responsibility of each branch in doing the part assigned to it in the carrying on of the business of the people in the government....

The true view of the Executive functions is, as I conceive it, that the President can exercise no power which cannot be fairly and reasonably traced to some specific grant of power or justly implied and included within such express grant as proper and necessary to its exercise. Such specific grant must be either in the Federal Constitution or in an act of Congress passed in pursuance thereof. There is no undefined residuum of power which he can exercise because it seems to him to be in the public interest, and there is nothing ...warranting such an inference. The grants of Executive power are necessarily in general terms in order not to embarrass the Executive within the field of action plainly marked for him, but his jurisdiction must be justified and vindicated by affirmative constitutional or statutory provision, or it does not exist. There have not been wanting, however, eminent men in high public office holding a different view and who have insisted upon the necessity for an undefined residuum of Executive power in the public interest. They have not been confined to the present generation. We may learn this from the complaint of a Virginia statesman, Abel P. Upshur, a strict constructionist of the old school, who succeeded Daniel Webster as Secretary of State under President Tyler. He was aroused by Story's commentaries on the Constitution to write a monograph answering and criticizing them, and in the course of this he comments as follows on the Executive power under the Constitution:

> The most defective part of the Constitution beyond all question, is that which related to the Executive Department. It is impossible to read that instrument, without being struck with the loose and unguarded terms in which the powers and duties of the President are pointed out. So far as the legislature is concerned, the limitations of the Constitution, are, perhaps, as precise and strict as they could safely have been made; but in regard to the Executive, the Convention appears to have studiously selected such loose and general expressions, as would enable the President, by implication and construction either to neglect his duties or to enlarge his powers. *We have heard it gravely asserted in Congress that whatever power is neither legislative nor judiciary, is of course executive, and, as such, belongs to the President under the Constitution.* How far a majority of that body would have sustained a doctrine so monstrous, and so utterly at war with the whole genius of our government, it is impossible to say, but this, at least, we know, that it met with no rebuke from those who supported the particular act of Executive power, in defense of which it was urged. Be this as it may, it is a reproach to the Constitution that the Executive trust is so ill-defined, as to leave any plausible pretense even to the insane zeal of party devotion, for attributing to the President of the United States the powers of a despot; powers which are wholly unknown in any limited monarchy in the world.

The view that he takes as a result of the loose language defining the Executive powers seems exaggerated. But one must agree with him in his condemnation of the view of the Executive power which he says was advanced in Congress. In recent years there has been put forward a similar view by executive officials and to some extent acted on. Men who are not such strict constructionists of the Constitution as Mr. Upshur may well feel real concern if such views are to receive the general acquiescence. Mr. Garfield, when Secretary of the Interior, under Mr. Roosevelt, in his final report to Congress in reference to the power of the Executive over the public domain, said:

> Full power under the Constitution was vested in the Executive Branch of the Government and the extent to which that power may be exercised is governed wholly by the discretion of the Executive unless any specific act has been prohibited either by the Constitution or by legislation.

In pursuance of this principle, Mr. Garfield, under an act for the reclamation of arid land by irrigation...made contracts with associations of settlers by which it was agreed that if these settlers would advance money and work, they might receive certificates from the government engineers of the labor and money furnished by them, and that such certificates might be received in the future in the discharge of their legal obligations to the government for water rent and other things under the statute. It became necessary for the succeeding administration to pass on the validity of these government certificates. They were held by Attorney-General Wickersham to be illegal, on the ground that no authority existed for their issuance.... The Court held that they were void because the Secretary of War had no statutory authority to issue them. Mr. Justice Miller, in deciding the case, said:

> The answer which at once suggests itself to one familiar with the structure of our government, in which all power is delegated, and is defined by law, constitutional or statutory, is, that to one or both of these sources we must resort in every instance. We have no officers in this government, from the President down to the most subordinate agent, who does not hold office under the law, with prescribed duties and limited authority.

In the light of this view of the Supreme Court it is interesting to compare the language of Mr. Roosevelt in his "Notes for a Possible Autobiography" on the subject of "Executive Powers," in which he says:

> The most important factor in getting the right spirit in my Administration...was my insistence upon the theory that the executive power was limited only by specific restrictions and prohibitions appearing in the Constitution or imposed by Congress under its constitutional powers. My view was that every Executive officer and above all every Executive officer in high position was a steward of the people bound actively and affirmatively to do all he could for the people and not to content himself with the negative merit of keeping his

talents undamaged in a napkin. I declined to adopt this view that what was imperatively necessary for the Nation could not be done by the President, unless he could find some specific authorization to do it. My belief was that it was not only his right but his duty to do anything that the needs of the Nation demanded unless such action was forbidden by the Constitution or by the laws. Under this interpretation of executive power I did and caused to be done many things not previously done by the President and the heads of the departments. I did not usurp power but I did greatly broaden the use of executive power. In other words, I acted for the common well being of all our people whenever and in whatever measure was necessary, unless prevented by direct constitutional or legislative prohibition.

I may add that Mr. Roosevelt, by way of illustrating his meaning as to the differing usefulness of Presidents, divides the Presidents into two classes, and designates them as "Lincoln Presidents" and "Buchanan Presidents." In order more fully to illustrate his division of Presidents on their merits, he places himself in the Lincoln class of Presidents, and me in the Buchanan class. The identification of Mr. Roosevelt with Mr. Lincoln might otherwise have escaped notice, because there are many differences between the two, presumably superficial, which would give the impartial student of history a different impression. It suggests a story which a friend of mine told of his little daughter Mary. As he came walking home after a business day, she ran out from the house to greet him, all aglow with the importance of what she wished to tell him. She said, "Papa, I am the best scholar in the class." The father's heart throbbed with pleasure as he inquired, "Why, Mary, you surprise me. When did the teacher tell you? This afternoon?" "Oh, no," Mary's reply was, "the teacher didn't tell me—I just noticed it myself."

My judgment is that the view of Mr. Garfield and Mr. Roosevelt, ascribing an undefined residuum of power to the President is an unsafe doctrine and that it might lead under emergencies to results of an arbitrary character, doing irremediable injustice to private right. The mainspring of such a view is that the Executive is charged with responsibility for the welfare of all the people in a general way, that he is to play the part of a Universal Providence and set all things right, and that anything that in his judgment will help the

people he ought to do, unless he is expressly forbidden not to do it. The wide field of action that this would give to the Executive one can hardly limit....

Mr. Roosevelt in his subsequent remarks seems to find a justification for his general view of the limitations of Executive power in what Mr. Lincoln did during the Civil War. That Mr. Lincoln with the stress of the greatest civil war in modern times felt called upon to do things, the constitutionality of which was seriously questioned, is undoubtedly true. But Mr. Lincoln always pointed out the source of the authority which in his opinion justified his acts, and there was always a strong ground for maintaining the view which he took. His claim of right to suspend the writ of habeas corpus I venture to think was well founded. Congress subsequently expressly gave him this right and the Supreme Court sustained his exercise of it under the act of Congress. His Emancipation Proclamation was attacked as an unconstitutional exercise of authority, but he defended it as an act of the Commander-in-Chief justified by military necessity to weaken the enemies of the Nation and suppress their rebellion. Certainly the arguments that he and those who supported his action brought to sustain it have great weight. But Mr. Lincoln never claimed that whatever authority in government was not expressly denied to him he could exercise....

I have now concluded a review of the Executive power, and hope that I have shown that it is limited, so far as it is possible to limit such a power consistent with that discretion and promptness of action that are essential to preserve the interests of the public in times of emergency, or legislative neglect or inaction.

There is little danger to the public weal from the tyranny or reckless character of a President who is not sustained by the people. The absence of popular support will certainly in the course of two years withdraw from him the sympathetic action of at least one House of Congress, and by the control that that House has over appropriations, the Executive arm can be paralyzed, unless he resorts to a coup d'état, which means impeachment, conviction and deposition. The only danger in the action of the Executive under the present limitations and lack of limitation of his powers is when his popularity is such that he can be sure of the support of the electorate and therefore of Congress, and when the majority in the legislative halls respond with alacrity and sycophancy to his will. This condition cannot probably be long continued. We have had Presidents who felt the public pulse with accuracy, who played their parts upon the political stage with histrionic genius and commanded the people almost as if they were an army and the President their Commander-in-Chief. Yet in all these cases, the good sense of the people has ultimately prevailed and no danger has been done to our political structure and the reign of law has continued. In such times when the Executive power seems to be all prevailing, there have always been men in this free and intelligent people of ours, who apparently courting political humiliation and disaster have registered protest against this undue Executive domination and this use of the Executive power and popular support to perpetuate itself....

The Presidency: Making an Old Party Progressive

Theodore Roosevelt

[N]othing could have been done in my administration if it had not been for the zeal, intelligence, masterful ability, and downright hard labor of...men in countless positions under me. I was helpless to do anything except as my thoughts and orders were translated into action by them; and, moreover, each of them, as he grew specially fit for his job, used to suggest to me the right thought to have, the right order to give, concerning that job. It is of course hard for me to speak with cold and dispassionate partiality of these men, who were as close to me as were the men of my regiment. But the outside observers best fitted to pass judgment about them felt as I did....

My view was that every executive officer, and above all every executive officer in high position was a steward of the people bound actively and affirmatively to do all he could for the people, and not to content himself with the negative merit of keeping his talents undamaged in a napkin. I declined to adopt the view that what was imperatively necessary for the nation could not be done by the President unless he could find some specific authorization to do it. My

belief was that it was not only his right but his duty to do anything that the needs of the nation demanded unless such action was forbidden by the Constitution or by the laws. Under this interpretation of executive power I did and caused to be done many things not previously done by the President and the heads of the departments. I did not usurp power, but I did greatly broaden the use of executive power. In other words, I acted for the public welfare, I acted for the common well-being of all our people, whenever and in whatever manner was necessary, unless prevented by direct constitutional or legislative prohibition....

The course I followed, of regarding the Executive as subject only to the people, and, under the Constitution, bound to serve the people affirmatively in cases where the Constitution does not explicitly forbid him to render the service, was substantially the course followed by both Andrew Jackson and Abraham Lincoln. Other honorable and well-meaning Presidents, such as James Buchanan, took the opposite and, as it seems to me, narrowly legalized view that the President is the servant of Congress rather than of the people, and can do nothing, no matter how necessary it be to act, unless the Constitution explicitly commands the action. Most able lawyers who are past middle age take this view, and so do large numbers of well-meaning, respectable citizens. My successor in office took this, the Buchanan, view of the President's powers and duties.

For example, under my administration we found that one of the favorite methods adopted by the men desirous of stealing the public domain was to carry the decision of the secretary of the interior into court. By vigorously opposing such action, and only by so doing, we were able to carry out the policy of properly protecting the public domain. My successor not only took the opposite view, but recommended to Congress the passage of a bill which would have given the courts direct appellate power over the secretary of the interior in these land matters.... Fortunately, Congress declined to pass the bill. Its passage would have been a veritable calamity.

I acted on the theory that the President could at any time in his discretion withdraw from entry any of the public lands of the United States and reserve the same for forestry, for water-power sites, for irrigation, and other public purposes. Without such action it would have been impossible to stop the activity of the land-thieves. No one ventured to test its legality by lawsuit. My successor, however, himself questioned it, and referred the matter to Congress. Again Congress showed its wisdom by passing a law which gave the President the power which he had long exercised, and of which my successor had shorn himself.

Perhaps the sharp difference between what may be called the Lincoln-Jackson and the Buchanan-Taft schools, in their views of the power and duties of the President, may be best illustrated by comparing the attitude of my successor toward his Secretary of the Interior, Mr. Ballinger, when the latter was accused of gross misconduct in office, with my attitude toward my chiefs of department and other subordinate officers. More than once while I was President my officials were attacked by Congress, generally because these officials did their duty well and fearlessly. In every such case I stood by the official and refused to recognize the right of Congress to interfere with me excepting by impeachment or in other constitutional manner. On the other hand, wherever I found the officer unfit for his position, I promptly removed him, even although the most influential men in Congress fought for his retention. The Jackson-Lincoln view is that a President who is fit to do good work should be able to form his own judgment as to his own subordinates and, above all, of the subordinates standing highest and in closest and most intimate touch with him. My secretaries and their subordinates were responsible to me, and I accepted the responsibility for all their deeds. As long as they were satisfactory to me I stood by them against every critic or assailant, within or without Congress; and as for getting Congress to make up my mind for me about them the thought would have been inconceivable to me. My successor took the opposite, or Buchanan, view when he permitted and requested Congress to pass judgment on the charges made against Mr. Ballinger as an executive officer. These charges were made to the President: the President had the facts before him and could get at them at any time, and he alone had power to act if the charges were true. However, he permitted and requested Congress to investigate Mr. Ballinger. The party minority of the committee that investigated him, and one member of the majority, declared that the charges were well-founded

and that Mr. Ballinger should be removed. The other members of the majority declared the charges ill-founded. The President abode by the view of the majority. Of course believers in the Jackson-Lincoln theory of the presidency would not be content with this town-meeting majority and minority method of determining by another branch of the government what it seems the especial duty of the President himself to determine for himself in dealing with his own subordinate in his own department....

There was one cartoon made while I was President, in which I appeared incidentally, that was always a great favorite of mine. It pictured an old fellow with chinwhiskers, a farmer, in his shirt-sleeves, with his boots off, sitting before the fire, reading the President's message. On his feet were stockings of the kind I have seen hung up by the dozen in Joe Ferris's store at Medora, in the days when I used to come in to town and sleep in one of the rooms over the store. The title of the picture was "His Favorite Author." This was the old fellow whom I always used to keep in my mind. He had probably been in the Civil War in his youth; he had worked hard ever since he left the army; he had been a good husband and father; he had brought up his boys and girls to work: he did not wish to do injustice to any one else, but he wanted justice done to himself and to others like him; and I was bound to secure that justice for him if it lay in my power to do so.

READING 47

The Power to Persuade

Richard Neustadt

Richard Neustadt is a political scientist at the Kennedy School at Harvard whose career has also included periodic service as a presidential advisor.

From "The Power to Persuade" by R. Neustadt, 1976, *Presidential Power: The Politics of Leadership with Reflections on Johnson and Nixon,* by R. Neustadt, John Wiley and Sons. Copyright © 1976 by R. Neustadt. Reprinted by permission.

The Power to Persuade is required reading for anybody with an interest in furthering their understanding of the American presidency, its limits, and opportunities.

Neustadt argues that presidents are met both in and out of government by individuals and institutions that are not likely to jump automatically at their bidding. Presidential orders are generally not self-executing and, to be successful, he must persuade those with whom he interacts that what he desires of them is, fundamentally, in their own self-interest. Presidential power is the power to persuade, and the power to persuade is the power to bargain. Clearly, the president is at an advantage in his persuasive relationships because of the status of his office as well as his formal powers. He simply has more vantage points in power relationships and the potential to be first among equals in interactions premised on mutual dependency.

While Neustadt's thesis may not seem shocking when the president is dealing with functionaries outside the executive realm, interestingly, the most precarious presidential relationships may be with individuals within the executive branch. Neustadt's argument may be most compelling, for example, in discussing White House aides who, lacking status and authority in their own right, are seemingly most likely to be responsive to the president. Yet, given their position, "lifted eyebrows may suffice to set an aide in motion" as they attempt to anticipate what the president wants. Such an explanation has been used to understand much of what transpired, for example, in Watergate and the Iran–Contra affair. On another level, some aides may become central to policymaking independent of their chief. "Nothing...keeps a well-placed aide from converting status into power of his own."

At bottom, Neustadt's presidential primer is a call for caution and sensitivity in command and advisory relationships. Presidents must recognize that every choice made today has implications for tomorrow and that their perspective is, of necessity, a uniquely holistic one shared by no one with whom they interact. Presidents have advantages in dealing with others yet, "Bargaining advantages convey no guarantees." Consequently, presidents must

continually guard their power prospects in all their relationships and all the choices that they make.

I

The limits on command suggest the structure of our government. The constitutional convention of 1787 is supposed to have created a government of "separated powers." It did nothing of the sort. Rather, it created a government of separated institutions *sharing* powers. "I am part of the legislative process," Eisenhower often said in 1959 as reminder of his veto. Congress, the dispenser of authority and funds, is no less part of the administrative process. Federalism adds another set of separated institutions. The Bill of Rights adds others. Many public purposes can only be achieved by voluntary acts of private institutions; the press, for one, in Douglass Cater's phrase, is a "fourth branch of government." And with the coming of alliances abroad, the separate institutions of a London, or a Bonn, share in the making of American public policy.

What the Constitution separates our political parties do not combine.... Our national parties are confederations of state and local party institutions.... These confederacies manage presidential nominations. All other public offices depend upon electorates confined within the states. All other nominations are controlled within the states. The President and congressmen who bear one party's label are divided by dependence upon different sets of voters. The differences are sharpest at the stage of nomination. The White House has too small a share in nominating congressmen, and Congress has too little weight in nominating Presidents for party to erase their constitutional separation. Party links are stronger than is frequently supposed, but nominating processes assure the separation.

The separateness of institutions and the sharing of authority prescribe the terms on which a President persuades. When one man shares authority with another, but does not gain or lose his job upon the other's whim, his willingness to act upon the urging of the other turns on whether he conceives the action right for him. The essence of a President's persuasive task is to convince such men that what the White House wants of them is what they ought to do for their sake and on their authority.

Persuasive power, thus defined, amounts to more than charm or reasoned argument, These have their uses for a President, but these are not the whole of his resources. For the men he would induce to do what he wants done on their own responsibility will need or fear some acts by him on his responsibility. If they share his authority, he has some share in theirs. Presidential "powers" may be inconclusive when a President commands, but always remain relevant as he persuades. The status and authority inherent in his office reinforce his logic and his charm.

Status adds something to persuasiveness; authority adds still more. When Truman urged wage changes on his Secretary of Commerce while the latter was administering the steel mills, he and Secretary Sawyer were not just two men reasoning with one another. Had they been so, Sawyer probably would never have agreed to act. Truman's status gave him special claims to Sawyer's loyalty, or at least attention.... [F]ew men—and exceedingly few Cabinet officers—are immune to the impulse to say "yes" to the President of the United States. It grows harder to say "no" when they are seated in his oval office at the White House, or in his study on the second floor, where almost tangibly he partakes of the aura of his physical surroundings. In Sawyer's case, moreover, the President possessed formal authority to intervene in many matters of concern to the Secretary of Commerce. These matters ranged from jurisdictional disputes...to legislation...and, ultimately, to the tenure of the Secretary, himself. There is nothing in the record to suggest that Truman voiced specific threats when they negotiated over wage increases. But given his *formal* powers and their relevance to Sawyer's other interests, it is safe to assume that Truman's very advocacy of wage action conveyed an implicit threat.

A President's authority and status give him great advantages in dealing with the men he would persuade. Each "power" is a vantage point for him in the degree that other men have use for his authority. From the veto to appointments, from publicity to budgeting, and so down a long list, the White House now controls the most encompassing array of vantage points in the American political system. With hardly an exception, the men who share in governing this country are aware that at some time, in some de-

gree, the doing of *their* jobs, the furthering of *their* ambitions, may depend upon the President of the United States. Their need for presidential action, or their fear of it, is bound to be recurrent if not actually continuous. Their need or fear is his advantage.

A President's advantages are greater than mere listing of his "powers" might suggest. The men with whom he deals must deal with him until the last day of his term.... Even though there is no need or fear of him today, what he could do tomorrow may supply today's advantage.... When he induces other men to do what he wants done, a President can trade on their dependence now *and* later.

The President's advantages are checked by the advantages of others. Continuing relationships will pull in both directions. These are relationships of mutual dependence. A President depends upon the men he would persuade; he has to reckon with his need or fear of them. They too will possess status, or authority, or both, else they would be of little use to him. Their vantage points confront his own; their power tempers his.

Persuasion is a two-way street. Sawyer, it will be recalled, did not respond at once to Truman's plan for wage increases at the steel mills. On the contrary, the Secretary hesitated and delayed and only acquiesced when he was satisfied that publicly he would not bear the onus of decision. Sawyer had some points of vantage all his own from which to resist presidential pressure. If he had to reckon with coercive implications in the President's "situations of strength," so had Truman to be mindful of the implications underlying Sawyer's place as a department head, as steel administrator, and as a Cabinet spokesman for business. Loyalty is reciprocal. Having taken on a dirty job in the steel crisis, Sawyer had strong claims to loyal support. Besides, he had authority to do some things that the White House could ill afford.... [H]e might have resigned in a huff (the removal power also works two ways).... [H]e might have declined to sign necessary orders. Or he might have let it be known publicly that he deplored what he was told to do and protested doing. By following any of these courses Sawyer almost surely would have strengthened the position of management, weakened the position of the White House, and embittered the union.... Although Sawyer's status and authority did not give him the power to prevent an increase outright, they gave him capability to undermine its purpose. If his authority over wage rates had been vested by a statute, not by revocable presidential order, his power of prevention might have been complete....

The power to persuade is the power to bargain. Status and authority yield bargaining advantages. But in a government of "separated institutions sharing powers," they yield them to all sides. With the array of vantage points at his disposal, a President may be far more persuasive than his logic or his charm could make him. But outcomes are not guaranteed by his advantages. There remain the counter pressures those whom he would influence can bring to bear on him from vantage points at their disposal. Command has limited utility: persuasion becomes give-and-take. It is well that the White House holds the vantage points it does. In such a business any President may need them all—and more.

II

This view of power as akin to bargaining is one we commonly accept in the sphere of congressional relations. Every textbook states and every legislative session demonstrates that...a President will often be unable to obtain congressional action on his terms or even to halt action he opposes. The reverse is equally accepted: Congress often is frustrated by the President. Their formal powers are so intertwined that neither will accomplish very much, for very long, without the acquiescence of the other. By the same token, though, what one demands the other can resist. The stage is set for that great game, much like collective bargaining, in which each seeks to profit from the other's needs and fears. It is a game played catch-as-catch-can, case by case. And everybody knows the game, observers and participants alike.

The concept of real power as a give-and-take is equally familiar when applied to presidential influence outside the formal structure of the Federal government....

In spheres of party politics the same thing follows, necessarily, from the confederal nature of our party organizations. Even in the case of national nominations a President's advantages are checked by those of others. In 1944 it is by no means clear that Roosevelt got his first choice as his running mate. In 1948 Truman, then the President, faced serious revolts against his nomination. In 1952 his intervention from the White House helped the choice of Adlai Stevenson, but it is far from clear that Truman could have done as much for any other candidate acceptable to him. In 1956 when Eisenhower was President, the record leaves obscure just who backed Harold Stassen's effort to block Richard Nixon's renomination as Vice-President. But evidently everything did not go quite as Eisenhower wanted, whatever his intentions may have been. The outcomes in these instances bear all the marks of limits on command and of power checked by power that characterize congressional relations. Both in and out of politics these checks and limits seem to be quite widely understood.

Influence becomes still more a matter of give-and-take when Presidents attempt to deal with allied governments. A classic illustration is the long unhappy wrangle over policy in 1956. In dealing with the British and the French before their military intervention, Eisenhower had his share of bargaining advantages but no effective power of command. His allies had their share of counter pressures, and they finally tried the most extreme of all: action despite him. His pressure then was instrumental in reversing them. But had the British government been on safe ground at *home*, Eisenhower's wishes might have made as little difference after intervention as before. Behind the decorum of diplomacy—which was not very decorous in the Suez affair—relationships among allies are not unlike relationships among state delegations at a national convention. Power is persuasion and persuasion becomes bargaining....

In only one sphere is the concept unfamiliar: the sphere of executive relations. Perhaps because of civics textbooks and teaching in our schools, Americans instinctively resist the view that power in this sphere resembles power in all others. Even Washington reporters, White House aides, and congressmen are not immune to the illusion that administrative agencies comprise a single structure, "the" Executive Branch, where presidential word is law, or ought to be. Yet...when a President seeks something from executive officials his persuasiveness is subject to the same sorts of limitations as in the case of congressmen, or governors, or national committeemen, or private citizens, or foreign governments. There are no generic differences, no differences in kind and only sometimes in degree.... [H]ere as elsewhere influence derives from bargaining advantages; power is a give-and-take.

Like our governmental structure as a whole, the executive establishment consists of separated institutions sharing powers. The President heads one of these; Cabinet officers, agency administrators, and military commanders head others. Below the departmental level, virtually independent bureau chiefs head many more. Under mid-century conditions, Federal operations spill across dividing lines on organization charts; almost every policy entangles many agencies, almost every program calls for interagency collaboration. Everything somehow involves the President. But operating agencies owe their existence least of all to one another—and only in some part to him. Each has a separate statutory base; each has its statutes to administer; each deals with a different set of subcommittees at the Capitol. Each has its own peculiar set of clients, friends, and enemies outside the formal government. Each has a different set of specialized careerists inside its own bailiwick. Our Constitution gives the President the "take-care" clause and the appointive power. Our statutes give him central budgeting and a degree of personnel control. All agency administrators are responsible to him. But they *also* are responsible to Congress, to their clients, to their staffs, and to themselves. In short, they have five masters. Only after all of those do they owe any loyalty to each other.

"The members of the Cabinet," Charles G. Dawes used to remark, "are a President's natural enemies." Dawes had been Harding's Budget Director, Coolidge's Vice-President, and Hoover's Ambassador to London.... The words are highly colored, but Dawes knew whereof he spoke. The men who have to serve so many masters cannot help but be somewhat the "enemy" of any one of them. By the same token, any master wanting service is in some degree the "enemy" of such a servant.... Many a Cabinet officer, with loyalty ill-rewarded by his lights and help with-

held, has come to view the White House as innately hostile to department heads. Dawes's dictum can be turned around.

A senior presidential aide remarked to me in Eisenhower's time: "If some of these Cabinet members would just take time out to stop and ask themselves 'What would I want if I were President?', they wouldn't give him all the trouble he's been having." But even if they asked themselves the question, such officials often could not act upon the answer. Their personal attachment to the President is all too often overwhelmed by duty to their other masters.

Executive officials are not equally advantaged in their dealings with a President. Nor are the same officials equally advantaged all the time.... The vantage points conferred upon officials by their own authority and status vary enormously. The variance is heightened by particulars of time and circumstance....

And when officials have no "powers" in their own right, or depend upon the President for status, their counter pressure may be limited indeed. White House aides...are among the most responsive men of all, and for good reason. As a Director of the Budget once remarked to me, "Thank God I'm here and not across the street. If the President doesn't call me, I've got plenty I can do right here and plenty coming up to me, by rights, to justify my calling him. But those poor fellows over there, if the boss doesn't call them, doesn't ask them to do something, what can they do but sit?" Authority and status so conditional are frail reliances in resisting a President's own wants. Within the White House precincts, lifted eyebrows may suffice to set an aide in motion: command, coercion, even charm aside. But even in the White House a President does not monopolize effective power. Even there persuasion is akin to bargaining. A former Roosevelt aide once wrote of Cabinet officers:

> Half of a President's suggestions, which theoretically carry the weight of orders, can be safely forgotten by a Cabinet member. And if the President asks about a suggestion a second time, he can be told that it is being investigated. If he asks a third time, a wise Cabinet officer will give him at least part of what he suggests. But only occasionally, except about the most important matters, do Presidents ever get around to asking three times.

The rule applies to staff as well as to the Cabinet, and certainly has been applied *by* staff in Truman's time and Eisenhower's.

Some aides will have more vantage points than a selective memory. Sherman Adams, for example, as The Assistant to the President under Eisenhower, scarcely deserved the appellation "White House aide" in the meaning of the term before his time or as applied to other members of the Eisenhower entourage. Although Adams was by no means "chief of staff" in any sense so sweeping—or so simple—as press commentaries often took for granted, he apparently became no more dependent on the President than Eisenhower on him. "I need him," said the President when Adams turned out to have been remarkably imprudent in the Goldfine case, and delegated to him even the decision on his own departure. This instance is extreme, but the tendency it illustrates is common enough. Any aide who demonstrates to others that he has the President's consistent confidence and a consistent part in presidential business will acquire so much business on his own account that he becomes in some sense independent of his chief. Nothing in the Constitution keeps a well-placed aide from converting status into power of his own, usable in some degree even against the President—an outcome not unknown in Truman's regime or, by all accounts, in Eisenhower's.

The more an officeholder's status and his "powers" stem from sources independent of the President, the stronger will be his potential pressure on the President. Department heads in general have more bargaining power than do most members of the White House staff; but bureau chiefs may have still more, and specialists at upper levels of established career services may have almost unlimited reserves of the enormous power which consists of sitting still. . . .

In the right circumstances, of course, a President can have his way with any of these people. . . . But one need only note the favorable factors giving . . . orders their self-executing quality to recognize that as between a President and his "subordinates," no less than others on whom he depends, real power is reciprocal and varies markedly with organization, subject matter, personality, and situation. The mere fact that persuasion is directed at executive officials signifies no

necessary easing of his way. Any new congressman of the Administration's party, especially if narrowly elected, may turn out more amenable (though useful) to the President than any seasoned bureau chief "downtown." *The probabilities of power do not derive from the literary theory of the Constitution.*

III

There is a widely held belief in the United States that were it not for folly or for knavery, a reasonable President would need no power other than the logic of his argument. . . . But faulty reasoning and bad intentions do not cause all quarrels with Presidents. The best of reasoning and of intent cannot compose them all. For in the first place, what the President wants will rarely seem a trifle to the men he wants it from. And in the second place, they will be bound to judge it by the standard of their own responsibilities, not his. However logical his argument according to his lights, their judgment may not bring them to his view.

The men who share in governing this country frequently appear to act as though they were in business for themselves. So, in a real though not entire sense, they are and have to be. When Truman and MacArthur fell to quarreling, for example, the stakes were no less than the substance of American foreign policy, the risks of greater war or military stalemate, the prerogatives of Presidents and field commanders. . . . Intertwined, inevitably, were other stakes, as well: political stakes for men and factions of both parties; power stakes for interest groups with which they were or wished to be affiliated. And every stake was raised by the apparent discontent in the American public mood. There is no reason to suppose that in such circumstances men of large but differing responsibilities will see all things through the same glasses. On the contrary, it is to be expected that their views of what ought to be done and what they then should do will vary with the differing perspectives their particular responsibilities evoke. Since their duties are not vested in a "team" or a "collegium" but in themselves, as individuals, one must expect that they will see things *for* themselves. Moreover, when they are responsible to many masters and when an event or policy turns loyalty against loyalty—a day by day occurrence in the nature of the case—one must assume that those who have the duties to perform will choose the terms of reconciliation. This is the essence of their personal responsibility. When their own duties pull in opposite directions, who else but they can choose what they will do?...

Reasonable men, it is so often said, *ought* to be able to agree on the requirements of given situations. But when the outlook varies with the placement of each man, and the response required in his place is for each to decide, their reasoning may lead to disagreement quite as well—and quite as reasonably....

Outside the Executive Branch the situation is the same, except that loyalty to the President may often matter *less*.... And when one comes to congressmen who can do nothing for themselves (or their constituents) save as they are elected, term by term, in districts and through party structures *differing* from those on which a President depends, the case is very clear. An able Eisenhower aide with long congressional experience remarked to me in 1958: "The people on the Hill don't do what they might *like* to do, they do what they think they *have* to do in their own interest as *they* see it...." This states the case precisely.

The essence of a President's persuasive task with congressmen and everybody else, *is to induce them to believe that what he wants of them is what their own appraisal of their own responsibilities requires them to do in their interest, not his.* Because men may differ in their views on public policy, because differences in outlook stem from differences in duty—duty to one's office, one's constituents, oneself—that task is bound to be more like collective bargaining than like a reasoned argument among philosopher kings.... [P]ersuasion deals in the coin of self-interest with men who have some freedom to reject what they find counterfeit.

IV

A President draws influence from bargaining advantages. But does he always need them? The episodes described...were instances where views on public policy diverged with special sharpness. Suppose such sharp divergences are lacking, suppose most players of the governmental game see policy objectives much alike, then can he not rely on logic (or on charm) to get him what he wants? The answer is that even then most outcomes turn on bargaining. The reason for this answer is a simple one: most men who share in governing have interests of their own beyond the realm of policy *objectives.* The sponsorship of policy, the form it takes, the conduct of it, and the credit for it separate their interest from the President's despite agreement on the end in view. In political government, the means can matter quite as much as ends; they often matter more. And there are always differences of interest in the means....

[T]he help accorded Truman in obtaining action on the Marshall Plan...was not extended to the President for his own sake. He was not favored in this fashion just because they liked him personally, or were spellbound by his intellect or charm. They might have been as helpful had all held him in disdain, which some of them certainly did.... [A]ll...played the parts they did because they thought they had to, in their interest, given their responsibilities, not Truman's. Yet they hardly would have found it in their interest to collaborate with one another, or with him, had he not furnished them precisely what *they* needed from the White House. Truman could not do without their help, but he could not have had it without unremitting effort on his part.

The crucial thing to note about this case is that despite compatibility of views on public policy, Truman got no help he did not pay for....

Truman paid the price required for their services. So far as the record shows, the White House did not falter once in firm support for Marshall and the Marshall Plan. Truman backed his Secretary's gamble on an invitation to all Europe. He made the plan his own.... He lost no opportunity to widen the involvements of his own official family in the cause.... [A]ll were made responsible for studies and reports contributing directly to the legislative presentation. Thus these men were committed in advance. Besides, the President continually emphasized to everyone in reach that he did not have doubts, did not desire complications and would foreclose all he could.... [T]ruman employed the sparse advantages his "powers" and his status then accorded him to gain the sort of help he had to have.

Truman helped himself in still another way. Traditionally and practically no one was placed as well as he to call public attention to the task of *Congress* (and its Republican leadership).... [H]e made repeated use of presidential "powers" to remind the country that congressional action was required. Messages, speeches, and an extra session were employed to make the point. Here, too, he drew advantage from his place. However, in his circumstances, Truman's public advocacy might have hurt, not helped, had his words seemed directed toward the forthcoming election. Truman gained advantage for his program only as his own endorsement of it stayed on the right side of that fine line between the "caretaker" in office and the would-be candidate....

It is symptomatic of Truman's situation that "bipartisan" accommodation by the White House then was thought to mean congressional consultation and conciliation on a scale unmatched in Eisenhower's time. Yet Eisenhower did about as well with opposition Congresses as Truman did, in terms of requests granted for defense and foreign aid. It may be said that Truman asked for more extraordinary measures. But it also may be said that Eisenhower never lacked for the prestige his predecessor had to borrow.... The plain fact is that Truman had to play bipartisanship as he did or lose the game.

V

Had Truman lacked the personal advantages his "powers" and his status gave him, or if he had been maladroit in using them, there probably would not have been a massive European aid program in 1948. Something of the sort, perhaps quite different in its emphasis, would almost certainly have come to pass before the end of 1949. *Some* American response to European weakness and to Soviet expansion was as certain as such things can be. But in 1948 temptations to await a Taft Plan or a Dewey Plan might well have caused at least a year's postponement of response had the "outgoing" Administration bungled its congressional, or public, or allied, or executive relations.... The President's own share in this accomplishment was vital. He made his contribution by exploiting his advantages. Truman, in effect, lent Marshall and the

rest the perquisites and status of his office. In return they lent him their prestige and their own influence. The transfer multiplied *his* influence despite his limited authority in form and lack of strength politically. Without the wherewithal to make this bargain, Truman could not have contributed to European aid.

Bargaining advantages convey no guarantees. Influence remains a two-way street. In the fortunate instance of the Marshall Plan, what Truman needed was actually in the hands of men who were prepared to "trade" with him. He personally could deliver what they wanted in return. Marshall, Vandenberg, Harriman, *et al.,* possessed the prestige, energy, associations, staffs, essential to the legislative effort. Truman himself had a sufficient hold on presidential messages and speeches, on budget policy, on high-level appointments, and on his own time and temper to carry through all aspects of his necessary part. But it takes two to make a bargain. It takes those who have prestige to lend it on whatever terms.... Truman was not guaranteed more power than his "powers" just because he had continuing relationships with Cabinet secretaries and with senior senators. Here, as everywhere, the outcome was conditional on who they were and what he was and how each viewed events, and on their actual performance in response.

Granting that persuasion has no guarantee attached, how can a President reduce the risks of failing to persuade? How can he maximize his prospects for effectiveness by minimizing chances that his power will elude him? The Marshall Plan suggests an answer: he guards his power prospects in the course of making choices.... What Truman needed...he received, in part, because of his past choice of men and measures. What they received in turn were actions taken or withheld by him, himself. The things they needed from him mostly involved his own conduct where his current choices ruled. The President's own actions in the past had cleared the way for current bargaining. His actions in the present were his trading stock. Behind each action lay a personal choice, and these together comprised *his* control over the give-and-take that gained him what he wanted. In the degree that Truman, personally, affected the advantages he drew from his relationships with other men in government, *his power was protected by his choices.*

By "choice" I mean no more than what is commonly referred to as "decision": a President's own act of doing or not doing.... "Choice" has its share of undesired connotations. In common usage it implies a black-and-white alternative. Presidential choices are rarely of that character. It also may imply that the alternatives are set before the choice-maker by someone else. A President is often left to figure out his options for himself....

If Presidents could count upon past choices to enhance their current influence, as Truman's choice of men had done for him, persuasion would pose fewer difficulties than it does. But Presidents can count on no such thing. Depending on the circumstances, prior choices can be as embarrassing as they were helpful in the instance of the Marshall Plan....

Assuming that past choices have protected influence, not harmed it, present choices still may be inadequate. If Presidents could count on their own conduct to provide *enough* bargaining advantages...effective bargaining might be much easier to manage than it often is. In the steel crisis, for instance. Truman's own persuasiveness with companies and union, both, was burdened by the conduct of an independent Wage Board and of government attorneys in the courts, to say nothing of Wilson, Arnall, Sawyer, and the like. Yet in practice, if not theory, many of *their* crucial choices never were the President's to make. Decisions that are legally in other's hands, or delegated past recall, have an unhappy way of proving just the trading stock most needed when the White House wants to trade. One reason why Truman was consistently more influential in the instance of the Marshall Plan than in the steel case, or the MacArthur case, is that the Marshall Plan directly involved Congress. In congressional relations there are some things that no one but the President can do. His chance to choose is higher when a message must be sent, or a nomination submitted, or a bill signed into law, than when the sphere of action is confined to the Executive, where all decisive tasks may have been delegated past recall.

But adequate or not, a President's own choices are the only means *in his own hands* of guarding his own prospects for effective influence. He can draw power from continuing relationships in the degree that he can capitalize upon the needs of others for the Presidency's status and authority. He helps himself to do so, though, by nothing save ability to recognize the pre-conditions and the chance advantages and to proceed accordingly in the course of the choice-making that comes his way. To ask how he can guard prospective influence is thus to raise a further question: what helps him guard his power stakes in his own acts of choice?

READING 48

The Paradoxes of the Presidency
Thomas E. Cronin

Thomas Cronin is a prominent presidential scholar who is currently the President of Whitman College. In this essay, Cronin underscores the schizophrenic nature of the presidential condition. At bottom, there are numerous and inevitable sources of conflicting expectations placed on the shoulders of the president that serve as an invitation to presidential failure.

We want our presidents to be gentle and decent yet forceful and decisive. We want them to be sharing and open but, at the same time, to act independently. We want them to be zealously programmatic and yet to act pragmatically. We value their innovativeness and originality, while we demand their responsiveness and regard for the public. We seek leaders who will unify the country from among partisans who underline the bases of societal division. We desire an uncommon performance from individuals whose very commonness we find appealing. Under such circumstances it is little wonder that Cronin finds an additional paradox: The longer a president is in office, the less we like him.

Cronin reveals a unique hybrid figure who is not only the working head of our government, the chief executive in a very real sense, but also chief of state

---

in symbolizing America to the world and chief politician in serving the interests of the party coalition under whose banner he was elected. These roles are all performed by an individual laboring under the ultimate paradox of a selection process that does little to prepare him for office.

While Cronin recognizes that the presidential paradoxes are, by and large, irreconcilable, it remains important to understand them. First, it is critical that public expectations of the presidency be more realistic so that the occupants of the office are not encouraged to promise and attempt more than can be accomplished. Equally important from the perspective of the presidency itself, understanding the paradoxes can lead presidents to better utilize their "vantage points," in Neustadt's terms, to pursue the possible. Successful presidents cannot solve the presidential paradoxes, but they may be able to manage them.

Why is the presidency such a bewildering office? Why do presidents so often look like losers? Why is the general public so disapproving of recent presidential performances, and so predictably less supportive the longer a president stays in office?

The search for explanations leads in several directions. Vietnam and the Watergate scandals must be considered. Then too, the personalities of Lyndon Johnson and Richard Nixon doubtless are factors that soured many people on this office. Observers also claim that the institution is structurally defective; that it encourages isolation, palace guards, "group-think" and arrogance.

Yet something else seems at work. Our expectations and demands are frequently so paradoxical as to invite two-faced behavior by our presidents. We seem to want so much so fast that a president, whose powers are often simply not as great as many of us believe, gets condemned as ineffectual. Or a president will overreach or resort to unfair play while trying to live up to our demands. Either way, he seems to become locked into a rather high number of no-win situations.

The Constitution is of little help in explaining any of this. Our Founding Fathers purposely were vague and left the presidency defined imprecisely. They knew well that the presidency would have to provide the capability for swift and competent executive action, yet they went to considerable length to avoid enumerating specific powers and duties, so as to calm the then ever-present popular fear of monarchy.

Plainly, the informal and symbolic powers of the presidency today account for as much as the formal ones. Too, presidential powers expand and contract in response to varying situational and personality changes. Thus the powers of the presidency are interpreted in ways so markedly different as to seem to describe different offices. In some ways the presidency today is an open mandate for nearly anything its occupant chooses to do with it. In other ways, however, our beliefs and hopes about the presidency very much shape the character and quality of the presidential performances we get.

The modern (post-Roosevelt II) presidency is riddled through with various expectations that are decidedly paradoxical. Presidents and presidential candidates must constantly balance themselves between conflicting demands.... [V]ery often we simultaneously expect contradictory kinds of performances, contradictory kinds of personalities. It is not unreasonable to conclude that these paradoxes may sometimes make for schizophrenic presidential performances.

We may not be able to resolve the inherent contradictions and dilemmas these paradoxes point up. Still, a more rigorous understanding of these conflicts and no-win or near no-win situations should encourage more sensitivity to the limits of what a president can achieve. Exaggerated or hopelessly contradictory public expectations doubtless encourage a president to attempt more than he can accomplish and to overpromise and overextend himself.

Perhaps, too, an assessment of *the paradoxed presidency* may impel us anew to revise some of our unrealistic expectations of the institution of the presidency and encourage in turn the nurturing of alternative sources or centers for national leadership.

A more realistic appreciation of presidential paradoxes might help presidents concentrate on the practicable among their priorities. A more sophisticated and tolerant consideration of the modern presidency and its paradoxes might relieve the load so that a president can better lead and administer in those critical realms in which the nation has little choice but to turn to him. Like it or not, the vitality of our democracy still depends in large measure on the sensitive interaction of presidential leadership and an understanding public willing to listen and willing to support when a president can persuade....

Each of the paradoxes is based on apparent logical contradictions. Each has important implications for presidential performance and public evaluation of presidential behavior. A better understanding may lead to the removal, reconciliation, or more enlightened tolerance of the initial contradictions to which they give rise.

THE GENTLE AND DECENT/BUT FORCEFUL AND DECISIVE PRESIDENT

Opinion polls time and again indicate that people want a just, decent, humane "man of good faith" in the White House. Honesty and trustworthiness repeatedly top the list of qualities the public values most highly in a president these days. However, the public just as strongly demands the qualities of toughness, decisiveness, even a touch of ruthlessness.

Adlai Stevenson, George McGovern and Gerald Ford were all criticized for being "too nice," "too decent."... Being a "Mr. Nice Guy" is too easily equated with being too soft. The public dislikes the idea of a weak, spineless or sentimental person in the White House....

[T]his paradox may explain the unusual extraordinary public fondness for President Eisenhower. For he was at one and the same time blessed with a benign smile and a reserved, calming disposition. Yet he also was the disciplined, strong, no-nonsense, five-star general. Perhaps his ultimate resource as president was this reconciliation of decency and decisiveness, likeability alongside demonstrated valor....

Thus this paradox highlights one of the distinctive frustrations for presidents and would-be presidents. We demand the *sinister* as well as the *sincere*. President *Mean* and President *Nice;* tough and hard enough to stand up to a Khrushchev or to press the nuclear button, compassionate enough to care for the ill-fed, ill-clad, ill-housed. The public in this case seems to want a softhearted son of a bitch. It's a hard role to cast and a harder role to perform for eight years.

THE OPEN AND SHARING/BUT COURAGEOUS AND INDEPENDENT PRESIDENCY

We unquestionably cherish our three-branched system with its checks and balances and its theories of dispersed and separated powers. We want our presidents not only to be sincere but to share their powers with their cabinet, the Congress and other "responsible" national leaders. In theory, we oppose the concentration of power, we dislike secrecy and we resent depending on any one person to provide for all our leadership. In more recent years...there have been repeated calls for a more open, accountable and deroyalized presidency.

The other side of the coin, however, rejects the call for deroyalization. It rejects as well the idea that openness is the solution; indeed it suggests instead that the great presidents have been the strong presidents, who stretched their legal authority, who occasionally relied on the convenience of secrecy and who dominated the other branches of government. This point of view argues that the country in fact often yearns for a messiah, that the human heart ceaselessly reinvents royalty and that Roosevelts and Camelots, participatory democracy notwithstanding, are vital to the success of America.

Some people feel we are getting to the point where all of us would like to see a deroyalized, demythologized presidency. Others claim we need myth, we need symbol....

The clamor for a truly open or collegial presidency was opposed...by the late Harold Laski when he concluded that Americans in practice want to rally round a president who can demonstrate his independence and vigor:

> A president who is believed not to make up his own mind rapidly loses the power to maintain the hold. The need to dramatize his position by insistence upon his undoubted supremacy is inherent in the office as history has shaped it. A masterful man in the White House will, under all circumstances, be more to the liking of the multitude than one who is thought to be swayed by his colleagues.

Thus it is that we want our president not only to be both a lion and a fox, but more than a lion, more than a fox. We want simultaneously a secular leader and a civil religious mentor; we praise our three-branched system but we place capacious hopes upon and thus elevate the presidential branch. Only the president can give us heroic leadership. Only a president can dramatize and symbolize our highest expectations of ourselves as a chosen people with a unique mission. If it seems a little ironic for a semi-sovereign people (who have so recently celebrated the bicentennial of the power-to-the-governed experiment) to delegate so much hierarchical and semiautocratic power to their president, this is nonetheless precisely what we continually do.

We want an open presidency and we oppose the concentration of vast power in any one position. Still, we want forceful, courageous displays of leadership from our presidents. Anything less than that is condemned as aimlessness or loss of nerve. Further, we praise those who leave the presidency stronger than it was when they entered the institution.

THE PROGRAMMATIC/BUT PRAGMATIC LEADER

We want both a *programmatic* and a *pragmatic* person in the White House. We want a *moral* leader, yet the job forces the president to become a *constant compromiser.*

On the one hand, Franklin Roosevelt proclaimed that the presidency is preeminently a place for moral leadership. On the other hand, Governor Jerry Brown aptly notes that "a little vagueness goes a long way in this business."

A president who becomes too committed risks being called rigid; a president who becomes too pragmatic risks becoming called wishy-washy. The secret, of course, is to stay the course by stressing character, competence, rectitude and experience, and by avoiding strong stands that offend important segments in the population.

Jimmy Carter was especially criticized by the press and others for avoiding commitments and stressing his "flexibility" on the issues. This prompted a major discussion of what became called the "fuzziness issue."... Still, his "maybe I will and maybe I won't" strategy (as well as his talking softly about the issues while carrying a big smile) proved very effective in

overcoming critics and opponents who early on claimed he didn't have a chance.

What strikes one person as fuzziness or even duplicity appeals to another person as remarkable political skill, the very capacity for compromise and negotiation that is required if a president is to maneuver through the political minefields that come with the job.

Most candidates view a campaign as a fight to win office, not an opportunity for adult education. Barry Goldwater in 1964 may have run with the slogan "We offer a *choice* not an echo," but many Republican party regulars who, more pragmatically, aspired to win the election, preferred "a *chance* not a *choice.*" Once in office, presidents often operate the same way; the electoral connection looms large as an issue-avoiding, controversy-ducking political incentive.

AN INNOVATIVE AND INVENTIVE/ YET MAJORITARIAN AND RESPONSIVE PRESIDENCY

One of the most compelling paradoxes at the very heart of our democratic system arises from the fact that we expect our presidents to provide bold, innovative leadership and yet respond faithfully to public opinion majorities.

Walter Lippmann warned against letting public opinion become the chief guide to leadership in America, but he just as forcefully warned democratic leaders: Don't be right too soon, for public opinion will lacerate you! So most presidents fear being in advance of their times. They must *lead us,* but also *listen to us.*

We want our presidents to offer leadership, to be architects of the future, providers of visions, plans and goals. At the same time we want them to stay in close touch with the sentiments of the people. To *talk* about high ideals, New Deals, Big Deals and the like is one thing. But the public resists being *led* too far in any one direction.

Most of our presidents have been conservatives or at best "pragmatic liberals." They have seldom ventured much beyond the crowd. John Kennedy, the author of the much acclaimed *Profiles in Courage,* was often criticized for presenting far more profile than courage; if political risks could be avoided, he shrewdly avoided them. Kennedy was fond of pointing out that he had barely won election in 1960 and that great innovations should not be forced upon a leader with such a slender mandate.... Kennedy more often than not reminded Americans that caution was needed, that the important issues are complicated and technical, and best left to the administrative and political experts.

Presidents can get caught whether they are coming or going. The public wants them to be both *leaders* of the country and *representatives* of the people. We want them to be decisive and rely mainly on their own judgment, yet we want them to be very responsive to public opinion, especially to the "common sense" of our own opinions. It was perhaps with this in mind that an English essayist once defined the ideal democratic leader as "an uncommon man of common opinions."

TAKING THE PRESIDENCY OUT OF POLITICS

The public yearns for a statesman in the White House, for a George Washington or a second "era of good feelings," anything that might prevent partisanship or politics-as-usual in the White House. In fact, however, the job demands a president to be a gifted political broker, ever-attentive to changing political moods and coalitions.

Franklin Roosevelt illustrates well this paradox. Appearing so remarkably nonpartisan while addressing the nation, he was in practice one of the craftiest political coalition builders to occupy the White House. He mastered the art of politics—the art of making the difficult and desirable possible.

A president is expected to be above politics in some respects and highly political in others. A president is never supposed to act with his eye on the next election; he's not supposed to favor any particular group or party. Nor is he supposed to wheel and deal or twist too many arms. That's politics and that's bad! No, a president, or so most people are inclined to believe, is supposed to be "president of all the people." On the other hand, he is asked to be the head of his party, to help friendly members of Congress get elected or re-elected, to deal firmly with party barons and congressional political brokers. Too, he must build political coalitions around what he feels needs to be done....

In his reelection campaign of 1972, Richard Nixon in vain sought to reveal himself outwardly as too busy to be a politician; he wanted the American people to believe he was too preoccupied with the Vietnam War to have any personal concern about his election. In one sense, Mr. Nixon may have destroyed this paradox for at least a while. Haven't the American people learned that we *cannot* have a president *above* politics?

If past is prologue, presidents in the future will go to considerable lengths to portray themselves as unconcerned with their own political future. They will do so in large part because the public applauds the divorce between presidency and politics. People naively think that we can somehow turn the job of president into that of a managerial or strictly executive post. Not so. The presidency is a highly political office, and it cannot be otherwise. Moreover, its political character is for the most part desirable. A president separated from or somehow above politics might easily become a president who doesn't listen to the people, doesn't respond to majority sentiment or pay attention to views that may be diverse, intense and at variance with his own. A president immunized from politics would be a president who would too easily become isolated from the processes of government and too removed from the thoughts and aspirations of his people.

In all probability this paradox will be an enduring one. The standard diagnosis of what's gone wrong in an administration will be that the presidency has become too politicized. But it will be futile to try to take the president out of politics. A more helpful approach is to realize that certain presidents try too hard to hold themselves above politics—or at least to give that appearance—rather than engaging in it deeply, openly and creatively enough. A president in a democracy has to act politically in regard to controversial issues if we are to have any semblance of government by the consent of the governed.

THE COMMON MAN/WHO GIVES AN UNCOMMON PERFORMANCE

We like to think that America is the land where the common sense of the common man reigns. We prize the common touch, the "man of the people." Yet few of us will settle for anything but an uncommon performance from our presidents.

This paradox is splendidly summed up by some findings of a survey conducted by Field Research Corp., the California public opinion organization. Field asked a cross section of Californians in 1975 to describe in their own words the qualities a presidential candidate should or should not have. Honesty and trustworthiness topped the list. But one of his more intriguing findings was that "while most (72 percent) prefer someone with plain and simple tastes, there is also a strong preference (66 percent) for someone who can give exciting speeches and inspire the public."

It has been said that American people crave to be governed by men who are both Everyman and yet better than Everyman. The Lincoln and Kennedy presidencies are illustrative. We might cherish the myth that anyone can grow up to be president, that there are no barriers, no elite qualifications. But the nation doesn't want a person who is too ordinary. Would-be presidents have to prove their special qualifications—their excellence, their stamina, their capacity for uncommon leadership.

The Harry Truman reputation, at least as it flourishes now, demonstrates the apparent reconciliation of this paradox. Fellow-commoner Truman rose to the demands of the job and became a gifted decision-maker, or so his supporters would have us believe.

Candidate Carter in 1976 nicely fit this paradox as well. Local, down-home, farm boy next door, makes good! The image of peanut farmer turned gifted governor and talented campaigner contributed greatly to Carter's success as a national candidate, and he used it with consummate skill.

A president or would-be president must be bright, but not too bright; warm and accessible, but not too folksy; down to earth, but not pedestrian. Adlai Stevenson spoke too eloquently, and President Ford's talks dulled our senses with the banal. Both suffered because of this paradox. The Catch 22 here, of course, is that the very fact of an uncommon performance puts distance between a president and the truly common man. We persist, however, in wanting both at the same time.

THE INSPIRATIONAL/BUT DON'T-PROMISE-MORE-THAN-YOU-CAN-DELIVER LEADER

We ask our presidents to raise hopes, to educate us, to inspire. But too much inspiration will invariably lead to disillusion and cynicism.

We enjoy the upbeat rhetoric and promises of a brighter tomorrow. We genuinely want to hear about New Nationalism, New Deals, New Frontiers, Great Societies, and New American Revolutions; we want our fears to be assuaged during "fireside chats" or "a conversation with the president"; to be told that "we are a great people," that the "only fear we have to fear is fear itself," and that a recession has "bottomed out." So much do we want the drive of a lifting dream, to use Mr. Nixon's corny phrase, that the American people are easily duped by presidential promises.

Do presidents overpromise because they are congenital optimists or because they are pushed into it by the demanding public? Surely it is an admixture of the two. But whatever the source, few presidents in recent times were able to keep their promises and fulfill their intentions. Poverty was not ended, a Great Society was not realized. Vietnam dragged on and on. Watergate outraged a public that had been promised an open presidency. Energy independence remains an illusion just as crime in the streets continues to rise.

A president who does not raise hopes is criticized as letting events shape his presidency, rather than making things happen. A president who eschewed inspiration of any kind would be rejected as un-American. For as a poet once wrote, "America is promises." For people everywhere cherishing the dream of individual liberty and self-fulfillment, America has been the land of promises, of possibilities, of dreams. No president can stand in the way of this truth, no matter how much the current dissatisfaction about the size of big government in Washington, and its incapacity to deliver the services it promises....

THE NATIONAL UNIFIER/NATIONAL DIVIDER

One of the most difficult to alleviate paradoxes arises from our longing simultaneously for a president who will pull us together again and yet be a forceful priority setter, budget manager and executive leader. The two tasks are near opposites.

We remain one of the few nations in the world that calls upon our chief executive to also serve as our symbolic, ceremonial head of state. Elsewhere these tasks are spread around. In some nations there is a monarch and a prime minister; in other nations there are three visible national leaders—the head of state, a premier, and a powerful party head.

In the absence of an alternative, we demand that our presidents and our presidency act as a unifying force in our lives. Perhaps it all began with George Washington, who so artfully performed this function. At least for a while, he truly was above politics and an ideal symbol for our new nation. He was a healer, a unifier and an extraordinary man for all seasons. Today we ask no less of our presidents than that they should do as Washington did.

However, we have designed a presidential job description that compels our contemporary presidents to act as national dividers. They necessarily divide when they act as the leader of their political party; when they set priorities that advantage certain goals and groups at the expense of others; when they forge and lead political coalitions when they move out ahead of public opinion and assume the role of national educator; when they choose one set of advisers over another. A president, if he is to be a creative executive, cannot help but offend certain interests. When Franklin Roosevelt was running for a second term some garment workers unfolded a great sign that said, "We love him for the enemies he has made." Such is the fate of a president on an everyday basis if he chooses to use power he usually will lose the good will of those who preferred inaction over action. The opposite is of course true if he chooses not to act.

Look at it from another angle. The nation is torn between the view that a president should primarily preside over the nation and merely serve as a referee among the various powerful interests that actually control who gets what, when and how, and the view which holds that a president should gain control of governmental processes and powers so as to use them for the purpose of furthering public, as opposed to private, interests.

Harry Truman said it all very simply. He once said there are 14 or 15 million Americans who have the resources to have representatives in Washington to protect their interests, and that the interests of the 160 million or so others are the responsibility of the president.

Put another way, the presidency is sometimes seen as the great defender of the people, the ombudsman or advocate-general of "public interests." Yet it is sometimes also (and sometimes at the same time) viewed as the enemy—hostile to the people, isolated from them, wary of them, antagonistic.

This debate notwithstanding, however, Americans prize the presidency as a grand American invention. As a nation we do not want to change it. Proposals to weaken it are dismissed. Proposals to reform or restructure it are paid little respect. If we sour on a president, the conventional solution has been to find and elect someone better.

THE LONGER HE IS THERE/THE LESS WE LIKE HIM

Every four years we pick a president and for the next four years we pick on him, at him, and sometimes pick him entirely apart. There is no adequate pre-presidential job experience, so much of the first term is an on-the-job learning experience. But we resent this. It is too important a position for on-the-job learning, or at least that's how most of us feel.

Too, we expect presidents to grow in office and to become better acclimated to the office. But the longer they are in office, the more they find themselves with more crises and less public support....

Simply stated, the more we know of a president, or the more we observe his presidency, the less we approve of him. Familiarity breeds discontent. Research on public support of presidents indicates that presidential approval peaks soon after a president takes office, and then slides downward at a declining rate over time until it reaches a point in the latter half of the four-year term, when it bottoms out. Thereafter it rises a bit, but never attains its original levels. Why this pattern of declining support afflicts presidents is a subject of debate among social scientists. Unrealistic early expectations are, of course, a major factor.

These unrealistic expectations ensure a period of disenchantment.

Peace and prosperity, of course, can help stem the unpleasant tide of ingratitude, and the Eisenhower popularity remained reasonably high in large part because of his (or the nation's) achievements in these areas. For most presidents, however, their eventual downsliding popularity is due perhaps as much to the public's inflated expectations of the presidency as to a president's actions. It is often as if their downslide in popularity would occur no matter what the president did. If this seems unfair, even cruel, this is nonetheless what happens to those lucky enough to win election to the highest office in the land.

And all this occurs despite our conventional wisdom that the *office makes the man,* "that the presidency with its built-in educational processes, its spacious view of the world, its command of talent, and above all its self-conscious historic role, does work its way on the man in the Oval Office," as James MacGregor Burns put it. If we concede that the office in part does make the man, we must admit also that time in office often unmakes the man.

WHAT IT TAKES TO BECOME PRESIDENT/ MAY NOT BE WHAT IS NEEDED TO GOVERN THE NATION

To win a presidential election it takes ambition, ambiguity, luck, and masterful public relations strategies. To govern the nation requires all of these, but far more as well. It may well be that too much ambition, too much ambiguity and too heavy a reliance on phony public relations tricks actually undermine the integrity and legitimacy of the presidency.

Columnist David Broder offers an apt example: "People who win primaries may become good presidents—but 'it ain't necessarily so.' Organizing well is important in governing just as it is in winning primaries. But the Nixon years should teach us that good advance men do not necessarily make trustworthy White House aides. Establishing a government is a little more complicated than having the motorcade run on time."

Likewise, ambition (in very heavy doses) is essential for a presidential candidate, but too much hunger for the office or for "success-at-any-price" is a danger to be avoided. He must be bold and energetic, but carried too far this can make him cold and frenetic. To win the presidency requires a single-mindedness of purpose, and yet we want our presidents to be well rounded, to have a sense of humor, to be able to take a joke, to have hobbies and interests outside the realm of politics—in short, to have a sense of proportion.

Another aspect of this paradox can be seen in the way candidates take ambiguous positions on issues in order to increase their appeal to the large bulk of centrist and independent voters. Not only does such equivocation discourage rational choices by the voters, but it also may alienate people who later learn, after the candidate has won, that his views and policies are otherwise. LBJ's "We will not send American boys to fight the war that Asian boys should be fighting," and Richard Nixon's "open presidency" pledges come readily to mind. Their pre-presidential centrist stands were later violated or ignored.

Political scientist Samuel Huntington calls attention to yet another way this paradox works. To be a winning candidate, he notes, the would-be president must put together an *electoral coalition* involving a majority of voters appropriately distributed across the country. To do this he must appeal to all regions and interest groups and cultivate the appearance of honesty, sincerity and experience. But once elected, the electoral coalition has served its purpose and a *governing coalition* is the order of the day. This all may sound rather elitist, but presidential advisor Huntington insists that this is what has to be:

> The day after his election the size of his majority is almost—if not entirely—irrelevant to his ability to govern the country. What counts then is his ability to mobilize support from the leaders of the key institutions in society and government. He has to constitute a broad governing coalition of strategically located supporters who can furnish him with the information, talent, expertise, manpower, publicity, arguments, and political support which he needs to develop a program, to embody it in legislation, and to see it effectively implemented, This coalition must include key people in Congress, the executive branch, and the private-sector "Establishment." The governing coalition need have little relation to the electoral coalition. The fact that the president as a candidate put together a

successful electoral coalition does not insure that he will have a viable governing coalition.

Presidential candidate Adlai Stevenson had another way of saying it in 1956. He said that he had "learned that the hardest thing about any political campaign is how to win without proving that you are unworthy of winning." The process of becoming president is an extraordinarily taxing one that defies description. . . .

What it takes to *become* president may differ from what it takes to be president. It takes a near-megalomaniac who is also glib, dynamic, charming on television and relatively hazy on the issues. Yet we want our presidents to be well rounded, not overly ambitious, careful in their reasoning and clear and specific in their communications. It may well be that our existing primary and convention system adds up to an effective testing or obstacle course for would-be presidents. Certainly they have to travel to all sections of the country, meet the people, deal with interest group elites and learn about the bracing issues of the day. But with the Johnson and Nixon experiences in our not-too-distant past, we have reason to reappraise whether our system of producing presidents is adequately reconciled with what is required to produce a president who is competent, fair-minded, and emotionally healthy.

Perhaps the ultimate paradox of the modern presidency is that it is always too powerful and yet it is always too inadequate. Always too powerful, because it is contrary to our ideals of a government by the people and because it must now possess the capacity to wage nuclear war (a capacity that unfortunately doesn't permit much in the way of checks and balances and deliberative, participatory government). Always too inadequate, because it seldom achieves our highest hopes for it, not to mention its own stated intentions.

The dilemma for the attentive public is that curbing the powers of a president who abuses the public trust will usually undermine the capacity of a fair-minded president to serve the public interest. In the 187 years since Washington took office, we have multiplied the requirements for presidential leadership and we have made it increasingly more difficult to lead. Certainly this is not the time for mindless retribution against the already fragile institution of the presidency.

Neither presidents nor the public should be relieved of their responsibilities of trying to fashion a more effective and fair-minded leadership system simply because these paradoxes are widely agreed upon. Nor is it enough to throw up our hands and say: "Well, no one makes a person run for that crazy job in the first place." These paradoxes are enduring ones. We shall have to select as our presidents persons who understand these contrary demands and who have a gift for the improvisation that these paradoxes demand. It is important for us to ask our chief public servants occasionally to forgo enhancing their own short-term political fortunes for a greater good of simplifying the paradoxes of the presidency.

While the presidency will doubtless remain one of our nation's best vehicles for creative policy change, it will also continue to be an embattled office, fraught with the cumulative weight of these paradoxes. We need urgently to probe the origins and assess the consequences of these paradoxes and to learn how presidents and public can better coexist with them. For it is apparent that these paradoxes serve to isolate and disconnect a president from the public. Like it or not, the growing importance of the presidency and our growing dependence on presidents seem to ensure that presidents will be less popular and increasingly the scapegoat when anything goes wrong.

Let us ask our presidents to give us their best, but let us not ask them to deliver more than the presidency—or any single institution—has to give.

READING 49

The Clinton Administration in the Separated System: A Presidency at Risk?

Charles O. Jones

Charles O. Jones of the University of Wisconsin is a past president of the American Political Science Association and a prominent analyst of the American presidency. His recent writing has focused on the institution's role in the "separated" American political system in which there is a widespread sharing of and a competition for the exercise of power.

In this selection, Jones moves from a general discussion of our separated system to a more specific focus on the Clinton administration's efforts to govern in such a context. The Clinton case study offers an interesting analogue and companion piece to Tom Cronin's evaluation of the paradoxes of the presidency with one important difference. Whereas Cronin's focus is on the unrealistic expectations thrust upon the presidency, Jones argues that the Clinton administration erred, in part, by adopting publicly an all too ambitious agenda and set of expectations for itself.

Jones documents, for example, the president's overly aggressive stance early in his first term in personally drawing accountability into the White House for successful passage of health care reform, an exceedingly problematic strategy in view of the administration's weak political base. The health care example underscores the manner in which Clinton exacerbated the inherent problems that presidents face in managing expectations in a separated system.

As Jones notes, Clinton's problems grew more complex midway through his first term when, with a Republican majority gaining control of Congress, the separated system was joined with divided government, in which different parties control the executive and legislative branches. Jones suggests that Clinton's behavior has adjusted to this new political context as he has become more of a moderating "prospector" and less of an aggressive "campaigner" in managing his presidency. At the time of this writing (early in Clinton's second term) it is too soon to tell whether the president has arrived at a successful strategy for governing.

Reprinted by permission from the Spring 1996 issue of *Extensions,* a copyrighted publication of the Carl Albert Congressional Research and Studies Center, University of Oklahoma. This essay is a summary of Professor Jones's discourse in the 1995 Julian J. Rothbaum Distinguished Lecture in Representative Government. The lecture will be fully developed in a book to be published by the University of Oklahoma Press.

Shortly after his inauguration, President Clinton reiterated an extravagant campaign promise, accompanied by a dramatic announcement:

> As a first step in responding to the demands of literally millions of Americans, today I am announcing the formation of the President's Task Force on National Health Reform. Although the issue is complex, the task force's mission is simple: Build on the work of the campaign and the transition, listen to all parties, and prepare health care reform legislation to be submitted to Congress *within 100 days of our taking office.* This task will be chaired by the First Lady, Hillary Rodham Clinton...

The effect was to draw accountability clearly, unmistakably to the White House, indeed, into the residence itself. The president and his partner by marriage would be held directly accountable for what happened. Yet as political scientist Hugh Heclo observed, "Never in the modern history of major social reform efforts had a president with so few political resources tried to do so much."

Ours in not a unified political and governmental system. Setting ambitious goals, promising swift action, and assuming complete management for dramatic change, taken together represent a huge political gamble for a leader in a government of truly separated institutions. To do so having won 43 percent of the popular vote is surely one definition of derring-do. By drawing accountability to himself, Clinton accentuated a problem inherent in a separated system. A prime challenge to presidents is to manage the often lavish expectations of their accountability under conditions of distributed power.

ACCOUNTABILITY IN A SEPARATED SYSTEM

Though a government of separated institutions sharing or competing for powers has many virtues, *focused responsibility is not one of them.* Accountability is highly diffused in a separated system. And though some observers argue that to have accountability everywhere is to have it nowhere, that is not so. A system like ours has substantial *individual accountability* but limited *collective accountability.*

Accountability for presidents is primarily rhetorical; presidents speak of representing the public. The media often act as enforcers, holding presidents accountable to an inexact public interest standard. Because they operate in a separated system, however, presidents are held responsible for that over which they have limited control. This reality is central to the governing strategy of modern presidents. The White House cannot depend for support on what happened in the last election but must account for how the members' policy preferences relate to the next election. The president must develop and redevelop policy strategies that acknowledge the ever-shifting coalitional base. Serious and continuous in-party and cross-party coalition building thus typifies policy-making in the separated system.

The defining challenge for a new president, therefore, is to capitalize on his freshness without elevating further the lofty expectations of his position. The president is well advised to resist the efforts by others, or himself, to assign him the heady charge of being the commander of government.

MANAGING HIGH EXPECTATIONS: THE FIRST CLINTON PRESIDENCY

Imagine that the fires of ambition burn so strongly that sleep is your enemy. Success by most measures comes easily but it does not provide solace. The need to do more is all-consuming. There is no reward great enough; an obstacle overcome is less valued than the identification of a new challenge. Conceive, if you can, the challenge involved in making everyone happy and getting credit for having done so, and then you will understand why there is little time or patience for sleep. Meet Bill Clinton, "first in his class," bound to be President.

Bill Clinton's ambition is for a kind of greatness as defined by approval. He wants to do good things for many people. He is a talker, engaged in a game-like process of exploration. As such he is puzzled by listeners who hear the talk as commitment. Talkers find satisfaction in the immediate response. They are unlikely to make a strong distinction between campaigning and governing. Nor are they likely to be intrigued by the intricacies of the lawmaking process. Bill Clinton is the quintessential campaigner as president. He most assuredly is not a lawmaker president in the Lyndon Johnson mold; had he been so, he may have had a

more successful two years. What follows, then, is a description and analysis of a presidency increasingly at risk, one persistently "on the edge" as Elizabeth Drew entitles her book on the Clinton Administration.

The 1992 campaign and election were bound to encourage a parliamentary-style accounting. A youthful, new-generation Democratic team won after twelve years of Republican dominance of the White House. Clinton promised to work hardest at economic recovery and on issues generally acknowledged to form the contemporary agenda. Moreover, one party would now be in charge of both ends of Pennsylvania Avenue; "gridlock" would end.

Contributing to high expectations were political analysts, especially those who adhere to the perspective on national elections I term "unitarian" (as opposed to "separationist"). At root, the unitarians disagree with the separation of powers. They propose reforms designed to ensure one-party government so as to achieve collective accountability. For the unitarian, the best possible election result is that in which one political party wins the White house and majority control of both houses of Congress. That party is then expected to display unity on policy issues and to produce a record for which it can be held responsible at the next election. I'll wager that most political analysts are unitarians.

In contrast, the general voting public and most members of Congress are practicing "separationists." For the separationist the best possible election result is one that reinforces the legitimacy of independent participation by each branch. Party leaders, including presidents, are then expected to build cross-partisan support within and between the elected branches whether or not one party has majorities in Congress and a president in the White House. A separationist perspective of the 1992 election would have stressed the rejection of Bush without identifying a mandate for Clinton. By this view, voters continued to split their tickets, albeit in new and interesting ways, making it difficult to spot a "mandate."

Evidence for this separationist interpretation abounds. Ross Perot garnered the most votes for an independent or a third-party candidate since Theodore Roosevelt in 1912. A president won in a three-way contest by designating a credible agenda and projecting a sufficiently moderate policy posture as to be reassuring to just over half of the Reagan (1984) and Bush (1988) voters who were disillusioned with the Bush presidency. Indeed, Clinton's campaign strategy sought to "convince middle-class voters that Democrats could work within the Reagan-Bush consensus." Moreover, House Republicans had a net gain of the national vote for the House, compared to Bush's 37 percent of the national vote for president.

It follows from these assertions that a partisan, unitarian approach was unlikely to succeed. Yet that is the approach Clinton employed. Not only that, but Clinton's activist style drew accountability to himself. A book of promises, entitled *Putting People First,* was published during the campaign and was bound to raise hopes while defining awesome challenges and providing a scorecard for the media. In reading from this text of pledges, little was to be left untouched by a Clinton-Gore administration—a total of 35 proposals for the "national economic strategy," and 577 proposals for "other crucial issues."

Absent was an understanding of how ours is truly the most elaborate lawmaking system in the world. It does not submit to enthusiasm alone. Effective leadership starts with knowing how the system works. Moreover, the 1992 election produced exceptionally challenging conditions for lawmaking, requiring extraordinary sensitive strategies for producing cross-party majorities on Capitol Hill. Bill Clinton lacked the skills for devising these strategies and therefore had to learn then or, like Reagan, rely on those with that competence.

In understanding the centrist underpinnings of Clinton's pre-inaugural support, one can comprehend the problems the new president faced during his first two-year presidency. For the actions that could be taken early in order to demonstrate momentum—executive orders regarding abortions performed in military hospitals, federal funding of fetal tissue transplant research, the importation of abortion pill RU-486, and ending the ban on gays in the military—were likely to project a substantially more liberal cast than could be justified by public opinion as expressed either in the election or in subsequent polls.

Moreover, actions that were more moderate-to-conservative in nature—reducing the federal work-force, terminating advisory committees, seeking to make government more efficient—were overshadowed at the start by the more liberal actions cited above. Why? They were noncontroversial, not newsworthy, and therefore unavailable as ballast to the liberal tilt on controversial issues.

As if these developments were not sufficient to ensure Republican unity, Democrats in the House of Representatives used the rules of that chamber to prevent Republicans from effective participation in the amending process. Senate Republicans were in a substantially stronger position than their colleagues in the House due to the fact that they had sufficient numbers to prevent closing debate, an advantage used early against the president's economic stimulus package and late in 1994 to kill much of the president's program.

With all of these problems and miscalculations, the first year was moderately productive under contentious political circumstances in which partisan lines hardened. Several Bush-vetoed bills were passed again and signed by the president, a deficit-reduction package was enacted by a tie-breaking vote by Vice President Gore in the Senate and by two votes in the House, NAFTA was approved with the crucial support of Republicans, and the president got a modified version of his National Service Program.

However, many of the most contentious issues were carried over. As a result, the second year was among the least productive of major legislation in the post-World War II period. Of the ten presidential priorities mentioned in the State of the Union Message, four became law—the GATT (again with Republican support), Goals 2000, anti-crime, and community development loans. Each was important but none was as important for the president as the health care system—a matter that dominated the politics of the year. "We will make history by reforming the health-care system," was the president's promise in his January, 1994, State of the Union Message. Yet by September 26, Senate Majority Leader George Mitchell had issued the last rites.

Perhaps most stunning as a measure of political mismanagement was the fact that by raising expectations, inviting responsibility, and yet failing to produce, the president and his leaders in Congress deflected criticism of Republicans for having obstructed much of the president's legislative program. As was noted in a *New York Times* editorial, Republican cooperation "was never part of the original promise." Democratic leaders had informed the president that they could deliver without Republican support. Republicans, however, were content to accept being excluded. In the end it permitted them to avoid the accountability that was solicited by the administration.

Clinton's personal strengths are many. He is a superb campaigner—an effective and empathetic communicator with the public and a man with an "upbeat personality." He is, unquestionably, highly intelligent, possessed of an extraordinary capacity to identify and explore public policy issues. We also know from David Maraniss' fine biography that Clinton knows how to cram for an exam—a characteristic displayed in his role in lawmaking, as he often waits to the last minute to engage the issue to the extent of making a choice.

But it is generally conceded that Bill Clinton also has a number of weaknesses. He never held a position in the federal government. While governor, he worked with a Democratic legislature, seldom having to take Republicans into account or to display the kind of lawmaking prowess of a governor from a more competitive two-party state. As with most governors, he lacked direct experience in foreign and national security policy. He is an admitted "policy talk wonk" who finds it difficult to concentrate on a limited agenda. And there is ample evidence that Bill Clinton lacks direct experience in forming and accommodating an effective staff. Clinton's strengths are more intellectual than managerial.

Moreover, instead of compensating for his weaknesses, Clinton preferred to capitalize on his strengths. He sought to govern by campaigning, not lawmaking, virtually melding the two in his own mind and through his behavior. In his first two years the president visited 194 places, making 264 appearances (excluding foreign travel, visits to Arkansas, and vacations). Bill Clinton is the most traveled president in history, exceeding even President George Bush. One effect of all this travel was to reinforce the distorted view of the president as the government, holding him accountable

for what is and has ever been a separated system of diffused accountability. As a consequence, Bill Clinton became a major issue in the midterm election. The result was to produce a very different presidency for his second two years in office.

THE MIDTERM EARTHQUAKE

It is standard wisdom that congressional elections are state and local events, albeit with important national effects. In 1994, however, there were two bids to nationalize the midterm elections: one by the president who seemingly could not resist joining the fray and one by Newt Gingrich, the House Republican Leader in waiting, who harbored national crusade-like ambitions.

As the election approached, the president might well have followed the advice given Harry Truman by the Democratic National Committee chairman in 1946—i.e., stay out of midterm politics! Truman, whose standing in the polls was at 40 percent, accepted this advice. "He kept silent on politics." Few, if any, Democratic candidates invoked his name.

Clinton was in a similar situation, with approximately the same poll results. And, in fact, his pollster, Stanley Greenberg, issued a memorandum to Democratic candidates advising that they run on their own accomplishments, not those of the president. "There is no reason to highlight these as Clinton or Democratic proposals. Voters want to know that you are fighting to get things done for them, not that you are advancing some national agenda."

A flurry of foreign and national security policy decisions on North Korea, Haiti, and Iraq—all judged to be successful—resulted in a boost in the president's approval rating to 50 percent, exceeding his disapproval rating for the first time in six months. That was the good news; the bad news was that the good news encouraged him to reenter the campaign. He launched a last-minute, furious schedule of appearances, drawing attention to his record and attacking the Republican "Contract *on* America." By campaigning so energetically in the last week, the president naturally attracted press attention to himself as an issue. The effect was to ensure that dramatic Republican gains would be interpreted as a rejection of Clinton's presidency, whether or not that conclusion was merited in terms of actual voting behavior.

The other half, or more, of the nationalization of the 1994 elections is explained by what the Republicans did. As political scientist Gary C. Jacobson pointed out: "All politics was *not* local in 1994. Republicans succeeded in framing the local choice in national terms, making taxes, social discipline, big government, and the Clinton presidency the dominant issues." The Republicans tied "congressional Democrats to Clinton, a discredited government establishment, and deplorable status quo."

Gingrich, too, deserves notice for his daring strategy of committing Republican candidates to a bold midterm party platform, the "Contract with America." It is true that most voters knew little or nothing about the contract. But the act of getting over 300 Republican candidates to commit themselves in a media show at the Capitol on September 27 had profound effects on how the election results would then be interpreted.

The new Republican leaders were also not in the least bothered by Democratic claims that the contract tied "Republican candidates back into their congressional leadership." That was precisely the point. Gingrich and company would be strengthened in their effort to establish firm control of the agenda if the new members supported them. Meanwhile, the Democrats were in considerable disarray. Bill Clinton was still president, but he was not leader of the Democrats in any serious or meaningful sense. One study concluded that: "The more the Democratic incumbent voted to support the president's policies, the more likely he or she was to be defeated."

Justified or not in terms of what the voters actually wanted, a new agenda had been created. "Change isn't Bill Clinton's friend anymore," is how two reporters put it. A *Washington Post* editorial referred to a "sea change," pointing out that:"This was not just an 'anti-incumbent' vote. The incumbents who were defeated this year were Democrats" and "the change called for went almost uniformly in one direction, and that was against liberalism and toward the right." A mandate had been declared, centered in just one of the three elected branches—the House of Representatives.

RECLAIMING LEADERSHIP: THE SECOND CLINTON PRESIDENCY

How then did this policy ambitious president—one who wanted government to do more, not less; and to do it better, not worse—how did he respond to dramatically new political conditions? I have made the point that Bill Clinton is not a lawmaker president. Yet there are functions that cannot be avoided, choices that have to be made—notably whether to sign or to veto a bill. How is the president coping? He has altered his governing style from that of a *campaigner* to that of a *prospector,* searching for a role that is compatible with the unusual politics of the time. The strategy devised in 1995 contains these tenets:

- Associate the president with the change seemingly demanded by the voters.
- Remind the public that the president was there first with many of the issues in the Contract.
- Argue that the Republicans are going too far. It is not necessary to destroy programs in order to improve government. Be the voice of moderation against the extremist Republicans. "I'm for that, but not so much."
- Search for high profile issues subject to executive order, pushing the limits of that power (as with the anti-teenage smoking measures and barring government contracts with firms replacing strikers).
- Await the completion of lawmaking, then exercise the veto while imploring Republicans to meet on "common ground." Avoid specifics in favor of a "no, that's not it" response.
- Travel, taking your presidency to the people, posturing as the voice of reason, the interpreter of change.
- Take full advantage of the uniquely presidential status in foreign and national security issues.

Taken as a whole, this strategy is defensible and rational given the president's political status. And there is evidence of effectiveness as measured by the opinion polls. Meanwhile there is a moderately strong chance that congressional Republicans will deliver in the 104th Congress what congressional Democrats could not in the 103rd; namely the fulfilling of many of the campaign promises of Bill Clinton—balancing the budget, welfare reform, health care reform, lobbying reform, government reorganization and downsizing, perhaps even a tax cut and campaign finance reform. Should the economy stay basically sound in 1996, it would not be the first time that the voters returned the whole split-party government—a president of one party, a Congress (one house or both) of another (e.g., 1956, 1972, 1984).

BILL CLINTON IN HISTORICAL PROSPECTIVE

Bill Clinton joins others whose presidencies have been at risk. Indeed, the imbalance between expectations and authority perpetuates political peril for presidents.

Bill Clinton amplified the inherent risk for the president by raising expectations despite weak political advantages. He invited accountability for the failures that were likely to come, given the overreaching that characterized his early months in office. A dramatically new politics was created as a result.

Now freed from the exacting demands of his original ambitious agenda, the president is settling into the role of moderating the striking, even threatening, policy changes proposed by Republicans. Though not a leadership role, it is a mode that becomes him. As the nation's moderator in the serious policy debates at hand, he can justify the travel and public exposure that he finds personally and intellectually rewarding. He displayed patience in 1995, permitting Republicans to dominate the agenda and awaiting the time when his veto power would inevitably attract their lawmaking efforts—inexorably drawing them into the public arena where he excels. The campaigner could not reinsert himself into the policy process. But having been more an observer than a participant during the active congressional session, it was no simple matter for President Clinton to reconnect with the lawmaking process. Therefore negotiations with congressional leaders have been protracted and disorderly.

Control of his political destiny was taken from the president in the 1994 elections and so he has positioned himself to take advantage of what others do or fail to do. He has recovered somewhat in the polls but, no doubt, he would agree that the separated system works best when success is measured less by recovery than be effective participation throughout. However impressive it is to be the "Come Back Kid," it is substantially more imposing to be a president who needs no recuperation.

┌─────────────────────────────────┐
│   **R E A D I N G 5 0**   │
└─────────────────────────────────┘

Short-Term Success without Strategy: An Assessment of Clinton Foreign Policy

Jeffrey S. Lantis

Charles Jones's analysis of the Clinton administration's aggressive initiatives in the domestic realm at the beginning of his presidency suggests that this was a problematic strategy; perhaps somewhat ironically, this selection by Jeffrey Lantis, a political scientist at the College of Wooster, underscores that the Clinton administration has achieved some noteworthy successes in the foreign policy arena, at least in the short run, in the virtual absence of presidential strategy that, for Lantis, is equally problematic.

In this essay, Lantis examines the puzzle of how the administration could be successful in accomplishing things such as the North American Free Trade Agreement (NAFTA), the Dayton Peace Accords for Bosnia, and proximate successes in Palestinian–Israeli relationships in the absence of the articulation of any "Clinton Doctrine." Lantis's answer, which can only be assessed by the test of time, is that Clinton's foreign policy successes may prove to be short-lived.

Lantis portrays a setting where, despite President Clinton's relative disinterest in foreign policy, his clear penchant for trying to please everyone (often alluded to in analyses of his domestic policy behavior) and, as importantly, his effort to address domestic concerns often drive his foreign policy choices. Fortuitous political events and timing are credited with coming together in several instances to bring about policy successes despite the administration's false starts, changes in direction, and lack of an overall plan. While this approach to foreign policy decision making can, of course, be criticized, it remains possible, nevertheless, that for a president as domestically focused as Clinton appears to be, the behavior Lantis documents can be considered a strategy of sorts. This is particularly the case if the president's choices do, indeed, serve his primary domestic policy goals.

If the president does not want to leave his legacy to chance or be merely a caretaker in office, he must take a self-conscious strategic approach to the presidency.

—James Pfiffner, *The Strategic Presidency,*
1988

In 1993, William Jefferson Clinton became the first post-Cold War president of the United States of America. A review of the Clinton foreign policy record in the first term finds some notable successes including the completion of the North American Free Trade Agreement (NAFTA), the Palestinian-Israeli peace treaty, and the Dayton Accords for Bosnia. The administration successfully portrayed these developments as foreign policy victories in the 1996 presidential campaign against Republican challenger Bob Dole, and Clinton's selection of new advisors for his second term—Secretary of State Madeline Albright, Secretary of Defense William Cohen, and National Security Adviser Samuel Berger—emphasized consistency and strength for U.S. foreign policy on the road to the new millennium.

Critics have charged, however, that the administration has been quite inconsistent in its approach to foreign affairs and lacks an overarching foreign policy strategy for the new era. The irony of success in spite of the absence of a "Clinton Doctrine" raises a puzzle in understanding the president's record. Indeed, how could foreign policy achievements come from a president who was so openly disinterested in foreign policy? This article examines the Clinton record in light this puzzle and argues that the president only secured short-term solutions to major for-

eign policy challenges in the first term as a function of a special combination of political events and timing. These successes (and a number of failures) derived from the president's efforts to simultaneously satisfy both international and domestic constituencies in order to ensure an historical image of success.

THE RELUCTANT FOREIGN POLICY PRESIDENT

During the presidential race of 1992, Clinton campaigned on the promise that he would "focus like a laser beam" on domestic issues and economic woes. His pollsters knew that the public felt as if America had won the Cold War at the cost and neglect of economic and social conditions at home. Thus, candidate Clinton portrayed himself as a New Democrat—as one who would establish more centrist positions on major domestic issues and would meet the needs of his various constituencies. He also knew that President Bush had a distinct advantage in the foreign policy arena, so he played a game of foreign policy poker with Bush during the campaign. At various stops on the road to the presidency, Clinton pledged to cut defense spending more dramatically than Bush, to press China harder on its human rights record, to reform U.S.-Russian relations, and to increase the U.S. contribution to international peacekeeping. These were all parts of candidate Clinton's call for a new and improved world order, but they were more tactics than strategy.

Once in office, President Clinton had to face the task of ordering and prioritizing this ambitious foreign policy agenda. Like Presidents Harding and Truman before him, he took power at the end of a major transition in world politics and was given the opportunity to choose between an internationalist or isolationist foreign policy agenda. Characteristically, Clinton chose both. On one hand, the new president pledged that the United States would remain actively engaged in world affairs and serve as a moral leader in foreign policy. Secretary of State Christopher was immediately dispatched to all corners of the globe to deliver mixed messages to foreign leaders. At the same time, the president directed his new National Security Advisor, Anthony Lake, to draw up plans for intensifying the U.S. commitment to United Nations (UN) peacekeeping operations around the world. In a candid statement about the Clinton agenda in 1993, Lake said that he and the president wanted "to work to end every conflict...to save every child out there." One critic, Michael Mandelbaum, termed this a "Mother Teresa-like" agenda of humanitarian concerns that was devoid of strategic considerations and reminiscent of the Carter administration.

On the other hand, the president was also sensitive to isolationist pressures on American foreign policy in the post-Cold War era. Clinton worked quite hard to maintain his domestic affairs focus by attending primarily to his agenda of social and economic programs, and his preoccupation with domestic concerns largely kept him away from the foreign policy planning process. When he did return to such strategy discussions, it was only sporadically, and his personal penchant for the details often got in the way of strategic thinking. To the extent that the president considered foreign affairs, such issues were most often approached in terms of how they might impact domestic constituencies. Thus, the foreign policy agenda reflected the administration's commitment to domestic politics and problem solving rather than strategy development.

The president's Janus-faced foreign affairs profile combined to derail the development of coherent foreign policy initiatives throughout his first term. On trade, for example, the administration's preoccupation with the domestic implications of its foreign policy meant that it focused more on how sanctions on China might affect American industry than on the consistency of its trade profile. In responding to the crisis in Bosnia, the administration's concern for public opposition to involvement in the region kept America firmly on the sidelines of the conflict from 1993 to 1995. And other foreign policy challenges—from refugee crises in the Caribbean to political instability in Russia—produced similar inconsistencies in policy. In seeking to be all things to all people, Clinton's foreign policy style actually satisfied very few.

A FRAGILE BALANCE OF SHORT-TERM SUCCESSES

The Clinton administration did achieve some foreign policy victories in the first term, but a close examination of the foreign policy making process reveals the fragile and short-term nature of these achievements.

Defense Policy and Military Strategy for the Post-Cold War Era

Clinton's defense policy record is an example of how the administration's effort to respond to both international and domestic pressures combined to produce policy and doctrinal inconsistency. Three important documents, the *Bottom-Up Review* (BUR), the *National Security Strategy of Engagement and Enlargement,* and the *Quadrennial Defense Review* (QDR), were developed by the administration between 1993 and 1997 to articulate a new American defense strategy. The BUR was conducted during the first seven months of the Clinton presidency and posed basic questions about the criteria for the use of force and military requirements for the new era. Pentagon officials argued through the BUR that the United States must be prepared to respond to many new types of threats to security including "two, nearly simultaneous major regional conflicts (MRCs)," the proliferation of weapons of mass destruction, and challenges to democratic stability and market reforms. Second, the *National Security Strategy of Engagement and Enlargement* was prepared by Lake and released in July 1994. It argued that "the successor to a doctrine of containment must be a strategy of enlargement of the world's free community of market democracies." Like the BUR, this strategy also called for an active, engaged United States to "build a world of security, freedom, democracy, free markets, and growth." And in May 1997, the QDR was released under new Defense Secretary Cohen. Once again, the Pentagon maintained a commitment to the two-MRC strategy and called for relatively modest cuts in force structures worldwide.

The strong internationalist orientation of these statements on defense policy seemed impressive. It was, however, offset by the realities of economic trouble and political challenges at home. At the same time the administration was calling for active engagement in global affairs, it was proposing deep cuts in defense spending and personnel. In 1993, Secretary Aspin's first defense budget request called for $263.7 billion in spending, marking the tenth consecutive year of declining defense budgets, a reduction of defense outlays to the lowest level of annual defense expenditure in seventy years, and a reduction of active duty military strength to 1,526,000 soldiers by 1995. These cuts continued throughout Clinton's first term, leading one critic, William Odom, to argue that the three doctrinal statements were all guilty of "faulty rationalizations for inappropriate force structures." The incompatibility of Clinton's global defense agenda and its deep defense spending cuts was becoming ever more clear.

Administration officials began to confront the fact that allocations would not support full American "engagement" in international security affairs and that, at best, they had articulated a short-term solution to a much deeper problem. In the buildup to the 1994 Congressional elections, administration officials admitted that their defense spending programs were "severely underfunded" and would produce a deficit of as much as $100 billion for budgets from 1996 to 2000. Others warned that the defense plan to fight and win two MRCs would not be possible with a new force structure of only ten Army divisions and twelve Air Force combat wings. When the Republicans gained control of Congress in 1994, they became highly critical of inconsistencies in Clinton defense policy and began pressuring the administration to seek higher appropriations levels and revise its military strategy. In response, Clinton's chairman of the Joint Chiefs of Staff, General Shalikashvili, and Secretary of Defense Perry proposed several short-term spending programs in 1994 that would add $25 billion to the long range defense budget. In 1995, Congress moved to add an additional $20 billion to what the Pentagon requested, and the administration supported the joint defense budget resolution that would increase military expenditures through fiscal year 2000.

Debates over security policy and military spending during the Clinton presidency were testament to the fragile balance between internal and external political pressures. Three successive Defense Secretaries believed that it was imperative to maintain a strong internationalist orientation, but major policy reviews did not produce a plan that matched the orientation to fiscal and political realities. Calls from Republican leaders to increase defense spending after the 1994 elections produced budget increases, but

the administration missed another opportunity in the 1997 QDR to articulate a true defense strategy for the new millennium.

The Development of American Trade Policy

Trade was an area of Clinton foreign policy where success was achieved only after a rocky and problematic start. During the presidential campaign, Clinton had identified the economy as the Bush administration's weak spot and emphasized his own commitment to restore American economic security. For candidate Clinton, this entailed focusing on domestic economic conditions while at the same time attempting to ride the fence on the specifics of trade-related themes such as China policy and the NAFTA during the campaign.

Once in office, Clinton's inconsistency on trade showed through in his nominations for top trade posts and in policy statements. Even though the president claimed to support lower tariff barriers to trade in his first term, he nominated Mickey Kantor to serve as Special U.S. Trade Representative and Ron Brown as Commerce Secretary—neither of whom had any professional trade experience—and Laura Tyson as the Chairperson of the Council of Economic Advisers. Tyson was known as an advocate of a "managed trade" approach that called for increased government intervention in the markets under certain conditions (such as providing special tariffs on imports to encourage consumers to "buy American"). Meanwhile, the new president's election manifesto, *Putting People First,* promised to "stand up for American workers by standing up to countries that don't play by the rules of free and fair trade." This protectionist sentiment played out in the early days of the new administration when the president and his top advisers indelicately challenged countries like Japan, Mexico, and even the European Union on trade matters. In spite of its free trade rhetoric, the administration seemed to view the bilateral trade balance as the most important measure of relations between the United States and others.

From 1993 to 1997, trade relations with China presented a special challenge. While candidate Clinton had pledged that human rights would be a fundamental concern for his presidency and that "he would not hesitate to use American clout to force social change in nations where the United States conducts business," he faced a real dilemma once in office about whether or not to renew China's most-favored-nation (MFN) trade status in light of severe human rights violations in that country. The president was confronted by human rights groups who opposed the special trade status on one side and, on the other, by strong pressure to maintain the growing bilateral trade relationship with China (worth an estimated $40 billion). In May 1994, the internationalist imperative won out when Clinton approved MFN status for China and de-linked human rights concerns there from trade issues. The president justified his action by saying that "the United States should integrate rather than isolate China...[as] the best opportunity to lay the basis for long-term sustainable progress in human rights." This rationale continued to dominate U.S. trade policy toward China into the second term, even though Congressional opposition to the arrangement became much more vocal. In 1997, the Clinton administration once again supported MFN status in spite of Chinese government plans to crackdown on political dissent and democracy in Hong Kong after the 1997 handover from British control. The same presidential candidate who had accused the Bush administration of "coddling dictators" in 1992 had actually intensified U.S.-Chinese relations by 1997.

The MFN decision in the first term seemed to strengthen resolve on the part of the administration to pursue a broader free trade agenda. Soon thereafter, the Clinton administration reached a compromise with other world leaders on the Uruguay Round of negotiations on the General Agreement on Tariffs and Trade (GATT) and formalized the 112-nation agreement in the fall of 1994. Clinton advisers also turned their attention to another initiative carried over from the Bush administration, the NAFTA, which was designed to reduce barriers to trade between the United States, Canada, and Mexico in thousands of product categories by 2009. While the president had publicly endorsed NAFTA during the campaign, he called for specific "side agreements" on labor and environmental issues. Clinton was very sensitive to public uncertainty about the agreement (some public opinion polls showed that more than 60% of Americans were opposed to the plan) and to concerns from specific con-

stituencies of the Democratic party that were opposed to the treaty. Organized labor, for example, feared that the United States would lose jobs to lower-wage areas south of the border, and environmental groups were very concerned about the potential negative environmental impact of the NAFTA.

In this case the president demonstrated leadership on the treaty by creating a bipartisan coalition in support of Senate ratification, and administration efforts were helped along by dramatically improved economic conditions. In the fall of 1994, the president held a highly publicized pro-NAFTA rally at the White House which included several former American presidents and leading economists who supported the treaty. The administration also endeavored to accommodate interest group concerns by confronting them head-on and by promising to address specific concerns in the final draft agreement. Clinton was able to secure ratification of NAFTA in the Senate in December 1994, and a few weeks later the president used that momentum to propose a free trade zone for the entire western hemisphere at the Summit of the Americas. By 1997, the economy was in high gear, and the administration sought special authority from Congress to negotiate a broader Free Trade Area of the Americas (FTAA).

Responding to Regional Crises: Bosnia Policy

The Dayton Peace Agreement in November 1995 ended the civil war in the former Yugoslavia, and it was touted as a major foreign policy success for the Clinton administration. Indeed, the treaty did stop the war in the Balkans, end the genocide, save face for the UN peace mission there, and forestall mass migration and refugee crises. But once again, this success can best be characterized as a short-term solution that came about only after four years of inconsistency, vacillation, and double-takes in U.S. foreign policy toward the region.

When the civil war began in June 1991, the Bush administration attempted to distance itself from the situation by supporting a unified Yugoslavia and labeling the crisis a "European problem." Candidate Clinton seized on this inaction during the 1992 campaign and tried to trump the president by pledging that the United States should support the United Nations in "doing whatever it takes to stop the slaughter of civilians." Clinton promised to lift the arms embargo on Bosnia and to conduct airstrikes on Bosnian Serb artillery positions if necessary. Once in office, however, the president's internationalist orientation toward the crisis was supplanted by domestic pressures to avoid entanglement in the Balkans. The president articulated his new "lift and strike" formula—a plan to lift the arms embargo on Bosnia and carry out airstrikes against Bosnian Serb targets—but the idea soon fell victim to resistance from the military, Congressional leaders, the American public, and European allies. Outspoken critics also warned that any ground deployment of U.S. troops could become another Vietnam. Administration officials like Undersecretary of State Peter Tarnoff even suggested that non-involvement in the war in Bosnia would exemplify U.S. foreign policy in the post-Cold War era because "we certainly don't have the money" to address all international crises. While Clinton dismissed this characterization as inaccurate, American foreign policy toward the crisis was quite reserved from 1993 to 1995.

A special combination of developments and personalities finally brought needed relief and short-term success to the Clinton administration's Balkan policy in 1995. In the spring, Jacques Chirac, the new Gaullist president of France, pushed for a tougher Western position to conduct airstrikes against Bosnian Serb targets. Croatian and Muslim military advances in the region soon thereafter also put pressure on the Serbs to enter into negotiations to attain the best possible settlement of the situation. And in July, the Senate voted by a wide margin to abandon American participation in the UN arms embargo against the former Yugoslav republics and threatened to engage the United States in support of Bosnia. The president faced external and internal pressures to try to take the lead in forcing a peaceful settlement to the crisis. This time, a more assertive president, a doggedly persistent Assistant Secretary of State Richard Holbrooke, a confident Croatian President Franjo Tudjman, and a chastened Serbian President Slobodan Milosevic (representing the Bosnian Serbs) all came together in Dayton, Ohio, to negotiate an end to the conflict in the Balkans.

To support the implementation of the Dayton agreements, a NATO-led Implementation Force (IFOR) peace operation was established in the former Yugoslavia. IFOR would ensure stability in the region while all the political, social, and economic arrangements for peace in the Balkans were finalized. President Clinton ordered the deployment of 20,000 U.S. soldiers to IFOR and pledged that they would only be in the Balkans for one year. While the IFOR deployment throughout 1996 was successful, it was clear by the time of the November elections that the political foundations for peace in that region were not yet established. Soon after Clinton's election victory, administration officials announced that U.S. soldiers would stay there for another eighteen months.

There are an increasing number of signs that peace in the Balkans may be short-lived. For example, the Dayton agreements called for a temporary partition of Bosnia and the creation of political power-sharing arrangements, but post-conflict zones of occupation have condensed into long-term arrangements allowing the continued displacement of hundreds of thousands of civilians. There are doubts about compliance with all parts of the Dayton agreements in these zones, and military training continues for all factions (with some groups being aided by retired U.S. military officers). The very act of extension of the IFOR commitment was a sign that political and economic restructuring in the Balkans was going excruciatingly slowly. In early 1997, Clinton even suggested that U.S. troops might have to stay on beyond the summer of 1998, continuing to maintain the fragile peace in the region until the end of the decade.

Other Foreign Policy Challenges

The characteristics of the Clinton record noted above apply to a wide range of other concerns on the U.S. foreign policy agenda. At the global level, U.S. relations with the United Nations were quite inconsistent in the first Clinton administration—again reflecting efforts to balance internal and external pressures to secure short-term solutions to foreign policy problems. Once a supporter of "empowering" the UN to conduct more assertive peacekeeping and peace-making missions, the Clinton administration had to reverse course in 1993 after an attack on U.S. soldiers in the Somalia operation produced popular disillusionment with (and heavy Congressional opposition to) such undertakings. U.S.-UN relations worsened significantly between 1994 and 1997. This was evidenced by a series of developments including the release of Presidential Directive #25 (which tightly circumscribed future U.S. involvement in peacekeeping operations), the refusal of the U.S. government to pay $1.5 billion in back dues to the UN, reluctance to support peace missions to Central Africa, and increasingly harsh demands for deep structural reform of the organization. This decay in relations was punctuated by President Clinton's announcement in June 1996 that the U.S. would not support a second term for UN Secretary General Boutros Boutros-Ghali, a direct response to domestic pressures in an election year. Another sign of changing priorities in this area was the steady decrease in U.S. foreign assistance to less developed countries during Clinton's first term. In 1997, the U.S. government devoted less than .1% of its gross national product to overseas development assistance, falling far behind most other advanced industrialized nations.

At the regional level, U.S. relations with Latin American countries have also been problematic. In 1994, Clinton ordered that Cuban refugees flocking to the U.S. across the Florida Straits be held in detention camps instead of being granted immediate asylum—a reversal of long standing policy. But heavy pressure from the Cuban-American lobby soon forced the president to reverse this reversal and allow the Cuban refugees into the country. In early 1996, just as some administration officials were warming to the idea of improved ties with Cuba, two civilian planes flown by Cuban-Americans were shot down by Cuban fighters, provoking public outrage. The Clinton administration quickly condemned the attack, tightened sanctions against Cuba, and backed away from all efforts to normalize relations. In an extreme effort to balance internal and external pressures, Clinton even supported the Helms-Burton Act, a Republican initiative that allows private citizens to sue companies doing business in Cuba with nationalized assets. In this case, regional policy seemed to be dictated by the actions of a few private citizens and conservative pressure in Congress,

rather than a comprehensive strategy for U.S.-Latin American relations.

CONCLUSION

President Clinton's strategy for success in the 1996 election hinged on his short-term foreign policy achievements abroad and economic stability at home. But this remained an electoral strategy—not a Clinton Doctrine which set out consistent policy goals for the future. While some notable foreign policy successes have emerged in the second term, including the completion of a global Comprehensive Nuclear Test Ban Treaty and the NATO expansion deal with Russia, there is little evidence to suggest that a new grand strategy will arise in the 1990s.

Meanwhile, the foreign policy troubles of the first term can be attributed to an inherent contradiction in the Clinton administration between internationalist and isolationist foreign policy pressures and between ends and means. If the president intends to do more than ride out the millennium on short-term foreign policy successes, he and his new advisers must reflect on first term experience. They must move beyond a bottom-up calculation of domestic pressures, and articulate a clear, focused set of national interests to guide American foreign policy strongly into the 21st century.

FOOD FOR THOUGHT

1. What are the fundamental differences in the conceptions of the scope of presidential power offered by Presidents Taft and Roosevelt? Which view of the presidency is most appropriate for governance in contemporary American politics? Why?

2. Richard Neustadt characterizes presidential power as the power to persuade. Utilizing an example of a policy issue faced by the current administration, how effectively has the president exercised this power and utilized his vantage points?

3. Thomas Cronin argues that while the paradoxes of the presidency are ultimately irreconcilable, presidents may, with different levels of success, learn to coexist with and manage them. Compare and contrast the manner in which two different presidents have

handled the presidential paradoxes. How would Charles Jones characterize President Clinton's effect on the expectations the paradoxes of the presidency create?

4. Charles Jones offers the reader a unitarian and separationist model of American government. What are the differences between them? Which is a preferable model for American governance? Why?

CHAPTER 11

BUREAUCRACY

Bureaucracy does the day-to-day work of the federal government. Bureaucratic agencies and their employees are the central players in the implementation of government programs. They also play key roles in the development of legislative proposals and in the evaluation of program results. They are the chosen instrument for addressing most matters defined to be part of the public's business. They administer programs that are large, complex, and serve a wide range of substantive purposes.

Over the course of the nation's history the size and scope of bureaucratic responsibility have increased. There were large bursts of growth triggered by major national crises, especially World War I, the Great Depression of the 1930s, and World War II. Industrialization and the growing political commitment to activist government also propelled major growth. However, federal employment as a percentage of the total labor force has been going down in recent years.

As the scope of government activity has expanded and/or shifted in focus, different types of agencies were created and added to the total bureaucratic mix. From its inception in 1789 to the late 19th century the federal government was principally committed to internal improvements and development of resources through encouraging and subsidizing certain kinds of private activities. It created bureaucracies devoted to those ends, such as the Department of Agriculture and the Department of the Interior. Beginning in the late 19th century the federal government evinced more interest in regulating private behavior. It created agencies appropriate for working in the regulatory arena, such as the Interstate Commerce Commission and, later, the Food and Drug Administration, the Federal Trade Commission, the Federal Aviation Agency, and the Environmental Protection Agency. In the 1930s the federal government became intent on

creating and/or refining various social welfare functions and created yet another set of agencies, such as the Social Security Administration, the Department of Health and Human Services, the Department of Housing and Urban Development, and the Department of Education.

Bureaucracies with different programmatic aims also had different growth dynamics. James Wilson, in "The Rise of the Bureaucratic State," the first reading in this chapter, identifies different patterns of growth among what he calls service bureaucracies (e.g., the postal service and the military establishment), clientele-oriented bureaucracies (e.g., the Department of Agriculture), and regulatory bureaucracies (e.g., the Food and Drug Administration).

Do elected officials—both the president and members of Congress—control the bureaucracy? Along with the expansion of activities, responsibilities, and programs on the part of the federal government over time, Congress has delegated more power to the bureaucracies. The independent, discretionary power of bureaucrats has grown.

Presidential appointees to bureaucratic positions (for example, department secretaries, undersecretaries, and assistant secretaries) are formally identified as political officials. Presidents hope they can rely on them to carry out presidential policy preferences and exercise control over the bureaucracy. However, many of them have their substantive and political agendas, their own connections with senators and representatives, and their own ties with powerful figures in the private sector.

The larger problem for presidents, however, is that their appointees can be overwhelmed by their reliance on long-time career bureaucrats. Many presidential appointees, both at the cabinet and subcabinet level, become captives of the bureaucracies they are supposed to manage in accord with the policy preferences of the White House.

In short, presidents cannot rely solely on their own appointees to high-ranking bureaucratic positions to effect change. These appointees may not be totally reliable. And they are short-timers who have to deal with politically active long-timers with civil service tenure. The second reading in this chapter, "Executive Politics in Washington" by Hugh Heclo, explores the behavior and political standing of presidential appointees in federal agencies in Washington.

American career bureaucrats, especially at the middle and senior levels, are heavily engaged in the political process. They are not simply neutral implementers of programs designed and mandated by others. They build alliances with other bureaucrats, political officials, members and staff members in Congress, and representatives of various interest groups in pursuing preferred policy options. The third reading in the present chapter, "In Search of a Role: America's Higher Civil Service," also by Heclo, makes clear that the United States is unusual among the developed, industrialized, democratic nations in viewing a politically active senior bureaucracy as normal. There is no senior civil service with a tradition of political neutrality. The highest level civil servants generally pursue careers in single agencies and build enduring ties with members of Congress and interest groups. Presidents and secretaries come and go. The personal political beliefs of bureaucrats, as well as their pursuit of personal and agency interests, help shape both the formulation and implementation of policy.

Bureaucracy is often portrayed as unchanging. That is inaccurate. Some incremental, cyclical change is predictable, although slow. Bureaucratic resistance to planned substantial change is usually strong. The resistance comes not just from the bureaucrats but also from their friends and allies in Congress and the private sector who have well-established working relationships they do not want to see disturbed.

One source of opposition to change in any mature organization, including governmental bureaucracies, is based on the dominant culture in the organization. In this case, *culture* refers simply to "the way things get done around here." The senior career members of the organization typically believe in the culture, may have helped create it, and help perpetuate it by socializing new members of the organization. The fourth reading in this chapter, "The C.I.A.'s Most Important Mission: Itself" by Tim Weiner, deals specifically with a case of the dominant culture of a specific organization, the Central Intelligence Agency, being challenged by the formal leader of that organization, a new Director in 1995.

Change occurs in the structure of American bureaucracy over time in several different ways. First, federal agencies come and go. The image of an unchanging federal bureaucracy at the gross organizational level is inaccurate.

Second, even in agencies that persist in recognizable form, internal change is constant, even if not always rapid or dramatic.

Third, changes in bureaucracy often stem, at least in part, from the actions of external agents. Public bureaucracies are particularly dependent on others (especially the president, institutional presidency, and Congress) for resources to operate. Change in a specific bureaucracy is often initiated or inhibited by these external agents.

These agents themselves, of course, will presumably be aware of major changes in the external system that may require major policy and program changes. But the general treatments of bureaucratic politics typically do not examine major changes in the external system. Treatments of bureaucracy and policy often have an inbuilt incrementalist bias that assumes that all changes will be modest in size and slow to evolve. That situation is, no doubt, most likely most of the time. But it is not necessarily universal and unchanging.

Fourth, the nature of external environmental change, although occurring over a period of time, promotes bureaucratic change. Even if a specific bureaucracy favors a fairly dramatic course of changed policy in response to external environment, its immediate environment of other actors may not foster or permit such change. In other cases a bureaucracy completely opposed to policy change may be pushed into at least some change by other actors who perceive dramatically altered external circumstances that require new policy responses.

There is constant interaction between Congress and the bureaucracy in policy formulation and also in policy implementation. These help determine the details of a great deal of policy through the processes of formulating legislative alternatives, choosing one of them for formal adoption, and implementing the program or programs based on the legislation. Congress does not treat all agencies the same.

The final reading in the chapter, "Bureaucratic–Congressional Relations: Separate Institutions, Shared Powers" by Randall Ripley and Grace Franklin, explores three major aspects of the relationship between Congress and the bureaucracy: conflict and cooperation over policy, the delegation of authority from Congress to the bureaucracy, and congressional oversight of the performance of the bureaucracy.

How does the public view bureaucracy? People often condemn the bureaucracy in general but are pleased with their personal interactions with bureaucrats.

On the basis of evidence from public opinion surveys, it is clear that the general public has little confidence in bureaucracy, although it is usually more highly regarded than Congress.

Surveys reveal a public stereotype of bureaucrats as inefficient, lazy, overpaid, incompetent, and unethical. The electoral campaigns of a large number of politicians, including presidents Nixon, Carter, and Reagan, have reinforced the stereotype. Some mass media have also reinforced this negative image.

What are the consequences of negative public opinion about bureaucracies and bureaucrats? Low confidence in bureaucracies enhances the public's natural tendency to oppose taxes, even though the demand for services is undiminished by such negative attitudes. Attacks on the bureaucracy also make recruiting and retaining employees of high quality more difficult.

The link between public opinion and specific actions or decisions by bureaucrats is much more difficult to pinpoint. The links are probably indirect. Public opinion influences bureaucracies through pressure placed on them by interest groups, the media, legislatures, and the White House (president and staff) rather than directly. Public opinion is mediated by these other institutions. Short-term, intense public

reaction to controversy may also affect a bureaucratic decision more directly or be instrumental in the establishment, abolition, or modification of a program.

READING 51

The Rise of the Bureaucratic State
James Q. Wilson

The essay from which this selection is taken both describes "the rise of the bureaucratic state" in the United States and, from a conservative perspective, criticizes the particular form of it that has evolved. Wilson offers a capsule history of the growth of American federal bureaucracy since the beginning of the republic to the mid-1970s. More importantly, he explores the reasons behind different kinds of growth, particularly since the Civil War, and offers an analysis of the relationship of the bureaucracy to our political system in broader terms.

It should be noted that in the years since Wilson, a political scientist at the University of California at Los Angeles, wrote this piece the federal bureaucracy has shrunk in terms of its relationship to the size of the total population. That is, a smaller proportion of the workforce is in the federal bureaucracy now than several decades ago. This fact alone, however, does not alter Wilson's argument that our bureaucracies are client-dominated.

Politicians of both major parties have encouraged shrinkage of the bureaucracy in comparison to the size of the population. In general, Republicans are more devoted to the effort than Democrats. Republicans tend to be relatively suspicious of government because, in the view of many of them, it puts unnecessary restrictions on the private sector and, therefore, hampers economic

From "The Rise of the Bureaucratic State" by J. Q. Wilson, 1975. Reprinted with permission of the author from: *The Public Interest*, No. 41 (Fall, 1975), pp. 77–103. © 1975 by National Affairs, Inc.

growth. In general, Democrats are more likely to view governmental programs positively and, therefore, are less likely to be automatically suspicious of bureaucracy.

Three broad issues Wilson raises during the course of his essay are worth particular attention. First, is a large bureaucracy that has considerable independent power compatible with a Madisonian political system, a system he defines in the text?

Second, Wilson's concern is not simply with size of bureaucracy, an issue that politicians usually raise in simpleminded terms. Rather, it is the independent power of bureaucracy—especially when it is realized that that power is enhanced by the linkage of bureaucracy with Congress and interest groups—that concerns him. He would not object to a large bureaucracy if it were clearly controlled and accountable.

Third, he carefully analyzes the differing dynamics of growth of bureaucracies serving different major functions: general service functions, service to identified clienteles, and general regulatory functions.

THE "BUREAUCRACY PROBLEM"

The original departments were small and had limited duties. The State Department, the first to be created, had but nine employees in addition to the Secretary. The War Department did not reach 80 civilian employees until 1801; it commanded only a few thousand soldiers. Only the Treasury Department had substantial powers—it collected taxes, managed the public debt, ran the national bank, conducted land surveys, and purchased military supplies. Because of this, Congress gave the closest scrutiny to its structure and its activities.

The number of administrative agencies and employees grew slowly but steadily during the 19th and early 20th centuries and then increased explosively on the occasion of World War I, the Depression, and World War II. It is difficult to say at what point in this process the administrative system became a distinct locus of power or an independent source of political initiatives and problems....

BUREAUCRACY AND SIZE

During the first half of the 19th century, the growth in the size of the federal bureaucracy can be explained, not by the assumption of new tasks by the government or by the imperialistic designs of the managers of existing tasks but by the addition to existing bureaus of personnel performing essentially routine, repetitive tasks for which the public demand was great and unavoidable. The principal problem facing a bureaucracy thus enlarged was how best to coordinate its activities toward given and noncontroversial ends.

The increase in the size of the executive branch of the federal government at this time was almost entirely the result of the increase in the size of the Post Office....

THE MILITARY ESTABLISHMENT

Not all large bureaucracies grow in response to demands for service. The Department of Defense, since 1941 the largest employer of federal civilian officials, has become, as the governmental keystone of the "military-industrial complex," the very archetype of an administrative entity that is thought to be so vast and so well-entrenched that it can virtually ignore the political branches of government, growing and even acting on the basis of its own inner imperatives. In fact, until recently the military services were a major economic and political force only during wartime....

A "MILITARY-INDUSTRIAL COMPLEX"?

The argument for the existence of an autonomous, bureaucratically-led military-industrial complex is supported primarily by events since 1950. Not only has the United States assumed during this period world-wide commitments that necessitate a larger military establishment, but the advent of new, high-technology weapons has created a vast industrial machine with an interest in sustaining a high level of military expenditures, especially on weapons research, development, and acquisition....

The bureaucratic problems associated with the military establishment arise mostly from its internal management and are functions of its complexity, the uncertainty surrounding its future deployment, conflicts among its constituent services over mission and role, and the need to purchase expensive equipment without the benefit of a market economy that can control costs. Complexity, uncertainty, rivalry, and monopsony are inherent (and frustrating) aspects of the military as a bureaucracy, but they are very different problems from those typically associated with the phrase, "the military-industrial complex." The size and budget of the military are matters wholly within the power of civilian authorities to decide—indeed, the military budget contains the largest discretionary items in the entire federal budget....

BUREAUCRACY AND CLIENTELISM

After 1861, the growth in the federal administrative system could no longer be explained primarily by an expansion of the postal service and other traditional bureaus. Though these continued to expand, new departments were added that reflected a new (or at least greater) emphasis on the enlargement of the scope of government. Between 1861 and 1901, over 200,000 civilian employees were added to the federal service, only 52 per cent of whom were postal workers. Some of these, of course, staffed a larger military and naval establishment stimulated by the Civil War and the Spanish-American War. By 1901 there were over 44,000 civilian defense employees, mostly workers in government-owned arsenals and shipyards. But even these could account for less than one fourth of the increase in employment during the preceding 40 years.

What was striking about the period after 1861 was that the government began to give formal, bureaucratic recognition to the emergence of distinctive interests in a diversifying economy....

The original purpose behind these clientele-oriented departments was neither to subsidize nor to regulate, but to promote, chiefly by gathering and publishing statistics and (especially in the case of agriculture) by research. The formation of the Department of Agriculture in 1862 was to become a model, for better or worse, for later political campaigns for

government recognition. A private association representing an interest—in this case the United States Agricultural Society—was formed. It made every President from Fillmore to Lincoln an honorary member, it enrolled key Congressmen, and it began to lobby for a new department. The precedent was followed by labor groups, especially the Knights of Labor, to secure creation in 1888 of a Department of Labor. It was broadened in 1903 to be a Department of Commerce and Labor, but 10 years later, at the insistence of the American Federation of Labor, the parts were separated and the two departments we now know were formed.

There was an early 19th-century precedent for the creation of these client-serving departments: the Pension Office, then in the Department of the Interior. Begun in 1833 and regularized in 1849, the Office became one of the largest bureaus of the government in the aftermath of the Civil War....

PUBLIC POWER AND PRIVATE INTERESTS

It was at the state level, however, that client-oriented bureaucracies proliferated in the 19th century. Chief among these were the occupational licensing agencies....

The New Deal was perhaps the high water mark of at least the theory of bureaucratic clientelism. Not only did various sectors of society, notably agriculture, begin receiving massive subsidies, but the government proposed, through the National Industrial Recovery Act (NRA), to cloak with public power a vast number of industrial groupings and trade associations so that they might control production and prices in ways that would end the depression. The NRA's Blue Eagle fell before the Supreme Court— the wholesale delegation of public power to private interests was declared unconstitutional. But the piecemeal delegation was not, as the continued growth of specialized promotional agencies attests. The Civil Aeronautics Board, for example, erroneously thought to be exclusively a regulatory agency, was formed in 1938 "to promote" as well as to regulate civil aviation and it has done so by restricting entry and maintaining above-market rate fares.

Agriculture, of course, provides the leading case of clientelism. Theodore J. Lowi finds "at least 10 separate, autonomous, local self-governing systems" located in or closely associated with the Department of Agriculture that control to some significant degree the flow of billions of dollars in expenditures and loans. Local committees of farmers, private farm organizations, agency heads, and committee chairmen in Congress dominate policy-making in this area—not, perhaps, to the exclusion of the concerns of other publics, but certainly in ways not powerfully constrained by them.

"COOPERATIVE FEDERALISM"

The growing edge of client-oriented bureaucracy can be found, however, not in government relations with private groups, but in the relations among governmental units. In dollar volume, the chief clients of federal domestic expenditures are state and local government agencies. . . .

SELF-PERPETUATING AGENCIES

If the Founding Fathers were to return to examine bureaucratic clientelism, they would, I suspect, be deeply discouraged. James Madison clearly foresaw that American society would be "broken into many parts, interests and classes of citizens" and that this "multiplicity of interests" would help ensure against "the tyranny of the majority," especially in a federal regime with separate branches of government. Positive action would require a "coalition of a majority"; in the process of forming this coalition, the rights of all would be protected, not merely by self-interested bargains, but because in a free society such a coalition "could seldom take place on any other principles than those of justice and the general good." To those who wrongly believed that Madison thought of men as acting only out of base motives, the phrase is instructive: Persuading men who disagree to compromise their differences can rarely be achieved solely by the parceling out of relative advantage; the belief is also required that what is being agree[d] to is right, proper, and defensible before public opinion.

Most of the major new social programs of the United States, whether for the good of the few or the many, were initially adopted by broad coalitions appealing to general standards of justice or to conceptions of the public weal. This is certainly the case with most of the New Deal legislation—notably such programs as Social Security—and with most Great Society legislation—notably Medicare and aid to education; it was also conspicuously the case with respect to post-Great Society legislation pertaining to consumer and environmental concerns. State occupational licensing laws were supported by majorities interested in, among other things, the contribution of these statutes to public safety and health.

But when a program supplies particular benefits to an existing or newly-created interest, public or private, it creates a set of political relationships that make exceptionally difficult further alteration of that program by coalitions of the majority. What was created in the name of the common good is sustained in the name of the particular interest. Bureaucratic clientelism becomes self-perpetuating, in the absence of some crisis or scandal, because a single interest group to which the program matters greatly is highly motivated and well-situated to ward off the criticisms of other groups that have a broad but weak interest in the policy.

In short, a regime of separated powers makes it difficult to overcome objections and contrary interests sufficiently to permit the enactment of a new program or the creation of a new agency. Unless the legislation can be made to pass either with little notice or at a time of crisis or extraordinary majorities—and sometimes even then—the initiation of new programs requires public interest arguments. But the same regime works to protect agencies, once created, from unwelcome change because a major change is, in effect, new legislation that must overcome the same hurdles as the original law, but this time with one of the hurdles—the wishes of the agency and its client—raised much higher. As a result, the Madisonian system makes it relatively easy for the delegation of public power to private groups to go unchallenged and, therefore, for factional interests that have acquired a supportive public bureaucracy to rule without submitting their interests to the effective scrutiny and modification of other interests.

BUREAUCRACY AND DISCRETION

For many decades, the Supreme Court denied to the federal government any general "police power" over occupations and businesses, and thus most such regulation occurred at the state level and even there under the constraint that it must not violate the notion of "substantive due process"—that is, the view that there were sharp limits to the power of any government to take (and therefore to regulate) property. What clearly was within the regulatory province of the federal government was interstate commerce, and thus it is not surprising that the first major federal regulatory body should be the Interstate Commerce Commission (ICC), created in 1887....

REGULATION VERSUS PROMOTION

It was the ICC and agencies and commissions for which it was the precedent that became the principal example of federal discretionary authority. It is important, however, to be clear about just what this precedent was. Not everything we now call a regulatory agency was in fact intended to be one. The ICC, the Antitrust Division of the Justice Department, the Federal Trade Commission (FTC), the Food and Drug Administration (FDA), the National Labor Relations Board (NRLB)—all these were intended to be genuinely regulatory bodies created to handle under public auspices matters once left to private arrangements. The techniques they were to employ varied: approving rates (ICC), issuing cease-and-desist orders (FTC), bringing civil or criminal actions in the courts (the Antitrust Division), defining after a hearing an appropriate standard of conduct (NRLB), or testing a product for safety (FDA). In each case, however, Congress clearly intended that the agency either define its own standards (a safe drug, a conspiracy in restraint of trade, a fair labor practice) or choose among competing claims (a higher or lower rate for shipping grain).

Other agencies often grouped with these regulatory bodies—the Civil Aeronautics Board, the Federal Communications Commission, the Maritime Commission—were designed, however, not primarily to regulate, but to promote the development of various infant or threatened industries. However, unlike fostering agriculture or commerce, fostering civil aviation or radio broadcasting was thought to require limiting entry (to prevent "unsafe" aviation or broadcast interference); but at the time these laws were passed few believed that the restrictions on entry would be many, or that the choices would be made on any but technical or otherwise noncontroversial criteria. We smile now at their naïveté, but we continue to share it—today we sometimes suppose that choosing an approved exhaust emission control system or a water pollution control system can be done on the basis of technical criteria and without affecting production and employment.

MAJORITARIAN POLITICS

The creation of regulatory bureaucracies has occurred, as is often remarked, in waves. The first was the period between 1887 and 1890 (the Commerce Act and the Antitrust Act), the second between 1905 and 1915 (the Pure Food and Drug Act, the Meat Act, the Federal Trade Commission Act, the Clayton Act), the third during the 1930's (the Food, Drug, and Cosmetic Act, the Public Utility Holding Company Act, the Securities Exchange Act, the Natural Gas Act, the National Labor Relations Act), and the fourth during the latter part of the 1960's (the Water Quality Act, the Truth in Lending Act, the National Traffic and Motor Vehicle Safety Act, various amendments to the drug laws, the Motor Vehicle Pollution Control Act, and many others).

Each of these periods was characterized by progressive or liberal Presidents in office (Cleveland, T. R. Roosevelt, Wilson, F. D. Roosevelt, Johnson): one was a period of national crisis (the 1930's); three were periods when the President enjoyed extraordinary majorities of his own party in both houses of Congress (1914–1916, 1932–1940, and 1964–1968); and only the first period preceded the emergence of the national mass media of communication. These facts are important because of the special difficulty of passing any genuinely regulatory legislation: A single interest, the regulated party, sees itself seriously threatened by a law proposed by a policy entrepreneur who must appeal to an unorganized majority, the members of which may not expect to be substantially or directly benefitted by the law. Without special political circumstances—a crisis, a scandal, extraordinary majorities, an especially vigorous President, the support of media—the normal barriers to legislative innovation (i.e.. to the formation of a "coalition of the majority") may prove insuperable.

Stated another way, the initiation of regulatory programs tends to take the form of majoritarian rather than coalitional politics. The Madisonian system is placed in temporary suspense: Exceptional majorities propelled by a public mood and led by a skillful policy entrepreneur take action that might not be possible under ordinary circumstances (closely divided parties, legislative-executive checks and balances, popular indifference). The consequence of majoritarian politics for the administration of regulatory bureaucracies is great. To initiate and sustain the necessary legislative mood, strong, moralistic, and sometimes ideological appeals are necessary—leading, in turn, to the granting of broad mandates of power to the new agency (a modest delegation of authority would obviously be inadequate if the problem to be resolved is of crisis proportions), or to the specifying of exacting standards to be enforced (e.g., *no* carcinogenic products may be sold, 95 per cent of the pollutants must be eliminated), or to both.

Either in applying a vague but broad rule ("the public interest, convenience, and necessity") or in enforcing a clear and strict standard, the regulatory agency will tend to broaden the range and domain of its authority, to lag behind technological and economic change, to resist deregulation, to stimulate corruption, and to contribute to the bureaucratization of private institutions.

It will broaden its regulatory reach out of a variety of motives: to satisfy the demand of the regulated enterprise that it be protected from competition, to make effective the initial regulatory action by attending to the unanticipated side effects of that action, to discover or stretch the meaning of vague statutory language, or to respond to new constituencies induced by the existence of the agency to convert what were once private demands into public pressures. For example, the Civil Aeronautics Board, out of a desire both to promote aviation and to protect the regulated price structure of the industry, will resist the entry into the industry of new carriers. If a Public Utilities Commission sets rates too low for a certain class of customers, the utility will allow service to those customers to decline in quality, leading in turn to a demand that the Commission also regulate the quality of service. If the Federal Communications Commission cannot decide who should receive a broadcast license by applying the "public interest" standard, it will be powerfully tempted to invest that phrase with whatever preferences the majority of the Commission then entertains, leading in turn to the exercise of control over many more aspects of broadcasting than merely signal interference—all in the name of deciding what the standard for entry shall be. If the Antitrust Division can prosecute conspiracies in restraint of trade, it will attract to itself the complaints of various firms about business practices that are neither conspiratorial nor restraining but merely competitive, and a "vigorous" antitrust lawyer may conclude that these practices warrant prosecution....

THE BUREAUCRATIC STATE AND THE REVOLUTION

The American Revolution was not only a struggle for independence but a fundamental rethinking of the nature of political authority. Indeed, until that reformulation was completed the Revolution was not finished. What made political authority problematic for the colonists was the extent to which they believed Mother England had subverted their liberties despite the protection of the British constitution, until then widely regarded in America as the most perfect set of governing arrangements yet devised. The evidence of usurpation is now familiar: unjust taxation, the weakening of the independence of the judiciary, the stationing of standing armies, and the extensive use of royal patronage to reward office-seekers at colonial expense. Except for the issue of taxation, which raised for the colonists major questions of representation, almost all of their complaints involved the abuse of *administrative* powers.

The first solution proposed by Americans to remedy this abuse was the vesting of most (or, in the case of Pennsylvania and a few other states, virtually all) powers in the legislature. But the events after 1776 in many colonies, notably Pennsylvania, convinced the most thoughtful citizens that legislative abuses were as likely as administrative ones: In the extreme case, citizens would suffer from the "tyranny of the majority." Their solution to this problem was, of course, the theory of the separation of powers by which, as brilliantly argued in *The Federalist* papers, each branch of government would check the likely usurpations of the other.

This formulation went essentially unchallenged in theory and unmodified by practice for over a century. Though a sizeable administrative apparatus had come into being by the end of the 19th century, it constituted no serious threat to the existing distribution of political power because it either performed routine tasks (the Post Office) or dealt with temporary crises (the military). Some agencies wielding discretionary authority existed, but they either dealt with groups whose liberties were not of much concern (the Indian Office) or their exercise of discretion was minutely scrutinized by Congress (the Land Office, the Pension Office, the Customs Office). The major discretionary agencies of the 19th century flourished at the very period of greatest Congressional domination of the political process—the decades after the Civil War—and thus, though their supervision was typically inefficient and sometimes corrupt, these agencies were for most practical purposes direct dependencies of Congress. In short, their existence did not call into question the theory of the separation of powers.

But with the growth of client-serving and regulatory agencies, grave questions began to be raised—usually implicitly—about that theory. A client-serving bureau, because of its relations with some source of private power, could become partially independent of both the executive and legislative branches—or in the case of the latter, dependent upon certain committees and independent of others and of the views of the Congress as a whole. A regulatory agency (that is to say, a truly regulatory one and not a clientelist or promotional agency hiding behind a regulatory fig leaf) was, in the typical case, placed formally outside the existing branches of government. Indeed, they were called "independent" or "quasi-judicial" agencies (they might as well have been called "quasi-executive" or "quasi-legislative") and thus the special status that clientelist bureaus achieved *de facto*, the regulatory ones achieved *de jure*.

It is, of course, inadequate and misleading to criticize these agencies, as has often been done, merely because they raise questions about the problem of sovereignty. The crucial test of their value is their behavior, and that can be judged only by applying economic and welfare criteria to the policies they produce. But if such judgments should prove damning, as increasingly has been the case, then the problem of finding the authority with which to alter or abolish such organizations becomes acute. In this regard the theory of the separation of powers has proved unhelpful.

The separation of powers makes difficult, in ordinary times, the extension of public power over private conduct—as a nation, we came more slowly to the welfare state than almost any European nation, and we still engage in less central planning and operate fewer nationalized industries than other democratic regimes. But we have extended the regulatory sway of our national government as far or farther than that of most other liberal regimes (our environmental and safety codes are now models for much of Europe), and the bureaus wielding these discretionary powers are, once created, harder to change or redirect than would be the case if authority were more centralized.

The shift of power toward the bureaucracy was not inevitable. It did not result simply from increased specialization, the growth of industry, or the imperialistic designs of the bureaus themselves. Before the second decade of this century, there was no federal bureaucracy wielding substantial discretionary powers. That we have one now is the result of political decisions made by elected representatives. Fifty years ago, the people often wanted more of government than it was willing to provide—it was, in that sense, a republican government in which representatives moderated popular demands. Today, not only does political action follow quickly upon the stimulus of public interest, but government itself creates that stimulus and sometimes acts in advance of it.

All democratic regimes tend to shift resources from the private to the public sector and to enlarge the size of the administrative component of government. The particularistic and localistic nature of American democracy has created a particularistic and client-serving administration. If our bureaucracy often serves special interests and is subject to no central direction, it is because our legislature often serves special interests and is subject to no central leadership. For Congress to complain of what it has created and it maintains is, to be charitable, misleading. Congress could change what it has devised, but there is little reason to suppose it will.

READING 52

Executive Politics in Washington

Hugh Heclo

This selection comes from two different chapters of George Mason University political scientist Hugh Heclo's book, A Government of Strangers. *The book is an examination of presidential appointees at policymaking levels throughout the executive branch: who they are, where they come from, how they behave, and, above all, how they fit into Washington politics. Those politics, of course, help determine what kinds of policies and programs emerge from the federal government. The title Heclo chose for his book encapsulates the general picture he paints: These political executives, of whom there are about 700 in the entire executive branch, are "strangers" in two senses.*

First, they do not know each other. The president personally knows only a few of them, although he appoints them and, necessarily, has to rely on them in many ways. Throughout their

From "Executive Politics in Washington" by Hugh Heclo, 1977. *A Government of Strangers: Executive Politics in Washington*, by H. Heclo. Copyright © 1977 by the Brookings Institution. Reprinted by permission.

typically short stays in Washington, usually between two and three years, they remain strangers to each other and to the president.

Second, and more important, they are also strangers to the layers of political institutions and individuals with which and with whom they must interact in conducting their daily business. They are especially uninformed about and unacquainted with Congress. To a somewhat lesser extent, they are also strangers to the web of interest groups that have an important impact on the policies of whatever agency employs them.

The situation portrayed by Heclo, even though his book appeared at the beginning of the Carter administration in 1977, has not changed fundamentally. Reagan and his top advisers were more insistent on loyal and aggressive "strangers" than were their predecessors. The Reagan administration had considerably greater success than previous administrations in using "strangers" to achieve a high degree of administrative control over many agencies. The zeal for control weakened late in the Reagan years, however. The effort to achieve greater central control through "strangers" returned to pre-Reagan levels during the Bush and Clinton Administrations.

POLITICAL EXECUTIVES

To speak of political appointees in Washington is obviously to embrace a wide variety of people and situations. Political appointments cover everything from the temporary file clerk recouping a campaign obligation to the cabinet secretary heading a department organization larger than many state governments or the national administrations of some foreign countries. . . .

The Political Executive System

From the outset political executives share one broad feature; all hold an ambivalent leadership position in what might loosely be termed the American "system" of public executives. To appreciate the peculiarity of their political situation, one must return to the basic rationale for having a number of nonelected political appointees in the executive branch in the first place. According to the Founding Fathers' design, power for the legislative functions of government was spread among the various representatives from states and congressional districts; for the executive function, power was deliberately unified in one elected chief executive. A single president to nominate and supervise the principal officers of the executive branch would promote the unity and vigor of executive operations, while requiring the Senate's consent to make appointments final would safeguard against any presidential abuse of the appointment power and would stabilize administration. Theorists of party government later elaborated on what some of the Founders only hinted at—that competition in the electoral marketplace would result in choices between alternative political teams and policies.

The idea of a single chief executive entering office to promote his measures through a band of loyal political supporters in the executive branch is an easily understood model. It fits well with the media's desire to focus on the central presidential personality, and the notion of undertaking public service at the call of the President attracts many new political appointees to Washington. Astute scholars have pointed out that in reality the President's formal power as the single chief executive is often illusory, that even within his own executive branch he must persuade others and calculate his power stakes rather than cudgel his minions. The revisionist view, however, has not altered the customary concentration on the President and, like the standard constitutional or party government models, it relegates the bulk of political executives to a secondary, derivative role in the executive branch.

As noted earlier, the problem with relying on such president-centered models of executive politics is that they all depend on a tenuous political chain of events. The links of this chain are unlikely to hold from a preelection formulation of intentions, through an election contest giving a clear mandate to a particular president and his measures, to the installation of his team of executives in positions of control over government actions, to faithful administrative implementation of the promised policies. Nevertheless, there is an underlying psychological validity to the president-centered models. In good times and bad the

President *is* the focus of national political attention. His popular following and public stature give him resources for bargaining and leadership that no political executive in the departments can hope to match....

U.S. federal executives...still find themselves in an extraordinarily difficult political situation. In theory political executives are supposed to provide departmental leadership and to work together under the President. But, there are no "natural" political forces bolstering such expectations. Where, after all, does the political strength of these executives lie?

In elections? Departmental appointees are supposed to be helping the President make and carry out public policies affecting millions of lives, but no one has elected them. Typically, in fact, they will have played little part in the election responsible for their presence in Washington. Can ties to the President supply political strength? The President's closest companions are those who have followed him—not necessarily the party—and they will often have done so throughout the long march to the White House. Knowing the source of their power, they usually prefer proximity as White House aides rather than isolation as executive appointees somewhere "out" in the departments. And in any event a president who calculates his own power stakes is unlikely to let department executives borrow heavily on his political resources. Might political executives look for strength in their managerial authority? Hardly. Their second-hand mandate from the President competes with the mandates of elected congressmen who call the hearings, pass the enabling legislation, and appropriate the money. What about interest groups and clienteles? Obviously they have power, and many new political appointees do arrive in office closely tied to one or another such group. But if this is the executives' exclusive source of political backing, any leadership role will be severely constrained. A public executive's responsibility is supposed to entail something more than advocacy for private groups.

Since these are "political" appointees, can strength perhaps be derived from political parties?... [N]ew political executives may be outsiders, but they are not outsiders who have been linked together politically during periods of opposition. Whatever central campaign machinery there is belongs largely to the individual president rather than to a set of national party leaders. At the vital state and local party level, those ambitious for their own elective careers know they must prepare their true political bases back home rather than in Washington bureaucracy. Political parties are in no position to reward appointed executives for their successes or punish them for their failures.

On all of these counts, Washington's political executives have as few incentives to pull together as they have resources to stand alone as political leaders. Like the President, they must persuade rather than command others, but they lack the President's preeminent position to improve their bargaining power. The glare of White House attention may occasionally sweep across their agencies' activity, but for most political executives the President's traditional handshake and photograph will be his way of saying both hello and goodbye. In the constitutional structure and in the public eye, they are distinctly secondary figures to the single chief executive, yet the President's limited time, interests, and fighting power will make him utterly dependent on them for most of what is done by the executive branch. That they exist in such a twilight zone of political leadership is the first and primary fact of life shared by political appointees....

Any commitment to democratic values necessarily means accepting a measure of instability in the top governing levels. Democratic elections are, after all, "a political invention to assure uncertainty of leadership, in what are deemed to be optimum amounts and periods of time." But to the inherent electoral changes, the American executive political system adds a considerably greater range of nonelectoral uncertainty to political leadership. This system produces top executives who are both expendable over time and in a relatively weak, uncertain position at any one time.

The number of political executives is small vis-à-vis the bureaucracy but large and fragmented in relation to any notion of a trim top-management structure. To the normal confusions of pluralistic institutions and powers in Washington, the selection process contributes its own complexities. White House personnel efforts have rarely been effectively organized. Political forces intervene from many quarters, and their interests in political appointments often bear little relation to presidential needs or to qualifications required for effective performance by public executives. White House efforts at political recruitment can be effective, but the organizational requirements are difficult to master. A White House operation that veers too far in the direction of centralized control can easily become self-defeating by overlooking the need for political executives to balance their responsiveness to the President with their usefulness to the departments.

While political appointees are more experienced in government than might be assumed, their government service does not usually provide continuity of experience, either through periodic spells of office-holding or long tenure in particular jobs. This is especially true at the higher political levels. Hence without a very steep learning curve, political appointees are likely to find that their capacities for effective action have matured at just about the time they are leaving office. As one assistant secretary said, "You're given this particular situation for one moment in time...you've got to get on your feet quickly." The entire process does not produce long-suffering policymakers who realize their major changes will come gradually through persistence. Most political appointees are more impatient. Any civil servant who offers the standard and often sensible bureaucratic advice to watch, wait, and be careful can expect to arouse more than a little suspicion.

All these tendencies are vastly intensified by the instability and uncertainty of working relationships among political appointees as a group. Over time, changes in the Washington community, particularly the declining role of parties, have provided even fewer points of political reference to help orient leadership in the executive branch. Despite the conventional models, political interaction is less like regularly scheduled matches between competing teams of partisans (President versus Congress, Republicans versus Democrats) and more like a sandlot pick-up game, with a variety of strangers, strategies, and misunderstandings. Such working relationships as exist are created and recreated sporadically as the political players come and go. Each largely picks up his lore anew—how to make his way, look for support, and deal with officialdom. It is circumstances such as these that lead many civil servants and experienced political executives to echo the words of one presidential appointee (in fact a Nixon placement in the supposedly enemy territory of the Department of Health, Education, and Welfare): "In my time I've come to the conclusion you can't say it's the damn bureaucrats. With some exceptions, that's not the problem. What's lacking is the political leadership." Political executives have no common culture for dealing with the problems of governing, and it is seldom that they are around long enough or trust one another enough to acquire one.

Weaknesses among political executives lead inevitably to While House complaints about their "going native" in the bureaucracy. The image is apt. To a large extent the particular agencies and bureaus *are* the native villages of executive politics. Even the most presidentially minded political executive will discover that his own agency provides the one relatively secure reference point amid all the other uncertainties of Washington. In their own agencies, appointees usually have at least some knowledge of each other and a common identity with particular programs. Outside the agency it is more like life in the big city among large numbers of anonymous people who have unknown lineages. Any common kinship in the political party or a shared political vocation is improbable, and in the background are always the suspicions of the President's "true" family of supporters in the White House. Political appointees in the larger Washington environment may deal frequently with each other, but these are likely to be the kind of ad hoc, instrumental relations of the city, where people interact without truly knowing each other.

Yet the political appointee's situation is not so simple that he can act as if he is surrounded by a random collection of strangers outside the confines of his agency village. Everywhere extensive networks of village folk in the bureaucracy, Congress, and lobby organizations share experiences, problems, and readings on people and events. An appointee may or may not be in touch with people in these networks, but they are certain to be in touch with each other independently of him. In sociological terms his networks are thin, transient, and single-stranded; theirs are dense, multiple, and enduring. Among public executives themselves there is little need to worry about any joint action to enforce community norms, because there is no community. In dealing with outside villagers who know each other, however, appointees can find that reprisals for any misdeeds are extraordinarily oblique and powerful. The political executive system may be a government of strangers, but its members cannot act as if everyone else is.

Now one can begin to see the real challenge to the political executives' statecraft in Washington. They must be able to move in two worlds—the tight, ingrown village life of the bureaucratic community and the open, disjointed world of political strangers. A public executive in Washington needs the social sensitivity of a villager and the political toughness of a city streetfighter. It is an increasingly unlikely combination. Despite all the resources devoted to more topside staff, new management initiatives, more elaborate analytic techniques, and so on, there remain few—probably fewer than ever—places where political executives can look for reliable political support in any efforts at leadership in the bureaucracy. Political appointees in Washington are substantially on their own and vulnerable to bureaucratic power. . . .

WORKING RELATIONS

Once political executives have learned to qualify their initial distrust and have established preliminary working relations in the Washington bureaucracy, they are ready to move on to the main event: using these relationships and networks in a strategic way. Political appointees are not and should not be in a position to gain absolute power over their agencies, but they can strengthen their hands for political leadership.

Experts writing about private organizations have described two different orientations toward management control. Under so-called Theory X it is assumed that an average subordinate avoids work if he can, loathes responsibility, covets security, and must be directed and threatened with punishment in order to put forth sufficient effort to achieve managerial goals. Theory Y emphasizes a worker's need for identity and personal growth through work, rewards rather than punishment as a means of motivation, and the cooperation toward objectives that can be gained by commitments to mutually agreed upon goals rather than by strict supervision from above....

The basic theme of this chapter is that experience reveals the shortcomings of both Theory X and Theory Y and suggests the value of a third approach to working relations between political executives and ranking bureaucrats. It is what might be termed "conditionally cooperative behavior." Any premise of compassionate cooperation and participatory management overlooks the bureaucracy's divided loyalties, its needs for self-protection, and its multiple sources of resistance. Unconditionally negative approaches fail to recognize the enduring character of bureaucratic power and a political leader's need to elicit the bureaucracy's help in governing.

Conditional cooperation emerges between these extremes. It implies a kind of cooperation that is conditional on the mutual performance of the political appointees and the civil servants. It emphasizes the need of executives and bureaucrats to work at relationships that depend on the contingencies of one another's actions, not on preconceived ideas of strict supervision or harmonious goodwill. Conditional cooperation rejects any final choice between suspicion and trust, between trying to force obedience and passively hoping for compliance. By making their reactions conditional on the performance of subordinates, political appointees create latitude for choice—possibilities for various types of exchanges with different bureaucrats. The basis for the executives' leadership becomes strategic rather than "take it or leave it."

As opposed to a set formula that assures success, conditional cooperation is a strategy that suggests a variety of resources and methods for trading services. It increases the likelihood that some political executives will do better than others in getting what they need from Washington's bureaucracies. Superficially, conditional cooperation might seem to be simply a matter of exchanging favors with the bureaucracy on a quid pro quo basis. The reality of executive leadership is more subtle. It involves bringing others to appreciate not so much what they have gotten as what they might get. Would-be executive leaders, remember, are like poor credit risks in a well-established credit market; they have had little chance to acquire a favorable standing or reputation in the eyes of other participants

who are used to dealing with each other. The new political strangers have to work at building credit in the bureaucracy precisely because they have not had—and will only briefly enjoy—a chance to put anyone in their debt. Even so, memories are short and debts are often not repaid in Washington. The real basis of conditional cooperation lies in making bureaucrats creditors rather than debtors to the political executives: that is, giving them a stake in his future performance. Any past exchange of favors between appointees and careerists is far less influential than the general hope of grasping future returns. It is the grasping rather than the gratitude that drives executive politics....

CONCLUSIONS

As demand exceeds the supply of mutual performance between appointees and bureaucrats, tempers rise in the government marketplace. Although the alienation of executive leadership from operations can catch up with a private company by forcing it into bankruptcy, barring revolution, the government's business always continues in some form. Exchanges of conditional cooperation between political executives and higher civil servants simply break down or are never created in the first place. So what difference does it all make?

The failure to establish constructive working relationships usually produces obscure and indirect effects. This is not only because politicians and government agencies try to hide deficiencies in their operations, but also because of the nature of government activity. Since it is usually difficult to know how or when a policy emerges, it is doubly difficult to identify the effect of only one linkage—that between political executives and bureaucrats—among the many involved in public policymaking. So great are the contingencies among people, institutions, and outside events that it is better to think of probabilities than to expect straightforward one-for-one effects.

When exchanges between political appointees and civil servants break down, there is often more hedging in the recommendations flowing up to the political levels, even though few may be able to identify the consequence of a recommendation or warning not given. Frequently signals sent down to middle- and lower-level officials become more garbled, although again it is difficult to trace the consequences of a higher civil servant's failure to implement and follow through. Presidents and political executives usually seem adept at calling on a variety of political forces to help sell the idea for some kind of action; where the civil service matters to politicians is not so much in marshaling these forces as in helping to work out a program that makes administrative sense and getting something down once it has been politically sold.

It may, for example, take some years to show the self-defeating consequences of decisions that are taken without the participation of professional specialists in the bureaucracy. Political executives can find themselves taking more time to become oriented, operating with less understanding of a policy, and failing to mobilize the varieties of bureaucrats. Where changes remain unconsolidated in political administration, zigs and zags in grand policy at the top echelons can be mere switchbacks in the bureaucracy's slow progress toward its own inertial goals.

Whatever the difficulties of tracing a given policy effect, there is no mistaking the lessons learned by many participants. As noted at the beginning of this chapter, perceptive appointees from both the Theory X and Theory Y schools of management eventually see that the political executive's real job lies between the extremes of giving orders and of taking cooperation for granted. They learn that political leadership in the Washington bureaucracy is not a task for martinets or presiding officers. For those both tough and sensitive enough, it is a job of managing a pluralistic, changing consensus with limited strategic resources.

There is no need to overdramatize the difficulties that occur. People in government can manage without conditional cooperation at the political-bureaucratic interface. When political appointees have little sense of direction or statecraft, the failure to establish a constructive working relationship with higher civil servants may be inconsequential, except that the bureaucracy is left freer to pursue its own agenda. Experienced bureaucrats become quite expert at helping themselves in the Washington scramble. Similarly, some political managers may feel no great loss if the careerists with whom they fail to build working rela-

tions have few analytic or administrative capabilities to offer or withhold; they become adept at creating their own personal teams in place of career civil servants. Appointees and bureaucrats can and do try to compensate for each other's inadequacies.

Yet as each side maximizes its own convenience in this way, the overall quality of American democratic institutions is likely to decline. It is no consolation that appointees and top bureaucrats can compensate for having little that is worth exchanging with each other. If officialdom and professional specialists can get along very well despite an absence of political leadership above them, that should not reassure citizens who expect government bureaucracies to be guided by publicly accountable and removable political representatives. Likewise, political executives may manage without the institutionalized knowledge, continuity, and impartiality that government civil services are created to supply. That, too, is little consolation since the real strength of government machinery in a democracy is its ability to serve effectively, not just one particular set of political leaders, but any succession of leaders with a legitimate popular mandate. If democratic government did not require bureaucrats and political leaders to need each other, it might not matter so much when in practice they discover they do not.

READING 53

In Search of a Role: America's Higher Civil Service

Hugh Heclo

All of the major western European democracies, Japan, and Canada have recognizable professional senior civil services. The members are stable and identifiable. They have a regular career ladder. Not only are they loyal to the political leaders of the day, but they also serve the leaders directly in sensitive policy positions. This service is reliable and of high quality. Successive governments with different political beliefs and agendas rely on the same people in the senior career administrative positions and have every reason to expect very satisfactory performance.

The United States, however, presents a very different picture, which is examined by George Mason political scientist Hugh Heclo in this selection. He addresses three themes. First, there is no central management of the higher civil service in the United States. Second, the higher civil service has no formal presence in most important administrative bodies in Washington. Third, and most important, there is a "two-track system of top bureaucratic manpower, a formal civil service bureaucracy and an informal political technocracy." The existence of the two tracks creates some additional tensions.

The most significant feature of American higher bureaucracy is that individuals in both tracks are expected to be political actors. The policy neutrality and apolitical posture expected of higher civil servants in other developed democracies are not expected in the United States. In fact, other governmental actors—the president, presidential appointees, members of the House and Senate—and interest group representatives expect higher civil servants to be skilled political operatives. The civil servants form alliances with other actors and are part of various policy coalitions and networks. Loyalty to the president of the day is the weakest loyalty of all, which helps explain why presidents generally have such a difficult time in framing a policy agenda and making headway in achieving it.

The higher civil service in the United States is a study in ambiguities. Top bureaucrats' status, their role in policy making and politics, their relationship to the larger society—all these features are poorly defined in American central government and subject to immense counter-pressures. It is even questionable

whether or not there actually is a higher civil service in the United States, at least in the sense in which that term is used in other countries. To study the higher civil service in Washington, we need to think not only of hierarchies with formal, clear career lines, but also loose groupings of people where the lines of policy, politics, and administration merge in a complex jumble of bodies....

And yet to think that the senior bureaucracy is simply a random collection of people and styles would be obtuse. Like any montage, the U.S. higher civil service is best appreciated by its themes, not its individual pictures.

One such theme is the unmanaged quality of America's higher civil service. By that I do not mean that there is runaway growth or absence of legalistic constraints. Far from it. Growth in personnel has been meager, and restrictive personnel regulations abound. I mean that no one looks after the higher civil service as such, and certainly senior bureaucrats themselves do not (as in other countries) oversee its workings, traditions, and fate.

A second theme, related to the first, is the peculiar absence of a formal civil service presence in the central executive institutions of government, especially the president's office and the offices of major department heads. This situation appears to have been a gradual development of the last forty years or so: one part a "disappearing act" by senior officials who once made up such a presence, and one part a failure to discover effective new ways of using senior careerists as these central offices have grown over the years. But whatever the explanation, the result is clear. Compared to its counterparts in other countries, the U.S. higher civil service seems hollow at the center.

A final theme explored in this paper concerns a profound and probably growing duality in the higher civil service as an informal personnel system. Certainly, it is possible to identify a schizoid quality in the upper level bureaucracy of every country. This condition is the natural by-product of having to accommodate twin tasks in any higher civil service: overall supervision of the administrative machinery below and personal advisory relations with political ministers above.... The United States, on the other hand, has erected this dual need into a two-track system of top bureaucratic manpower, a formal civil service bureaucracy and an informal political technocracy.

The three themes are, of course, related. If the system as a whole tends to be unmanaged, how can there be any reliable civil service presence at the center of any coherent organization of the dual tasks at the top of the bureaucracy? If the civil service is largely excluded from the executive center, i.e., presidency, how can it be managed or even imagined to have a topside structure? With no real top but instead a duality of senior bureaucratic manpower, what is there to be represented at the center? And so the circle of ambivalence about the higher civil service continue[s] unbroken in Washington. In the past several years, a new attempt has been made to reconstitute the senior executive personnel system of the bureaucracy, but as we shall see there are powerful historical and political forces working against any movement in the direction of a European or Japanese style of higher civil service. The real definition of America's higher civil service is being written, not in the language of formal personnel statutes, but in the quiet, informal understandings that shape people's careers in public service. In this as perhaps in no other country, the higher civil service is molded by forces external to itself. Its emerging structure, broadly understood, is shaped by changes in the larger political society, its character stamped by the unwritten no less than the written political constitution. . . .

THE DUAL STRUCTURE

Seen as a whole, the Washington bureaucracy has a dual, or two-track system of administrative management: one growing out of the formal civil service rules of the personnel system and one based on an informal, but also technocratic quasi-bureaucracy of appointed manpower. . . .

The general distribution is more important than the exact numbers and job titles. These American images of departmental management contrast with the situation found in other developed countries in these respects: there are (1) more appointive political positions that, (2) extend farther down into the administrative structure and, (3) commingle career and political appointments at some of the same levels in the agency hierarchy. . . .

Yet there are people today who are regularly counted on to service cabinet secretaries and other top appointees and who oversee the working of departmental machinery. Indeed, it would be difficult to imagine how the work of government could go on if there were not such people. If we loosen our concept of the higher civil service so as to include indeliberately organized, loosely woven career lines, then the outlines of a second, de facto higher civil service begin to emerge.

The unilluminating term generally used for these persons is "In and Outers." This is not a helpful concept because it can apply to anyone with a temporary stint in government, especially the top political appointees whose tenures are short and sometimes (as one U.S. senator put it) possessing all the impact of a snowflake on the bosom of the Potomac. The *public careerists,* as I will call them, do occasionally rise to the ranks of secretary or agency head. In fact, as the role of political parties and their patronage power has declined, public careerists have become a more prominent source of senior political appointments. Approximately one-half of President Reagan's top appointees in the winter of 1980–1981 had held subordinate appointments in earlier administrations. But what truly distinguishes public careerists is not that they are part of any coherent, political career ladder, as is the case, for example, with the progression of British political executives (from parliamentary secretary, to junior minister, to senior minister).

What distinguishes the de facto, higher civil service of public careerists is their ability to combine top-level assistance to senior presidential appointees with some measure of familiarity about the issues and processes of government. What they know about policies—and public policy issues have become an increasingly complex area of technical specialization—makes the public careerists useful to the senior political executives. What the public careerists know about the ins and outs of government work and their own network of personal contacts in Washington helps this de facto higher civil service use, if not administratively control in a classic bureaucratic sense, the machinery of government.

It would be fruitless to try to draw clear lines around the careers of those participating in this informal system of bureaucratic executives. Some who participate in it are former career civil servants, especially those who are ambitious to expand their careers beyond the boundaries of their agencies. Some have worked in congressional staff positions. Some are academic experts with a penchant for government affairs. Any attempt to apply a single label, such as public careerists, does some injustice to the complexities involved. But the key point is that these are people who build their careers around problems of public policy and do so outside the confines of the formal civil service personnel system. They are not like career executives, who spend their lives within one or another government agency. Neither are they exactly like senior political appointees, who are often transient on the scene of public affairs and have little prospect for reentering government.... [P]ublic careerists [are] less experienced in government jobs than career executives but far better grounded than the normal run of presidential appointees. This latter feature is particularly striking inasmuch as the information shown is for a time when a new Republican administration had been in office less than two years and after a preceding eight years of control by the Democrats; yet over one-half of the noncareer executives had already had more than five years' prior experience in government at one time or another.

The potential recruitment pool for the de facto civil service is, indeed, immense. Since the mid-1950s the number of full-time permanent federal employees has remained unchanged at approximately 3 million persons, but the size of the so-called indirect federal work force has grown to an estimated 8 million persons; of these, an estimated 3 million are doing work that federal employees would have to do themselves to keep the government operating if the indirect employees were not there. I am certainly not suggesting that these millions of people themselves are public careerists as I have been using the term. But if one could look behind the numbers, deep into the tangle of relationships that is implied by this indirect or third-party government, what one would find are significant numbers who learn a great deal about particular policies and the administrative processes that go with them. Because of what they know and can do, at least by reputation if not in practice, they are likely to be called on

when a new administration or new secretary begins "staffing up" and looking for "some good people who can help us," as the sayings go.

When not holding temporary positions in the executive branch or mushrooming congressional bureaucracy, public careerists can be found in academic departments, think tanks, interest group associations and public interest lobbies, law firms, consulting and policy research firms, and so on (rarely in state and local governments but sometimes in the lobby organizations for state and local governments!). The one thing that these places have in common is a stake in concrete problems of public policy and programming. The number of potential roosts for public careerists has grown phenomenally in recent years as the federal government has intervened in more policy areas and used various profit and nonprofit organizations—rather than the government work force—to do its work. The largely inadvertent result has been to expand a kind of on-the-job training by which persons outside the formal civil service system acquire policy expertise and a working familiarity with many aspects of government administration....

POLICY AND POLITICS IN THE DUAL STRUCTURE

By now it should be clear that there can be no simple model describing the role of America's higher civil service in politics and policy making. Even the concept of a higher civil service is diffuse and subject to differing interpretations. "The" higher civil service is really an inadvertent byproduct shaped by four immensely powerful political forces.

First, the higher civil service is part of an executive branch that the framers of the Constitution designed to have a single executive head, the president. Second, however, it is also part of an administrative structure that is beholden to a legislature—or more accurately various specialized parts (committees and subcommittees) of a legislature—that has enduring and independent power to shape administration. Congress can deny the civil servant and his organization funds, overturn decisions, specify actions, and generally make the bureaucrat's life miserable in a dozen ways. Third, administrative leadership is vested in a mix of permanent careerists and transient appointees who have only the most tenuous attachment to either presidents or congressmen as party politicians. Finally, the Washington bureaucracy has depended more and more on largely independent third parties in the private sector and subnational government level to accomplish its purposes.

One way of summarizing all this is to say that the basic organizing principle—more unintentional than planned—of the higher civil service is horizontal. For members of both de jure and de facto systems, the lines of loyalty run outward through programs and policies rather than upward to bureaucratic or political superiors. That is, of course, a gross simplification of a very complex system, but it does encapsulate the essential difference of higher civil service work in the United States compared to other Western nations....

The horizontal rather than vertical principle also applies to public careerists. Those closest to the cabinet secretary or agency head are not so much his political lieutenants as they are members of his personal entourage or liaison staff to outside groups. Public careerists mixed elsewhere in the administrative structure are political subordinates only in the most formalistic sense (job titles and pay scales) of that term. More realistically, they should be seen as peers drawn from collateral networks of analysts, lobbyists, and other activists in public affairs for whom politics is policy. This is true in foreign affairs no less than in domestic policy, where the horizontal alliances tend to be more obvious....

Missing from this picture of mixed career bureaucracies and policy technocracies is "politics" in the traditional party-political meaning of that term. Neither career nor political executives have any tradition of serving in the national legislature, although some movement back and forth between legislative staff positions and the executive bureaucracy has become more common in recent decades. There is also little experience with senior bureaucrats serving in elective or appointive positions in state and local government (contra France and West Germany, for example). Career officials in the federal civil service are prohibited from engaging in all but the most routine grassroots, nonpartisan political activity. Public careerists face no such prohibition but their policy inter-

ests generally lead them to shun the "nonsubstantive" and often tedious work associated with congressional careers or state and local government service. Likewise, career civil servants almost never rise to the top ranks of political appointments although, as we have seen, they can be found migrating into lower-level political executive positions, and there is some tendency for public careerists to form part of the potential pool for senior presidential appointments....

THE HOLLOW CENTER

It is at this point—the nature of policy and administration as an up-and-down conversation within the machinery of government—that we come to the core problem in the search for a role in any higher civil service in Washington. The one institution with an inherent interest in taut vertical strength in the executive branch is the presidency. That is the inevitable consequence of a Constitution vesting the executive function in a single rather than a plural head chosen independently of the legislature. As the *Federalist Papers* put it,

> Energy in the Executive is a leading character of good government.... The ingredients which constitute energy in the Executive are, first, unity.... This unity may be destroyed in two ways: either by vesting the power in two or more magistrates of equal dignity and authority; or by vesting it ostensibly in one man, subject, in whole or in part, to the control and co-operation of others in the capacity of counsellors to him.

The logic of the Constitution means that there can be no governmentwide, coherent higher civil service unless it is somehow attached to and led from the presidency. Anything less *must* represent less than the executive branch as a whole. Only the presidential office has a vested interest in integrating the diverse parts.

And yet there is a powerful political logic that has militated against the constitutional logic for the higher civil service. Everything said earlier about the difficulty of career executives working in close relations with senior political executives applies *in extremis* to the presidency. Secure in their horizontal loyalties, congressmen, departmental bureaucrats, and outside groups are deeply hostile to anything that smacks of permanent officialdom near the president. Likewise, presidents and their transient aids suspect any official who has been closely identified with the work of a preceding administration. And always in the background is the pervasive historical attitude that civil servants are at their best on narrowly technical matters and unfit for working in a political environment on questions of general policy—precisely the situation in the White House. It seems strange to say but it is true: the surest way for a higher civil servant to cut short his career in government is to work faithfully as a higher civil servant to the president.

This political logic means that the closer one approaches the person of the president, the farther into the background recede higher civil servants in both the de facto and de jure senses of that term. One searches in vain for anything even approaching a higher civil service presence in the Executive Office of the President as a whole. A closer look at the president's executive office will help clarify the paradox of a hollow center in the American higher civil service....

Taking these four units of central EOP machinery as a whole (the Office of Management and Budget, the National Security Council, the Council of Economic Advisers, and the Domestic Council) one can say that each is (on the record of the past decade) likely to be headed by a senior personal assistant to the president, supported by a staff whose leading members are policy specialists drawn from outside and the fringes of the federal government. One might stretch terms and call these people informal higher civil servants (their careers are not heavily government based), but three things should be recalled before going very far with that label. First, their service is highly compartmentalized, limited to one of these four units at present or at anytime in the future. An NSC staffman simply will not turn up later as a CEA, OMB, or domestic policy staffer, and the same applies for each of the other offices. Even if one accepts that there can be an informal type of higher civil service, that clearly does not apply to the EOP as a central entity, only to its parts.

A second reservation is that in all these offices, the general preoccupation is with policy problems and decisions, not with the administrative workings of government. Where there is administrative involvement it is likely to be concerned with checking to see that painfully arrived at presidential decisions are, in fact, being carried out. But this kind of "checking for obedience" hardly amounts to the oversight of administrative machinery normally associated with the functioning of a higher civil service....

The third problem in speaking of an informal higher civil service within the perimeters of OMB/NSC/CEA/DC professional staffs is that these people simply do not interact directly with their chief client, the president....

A PROLOGUE TO DEMOCRATIC TECHNOLOGY

America's higher civil service is an unmanaged affair, weak in the central executive apparatus and extensive in horizontal links to the larger political society. The two faces of the higher civil service, de facto and de jure, are really both reflections of the profound duality in modern government—at once inward-oriented by the immense technical complexity of modern policy *and* outward-directed by the broader social cooperation on which its policies depend.

The profile of the senior bureaucracy is, therefore, etched by the interaction of powerful external agents on the hard surface of government expertise. The great strength of this system is its capacity to make government accessible to those who are actively interested in affecting its work. The great dangers are that the government will be unable to act as a collective enterprise with institutional continuity and with some sense of purpose that is more than a reflection of the preferences held by those who happen to be mobilized to affect its work. No nation seems likely to reverse the growing need for technical expertise at all government levels. What America's "non system" of public careerists may have to offer are some hints about tilting the inevitable technocracy in more broadly democratic directions. What Washington has yet to discover is a means of meshing its formal and informal higher civil service with presidential leadership and with the need for a longer and broader attention span in government.

In 1978, President Carter signed into law the first comprehensive Civil Service Reform Act since the passage of the original statute in 1883. It would clearly be premature to try and judge the full impact of this major act, but there are four features that reaffirm the thesis of this paper. The real definition of America's higher civil service is being written not so much in formal personnel laws as in the ambiguous, informal understandings that shape people's careers in public service.

First, the new law has disbanded the old Civil Service Commission. In its place is an Office of Personnel Management, headed by a director appointed by the president and confirmed by the Senate to a four-year term, and a separate bipartisan board to police the mass of routine civil service jobs. But the new personnel office was not placed in the Executive Office of the President, largely because of the congressional criticism that was feared from increasing the number of staff in the presidency.

Second, the new law places considerable emphasis on competition for financial rewards at both the middle and the upper levels of the formal civil service system. Each department and agency develops its own performance appraisal system and pays out cash rewards to the top "performers" from a limited pool of funds. Here again are the familiar echoes of technical efficiency and scientific management in government personnel policy, as if the work of higher civil servants were an unambiguous product to be measured and ranked....

Third, a new Senior Executive Service was created...to provide more mobile and systematic management of career and political executives below the level of top presidential appointees. What is noteworthy so far is that management of the new system has devolved mainly to the bureau level within the separate departments and agencies. No central means exists to control or even facilitate the assignment of senior executives on anything like a department-wide—much less a governmentwide—basis.

Finally, there is simply no meaningful system for using the higher civil servants of the Senior Executive Service in the Executive Office of the President. The Office of Management and Budget, with 40 percent of all Executive Office staff, has its own procedures for its own purposes. Several other units do likewise, and the White House Office, with 30 percent of total Executive Office manpower, has no systematic means for using Senior Executive manpower. As far as the operation of the presidency is concerned, the new, reformed civilian career system is largely a nonevent.

The conclusion seems inescapable. Neither the historic constraints, nor the 1978 reforms, nor current practice, point toward a significantly different future for the formal, de jure concept of a higher civil service in American government. Yet there is a system, and it carries with it the strengths and dangers of a democratic technocracy. To find a higher civil service function developing we must loosen our categories, take a deep breath, and keep an eye on the public careerists.

READING 54

The C.I.A.'s Most Important Mission: Itself

Tim Weiner

It is a favorite theme with journalists, editorial cartoonists, and politicians to portray bureaucracy as immovable and unchanging. These characteristics are usually embellished by allegations, or at least implications, that the bureaucracy is also inefficient, unresponsive, overpaid, and underworked.

Political scientists who study bureaucracy usually paint a more subtle picture. Change is slow, but not absent. Over time the amount of change that accumulates is substantial. There are usually powerful forces working against change, but bureaucracies are not immutable.

In the article that follows, Tim Weiner, a Washington correspondent for The New York Times, *focuses on one specific federal bureaucracy—the Central Intelligence Agency. Within the C.I.A. he pays most attention to the "spooks," the clandestine service within the agency.*

He portrays an agency in deep internal trouble in several ways. The end of the cold war has left it without a clear mission. This fact alone cries out, in a rational world, for programmatic change. A series of scandals—long-standing undetected treason on the part of Aldrich Ames and complicity in brutal behavior on the part of foreign nationals in the pay of the C.I.A. in their home countries stand out—seems unrelenting. It is also an agency with a core of "old boys" who have dominated the norms and behavior of the agency for decades and are generally opposed to change. This is, in short, a dramatic case of an agency in need of change, yet one with great internal resistance to change.

The drama of the situation is enhanced because of the secret nature of much of the work of the C.I.A. It is also enhanced because President Bill Clinton appointed a new director, John Deutch, in part because the two agreed that significant change was the order of the day.

This case does not offer general explanations or predictions of what ultimately will happen. But it offers insights into the internal dynamics among those in conflict over the mission of the agency. Some of these individuals promote change; many resist it. The president and the director recognize the need for serious change. Whether the employees whom the director is supposed to lead will respond positively remains to be seen.

On an autumn evening, in a private plane approaching Washington, John Deutch, the new Director of Central Intelligence, sprawled wearily in an armchair and worried aloud about the nation's spies. He compared them to a defeated force—the United States Army after the fall of Saigon.

"What happened with the Army?" Deutch said. "The young officers looked at each other and said: 'We're in trouble. We've got to change. We've got to figure out a way to do this differently. We're either leaving or we're going to change the system.' And the people who stayed did change the system."

Deutch's struggle to transform the Central Intelligence Agency, the world's greatest and most reviled spy service, has become a war in itself, a battle against the history and the culture of the C.I.A. The opening shot came early one morning last May when Deutch first walked onstage at the Bubble, the agency's once-futuristic amphitheater, and looked out at 500 frightened people. Fear was the watchword of the day. The agency was taking a terrible beating, lampooned by cartoonists, lambasted by pundits and politicians. Its last chief had quit abruptly. Its best people were fleeing. Its great enemy, the Soviet Union, had disappeared. It had been betrayed by Aldrich Ames, the unctuous apparatchik who had blown a hundred secret missions and exposed scores of American spies. He helped Moscow create a team of double agents who manipulated American perceptions of the Kremlin for years, a fact the C.I.A. concealed from three Presidents and the Pentagon.

The agency's scarred heart—the spies in the D.O., the directorate of operations—needed surgery. Republican Senators, three-star generals and National Security Council officials were talking in public about whether merely to "overhaul" or to "eviscerate" or "blow up" the agency. A Presidential commission was debating whether the C.I.A. should live or die. The agency's very existence depended on what Deutch did—and he had vowed to change it, if needed, "down to the bare bones." No wonder the spooks were spooked.

The new leader told a little joke to put them at ease. He recalled that his connections with the agency went back to 1976, when George Bush, then the director, put him on a panel of expert advisers on spy satellites and other technical wizardry. "And ever since that time," he said "I always harbored a secret desire to be the Director of Central Intelligence."

The spies laughed, knowing the truth. In January, the President had gazed fondly upon Deutch, his brainy and ebullient Deputy Secretary of Defense, and said, John, your country needs you. Deutch, astute fellow, said no. His punishment was to find someone willing and able to say yes. The search went on for six weeks. Finally Deutch came up with an obscure Air Force general whose nomination wobbled, plummeted and crashed. And then the President gazed with something less than fondness upon John Deutch.

"The President pressed on me the view that I really had to do it," he recalls. Thus was a 57-year-old physical chemistry professor from the Massachusetts Institute of Technology given the most difficult experiment of his life. . . .

The clandestine service is the heart and soul of the agency," says Robert M. Gates, Director of Central Intelligence from 1991 to 1993. "It is also the part that can land you in jail." The operations directorate was in such deep trouble that it was facing a life sentence—or execution. It had "to change its nature and character," says Adm. William O. Studeman, acting director from January to May, 1995. Under enormous pressure, it had to be transformed.

The agency would live, Deutch told his audience that May morning, his first full day on the job. There would always be a C.I.A., he assured them, despite past calls to shut it down from people like Senator Daniel Patrick Moynihan. And there would always be spies within it, despite proposals to the contrary from retired generals and would-be wise men ready to give the job to the military.

Deutch knew that the congressional intelligence committees and the Presidential commission re-evaluating the agency were beginning with a blank sheet of paper. He had their trust to fill in the blanks—if they first could be convinced that the agency's 5,000 spies had the capacity to change, and the morale, the motivation and the mental wherewithal to perform vital missions. Deutch has had to convince himself. This is taking time.

The least difficult part of the equation was: which missions? There remains a widespread belief that the C.I.A., without a cold war to fight, is wandering around looking for work. The reality is different. The Clinton Administration has been using the agency as its own private Internet, a kind of secret adjunct to the Library of Congress, asking thousands of questions about ravaged rain forests, compact-disk counterfeiters, the opium crop in Afghanistan and the crooked ruler of Zaire. But many of the answers can be found in newspapers—"and in many cases I get a better presentation in the newspapers than I do in a secret briefing from the C.I.A.," says Senator Bob Kerrey of Nebraska, vice chairman of the Senate intelligence committee.

The clandestine service, unhappy at being thought of as billion-dollar news bureau, conceived a plan. Shortly after Deutch arrived, it presented him with a glossy brochure titled "A New Direction. A

New Future." It said, in essence, forget about ecology and human rights and epidemics and sociology. That's soft stuff. The spies proposed narrowing and sharpening their focus on what the C.I.A. calls hard targets.

Most of the top 10 targets were obvious—though nobody knew where the next Somalia or Haiti would pop up, and everyone knew the agency would be crucified for failing to see it coming. The specter of loose nukes, the whole Pandora's box of weapons proliferation, was high on the list. So was terrorism in all its faces, including armed Islamic fundamentalism. The C.I.A. always had to satisfy the military's thirst for intelligence, from the order of battle in the Balkans to the latest intrigues in Libya.

Five nations pose endless questions. What's going on in the high councils of Iran, Iraq and North Korea? Who really understands China's future directions and leadership? What will happen in Russia, a minefield of out-of-work weapons designers and wild visionaries? . . .

Last on the priority list was the thorny problem of economic intelligence. Inevitably, that means spying on Japan, Germany, and France. . . .

Deutch had reservations about the spies' new vision. He would not have laid it out quite the same way. Now, he says, he embraces it as the "road map for the future." One of his deputies says the message for the clandestine service is blunt: "Let me explain life to you. Here are the 10 or 15 things that we cannot tolerate to fail against to advance the national-security interests of the United States. This is what we want you to devote your money, your people, your language training and your skills to. We want to get this right."

In order to get it right, the clandestine service has to change its ways. . .

If terrorists, thugs and tribes with flags were the hardest targets, then the spies had better be good. The alternative is to start from scratch and build a completely different clandestine service. . . .

Deutch soon learned that though the clandestine service consumes only 3 percent of his budget, it would occupy half his waking hours, and more than a few restless nights. The Director of Central Intelligence is chairman of all the intelligence agencies as well as the C.E.O. of the C.I.A. Nearly 90 percent of the $28 billion or so Deutch will spend this year goes to military intelligence services like the National Security Agency, which conducts signals intelligence, or sigint, with satellites and ground stations, and the National Reconnaissance Office, which builds the fantastically expensive satellites. Deutch loves this stuff—"I'm a technical guy. I'm a satellite guy. I'm a sigint guy," he says—and orchestrating the instruments of intelligence to perform like an symphony was a task he could handle.

Making the clandestine chorus sing his tune was a different problem. From his first days, he went walking around the agency's headquarters, shaking hands, lunching in the cafeteria, semi-spontaneously dropping into people's offices, and then flying off around the world to C.I.A. stations, listening, nodding, questioning.

His initial impressions of the spies were unsettling. He says he was "shocked by their inability to formulate solutions" to their problems. He says he heard "a defensiveness, and almost panic, about what should be done" to reassert the C.I.A.'s credibility. He heard a lot of complaints, a lot of pleas to save the clandestine service—but few ideas about how to do it. Though the spies had been through their own Vietnam, through two decades of scandals and snafus and self-inflicted wounds, the clandestine service did not appear to have the ability or desire to reinvent itself the way the Army did. Deutch did not find many first-class minds in the ranks. "Compared to uniformed officers," he said in September, "they certainly are not as competent, or as understanding of what their relative role is and what their responsibilities are."

He figured out later that the spies knew what he thought of them, and began to rethink his first impressions. He started to search for the talented younger officers who were unhappy with the clandestine service but had stuck it out, hoping for a change. He started saying "we" instead of "they." This, again, took time.

The directorate of operations' initial response to Deutch was not wholly favorable either. Antipathy boiled over in the Bubble on Sept. 29. That morning, Deutch was forced to confront the C.I.A.'s history. There are places where the agency has done good—like smuggling money and fax machines to the Solidarity movement in Poland or securing Vaclav Havel's Velvet Revolution in Czechoslovakia—but Latin America is not one of them. Nowhere is the agency's record worse than Guatemala, where it

overthrew the Government in a 1954 coup and for the next 40 years supported a brutal military that has killed more than 100,000 civilians.

Prompted by the disclosure that one of the C.I.A.'s foreign agents, a Guatemalan colonel, might have been implicated in the murder of an American, Deutch ordered a worldwide re-evaluation of thousands of paid informers. The orders were to identify the crooks and the fingernail-pullers, to weigh the information they provided against their records, and to sack them if they failed the test. Then he reviewed the C.I.A.'s recent performance in Guatemala, and found what he politely called "tremendous deficiencies in the way the agency carried out its business." Above all, he found "a lack of candor—between the chief of station and the Ambassador, between the station and the directorate of operations' Latin America division, between the directorate of operations' Latin America division and the deputy director for operations, and between the C.I.A. and the Congress." Guatemala proved to be a core sample of a deep rot.

In the World-of-Tomorrow setting of the Bubble, Deutch announced he was firing the former chief of the Latin America division and a former station chief. It is very hard to get fired from the C.I.A.—no one was dismissed after the Ames debacle—and the discipline did not go over well. The hundreds of officers gathered there were deeply unhappy, and they told Deutch so. They said he was moving the goal posts on them. They saw their job in Guatemala as getting rid of Communists, not providing grist for Amnesty International reports. They saw the affair as a supremely pointless scandal, a left-wing revisionist history of the cold war.

Deutch said O.K., this was a setback, but you can't be afraid of failure. You can't be afraid of controversy. You've got to go out there and keep taking risks in the service of your country. And then a low, rumbling growl started from the back of the Bubble, a bitter, sardonic, self-pitying chuckle signifying: Yeah. Sure. They were laughing at him. The curse of the Old Boys was upon John Deutch.

The curse is the patrimony of an elite secret society that degenerated into an elitist bureaucracy, an inbred tribal culture. The old boys were the Knights Templar of America. Secrecy was their sword and shield. They had billions of dollars; they could buy kings and break them; they were saving the world. They were different. Rules and laws were not for them.

Their legacy is an arrogation of power through secrecy, a we-know-what's-best-for-America imperiousness, a "lack of candor"—lying to Presidents, to the Pentagon, to the Congress and to each other. It's a suicidal habit; it keeps threatening to do the spies in. Deutch must break the tradition.

"It's a tradition to keep in mind, because I'm certainly flowing against that tide," Deutch says. "They were careless. Not being fully forthcoming with—never mind the Congress—with the President? With the Secretary of State? With the Secretary of Defense? It's unimaginable." It dies hard. The old boys' heirs "have habits, they have practices, they have attitudes which are just not reasonable," he says. "There is a wish that somebody would come in and in one fell swoop replace what they see as the dignity of the past."

To better understand that past, Deutch stays in touch with the last great spymaster, the vicar of dirty tricks, who once said he wore his conviction for failing to testify truly to Congress as a badge of honor: the Honorable Richard McGarrah Helms, Director of Central Intelligence from 1966 to 1973...

Helms's day ended in congressional hearings that paraded a generation's worth of skeletons before the public—the assassination plots, the coups, the spying on Americans. Then came a brief reformation in the late 1970's. Then came the counterrefomation. In the 1980's, the C.I.A. expanded mightily under William J. Casey, President Reagan's Director of Central Intelligence. Casey hired thousands of new spies, but quantity was not matched with quality. He lowered the intelligence quotient of the C.I.A., said Gates, his deputy director. And when Casey was caught running guns to Iran and Nicaragua on orders from the White House in 1986, in defiance of law and common sense, the clandestine service took another flaying in the form of indictments and investigations. These left permanent scars, in the form of "a risk-avoidance mentality, a lack of boldness and imagination," Gates says.

The most recent beating, still being administered, began last year after the arrest of Aldrich Ames. For seven years after Ames walked out of headquarters with a six-pound stack of secret papers, no one at the agency investigating the betrayal ever told Gates or his predecessor, William Webster, any-

thing close to the truth about the case. The chain of command was broken....

Come what may, the agency will always have a role supporting the military, especially in helping the Pentagon create a 3-D map of the theater of war that overwhelms the enemy's two-dimensional vision. The failure to deliver timely, accurate information to battlefield commanders was one of the main shortcomings in the 1991 gulf war. Deutch's Pentagon experience and connections will create permanent channels to insure better performance the next time.

But on a typical, Sunday morning, the United States is not at war. And its enemies sit not in the Kremlin or any other capital, but in the Bekaa Valley, the outskirts of Kabul, the nouveau-riche estates above Bogotá and the mosques outside Teheran. As borders blur and states collapse, the threats are less nations than gangs. The harm they can do the United States is less a military matter than a law-enforcement problem.

The F.B.I. thinks this is a job for the F.B.I. The C.I.A. begs to differ.

The bureau and the agency have a lifetime of mutual mistrust to overcome, another legacy from the old boys, and one of Deutch's biggest burdens. The C.I.A. wants to keep control of overseas intelligence missions, seeing the F.B.I. as a bunch of cops in Ninja suits with certain lack of savoir-faire. The bureau wants to wrest control from the agency, seeing it as unskilled in the basics of busting bad guys. They are forced to cooperate, and this requires working hard to avoid colliding. This struggle either will end in an amicable truce or a catastrophic loss of power and prestige for the clandestine service.

"The problem we face today," Deutch says, "is getting both these communities to work together and build on each other's strength and forget about the fact that this tussle goes back to the time of Allen Dulles and J. Edgar Hoover."...

It will take a very long time to turn the C.I.A. around, if it can be done at all. Deutch is talking about three or four years. But it may be far longer. "We didn't get to the position we're in overnight and we aren't going to get out of it overnight," said Nora Slatkin, whom Deutch brought in from the Pentagon to serve as the agency's executive director, its day-to-day manager and by far the highest-ranking woman in its history. "Change isn't easy. There's always going to be some resistance to change. Always. If it takes a decade or so to build a new satellite, it's not unreasonable to take that long to build a new generation of C.I.A. officers.". . .

Deutch wanted to become president of M.I.T. in 1990, but did not win the prize. He stepped down as provost and returned to teaching, one of a dozen among the more than 900 given the title of institute professor. He had become rich from patents and consultancies and companies and investments and a partnership with William Perry, an old friend and colleague from the Pentagon. When the Democrats returned to power in 1993, there was a limited universe of people deemed capable of running the Defense Department. Deutch and Perry were in it, as was another friend from M.I.T, Les Aspin, a whiz kid who was chairman of the House Armed Services Committee. Aspin became Defense Secretary, Perry his deputy. Deutch became the procurement czar and by most accounts, did very well. He cut $90 billion out of President Bush's five-year military plan. He took a ruinously expensive and fouled-up program—the new C-17 transport plane—and made it fly.

In March 1994, Perry became Defense Secretary and Deutch his deputy. And now that Deutch holds what Perry says "may be the toughest job in Washington"—tougher than running the Defense Department or, for that matter, the White House—Deutch looks back and sees his experiences in stark relief.

"The Pentagon, this time around, was an organization equipped to take on change and well aware that it was necessary because of the fall of the Soviet empire," he says. "It was a huge organization whose leadership and all of its different parts said: 'We need to change, and to organize our resources and our people to accomplish this change.'

"The C.I.A. is an organization suffering because it's had tremendous criticism because of its own mistakes, and part of the problem is for the core work force to recognize that they are responsible for some of these problems and that it's in their power to change," he says. "There's been some tendency to say, 'It's the world that's wrong, not us, and if only we could revert to the good old days things would be better.' It's very much harder for an outsider to come in and make progress, especially when a great fraction of my time has been spent explaining these inexplicable past er-

rors. It's a very, very different management challenge and by far the most difficult, running the C.I.A. By far."

It is the business of intelligence to replace ignorance and fear with knowledge and confidence. The C.I.A has been imprisoned by its own lies, living in fear, unsure of its history, uncertain of its future. Deutch is trying to force the agency to face its sins and shortcomings. If the C.I.A. has a future, this is how it must begin.

At 8:30 on Halloween morning, John Deutch returned to address the spies in the Bubble, once again trying to explain the inexplicable. The agency had suffered yet another self-inflicted wound, this time to its soul.

For eight years, the agency had knowingly given the White House and the Pentagon reports from Soviet agents it knew to be under Moscow's control—a stupid and self-destructive decision. It was the most important job of the C.I.A. to speak truth to power. But the agency had simply picked the most plausible-sounding stories told by paid liars. Passing along information without revealing that its source works for the other side is putting poison in the well. The officers in question figured that they knew best. They thought the information was probably true, so they did not have to tell anyone that it came from double agents. They concealed that salient fact from three Presidents—whose policy judgments may have been swayed by the reports. This deception reflected supreme arrogance, Deutch says, "an arrogance that let them ignore the fundamentals of their profession."

The double agents existed thanks to the treason of Aldrich Ames, and his treason sprang from that same arrogance. Ames was a child of the C.I.A., the son of an agency man, a living emblem of the malevolent mediocrity in its ranks. His treason has forced the agency to live in a state of fear, not knowing which of its secrets are secret. And this latest disaster shows that his spirit lives on. In a jailhouse interview last year, he spelled out why he sold out the agency's crown jewels to the Kremlin. "Call it arrogance, if you will, but I'd say: 'I know what's damaging, and I know what's not damaging, and I know what the Soviet Union is really all about, and I know what's best for foreign policy and national security.' And I do."

In the Bubble, Deutch discussed the disaster in detail for 15 minutes, then answered questions. And then he talked to the spies about the future. He said he understood the damage to their morale. He exhorted them not to let it bring them down. There are ways to fix it, he said. We're going to pull together. We're going to stand as one and move on.

They rose and applauded, long and loud.

Deutch received a similar reception the next day at a convocation of station chiefs from around the world down at the Farm, the agency's training grounds at Camp Peary, outside Williamsburg, Va. After his return, a sense of wonder began showing through his deep weariness.

As he talked about it the next night, in his suite of offices up on the seventh floor, he began to think aloud again: maybe he was getting through to the spies. Perhaps this last chapter of the Ames affair had shocked them into consciousness.

"This one got to them, on their own terms," he said. "It was such a violation of their own rules. They've realized what happened here. And I think it's shaken them very considerably. They're a lot more ready to say: 'Tell us what to do. We're going to work.'"

READING 55

Bureaucratic-Congressional Relations: Separate Institutions, Shared Powers

Randall B. Ripley and Grace A. Franklin

Congress and the federal bureaucracy have an ongoing, close relationship in the making of national policy and programs. They also have an important relationship, although more sporadic, in the implementation of national programs. This relationship is often given less attention than it deserves, both by journalists and even by political

scientists, both of whom are more fascinated by the congressional–presidential relationship.

However, a great deal of the day-to-day policy and program development business of the federal government cannot be properly understood without a good grasp of the bureaucratic–congressional relationship.

This reading, by Randall Ripley, a political scientist at Ohio State University, and Grace Franklin, a political scientist affiliated with the Columbus Metropolitan Library, addresses three principal topics: the mix of cooperation and conflict between Congress and the bureaucracy, the nature and scope of the delegation of authority from Congress to the bureaucracy, and congressional oversight of bureaucratic performance.

The conditions that promote either conflict or cooperation are addressed in the first section. Note also the assertion that cooperation is more prevalent than conflict in this relationship, although the latter gets more attention because it is generally more interesting, both to journalists—who don't usually look at the relationship much at all—and to many political scientists.

The section stresses the prevalence and fairly open-ended nature of much delegation of authority. The judiciary continues not to make decisions that limit delegation.

The final section indicates that, at least in principle, broad delegation of authority presents no particular danger of irresponsible behavior because Congress has multiple opportunities to engage in oversight. How well Congress conducts that oversight is another question. The motivations to engage in broad-gauged, policy oriented oversight of programs are sporadic. A great deal of bureaucratic behavior goes without that kind of oversight, even though Congress may submit some bureaucrats to random, nit-picking questions.

COOPERATION AND CONFLICT

The Constitution created three branches of government that have distinct identities in terms of their powers and the way in which officeholders are chosen. It also distributed powers in such a way that interaction and cooperation between the branches are necessary if anything is to be accomplished. Institutional jealousies about preserving powers and competition to serve different constituencies mean that the three branches will inevitably have some conflicts. But an overriding desire to achieve some policy goals also means that most participants in all three branches understand and operate on the values of cooperation and compromise much of the time. The existence of subgovernments serves to reinforce the values of cooperation and compromise for the participants. Institutional jealousies and competition among constituencies remain even within individual subgovernments, but the effects of those jealousies and competition are muted in day-to-day operations. A premium is placed on generating policy that is usually either an extension of the status quo or some small variant of it. More policy generation also creates more bureaucracy, which, in the course of implementing programs, creates more occasions for members of Congress to serve their constituents in dealings with the bureaucracy. Such service benefits the members at election time.

Most of the literature dealing with Congress and the bureaucracy usually focuses on the conflictive aspects of the relationship, and although conflict is a more exciting topic than cooperation, the bulk of policy making is nevertheless based on cooperation. One of the tasks of this volume will be to develop suggestions in the literature about the conditions that promote cooperation or conflict.

A few generalizations specify some of the major conditions promoting either cooperation or conflict.

First, personal compatibility between key agency personnel and key congressional personnel, especially at the subcommittee level, is important. A high degree of compatibility promotes cooperation. Less compatibility (or greater amounts of hostility) promotes conflict.

Second, the degree of ideological and programmatic agreement between key individuals in Congress (usually those on the relevant subcommittee) and in the agency is important. A high degree of agreement promotes cooperation. A low degree of agreement promotes conflict. Similarly, a high degree of unity *between* the individual members of Congress thought by bureaucrats to be important is likely to make the bureaucrats less inclined to pursue interests that may conflict with united congressional opinion. Disunity among members of Congress may tempt bureaucrats to form alliances with those agreeing with them, thus provoking conflict with the other congressional faction.

Third, the amount of genuine participation by Congress (primarily members of a subcommittee) in the development of programs is important. If executive branch officials simply present Congress with finished products—either in the form of proposed legislation or in the form of major administrative decisions—conflict may result. If the executive officials adopt the habit of consultation as they undertake either legislative or administrative courses of action, they enhance the chances of cooperation.

Fourth, if an issue is relatively unimportant to constituents or interest groups, then the chances of congressional–bureaucratic cooperation are enhanced. However, if constituents or interest groups are heavily involved, the potential for conflict increases.

Fifth, agencies that are highly aggressive in seeking to expand their authority and their funding run a greater risk of conflict with Congress, especially committees and subcommittees, than agencies that are less aggressive.

Sixth, if the presidency and Congress are controlled by the same political party, the chances for cooperation are enhanced. If different parties control the two branches, the chances for conflict increase.

DELEGATION OF AUTHORITY

Delegation of authority occurs when Congress writes general statutes that necessitate further elaboration before they can be implemented. Career civil servants in executive branch agencies must supplement general statutory language with more specific language in a variety of regulations. The regulation writing process is, in effect, a second legislative process. The process of writing regulations can take a long time, and, over the course of time, the regulations can alter substantially the presumed purposes of the statutes on which they are based.

There is nothing disreputable or unusual about delegation of authority. Some degree of delegation is necessary because of the volume of legislation and because of the complicated nature of individual statutes and the topics they address. In theory, Congress sets clear standards and guidelines in the legislation for the bureaucracy to follow in elaborating the statute through regulations. In practice, however, the clarity and specificity of the standards and guidelines vary a great deal. For example, Congress may direct the National Labor Relations Board (NLRB) to ascertain that the parties in labor negotiations adhere to "fair standards." The meaning of "fair standards" is, however, not provided by Congress but is, instead, left to the determination of the NLRB. Similarly, the interpretation of "maximum feasible participation" of the poor mandated in the Economic Opportunity Act of 1964 was left to the Office of Economic Opportunity and not provided in any way by Congress. On the other hand, Congress may specify precise standards that allow little agency leeway, as was the case with the Securities Act of 1933. The large size of the *Federal Register,* in which regulations generated by the bureaucracy must be published, testifies to the importance of agency-generated regulations. There is also a large amount of informal, unrecorded administrative rule making on the part of agencies.

Congress sometimes intentionally uses delegation to delay making a final decision. A clear-cut policy decision may penalize or anger some groups. These groups can then manifest their unhappiness by withdrawing their support from selected members of Congress. If the members perceive that they would lose a great deal of support, they may choose not to state a clear policy and leave the policy outcome ambiguous by delegating decision making to parts of the bureaucracy, or to regulatory commissions, or to the courts, with only vague congressional guidance. This way, the perceived winners and losers defined by the policy decision are less clear, and the responsibility for the decision is deflected from Congress to others.

The propriety of congressional delegation of authority was challenged during the New Deal, and the Supreme Court ruled on a few occasions that specific delegations were unconstitutional because of vagueness. But the judicial check has not been exercised since the 1930s. In effect, Congress can follow whatever course it wishes with respect to delegation. In summarizing this fact and the continuing trend toward very broad delegations, Woll wrote that "it is possible to conclude that there are no constitutional or legal restrictions that have impeded in any substantial way the trend toward greater delegation. This situation has not, of course, resulted from administration usurpation, but from congressional desire." Delegation, in sum, is a result of necessity; but it is also a matter of will, not coercion.

Although the principle of delegation of authority is well established, the question of what form delegation ought to take is not so well settled. Some scholars argue that Congress should be only minimally involved in administration. They imply that its delegations of authority should be broad and vague to allow bureaucrats to make interpretations best suited to meeting problems faced in program administration. Other scholars argue that delegation of authority without accompanying clear guidelines limits congressional policy impact to relatively marginal details and represents, in effect, a congressional abdication of responsibility. Congress, in this view, should publish clear expectations and guidelines along with its delegations.

The forms of delegation vary. The reasons for relatively clear guidelines in statutory language in some cases and very broad and vague language in others are numerous and vary from case to case. One important consideration may be the mood of Congress at any given time with reference to the agency to which the delegation is being made. More precisely, the most important consideration may be the attitude of the responsible congressional subcommittees toward the relevant agencies.

A striking example of how patterns of delegation are affected by changing congressional attitudes is provided by comparing the degree of discretionary power allocated to the Federal Trade Commission (FTC) in the Securities Act of 1933 with the degree of power allocated to the Securities and Exchange Commission (SEC) in the Securities and Exchange Act of 1934. The FTC's discretionary power was severely limited in part because of congressional lack of confidence in the agency's membership. Its duties were defined so precisely that administration was almost a matter of mechanical routine. In contrast, attitudes toward the FTC had changed in a more favorable direction by 1934, and the new confidence was reflected in the broader administrative authority granted to the new SEC.

The type of issue involved also affects the nature of congressional delegation. In dealing with complex issues, especially those in the jurisdictions of the independent regulatory commissions, Congress is often unable or unwilling to arrive at specific language. The result is that the regulatory commissions have a great deal of discretion in interpreting statutes.

A desire to shift responsibility for decision making may also be a factor in congressional delegations of authority to the bureaucracy. Unpopular decisions can be laid at the bureaucracy's door, rather than reflecting negatively on Congress. Landis makes the point that Congress can shift the focus of conflict to administrative agencies and away from itself by avoiding clear policy statements in statutes.

The bottom line with reference to delegation of authority is that a good deal of the detail of public policy gets made by the bureaucracy without any explicit attention from Congress. Congressional access to routine policy matters is limited in practice, if not in theory. Even in initiating new formal statutes, the bureaucracy is important and sometimes dominant.

LEGISLATIVE OVERSIGHT

Congressional delegation of authority does not necessarily mean congressional abdication, however. Congress has access to administrative policy making through a variety of activities collectively known as legislative oversight. This oversight can serve as a counterbalance to congressional grants of policy making authority to the bureaucracy. On the one hand, Congress gives away part of its powers to the executive branch through delegation. On the other hand, it reserves the right to monitor the way the executive branch is exercising that authority. We use "oversight" as a neutral word. Oversight in general is necessary in a representative government. But we do not prejudge any specific exercise of it as either good or bad.

Legislative oversight is not just a single activity that occurs on a regular basis. Oversight, broadly conceived, consists of all of Congress's involvement in the affairs of the bureaucracy. The oversight activities of Congress focus on five objects: the substance of policy, agency personnel, agency structure, agency decision-making processes, and agency budgets. A brief survey of the techniques of oversight follows....

Congressional concern with the substance of policy is manifested in any of three stages: passage of legislation, implementation of programs, and societal impact of the programs. The content of legislation at the time of its passage identifies congressional intents as modified during the legislative process. The legislation may allow the bureaucracy considerable discretion in interpreting and applying the law. To monitor administrative interpretation, Congress can hold regular hearings in connection with both authorization and appropriation decisions and focus on aspects of this issue; it can hold special investigatory hearings or it can make a variety of personal contacts. If Congress determines that it has overdelegated or underdelegated, it can rewrite a statute. To monitor the impact of legislation on society, Congress can require program evaluations, usually either by the agency itself or by an outside agency such as the General Accounting Office.

The personnel who develop and implement government programs are just as important to policy impact as the content of legislation. Congress is involved with a variety of agency personnel matters—size of total staff or specific components, confirmation of top administrators appointed by the president, compensation for federal employees, and the conduct of personnel in areas such as political activity, loyalty, and conflict of interest.

Congress is involved in agency structure and organization in a fundamental life-and-death sense because it is responsible for creating new agencies or for granting the president reorganization powers while retaining a congressional option for disapproving presidential initiatives. Congress also controls the lifeblood of all agencies—budget—and can kill an agency by refusing to fund it, as it did with the Area Redevelopment Administration in 1963. In addition, Congress becomes involved in the details of agency organization when the president submits reorganization plans. Congressional action killed President John Kennedy's proposal for a Department of Urban Affairs in 1962, for example.

Congress inserts itself into the internal decision-making processes of agencies in at least two ways. First, Congress requires many reports and submissions of data. Congress can review these materials to oversee agency behavior. Second, Congress can use various forms of the legislative veto, which requires an agency to submit its proposals either to Congress as a whole or to a particular committee for approval or disapproval. Although the Supreme Court ruled that the legislative veto was unconstitutional in a 1983 decision, that decision has been largely ignored by both Congress and the executive branch in practice.

Congressional budgetary oversight can involve authorizations, appropriations, and expenditures. Authorizations establish the legitimacy of a program and set a ceiling on appropriations for subsequent years. Authorizations must be passed before a program can receive appropriations. The authorization process for a new or existing program requires hearings before the relevant House and Senate legislative committees. At these hearings, members review past and expected future program performances by agencies. The frequency of authorization hearings varies from yearly to longer periods, depending on the program. The appropriations hearings held by subcommittees of the House and Senate Appropriations Committees are an annual event for most agencies. These hearings also review agency performance.

It has been difficult for Congress to coordinate the program reviews that occur in the separate authorization and appropriation hearings. The quality of oversight has been criticized for focusing too much on detail and too little on program effectiveness and impact. Detailed questions about spending ("How did you spend the $10,000 for chicken wire at your field office in Ogden?") are raised in appropriation hearings and also in special audits and investigations by the General Accounting Office, an arm of Congress. Considerable funding of agencies also takes place through forms other than appropriations, which further diffuses the congressional potential for focused oversight.

FOOD FOR THOUGHT

1. The Civil War, the Progressive era, and the New Deal period are considered to be critical points in the growth of the federal bureaucracy. What does Wilson add to this account in regard to the link between bureaucratic growth and its subservience to clienteles or the government's agenda more generally? To what other factors does he attribute a larger and more powerful bureaucracy?

2. In the reading entitled "Executive Politics in Washington," Heclo indicates the weaknesses of president-centered models of executive politics by focusing on the behavior of the president's departmental appointees. What difficulties do these appointees face in their positions? How do they make decisions; to what forces or influences do they respond? In the related reading, "In Search of a Role: America's Higher Civil Service," Heclo notes the expectations of other politicians for higher civil servants to be political actors. Why do these bureaucratic actors lack incentives to work closely with the president?

3. John Deutch, director of the C.I.A., believes that the clandestine service within the agency must be fundamentally changed in order to be effective in the post-cold war era. Instead of focusing on the former Soviet Union or issues such as ecology and human rights violations, the C.I.A. now proposes to gather intelligence on nuclear weapons proliferation, terrorism, and "hot spots" such as Somalia and Haiti. In the reading "The C.I.A.'s Most Important Mission: Itself," Tim Weiner chronicles Deutch's difficulties in dealing with scandal and convincing his officers of the need to change. Describe the institutional culture of the C.I.A. and some of Deutch's efforts to change it. How does the C.I.A. compare to the Department of Defense in this regard? Offer an example of another executive branch agency or department that might face such substantial change in the future. Explain both why change is necessary and how it might be difficult.

4. Randall Ripley and Grace Franklin describe three aspects of the relationship between Congress and the bureaucracy in the reading "Bureaucratic–Congressional Relations: Separate Institutions, Shared Powers." Can you give a recent example of conflict between Congress and the bureaucracy? Under what conditions is Congress likely to delegate authority to the bureaucracy? The Clinton administration undertook the National Performance Review (1993) of the bureaucracy in part to reform complex regulations developed during the Reagan–Bush era. Do you agree with critics of this effort that such complex regulations were the result of a Democratic congress attempting to control bureaucrats appointed by Republican presidents? How does Congress exercise its oversight of bureaucracy? What are the problems or difficulties of its oversight activities?

5. Many observers of government view an independent bureaucracy as problematic. Through the readings, we have seen that both the president and congress have difficulties overseeing its activities. Would a return to the spoils system enhance presidential control over the bureaucracy and strengthen political parties? Do you support such a shift away from the merit system?

6. James Carville, a political consultant in President Clinton's 1992 campaign, makes the case that, al-though there are a number of things that government does poorly, there are many more things that government does well. For him, programs and projects such as Medicare, the GI bill, Head Start, and the Clean Water Act are examples of bureaucratic action that benefited millions of Americans. In sum, he argues that the federal government, acting through its client-dominated bureaucracy, accomplished goals that could not be met without governmental intervention. Still, public opinion often runs against the federal bureaucracy and many citizens rate its performance as poor. Do you agree with Carville? Offer an argument to support or attack his case. In light of this argument, why do you think that there is an antibureaucratic sentiment in the United States? Does this affect Wilson's notion of the bureaucracy as client oriented? In keeping with the Clinton administration's effort to "reinvent government," discuss ways in which the bureaucracy might be made more "customer friendly."

CHAPTER 12

THE JUDICIARY

The U. S. Supreme Court and the lower federal bench consisting of U. S. District Courts and U. S. Courts of Appeals constitute what is undoubtedly the most invisible branch of American government and policymaking institutions, about which the citizenry has relatively little knowledge and understanding. Indeed, we suspect that many students enrolled in this course did not, at the outset, even think of the courts as "political" institutions but, by now, that presumption may have been sorely tested. In your readings on constitutional interpretation and the Court's actual decisions in cases such as *Marbury* and *McCulloch* we have seen some of the important consequences for judicial policymaking of different approaches to defining the Court's constitutional authority as well as some of the implications of the great potential for policymaking enjoyed by judges. In Chapter 13, additional landmark cases spanning a range of issues are offered as further testimony to the scope of the Court's policymaking role in America. While that role has been and remains controversial it is, nevertheless, real and substantial.

To take note that courts make policy does not suggest that they "do" the same thing that legislators do when they pass a bill or that a president does as Chief Executive. Both the manner in which judicial policy is made and implemented as well as the nature of the authority attached to judicial rulings and the way in which judges are viewed differ significantly from other governmental branches. This chapter offers a series of readings aimed at unravelling and exploring the nature of U. S. judicial politics starting with attempts to examine federal judicial selection, ranging through efforts to understand the aftermath and consequences of Supreme Court rulings.

In politics it is a truism to observe that the decision as to who will make decisions has an important part to play in deciding what decisions are made. This

is certainly true of the courts and we begin with two readings on the politics of federal judicial selection. One of the most important decisions a president can make, the implications of which can far outlast a presidency, concerns the choice of a nominee to fill a vacancy on the Supreme Court. Many variables enter into this appointment process including numerous representational, professional, and ideological concerns. Thus, a president may consider a potential nominee's race, gender, ethnicity, regional background, and party affiliation as factors that might facilitate or impede eventual appointment as well as aid or complicate other facets of presidential politics. A president's professional concern may extend to a potential nominee's intellectual capacity, sense of fairness, judicial temperament, and legal experience. Ideological concerns may be raised at a very broad level with regard to a potential nominee's general outlook on the place of the Court in our tripartite governmental system. Alternatively, as may have been the case in President Reagan's failing effort to appoint Robert Bork to the Supreme Court, ideological concerns can be very specifically focused and lead to the nomination of individuals whose views on specific past and future Supreme Court cases appear to be well known.

As Michael Kahn illustrates through numerous historical examples in "The Appointment of a Supreme Court Justice: A Political Process From Beginning to End," the weight a president gives to each of the above considerations in making a nomination may vary depending on the political context at the time of the vacancy, the president's own goals and agenda, and several other possible factors. Robert Bork was not the first nor will he be the last Supreme Court nominee for whom politics played a key role in both presidential nominating and senatorial confirmation processes. Sheldon Goldman and Elliot Slotnick's piece, "Clinton's First Term Judiciary: Many Bridges to Cross," expands our gaze to lower federal court judicial recruitment. Their study offers historical context comparing Clinton's selection processes and nomination record with those of President's Bush, Reagan, and Carter. In addition, the article underscores some of the problems that can confront judicial selection processes during periods of divided government when one party controls the presidency and the other party holds a majority in the Senate.

The politics of judicial selection remains central in David Garrow's fascinating study, "Justice Souter Emerges," which documents the ascendancy of the one-time "stealth nominee" to a position of power and influence on the Court. Garrow's account demonstrates that Supreme Court appointments do not arise out of thin air but, rather, culminate a process which may (and in Souter's case did) take many unpredictable twists and turns. Garrow opens a window on the Court's operation through which we get a glance at the role an individual justice can play in the Court's collegial decision making. The portrait drawn of Justice Souter is a revealing one both for what it tells us about him, a sitting justice, and for what it reveals about the Supreme Court and the judicial process. Certainly after reading Garrow's article, readers will pause before characterizing the Court and its members through simplistic labels such as "liberal" and "conservative."

Johnson and Canon's study, "Responses to Judicial Policies," takes us beyond judicial decisions per se to a consideration of their aftermath. The article opens with a case study of abortion policy in the wake of the Court's ruling in *Roe* v. *Wade.* In the second half of the selection, the authors follow the path of much social science research in their effort to move from the specifics of *Roe* to the broader theoretical questions about implementation and impact that *Roe* raises. In this manner researchers hope to isolate those factors associated with judicial rulings that facilitate effective implementation and intended impact, while also recognizing those factors that lead to noncompliance and evasion. Although Johnson and Canon focus primarily on the actors responding to a judicial ruling and on the political context in which they operate, we should not lose sight of the importance of the qualities

of the decision itself for understanding its implementation and impact. How clear is the directive in the Court's majority opinion? Is it consistent with the line of earlier case development? Are there any dissenting justices, and how vocal and divisive are the dissenters? How effectively has the ruling been spread? These and other questions demonstrate that understanding the consequences of a judicial ruling is a difficult and complex enterprise. It is a critical one, however, in its recognition of the fact that judicial policies constitute more than simply the legal pronouncements rendered by judges. Those decisions are merely the starting point in a larger political process involving multiple actors playing numerous political roles.

The chapter concludes with Donald Horowitz's important essay on "Social Policy and Judicial Capacity," an analysis suggesting that the courts are ill-suited, that is, lack the capacity, for the policymaking role they currently play in American society. Horowitz traces the growth of judicial power to the aftermath of the historic school desegregation cases, which "created a magnetic field around the courts" for new policymaking initiatives. The courts loosened their rules of access, thus facilitating their expanded role. Further, the traditional American penchant for litigation exacerbated existing trends. At bottom, Horowitz asserts that the courts' lack of capacity, as well as the convergence of judicial policymaking with other forms of policymaking, creates a situation in which the supposed benefits of judicial decision making, the ability to deal with a case at hand and not in the realm of prophecy, may not actually exist.

Needless to say, Horowitz's thesis is a controversial one. On one level, it can be argued that the judiciary's current posture is less novel than Horowitz makes it appear. New turns in judicial policymaking may reflect the dominance of new concerns in the polity, where questions of democratic theory now focus on what government must do for the individual as much as on questions of governmental restraints. Horowitz appears to give short shrift to "preferred freedoms" conceptions of the judicial function that could serve to justify an expanded judicial role in some areas. Perhaps too little attention is given to the causes of judicial expansion. As Justice Powell wrote in one case decision, "Congress's failure to make political judgments can distort our system of separation of powers by encouraging other branches to make essentially legislative decisions." Further, the question of judicial impact, what courts can actually accomplish as the "least dangerous branch," remains paramount in any discussion of the judicial role. Finally, it should be underscored that there are, indeed, many forms of judicial accountability and that it has also been suggested that judicial capacity, while imperfect, holds up relatively well in comparisons with the policymaking capacities of other branches of government.

READING 56

The Appointment of a Supreme Court Justice: A Political Process From Beginning to End

Michael A. Kahn

The context of contemporary Supreme Court nomination battles including, most specifically the protracted and heated struggles over the designations of Robert Bork and Clarence Thomas to seats on the high court, has led to the charge by some analysts that Supreme Court appointment processes have become both unduly as well as all too frequently political in nature. Michael Kahn argues below that this assessment is inaccurate on both counts.

Historically, Kahn demonstrates, heated political struggles have occurred over many nominees, and justices have been nominated (and passed over for nomination) for clearly political reasons. Among the political criteria presidents have employed in nominating Supreme Court justices have been numerous representational concerns

---

From "The Appointment of a Supreme Court Justice: A Political Process from Beginning to End" by M. A. Kahn, 1995, *Presidential Studies Quarterly* 25(1):25–39. Copyright © 1995 by the Center for the Study of the Presidency. Permission granted by the Center for the Study of the Presidency, publisher of *Presidential Studies Quarterly.*

(such as political party, gender, race, religion, and geographical region) as well as doctrinal and ideological considerations. Indeed, as Kahn suggests, seemingly apolitical, "statesmanlike" appointments (such as those of William Brennan by President Eisenhower and, more recently, John Paul Stevens by President Ford) can be understood best from a strategic, political perspective.

Kahn's analysis goes beyond simply taking note of the political nature of Supreme Court appointment processes to make the more normative judgment that political considerations are both reasonable and desirable criteria by which to assess Supreme Court nominees. Left unexamined here, however, are the nuts and bolts of the advice and consent process, the Senate Judiciary Committee's confirmation hearings, through which the politics of Supreme Court appointment processes are now played out on television before a mass public. One might argue that political considerations are appropriate in both presidential nominations and senatorial confirmations of Supreme Court justices without necessarily endorsing the view that there are no constraints on the kinds of questions senators can legitimately ask nominees or that nominees must answer every question posed to them during the confirmation process.

JUDGE BORK'S THESIS

In his personal postmortem of his failed 1987 nomination to the Supreme Court Robert Bork complains bitterly that he was unfairly denied a seat on the Supreme Court by politicians strictly for political reasons. Bork excoriates these politicians (particularly Senators Kennedy and Metzenbaum) and laments the unwarranted intrusion of political considerations into the sacred process of selecting a Supreme Court Justice. Bork argues that only altruistic and pure criteria should be employed by Presidents and Senators in anointing Supreme Court Justices. Such valid reasons include competence, integrity and judicial temperament. Bork leaves no doubt that if valid criteria had been utilized he would have been deciding cases on the High Court since the early 1980s. Bork, quoting Senator Hatch, claims that the reason his nomination generated controversy "is found in one word, which is tragic in this judicial context, and that word is 'politics'."

Bork's complaint flows entirely from his professed belief in the myth that in choosing Supreme Court Justices and in confirming them Presidents and Senators are not supposed to and in the main historically have not used political criteria. By political criteria Bork means ideological bias or result orientation. It is not hard to understand why Bork embraces this view—it validates his belief that he is a victim of some unique wrongdoing which has deprived him of his rightful place in American life. Bork, indeed, asserts that his confirmation process was "politicized more than ever before in America's history."

Bork is not the first unsuccessful nominee to the Court to cry foul over his fate at the hands of politicians. Indeed, virtually all rejected Supreme Court appointees claim to be victims of venal political interests. Over one hundred and fifty years before the Bork affair John Crittenden complained to his friend Henry Clay that his nomination to the Court would be rejected for purely political reasons. He was right. Crittenden was nominated by John Quincy Adams in 1828 after Adams was defeated by Jackson. Jackson forces in the Senate blocked the nomination for purely political reasons, without even offering the pretense of a reason that Bork would find valid. Crittenden's confirmation floor manager in the Senate, John Chambers, described the rejection as pervaded by "disgraceful and degrading party feeling." Crittenden's reaction to his Senate defeat was identical to Bork's: he wrote Clay "there is a taste of dishonor which my nature revolts at."

It seems that at approximately fifty year intervals the Senate bares its political teeth and rejects a nominee exclusively for political reasons. In 1881, President Hayes' nomination of Stanley Matthews met this fate; and, in 1930 Judge John Parker was rejected because his political views were unacceptable to the Senate. The Parker Senate fight was every bit as political and nasty as the Bork fight and the vote in the Senate was even closer. Parker was rejected 41–39, as aptly summarized by Professor Kaufman of Harvard Law School, "primarily on ideological grounds, from liberals and progressives within the Senate. . . ."

Supreme Court Justices have always been appointed for political reasons by politicians and their confirmation process has always been dictated by politicians for political purposes.

Indeed, by requiring Supreme Court Justices to be confirmed by the Senate, the founding fathers designed the system to make the appointment process a highly political one. Moreover, this plan has served the country well as the vibrancy, flexibility and resiliency of the American political system [have] enhanced the Court's legitimacy by making this highly undemocratic instruction responsive to democratic pressures.

The surprising phenomenon is not the political nature of this process but rather the strength of the myths that politics is *not*, and *is not supposed to be,* the engine that drives the appointment machine. Bork's criticism of the Senate for politicizing the Supreme Court appointment process is reminiscent of Nixon's complaint about the Senate in 1970:

> With the Senate presently constituted, it is not possible to get confirmation for a Judge on the Supreme Court of any man who believes in the strict construction of the Constitution, as I do, if he happens to come from the South.
>
> Judge Carswell, and before him, Judge Haynsworth, have been submitted to vicious assaults on their intelligence, on their honesty and on their character. They have been falsely charged with being racists. But when you strip away all the hypocrisy, the real reason for their rejection was their legal philosophy, a philosophy that I share, of strict construction of the Constitution.
>
> With yesterday's action, the Senate has said that no southern Federal appellate judge who believes in a strict interpretation of the Constitution can be elevated to the Supreme Court.
>
> As long as the Senate is constituted the way it is today, I will not nominate another Southerner and let him be subjected to the kind of malicious character assassination accorded both Judges Haynsworth and Carswell. . . .

Criticism of the Senate by a President for making Supreme Court appointments a political football is ironic because it is a time-honored tradition for Presidents to complain about the actions of the Supreme Court to enhance their own political standing. By attacking an institution that cannot publicly strike back,

Presidents find an easy target to chastise for political purposes. Nixon himself made the Supreme Court a centerpiece of his 1968 election campaign proclaiming that the Supreme Court's decisions were "seriously hamstringing the peace forces in our society and strengthening the criminal forces." In playing politics with the Court, Nixon was only following the examples of Eisenhower, who chastised the Warren Court's early decisions and Franklin Roosevelt, who complained that nine old men were crippling the New Deal.

Moreover, presidential candidates such as Nixon and Bork's own sponsor, Reagan, often campaign on platforms promising the appointment of correct thinking Supreme Court Justices. Not surprisingly, Presidents who during the election campaign made an issue of the politics of the Supreme Court find themselves once elected required to use consistent political criteria when they are able to make Supreme Court appointments. Thus, Franklin Delano Roosevelt appointed young men who were staunch New Dealers to solve the nine old men problem. Eisenhower, who claimed that the problem with the Court was its "nonjudicial conduct" promised to appoint persons with "real judicial experience in the Court," and he did so with Harlan and Brennan. Nixon, whose anti-Warren Court rhetoric in 1968 was part of a southern strategy (where Warren had been especially vilified), made his first two appointments Southerners (Haynsworth and Carswell) for clearly political reasons.

Each of these appointments underscores the value of injecting political (defined as criteria other than intellectual and character traits) criteria into the appointment process. These Presidents and presidential candidates clearly believed that the means of restoring public confidence in the Court was to appoint politically correct justices. There is little doubt that they were right.

JUSTICE STEVENS: A CLASSIC POLITICAL APPOINTMENT

A good example of the enduring nature of the myth that Justices are appointed on the basis of merit, not politics, is the recent account of Justice Stevens' appointment by David O'Brien.... O'Brien seems to agree that the "practices and priorities" of recent Pres-

idents resulted in the utilization of political criteria for the selection of Supreme Court Justices. Nevertheless, he asserts that President Ford "had little truck with either the personal politics practiced by Democratic Presidents,...or the kind of White House politics calculated...to advance an administration legal-policy agenda." O'Brien asserts that Ford utilized professional criteria to select Justice Stevens, not personal or political criteria. Moreover, O'Brien clearly sees Stevens' non-controversial 98–0 confirmation vote as vindication of the nonpolitical nature of the appointment.

Contrary to his interpretation, O'Brien's recitation of the history of the Stevens appointment reveals that Stevens emerged as Ford's nominee out of an intensely political process. Moreover, Stevens' success in the Senate was proof of the political acumen of his political sponsors, President Ford and Attorney General Levi. Ford and Levi set out to select a non-controversial, preferably unknown, middle-aged Republican male, preferably from the Midwest and with judicial experience. Not surprisingly, the man they chose fit all these criteria and was, not coincidentally, a friend and ex-law school colleague of Levi.

O'Brien admits that because of Ford's unique elevation to the Presidency and his desire to run for President in 1976, Ford had to make an appointment that would avoid alienating hard line conservatives, avoid incurring the wrath of special interest groups and avoid antagonizing Democratic Senators. Accordingly, Attorney General Levi, working under Ford's instructions, compiled a list of non-controversial, middle-aged white male federal judges. Ford and Levi's political goals were obvious: they wanted a completely non-controversial appointment to enhance Ford's image of restoring competence and integrity to the White House.

[These] political criteria resulted in the elimination of a number of logical candidates. Ironically, Robert Bork's nomination would have inspired more political furor in 1975 than it did in 1987 because the memory of his participation in President Nixon's Friday night massacre was fresh in the public mind. Strike Bork for political reasons.

Stricken also for political reasons was President Ford's friend, Senator Griffin, who ardently wanted the nomination. O'Brien admits that Griffin could not be seriously considered by Ford because the Republicans had complained about President Johnson's cronyism in selecting Justice Fortas. For political reasons, Ford could not tolerate a similar charge against his appointment.

Gerald Ford's presidency in 1975 stood on the political quicksand of Watergate. From that precarious roost, Ford's chief goal was to be elected to a full term of his own in 1976. O'Brien's article shows that Ford's overriding goal in selecting a Supreme Court Justice was to enhance his political prospects in 1976. Ford believed he could do so by adopting the strategy of purporting to select all judges on the basis of professional criteria (intelligence, temperament, experience) rather than on the basis of political criteria (e.g., ideology) or personal criteria (e.g., selecting a crony). Ford's conclusion that the most astute political position in the aftermath of the political scandals in the White House was to purport to take politics out of the appointment process was not unique. President Coolidge, on the heels of the Harding scandals, proclaimed piously that the federal bench must be staffed with the best men regardless of their judicial outlook. Coolidge believed his appointment to the Court of Attorney General Harlan Stone, a highly regarded corporate lawyer and former Law School Dean, fit this bill.

In 1975, Ford concluded, wisely, that the most expedient political move was to avoid a political fight over the nomination by not alienating any special interest group and by not making a selection that would aggravate and activate political groups on the right or the left. In making this choice Ford made the political judgment not to make the politically bolder but riskier decision of appointing a hero of the right (such as Bork) or a woman. In selecting Stephen Breyer over Bruce Babbitt in May of 1994 President Clinton appears to have made the same political calculation.

In using political criteria designed to enhance his electability, Ford was following in the footsteps of his predecessors. Virtually every President who has made an appointment to the Supreme Court at the time he was actively running for reelection has used his appointment similarly. The classic examples are Eisenhower's 1956 appointment of Brennan, Hoover's 1932

selection of Cardozo, and Wilson's 1916 selection of Clarke.

When Sherman Minton resigned from the Court in early September 1956 to be effective October 15, Eisenhower was in the middle of his re-election campaign. The Senate was composed of a majority of Democrats, and the Supreme Court was controversial because of the recent desegregation cases. Throughout the academic world and the political world, the Court was under heavy attack; criticized for being political and policy oriented. One remedy often proposed was to require that Justices be selected from the lower Courts to ensure that men with more "judicial" orientations were elevated. Senator Smathers even made this proposal in the Senate.

Eisenhower was making an appointment extremely close to the election. Therefore, it was natural for him to be sensitive to the salient representational claims made upon the seat. First, since the death of Justice Murphy in 1949, there had not been a Catholic on the Court for the first time since President Cleveland had appointed Edward White to the Court in 1894; of course, there were millions of Catholic voters. Second, though New England and the South were under-represented on the Court, there were a number of key states that Eisenhower felt needed a little extra attention in the remaining weeks of the election; New Jersey was one of them. Third, Eisenhower had said that he wanted a younger man to ensure proper judicial influence over a long period (Brennan at fifty became the youngest judge). Fourth, Eisenhower, a Republican, needed Democratic votes for re-election in November and for Senate confirmation in February: therefore, he wanted an apolitical, bi-partisan figure—preferably a Democrat.

Brennan satisfied all of these requirements. In appointing the Democratic, Catholic, Northeastern (New Jersey) Brennan, Eisenhower was specifically pandering to voters who were not his natural constituents.

In 1916, Wilson, and in 1932, Hoover, faced with similar re-election year appointments, attempted for political reasons to appear non-partisan and statesmanlike by appointing someone who could not be criticized as being an ideological or personal selection. Hoover selected the universally revered Cardozo, who like Brennan was from the opposite party.

Wilson selected Clarke, who like Brennan was from a key state in the election, Ohio. Clarke also contrasted nicely with Wilson's previous appointments, Brandeis and MacReynolds, appointments who had been criticized as cronyism. Clarke was a federal judge clearly outside of Wilson's inner circle.

In 1975, Ford and Levi, paralleling Eisenhower, Hoover and Wilson before them, constructed a short list of candidates by using political criteria to make a politically correct appointment. The mandateless Ford decided the most politically astute appointment would be an unknown but highly regarded Judge. Stevens fit Ford's political criteria and that is why he was selected rather than Bork, Griffin or many other professionally qualified candidates.

THE CASE OF LEARNED HAND: PROOF THAT POLITICS GOVERNS THE APPOINTMENT OF SUPREME COURT JUSTICES

Perhaps the most effective refutation of the Bork and Hoover thesis that the appointment of Supreme Court Justices is usually apolitical is found in the case of Learned Hand. . . .

How is it that for over twenty years perhaps the greatest legal mind of the century—Learned Hand—was not elevated to the Supreme Court? Could it be that five Presidents truly believed that the twenty persons they nominated while Hand was at an eligible age were better qualified than Hand? Did President Harding believe that Senator Sutherland and Judge Sanford were better suited intellectually and temperamentally for the Court than Learned Hand? Did President Hoover think that Judge Parker and Philadelphia lawyer Roberts would make better Supreme Court Justices than Learned Hand? Did Franklin Roosevelt believe that Franklin Murphy and Wiley Rutledge would be better at tackling the great judicial issues before the Supreme Court than Learned Hand?

The answers to these questions cannot be avoided by hypothesizing that Hand was not prominent enough nor his excellence publicized enough to grab the attention of these Presidents or their advisors. Indeed. . .Hand had achieved a level of public prominence early in his career. Moreover, his brilliant performance as a District Court and Circuit Judge from 1909 until 1951 brought him praise and recognition

throughout the legal world. In 1923, Holmes spoke of Hand as a desirable fellow Justice; and by the end of that year Hand was given a seat on the Holmes-Laski ideal Supreme Court. In short, even early in his career Learned Hand had gained a place in the pantheon of great legal minds of the day alongside Holmes, Cardozo, and Brandeis.

Some scholars and Hand partisans who are unable or unwilling to believe that Hand was denied his rightful seat on the Court for logical or appropriate reasons, have postulated that "luck or the lack of it" explains this miscarriage of appointment justice. Harold Laski wrote to Justice Holmes on Justice Clarke's resignation, "If God is good, you will have Learned Hand."

Neither God, nor lady luck, was making the appointment in 1922 or at any time before or since. Woodrow Wilson, Warren Harding, Calvin Coolidge, Herbert Hoover, and Franklin Roosevelt all had the power and opportunity to elevate Learned Hand to the Supreme Court. There is no doubt that these Presidents and their advisors realized that Hand was more intelligent, more judicially experienced, and better temperamentally suited for the High Court than some of their nominees. In short, between 1914 and 1942, Hand was often the "best man" for the job and the President and his advisors knew it.

So why wasn't Hand nominated? The answer seems obvious: For *political* reasons. Wilson, Harding, Hoover, and Roosevelt all either disqualified Hand because he was politically unacceptable—too Republican for Wilson, too progressive for Harding, and too even-handed and old for Roosevelt—or chose other people because their selection was politically more profitable than a Hand appointment would have been. Learned Hand's political disqualification from Supreme Court appointment was not an accident—it was a logical consequence of his political and personal career and life style decisions.

Hand's political party affiliation was an ambiguous Republicanism. In 1913, he bolted the Republican Party to be the Bull Moose candidate for the Court of Appeal—a decision which President Taft resented until his death. Hand's political and judicial ideology was a complex mixture of libertarianism and judicial restraint, muted by his balanced, tempered judicial style. Unfortunately, the Supreme Court appointment process is such that a man with these characteristics was not a likely candidate in the first half of the twentieth century. Hence, it was not luck, but political reality—determined in twenty different ways for the twenty times that Hand was passed over—that kept Hand off the Court.

The political arena, however, was flexible enough to produce the appointments of men whose stature and ideology were similar to Hand's: Brandeis, Cardozo, and Frankfurter. Indeed, a strong argument can be made that the political nature of the appointment process has well served the Court and nation by causing (or at least not blocking) the elevation of numerous brilliant and qualified persons to the Court. Nevertheless, the question remains: why was it that Brandeis, Cardozo, and Frankfurter were selected and Hand was not?

A large part of the answer is to be found in Hand's personality and in the personal and political decisions he made throughout his life. Learned Hand never campaigned for a seat on the Supreme Court, and his life style and interests were not such that large numbers of influential people were moved to advocate his appointment ardently. Hand did not cultivate the friendship of politicians or people with political influence as did Brandeis and Frankfurter, whose friendships with the ultimate politicians—Presidents Wilson and Roosevelt—eventually led to their appointment.... Hand became a central figure in the intellectual, academic, and judicial worlds, but not in the political world. By contrast, Cardozo and Frankfurter had become such prominent public figures that their appointments by Hoover and Roosevelt were thought to be brilliant political maneuvers.

In 1932, Benjamin Cardozo was the only judge in America that "had a judicial reputation anywhere near approaching that of Holmes" whose seat Hoover was filling. Hoover succumbed to political pressure and public expressions of support for a unanimously respected jurist in selecting Cardozo.

Roosevelt, in replacing Cardozo with Frankfurter, similarly acquiesced in political and public pressure. In 1938, the Gallup poll had conducted a unique survey among the 175,000 members of the American Bar Association and had found (in results published in *The New York Times*), that five times as many respondents favored Felix Frankfurter, the Harvard law professor, for the appointment than the next most mentioned in-

dividuals, John Davis, Learned Hand, and Senator Walter George. On the evening of January 4, 1939, Roosevelt called Frankfurter and said, "I told you that I can't name you, but wherever I turn, wherever I turn, and to whomever I talk that matters to me, I am made to realize that you're the only person fit to succeed Holmes and Cardozo." Confirming the political wisdom of the Presidents, the Senate unanimously confirmed both Cardozo and Frankfurter.

The political forces and factors which conspired to elevate Cardozo, Frankfurter, and eighteen other men over Learned Hand were not unique to Hand's tenure in American life. These same forces and factors have been present since the Court's inception and they came into play in Bork's rejection. Judge Bork is in good company with Learned Hand in being denied a seat on the Court by political criteria which have always been used by Presidents in appointing Supreme Court Justices.

POLITICAL CRITERIA FOR APPOINTMENT

How politics drives the appointment process depends upon the political context in which the appointment opportunity arises: As we have seen, Presidents in election years face different political issues than lame duck Presidents or newly elected Presidents. However, there are certain types of political criteria that invariably come into play. These political criteria usually work to disqualify persons (e.g., all persons not in the President's political party are usually disqualified) rather than to identify the ultimate selection, and some of these criteria have changed dramatically over time.

The political criteria used by Presidents and their advisors (usually their attorneys general) can be grouped into three categories: representational, doctrinal, and professional. The degree to which a President utilizes these criteria depends upon the political environment at the time, however all Presidents use these three types of criteria to some degree.

Representational Criteria

These criteria—race, gender, political party, religion, and geographical origin—are the most unambiguously political criteria because it is impossible to argue that in using them a President is seeking to appoint the person most intellectually or temperamentally qualified to serve on the Court. Moreover, these criteria often serve to exclude entire classes of extremely qualified persons simply because they do not fit a particular demographic characteristic.

Persuasive proof that the business of appointing Justices is a political enterprise is found in the most obvious place—by looking at the political party of the nominees. It is hardly a coincidence that since President Cleveland's time, over ninety percent of the Court's appointees have been from the same political party as the President. Presidents clearly have seen the Court as the ultimate political patronage to their party. . . .

The practice of using a Court vacancy as a spoil of partisan politics is also demonstrated by the selection of six attorneys general (and several assistant attorneys general, e.g., Byron White and Rehnquist) by five different Presidents in this century. When Presidents so obviously play politics with the Court, their fellow politicians and the press piously complain that the appointment is improperly political. For example, the appointment of attorney general Thomas Clark to the Court was greeted by critical editorials in the *Washington Star* (8/1/49), *The New York Times* (8/2/49), *St. Louis Post Dispatch* (7/29/49), *Detroit Free Press* (8/3/49), and *New York Sun* (7/29/49) among others. Typical of the remarks was one paper's rebuke that, "President Truman, names to [the Court] a political hack who did dirty work for him, as attorney general, who is not learned in law or common ethics" (*Detroit Free Press* (8/12/49)). Another paper commented that "President Truman, of course, likes his appointee. Both are folksy, friendly, and politically molded. Mr. Clark has been a Truman man all the way" (*New York Herald* (8/11/49)). Finally, Representative J. Caleb Boggs of Delaware complained in the *Congressional Record* on August 1, 1949, "It is most certainly apparent that this appointment is purely a political appointment and ignores many of tried and proven judicial temperament and experience."

The appointment philosophy promoted by Congressman Boggs as translated by President Eisenhower into a judicial experience requirement has become the dominant practice since Justice Stevens' elevation from the Circuit Court in 1975. Indeed, including Justice Breyer, every member of the current Court, except Justice Rehnquist, was a judge before

his or her elevation. But there are signs this particular worm may turn again as President Clinton has spoken warmly of the value of appointing a Supreme Court Justice from the ranks of pure politicians (like Governor Cuomo, Senator Mitchell or Secretary Babbitt) to add a more worldly and practical viewpoint to the Court.

After political party, perhaps the most frequently cited representation qualification is geography. The utilization of geographical criteria has its origins in the original necessity of appointing Justices from different circuits to allocate the circuit riding responsibilities of the Justices. Subsequently, certain states claimed a "seat" on the Court, which, for example, was a controlling principle in the selection of Oliver Wendell Holmes to the Massachusetts seat in 1902. Moreover, maintaining a geographical balance on the Court remains a legitimate goal of the appointment process to this day. The Nixon excerpt quoted above demonstrates that Presidents often curry political favor by pandering to a particular region of the country.

The pressure to nominate someone from a region or state unrepresented on the Court usually comes from the Congress. An extreme example was the insistence in the middle 1950s of Senate Judiciary Committee member William Langer of North Dakota that he would oppose any nominee not from his home state on the grounds that North Dakota was entitled to its first representative on the Court. Senator Langer died with his goal still unrequited.

More typically, throughout the Court's history Western and Southern partisans have believed their regions under-represented. Hoover's selection of John Parker in 1930, Nixon's selection of Haynsworth and Carswell in 1969 and 1970, and Roosevelt's nomination of Douglas in 1939 all fulfilled presidential promises to select persons from the South and West. . . .

Religion, race, and gender have also played roles in the selection process—at first negative and later positive. Until the barriers were broken, Catholics, Jews, African-Americans, and women were not appointed by Presidents. Later, however, these arbitrary characteristics appeared to become requirements for appointment. At various times there was thought to be a Catholic seat and Jewish seat though both seats have lapsed at least once. Moreover, it is highly likely that if Justice Thomas left the Court and if another

African-American has not yet been seated, there will be extreme political pressure on the President to continue African-American representation. The appointment of Justice Ginsburg virtually assures permanent female representation on the Court; however it remains to be seen at what level (two? three? four?) the pressure for a gender selection criteria will abate.

Representational criteria alone never dictate the nominee. Nevertheless, these criteria often eliminate extremely qualified candidates as the President narrows his choices to politically acceptable or advantageous choices. The universal presidential practice of considering and usually employing these criteria is proof that Bork's complaint against Senators injecting political considerations into the appointment process misses the historical mark.

Doctrinal Criterion

Doctrinal criteria take into account the future Justice's political and judicial ideology. Basically, the process involves the President's attempt to appoint a Justice whose views most closely approximate his own.

The importance of this criterion cannot be exaggerated. Presidents realize that their most enduring legacy may be the decisions of the lifetime Justices they appoint. Moreover, the fact that Presidents often fail in the prediction of judicial behavior (as Eisenhower did with Brennan; Kennedy with White; Nixon with Blackmun, to cite three examples) does not lessen their political ambition to direct the ideological course of the Court.

Doctrinal criteria most certainly kept Hand off the Court during Harding's administration. Taft who desired the "right to warn" Harding of candidates whose views did not correspond to Taft's own, described Hand to be

> of proper age. . . an able judge and a hard worker [but] he turned out to be a wild Roosevelt man and a progressive, and though on the bench, he went into the campaign. If promoted he would almost certainly herd with Brandeis and be a dissenter. I think it would be risking too much to appoint him.

In activities such as this, Taft, according to his biographer, "merely confirmed the Supreme Court for what it was and always had been—a political institution."

Presidents and presidential aspirants seem to have a habit of making the decisions of the Court the object of continued political attacks. Whether they are complaining about unwarranted assaults on their program (as did FDR), unwarranted legislation by the Court (as did Eisenhower), unwarranted coddling of criminals (as did Nixon), or unwarranted attacks on our values (as did Bush in criticizing the abortion and flag-burning decisions), Presidents seek to increase their own political standing by flailing at the Court.

What is the logical presidential cure for this Supreme Court disease—which every President advocates? The appointment of correct-thinking Supreme Court Justices. Justices who will make the right decision, Justices who will reach the right results? In short, a completely legitimate political means of imposing the President's views on the country is to appoint Justices who share and will implement his views. As Chief Justice Rehnquist said in a 1985 speech in which he acknowledged the legitimacy of the President attempting to place persons on the Court with a particular philosophy

> The [governmental system] has been constructed in such a way that the public will, in the person of the President of the United States. . .have something to say about the membership of the Court, and thereby indirectly about its decisions.

The battle for ideological supremacy on the Court is exactly what the Bork nomination was all about. No one can seriously doubt that Reagan appointed Bork to the Court because he wanted to continue fulfilling his campaign pledge to appoint conservative thinkers to the Court. Indeed,. . . both sides in the Bork fight realized they were fighting a political holy war over the future political philosophy of the Court.

The presidential quest to extend doctrinal influence over the Court often imposes another requirement on the nominee. Most Presidents like President Ford in 1975 desire to guide the Court's ideology for as far into the future as possible. Accordingly, age is usually a criterion as Presidents seek to appoint a Justice who will impose his doctrine for decades. There have only been three appointees in the Court's history over age sixty-five and none over age seventy.

Professional Criteria

Professional criteria—intelligence, experience, temperament—are presumably the criteria Bork believes are legitimate. Indeed, every President proclaims his nominee—no matter how abysmal the selection—well-suited on the basis of professional criteria. To date, no President has invoked Senator Hruska's famous belief that "mediocre" people "are entitled to a little representation in the Court."

There are, unfortunately, no universal tests for professional criteria. Presidents, accordingly, look for any test they can find. Eisenhower decided that judicial experience was required to prove professional competence. He also began the policy of seeking the ABA's views on professional competence. Nixon, however, discarded the ABA's screening because he did not like the results....

Undoubtedly post hoc arguments can be made that virtually every nominee has been professionally qualified. Thus, though Presidents usually parade the professional qualifications of their nominees, these criteria almost never dominate the process. Only after representational and doctrinal criteria dramatically narrow the field does the President employ his professional litmus test—whatever it may be.

The virtue of professional qualifications is that they give the President a high ground from which to defend the discharge of what Hoover called a President's "sacred duty." Moreover, those rare occasions when a selection is made in which professional qualifications appear to the public and press to predominate reward the President with increased stature. Justice Stone's assessment of the Cardozo appointment demonstrates this political axiom:

> The appointment is so obviously non-political that it will, paradoxically enough be of great political advantage to the President. But, of course, that is always good Presidential politics.

The unambiguously political nature of the appointment process is proved finally and irrevocably by the confirmation process.... It seems abundantly clear that because of the Senate confirmation process, which subjects the nominee to the vagaries of a vote by one hundred democratically elected officials, the appointment process is inexorably dictated by political considerations, not by professional ones.

SENATE POLITICS

There is great risk of embarrassment in the appointment of a Supreme Court Justice. The President must submit a person who will be thoroughly scrutinized by roughly fifty hostile Senators whose fondest wish is usually to have the President replaced by someone of their own party. Thus, the most obvious and immediate goal of every Supreme Court appointment decision is to select someone who will be confirmed—hopefully, swiftly and without controversy.

Presidential fear of the Senate is well founded. Since Washington's time twenty-eight nominees have been rejected, withdrawn or postponed. Moreover, several other nominees have been confirmed only after bitter battles in the Senate which have cost the President dearly. The nomination of Lucius Laman in 1887 as well as the nominations of Brandeis, Hughes, Black and Thomas experienced unpleasant and divisive battles in the Senate though each was confirmed.

As discussed earlier, the going gets the roughest for a President at the end of his term. John Adams, Rutherford Hayes, Lyndon Johnson, and Ronald Reagan all shared this experience. The reason is clear: usually the President's power is weakest at the end of his term and his political enemies have the most to gain by wounding his party at that juncture.

One or more of the following factors can constrain a President's freedom of appointment: (1) the President is a "lame duck" near the end of his term; (2) the majority in the United States Senate is from the opposite party, or the actual majority in the Senate (disregarding party labels) is hostile to the President; (3) the President is running for re-election; (4) the appointment is overshadowed by a national crisis and the President must use his patronage to gain political advantages in other areas.

There are two political solutions to the dilemma of making an appointment at the time of presidential vulnerability. One is to co-opt the political rules of the game by appointing a Senator. It is said that Roosevelt selected Black because he knew the Senate had to confirm him and he wanted the enemies of his Court packing scheme to swallow a bitter pill. No Senator, no matter how unqualified, has ever been rejected by the Senate. Indeed, Senator Sutherland sailed through unanimously while Brandeis and Hughes were vilified and confirmed only after bitter battles. No doubt confirmation was on President Clinton's mind in his early support of Senator Mitchell.

A second strategy of a President in a vulnerable position is to appoint a person from the opposite party. Brennan's selection in 1956 and Cardozo's in 1932 are excellent examples.

Why is it that a weak President has less latitude in selecting his nominees than a politically powerful President? The answer is clear: From the time George Washington established specific representational, doctrinal, and professional qualifications for his appointments in 1789 and the Senate rebuked him by rejecting his nominee John Rutledge to replace John Jay as Chief Justice in 1796 for the political reason that Rutledge opposed the Jay treaty, the nomination and confirmation process has always been an essentially political battlefield where political goals, strategy and tactics dictate the results....

[T]he simple fact is that, despite Bork's almost unprecedented professional qualifications for the Supreme Court, Ronald Reagan did not have the political clout to impose him on the Senate Democrats in 1987. Of course, the Democrats did not have the power to block every Reagan selection or to dictate a choice. This political stalemate resulted in the unanimous elevation of Judge Kennedy (like Judge Stevens before him), a politically neutral and therefore politically acceptable choice.

CONCLUSION

Robert Bork did not lose his seat on the Court because the Democrats changed the rules of the game. He lost because the rules of the game make the appointment process essentially a bare knuckle political fight. John Parker, Clement Haynsworth, Abe Fortas, and others could have told him so.

In 1969 Professor Kohlmeier complained that the Republicans were ruining the Court and the nation by politicizing the appointment process; Bork

put this shoe on the other foot in his 1990 book. In fact, however, not despite the politicization of the appointment and confirmation process, but because of it, the Supreme Court has endured as a flexible, viable force in the American democracy for over 200 years. Undoubtedly, driven by the engine of politics, the Court will continue to play this critical role regardless of how loudly politicians, failed nominees or scholars pronounce that the Court is dying of dread political diseases.

| READING 57 |

Clinton's First Term Judiciary: Many Bridges to Cross
Sheldon Goldman and Elliot Slotnick

Unlike the widespread attention generally paid to appointments to the Supreme Court, recruitment to the lower federal bench (U. S. District Courts and U. S. Courts of Appeals) has been, with isolated exceptions, a relatively invisible affair. Nevertheless, because most cases are definitively resolved in the lower courts, never receiving Supreme Court review, it is clear that the lower courts play a critical role in the making of American public policy. Indeed, it is at this level of the American judiciary that an American president can leave his mark with a great deal more subtlety than in the fishbowl process of appointing Supreme Court justices.

In this selection, political scientists Goldman (University of Massachusetts) and Slotnick (Ohio State University) focus primarily on the appointment processes followed and the record developed by President Clinton during his first term in office, comparing the Clinton record to that of Presidents Bush, Reagan, and Carter. The analysis reveals both

*the President's commitment to as well as the clear
success of (at least as judged by ABA ratings)
his pursuit of affirmative action in judicial
recruitment, with an unprecedented proportion of
vacancies filled by "nontraditional" judges (women
and minorities). At the same time, however, the
President has avoided nominating ideologically
controversial candidates to the bench, while
emphasizing consultation with the Republican
opposition, even before they became the majority
party in the Senate.*

*In highlighting dramatically different
appointment outcomes in the second half of Clinton's
first term (when Republicans controlled the Senate)
compared to Clinton's first two years, the analysis
underscores the political nature of the judicial
selection process and some of the potential
consequences of divided government. Indeed, the
authors suggest, the virtual stoppage of confirmation
processes in 1996 (attributable to presidential
election politics) and the continued snail's pace of
confirmations at the beginning of Clinton's second
term, threaten to strike at the institutional integrity of
the American judiciary while hearkening back to
earlier infamous struggles over the courts in
American history.*

Bill Clinton's first term as president was an eventful
one for judicial selection. The Democratic 103rd Congress, which was hospitable to Clinton's nominees,
gave way to the Republican 104th Congress, which
was much less so. The 1996 election resulted in Republican control of both houses of Congress, the first
time in American history that a Democratic president
was elected with a Republican Congress.

This article surveys the judicial selection mile-
stones from the first term with emphasis on the second
half of that term. The Clinton judicial selection process, particularly the relationship with the Republican
leadership on the Senate Judiciary Committee, is discussed as well as the implications for continued Republican control of the confirmation process. The
centerpiece of this survey consists of the demographic
profiles of the Clinton appointees to lifetime judgeships on the lower courts of general jurisdiction....

THE SELECTION PROCESS

Judicial selection during Clinton's first term was
jointly conducted by the Office of Policy Development and the White House Counsel's Office. Eleanor
D. Acheson, assistant attorney general for policy
development, oversaw the Justice Department's selection activity. Her deputy, Peter Erichsen, worked
full-time on judicial selection until he moved in 1996
to the Office of White House Counsel where he coordinated judicial selection efforts for the remainder of
the 104th Congress....

The process within the Justice Department began with the assignment of each candidate to a Justice Department lawyer who analyzed the candidate's
professional credentials, including any relevant judicial decision making. Candidates for the district
bench came from recommendations by Democratic
senators, or in the absence of a Democratic senator,
from the Democratic members of the House of Representatives or other high-ranking Democratic Party
politicians. Screening began with a lengthy in-depth
telephone interview with the candidate and dozens of
follow-up calls to those who had professional dealings with the individual. Overseeing the screening
process was a judicial selection committee within the
Justice Department....

At the Office of White House Counsel more political matters were considered. The counsel's office
sounded out Republican senators, working closely
with the ranking Republican on the Senate Judiciary
Committee during the 103rd Congress, Orin Hatch,
who became chair during the 104th Congress....

The Judicial Selection Group, a joint White
House-Justice Department committee, met regularly
to discuss candidates for judgeships and to decide
whom to recommend to the president. The chair of the
committee was the White House counsel. Other members included the associate White House counsel with
responsibility for judicial selection, the deputy White
House counsel Joel Klein and later his replacement
James Castello, and deputy Bruce R. Lindsey. Other
members from the White House staff included a representative from the Office of Legislative Affairs, the
vice-president's counsel, and an assistant to the president, who is also deputy chief of staff for the first

lady. Committee members from the Justice Department included Eleanor Acheson, Peter Erichsen, Roslyn Mazer, and a former deputy who later became counselor and chief of staff in the Civil Rights Division, Susan Liss. Although Attorney General Janet Reno was an ex officio member, she did not attend meetings.

District court candidates were screened by the Office of Policy Development with little involvement from the White House counsel's office. Courts of appeals candidacies were often initiated at the White House counsel's office and some screening occurred there as well. For the filling of the two Supreme Court positions, the White House counsel's office took the principal role in screening.

During Clinton's first two years in office, with a Democratic Senate in the 103rd Congress, 118 people were nominated for lifetime judgeships on the district courts and 107 were confirmed (approximately 91 percent). During the Republican controlled 104th Congress, 85 people were nominated to the district bench and 62 were confirmed (about 73 percent). For courts of appeals nominations to courts of general jurisdiction during the 103rd Congress, 21 individuals were nominated and 18 were confirmed (about 86 percent). During the 104th Congress, 18 were nominated to the appeals courts and 11 were confirmed, all within the first session (61 percent). As these figures suggest, the confirmation process underwent a stunning transformation from a Senate controlled by Democrats to one controlled by Republicans.

THE CONFIRMATION PROCESS

In assessing the "success" of an administration's appointments, one must focus on more than the few or rare instances of nominees being defeated in an actual confirmation vote. Rather, the president's difficulties may best be assessed by criteria such as the extent of delay in confirmation processes or the failure to gain final votes on nominees. From such a perspective the 104th Congress and, in particular, its second session in 1996, proved an inhospitable setting for Bill Clinton.

Indeed, combining all of Clinton's first term district and appeals court nominations reveals that in the

103rd Congress almost 90 percent of the nominations received in the Senate, and 100 percent of those reported out of committee, resulted in eventual confirmation. In the Republican 104th Congress, slightly more than 70 percent of all nominations received resulted in confirmation, while 6.4 percent of those reported favorably out of committee were not confirmed. The data also reveal that the president's track record was considerably stronger in the first session of the 104th Congress than in 1996's second session.

The two key watchwords for characterizing confirmation processes in the 104th Congress proved clearly to be delay in the Senate and, concurrently, consultation between the president's judicial selection team and the Senate's Judiciary Committee chair. That things did not run smoothly in the 104th Congress should not have come as a great surprise, since the fundamental changes in the judicial selection environment were fraught with enormous potential for divisiveness. "Payback time" was anticipated for attacks on Supreme Court nominees Robert Bork and Clarence Thomas, as well as for the alleged sabotaging of several lower court nominations or potential nominations by a Democratic Senate during the Republican Reagan-Bush presidencies. A vindictive and meanspirited Congress appeared to be in the offing for Bill Clinton.

The Senate was now led by presidential candidate Bob Dole (until his resignation in June 1996) who stood to gain a great deal by making Clinton's life difficult on the judgeship front. Further, the all important Senate Judiciary Committee witnessed a critical changing of the guard when Delaware Senator Joseph R. Biden Jr. was replaced by Utah Senator Orrin G. Hatch as the committee's chair. Hatch had been a major player in previous judicial selection battles (and had been strongly behind both Bork and Thomas).

While the Senate in the 104th Congress seemed uniquely positioned to "do battle" in the judicial selection arena, the Clinton administration emerged as a curious and unlikely adversary. For, unlike administrations dating back at least as far as Richard Nixon's, judgeships did not take center stage in the president's domestic policy agenda. Assistant Attorney General Eleanor Dean Acheson, responsible for judicial selection within the Justice Department, explained the administration's philosophy:

> The process has been wildly disserved by this idea that this is a huge ideological battle for the courts and...there is no middle ground and, somehow whatever else anybody is, they are primarily and most importantly for judicial selection somewhere on this ideological axis. And I think that concept...and the practicing of it for the last twenty years has been the single most undermining factor of the judiciary. We have done huge damage and the higher up it goes the greater damage we do.

Putting the matter equally bluntly, a key member of the president's judicial selection team, who had labored in both the Justice Department and White House facets of the process, indicated that ideological concerns did not dictate things in either locale: "Neither side is running an ideology shop. Neither of us consider ourselves to be the guardians of some kind of flame.... [T]his is not a do or die fight for American culture. This is an attempt to get...highly competent lawyers on the federal bench so they can resolve disputes."

Despite the existence of divided government, things appeared to have functioned relatively smoothly, at least on the surface, in the relationship between the Clinton administration and the Hatch-led Judiciary Committee. Indeed, commenting on the unusual amount of consultation and, some would argue, compromise and accommodation between the administration, individual senators, the Judiciary Committee and, most specifically, its chair, one analyst credited the White House with "using an approach that would have been unthinkable in recent administrations."

The collaborative relationship between the Democratic White House and Republican-led Judiciary Committee appeared to flow from a number of sources. Senator Hatch exhibited substantial professionalism and, as attested to by administration sources as well as by both Republican and Democratic Senate staff, he pursued a commitment to work with the administration to see nominations through to confirmation. Administratively, the rhythm of judicial selection processes in the committee operated with regularity and predictability. While there were extended periods during the 104th Congress when no judges were con-

firmed by the Senate as a whole (more than four months in 1995 and about 11 months in 1996) this did not appear to be the result of Judiciary Committee stonewalling but, rather, inaction on the Senate floor.

Divided government did not lead to greater surface changes in judicial confirmation processes at the committee level during Clinton's first term in part because the Senate remained a more collegial institution than the House. As one senior Senate aide put it, "Kennedy gets along with Hatch. Hatch gets along with Biden and everybody sort of slaps each other on the back. And it's natural that the Chairman of the Judiciary Committee would develop a close working relationship with the administration nominating these people." This is not meant to suggest that the nature of the consultation was the same with Senator Hatch as it had been with Senator Biden.

> [W]ith Biden the...consultation was...in the nature of...we're working together...[W]e all want to get as many judges, and as progressive judges through as we can. We'll work together to figure out what we can do. Now with Hatch it is more of a dance, a negotiation.

Because ideology was not the basis for Clinton's selection process, it was possible for there to be a nonconfrontational mode of operation with the Republican majority. As an administration source underscored, "[Y]ou can't consult about ideology. If we were going to appoint activist liberals it would be a waste of time to go up there and say, 'Gee, I really think you should meet this person.'" Things operate quite differently in a nonideological, nonconfrontational setting.

The value of consulting with Senator Hatch, as well as other senators from both parties on nominations, was underscored by Eleanor Acheson. "It is just a better way of doing business.... [H]e gives good advice and a good sense of what's going to work and what's not going to work." Acheson stressed, however, that all such advice is just that, advisory to, not determinative of the administration's decisions. Critical to understanding the role that consultation with the Republicans and, in particular, their Judiciary Committee leadership played in the 104th Congress is the recognition that the administration pursued a similar consultative posture during the 103rd Congress with its Republican minority.

If the administration can be characterized as having avoided controversy in judicial selection with a Democratic majority in the Senate in the 103rd Congress, that characterization was even more pronounced in the Republican controlled 104th Congress. Assistant Attorney General Acheson described the change in the administration's behavior in the altered congressional setting at the outset of the 104th Congress:

> I think we were much more reactively cautious.... Right after the [1994] elections...I think the rule that...was only fair and responsible for the President to operate with was until this thing settles out and we have a better sense of where we're going we just have to be very cautious. And then I think we sort of felt out...the sort of environment and...our relationships with Senator Hatch and his staff. You know we don't agree on everything...but we also know, which we didn't know then, that you can have...absolutely candid conversations about what is going to happen with a situation.

What some would characterize as the president's unwillingness to fight for his judicial nominees was assessed by the administration in cost-benefit terms. As noted by Eleanor Acheson: "There are a couple of cases in which we decided that even if we thought we had a shot at winning a fight...that it was not worth the time and resources...because these fights go for months and months, and during that period it is very difficult to concentrate."

In effect, the administration did not view judicial selection as a test of its strength but, rather, as a responsibility to appoint good judges and to see them seated on the federal bench. According to Acheson, "It's not that we doubt that people would be excellent if you could ever get them into the position. It's a question...of at what cost?"

PRESIDENTIAL POLITICS

In analyzing the operation of the advice and consent process in the Clinton administration, it is important to highlight the diminished activity during the second session of the 104th Congress in 1996, a presidential election year. Indeed, judicial appointments were confirmed on the Senate floor on only a few days and only in small numbers throughout 1996 despite the

fact that nominees were being processed and sent forward for confirmation by the Judiciary Committee. The major logjam on the Senate floor broke only temporarily in July 1996, the month after Senator Dole relinquished his position as Senate majority leader and resigned from his Senate seat to pursue his presidential ambitions.

While it is natural for the pace of judicial confirmations to slow as a presidential election approaches, it is not typical for the pace to stop completely. In 1996, however, the confirmation of federal judges was held hostage by presidential electoral politics and the power of the majority leader/presidential candidate to control the flow of Senate business in the interest of his campaign. Quite clearly, Dole attempted to make judgeships a major theme of his presidential campaign. In a prominent speech on April 19, 1996, he charged, among other things, that Clinton was promoting "an all star team of liberal leniency" and that the president's re-election "could lock in liberal judicial activism for the next generation." Senator Hatch had previously taken to the Senate floor to complain about some of Clinton's appointments, but that was likely designed to pave the way for Dole's public stance rather than a justification for stalling the process. Indeed, an aide to a liberal Democrat on the Judiciary Committee noted in March of 1996 that Hatch even sent Dole a letter expressing his belief that it was necessary to move judicial nominations to the Senate floor for confirmation votes.

If Hatch's public statements about the confirmation process, as well as those of other sources in the administration and on both sides of the congressional aisle are to be taken at face value, the conclusion is inescapable that Hatch's authority was undermined by his inability to translate committee processing of nominees to Senate floor action on their confirmations. At bottom, the normal functioning of Senate processes, whereby committee actions are legitimated on the Senate floor, may have been trumped in 1996 by presidential politics.

The portrait of Senate floor action on judgeships in 1996 revealed an institution that, initially, was rendered immobile by the politically driven choice of the majority leader/presidential candidate to make judgeships a prime campaign issue while holding the president's nominees (even those endorsed by the Republican led Judiciary Committee) hostage on the Senate floor. By the time Dole resigned from the Senate, summer had arrived and with it the traditional election year slow-down that normally brings the curtain down on judgeship nominations. Nevertheless, the administration continued to send names to the Senate. Eleanor Acheson characterized the continuing work of the administration in nominating judges as necessary to keep the pressure on and to prepare for the future. "Certainly if the president is re-elected…we don't want to create for ourselves a situation where we slip behind. We want to be as ready to go as possible in the 105th Congress." But with the election of more militantly conservative Republican senators in the election of 1996, the opening months of the 105th Congress saw an unprecedented move by Republicans to stall the confirmation of nominees of a newly re-elected president.

DISTRICT COURT APPOINTEES

Tables 12.1, 12.2, and 12.3 present background data on persons appointed to lifetime positions on the federal district courts. Table 12.1 compares the 107 individuals confirmed during the Democratic 103rd Congress in 1993–1994 (Clinton 1) with the 62 persons confirmed by the Republican 104th Congress in 1995–1996 (Clinton 2). Table 12.2 compares Clinton's 89 non-traditional (women and minorities) to his 80 traditional (white male) appointees…. Table 12.3 compares Clinton's district court appointments to those of the three previous administrations.

Occupation

When the occupations of Clinton 1 appointees are compared to Clinton 2 appointees we find only modest differences…. When the nontraditional appointees are compared to the traditional appointees, however, more substantial differences emerge. Over two thirds of nontraditional appointees were government employees—mostly in the judiciary—compared to only 40 percent of the traditional appointees. Slightly less than one in seven nontraditional appointees practiced law in large law firms compared to more than one in five traditional appointees (and twice as high a proportion of traditional appointees were practicing in superfirms employing more than 100 lawyers). Overall, slightly more than one in four non-traditional appointees as compared to well over half the traditional appointees were engaged in the private practice of law. The most promising professional career opportunities for women and minorities have been in the public sector, and these findings reflect that.

Comparing all the Clinton district court appointees to the appointees of Bush, Reagan, and Carter (Table 12.3), we observe that well over half of Clinton's appointees held public service positions at the time of their appointment, a slightly higher proportion than that of his immediate three predecessors.

Of the 75 who were judges at the time of appointment, 20 were U.S. magistrates (or U.S. bankruptcy judges) when they were tapped for the district bench. This represents a career path to the district bench that has recently emerged. Of the 20 U.S. magistrates or bankruptcy judges promoted to U.S. district judge, 16 were nontraditional appointees.

More than two in five Clinton appointees were serving in the judiciary when they were named to the federal bench, continuing the trend of a career judiciary that began with Carter. The judiciary seems to have become a favored source in the selection process, likely because candidates who are judges have judicial track records that can be studied in terms of judicial philosophy and temperament.

The U.S. attorney's office accounted for exceedingly few Clinton first term appointees. Only seven individuals, or 4 percent of the Clinton district court appointments, were serving in some capacity in the U.S. attorney's office at the time of appointment. By comparison, Bush named about 8 percent, and Reagan even more, exceeding 10 percent of his appointees.

Interestingly, approximately one out of 12 Clinton appointees came from superfirms, more than four times as great a proportion as was appointed by Democrat Carter and, indeed, even slightly more than had been appointed by Republican Reagan. However, when all large firms (over 24 members) are considered, Clinton's appointments are far surpassed by Bush's and slightly exceeded by Reagan's. The general point, however, is clear. It is inaccurate to think of the large Wall Street-type law firms as the bastions of Republicanism. Pronounced numbers of Democratic appointees have emerged from their ranks.

TABLE 12.1 U.S. district court appointees confirmed in 1993–1994 (Clinton 1) compared with appointees confirmed in 1995–1996 (Clinton 2)

	CLINTON 1 APPOINTEES		CLINTON 2 APPOINTEES	
	%	(N)	%	(N)
Occupation				
Politics/government	11.2%	(12)	9.7%	(6)
Judiciary	43.9%	(47)	45.2%	(28)
Large law firm				
100+ members	11.2%	(12)	3.2%	(2)
50–99	5.6%	(6)	4.8%	(3)
25–49	4.7%	(5)	1.6%	(1)
Moderate size firm				
10–24 members	6.5%	(7)	11.3%	(7)
5–9	4.7%	(5)	14.5%	(9)
Small firm				
2–4	7.5%	(8)	1.6%	(1)
solo	0.9%	(1)	4.8%	(3)
Professor of law	2.8%	(3)	1.6%	(1)
Other	0.9%	(1)	1.6%	(1)
Experience				
Judicial	48.6%	(52)	51.6%	(32)
Prosecutorial	35.5%	(38)	41.9%	(26)
Neither	32.7%	(35)	29.0%	(18)
Undergraduate education				
Public	43.0%	(46)	46.8%	(29)
Private	42.0%	(45)	38.7%	(24)
Ivy League	15.0%	(16)	14.5%	(9)
Law school education				
Public	38.3%	(41)	50.0%	(31)
Private	38.3%	(41)	35.5%	(22)
Ivy League	23.4%	(25)	14.5%	(9)
Gender				
Male	68.2%	(73)	72.6%	(45)
Female	31.8%	(34)	27.4%	(17)
Ethnicity/race				
White	64.5%	(69)	85.5%	(53)
African American	25.2%	(27)	9.7%	(6)
Hispanic	8.4%	(9)	3.2%	(2)
Asian	0.9%	(1)	1.6%	(1)
Native American	0.9%	(1)	—	
Percentage white male	39.2%	(42)	61.3%	(38)
ABA Rating				
Well Qualified	60.7%	(65)	69.4%	(43)
Qualified	36.4%	(39)	30.6%	(19)
Not Qualified	2.8%	(3)	—	

(continued)

TABLE 12.1 Continued

	CLINTON 1 APPOINTEES		CLINTON 2 APPOINTEES	
	%	(N)	%	(N)
Political Identification				
Democrat	88.8%	(95)	93.6%	(58)
Republican	2.8%	(3)	1.6%	(1)
Other	0.9%	(1)	—	
None	7.5%	(8)	4.8%	(3)
Past party activism	53.3%	(57)	54.8%	(34)
Net worth				
Less than $200,000	15.9%	(17)	19.4%	(12)
$200–499,999	27.1%	(29)	14.5%	(9)
$500–999,999	28.0%	(30)	29.0%	(18)
$1+ million	29.0%	(31)	37.1%	(23)
Total number of appointees	107		62	
Average age at nomination	48.7		48.6	

TABLE 12.2 Clinton's nontraditional appointees compared to his traditional appointees to the federal district courts, first term

	NONTRADITIONAL APPOINTEES		TRADITIONAL APPOINTEES	
	%	(N)	%	(N)
Occupation				
Politics/government	13.5%	(12)	7.5%	(6)
Judiciary	55.1%	(49)	32.5%	(26)
Large law firm				
100+ members	5.6%	(5)	11.2%	(9)
50–99	6.7%	(6)	3.8%	(3)
25–49	1.1%	(1)	6.2%	(5)
Moderate size firm				
10–24 members	4.5%	(4)	12.5%	(10)
5–9	3.4%	(3)	13.8%	(11)
Small firm				
2–4	4.5%	(4)	6.2%	(5)
solo	1.1%	(1)	3.8%	(3)
Professor of law	3.4%	(3)	1.2%	(1)
Other	1.1%	(1)	1.2%	(1)
Experience				
Judicial	60.7%	(54)	37.5%	(30)
Prosecutorial	41.6%	(37)	33.8%	(27)
Neither	21.3%	(19)	42.5%	(34)
Undergraduate education				
Public	44.9%	(40)	43.8%	(35)
Private	38.2%	(34)	43.8%	(35)
Ivy League	16.9%	(15)	12.5%	(10)

	NONTRADITIONAL APPOINTEES		TRADITIONAL APPOINTEES	
	%	(N)	%	(N)
Law school education				
Public	40.4%	(36)	45.0%	(36)
Private	41.6%	(37)	32.5%	(26)
Ivy League	18.0%	(16)	22.5%	(18)
Gender				
Male	42.7%	(38)	100.0%	(80)
Female	57.3%	(51)	—	
Ethnicity/race				
White	47.2%	(42)	100.0%	(80)
African American	37.1%	(33)	—	
Hispanic	12.4%	(11)	—	
Asian	2.2%	(2)	—	
Native American	1.1%	(1)	—	
ABA Rating				
Well Qualified	55.1%	(49)	73.8%	(59)
Qualified	43.8%	(39)	23.8%	(19)
Not Qualified	1.1%	(1)	2.5%	(2)
Political Identification				
Democrat	92.1%	(82)	88.8%	(71)
Republican	1.1%	(1)	3.8%	(3)
Other	—		1.2%	(1)
None	6.7%	(6)	6.2%	(5)
Past party activism	38.2%	(34)	71.2%	(57)
Net worth				
Less than $200,000	19.1%	(17)	15.0%	(12)
$200–499,999	30.3%	(27)	13.8%	(11)
$500–999,999	27.0%	(24)	30.0%	(24)
$1+ million	23.6%	(21)	41.2%	(33)
Average age at nomination	46.9		50.7	
Total number of appointees	89		80	

TABLE 12.3 U.S. district court appointees compared by administration

	CLINTON		BUSH		REAGAN		CARTER	
	%	(N)	%	(N)	%	(N)	%	(N)
Occupation								
Politics/government	10.7%	(18)	10.8%	(16)	13.4%	(39)	5.0%	(10)
Judiciary	44.4%	(75)	41.9%	(62)	36.9%	(107)	44.6%	(90)
Large law firm								
100 + members	8.3%	(14)	10.8%	(16)	6.2%	(18)	2.0%	(4)
50–99	5.3%	(9)	7.4%	(11)	4.8%	(14)	6.0%	(12)
25–49	3.6%	(6)	7.4%	(11)	6.9%	(20)	6.0%	(12)
Moderate size firm								
10–24 members	8.3%	(14)	8.8%	(13)	10.0%	(29)	9.4%	(19)
5–9	8.3%	(14)	6.1%	(9)	9.0%	(26)	10.4%	(21)
Small firm								
2–4	5.3%	(9)	3.4%	(5)	7.2%	(21)	10.9%	(22)

(continued)

TABLE   12.3   Continued

	CLINTON		BUSH		REAGAN		CARTER	
	%	(N)	%	(N)	%	(N)	%	(N)
solo	2.4%	(4)	1.4%	(2)	2.8%	(8)	2.5%	(5)
Professor of law	2.4%	(4)	0.7%	(1)	2.1%	(6)	3.0%	(6)
Other	1.2%	(2)	1.4%	(2)	0.7%	(2)	0.5%	(1)
Experience								
Judicial	49.7%	(84)	46.6%	(69)	46.2%	(134)	54.0%	(109)
Prosecutorial	37.9%	(64)	39.2%	(58)	44.1%	(128)	38.1%	(77)
Neither	31.4%	(53)	31.8%	(47)	28.6%	(83)	30.7%	(62)
Undergraduate education								
Public	44.4%	(75)	44.6%	(66)	36.6%	(106)	56.4%	(114)
Private	40.8%	(69)	41.2%	(61)	49.7%	(144)	33.7%	(68)
Ivy League	14.8%	(25)	14.2%	(21)	13.8%	(40)	9.9%	(20)
Law school education								
Public	42.6%	(72)	52.7%	(78)	42.4%	(123)	50.5%	(102)
Private	37.3%	(63)	33.1%	(49)	45.9%	(133)	32.7%	(66)
Ivy League	20.1%	(34)	14.2%	(21)	11.7%	(34)	16.8%	(34)
Gender								
Male	69.8%	(118)	80.4%	(119)	91.7%	(266)	85.6%	(173)
Female	30.2%	(51)	19.6%	(29)	8.3%	(24)	14.4%	(29)
Ethnicity/race								
White	72.2%	(122)	89.2%	(132)	92.4%	(268)	78.7%	(159)
African American	19.5%	(33)	6.8%	(10)	2.1%	(6)	13.9%	(28)
Hispanic	6.5%	(11)	4.0%	(6)	4.8%	(14)	6.9%	(14)
Asian	1.2%	(2)	—		0.7%	(2)	0.5%	(1)
Native American	0.6%	(1)	—		—		—	
Percentage white male	47.3%	(80)	73.0%	(108)	84.8%	(246)	68.3%	(138)
ABA rating								
Exceptionally Well Qualified/Well Qualified	63.9%	(108)	57.4%	(85)	53.5%	(155)	51.0%	(103)
Qualified	34.3%	(58)	42.6%	(63)	46.6%	(135)	47.5%	(96)
Not Qualified	1.8%	(3)	—		—		1.5%	(3)
Political Identification								
Democrat	90.5%	(153)	5.4%	(8)	4.8%	(14)	90.6%	(183)
Republican	2.4%	(4)	88.5%	(131)	91.7%	(266)	4.5%	(9)
Other	0.6%	(1)	—		—		—	
None	6.5%	(11)	6.1%	(9)	3.4%	(10)	5.0%	(10)
Past party activism	53.9%	(91)	60.8%	(90)	59.0%	(171)	60.9%	(123)
Net worth								
Less than $200,000	17.2%	(29)	10.1%	(15)	17.6%	(51)	35.8%*	(53)
$200–499,999	22.5%	(38)	31.1%	(46)	37.6%	(109)	41.2%	(61)
$500–999,999	28.4%	(46)	26.4%	(39)	21.7%	(63)	18.9%	(28)
$1+ million	32.0%	(54)	32.4%	(48)	23.1%	(67)	4.0%	(6)
Average age at nomination	48.7		48.1		48.7		49.6	
Total number of appointees	169		148		290		202	

*These figures are for appointees confirmed by the 96th Congress for all but six Carter district court appointees (for whom no data were available).

Sources: for Carter and Reagan appointees—Goldman, *Picking Federal Judges: Lower Court Selection from Roosevelt through Reagan* 348–350 (New Haven: Yale University Press, 1997); for Bush appointees—Goldman, *Bush's judicial legacy: the final imprint,* 76 *Judicature* 287 (1993).

Law school faculties were the source of few district court judges, as they had been in the Bush, Reagan, and Carter administrations. Just as the seated bench may be favored for housing potential appointees with a proven adjudicating record, legal academicians may be disfavored because of the lack of such a record coupled with a greater propensity for having authored pointed, provocative, sometimes partisan, and possibly controversial scholarly works.

Experience

Table 12.1 shows that the Clinton 2 appointees had more judicial and prosecutorial experience than Clinton 1 appointees. Table 12.2 strongly suggests that the nontraditional appointees had considerably more judicial experience than did the traditional appointees. Overall, as shown in Table 12.3, almost half the Clinton appointees had prior judicial experience, a record second only to that of Carter. Beginning with the Carter administration, a larger proportion of judges had judicial than had prosecutorial experience. With Clinton, the backgrounds of the nontraditional appointees primarily account for this....

Fewer than one in three Clinton appointees had neither judicial nor prosecutorial experience, with traditional appointees lacking such experience outpacing nontraditional appointees by about two to one. Overall, the Clinton, Bush, and Carter records of appointing district court judges with neither judicial nor prosecutorial experience are virtually identical, with President Reagan even less likely to place such individuals on the bench.

Together with the findings on occupation upon appointment, there clearly appears to be a movement toward a career judiciary. This can also be seen at the Supreme Court level with Clinton's two appointments being elevations from the appeals courts, and the six preceding appointments to associate justice also going to individuals with judicial experience....

Gender and Ethnicity

In several respects, appointees from the latter half of Clinton's first term differ from those appointed during his first two years in office. In 1995 and 1996 there was a substantial increase in white appointees and a dramatic decline in he appointment of African Americans to the district court bench. Indeed, the proportion of traditional nominees appointed by Clinton rose by close to 50 percent in the latter half of his first term. Coupled with the higher percentage of appointees receiving the highest rating from the ABA in 1995 and 1996, the data clearly suggest a tendency to "play it safe" in the context of a Republican controlled Senate with the appointment of more traditional candidates with established career paths valued by the ABA committee.

If the 20 district judge nominees who were not acted upon by the 104th Congress are included in the figures for gender and ethnicity, the proportion of women rises only marginally—from about 32 percent to about 35 percent. The proportion of whites, however, drops to about the same proportion for the Clinton 1 appointees, while the proportion of African Americans remains at two-fifths the rate of Clinton 1 African American appointees. The proportion of Hispanics remains considerably lower than Clinton 1 appointees and only the proportion of Asian Americans rose substantially.

The decrease in nontraditional appointees in the second half of Clinton's first term takes on added importance (beyond concerns with representativeness of the federal bench per se) to the extent that traditional appointees differ in meaningful ways from the white males who are appointed. Overall, Clinton's 89 nontraditional appointees constituted a slight majority (52.7 percent) of the 169 district court seats filled during his first term in office, a presidential first despite the clear move away from the seating of nontraditional judges in 1995 and 1996.

The Clinton record on diversifying the bench by gender and ethnicity has set a historic precedent. During his first term, Clinton appointed 42 white women, seven black women, and two Hispanic women for a total of 51 women, far exceeding the 29 women appointed by Bush, the 29 named by Carter, and the 24 women appointed by Reagan (during his two terms). About three in ten Clinton appointees were women. Thus, both the proportion and the absolute numbers of women Clinton placed on the district court established a new record.

Clinton named 33 African Americans (including seven women), 11 Hispanics (including two women), two Asian American males, and one Native American (male) to the federal district bench. Clinton picked more African Americans (5) than Carter and three fewer Hispanics than Reagan or Carter. The proportions of African American appointees, however, constitutes a new milestone while the proportion of Hispanics, at present, only slightly trails the record of Jimmy Carter. Overall, less than half of Clinton's judges were white males, the first time ever that nontraditional appointees were a majority of those chosen for the federal bench. While the magnitude of this achievement is largely a reflection of Clinton's appointments during his first two years in office with a Democratic Senate, it should be pointed out that the proportion of nontraditional appointees seated by Clinton in 1995 and 1996 still far exceeded that of Presidents Bush, Reagan and even Carter. It remains the case, however, that white males dominate the ranks of the active service judiciary. (See "Nontraditional judges in active service," Table 12.4.)

ABA Ratings

Clinton 2 appointees had a higher percentage of those given the highest rating by the American Bar Association Committee on Federal Judiciary than Clinton 1 appointees. When nontraditional appointees are compared to traditional appointees, we see that the proportion of nontraditional Clinton appointees with the highest ABA rating was about 55 percent, compared to about 74 percent for the traditional appointees. Although Clinton's traditional appointees tended to receive higher ABA ratings than his nontraditional ones, Clinton's nontraditional appointees still earned the highest ABA ratings in greater proportion than all judges (traditional and nontraditional combined) appointed by Reagan and Carter, while earning the highest ratings at only a slightly lower pace than all judges appointed by Bush. If, indeed, the ABA ratings are a valid measure of quality, the nontraditional judges appointed by Clinton were generally of very high quality.

Table 12.3 shows that the Clinton appointees' highest ABA ratings well surpass those from the three previous administrations. Indeed, when the district and appeals court appointees are combined, the proportion of Clinton appointees receiving the highest ratings (two out of three) is the highest since the ABA began rating federal judicial appointees.... As has been typical, the highest ratings were generally given to white males.

Political Party

It is no surprise that the overwhelming majority of Clinton's appointees were Democrats. When the entire first term appointees are examined, the proportion of those appointed with a party affiliation of the president's is about the same as that of Clinton's three immediate predecessors....

Dramatic differences are found when we examine the Clinton nominees' records of past party activism. The overwhelming majority of the traditional appointees (more than seven out of ten) exhibited an activist political past, while fewer than two in five of the nontraditional appointees could be characterized in those terms. More generally, the proportion of Clinton appointees with records of past party activism is lower than that of the Bush, Reagan, and Carter appointees. For nontraditional appointees, past party activity was relatively unimportant.

Net Worth

A greater proportion of nontraditional than traditional appointees had net worths under $200,000 and, when the bar is raised to a net worth of half a million dollars or less, the differences between nontraditional and traditional appointees loom even greater. At the other end of the net worth scale, fewer than one in four nontraditional appointees were millionaires compared to more than two out of five traditional appointees. More generally, nearly one in three Clinton appointees were millionaires. Virtually matching Bush's record of appointing judges of considerable means. But also note that about two in five Clinton appointees (as was the case with Bush) had net worths of less than half a million dollars and could not be characterized as having great worth. Quite clearly, Jimmy Carter appointed the greatest proportion of judges of modest means and the smallest proportion of millionaires.

TABLE 12.4 Proportion of nontraditional lifetime judges in active service on courts of general jurisdiction—November 3, 1992 through January 1, 1997

	1992		1997		% INCREASE
	%	(N)	%	(N)	
U.S. district courts					
Women	10.5%*	(68)	17.4%*	(112)	64.7%
African American	5.3%	(34)	9.3%	(60)	76.5%
Hispanic	4.5%	(29)	4.7%	(30)	3.4%
Asian	0.6%	(4)	0.5%	(3)	(− 25.0%)
Native American	0.0%	(0)	0.2%	(1)	100.0%
Total nontraditional	19.1%	(123)	29.0%	(187)	52.0%
U.S. courts of appeals					
Women	13.2%**	(22)	15.6%**	(29)	31.8%
African American	5.4%	(9)	5.4%	(9)	—
Hispanic	2.4%	(4)	3.6%	(6)	50.0%
Asian	0.6%	(1)	0.6%	(1)	—
Total nontraditional	20.9%	(35)	25.8%	(43)	22.9%
U.S. Supreme Court					
Women	11.1%***	(1)	22.2%***	(2)	100.0%
African American	11.1%	(1)	11.1%	(1)	—
Total nontraditional	22.2%	(2)	33.3%	(3)	50.0%
All three court levels					
Women	11.1%	(91)	17.4%	(143)	57.1%
African American	5.4%	(44)	8.5%	(70)	59.1%
Hispanic	4.0%	(33)	4.4%	(36)	9.1%
Asian	0.6%	(5)	0.5%	(4)	(− 20.0%)
Native American	0.0%	(0)	0.1%	(1)	100.0%
Total nontraditional	19.5%	(160)	28.4%	(233)	45.6%

The total does not double count those who were classified in more than one category. Also note that from November 3, 1992 through January 1, 1997, 23 nontraditional district court judges and 7 nontraditional appeals court judges left active service. An additional three nontraditional district court judges were elevated by Clinton to the appeals bench. Also, Ruth Bader Ginsburg was elevated from the U.S. Court of Appeals for the District of Columbia to the U.S. Supreme Court.

*Out of 645 authorized lifetime positions on the U.S. district courts.

**Out of 167 authorized lifetime positions on the numbered circuits and the U.S. Court of Appeals for the District of Columbia Circuit, all courts of general jurisdiction.

***Out of nine authorized positions on the U.S. Supreme Court.

Age

...Overall...the Clinton appointees were nominated, on average, at approximately the same age as those of the previous three presidential administrations. The proportion of those under 45 was about 24 percent, the smallest proportion of all four administrations. About three in five of the Clinton appointees under 45 were nontraditional. The evidence suggests that age has not been a deliberate consideration by the Clinton administration for extending Clinton's legacy. This is quite different from the Bush and Reagan record (the proportion of Bush's appointees during his last two years who were under 45 was 44 percent; for Reagan's second term, 37 percent).

APPEALS COURT APPOINTEES

During the 103rd Congress, 18 appeals court judges were confirmed by the Senate. During the 104th Congress, only 11 were confirmed, all during the first session. The Republican leadership during the second session refused to move on the seven appeals court nominations submitted, and as a result they died at the end of the session. . . .

Occupation and Experience

. . .Clinton's judges had about the same proportion who were sitting judges at the time of appointment as the Bush judges and a larger proportion than the Reagan and Carter appointees. In terms of experience, however, in excess of two-thirds of the Clinton appointees had judicial experience and more than one-third had prosecutorial experience. Only about one in five had neither judicial nor prosecutorial experience. In terms of judicial and prosecutorial experience, the Clinton first term appeals court appointees set a modern record.

Gender and Ethnicity

Although in proportions nontraditional appointees to the appeals court (with the exception of that of African Americans) were the largest in American history, the absolute numbers of women and African Americans were fewer than Carter's. . . . The total impact of Clinton's appointments on the diversification of the bench is seen in "Nontraditional judges in active service" (Table 12.4).

ABA Ratings

. . .Traditional appointees tended to receive the highest ABA rating. However, it must be emphasized that three out of four nontraditional appointees were awarded the highest ABA rating. . . . Clinton's pro-portion of those with the highest ABA rating is larger than that of his three immediate predecessors.

Political Party

Not a single Republican was among the Clinton 2 appointees (or nominees); there was only one Clinton 1 Republican. This degree of partisanship was reminiscent of Ronald Reagan's (Reagan failed to name even one Democrat). However, the level of previous political activism of the Clinton appointees was the lowest of all four administrations. . . .

Net Worth

Half the nontraditional appointees were millionaires but less than one fourth of the traditional appointees were in that income bracket. As a whole, the Bush appointees accounted for a larger proportion of millionaires than the Clinton appointees.

Age

The average age of the nontraditional appointees was lower than that of the traditional appointees, which was consistent with the findings for district court appointees. The average age of all of Clinton's appeals court appointees was 51.3, more than two and a half years older than the Bush appointees and more than a year older than the Reagan appointees. Only the Carter appointees were older on average. Only about 17 percent of the Clinton appointees were under 45. In contrast, almost one quarter of the Bush and Reagan appointees were under 45. Age, apparently, is not the consideration that it was in the Reagan and Bush administrations.

THE COMING STRUGGLE

What lies ahead for Clinton's second term? What appeared to be a presidential election-year slowdown in confirmations in 1996 may well have been the opening round of an audacious and bold plan by Republicans to block Clinton's appointments as a means of wresting judicial patronage from the Democrats. This court-blocking strategy, unprecedented in its scope, is a congressional analogue of President Franklin Roosevelt's court-packing plan of 1937. Both Roosevelt's court-packing and the Republican's court-blocking plans had their genesis in displeasure with court decisions. And both plans were justified publicly, in part, by deceptive uses of court workload statistics. Roosevelt claimed the Supreme Court was behind in its work. Republicans claimed that judicial workloads did not justify the filling of certain judgeships, particularly on the circuit courts. Roosevelt was roundly attacked for trying to make an end-run around the Constitution, and his plan ultimately failed. Republicans indignantly deny any such court-blocking strategy and as such it has not attracted much public scrutiny. It remains to be seen if the Republican senatorial leadership in 1997 will continue the current end-run around the Constitution (in terms of the president's ability to name people to the federal courts) and whether a constitutional confrontation between Clinton and Senate Republicans is in the offing.

During the Senate debate, on March 19, 1997, on the first appeals court nomination to come to the Senate floor in more than 14 months, Senator Orrin Hatch, a supporter of the nominee, Merrick B. Garland, for a position on the U.S. Court of Appeals for the District of Columbia, said in apparent exasperation at the tactics of some of his Republican colleagues, "[P]laying politics with judges is unfair, and I am sick of it...the statistics that have been cited, with all due respect, they are not a fair or accurate characterization of the D.C. circuit's caseload relative to the other circuits' caseloads." Former Senate Judiciary Committee Chair Joseph R. Biden, even more exercised than his successor, spoke bluntly and noted: "This is about trying to keep the President of the United States of America from being able to appoint judges, particularly as it relates to the courts of appeals." He asserted that what really was going on was that Republican senators wanted a certain proportion of judgeships to fill for themselves and that allegations that Clinton's nominees were activists (which Republicans used to justify the pace of the confirmation process) were a smokescreen. Biden made it clear that he thought it was "not...appropriate not to have hearings on them [Clinton's nominees], not to bring them to the floor and not to allow a vote..." And

Biden charged that what the Republicans were doing "is not in line with the last 200 years of tradition."

Assuming that Republicans choose not to end their court-blocking tactics entirely (although the Republican conference on April 29, 1997, rejected more extreme court-blocking proposals), it seems that the Clinton administration has two major options. First, it can make deals with Republicans, allowing them to suggest and/or approve candidates to be formally nominated. This would mean an end to the virtual shut-out of Republicans from becoming Clinton appointees. The administration could tie this to enactment of a new omnibus judgeships bill (the only other 20th century president denied the opportunity to fill new judgeships was Gerald Ford).

The concept of a bipartisan deal on new judgeships has a precedent. During 1960, the last year of President Dwight Eisenhower's second term, the Republican administration was stymied by the refusal of the Democratic leadership in Congress to enact a new judgeships bill. The administration offered to let Democrats name half the new judges but they preferred to take their chances on a Democrat being elected in 1960. Democrat John F. Kennedy was elected and the Democratic Congress speedily enacted the largest omnibus judgeships act up to that time. Of course the Clinton administration is in its *first* year of its second term and might be able to negotiate such a deal for the filling of newly created judgeships (the Republican leadership in Congress has otherwise indicated no interest in creating any new judgeships). The concept of a bipartisan (and nonpartisan) judiciary has been championed in the past by the organized bar and perhaps the current political climate can provide fertile ground for this concept.

A second option for the administration, assuming court-blocking is not voluntarily ended by the Republicans, is for Clinton to reinstitute the practice of making recess appointments to those nominated for judgeships. Last used by President Carter in 1980, recess appointments and reappointments (in the event that subsequent sessions of the Senate have not acted on the nominations) would immediately help to reduce the burdens on overworked courts and at the same time would bring pressure on Republicans to vote judicial nominations up or down. This strategy could also bring court-blocking to public attention and set the stage for a major campaign issue in 1998 and 2000. Interestingly, before the events of 1996 and 1997, a bipartisan commission on judicial selection organized by the Miller Center of Public Affairs at the University of Virginia concluded that the confirmation process takes too long and that recess appointments should once again be utilized.

If Republican court-blocking continues, it surely will test the Clinton administration's well-known aversion to expending political capital on judicial confirmation fights. But the administration may be unable to avoid a confrontation and may have to take the offensive by going public as well as by working with Senate Democrats in fashioning a response. Also, the third branch will be unable to sit by quietly as vacancies mount and caseloads build. Indeed, if history repeats itself, Chief Justice William H. Rehnquist may have as critical a role to play in breaking the court-blocking plan as Chief Justice Charles Evan Hughes had in breaking Roosevelt's court-packing plan.

It is reasonable to expect that when the dust settles, there will be a fair number of Clinton judges confirmed by the 105th Congress, although nothing on the order of the number confirmed by the 103rd Congress. There is every reason to believe that the

profile of judges seen during the first term will continue through the second. That means a heavy emphasis on gender and racial diversification and those with judicial experience and high ABA ratings. Also it can be expected that the administration will continue to consult Senator Hatch before sending nominations to the Senate and that the administration will continue to avoid deliberately provoking Republicans by not submitting nominees with a high profile of liberal activism. The ranks of Clinton's essentially centrist judiciary should continue to receive judicial troops. Even without deals with Republicans, it is likely that more Republicans will be named by Clinton. But even if Clinton were to name only Democrats, the partisan balance on the lower federal courts will not approach the level of imbalance that resulted from 12 years of Reagan and Bush appointments (see "Clinton's impact," Table 12.5).

There is always the possibility the president will have the opportunity to fill a Supreme Court vacancy. If so, it is likely he would turn to a Hispanic. Clinton's first term record in naming Hispanics on the district court level was not as good as Carter's (both proportionately and in absolute numbers) and on the appeals court level the record was only slightly better than Clinton's predecessors in absolute numbers; in per-

TABLE 12.5 Make-up of federal bench by appointing president, January 1, 1997 (lifetime positions on lower courts of general jurisdiction)

	DISTRICT COURTS				COURTS OF APPEALS			
	ACTIVE		SENIOR		ACTIVE		SENIOR	
	%	(N)	%	(N)	%	(N)	%	(N)
Clinton	26.0%	(168)	—	—	16.8%	(28)	—	—
Bush	21.9%	(141)	—	—	20.9%	(35)	—	—
Reagan	31.3%	(202)	12.0%	(35)	34.1%	(57)	16.0%	(12)
Carter	9.3%	(60)	31.8%	(93)	13.8%	(23)	30.7%	(23)
Ford	0.9%	(6)	8.9%	(26)	1.2%	(2)	9.3%	(7)
Nixon	1.9%	(12)	21.9%	(64)	1.2%	(2)	22.7%	(17)
Johnson	0.3%	(2)	15.8%	(46)	0.6%	(1)	17.3%	(13)
Kennedy	0.2%	(1)	5.5%	(16)	0.6%	(1)	—	—
Eisenhower	—	—	3.4%	(10)	—	—	4.0%	(3)
Truman	—	—	0.7%	(2)	—	—	—	—
Vacancies	8.2%	(53)	—	—	10.8%	(18)	—	—
TOTALS	100.0%	(645)	100.0%	(292)	100.0%	(167)	100.0%	(78)

centage terms the Clinton record was a historic high. The Hispanic vote was important for Clinton's reelection in 1996 and in political terms alone Hispanic representation on the Supreme Court is compelling. There are a number of very well qualified jurists of Hispanic background that are likely to be considered, including Jose Cabranes, whom Clinton elevated to the Second Circuit, and for whom there appears to be broad-based bipartisan support.

There are many unanswered questions about how judicial selection will unfold during Clinton's second term. The stakes are high for the administration in terms of its judicial legacy and high for the judiciary in terms of its institutional integrity and independence.

CLINTON'S IMPACT

At the conclusion of his first term, President Clinton's appointees occupied approximately one out of every four (26 percent) allocated federal district judgeship seats. Appointees from the 12 year tenure of Presidents Reagan and Bush still accounted for an absolute majority (53 percent) of the active district court bench seats. When the remaining active appointees of Presidents Kennedy, Johnson, Nixon, Ford, and Carter are taken into account, slightly more than a third (36 percent) of all allocated federal district judgeships have been appointed by Democrats, while a clear majority (56 percent) have been appointed by Republicans. Fifty-three (8 percent) allocated district court seats remained vacant.

On the appeals court, Clinton's appointees occupied only about 17 percent of allocated circuit judgeships reflecting, in part, the historic lack of any appeals court confirmations taking place during the second session of the 104th Congress. Again, Bush and Reagan appointees still dominated the appeals courts, occupying a majority (55 percent) of authorized seats. Democratic presidents, all told, have filled under a third (32 percent) of allocated appeals court judgeships, and more than one in ten appeals court seats (11 percent) remained vacant at the conclusion of President Clinton's first term.

More of a partisan balance is evident when the judges in senior service on January 1, 1997 are also considered. The appointments of Democratic presidents Truman, Kennedy, Johnson, and Carter accounted for a majority (54 percent) of the senior judges on the district courts and close to half (46 percent) of those still serving on the courts of appeals at the start of 1997.

READING 58

Justice Souter Emerges
David J. Garrow

The analyses by Kahn and Goldman and Slotnick clearly reveal the political nature of federal judicial selection and are suggestive of the manner in which presidents can use judgeship appointments as part of the pursuit of their domestic policy agendas. It should come as no surprise then, that many moderates and liberals greatly feared the consequences of the appointment of David Souter, President Bush's "stealth nominee," to the Supreme Court in 1990. Particularly because Souter was to replace liberal activist Justice William Brennan, it appeared certain that he would tip the Court's ideological balance squarely in a conservative direction, definitively completing a judicial transition that began during the Nixon presidency.

In this fascinating analysis, Pulitzer prize-winning author, historian, and journalist David Garrow details why the pundits were wrong as well as how Souter rose from relative obscurity to a seat (and eventually a pivotal position) on the U. S. Supreme Court. Garrow argues that, contrary to the stealth image, there were ample footprints in Souter's past that offered clues about the role he would play on the Court, including his central position in Planned Parenthood of Southeastern Pennsylvania *v.* Casey, *a plurality opinion upholding* Roe v. Wade*'s fundamental right to freedom of*

From "Justice Souter Emerges" by D. J. Garrow, September 25, 1994 *The New York Times Magazine.* Copyright © 1994 by D. J. Garrow. Reprinted by permission.

choice in abortion decisions. Well beyond the critical Casey *ruling, Garrow documents how Justice Souter's intellectual leadership, "liberal streak," and "moderate pragmatism" have evolved and blunted the Court's predicted move in a conservative direction. Throughout Garrow's portrait of Justice Souter, the reader witnesses the interplay between politics and judicial careers, as well as the unpredictable and unlikely events that have brought Souter to his current position of power and influence on the nation's highest Court.*

No public document—and probably only a single very private one—marks April 23, 1992, as one of the more momentous days in recent Supreme Court history. Nothing of apparent note transpired at the Court that Thursday; oral arguments had taken place the day before and the Justices' weekly private conference, where they vote on cases, would not begin until Friday morning.

In his chambers on the far southeastern corner of the main floor, the Court's then-second-newest justice spent the day in contemplation, pondering one of Wednesday's cases. A large portrait of Harlan Fiske Stone, a New Hampshire-born Republican Justice later named Chief Justice by a Democratic President, dominated the room. Many visitors would note that the office, unlike those of other Justices, had no computer terminal; only a few—particularly those visiting toward dusk—would realize that the office also had not a single electric desk lamp.

Only late in the day did the Justice reach a firm conclusion. Even though this was the case of the year, and perhaps of the decade, as of the day before, he had not—just as he had told the United States Senate and the American people almost two years earlier—decided what he would do. On Wednesday, during oral argument of the case, Planned Parenthood of Southeastern Pennsylvania v. Casey, he had listened intently from his seat on the bench as Planned Parenthood's attorney, Kathryn Kolbert, began her argument:

"Whether our Constitution endows government with the power to force a woman to continue or to end a pregnancy against her will is the central question in this case.

"Since this Court's decision in Roe v. Wade, a generation of American women have come of age secure in the knowledge that the Constitution provides the highest level of protection for their childbearing decisions.

"This landmark decision, which necessarily and logically flows from a century of this Court's jurisprudence, not only protects rights of bodily integrity and autonomy but has enabled millions of women to participate fully and equally in society."

But now Roe's survival was very much in doubt, as was starkly revealed by the Pennsylvania anti-abortion regulations under review in Casey. Three years earlier, Chief Justice William H. Rehnquist and Justices Byron R. White, Antonin Scalia and Anthony M. Kennedy had signaled their desire to overrule Roe at the first available opportunity, and few observers doubted that the Court's newest and most controversial member, Clarence Thomas, was eager to join them as the fifth and decisive vote.

Justice Sandra Day O'Connor, who three years earlier had infuriated Scalia by refusing to provide a fifth vote to jettison Roe, interrupted Kolbert with the hour's first question, and she was soon followed by Scalia, Kennedy and Rehnquist.

Pennsylvania's attorney general, Ernest D. Preate Jr., representing Gov. Robert P. Casey, followed Kolbert to the lectern, but almost before he could begin, Justice Harry A. Blackmun, the 82-year-old author of the Court's landmark 1973 abortion decision, asked whether Preate had even read Roe. Then O'Connor peppered Preate with a series of skeptical questions, followed by John Paul Stevens, a firm supporter of Roe, and even by Anthony Kennedy, before Scalia jumped in to provide some cover.

Only as Preate's time was about to expire did the 52-year-old David Hackett Souter speak up to ask Preate a statistical question about the Pennsylvania provision that would require married women facing unwanted pregnancies to notify their husbands, even if they were separated or estranged, before seeking an abortion. Then, after United States Solicitor General Kenneth W. Starr, representing the anti-abortion views of the Bush Administration, succeeded Preate to second the attack on Roe, Souter pressed Starr to concede that if his position prevailed, states could outlaw *all* abortions except perhaps those where a pregnancy directly threatened a woman's life.

None of Souter's comments had telegraphed a clear position on either Casey or Roe. Had any abortion-rights activists been inclined to interpret his exchange with Starr as promising, they had only to remember how Souter's encouraging comments from the bench 18 months earlier in the abortion "gag rule" case of Rust v. Sullivan had proved utterly misleading. Souter had joined Rehnquist, White, Scalia and Kennedy in a 5–4 decision upholding statutory restrictions on what doctors in federally financed clinics could say to female patients.

Not for many years will any outsiders likely see any notes that may have been taken that following Friday morning when the Justices met to vote on Planned Parenthood v. Casey. But while seven Justices indicated that they would uphold most of the Pennsylvania restrictions, only four—Rehnquist, White, Scalia and Thomas—wanted to explicitly vitiate Roe. O'Connor, Kennedy and Souter, however, all believed the restrictions could be upheld at the same time that Roe was left standing. While Rehnquist himself undertook the drafting of Casey's apparent majority opinion, Kennedy's surprising stance gave Souter and O'Connor the opening toward an intermediate outcome for which they had been hoping.

Well before Rehnquist's opinion was circulated to other Justices in late May, Kennedy privately joined Souter and O'Connor in preparing an extensive separate statement. Sometimes all three Justices, sitting on the couch in Souter's office, would jointly review their progress, and their cooperation led to a stunningly unexpected result: Rather than Rehnquist and Scalia having five votes to void Roe, there were five votes—Souter, O'Connor and Kennedy, plus Blackmun and Stevens, to *uphold* Roe.

In early June, Souter, O'Connor, and Kennedy distributed to their colleagues initial copies of their joint opinion. As David Savage later wrote in The Los Angeles Times, "Rehnquist and Scalia were stunned. So, too, was Blackmun." And so, on Monday morning, June 29, 1992, the final day of the term, commentators were unprepared for the result in Planned Parenthood v. Casey. Not since the famous 1958 Little Rock school desegregation case of Cooper v. Aaron,

when all nine Justices signed a ringing reaffirmation of Brown v. Board of Education, had any Supreme Court opinion been presented to the American people as formally authored by more than one Justice. But now, symbolically invoking the powerful precedent of Cooper, Justices O'Connor, Kennedy and Souter issued their plurality decision in Casey as an explicit trio opinion.

"[T]he essential holding of Roe v. Wade should be retained and once again affirmed," they wrote in language that also spoke for Blackmun and Stevens.

"Roe's essential holding, the holding we reaffirm, has three parts. First is a recognition of the right of the woman to choose to have an abortion before viability and to obtain it without undue interference from the State.... Second is a confirmation of the State's power to restrict abortions after fetal viability, if the law contains exceptions for pregnancies which endanger a woman's life or health. And third is the principle that the State has legitimate interests from the outset of the pregnancy in protecting the health of the woman and the life of the fetus that may become a child. These principles do not contradict one another; and we adhere to each."

When announcing decisions from the bench, Justices usually offer a summary or read brief excerpts. On this morning, however, each of the three—first O'Connor, then Kennedy and finally Souter—orally delivered major portions of the trio opinion. Journalists quickly realized they were witnessing an unprecedented event.

The most eloquent section of the opinion was the discussion of Roe and the principle of stare decisis—Latin for judicial respect of existing precedent—that had been crafted principally by David Souter. Souter's words in Casey spoke not only for the Court, but also for the essence of America's judicial heritage and for the very core of Souter's own judicial background. That background had not been fully understood by the commentators and Senators who had debated what his 1990 nomination meant for the future of Roe and other fundamental rights. If they had, what was now happening in Casey would not have come as a surprise.

Souter's analysis reflected a realism not always found in high court pronouncements:

"For two decades of economic and social developments, people have organized intimate relationships and made choices that define their views of themselves and their places in society, in reliance on the availability of abortion in the event that contraception should fail. The ability of women to participate equally in the economic and social life of the Nation has been facilitated by their ability to control their reproductive lives."

Then Souter moved to the core of his argument, two paragraphs that rank among the most memorable lines ever authored by an American jurist:

"Where, in the performance of its judicial duties, the Court decides a case in such a way as to resolve the sort of intensely divisive controversy reflected in Roe and those rare, comparable cases, its decision has a dimension that the resolution of the normal case does not carry. It is the dimension present whenever the Court's interpretation of the Constitution calls the contending sides of a national controversy to end their national division by accepting a common mandate rooted in the Constitution.

"The Court is not asked to do this very often, having thus addressed the Nation only twice in our lifetime, in the decisions of Brown and Roe. But when the Court does act in this way, its decision requires an equally rare precedential force to counter the inevitable efforts to overturn it and to thwart its implementation. Some of those efforts may be mere unprincipled emotional reactions; others may proceed from principles worthy of profound respect. But whatever the premises of opposition may be, only the most convincing justification under accepted standards of precedent could suffice to demonstrate that a later decision overruling the first was anything but a surrender to political pressure, and an unjustified repudiation of the principle on which the Court staked its authority in the first instance. So to overrule under fire in the absence of the most compelling reason to reexamine a watershed decision would subvert the Court's legitimacy beyond any serious question."

Souter closed by reiterating that Casey and Roe, were about far more than simply abortion: "A decision to overrule Roe's essential holding under the existing circumstances would address error, if error there was, at the cost of both profound and unneces-

sary damage to the Court's legitimacy, and to the Nation's commitment to the rule of law. It is therefore imperative to adhere to the essence of Roe's original decision, and we do so today."

Harry Blackmun's concurrence accurately termed the Souter-O'Connor-Kennedy joint opinion "an act of personal courage and constitutional principle," and Blackmun added that "what has happened today should serve as a model for future Justices and a warning to all who have tried to turn this Court into yet another political branch."

Casey *was* a watershed event in American history, the most institutionally significant decision for the Court since Brown. Although some abortion-rights activists failed to acknowledge their victory, expert observers like Laurence H. Tribe, the Harvard law professor, emphasized that the trio opinion "puts the right to abortion on a firmer jurisprudential foundation than ever before."

But the significance of Casey lay not just in its constitutional resolution of the 20-year battle over Roe, nor its long-term importance to the Court's own institutional reputation; Casey also signaled the unexpected failure of the right-wing judicial counter-revolution that the Reagan and Bush Administrations had hoped to bring about by naming staunch conservatives to the Federal bench.

After Casey, hard-right commentators like the columnist Robert Novak unleashed vituperative assaults on the trio of Republican Justices who had redeemed Roe, particularly the Roman Catholic Justice Kennedy. Gary L. McDowell, a Reagan Justice Department aide who had helped former Attorney General Edwin Meese articulate his harsh denunciations of Federal judges, lamented how "all that had been so vigorously fought for by Reagan and Bush, all that had been achieved was suddenly lost."

But there is one other remarkable thing about Casey, both in the context of today's uncertainty about where the Court is heading and in the context of 1990's debate over how "stealth nominee" David Souter would vote on Roe: namely that it is impossible to find anyone who has long known Souter who was surprised by his resolution of Casey. How could something so obvious to those who know Souter best have eluded 1990's army of politicians and prognosticators? In that seeming puzzle lies the rich story of a humble yet utterly self-confident man who, far from being an odd recluse from another age, possesses both exceptional intelligence and a warm circle of friends.

David Hackett Souter, the only child of a quiet bank officer and an equally reserved homemaker, was born in Melrose, Mass., on Sept. 17, 1939; in 1950, the Souters moved to an old family homestead in the rural village of East Weare, N.H., a few miles west of Concord. Souter's father worked at a Concord bank. Weare was too small to have its own secondary school so David commuted to Concord High School, from which he graduated in 1957 and won admission to Harvard.

Following Harvard, Souter received a two-year Rhodes scholarship to Magdalen College at Oxford where he completed a bachelor's degree in jurisprudence before entering Harvard Law School in 1963. Upon graduation in 1966, he happily returned home to New Hampshire to take an entry-level position with the well-respected Concord firm of Orr & Reno.

Law-office work gave Souter few opportunities for courtroom experience, and in late 1968 he eagerly enlisted as one of about 20 state assistant attorneys general. His first few years in the Attorney General's office were devoted more to crime than to civil cases, but the most important development in Souter's young career came in 1970 when Gov. Walter Peterson of New Hampshire named Warren Rudman, previously his own legal counsel, to a five-year term as the state's new Attorney General.

Rudman quickly came to appreciate Souter as a "lawyer's lawyer" and within a few months named Souter his deputy. A gregarious politician, Rudman delegated much of the running of the office to Souter. Rudman's own mentor, Governor Peterson, was defeated for re-election in the 1972 Republican primary by Meldrim Thomson, an unpredictable conservative. Thomson's victory set off a decade-long ideological battle among New Hampshire Republicans, and although Rudman and Thomson quickly reached a grudging accommodation, one of Souter's main responsibilities was to insure the utmost professionalism in the office. As Souter explained to one young lawyer joining the staff: "We don't win cases. We don't lose cases. We try cases."

In 1976, with Rudman's term as Attorney General expiring, Rudman convinced Thomson to name Souter as his successor. Souter responded to the appointment by stressing that "the legal issues I feel most strongly about are not political ones." When reporters asked if he viewed the Attorney General's job as a steppingstone to a judgeship, Souter replied, "I'd have to decide if I were temperamentally suited to it."...

Early in 1978, Governor Thomson sought to fill a vacancy on the five-member New Hampshire Supreme Court with former Congressman Louis C. Wyman, but the Executive Council, the Colonial-era body charged with ratifying judicial nominations, declined to approve Wyman and several councilors suggested naming Souter to the seat. Thomson resisted and, seeking to eliminate Souter as an alternative to Wyman, offered instead to nominate Souter to a newly authorized judgeship on the Superior Court trial bench.

Faced with the choice, Souter hesitated. Thomson was not going to name him to the high court, and under longtime New Hampshire norms, almost every Justice appointed to the Supreme Court had been promoted from Superior Court. Souter could remain Attorney General for another two and a half years, but there was no reason to believe that whoever might be governor in 1980 would offer him a judgeship. With some ambivalence about becoming a trial judge simply as a steppingstone to an appellate post, Souter accepted Thomson's offer to nominate him and name his close friend Tom Rath his successor....

Throughout Souter's years on the trial bench, Warren Rudman remained among his closest friends. Rudman won election to the United States Senate in 1980 after defeating a fellow Republican, John Sununu, in a hard-fought primary. After Sununu supported Rudman in the general election, Rudman returned the favor two years later in Sununu's successful gubernatorial campaign. Rudman never concealed his opinion that Souter was "the finest constitutional lawyer I've ever known," and when New Hampshire Supreme Court Justice Maurice P. Bois retired in mid-1983, Rudman immediately told Sununu that David Souter should be elevated to that court.

Sununu interviewed Souter and two other candidates before sending Souter's name to the Executive

Council, which unanimously approved the nomination. Souter told reporters that the past five years had been "a very happy time," and later he would view his trial court tenure as the best experience of his professional life. But the promotion was exactly what he had long aspired to. A few days before his 44th birthday, David Souter was sworn in as the Junior member of the New Hampshire Supreme Court. . . .

In mid-1986, Chief Justice King retired, opening the door for what threatened to be the emotional climax of Souter's professional life. Brock, as the senior associate justice was widely expected to be Governor Sununu's choice. . . . Senator Rudman, however, mounted what one participant called "quite an effort" on Souter's behalf, and inside the court no one doubted that Souter was very interested in the center chair. One equally desirous colleague says the Chief Justiceship was Souter's "life ambition" and that Souter wanted it "in the worst way." A second justice agrees that "David wanted to be Chief Justice," but adds that "everyone wanted to become Chief Justice."

Sununu held 45-minute interviews with both Brock and Souter and then, in advance of the announcement, called Souter to say he was choosing Brock. Publicly, Souter suffered no embarrassment, for he had not been named as a possible choice, and news reports simply noted how "Brock Nomination Signals Return to Tradition of Seniority." Privately, however, Souter was deeply disappointed, and perhaps acutely wounded. One close observer called it "something of a slap," since Souter already was "intellectually the leader," and another court insider thought Souter "deeply resented" Brock's selection. But Souter was inclined to think that things always happen for the best, and in the wake of his greatest professional disappointment, he began to ponder whether there might be life after the New Hampshire Supreme Court. . . .

[F]or Souter the late 1980's was a time of increased introspection. One colleague thought he was "very unhappy" on the New Hampshire court, and not so much with mundane cases as with being "doomed to be an associate under David Brock." By 1989, close friends were certain that Souter was "ready for a new challenge." Privately, Souter admitted to friends that he was toying with ideas for a second career or

extensive world travels, but Warren Rudman focused on a possibility much closer to home: New Hampshire's one judge on the Federal First Circuit-Court of Appeals, Hugh Bownes, was old enough to move to semiretired "senior status." When he did, Rudman, as New Hampshire's most influential Republican senator, would effectively control the Bush Administration's selection of his successor. Some intimates believe Souter initially was ambivalent about the Federal judgeship, but by the time that Bownes did "go senior" in the Winter of 1989–90, any hesitation had disappeared. The First Circuit would offer a greater variety of cases than New Hampshire, and Boston—the First Circuit's home city—featured cultural attractions and was a manageable drive from Weare. A brief, almost pro forma hearing before the Senate Judiciary Committee was soon followed by unanimous Senate confirmation, and on May 25, 1990, David Souter was sworn into office by First Circuit Chief Judge Stephen Breyer.

Souter spent the early summer setting up his new office in Concord's Federal building and in June he traveled to Boston for his first sitting as a circuit judge. Then, early one Sunday afternoon in late July, a telephone call interrupted him at his Concord office: C. Boyden Gray, George Bush's White House counsel, explained that the President wanted to see Souter on Monday and Souter should fly to Washington that evening.

Souter had heard Friday's news of the retirement of Supreme Court Justice William J. Brennan and he knew that three years earlier Rudman had placed his name on the Reagan White House's list of Court prospects prior to the nomination of Justice Anthony Kennedy. Gray's call, however, was totally unexpected, as was the prospect of a face-to-face Presidential interview the next day. Souter's first reaction was to phone Rudman: "What have you done to me now?" he asked his long-time patron. Rudman gave him a pep talk and explained how Gray had called on Saturday to request a recommendation letter; Souter was on a Presidential short list of just four names. Then, a few minutes later, Souter called Rudman back: was it possible to fly directly from Manchester to Washington? Yes, Rudman said. Finally, after some reflection, Souter called for a third time: the White House ought to know that he would *not* discuss how he might rule in future cases. Rudman assured him no such questions would be posed and told Souter he'd take him to the airport for his 6 P.M. flight.

An aide to Attorney General Dick Thornburgh met Souter's plane and took him to another staff member's home to have dinner and spend the night. The next morning, Thornburgh's aide took Souter to the White House, where Boyden Gray asked him personal background questions aimed at exposing any skeletons. Unbeknown to Souter, Federal Appellate Judge Edith H. Jones of Texas was also in the White House undergoing similar scrutiny; over the weekend George Bush had narrowed his short list to two by deleting Federal appellate Judges Clarence Thomas and Laurence Suberman, both of Washington.

At 1:30 P.M., Souter was ushered into the Oval Office for a 45-minute meeting with Bush, Thornburgh, Gray and the White House chief of staff, John Sununu, who as New Hampshire Governor had named him to the state Supreme Court but had also preferred David Brock for Chief Justice. Bush and his aides had already interviewed Jones, and at the conclusion of the Souter meeting, those four, joined by Vice President Dan Quayle, spent an hour debating the pros and cons of each finalist, with Bush asking Quayle and Sununu to make the case for Jones and Thornburgh and Gray for Souter. Jones had a more conservative reputation than Souter, but Bush's aides feared that her ideological renown would hamper confirmation and the President had been highly impressed by Souter's intellectual seriousness. Bush spent almost an hour pondering the choice privately before deciding, and at 4:15 P.M. Souter was summoned back to the Oval Office to be offered the nomination. At 5 P.M., with a visibly stunned David Souter at his side, George Bush announced the selection in the White House press room.

Souter's transformation from obscurity to national celebrity was the greatest emotional shock he had ever experienced. That evening, Warren Rudman took his dazed friend to dinner before Souter turned in on a cot in Rudman's Southwest Washington apartment. Having anticipated only a one-day visit to Washington, Souter had just the suit he'd worn on Monday, plus a second tie, to carry him through the following three days of senatorial courtesy calls. Only on Friday did a shellshocked David Souter return home.

After a visit to his mother, who now lived in a Concord retirement community, Souter spent one night in Weare before heading to Tom Rath's lakefront summer home to escape the journalists descending upon Concord. Reporters failed to distill any clear ideological messages from Souter's New Hampshire Supreme Court opinions, but some seemed unable to grasp even the vast political difference between being a protégé of Warren Rudman rather than of Meldrim Thomson or John Sununu. Rudman proclaimed that "history will prove this to be one of the greatest nominations of all time," but he admitted that Souter led "an almost monastic life." Rudman emphasized that if Souter "has any fault…it's that he's worked too hard all his life." Some journalists were more interested in Souter's personal life than in his professional record, and Souter's closest friends soon became intensely angry at several reporters' preoccupation with Souter's "bachelor" status.

Souter found the intrusive media scrutiny traumatic. "This is the biggest mistake I've made in my life," he told one friend and to another he confessed that "this has been the worst week of my life." By early August, with Senate Judiciary Committee confirmation hearings scheduled for mid-September, more and more speculation focused upon Souter's position on Roe v. Wade. New Hampshire's other United States Senator, Gordon Humphrey, an extreme conservative who barely knew Souter, anticipated that he would vote to overturn Roe. But the more astute James Duggan observed that even if Souter disagreed with Roe, "Whether he would be willing to overturn the decision…is a different proposition entirely." Liberal publications trumpeted the news that the conservative Free Congress Foundation had distributed a memo quoting John Sununu as telling one of its leaders that Souter's nomination was "a home run" for conservatives. Privately, as Sununu recently told this author, his belief that Souter would not uphold Roe was based upon "very detailed" confidential assurances from W. Stephen Thayer 3d, Souter's conservative junior colleague on the New Hampshire Supreme Court.

When the Senate Judiciary Committee hearing began on Thursday, Sept. 13, Senators and reporters quickly realized that Souter was an impressively erudite nominee. Souter spent three full days in front of the 14-member committee, and amid all the concepts and issues he was asked to address, two, in retrospect, stand out as most revealing: liberty and precedent. Most specifically, Souter stressed that in the due process clause language of the 5th and 14th Amendments, "the concept of liberty is not limited by the specific subjects" listed in the Bill of Rights. In protecting personal liberty, justices had to search for "principles that may be elucidated by the history and tradition of the United States. And ultimately the kind of search that we are making is a search for the limits of governmental power."

More generally, Souter explained that in reading the Constitution, "my interpretive position is not one that original intent is controlling, but that original meaning is controlling," in that Justices ought to identify the "principle that was intended to be established as opposed simply to the specific application that that particular provision was meant to have by, and that was in the minds of those who proposed and framed and adopted that provision in the first place." He summed up his perspective in one memorable sentence: "Principles don't change but our perceptions of the world around us and the need for those principles do."

Souter's comments about precedent were potentially inseparable from the looming issue of Roe. He highlighted the concept of reliance: "Who has relied upon that precedent and what does that reliance count for today?" If a court reconsidered a precedent, it was important for judges to ask "whether private citizens in their lives have relied upon it in their own planning to such a degree that, in fact, there would be a great hardship to overruling it now."

In his second day of testimony, Souter addressed Roe directly. "I have not got any agenda on what should be done with Roe v. Wade if that case were brought before me. I will listen to both sides of that case. I have not made up my mind." He added, however, that when an existing case was attacked, any reconsideration involved not only the correctness of the earlier decision but also "extremely significant issues of precedent." But regarding abortion itself, he emphasized that "whether I do or do not find it moral or immoral will play absolutely no role in any decision which I make, if I am asked to make it, on the question of what weight, should or legitimately may be given to the interest which is represented by the abortion decision."

Legal observers reacted favorably to Souter's testimony, with Walter Dellinger, then a Duke University law professor, commenting that Souter was "the most intellectually impressive nominee I've ever seen." Most Senators agreed, and in late September the Judiciary Committee ratified Souter's nomination by a vote of 13–1. On Oct. 2, the full Senate followed suit by a margin of 90 to 9, and on Oct. 8, 1990, David Hackett Souter was sworn in as an Associate Justice of the United States Supreme Court.

Unfortunately for Souter, the Court was already one week into its 1990–91 term, and from the first day he arrived Souter found himself playing an unwinnable game of catch-up. There was a huge volume of petitions to review and briefs to read, and Souter's relative unfamiliarity with Federal statutory issues made the process all the more difficult. He soon realized he was facing the most difficult professional challenge of his life.

Throughout the fall, Souter continued to room with Rudman before taking his own apartment at the same complex, but he spent almost all of his waking hours, on weekends as well as weekdays, at the Court. Asked about his Washington social plans by a New Hampshire magazine, Souter acknowledged that "I'm not a very sociable individual except among a fairly close circle of friends," most of whom lived in New Hampshire. And, he added, "I'm not going to change my personality as a result of getting a new job."

Souter's friends appreciated that the transition to Washington was more difficult than he had anticipated. Given Souter's "reverence" for the Court, Tom Rath explained, Souter was not only "in awe of the challenge" but also felt that "his first test was to satisfy himself that he was worthy of the job. Those who saw him thought he looked more exhausted than ever before; those who phoned him could sense he was worried about keeping up with the caseload. Rath identified the stress succinctly: "David Souter's harshest critic is David Souter."

By the spring of 1991, journalists were wondering if Souter was foundering; prior to late May, only *one* case in which he had written an opinion had been decided and as of mid-June, he had issued only five more opinions. Finally, in the last week of the term, another half-dozen Souter opinions appeared.

At the end of the term, a spent David Souter headed home to New Hampshire, grateful for a three-month respite from Washington. When he returned in September to begin the new term, he was fully pre-pared. The difference quickly showed in the pace and scale of Souter's output, and by the time Casey was argued in late April 1992, Souter had found his equi-librium. Even though he missed New Hampshire, he loved the Court and was a well-liked figure within the Court building.

Casey was the most important case of the 1991–92 term, but there were other impressive Souter successes. He, Kennedy and O'Connor also came to-gether, again joined by Blackmun and Stevens, in a crucial establishment clause case, Lee v. Weisman, where they struck down the recital of religious prayers at public school graduation ceremonies. Souter also stepped to the fore in humorously taking on the rhetorical excesses and interpretive shortcom-ings of Antonin Scalia, the intellectual leader of the Court's right wing. Indeed, of the term's 108 cases, Souter dissented in only 8. But Casey was the high-light of many a year, and both before the decision came down, as well as after, David Souter did not for a moment doubt the correctness or the importance of the trio's achievement.

In the immediate aftermath of Casey, no one who knew David Souter well, irrespective of their po-sition on abortion, was surprised by what Souter and his two allies had said and done. From Chuck Dou-glas ("I was not surprised by the Casey decision") to James Duggan ("It should not be a surprise to anyone that David Souter is not voting to overturn prece-dent") to all of Souter's close friends, the reactions were virtually identical.

What Casey boiled down to, Tom Rath said, was "how the judiciary can bind a society together." David Souter, he told one questioner, "has a vision of the Court as a moderating influence," as "a concilia-tor and legitimizer," and that perspective represented "the essence of David Souter. That's the David Souter I've heard many a night on porches."

Another close friend, echoing how Casey "wasn't a surprise," especially given "David's respect for precedent," stressed that people did not appreciate

how "David's a judicial conservative, not a political conservative, Jane Cetlin Pickrell—the former clerk who had received the thank-you note in Latin, and the bar of soap—felt similarly. He "may have had doubts about Roe," because "we debated that at some point," but "I knew what he would do with Roe v. Wade," and Casey had proved her correct.

David Souter was happy to have the constitutional battle over abortion behind him. The 1991–92 term had been vastly different from 1990-91, and in Casey the Court had triumphantly passed a crucial test. Given the workload, there was no way around having his clerks do some opinion drafting, but the amount of ink he added to almost every line of their drafts left the clerks with no doubts whose opinions they really were.

Neither the 1992–93 or 1993–94 terms would prove as significant as 1991–92. The most striking statistic of 1991–92, as Casey exemplified, was the degree to which Anthony Kennedy had shifted away from Rehnquist and toward Souter and O'Connor. But in the following year, as Kennedy reverted to greater agreement with the Chief Justice, Souter found him-self on the minority side of far more split decisions.

In New Hampshire, some defense attorneys were pleasantly stunned by Souter's majority opinion in a Miranda-related criminal case, Withrow v. Williams. But Souter's most important opinion of 1992–93 was a concurrence in Church of the Lukumi Babaiu Aye Inc. v. City of Hialeah, a free-exercise clause chal-lenge to a municipal prohibition of animal sacrifices that was targeted against Santeria religionists. Souter's long concurrence in Lee v. Weisman a year earlier had signaled his special interest in the First Amendment's separation of church and state; but Souter's Lukumi Babaiu concurrence was striking in how it explicitly called for the Court to reconsider its reigning free-exercise clause precedent, a 1990 deci-sion entitled Employment Division v. Smith.

At his confirmation hearing, Souter had said only that "my own religion is a religion which I wish to exercise in private and with as little…expression in the political arena as is possible," but he now made it clear that Smith insufficiently protected religion from government intrusion. Since earlier cases contained "a free-exercise rule fundamentally at odds with the rule Smith declared," there now existed "an intolerable ten-sion in free-exercise law." Quoting Felix Frankfurter's reminder that stare decisis "is a principle of policy and not a mechanical formula," Souter's message was obvious—Casey's affirmation of Roe notwithstanding—that Smith was a disposable precedent.

The 1992–93 decline of the Souter-O'Connor-Kennedy trio led some observers to highlight how Kennedy had moved back rightward but Paul Barrett of The Wall Street journal contended that actually the "most striking development" was Souter's "emerging liberal streak."

Once the 1993–94 term got under way, evidence seemed to mount that Barrett's characterization was no overstatement. James Duggan believed a Souter concurrence concerning the use of uncounseled convictions for cumulative sentencing in Nichols v. U.S. was almost "180 degrees different" from a 1984 Souter opinion, State v. Cook. A few weeks later, one New Hampshire Supreme Court insider, reacting joyously to a Souter concurrence on behalf of fellow Justices Blackmun, Stevens and Ruth Bader Ginsburg in a Miranda-oriented military murder case, Davis v. U.S., vehemently exclaimed that "that was not the David Souter that sat on this bench!"

But the most dramatic 1993–94 evidence of Souter's increasingly influential intellectual leadership of the Court's six mainstream members was the growing number of combative references that Antonin Scalia was directing to him in multiple opinions. Supreme Court insiders emphasize that in person, the two justices "like each other" and "kid around," but based upon the written record, there is little doubt that Scalia now realizes—much as Felix Frankfurter did after the advent of Earl Warren and William Brennan—that he has decisively lost the struggle for intellectual leadership of the Court to someone who was not supposed to be a major player.

In one late June habeas corpus ruling, Heck v. Humphrey, three contentious Scalia footnotes criticized Souter by name; three days later, in one of the term's leading cases, Board of Education of Kiryas Joel Village School District v. Grumet, Scalia in angry dissent dismissed Souter's majority opinion as "facile" and petulantly invoked Souter's name again and again in criticizing the outcome. Seemingly both provoked and bemused, Souter responded that "Justice Scalia's dissent is certainly the work of a gladiator, but he thrusts at lions of his own imagining."

The 1993–94 term witnessed Souter's highest output of his four years on the Court—25 opinions (8 majority, 12 concurrences and 5 dissents), more than double the number he wrote his first year. In part, Souter's increased productivity reflected what he told friends was a lesson he had learned in each of his three judgeships: only after three years does one get fully up to speed.

But even though Souter was now completely at ease, the results of the 1993–94 term showed that he and his three most regular allies—Blackmun, Stevens and Ginsburg, who had been together in 11 of the year's 14 5–4 cases—had been the losing foursome in 8 of those 11, prevailing only in 3 criminal cases where they were joined by Kennedy. And if one looked at the 35 cases where Blackmun and Rehnquist had come out on opposite sides, perhaps Souter's "emerging liberal streak" was no exaggeration at all: While Ginsburg had sided 19 times with Blackmun and 16 with Rehnquist (and O'Connor only 7 with Blackmun and 27 with Rehnquist), Souter had been with Blackmun in 24 of the cases and with Rehnquist in only 11.

Right-wing Court watchers rued Souter's evolution. Thomas Jipping of the Free Congress Foundation, reminding the conservative Washington Times that "John Sununu told me directly that Souter would be a 'home run' for conservatives," offered a sarcastically dismissive metaphor: "The first term, I thought he might be a blooper single. After last year, I thought he was a foul ball. Now I think he's a strikeout."

But Linda Greenhouse of The New York Times saw it differently: "Souter's brand of moderate pragmatism and his willingness to engage Justice Scalia in direct intellectual combat is probably as responsible as any single factor for the failure of the conservative revolution."

A chagrined John Sununu readily concedes that he is "very surprised"—and deeply disappointed—by David Souter's evolution. In sharp contrast, however, former President Bush tells this author that he is proud of Souter's "outstanding" service and "outstanding intellect." Some antagonists, Bush recalls, greeted the nomination by dismissing Souter as "a predictable, extreme rightwinger." Now Bush quietly exults over "how wrong his critics were. This quiet decent man will serve for years on the Court, and he will serve with honor always and with brilliance."

The arrival of new Justice Stephen Breyer will make for few changes in the Court's basic lineup. In controversial cases, Breyer likely will take his predecessor Harry Blackmun's place in the Souter-Stevens-Ginsburg quartet. Although Breyer will be more centrally involved in the Court's discussions than was Blackmun, the highly pragmatic Breyer likely will make few waves on what Harvard's Laurence Tribe calls a "fundamentally unadventuresome and cautious Court." The widely anticipated retirement of John Paul Stevens...is expected to result in his replacement with a similarly mainstream voice, and only an unanticipated departure from the more conservative ranks of O'Connor, Kennedy, Rehnquist, Scalia and Thomas is likely to generate any significant ideological shift in the Court's alignment. If none of those justices leave prior to the 1996 Presidential election, the eventual timing of William Rehnquist's departure as Chief Justice—generally expected to occur after, rather than before, the 1996 balloting—looms as the next turning point in the Court's history. Whoever replaces Rehnquist as Chief Justice—and whoever as President gets to make that choice—will be responsible for piloting the Court into the next century....

Personally happy and professionally fulfilled, David Souter likely will help lead the Court well into the second decade of the 21st century. Says one friend, "A man more comfortable with himself would be hard to find."

READING 59

Responses to Judicial Policies

Charles Johnson and Bradley Canon

When discussing the role of the judiciary in the American governmental system, Alexander Hamilton characterized it as "the least dangerous branch,"

From "Responses to Judicial Policies" by C. Johnson and B. Canon, 1984, *Judicial Policies: Implementation and Impact.* Copyright © 1984 by the Congressional Quarterly, Inc. Reprinted by permission.

lacking the power of the purse and sword. Courts had neither force nor will but merely judgment, suggesting that policymaking by the judiciary is quite problematic when compared with that of the other branches.

In this selection, political scientists Johnson (Texas A&M) and Canon (University of Kentucky) present a wide-ranging case study of the multiple consequences of the Court's landmark abortion ruling in Roe v. Wade *(1973).* Roe *demonstrates that immediately after a judicial decision interested individuals and groups will begin their efforts to facilitate implementation or, alternatively, to block or reshape the case's outcome. This may result in the development of additional litigation, efforts at legislative alteration of a decision at both the federal and state levels, and even efforts at passage of a constitutional amendment.*

Public reaction to a decision, like public opinion itself, runs the gamut of possible viewpoints. Public policy consequences can occur from a ruling, yet Roe *illustrates the potential fragmentary nature of those consequences.* Roe *allowed for freedom of choice while not mandating the availability of such choice in the private medical arena. Thus, the actual exercise of the freedom guaranteed in* Roe *occurred overwhelmingly in congenial environments generally associated with large metropolitan areas. For many women, however,* Roe *held out an unfulfilled promise. Further,* Roe's *aftermath demonstrates the potential long-term consequences of judicial rulings, as lower courts and the Supreme Court itself must continue to grapple with new litigation to address related though not identical issues to those already decided.*

John Marshall has made his decision, now let him enforce it.

—attributed to President Andrew Jackson

Does anybody know...where we can go to find light on what the practical consequences of these decisions have been?

—Justice Felix Frankfurter

Constitutional rights...are not to be sacrificed or yielded to the violence and disorder which have followed upon the actions of the Governor and Legislature.

> —U.S. Supreme Court, *Cooper v. Aaron* (1958)

President Jackson's remark reveals an important insight—that judicial policies rarely implement themselves. Justice Frankfurter's comment also underscores the fact that once a judicial policy is announced a court may have little control over what the policy's consequences are. Finally, the Supreme Court's decision in *Cooper* v. *Aaron,* which overturned moves by Arkansas's governor and legislature to block school desegregation, illustrates the frequently political nature of the events that follow judicial decisions....

[J]udicial policies are not self-implementing, and implementing judicial policies is a political process. In virtually all instances, the courts that formulate policies must rely on other courts or on nonjudicial actors to translate those policies into action....

STUDYING RESPONSES TO JUDICIAL POLICIES

...Although they differ from legislative actions and executive orders in their origin, judicial policies are also public policies: they too must be implemented before disputes or problems are resolved, and they have an impact on the public. Racial segregation, for example, did not end with the announcement of *Brown* v. *Board of Education* in 1954.... The Court's policy was given meaning only after considerable efforts by lower courts, the Department of Justice, the Department of Health, Education and Welfare, the Congress, and civil rights groups. Our knowledge about desegregation and the judiciary would be quite incomplete if we limited our analysis to the *Brown* decision....

To a certain degree, evaluating the implementation of judicial policies is in the mainstream of the emerging field of policy analysis.... Why are some policies implemented while others are not? Why do some organizations change policies while others do not? Why do some policies have the intended impact while others fail to do so or have unintended consequences? The varied outcomes of judicial policies provide ample opportunities to examine the impact of public policies.

Responses to some court decisions have been immediate and implementation almost complete. For example, in the years following the Supreme Court's 1973 abortion decision in *Roe* v. *Wade,* several million women ended their pregnancies with legal abortions and new pro- and antiabortion groups emerged as powerful forces in our political system, By contrast, the events following *Brown* v. *Board of Education* demonstrate that the implementation of other decisions may be prolonged. And the Supreme Court's decision in *Abington School District* v. *Schempp* (1963), declaring prayers in public schools unconstitutional, is an example of a decision that has been implemented in varying degrees across the nation. Almost two decades after the decision, prayers continue as a daily practice in some of the nation's schools, while other school systems have dropped all religious activities. The aftermaths of these decisions and others raise important questions about the ability of the judiciary to make public policy effectively and about how individual citizens and political institutions relate to the judiciary....

[M]any judicial decisions carry a great deal of latitude for interpretation and implementation. Political actors and institutions who follow through on these decisions make the judicial policy.... Like the Congress, the Supreme Court and lower courts must rely on others to translate policy into action. And like the processes of formulating legislative, executive, and judicial policies, the process of translating those decisions into action is often a political one subject to a variety of pressures from a variety of political actors in the system.

ROE v. *WADE:* A CASE STUDY OF JUDICIAL IMPACT

The best way to illustrate the political nature of the events that follow a judicial decision is to review the implementation and impact of a...decision that remains controversial. We will use the Supreme Court's 1973 abortion decision in *Roe* v. *Wade* to show what may happen after a judicial policy is announced....

The Decision

On Monday, January 22, 1973, Associate Justice Harry Blackmun announced the decision of the Court in two cases concerning the rights of women to end unwanted pregnancies with legal abortions, *Roe* v. *Wade* and *Doe* v. *Bolton*.... The decision came after almost a full year of research by Justice Blackmun, and the justices fully expected a public outcry after the decision was announced. They were not disappointed.

The cases before the Court challenged the laws prohibiting abortion in Texas and Georgia. The Court decided in favor of the plaintiffs in both cases.... The direct effect of the decision was to void the antiabortion laws in Texas and Georgia. Indirectly, of course, the Court also voided laws in every state that prohibited or limited abortion....

In effect, the Supreme Court had given women the right to abortion on demand during the first two trimesters of pregnancy and had allowed the state to regulate abortions only to protect the mother's health during these two trimesters. The Court held that during the third trimester the state could regulate or even prohibit abortions, except where the life or the health of the mother was endangered.

Immediate Responses

On the day the Court announced the abortion decision, former president Lyndon B. Johnson died of a heart attack, and a few days before the Court's announcement, President Richard Nixon had announced the end of American military participation in the Vietnam War. These two events diminished the newsworthiness of the Court's decision in *Roe* and *Doe*. Instead of being the lead story in the weekly news magazines, the abortion decision received only limited coverage. Nevertheless, the reactions from several corners of the political system were immediate, and they were mostly negative.

A few reactions were aimed directly at the justices....

> [T]housands of letters poured into the Court.... The most mail came to Blackmun, the decision's author, and to Brennan, the Court's only Catholic. Some letters compared the Justices to the Butchers of Dachau, child killers, immoral beasts, and Communists.... Whole classes from Catholic schools wrote to denounce the Justices as murderers. "I really don't want to write this letter but my teacher made me," one child

> said.... Southern Baptists and other groups sent over a thousand bitter letters to Justice Hugo Black, who had died sixteen months earlier. Some letters and calls were death threats.

But not all reactions were negative. The president of Planned Parenthood...called the decision a "courageous stroke for right to privacy and for the protection of a woman's physical and emotional health." A similar reaction came from women attorneys at the Center for Constitutional Rights, who cited the decision as a "victory for [the] women's liberation movement."...

Reactions also came from members of Congress. A week after the Supreme Court's decision, Rep. Lawrence J. Hogan, R-Md., introduced the first of several "right to life" amendments to the U.S. Constitution. By November 1973 over two dozen resolutions to overturn some aspect of the Court's decision were introduced in Congress....

Response was also immediate from women who sought abortions.... [D]uring the first year following the Supreme Court's decision a total of 742,460 abortions were performed nationwide. The overwhelming majority of abortions occurred in metropolitan areas, and 41 percent occurred in Middle Atlantic states. The variation in the number of abortions from state to state was considerable.... Data from the first year of nationwide legal abortions suggest that almost one of every five pregnancies was terminated with an abortion.

Whether a woman secured an abortion depended heavily on whether there was a physician or medical facility willing to provide abortion services.... The data seem to indicate that whether hospitals provided abortion services depended heavily on whether the hospital staff was in favor of abortions; factors such as community need or demand for abortion services and the hospital's financial situation were largely unrelated to the hospitals' decisions.

A national survey by the research division of Planned Parenthood...in 1973 revealed that less than one-third (30.1 percent) of the non-Catholic short-term general hospitals in the United States provided abortion services....

[I]n the 12 months following the Supreme Court's abortion decision, "the response of health institutions in many areas to the legalization of abortion in 1973 was so limited as to be tantamount to no response at all." This widespread nonresponse had a considerable effect on *Roe* v. *Wade's* impact—after being granted the *constitutional* right to an abortion, many women could not exercise that right because medical facilities in their communities refused to provide the services necessary to secure an abortion.

LATER RESPONSES

One year after the Supreme Court's announcement of the abortion decision, the first annual "March for Life" was held in Washington, D.C., to protest that decision. . . .

In the Senate a subcommittee began hearing testimony on several proposed constitutional amendments to overturn the decision. . . . There were also moves in Congress to limit the federal government's support of abortions. . . . [I]n 1976 Congress approved a restriction on Medicaid funding for abortions known as the Hyde Amendment (for its sponsor, Rep. Henry J. Hyde, R-Ill.). The amendment was the subject of considerable debate and political maneuvering. . . . The provision came under attack immediately in the courts, and its implementation was delayed almost a full year, until August 1977.

Congress was not the only legislative body acting to restrict the implementation of the Supreme Court abortion decision. From 1973 through 1976, 34 states adopted laws relating to abortions. Some of the laws concerned regulations that the Court indicated states could pass to protect the health of the mother—for example, requiring that abortions be performed by licensed physicians—and others called for reporting abortions to a state agency. Such laws were not considered to be restrictive or aimed at limiting the availability of abortions. Other laws, however, were clearly intended to limit the impact of the Court's decision or to discourage the use of abortions by women with unwanted pregnancies. Several states passed consent requirements under which the husband of a married woman or the parents of an unmarried minor would have to give their written approval before an abortion could be performed. A few states also required consultation or certification by a second physician during the third trimester. A majority of the states (29) adopted laws protecting physicians from

discriminatory, disciplinary, or recriminatory actions if they refused to perform abortions, and 31 states adopted "conscience clause" laws specifically authorizing physicians to refuse to perform abortions.

Abortion opponents used the judicial process as well. The most celebrated case involved a Boston physician, Kenneth C. Edelin, who was indicted in June 1974 for manslaughter for causing the death of a fetus after an abortion he performed on a woman in the sixth or seventh month of her pregnancy. The trial of Dr. Edelin received national media coverage. . . . Dr. Edelin was convicted of manslaughter by a jury but the conviction was overturned by a state appellate court. Nonetheless, the immediate result of the conviction was to increase the caution of some hospitals and clinics in performing second trimester abortions. . . .

In spite of intense opposition and various legal restrictions, the number of abortions performed in the United States continued to grow. By 1980 over 1.6 million legal abortions were performed annually. In contrast, the number of illegal abortions had shrunk from nearly 750,000 in 1969 to around 10,000 in 1980. . . .

As before, the overwhelming percentage of abortions were performed in metropolitan areas; one survey found that there were no facilities in 80 percent of the counties in the United States. . . .

Four years after *Roe* v. *Wade,* the political struggles surrounding the abortion issue had spilled beyond the Congress, the states, and the judiciary. Pro- and antiabortion groups, for example, organized, and other political actors became involved. The National Right to Life Committee . . . applauded the House of Representative's vote for a ban on using Medicaid funds for abortions, and the leaders of the committee pledged to oppose the reelection of the representatives who had voted against the amendment. Proabortion forces were also continuing their fight against limits on the implementation of the Court's decision. In August 1977, 27 women's and public interest groups sent a letter to President Carter expressing their support for the women in his administration who had publicly disassociated themselves from his advocacy of a ban on federally funded abortions. Another political agency, the U.S. Commission on Civil Rights, issued a report in 1975 urging Congress to reject "anti-abortion legislation and amendments, and repeal those which have been enacted, which undermine the constitutional right to limit childbearing."

Local politics were also affected. The Right to Life party formed in New York state and ran candidates for office. In other localities, candidates' stands on abortion were sometimes crucial to endorsements or support from blocs of voters. Even presidential politics was affected by the abortion controversy....

The Controversy Continues

The controversy over the abortion policy announced by the Supreme Court in 1973 and over how that policy was to be implemented continued unabated four years after the decision was announced. The intensity of the debate is best seen in Congress's annual consideration of amendments to appropriations bills deleting funds for abortion (for example, the Hyde Amendment).... Although Congress had not passed a constitutional amendment to overturn the 1973 Supreme Court decision, it had gone quite far to limit the impact of the original abortion decision.

While Congress enacted restrictions on abortion procedures, proabortion forces had some success in the judiciary. The Supreme Court anticipated several questions in *Roe* v. *Wade*.... Three years after *Roe,* the Supreme Court began refining its policy by addressing these...issues.

One of the major cases came out of a challenge to several restrictive laws enacted in Missouri. Overturning several provisions of the law in question, the Court held that states could not require a woman to obtain her husband's consent (or parents' permission, in the instance of an unmarried minor) before having an abortion. Also, states could not proscribe the use of a particular method for abortions, nor could they require that physicians make an effort to save an aborted fetus as if the fetus were a premature baby (*Planned Parenthood of Central Missouri* v. *Danforth,* 1976)....

These decisions seemed to imply that states could not place limits on a woman's right to have an abortion. But the Court was not completely supportive of proabortion policies. In 1977 the Court held that states and municipalities could refuse to fund nontherapeutic abortions, even if they funded all other medical services (*Maher* v. *Roe,* 1977). And in 1980 the Court upheld by a five-to-four vote the constitutionality of the Hyde Amendment's prohibition of federal expenditures for elective abortions (*Harris* v. *McRae,* 1980)....

> It simply does not follow that a woman's freedom of choice carries with it a constitutional entitlement to the financial resources to avail herself of the full range of protected choices.... Although government may not place obstacles in the path of a woman's exercise of her freedom of choice, it need not remove those not of its own creation. Indigency falls in the latter category.

...[T]he effect of the Court's decision was almost immediate. The Department of Health and Human Services announced a fund cutoff date which, by their estimate, would reduce the projected number of federally funded abortions from 470,000 to less than 2,000 per year....

Following *Harris,* which was considered to be a victory for the antiabortion forces, the Court moved in 1983 to underscore its commitment to its original decision in *Roe v. Wade.* At issue were several sections of an Akron, Ohio, ordinance aimed at setting roadblocks to the provision and use of abortion services in that community. Items struck down by the Court included requirements that minors under the age of 15 obtain parental permission for an abortion, that women be informed in detail about fetal development and alternatives to abortion, that there be a 24-hour waiting period, and that fetal remains be given "humane" disposal (*Akron* v. *Akron Center for Reproductive Health*). Three justices—Sandra Day O'Connor, Byron White, and William Rehnquist—dissented in this case. However, at the same time, the Court upheld a Missouri law requiring parental consent for "unemancipated" minors....

The continuing controversial nature of the abortion issue is also revealed in the general public's attitude on abortion. A Gallup poll on the abortion issue immediately prior to the Supreme Court's decision in 1973 found that 46 percent of the respondents favored permitting a woman "to go to a doctor to end pregnancy at any time during the first three months." Almost exactly the same percentage of the respondents, 45 percent, opposed granting such a right. After the Court announced its decision, there was a slight jump in the proportion of the population favoring abortion.... However, a strong division in public opinion on abortion remained, as is indicated by...another series of public opinion polls, conducted from 1972 to 1982.... [T]here was a jump in support for abortions after the Court's decision in *Roe,* but thereafter public opinion has consistently remained sharply divided....

In 1980 political conflict over abortion entered directly into the presidential campaign. While both Jimmy Carter and Ronald Reagan were personally opposed to abortion, their parties took opposing stands on the issue. The Republican platform recognized "differing views" on the abortion issue but supported a constitutional amendment "to restore protection of the right to life for unborn children." The platform also supported "congressional efforts to restrict the use of taxpayers' dollars for abortion." The Democratic platform took the opposing point of view, expressing support for the 1973 decision.... Reagan's landslide victory—accompanied by a significant increase in the number of Republican representatives and the first Republican majority in the Senate in 26 years—gave renewed vigor to efforts to outlaw abortion. Senator Jesse Helms, R-N.C., introduced a measure by which Congress would declare that life begins at conception. He argued that such a law would undermine the logic of *Roe* v. *Wade,* which was premised on the belief that there was no consensus as to when life begins. Senator Orrin Hatch, R-Utah...pushed for an amendment that would give Congress and the states the power to regulate abortion or prohibit it altogether....For various reasons, such as divisions within the antiabortionist ranks over strategy, the threat of a filibuster by senators favoring *Roe* v. *Wade,* and the press of other "Reagan reform" proposals, neither proposal passed. The opponents of abortion, however, are still very strong politically, and in the second decade after *Roe* it seems clear that the controversy it raised is not going to go away any time soon.

A MODEL OF THE IMPLEMENTATION AND IMPACT OF JUDICIAL POLICIES

Chronicling the events that followed the Supreme Court's abortion decision gives some idea of the range of reactions and actors that may become involved in the implementation of a judicial decision. Similar case histories could be supplied for other court decisions. But our aim is not to study the aftermath of *every* judicial decision; instead, we want to make general statements about what has happened or may happen after any judicial decision. That is, we hope to move away from idiosyncratic, case-by-case or policy-by-policy analyses toward a general theoretical understanding of the events that may follow a judicial decision....

The first step in understanding any political process is to develop a conceptual foundation upon which explanations may be built. We will organize our presentation of what happens after a court decision around two major elements: the *actors* who may respond to the decision and the responses that these actors may make. Focusing on these two elements enables us to define more precisely who is reacting and how.... Hence, when we discuss "impact," we are describing general reactions following a judicial decision. When we discuss "implementation," we are describing the behavior of lower courts, government agencies, or other affected parties as it relates to enforcing a judicial decision. When we discuss what many would call "compliance/noncompliance" or "evasion," we are describing behavior that is in some way consistent or inconsistent with the behavioral requirements of the judicial decision.

Figure 12.1 presents a schematic diagram of the different sets of actors, referred to as *populations,* that may respond to a judicial policy. The organization of these populations is essentially a functional one, in which their roles in shaping the impact of judicial decisions and their influence on the ultimate impact of judicial policy differ....

The Interpreting Population

For any appellate court decision, the actor most often charged with responding to a decision is a particular lower court, often a trial court.... [A] higher court's policy affects all lower courts within its jurisdiction. This set of courts (and in some instances government officials such as attorneys general) is known as the *interpreting population.* The interpreting population, as

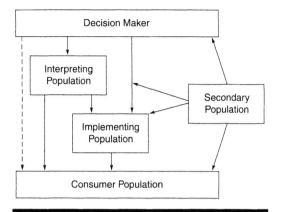

FIGURE 12.1 Populations and lines of communication involved in the implementation and impact of judicial policies.

Source: Adapted from Charles A. Johnson, "The Implementation and Impact of Judicial Policies: A Heuristic Model," in *Public Law and Public Policy,* ed. John A. Gardiner (New York: Praeger, 1977), 107–126, with the permission of the publisher.

the name implies, responds to the policy decisions of a higher court by refining the policy announced by the higher court. Such refinements could have the effect of enlarging or limiting the original policy. This population, in other words, interprets the meaning of the policy and develops the rules for matters not addressed in the original decision. Of course, all populations must "interpret" the decision in order to react to it. Interpretations of lower courts, however, are distinguished from the interpretations of others since theirs are viewed as authoritative in a legal sense by others in the political system. Hence, this population provides "official" interpretations of a court policy applicable to the other populations under their jurisdiction.

The Supreme Court's abortion decision launched the judiciary into a new area of the law, which required considerable refining before complete implementation. Shortly after the decision was announced, lower state and federal courts began hearing cases presenting issues that had not been directly addressed in the *Roe* or *Doe* opinions. In Florida, for example, the issue of a father's rights were raised by a father who brought legal action to restrain the mother of his unborn child from obtaining an abortion. . . .

Meanwhile, in Arizona, another matter was before the courts. Arizona law prohibited the advertisement of any medicine or procedures that facilitated abortions. New Times, Inc., a local publisher, was convicted under this statute and appealed to the state supreme court. . . .

In each of these instances the issue before the court had not been addressed directly in the original decision. Consistent with the common law tradition, the lower courts had the responsibility of making authoritative interpretations of policy in light of the original Supreme Court decision. . . .

The Implementing Population

The lower courts usually apply a higher court's policy only in cases coming before them. Higher court policies and their interpretation by lower courts quite often affect a wider set of actors. We refer to this set of actors as the *implementing population.* In most instances, this population is made up of authorities whose behavior may be reinforced or sanctioned by the interpreting population. The implementing population usually performs a policing or servicing function in the political system—that is, implementors apply the system's rules to persons subject to their authority. Prominent examples of this population are police officers, prosecutors, university and public school officials, and welfare and social security workers. In many instances, the original policy and subsequent interpretations by lower courts are intended to set parameters on the behavior of the implementing population. A clear example of this activity involves decisions concerning police behavior with regard to the rights of criminal suspects.

Occasionally, the implementing population is composed of private individuals or institutions. This is the case when services provided by private concerns are the subject of a judicial policy. The best example of such a circumstance involves the Supreme Court's abortion decision, for which physicians and hospitals were the actual implementors. . . . In the case of public implementing agencies, the court ordinarily *requires* that the agencies change behavior, stop a particular type of service, or provide some new service. Such was the obligation for school systems with regard to *Brown* v. *Board of Education* and the police with regard to *Miranda* v. *Arizona* (1966) and *Mapp* v. *Ohio* (1961). On the other hand, when private concerns are the implementing population, the compulsion to act affirmatively is substantially weaker, if it exists at all. For example, the abortion decision gave women the right to an abortion...but hospitals and physicians were not obliged to provide abortion services against their will. Thus, affirmation action implementing a judicial policy by private implementing groups is most often voluntary....

The degree to which a court decision actually benefits those it was intended to benefit depends on the actors and institutions who police the activities or provide the services called for in the decision. Women in communities where there were no physicians or hospitals willing to provide abortion services were effectively denied their newly granted right or were forced to go elsewhere to benefit from the judicial policy. As another example, where school officials sanctioned prayers after 1963, they often persisted for years....

The Consumer Population

Those for whom the policies are set forth by the court are identified as the *consumer population.* This population is the set of individuals...who would or should receive benefits or suffer disabilities as a result of a judicial decision; that is, they gain or lose desired rights or resources. Criminal suspects, for example, benefit from judicial policies announced by the Supreme Court in *Miranda,* and black students in newly desegregated schools benefit from the *Brown* decision. In other instances, some consumer populations may not benefit from a judicial policy. For example, juvenile court defendants suffer from not being extended the right of trial by jury.... And there are decisions under which members of the consumer population may either benefit or suffer, depending on their attitudes toward the policy. Under the *Schempp* decision on prayer in public schools, children who want to pray in pubic school suffer limitations and children who do not want to pray there gain benefits.

The consumer population, depending on the policy involved, may include the entire population of the

political system, as with judicial decisions concerning general tax legislation. On the other hand, a very limited population may be directly involved, such as criminal suspects under arrest....

In studying the reactions of consumers to judicial policies, several questions need to be addressed. Do the potential consumers of a judicial policy know of the policy? If they know of the policy, why and how do they modify their attitudes or behaviors because of it? What effect, if any, does the policy have on the attitudes and behavior of the consumer with regard to the judiciary or other political institutions?...

The Secondary Population

The populations we have discussed so far are those directly affected by a judicial policy or its implementation. The *secondary population* is a residual one. It consists of everyone who is not in the interpreting, implementing, or consumer population. Members of the secondary population are not directly affected by a judicial policy; however, some may react to a policy or its implementation. This reaction usually takes the form of some type of feedback directed toward the original policy maker, another policy maker, the implementing population, or the consumer population.

The secondary population may be divided into four subpopulations: government officials, interest groups, the media, and the public at large. First, there are *government officials.* This subpopulation includes legislators and executive officers who are not immediately affected by the decision. Though usually unaffected directly, these individuals are often in a position to support or hinder the implementation of the original policy. This subpopulation is distinguished from other secondary subpopulations in that its members have direct, legitimate authority in the political system, and they are often the recipients of political pressure from the public. The second subpopulation is *interest groups,* which are often activated by court policies even when they are not directly affected by them. Subsequent actions by these groups may facilitate or block effective implementation of the judicial policy. The third subpopulation is the *media,* which communicate the substance of judicial policies to potentially affected populations. Included here are general and specialized media, which may affect implementation by editorial stance or simply by the way of reporting judicial policies. Media attention to a policy, descriptions of reactions to it, and support or criticism of it can play a large role in determining the amount and direction of feedback behavior. The fourth subpopulation consists of members of the *public at large,* insofar as they do not fall within the consumer population. The most important segment of this subpopulation is attentive citizens—those who are most aware of a judicial policy....

For the Supreme Court's abortion decision, the secondary population is large and quite varied. Recall from our chronicle of the events following *Roe* that although there were apparently some minor moves in public opinion regarding abortions, most of the reaction came from interest groups and government officials. As to the former...[t]he efforts of these groups produced additional litigation, intensive lobbying, electoral maneuvering, and attempts to mobilize public opinion. Government officials also reacted to the abortion decision by passing restrictive laws, issuing restrictive orders, or, in a few cases, adopting policies that provided opportunities for women to obtain abortions....

Legislative and executive officials may have considerable influence on the implementation of a judicial policy, even though they are not members of the implementing population (that is, they do not provide policing or implementing services). Legislatures, for instance, may be generous or stinting in appropriating money to carry out a policy, as in funding legal services for the poor. The president and state governors may use their appointing authorize to select officials with power over members of the implementing population; or they may use their personal or official influence to encourage either maximum or minimum cooperation in the implementing process, as well as to mobilize public opinion....

Fluidity and Linkage among Populations

The basis for the foregoing classification of populations is primarily functional. We may, therefore, on some occasions find that particular individuals are members of different populations in different circumstances. For example, it is entirely possible for an attorney general to be an interpreter for one judicial policy and an implementor for another. In the former instance, the attorney general would be issuing an authoritative, legally binding statement interpreting a judicial decision; in the latter in stance, the attorney general would be charged with the responsibility of applying a judicial policy to some consumer population or of carrying out some order of the court. It is also possible that courts as members of the interpreting population may occasionally be in a position to direct the implementation of judicial policy. Such may be the case when a judge takes direct charge of the implementation of a school desegregation order, as happened in Boston in the 1970s.... Obviously, private citizens are in both consumer and secondary populations, depending on the nature of the judicial policy.

Attorneys constitute a special set of participants whose function may vary from one setting to another....

In a broad sense, attorneys...serve as linkages between various populations. They provide a link for the communication of decisions downward from higher courts to relevant actors as well as being unofficial interpreters of these decisions....

Acceptance Decisions and Behavioral Responses

We are interested in the responses to judicial policies by all of the populations identified above. We may observe a large variety of responses to judicial decisions, so precise distinctions are difficult to make. Nonetheless, we believe two general categories of responses are captured in the concepts of acceptance decisions and behavioral responses.

The *acceptance decision* involves psychological reactions to a judicial policy, which may be generalized in terms of accepting or rejecting the policy. The acceptance decision is shaped by several psychological dimensions: intensity of attitude, regard for the policy-making court, perceptions of the consequences of the decision, and the respondent's own role in society. . . .

Behavioral responses involve reactions that may be seen or recorded and that may determine the extent to which a court policy is actually realized. These responses are often closely linked to acceptance decisions. Persons who do not accept a judicial policy are likely to engage in behavior designed to defeat the policy or minimize its impact. They will interpret it narrowly, try to avoid implementing it, and refuse or evade its consumption. Those who accept a policy are likely to be more faithful or even enthusiastic in interpreting, implementing, and consuming it. . . .

Feedback behavior is another behavioral response to a judicial policy. It is directed toward the originator of the policy or some other policy-making agency. The purpose of feedback behavior is usually to provide support for or make demands upon other political institutions regarding the judicial policy. Almost immediately after the Supreme Court announced its abortion decision, feedback in the form of letters to the justices began. Also, some members of Congress let the Court know of their displeasure with the abortion decision by introducing amendments to the Constitution to overturn *Roe*. Frequent manifestations of displeasure, as well as some of support, by various interest groups have been directed at the Court and other political institutions, such as Congress and state legislatures. In varying degrees, these attempts at feedback have led to modifications of the policy—as we can see in the Court's approval of the Hyde Amendment passed by Congress, which terminated federal payment for abortions for poor women.

SUMMARY

[W]e have introduced the notion that judicial decisions are not self-implementing; courts must frequently rely on other courts or on nonjudicial actors in the political system to turn law into action. Moreover, the implementation of judicial decisions is a political process; the actors upon whom courts must rely to translate law into action are usually *political* actors and are subject to political pressures as they allocate resources to implement a judicial decision.

Social Policy and Judicial Capacity
Donald Horowitz

"Social Policy and Judicial Capacity" is the opening chapter of Duke law professor Donald Horowitz's important book, The Courts and Social Policy, *an exploration and critique of the American judiciary's contemporary judicial policymaking role. Horowitz's argument should be considered in light of your earlier readings on constitutional interpretation by Graglia, Brennan, and others who are also concerned with the judiciary's role. The difference in Horowitz's approach, however, is an important one. While your earlier readings were concerned with the legitimacy of the judiciary's policymaking role, Horowitz focuses more directly on judicial capacity, that is the judiciary's ability to handle effectively the kinds of issues being brought before it.*

As Horowitz notes, the scope of judicial authority in the United States lends our courts greater policymaking responsibility than any other national judiciary. Such policymaking, Horowitz documents, has led the courts into many unchartered areas in recent decades as they seize the initiative to handle cases regarding matters dealt with poorly elsewhere. Judicial remedies have also expanded in scope, and it is now commonplace for courts to affirmatively mandate massive expenditures of the public fisc in deciding cases and/or to render numerous compliance dictates in litigation processes that they retain open-ended control over for long periods of time. Litigation is treated, in effect, more as problem solving than as grievance answering. Judicial power expands to encompass all facets of governmental power, and the scope of judicial authority resembles that of the other branches, thus

From "Social Policy and Judicial Capacity" by D. Horowitz, 1977, *The Courts and Social Policy,* by D. Horowitz, pp. 1–21. Copyright © 1977 by The Brookings Institution. Reprinted with permission.

resulting in less institutional differentiation in our separation of powers.

Horowitz makes an important distinction between the legitimacy of the judiciary's decisions (a normative judgment) and the judiciary's capacity for making those decisions (a pragmatic assessment). Horowitz's charge that the judiciary lacks capacity for the kinds of judgments it is making serves as the focus for much of his book. Needless to say, his thesis is a provocative one.

"I care not," says Mr. Dooley, "who makes th' laws iv a nation if I can get out an injunction." With his accustomed acuity, the redoubtable Dooley lays bare in an epigram one of the prominent themes of American political history: the penchant for confiding to judges a large share of the lawmaking function.

The common law of England was judge-made law, law forged in the course of contested cases. The statute was a rather late and occasional interloper. In medieval England, legislation was often regarded as simply confirming what was already established as customary law. For a considerable time, states met with hostility at the hands of lawyers and judges. As Solicitor General of England, William Murray, later Lord Mansfield, argued that "a statute can seldom take in all cases, therefore the common law that works itself pure by rules drawn from the fountain of justice is for this reason superior to an Act of Parliament."

As Chief Justice of the King's Bench, Mansfield proved to be one of the most creative spirits of the common law, shaping, modifying, and adapting it to the changing conditions of the eighteenth century. For Mansfield, an act of Parliament was not infrequently regarded as an unwelcome excrescence on the venerated body of the common law, as well as an inferior instrument of reform. Mansfield accordingly became a target of the foremost social inventor of the following generation, Jeremy Bentham. Bentham had fixed his sights on intricate schemes of legislative reform, and he heaped scorn on what he saw as Mansfield's excesses on the bench.... Judges, said Bentham, make law after the fact, "just as a man makes laws for his dog. When your dog does anything you want to break him of, you wait till he does it, and then beat him for it."

Issue was thus joined between the concreteness of judge-made law and the generality of legislature-made law—or, to stress the critical side, between law that comes too late and law that comes too early. It was, in England, an unequal battle, the outcome perhaps foreordained by the Glorious Revolution, which settled the issue of parliamentary supremacy. With kings in check, who could doubt that judges would follow Parliament rather than lead? Small wonder that the dominant jurisprudential school in England has been the brand of legal positivism that, following John Austin, defines law as the "command of the Sovereign," the Sovereign being the Queen in Parliament.

In the United States, the outcome remains in doubt. A written Constitution, in need of judicial interpretation; a separation of powers that made each branch in theory the equal of the others; a profound distrust of popular legislative majorities; a strong current of natural rights; and a transplanted common-law tradition partly antedating the embodiment of natural right in Parliament: these were among the elements that sustained the creative lawmaking authority of judges.

As Parliament's place was becoming more firmly fixed in the early nineteenth century, in the United States "a contest between courts and legislatures began...which is comparable to the contests between courts and crown in seventeenth-century England...." Long after the Mansfieldian tradition had been relegated in England to a distinctly subordinate creativity, it could be echoed, untamed, in America—for example, by Roscoe Pound:

> Judicial finding of law has a real advantage in competition with legislation in that it works with concrete cases and generalizes only after a long course of trial and error in the effort to work out a practicable principle. Legislation, when more than declaratory, when it does more than restate authoritatively what judicial experience has indicated, involves the difficulties and the perils of prophecy.

...[W]hen legal positivism found expression in America, it was transmuted. For Holmes and Gray, unlike Austin and Bentham, law was not what the *legislature* ordered but what the *courts* decided in concrete cases.

The difference in the scope of judicial power in England and the United States should not be exaggerated. It is primarily a difference of emphasis. There have been periods of great judicial boldness and creativity in England and periods of great passivity in America. But still the difference remains. What it has meant, in the main, is that American courts have been more open to new challenges, more willing to take on new tasks. This has encouraged others to push problems their way—so much so that no courts anywhere have greater responsibility for making public policy than the courts of the United States.

THE EXPANSION OF JUDICIAL RESPONSIBILITY

The last two decades have been a period of considerable expansion of judicial responsibility in the United States. Although the kinds of cases judges have long handled still occupy most of their time, the scope of judicial business has broadened. The result has been involvement of courts in decisions that would earlier have been extended to welfare administration, prison administration, and mental hospital administration, to education policy and employment policy, to road building and bridge building, to automotive safety standards, and to natural resource management.

In just the past few years, courts have struck down laws requiring a period of in-state residence as a condition of eligibility for welfare. They have invalidated presumptions of child support arising from the presence in the home of a "substitute father." Federal district courts have laid down elaborate standards for food handling, hospital operations, recreation facilities, inmate employment and education, sanitation, and laundry, painting, lighting, plumbing, and renovation in some prisons; they have ordered other prisons closed. Courts have established equally comprehensive programs of care and treatment for the mentally ill confined in hospitals. They have ordered the equalization of school expenditures on teachers' salaries, established hearing procedures for public school discipline cases, decided that bilingual education must be provided for Mexican-American children, and suspended the use by school boards of the National Teacher Examination and of comparable tests for school supervisors. They have eliminated a high school diploma as a requirement for a fireman's job. They have enjoined the construction of roads and bridges on environmental grounds and suspended performance requirements for automobile tires and air bags. They have told the Farmers Home Administration to restore a disaster loan program, the Forest Service to stop the clear-cutting of timber, and the Corps of Engineers to maintain the nation's non-navigable waterways. They have been, to put it mildly, very busy, laboring in unfamiliar territory.

What the judges have been doing is new in a special sense. Although no single feature of most of this litigation constitutes an abrupt departure, the aggregate of features distinguishes it sharply from the traditional exercise of the judicial function.

First of all, many wholly new areas of adjudication have been opened up. There was, for all practical purposes, no previous judge-made law of housing or welfare rights, for example. To some extent, the new areas of activity respond to invitations from Congress or, to a much lesser extent, from state legislatures. Sometimes these take the form of judicial review provisions written into new legislation. Sometimes they take the form of new legislation so broad, so vague, so indeterminate, as to pass the problem to the courts. They then have to deal with the inevitable litigation to determine the "intent of Congress," which, in such statutes, is of course nonexistent.

If some such developments result from legislative or even bureaucratic activity (interpretation of regulations, for example), then it is natural to see the expansion of judicial activity as a mere concomitant of the growth of the welfare state. As governmental activity in general expands, so will judicial activity.

But that is not all that is involved. Much judicial activity has occurred quite independent of Congress and the bureaucracy, and sometimes quite contrary to their announced policies. The very idea is sometimes to handle a problem unsatisfactorily resolved by another branch of government. In areas far from traditional development by case law, indeed in areas often covered densely by statutes and regulations, the courts have now seized the initiative in lawmaking. In such areas, the conventional formulation of the judicial role has it that courts are to "legislate" only interstitially. With the important exception of judicial decisions holding legislative or executive action unconstitutional, this conventional formulation of what used to be the judicial role is probably not far from what judges did in fact do. It is no longer an adequate formulation.

What the courts demand in such cases, by way of remedy, also tends to be different. Even building programs have been ordered by courts, and the character of some judicial decrees has made them, de facto, exercises of the appropriation power. A district court order rendered in Alabama had the effect of raising the state's annual expenditure on mental institutions from $14 million before suit was filed in 1971 to $58 million in 1973, a year after the decree was rendered. Decisions expanding welfare eligibility or ordering special education for disturbed, retarded, or hyperactive pupils have had similar budgetary effects. "For example, it is estimated that federal court decisions striking down various state restrictions on welfare payments, like residency requirements, made an additional 100,000 people eligible for assistance." It is no longer even approximately accurate to say that courts exercise only a veto. What is asked and what is awarded is often the doing of something, not just the stopping of something,

To be sure, courts have always had some say in the way public funds were spent. How else could they award damages against the government? But even in the aggregate, decisions ordering a municipality to pay for an injury sustained by someone who trips over a loose manhole cover are not generally important enough to influence the setting of public priorities. The recent decisions that require spending to achieve compliance with a newly articulated policy are something else again.

It is also true that both affirmative and negative relief (orders to do something and orders to stop doing something) have a long history in English equity jurisprudence. The hoary remedies of mandamus and specific performance both require affirmative action–but action of a very circumscribed, precise sort, the limits of which are known in advance of the decree. . . .

Again, therefore, compelling the performance of certain affirmative acts is nothing new in principle, but it is new in degree. The decree of a federal district judge ordering mental hospitals to adhere to some eighty-four minimum standards of care and treatment represents an extreme in specificity, but it is representative of the trend toward demanding performance that cannot be measured in one or two simple acts but in a whole course of conduct, performance that tends to be open-ended in time and even in the identity of the parties to whom the performance will be owed. Remedies like these are reminiscent of the kinds of programs adopted by legislatures and executives. If they are to be translated into action, remedies of this kind often require the same kinds of supervision as other government programs do.

This leads to still another difference in degree between adjudication as it once was and as it now is. Litigation is now more explicitly problem-solving than grievance-answering. The individual litigant, though still necessary, has tended to fade a bit into the background. Courts sometimes take off from the individual cases before them to the more general problem the cases call up, and indeed they may assume—dubiously—that litigants before them typify the problem.

Once again, of course, it is all too easy to fabricate an idealized judicial past that consigned judges merely to resolving individual disputes. It has not been that way. . . . Some of the most formidable difficulties faced by common-law judges have arisen in cases that present the judges with an inescapable choice between doing justice in the individual case and doing justice in general.

For all that, however, the individual and his case remained indispensable. Courts paid particular attention to the interplay between the facts of the individual case and the facts of the class of cases they projected from it. Without the particular case, the task of framing standards was devoid of meaning. It is inconceivable, for example, that even a great, innovative common-law court like the New York Court of Appeals early in this century would have countenanced deciding a case that had become moot. That some issues might forever escape judicial scrutiny because of the doctrine that a moot case is not a case at all would have struck even bold judges of a few decades ago as entirely natural.

Today it is repellant to many judges. For the view has gained ground that the judicial power is, by and large, coterminous with the governmental power. One test of this is the withering of the mootness doctrine in the federal courts. The old prohibition on the decision of moot cases is now so riddled with exceptions that it is almost a matter of discretion whether to hear a moot case. The argument for deciding a case that has become moot is often the distinctly recent one that there is a public interest in the judicial resolution of important issues. In contrast, the earlier view was that there was a public interest in avoiding litigation. . . .

What this shift signifies is the increasing subordination of the individual case in judicial policymaking, as well as the expansion of judicial responsibility more nearly to overlap the responsibilities of other governmental institutions. The individual case and its peculiar facts have on occasion become mere vehicles for an exposition of more general policy problems. Consequently, somewhat less care can be devoted, by lawyers and judges alike, to the appropriateness of particular plaintiffs and to the details of their grievances.

At the same time, the courts have tended to move from the byways onto the highways of policymaking. Alexander M. Bickel has captured, albeit with hyperbole, the thrust of the new judicial ventures into social policy. "All too many federal judges," he has written, "have been induced to view themselves as holding roving commissions as problem solvers, and as charged with a duty to act when majoritarian institutions do not." The hyperbole is itself significant: many federal judges regard themselves as holding no such commission, yet even they have embarked on "problem-solving" ventures. This is the surest sign that the tendency is not idiosyncratic but systemic: it transcends, in some measure, individual judicial preference and calls for systematic explanation.

THE SOURCES OF JUDICIAL ROLE EXPANSION

As I have already suggested, the remote sources of the broad sweep of judicial power in America lie deep in English and American political history. The immediate origins of recent shifts in judicial emphasis are another matter. These are several, and they have tended to build on each other.

Most obvious has been the influence of the school desegregation cases. These decisions created a

magnetic field around the courts, attracting litigation in areas where judicial intervention had earlier seemed implausible. The more general judicial activism of the Warren Court signaled its willingness to test the conventional boundaries of judicial action. As this happened, significant social groups thwarted in achieving their goals in other forums turned to adjudication as a more promising course. Some organizations saw the opportunity to use litigation as a weapon in political struggles carried on elsewhere. The National Welfare Rights Organization, for example, is said to have turned to lawsuits to help create a state and local welfare crisis that might bring about a federal guaranteed income. The image of courts willing to "take the heat" was attractive, too, to legislators who were not. Such social programs as the poverty program had legal assistance components, which Congress obligingly provided, perhaps partly because they placed the onus for resolving social problems on the courts. Soon there were also privately funded lawyers functioning in the environmental, mental health, welfare rights, civil rights, and similar fields. They tended to prefer the judicial road to reform over the legislative. They raised issues never before tested in litigation, and the courts frequently responded by expanding the boundaries of judicial activity.

Major doctrinal developments both followed and contributed to the increase in number and the change in character of the issues being litigated. The loosening of requirements of jurisdiction, standing, and ripeness (to name just three) helped spread judge-made law out, moving it from the tangential questions to the great principles. If these doctrinal decisions mean anything, it is that the adjudicative format is less and less an inhibition on judicial action and that the lawsuit can increasingly be thought of [as] an option more or less interchangeable with options in other forums, except that it has advantages the other forums lack. . . . Hence the time-honored tradition that those who lose in the legislature or the bureaucracy may turn to the courts has lost none of its appeal. Only the identity of those who turn from one forum to another has undergone some change. Deprived social groups have joined the advantaged in the march to the courthouse.

Some major obstacles of a practical sort have also been cleared away. It still takes years to conclude most litigation, but some courts have shown a willingness to expedite hearing schedules to speed up the disposition of injunction cases. It still costs large sums of money to bring suit, and reductions in foundation funding of public-interest law firms are contracting their efforts. But decisions awarding attorneys' fees may have eased the hardship and proliferated the cases. In one decision, an attorney's fee was awarded even though the plaintiff's lawyer had agreed to represent him without charge. The court said the award would encourage lawyers to represent public-interest clients without fees in the hope that a fee will be awarded—and no doubt it would have that effect....

It is still true, too, that legislative remedies—when they are forthcoming—may be more systematic and inclusive than judicial remedies. Yet, more often than not, the judicial remedy has a directness, a concreteness, and a lack of equivocation notably absent in schemes that emerge from the political process. More and more, the courts have turned to decrees that afford comprehensive relief, often of a far-reaching sort. Support in the Anglo-American equity tradition for a decree as broad as the occasion warrants is unmistakable. The problem of school desegregation has tested this tradition, and the judges have sometimes proved as resourceful as the English chancellors from whom their equitable powers spring. In the process, the willingness to entertain remedies as inclusive as those a legislature might provide has grown, even to the point where the judicially ordered consolidation of school districts or equalization of tax burdens across districts—wholly beyond imagination not long ago—become debatable measures, indeed litigated issues.

All of this has taken place, perhaps could only take place, in a society given to an incomparable degree of legalism. In the United States, as Tocqueville observed long ago, "all parties are obliged to borrow, in their daily controversies, the ideas, and even the language, peculiar to judicial proceedings.... The language of the law thus becomes in some measure a vulgar tongue; the spirit of the law, which is produced in the schools and courts of justice, gradually penetrates beyond their walls into the bosom of society, where it descends to the lowest classes, so that at last the whole people contract the habits and the taste of the judicial magistrate." The American proclivity to think of social problems in legal terms and to judicialize everything from wage claims to community conflicts and the allocation of airline routes makes it only natural to accord judges a major share in the making of social policy. No doubt, this underlying premise in American thought was a necessary, though insufficient, condition for the expansion of judicial responsibility that has taken place over the last twenty years.

EXPANSION AND CONTRACTION, CONSTITUTIONAL AND STATUTORY

The tendency to commit the resolution of social policy issues to the courts is not likely to be arrested in the near future. The nature of the forces undergirding the tendency makes them not readily reversible. Doctrinal erosion in particular is not easily stopped. Ironically, perhaps, the traditional judicial conception of precedent makes it more difficult for courts to change course dramatically than for the other branches of government to do so. The generally greater stability of judicial personnel, appointed for life in the federal courts, appointed or elected to long terms in the states, also makes for continuity. The statutes already enacted and continuing to be enacted, lodging authority for policy-making in the courts by explicit provision or by default, are enough to propel judicial activity for some time to come. And the attractiveness of passing problems to the judges is unabated....

Even to the limited extent that judges can contract their recently expanded commitments, some curious twists are possible. Supreme Court Justices, appointed because a president thinks they will construe the Bill of Rights more narrowly than their predecessors, have a way of becoming entangled in institutional tradition. No contraction is likely to take place on all fronts.

Beyond that, expansive exercises in statutory construction may be untouched by a contraction in constitutional adjudication. As a matter of fact, judges who recoil at innovation in constitutional lawmaking may not see the same dangers at all in the interpretation of statutes. It is customary to think that judicial self-limitation in constitutional interpretation is important because constitutional law is a permanent inhibition on policy: a legislature cannot override an interpretation of the Constitution. In statutory law, judges may reason, basic policy choices have been made by other branches, and judicial construction may later be overridden by them. For these reasons, judges with a strong sense of institutional limitation are less likely to let it stand in the way of innovation short of constitutional interpretation. . . .

Judges concerned to avoid the excesses that are believed to have characterized the Supreme Court of the 1930s and 1960s may still embark on ambitious ventures of judicial reform in the name of statutory construction. . . .

LEGITIMACY AND CAPACITY

The appropriate scope of judicial power in the American system of government has periodically been debated, often intensely. For the most part, what has been challenged has been the power to declare legislative and executive action unconstitutional. Accordingly, the debate has been cast in terms of legitimacy. A polity accustomed to question unchecked power views with unease judicial authority to strike down laws enacted by democratically elected legislatures. Where, after all, is the accountability of life-tenured judges? This question of democratic theory has been raised insistently, especially in times of constitutional crisis, notably in the 1930s and again in the 1950s.

The last word has not been heard in these debates, and it will not soon be heard. The structure of American government guarantees the issue a long life. But, for the moment, the debate seems to have waned with the growing recognition that there are elements of overstatement in the case against judicial review. The courts are more democratically accountable, through a variety of formal and informal mechanisms, than they have been accused of being. Equally important, the other branches are in many ways less democratically accountable than they in turn were said to be by those who emphasized the special disabilities under which judges labor. . . .

As the debate over the democratic character of judicial review wanes, there is another set of issues in the offing. It relates not to legitimacy but to capacity,

not to whether the courts *should* perform certain tasks but to whether they *can* perform them competently.

Of course, legitimacy and capacity are related. A court wholly without capacity may forfeit its claim to legitimacy. A court wholly without legitimacy will soon suffer from diminished capacity. The cases for and against judicial review have always rested in part on assessments of judicial capacity: on the one hand, the presumably superior ability of the courts "to build up a body of coherent and intelligible constitutional principle"; on the other, the presumably inferior ability of courts to make the political judgments on which exercises of the power of judicial review so often turn. If the separation of powers reflects a division of labor according to expertise, then relative institutional capacity becomes relevant to defining spheres of power and particular exercises of power.

The recent developments that I have described necessarily raise the previously subsidiary issue of capacity to a more prominent place. Although the assumption of new responsibilities, can, as I have observed, be traced to exercises of the traditional power to declare laws unconstitutional, they now transcend that power. Traditional judicial review meant forbidding action, saying "no" to the other branches. Now the judicial function often means requiring action, and there is a difference between foreclosing an alternative and choosing one, between constraining and commanding. Among other things, it is this difference, and the problematic character of judicial resources to manage the task of commanding, that make the question of capacity so important.

AMENDMENT FROM THE JUDGMENT SEAT

Before proceeding any further, let me try to recapitulate what I have said so far and where it seems to me to lead. I have argued that judicial intervention in matters of social policy has greatly increased and will not soon decrease. This expansion of judicial responsibility means, first, a broadening of the sphere of judge-made law, into areas that might once have been called "social welfare" and were not considered "legal" at all. It also means an expansion of the scope for judicial initiative within these areas. Courts are no longer as confined to the interstices of legislation as they once were—now the statute is often a mere point of departure—and they are no longer as inhibited as they once were from delving into supervisory or administrative responsibilities in connection with the remedies they award. They are more often found requiring detailed, specific, and affirmative action than previously. They are less constrained, too, by the limitations of the cases and the litigants before them. More openly, self-consciously, and broadly than before, the courts are engaged in efforts to shape or control the behavior of identifiable social groups, groups not necessarily before the court: welfare administrators, employers, school officials, policemen. The expansion of the judicial sphere means there are more such groups whose behavior has become a subject of judicial attention.

This has not happened all at once, and the transition is anything but complete. Most courts, most of the time, are doing roughly what they did many years ago. Not a landslide but an erosion of some of the distinctive features of the judicial process is what seems to have been occurring.

What this means is that there is somewhat less institutional differentiation today than two decades ago. There is now more overlap between the courts and Congress in formulating policy and between the courts and the executive in both formulating and carrying out programs. That is, the types of decisions being made by the various institutions—their scope and level of generality—seem to be converging somewhat, though the processes by which the decisions are made and the outcomes of those processes may be quite different—as different as the groups who maneuver to place an issue before one set of decisionmakers rather than another, or who, defeated in one forum, turn hopefully to the next, believe them to be. Thus, to say that there is convergence in the business of courts and other institutions is not tantamount to saying that it makes no difference who decides a question. On the contrary, it matters a good deal, for the institutions are differently composed and organized. The real possibility of overlapping responsibilities but opposite outcomes makes the policy process a more complex and drawn-out affair than it once was.

The recency, the incompleteness, and the incremental history of these developments should not obscure their portentousness. It is just possible that these modifications in the scope of judicial power will one day amount to a major structural change. We regard as quaintly and unduly restrictive the medieval conception of legislation as mere restatement of customary law. Future generations may likewise view our distinctive association of adjudication with the grievances of individual litigants as an equally curious affectation.

It may be, of course, that something much less significant than this is in the offing. For the purposes of this discussion, it makes little difference. The changes of degree that are already visible are quite enough to raise important questions about the consequences of using the judicial process for the resolution of social policy issues.

If extensive judicial activity in matters of social policy is not a passing phenomenon, then Mansfield and Bentham have a new relevance for us. For we must confront Bentham's blunt assertion that "amendment from the judgment seat is confusion."

Nor is that all. Hybrid institutions run the risk of inheriting the disabilities of both parents. To the extent that institutional differentiation is in decline and courts are making policy of the scope formerly associated with legislatures, it must be asked not only whether Bentham's charge is true, but also whether Lord Mansfield's case against legislative foresight might not now be turned around on the courts. Do the putative advantages of "the common law that works itself pure" apply to judicial ventures into broad matters of social policy? Or do the courts now share the problem Mansfield attributes to Parliament: the inability to "take in all cases" in advance? Pound's "perils of prophecy," in other words, may now be on the other foot.

FOOD FOR THOUGHT

1. Imagine that you are an advisor to the president and have been asked to brief him on his options for filling a Supreme Court vacancy. In light of your knowledge of the president, the political context in which he currently serves, and the constraints operating in the Supreme Court selection process, what advice would you give him. Whom (or, more broadly, what kind of person) should he appoint? Why? What kinds of obstacles, if any, would you expect such an appointment to run into?

2. What should be the relative roles of the president and the Senate in federal judicial selection? Should these roles differ, depending on whether we are focusing on the U. S. District Courts, the Courts of Appeals, or the U. S. Supreme Court? Elaborate. What kinds of considerations are legitimate for the president to include as nomination criteria? Should precisely the same considerations apply when the Senate exercises advice and consent to a nomination?

3. Johnson and Canon's study of the aftermath of the *Roe* v. *Wade* decision demonstrates some of the difficulties of Supreme Court decisions moving from the level of doctrine to actual policy. What kinds of factors serve to differentiate between judicial decisions that are implemented effectively and those that do not have their intended policy effect? To what extent is the impact of a judicial ruling within the Court's control?

4. Suppose that you are a retired justice from the U. S. Supreme Court who was known for your liberal judicial activism. You have been asked to serve on a forum in which your role is to respond to a speech on Social Policy and Judicial Capacity given by Professor Donald Horowitz. The "text" of that speech is the reading you have done. What is your response?

CHAPTER 13

SELECTED LANDMARK SUPREME COURT RULINGS

Earlier chapters and selections in this volume have amply demonstrated the importance of constitutional interpretation for public policymaking in the United States, while also documenting the extraordinary controversy surrounding the very legitimacy of courts pursuing a policymaking role aggressively and purposefully. In this chapter we offer five "landmark" Supreme Court decisions, while fully recognizing both the folly and impossibility of even suggesting that these cases represent the five most "important" rulings the Court has rendered in two centuries of decision making. Clearly, however, the cases presented here are illustrative of the Court's policymaking role as well as the ongoing controversy that role has engendered. Further, while few analysts would likely place each of these cases in their "top five" for students of introductory American politics, we would venture to guess that some of these cases would make the list of any serious student of the American judiciary.

The introductions to the cases that follow, as well as the opinions themselves, place them in context and present important aspects of their factual settings. Importantly, however, we have chosen to present each of these cases because, in part, they serve to illustrate a good deal more about judicial policymaking than simply what they have to say about the substantive legal developments they bring about in their primary legal subject areas.

For example, perhaps no other ruling in the history of the Supreme Court has served as a symbol of an entire judicial era to the degree that *Brown* v. *Board of Education* signaled the egalitarian liberal activism that characterized the Court during the Chief Justiceship of Earl Warren from 1953 to 1969. Of equal or greater note, one would be hard pressed to identify a Supreme Court decision that is more central than *Brown* from the standpoint of the legal issues it examined, the rule it enunciated, and the policy implications it harbored.

Clearly, the Court's decision in *Brown* served as a primary catalyst for the American civil rights movement of the 1950s and 1960s. Prior to *Brown,* efforts to address the social, economic, and political plight of African Americans depended primarily on the good will and voluntary efforts of the American white people and the actions and initiatives of progressive individuals seeking to improve race relations in this country. *Brown,* however, changed the rules of America's race dilemma because, in the wake of this historic decision, African Americans found themselves in a quest for equality in which they were no longer in the position of supplicants asking for equal treatment but, rather, individuals who could now demand equality of the law as a clear matter of right. In effect, *Brown* can be credited, in part, with fostering a major social revolution in America.

Some fruits of that social revolution can be seen in the *Bakke* case and its examination of the legitimacy of affirmative action programs as well as in the ongoing political and social debate that surrounds affirmative action. If the invidious racial discrimination in *Brown* is unconstitutional, what of efforts to remedy such discrimination through ameliorative efforts in which race becomes a positive factor in governmental programs functioning in favor of identified racial minorities? The complexity of the affirmative action issue, and the shifting judicial coalitions leading to the Court's holding in the *Bakke* case, demonstrate that the Court can, at times, render judgments that few justices are comfortable with and that can leave the public even more confused than the justices themselves.

It is difficult to discuss the controversial nature of Supreme Court cases, their complexity, and their critical role in the policy process without talk turning to *Roe* v. *Wade,* the primary Supreme Court case examining the legitimacy of governmental efforts to constrain freedom of choice in abortion decisions. *Roe* exemplifies a case whose fundamental principle ("This right of privacy...is broad enough to encompass a woman's decision whether or not to terminate her pregnancy") remains intact (as of this writing) yet has been subjected to so much regulation and fine-tuning that the decision's author feels that, at worst, it has been rendered virtually meaningless or, at best, is in serious peril of extinction.

Critics of *Roe* would applaud such a characterization, labeling the decision as one of the most egregious examples of unwarranted "judicial legislation" and policymaking excess. Interestingly, both supporters and opponents of abortion rights may have some difficulty with the issue being resolved by resort to a constitutional right to privacy, a right some would argue cannot be found anywhere in the Constitution. Others would contend that, while such a right may exist, it bears no central or discernible relationship to the question of the legality of abortions.

Like *Roe, Texas* v. *Johnson* well demonstrates the close interplay between law and politics and, in particular, the political aftermath of some Supreme Court rulings with the championing of a constitutional amendment to ban flag burning continuing to have political cache for many political candidacies and public officeholders. Interestingly, the case serves to demonstrate the different considerations that may go into the freewheeling policy choices that can be made, for example, by legislators, and the legal decisions that must be rendered by the "good" judge (who, admittedly, often has a wide range of discretion). Note, however, the telling words of Justice Kennedy, who supplied the critical fifth vote overturning Johnson's conviction and finding the Texas statute unconstitutional. Kennedy laments, "The hard fact is that sometimes we must make decisions we do not like. We make them because they are right, right in the sense that the law and the Constitution...compel the result."

We conclude this chapter, appropriately we think, with *U.S.* v. *Nixon,* a case that demonstrates the

Court's awesome power as well as its unusual vulnerability. That power, of course, resides in the Court's definitive interpretation of the Constitution's meaning as, in this instance, when its refusal to recognize a president's claim of executive privilege ultimately brought the Nixon presidency to heel and contributed immeasurably to the resolution of the Watergate crisis and Nixon's resignation from the presidency. The Court's vulnerability, of course, can be seen, as Hamilton noted, in its lack of the power of the purse and the power of the sword. What, for example, would have transpired if Nixon had defied the Court? Would the unique stature of a judicial ruling have been successful against a president denying the legitimacy of the Court's ruling? While we cannot answer this question with certainty, its mere posing is illustrative of the potential precariousness of the judicial condition.

READING 61

Brown v. *Board of Education* (1954)
Earl Warren (Opinion of the Court)

Chief Justice Warren's opinion in Brown v. Board of Education *is often viewed as the Court's most important decision in the area of race relations and, indeed, some would even characterize* Brown *as the most critical constitutional ruling ever made in any substantive domain. Until* Brown, *the 14th Amendment's command that states offer their citizenry the "equal protection of the laws" was met by the "separate but equal" standard enunciated by the Court in* Plessy v. Ferguson *in 1896. In the wake of* Plessy, *society's emphasis (as well as the Court's) was placed almost exclusively on the "separate" part of the formula with little effort made to assure meaningful equality under the law. Thus,* Plessy *became the legal justification for, among other things, racial discrimination through the establishment of segregated public schools.*

From *Brown* v. *Board of Ed.,* 347 U.S. 483 (1954).

*The legal attack on the "separate but equal"
doctrine and segregated schooling was orchestrated
by the NAACP and its chief strategist, future
Supreme Court Justice Thurgood Marshall. In a
series of cases leading up to* Brown, *"separate but
equal" was attacked in graduate and professional
educational settings where a number of intangible
factors (such as the historic status of the separate
institutions and the professional prestige of their
alumni) were seized on by sympathetic but cautious
Courts to demonstrate that the separate schools were
not, in fact, equal. In* Brown, *however, Marshall and
the NAACP brought suit in an educational setting
where, on the surface, the separate "black" schools
were at least as good as their "white" counterparts.
Consequently, the Court would have to meet* Plessy's
"separate but equal" formula head on.

*It is a tribute to Earl Warren's leadership skills
that his determination that "separate educational
facilities are inherently unequal" was supported by a
unanimous Court. While the promise of* Brown *has
yet to be fully met, Warren's opinion served as a
beacon for the civil rights movement it helped to
foster and remains the starting point for analysis of
legal matters involving the issue of race in America.*

Mr. Chief Justice Warren delivered the opinion of the
Court.

These cases come to us from the States of Kansas, South Carolina, Virginia, and Delaware. They are
premised on different facts and different local conditions, but a common legal question justifies their consideration together in this consolidated opinion.

In each of the cases, minors of the Negro race,
through their legal representatives, seek the aid of the
courts in obtaining admission to the public schools of
their community on a nonsegregated basis. In each instance, they had been denied admission to schools attended by white children under laws requiring or
permitting segregation according to race. This segregation was alleged to deprive the plaintiffs of the equal
protection of the laws under the Fourteenth Amendment. In each of the cases other than the Delaware
case, a three-judge federal district court denied relief
to the plaintiffs on the so-called "separate but equal"

doctrine announced by this Court in *Plessy* v. *Ferguson,* 163 U.S. 537. Under that doctrine, equality of
treatment is accorded when the races are provided substantially equal facilities, even though these facilities
be separate. In the Delaware case, the Supreme Court
of Delaware adhered to that doctrine, but ordered that
the plaintiffs be admitted to the public schools because
of their superiority to the Negro schools.

The plaintiffs contend that segregated public
schools are not "equal" and cannot be made "equal,"
and that hence they are deprived of the equal protection of the laws. Because of the obvious importance
of the question presented, the Court took jurisdiction.
Argument was heard in the 1952 Term, and reargument was heard this Term on certain questions propounded by the Court.

Reargument was largely devoted to the circumstances surrounding the adoption of the Fourteenth
Amendment in 1868. It covered exhaustively consideration of the Amendment in Congress, ratification by
the states, then existing practices in racial segregation,
and the views of proponents and opponents of the
Amendment. This discussion and our own investigation convince us that, although these sources cast some
light, it is not enough to resolve the problem with
which we are faced. At best, they are inconclusive. The
most avid proponents of the post-War Amendments
undoubtedly intended them to remove all legal distinctions among "all persons born or naturalized in the
United States." Their opponents, just as certainly, were
antagonistic to both the letter and the spirit of the
Amendments and wished them to have the most limited effect. What others in Congress and the state legislatures had in mind cannot be determined with any
degree of certainty.

An additional reason for the inconclusive nature
of the Amendment's history, with respect to segregated schools, is the status of public education at that
time. In the South, the movement toward free common
schools, supported by general taxation, had not yet
taken hold. Education of white children was largely in
the hands of private groups. Education of Negroes was
almost non-existent, and practically all of the race
were illiterate. In fact, any education of Negroes was
forbidden by law in some states. Today, in contrast,
many Negroes have achieved outstanding success in the

arts and sciences as well as in the business and professional world. It is true that public school education at the time of the Amendment had advanced further in the North, but the effect of the Amendment on Northern States was generally ignored in the congressional debates. Even in the North, the conditions of public education did not approximate those existing today. The curriculum was usually rudimentary; ungraded schools were common in rural areas; the school term was but three months a year in many states; and compulsory school attendance was virtually unknown. As a consequence, it is not surprising that there should be so little in the history of the Fourteenth Amendment relating to its intended effect on public education.

In the first cases in this Court construing the Fourteenth Amendment, decided shortly after its adoption, the Court interpreted it as proscribing all state-imposed discriminations against the Negro race. The doctrine of "separate but equal" did not make its appearance in this Court until 1896 in the case of *Plessy* v. *Ferguson, supra,* involving not education but transportation. American courts have since labored with the doctrine for over half a century. In this Court, there have been six cases involving the "separate but equal" doctrine in the field of public education. In *Cumming* v. *County Board of Education,* 175 U.S. 528, and *Gong Lum* v. *Rice,* 275 U.S. 78, the validity of the doctrine itself was not challenged. In more recent cases, all on the graduate school level, inequality was found in that specific benefits enjoyed by white students were denied to Negro students of the same education qualifications. *Missouri ex rel. Gaines* v. *Canada,* 305 U.S. 337; *Sipuel* v. *Oklahoma,* 332 U.S. 631; *Sweatt* v. *Painter,* 339 U. S. 629; *McLaurin* v. *Oklahoma State Regents,* 339 U.S. 637. In none of these cases was it necessary to re-examine the doctrine to grant relief to the Negro plaintiff. And in *Sweatt* v. *Painter, supra,* the Court expressly reserved decision on the question whether *Plessy* v. *Ferguson* should be held inapplicable to public education.

In the instant cases, that question is directly presented. Here, unlike *Sweatt* v. *Painter,* there are findings below that the Negro and white schools involved have been equalized, or are being equalized, with respect to buildings, curricula, qualifications and salaries of teachers, and other "tangible" factors. Our decision, therefore, cannot turn on merely a comparison of these tangible factors in the Negro and white schools involved in each of the cases. We must look instead to the effect of segregation itself on public education.

In approaching this problem, we cannot turn the clock back to 1868 when the Amendment was adopted, or even to 1896 when *Plessy* v. *Ferguson* was written. We must consider public education in the light of its full development and its present place in American life throughout the Nation. Only in this way can it be determined if segregation in public schools deprives these plaintiffs of the equal protection of the laws.

Today, education is perhaps the most important function of state and local governments. Compulsory school attendance laws and the great expenditures for education both demonstrate our recognition of the importance of education to our democratic society. It is required in the performance of our most basic public responsibilities, even service in the armed forces. It is the very foundation of good citizenship. Today it is a principal instrument in awakening the child to cultural values, in preparing him for later professional training, and in helping him to adjust normally to his environment. In these days, it is doubtful that any child may reasonably be expected to succeed in life if he is denied the opportunity of an education. Such an opportunity, where the state has undertaken to provide it, is a right which must be made available to all on equal terms.

We come then to the question presented: Does segregation of children in public schools solely on the basis of race, even though the physical facilities and other "tangible" factors may be equal, deprive the children of the minority group of equal education opportunities? We believe that it does.

In *Sweatt* v. *Painter, supra,* in finding that a segregated law school for Negroes could not provide them equal educational opportunities, this Court relied in large part on "those equalities which are incapable of objective measurement but which make for greatness in a law school." In *McLaurin* v. *Oklahoma State Regents, supra,* the Court, in requiring that a Negro admitted to a white graduate school be treated like all other students, again resorted to intangible considerations: "...his ability to study, to engage in discussions and exchange views with other students, and, in general, to learn his profession." Such considerations apply with added force to children in grade and high schools. To separate them from others of similar age and qualifications solely because of their race generates a feeling of inferiority as to their status in the community that may affect their hearts and minds in a way unlikely ever to be undone. The effect of this separation on their educational opportunities was well stated by a finding in the Kansas case by a court which nevertheless felt compelled to rule against the Negro plaintiffs:

"Segregation of white and colored children in public schools has a detrimental effect upon the colored children. The impact is greater when it has the sanction of the law; for the policy of separating the races is usually interpreted as denoting the inferiority of the Negro group. A sense of inferiority affects the motivation of a child to learn. Segregation with the sanction of law, therefore has a tendency to retard the educational and mental development of Negro children and to deprive them of some of the benefits they would receive in a racially integrated school system."

Whatever may have been the extent of psychological knowledge at the time of *Plessy* v. *Ferguson*, this finding is amply supported by modern authority. Any language in *Plessy* v. *Ferguson* contrary to this finding is rejected. We conclude that in the field of public education the doctrine of "separate but equal" has no place. Separate educational facilities are inherently unequal. Therefore, we hold that the plaintiffs and others similarly situated for whom the actions have been brought are, by reason of the segregation complained of, deprived of the equal protection of the laws guaranteed by the Fourteenth Amendment....

READING 62

Regents of the University of California v. Bakke (1978)

Lewis Powell (Judgment of the Court) with Additional Partial Concurrences and Dissents

In Brown *the Supreme Court decided, in effect, that invidious discrimination could not be countenanced*

From *U.C. Board of Regents* v. *Bakke*, 438 U.S. 265 (1978).

under the equal protection clause of the Constitution's 14th Amendment. Subsequently, cases touching on race and the Constitution came to the Court with extraordinary frequency and in unusual guises. While Brown *was, by no means, a simple case, the cases reaching the Court in this domain, over time, raised issues that were exceedingly more complex than the legality of state-imposed segregation per se.*

One of the thorniest issues the Court wrestled with and, indeed, one which remains in a state of flux, is the legitimacy of "affirmative action" efforts aimed at being ameliorative and not invidiously discriminatory. The Court's first major substantive ruling on the affirmative action issue came in the case of Allan Bakke, a white male who claimed that he had been discriminated against in the admissions process of the University of California–Davis Medical School. UC–Davis's admissions procedures effectively guaranteed admission to 16 minority students in an entering class of 100. Minority student applicants were judged by a separate committee and processed in a separate pool from candidates such as Bakke. Bakke's application was never compared directly with applicants in the special admissions program, and the case's record revealed that his objective credentials were stronger than those of students admitted from the special pool.

The complexity of Bakke *is underscored by the voting breakdown of the justices, featuring opposing coalitions issuing partial concurrences and partial dissents. Only Justice Powell, whose opinion announces the judgment of the Court (but not its* majority *opinion!) agrees with all facets of the Court's holding. For some justices,* Bakke *required interpreting a statutory provision of the 1964 Civil Rights Act while, for others, it necessitated interpreting the Constitution.* Bakke's *complexity is also signaled by its bifurcated holding: The UC–Davis admissions policy is unconstitutional and Bakke must be admitted to the medical school, but the concept of affirmative action is also endorsed by the Court's majority.*

Mr. Justice POWELL announced the judgment of the Court.

This case presents a challenge to the special admissions program of the petitioner, the Medical School of the University of California at Davis, which is designed to assure the admission of a specified number of students from certain minority groups. [The Supreme Court of California held] the special admissions program unlawful, [enjoined] petitioner from considering the race of any applicant, [and ordered Bakke's] admission. For the reasons stated in the following opinion, I believe that so much of the judgment of the California court as holds petitioner's special admissions program unlawful and directs that respondent be admitted to the Medical School must be affirmed. For the reasons expressed in a separate opinion, my Brothers The Chief Justice, Mr. Justice Stewart, Mr. Justice Rehnquist. and Mr. Justice Stevens concur in this judgment. I also conclude for the reasons stated in the following opinion that the portion of the court's judgment enjoining petitioner from according any consideration to race in its admissions process must be reversed. For reasons expressed in separate opinions, my Brothers Mr. Justice Brennan, Mr. Justice White, Mr. Justice Marshall, and Mr. Justice Blackmun concur in this judgment.

Affirmed in part and reversed in part. . . .

II. [We] assume . . . for the purposes of this case that respondent has a right of action under Title VI [of The Civil Rights Act of 1964]. [In] view of the clear legislative intent, Title VI must be held to proscribe only those racial classifications that would violate [equal protection]. . . .

III. A. . . . .[T]he special admissions program is undeniably a classification based on race and ethnic background. To the extent that there existed a pool of at least minimally qualified minority applicants to fill the 16 special admissions seats, white applicants could compete only for 84 seats in the entering class, rather than the 100 open to minority applicants. Whether this limitation is described as a quota or a goal, it is a line drawn on the basis of race and ethnic status.

The guarantees of the 14th Amendment extend to persons. [The] guarantee of equal protection cannot mean one thing when applied to one individual and something else when applied to a person of another color. [Nevertheless], petitioner argues that the court

below erred in applying strict scrutiny [because white males] are not a "discrete and insular minority" requiring extraordinary protection from the majoritarian political process. [*Carolene Products,* n. 4.] This rationale, however, has never been invoked in our decisions as a prerequisite to subjecting racial or ethnic distinctions to strict scrutiny. [These] characteristics may be relevant in deciding whether or not to add new types of classifications to the list of "suspect" categories or whether a particular classification survives close examination. Racial and ethnic classifications, however, are subject to stringent examination without regard to these additional characteristics. We declared as much in the first cases explicitly to recognize racial distinctions as suspect [*Hirabayashi; Korematsu*]. Racial and ethnic distinctions of any sort are inherently suspect and thus call for the most exacting judicial examination.

B. This perception of racial and ethnic distinctions is rooted in our Nation's constitutional and demographic history. . . .

Over the past 30 years, this Court has embarked upon the crucial mission of interpreting [equal protection] with the view of assuring to all persons "the protection of equal laws," in a Nation confronting a legacy of slavery and racial discrimination. Because the landmark decisions in this area arose in response to the continued exclusion of Negroes from the mainstream of American society, they could be characterized as involving discrimination by the "majority" white race against the Negro minority. But they need not be read as depending upon that characterization for their results. It suffices to say that "[o]ver the years, this Court consistently repudiated '[d]istinctions between citizens solely because of their ancestry' as being 'odious to a free people whose institutions are founded upon the doctrine of equality.'" [*Loving* v. *Virginia,* quoting *Hirabayashi.*] Petitioner urges us to adopt for the first time a more restrictive view of [equal protection] and hold that discrimination against members of the white "majority" cannot be suspect if its purpose can be characterized as "benign." The clock of our liberties, however, cannot be turned back to 1868. *Brown.* It is far too late to argue that the guarantee of equal protection to *all* persons permits the recognition of special wards entitled to a degree of protection greater than that accorded [others].

Once the artificial line of a "two-class theory" of the 14th Amendment is put aside, the difficulties entailed in varying the level of judicial review according to a perceived "preferred" status of a particular racial or ethnic minority are intractable. The concepts of "majority" and "minority" necessarily reflect temporary arrangements and political judgments. [The] white "majority" itself is composed of various minority groups, most of which can lay claim to a history of prior discrimination at the hands of the state and private individuals. Not all of these groups can receive preferential treatment and corresponding judicial tolerance of distinctions drawn in terms of race and nationality, for then the only "majority" left would be a new minority of White Anglo-Saxon Protestants. There is no principled basis for deciding which groups would merit "heightened judicial solicitude" and which would not. Courts would be asked to evaluate the extent of the prejudice and consequent harm suffered by various minority groups. Those whose societal injury is thought to exceed some arbitrary level of tolerability then would be entitled to preferential classifications at the expense of individuals belonging to other groups. Those classifications would be free from exacting judicial scrutiny. As these preferences began to have their desired effect, and the consequences of past discrimination were undone, new judicial rankings would be necessary. The kind of variable sociological and political analysis necessary to produce such rankings simple does not lie within the judicial [competence].

Moreover, there are serious problems of justice connected with the idea of preference itself. First, it may not always be clear that a so-called preference is in fact benign.... Nothing in the Constitution supports the notion that individuals may be asked to suffer otherwise impermissible burdens in order to enhance the societal standing of their ethnic groups. Second, preferential programs may only reinforce common stereotypes holding that certain groups are unable to achieve success without special protection based on a factor having no relationship to individual worth. Third, there is a measure of inequity in forcing innocent persons in respondent's position to bear the burdens of redressing grievances not of their making. By hitching the meaning of [equal protection] to these transitory considerations, we would be holding, as a constitutional principle, that judicial scrutiny of classifications touching on racial and ethnic background may vary with the ebb and flow of political forces. Disparate constitutional tolerance of such classifications well may serve to exacerbate racial and ethnic antagonisms rather than alleviate them....

C. Petitioner contends that on several occasions this Court has approved preferential classifications without applying the most exacting scrutiny. Most of the cases upon which petitioner relies are drawn from three areas: school desegregation, employment discrimination, and sex discrimination. Each of the cases cited presented a situation materially different from the facts of this case.... Each involved remedies for clearly determined constitutional violations. Racial classifications thus were designed as remedies for the vindication of constitutional entitlement. Moreover, the scope of the remedies was not permitted to exceed the extent of the violations. Here, there was no judicial determination of constitutional violation as a predicate for the formulation of a remedial classification.... When a classification denies an individual opportunities or benefits enjoyed by others solely because of his race or ethnic background, it must be regarded as suspect.

IV. We have held that "in order to justify the use of a suspect classification, a State must show that its purpose or interest is both constitutionally permissible and substantial, and that its use of the classification is 'necessary [to] the accomplishment' of its purpose or the safeguarding of its interest." The special admissions program purports to serve the purposes of: (i) "reducing the historic deficit of traditionally disfavored minorities in medical schools and the medical profession"; (ii) countering the effects of societal discrimination; (iii) increasing the number of physicians who will practice in communities currently underserved; and (iv) obtaining the educational benefits that flow from an ethnically diverse student body. It is necessary to decide which, if any, of these purposes is substantial enough to support the use of a suspect classification.

A. If petitioner's purpose is to assure within its student body some specified percentage of a particular group merely because of its race or ethnic origin, such a preferential purpose must be rejected not as insubstantial but as facially invalid. Preferring members of any one group for no reason other than race or ethnic origin is discrimination for its own sake. This the Constitution forbids.

B.   The State certainly has a legitimate and substantial interest in ameliorating, or eliminating where feasible, the disabling effects of identified discrimination. [The] school desegregation cases [attest] to the importance of this state goal, [which is] far more focused than the remedying of the effects of "societal discrimination," an amorphous concept of injury that may be ageless in its reach into the past. We have never approved a classification that aids persons perceived as members of relatively victimized groups at the expense of other innocent individuals in the absence of judicial, legislative, or administrative findings of constitutional or statutory violations. After such findings have been made, the governmental interest in preferring members of the injured groups at the expense of others is substantial, since the legal rights of the victims must be vindicated. In such a case, the extent of the injury and the consequent remedy will have been judicially, legislatively, or administratively defined. Also, the remedial action usually remains subject to continuing oversight to assure that it will work the least harm possible to other innocent persons competing for the benefit. Without such finding of constitutional or statutory violations, it cannot be said that the government has any greater interest in helping one individual than in refraining from harming another. Thus, the government has no compelling justification for inflicting such harm.

Petitioner does not purport to have made, and is in no position to make, such findings. Its broad mission is education, not the formulation of any legislative policy or the adjudication of particular claims of illegality. Before...establishing a racial classification, a governmental body must have the authority and capability to establish, in the record, that the classification is responsive to identified discrimination. Lacking this capability, petitioner has not carried its burden of justification on this issue. Hence, the purpose of helping certain groups whom the faculty of the Davis Medical School perceived as vic-

tims of "societal discrimination" does not justify a classification that imposes disadvantages upon persons like respondent, who bear no responsibility for whatever harm the beneficiaries of the special admissions program are thought to have suffered. To hold otherwise would be to convert a remedy heretofore reserved for violations of legal rights into a privilege that all institutions throughout the Nation could grant at their pleasure to whatever groups are perceived as victims of societal discrimination. That is a step we have never approved.

C.   Petitioner identifies, as another purpose of its program, improving the delivery of health care services to communities currently underserved. [There] is virtually no evidence in the record indicating that petitioner's special admissions program is either needed or geared to promote that goal. [Petitioner] simply has not carried its burden of demonstrating that it must prefer members of particular ethnic groups over all other individuals in order to promote better health care delivery to deprived citizens. Indeed, petitioner has not shown that its preferential classification is likely to have any significant effect on the problem.

D.   The fourth goal asserted by petitioner is the attainment of a diverse student body. This clearly is a constitutionally permissible goal for an institution of higher education. Academic freedom, though not a specifically enumerated constitutional right, long has been viewed as a special concern of the First Amendment. The freedom of a university to make its own judgments as to education includes the selection of its student body. [Thus], in arguing that its universities must be accorded the right to select those students who will contribute the most to the "robust exchange of ideas," petitioner invokes a countervailing constitutional interest, that of the First Amendment. In this light, petitioner must be viewed as seeking to achieve a goal that is of paramount importance in the fulfillment of its mission. [Physicians] serve a heterogeneous population. An otherwise qualified medical student with a particular background—whether it be ethnic, geographic, culturally advantaged or disadvantaged—may bring to a professional school of medicine experiences, outlooks and ideas that enrich the training of its student body and better equip its graduates to render with understanding their vital service to humanity. [As] the interest of diversity is compelling in the context of a university's admissions program, the question remains whether the program's racial classification is necessary to promote this interest.

V.   A.   It may be assumed that the reservation of a specified number of seats in each class for individuals from the preferred ethnic groups would contribute to the attainment considerable ethnic diversity in the student body. But petitioner's argument that this is the only effective means of serving the interest of diversity is seriously flawed. In a most fundamental sense the argument misconceives the nature of the state interest that would justify consideration of race or ethnic background. It is not an interest in simple ethnic diversity, in which a specified percentage of the student body is in effect guaranteed to be members of selected ethnic [groups]. The diversity that furthers a compelling state interest encompasses a far broader array of qualifications and characteristics of which racial or ethnic origin is but a single though important element. Petitioner's special admissions program, focused *solely* on ethnic diversity, would hinder rather than further attainment of genuine diversity. Nor would the state interest in genuine diversity be served by expanding petitioner's two-track system into a multitrack program with a prescribed number of seats set aside for each identifiable category of applicants. Indeed, it is inconceivable that a university would thus pursue the logic of petitioner's two-track program to the illogical end of insulating each category of applicants with certain desired qualifications from competition with all other applicants.

The experience of other university admissions programs, which take race into account in achieving the educational diversity valued by the First Amendment, demonstrates that the assignment of a fixed number of places to a minority group is not a necessary means toward that end. An illuminating example is found in the Harvard College program: "In recent years Harvard College has expanded the concept of diversity to include students from disadvantaged economic, racial and ethnic groups. Harvard College now recruits not only Californians or Louisianans but also blacks and Chicanos and other minority stu-

dents. [In] practice, this new definition of diversity has meant that race has been a factor in some admission decisions. When the Committee on Admissions reviews the large middle group of applicants who are 'admissible' and deemed capable of doing good work in their courses, the race of an applicant may tip the balance in his favor just as geographic origin or a life spent on a farm may tip the balance in other candidates' cases. A farm boy from Idaho can bring something to Harvard College that a Bostonian cannot offer. Similarly, a black student can usually bring something that a white person cannot offer. In Harvard college admissions the Committee has not set target-quotas for the number of blacks, or of musicians, football players, physicists or Californians to be admitted in a given year. [But in] choosing among thousands of applicants who are not only 'admissible' academically but have other strong qualities, the Committee, with a number of criteria in mind, pays some attention to distribution among many types and categories of students."

In such an admissions program, race or ethnic background may be deemed a "plus" in a particular applicant's file, yet it does not insulate the individual from comparison with all other candidates for the available seats. The file of a particular black applicant may be examined for his potential contribution to diversity without the factor of race being decisive when compared, for example, with that of an applicant identified as an Italian-American if the latter is thought to exhibit qualities more likely to promote beneficial educational pluralism. Such qualities could include exceptional personal talents, unique work or service experience, leadership potential, maturity, demonstrated compassion, a history of overcoming disadvantage, ability to communicate with the poor, or other qualifications deemed important. In short, an admissions program operated in this way is flexible enough to consider all pertinent elements of diversity in light of the particular qualifications of each applicant, and to place them on the same footing or consideration, although not necessarily according them the same weight. [This] kind of program treats each applicant as an individual in the admissions process. [It] has been suggested that an admissions program which considers race only as one factor is simply a subtle and more sophisticated—but no less effective—means of according racial preference than the Davis program. A facial intent to discriminate, however, is evident in petitioner's preference program and not denied in this case. No such facial infirmity exists in an admissions program where race or ethnic background is simply one element—to be weighed fairly against other elements—in the selection process. [A] Court would not assume that a university, professing to employ a facially nondiscriminatory admissions policy, would operate it as a cover for the the functional equivalent of a quota system. In short, good faith would be presumed in the absence of a showing to the contrary in the manner permitted by our cases.

B.   In summary, it is evident that the Davis special admissions program involves the use of an explicit racial classification never before countenanced by this Court. It tells applicants who are not Negro, Asian, or "Chicano" that they are totally excluded from a specific percentage of the seats in an entering class. No matter how strong their qualifications, quantitative and extracurricular, including their own potential for contribution to educational diversity, they are never afforded the chance to compete with applicants from the preferred groups for the special admission seats. At the same time, the preferred applicants have the opportunity to compete for every seat in the class. The fatal flaw in petitioner's preferential program is its disregard of individual rights as guaranteed by the 14th Amendment. Such rights are not absolute. But when a State's distribution of benefits or imposition of burdens hinges on the color of a person's skin or ancestry, that individual is entitled to a demonstration that the challenged classification is necessary to promote a substantial state interest. Petitioner has failed to carry this burden. For this reason, that portion of the California court's judgment holding petitioner's special admissions program invalid under the 14th Amendment must be affirmed.

C.   In enjoining petitioner from ever considering the race of any applicant, however, the courts below failed to recognize that the State has a substantial interest that legitimately may be served by a properly devised admissions program involving the competitive consideration of race and ethnic origin. For this reason, so much of the judgment as enjoins petitioner

from any consideration of the race of any applicant must be reversed.

VI.   With respect to respondent's entitlement to an injunction directing his admission to the Medical School, petitioner has conceded that it could not carry its burden of proving that, but for the existence of its unlawful special admissions program, respondent still would not have been admitted. Hence, respondent is entitled to the injunction, and that portion of the judgment must be affirmed.

Opinion of Mr. Justice BRENNAN, Mr. Justice WHITE, Mr. Justice MARSHALL, and Mr. Justice BLACKMUN, concurring in the judgment in part and dissenting.

The Court…affirms the constitutional power…to act affirmatively to achieve equal opportunity for all. The difficulty of the issue presented…resulted in many opinions, no single one speaking for the Court. But this should not and must not mask the central meaning of today's opinions: Government may take race into account when it acts not to demean or insult any racial group, but to remedy disadvantages cast on minorities by past racial prejudice, at least when appropriate findings have been made by judicial, legislative, or administrative bodies with competence to act in this area.… Since we conclude that the affirmative admissions program [is] constitutional, we would reverse the judgment below in all respects. Mr. Justice Powell agrees that some uses of race in university admissions are permissible and, therefore, he joins with us to make five votes to reverse the judgment below insofar as it prohibits the University from establishing race-conscious programs in the future.

I.   [Even] today officially sanctioned discrimination is not a thing of the past. Against this background, claims that law must be "colorblind" or that the datum of race is no longer relevant to public policy must be seen as aspiration rather than as description of reality. [We cannot] let color blindness become myopia which masks the reality that many "created equal" have been treated within our lifetimes as inferior both by the law and by their fellow citizens.

II.   …[Title VI] prohibits only those uses of racial criteria that would violate the 14th Amendment if employed by a State or its agencies; it does not bar the preferential treatment of racial minorities as a means of remedying past societal discrimination to the extent that such action is consistent with the [14th Amendment].

III. A. [Our] cases have always implied that an "overriding statutory purpose" could be found that would justify racial classifications. We conclude, therefore, that racial classifications are not per se invalid under the 14th Amendment. Accordingly, we turn to the problem of articulating what our role should be in reviewing state action that expressly classifies by race.

B. Respondent argues that racial classifications are always suspect. [Petitioner] states that our proper role is simply to accept [its] determination that the racial classifications used by its program are reasonably related to what it tells us are its benign purposes. We reject petitioner's view, but, because our prior cases are in many respects inapposite to that before us now, we find it necessary to define with precision the meaning of that inexact term, "strict scrutiny." Unquestionably we have held that a government practice or statute which restricts "fundamental rights" or which contains "suspect classifications" is to be subjected to "strict scrutiny." [But] no fundamental right is involved here. Nor do whites as a class have any of the "traditional indicia of [suspectness]." Moreover, [this] is not a case where racial classifications are "irrelevant and therefore prohibited." Nor has anyone suggested that the University's purposes contravene the cardinal principle that racial classifications that stigmatize—because they are drawn on the presumption that one race is inferior to another or because they put the weight of government behind racial hatred and separatism—are invalid without more. On the other hand, the fact that this case does not fit neatly into our prior analytic framework for race cases does not mean that it should be analyzed by applying the very loose rational-basis [standard]. "'[T]he mere recitation of a benign, compensatory purpose is not an automatic shield which protects against any inquiry into the actual purposes underlying a statutory scheme.'" [*Webster,* quoting *Wiesenfeld.*] Instead, a number of considerations—developed in gender discrimination cases but which carry even more force when applied to racial classifications—lead us to conclude that racial classifications designed to further remedial pur-

poses "must serve important governmental objectives and must be substantially related to achievement of those objectives." [*Craig.*]....

In sum, because of the significant risk that racial classifications established for ostensibly benign purposes can be misused, causing effects not unlike those created by invidious classifications, it is inappropriate to inquire only whether there is any conceivable basis that might sustain such a classification. Instead, to justify such a classification an important and articulated purpose for its use must be shown. In addition, any statute must be stricken that stigmatizes any group or that singles out those least well represented in the political process to bear the brunt of a benign program. Thus our review under the 14th Amendment should be strict—not "'strict' in theory and fatal in fact," because it is stigma that causes fatality—but strict and searching nonetheless.

IV. Davis' articulated purpose of remedying the effects of past societal discrimination [is] sufficiently important to justify the use of race-conscious admissions programs where there is a sound basis for concluding that minority underrepresentation is substantial and chronic, and that the handicap of past discrimination is impeding access of minorities to the medical school.

A. At least since [*Green*], it has been clear that a public body which has itself been adjudged to have engaged in racial discrimination cannot bring itself into compliance with [equal protection] simply by ending its unlawful acts and adopting a neutral stance. Three years later, *Swann* [reiterated] that racially neutral remedies for past discrimination were inadequate where consequences of past discriminatory acts influence or control present decisions. And the Court further held both that courts could enter desegregation orders which assign students and faculty by reference to race and that local school boards could *voluntarily* adopt desegregation plans which made express reference to race if this was necessary to remedy the effects of past discrimination. Moreover, we stated that school boards. even in the absence of a judicial finding of past discrimination, could voluntarily adopt plans which assigned students with the end of creating racial pluralism by establishing fixed ratios of black and white students in each [school].

Finally, the conclusion that state educational institutions may constitutionally adopt admissions programs designed to avoid exclusion of historically disadvantaged minorities, even when such programs explicitly take race into account, finds direct support in our cases construing congressional legislation designed to overcome the present effects of past discrimination. Congress can and has outlawed actions which have a disproportionately adverse and unjustified impact upon members of racial minorities and has required or authorized race-conscious action to put individuals disadvantaged by such impact in the position they otherwise might have enjoyed. Such relief does not require as a predicate proof that recipients of preferential advancement have been individually discriminated against; it is enough that each recipient is within a general class of persons likely to have been the victims of discrimination....

Moreover, the presence or absence of past discrimination by universities or employers is largely irrelevant to resolving respondent's constitutional claims. [If] it was reasonable to conclude—as we hold that it was—that the failure of minorities to qualify for admission at Davis under regular procedures was due principally to the effects of past discrimination, then there is a reasonable likelihood that, but for pervasive racial discrimination, respondent would have failed to qualify for admission even in the absence of Davis' special admissions program. [In short,] States also may adopt race-conscious programs designed to overcome substantial, chronic minority underrepresentation where there is reason to believe that the evil addressed is a product of past racial [discrimination]. [We accordingly] conclude that Davis' goal of admitting minority students disadvantaged by the effects of past discrimination is sufficiently important to justify use of race-conscious admissions criteria.

B. Properly construed, therefore, our prior cases unequivocally show that a state government may adopt race-conscious programs if the purpose of such programs is to remove the disparate racial impact its actions might otherwise have and if there is reason to believe that the disparate impact is itself the product of past discrimination, whether its own or that of society at large. There is no question that Davis' program is valid under this test.... Davis had

a sound basis for believing that the problem of underrepresentation of minorities was substantial and chronic and that the problem was attributable to handicaps imposed on minority applicants by past and present racial [discrimination]. Davis clearly could conclude that the serious and persistent underrepresentation of minorities in medicine [is] the result of handicaps under which minority applicants labor as a consequence of a background of deliberate, purposeful discrimination against minorities in education and in society generally, as well as in the medical [profession]. The conclusion is inescapable that applicants to medical school must be few indeed who endured the effects of de jure segregation, the resistance to *Brown I,* or the equally debilitating pervasive private discrimination fostered by our long history of official discrimination, and yet come to the starting line with an education equal to [whites].

C. The second prong of our test—whether the Davis program stigmatizes any discrete group or individual and whether race is reasonably used in light of the program's objectives—is clearly satisfied by the Davis program. It is not even claimed that Davis' program in any way operates to stigmatize or single out any discrete and insular, or even any identifiable, nonminority group. Nor will harm comparable to that imposed upon racial minorities by exclusion or separation on grounds of race be the likely result of the program. It does not, for example, establish an exclusive preserve for minority students apart from and exclusive of whites. Rather, its purpose is to overcome the effects of segregation by bringing the races together. True, whites are excluded from participation in the special admissions program, but this fact only operates to reduce the number of whites to be admitted in the regular admissions program in order to permit admission of a reasonable percentage—less than their proportion of the California population—of otherwise underrepresented qualified minority applicants. Nor was Bakke in any sense stamped as inferior by the Medical School's [rejection]. Moreover, there is absolutely no basis for concluding that Bakke's rejection [will] affect him throughout his life in the same way as the segregation of the Negro school children in *Brown I* would have affected them. [This] does not mean that the exclusion of a white resulting from the preferential use of race is not sufficiently serious to require justification; but it does mean that the injury inflicted by such a policy is not distinguishable from disadvantages caused by a wide range of government actions, none of which has ever been thought impermissible for that reason alone.

In addition, there is simply no evidence that the Davis program discriminates intentionally or unintentionally against any minority group which it purports to benefit. The program does not establish a quota in the invidious sense of a ceiling on the number of minority applicants to be admitted. Nor can the program reasonably be regarded as stigmatizing the program's beneficiaries or their race as inferior. The Davis program does not simply advance less qualified applicants; rather it compensates applicants, whom it is uncontested are fully qualified to study medicine, for educational disadvantage which it was reasonable to conclude was a product of state-fostered discrimination. Once admitted, these students must satisfy the same degree requirements as regularly admitted students; and their performance is evaluated by the same standards by which regularly admitted students are judged. Under these circumstances, their performance and degrees must be regarded equally with the regularly admitted [students]. Since minority graduates cannot justifiably be regarded as less well qualified than nonminority graduates by virtue of the special admissions program, there is no reasonable basis to conclude that minority graduates [would] be stigmatized as inferior by the existence of such programs.

D.   We disagree with the lower courts' conclusion that the Davis program's use of race was unreasonable in light of its objectives. First, [there] are no practical means by which it could achieve it ends in the foreseeable future without the use of race-conscious measures. With respect to any factor (such as poverty or family educational background) that may be used as a substitute for race as an indicator of past discrimination, whites greatly outnumber racial minorities simply because whites make up a far larger percentage of the total population and therefore far outnumber minorities in absolute terms at every socioeconomic level. [Second], the Davis admissions program does not simply equate minority status with disadvantage. Rather, Davis considers on an individual basis each applicant's personal history to determine whether he or she has likely been disadvantaged

by racial discrimination.... [T]he procedure by which disadvantage is detected is informal, but we have never insisted that educators conduct their affairs through adjudicatory [proceedings]. A case-by-case inquiry into the extent to which each individual applicant has been affected, either directly or indirectly, by racial discrimination, would seem to be, as a practical matter, virtually impossible, despite the fact that there are excellent reasons for concluding that such effects generally exist. When individual measurement is impossible or extremely impractical, there is nothing to prevent a State from using categorical means to achieve its ends, at least where the category is closely related to the [goal].

E.   Finally, Davis' special admissions program cannot be said to violate the Constitution simply because it has set aside a predetermined number of places for qualified minority applicants rather than using minority status as a positive factor to be considered in evaluating the applications of disadvantaged minority applicants. For purposes of constitutional adjudication, there is no difference between the two approaches. In any admissions program which accords special consideration to disadvantaged racial minorities, a determination of the degree of preference to be given is unavoidable, and any given preference that results in the exclusion of a white candidate is no more or less constitutionally acceptable than a program such as that at Davis. Furthermore, the extent of the preference inevitably depends on how many minority applicants the particular school is seeking to admit in any particular year so long as the number of qualified minority applicants exceeds that number. There is no sensible, and certainly no constitutional, distinction between, for example, adding a set number of points to the admissions rating of disadvantaged minority applicants as an expression of the preference with the expectation that this will result in the admission of an approximately determined number of qualified minority applicants and setting a fixed number of places for such applicants as was done here. [That] the Harvard approach does [not] make public the extent of the preference and the precise workings of the system while the Davis program employs a specific, openly stated number, does not condemn the latter plan for purposes of 14th Amendment adjudication. It may be that the Harvard plan is more acceptable to the public than is the Davis "quota." If it is, any State [is] free to adopt it in preference to a less acceptable [alternative]. But there is no basis for preferring a particular preference program simply because in achieving the same goals that [Davis] is pursuing, it proceeds in a manner that is not immediately apparent to the [public].

Mr. Justice MARSHALL.

[It] must be remembered that, during most of the past 200 years, the Constitution as interpreted by this Court did not prohibit the most ingenious and pervasive forms of discrimination against the Negro. Now, when a State acts to remedy the effects of that legacy of discrimination, I cannot believe that this same Constitution stands as a barrier. [The] position of the Negro today in America is the tragic but inevitable consequence of centuries of unequal treatment. Measured by any benchmark of comfort or achievement, meaningful equality remains a distant dream for the Negro.... [I] do not believe that the 14th Amendment requires us to accept that fate. Neither its history nor our past cases lend any support to the conclusion that a University may not remedy the cumulative effects of society's discrimination by giving consideration to race in an effort to increase the number and percentage of Negro doctors. [While] I applaud the judgment of the Court that a university may consider race in its admissions process, it is more than a little ironic that, after several hundred years of class-based discrimination against Negroes, the Court is unwilling to hold that a class-based remedy for that discrimination is permissible. In declining to so hold, today's judgment ignores the fact that for several hundred years Negroes have been discriminated against, not as individuals, but rather solely because of the color of their skins. It is unnecessary in 20th century America to have individual Negroes demonstrate that they have been victims of racial discrimination; the racism of our society has been so pervasive that none, regardless of wealth or position, has managed to escape its impact. The experience of Negroes in America has been different in kind, not just in degree, from that of other ethnic groups. It is not merely the history of slavery alone but also that a whole people were marked as inferior by the law. And that mark has endured. The dream of America as the great melting pot has not been realized for the Negro; because of his skin color he never even made it into the pot. [Had] the Court been willing in

1896, in [*Plessy*], to hold that [equal protection] forbids differences in treatment based on race, we would not be faced with this dilemma in 1978. We must remember, however, that the principle that the "Constitution is color-blind" appeared only in the opinion of the lone dissenter. [For] the next 60 years, from *Plessy* to *Brown*, ours was a Nation where, *by law*, an individual could be given "special" treatment based on the color of his skin. It is because of a legacy of unequal treatment that we now must permit the institutions of this society to give consideration to race in making decisions about who will hold the positions of influence, affluence and [prestige].

I fear that we have come full circle. After the Civil War our government started several "affirmative action" programs. This Court in the *Civil Rights Cases* and [*Plessy*] destroyed the movement toward complete equality. For almost a century no action was taken, and this nonaction was with the tacit approval of the courts. Then we had *Brown* and the Civil Rights Acts of Congress, followed by numerous affirmative action programs. *Now,* we have this Court again stepping in, this time to stop affirmative action programs of the type used by the University of California.

Mr. Justice BLACKMUN.

[I] yield to no one in my earnest hope that the time will come when an "affirmative action" program is unnecessary and is, in truth, only a relic of the past. [At] some time, [the] United States must and will reach a stage of maturity where action along this line is no longer necessary. Then persons will be regarded as persons, and discrimination of the type we address today will be an ugly feature of history that is instructive but that is behind [us]. It is somewhat ironic to have us so deeply disturbed over a program where race is an element of consciousness, and yet to be aware of the fact, as we are, that institutions of higher learning, albeit more on the undergraduate than the graduate level, have given conceded preferences up to a point to those possessed of athletic skills, to the children of alumni, to the affluent who may bestow their largess on the institutions, and to those having connections with celebrities, the famous, and the powerful. [That] the 14th Amendment has expanded beyond its original 1868 [conception] does not mean for me that [it] has broken away from [its] original intended purposes. Those original aims persist. And that, in a distinct sense, is what "affirmative action" [is] all about. If this conflicts with idealistic equality, that tension is original 14th Amendment tension, [and] it is part of the Amendment's very nature until complete equality is achieved in the area. In this sense, constitutional equal protection is a shield. [I] suspect that it would be impossible to arrange an affirmative action program in a racially neutral way and have it successful. To ask that this be so is to demand the impossible. In order to get beyond racism, we must first take account of race. There is no other way. And in order to treat some persons equally, we must treat them differently. We cannot—we dare not—let the Equal Protection Clause perpetuate [racial supremacy].

Mr. Justice STEVENS, with whom The Chief Justice [BURGER], Mr. Justice STEWART, and Mr. Justice REHNQUIST join, concurring in the judgment in part and dissenting in part.

[This] is not a class action. [Bakke] challenged petitioner's special admissions program [and the] California Supreme Court upheld his challenge and ordered him admitted. If the state court was correct in its view that the University's special program was illegal, and that Bakke was therefore unlawfully excluded from the medical school because of his race, we should affirm its judgment, regardless of our views about the legality of admissions programs that are not now before the Court.... It is therefore perfectly clear that the question whether race can ever be used as a factor in an admissions decision is not an issue in this case, and that discussion of that issue is inappropriate....

| READING 63 |

Roe v. Wade (1973)

Harry Blackmun (Opinion of the Court) with Additional Concurrences and Dissents

It is, perhaps, both impossible and imprudent to rank Supreme Court decisions by the controversy they engender. Clearly, however, any such effort would

---

From *Roe* v. *Wade*, 410 U.S. 113 (1973).

place Roe v. Wade *at or near the top of the list. Indeed, more than two and a half decades after* Roe *was decided, the policy debate it reflected has, in many respects, not subsided. Annual commemorations of* Roe *continue to be held by both sides in the battle over abortion rights. Efforts persist, however doomed, to overturn* Roe *through a constitutional amendment. Litigation continues to work its way to the Supreme Court in an attempt to overturn* Roe *or, at least, to chisel away at and constrain its core protection for freedom of choice. Equally telling, candidates' positions on* Roe *continue to have important implications for their success in gaining public offices of every stripe—legislative, executive, and judicial.*

At issue in Roe *was the constitutionality of a Texas statute outlawing all "nontherapeutic" abortions, that is, those that were not necessary to save the life of the mother. Justice Blackmun, the Court's majority spokesperson, struggled for an unusually long time with the myriad of legal, medical, moral, and ethical questions the case raised before penning his opinion. Blackmun's labors even included considerable research at the Mayo Clinic where, earlier, he had been legal counsel. The trimester approach taken in* Roe *represents Blackmun's effort to balance the competitive interests he feels the decision should reconcile. Thus, the State may not premise abortion policy on the moral judgment that life begins at conception. Freedom of choice for women is greatest in the first trimester (when abortion is medically safer than childbirth), while state interests in maternal health and potential life grow weightier in the balance as the fetus moves closer to term. Judgments about all of these matters (and the trimester approach), of course, become even more problematic as continuing medical advances render abortion procedures (as well as childbirth) "safer" while making "fetal life" viable at earlier stages of pregnancy.*

Mr. Justice BLACKMUN delivered the opinion of the Court.

We forthwith acknowledge our awareness of the sensitive and emotional nature of the abortion controversy, of the vigorous opposing views, even among physicians, and of the deep and seemingly absolute convictions that the subject inspires. One's philosophy, one's experiences, one's exposure to the raw edges of human existence, one's religious training, one's attitudes toward life and family and their values, and the moral standards one establishes and seeks to observe, are all likely to influence and to color one's thinking and conclusions about abortion.

In addition, population growth, pollution, poverty, and racial overtones tend to complicate and not to simplify the problem.

Our task, of course, is to resolve the issue by constitutional measurement free of emotion and of predilection. We seek earnestly to do this, and, because we do, we have inquired into, and in this opinion place some emphasis upon, medical and medical-legal history and what that history reveals about man's attitudes toward the abortive procedure over the centuries. We bear in mind, too, Mr. Justice Holmes' admonition in his now vindicated dissent in *Lochner* v. *New York*, 198 U.S. 45, 76, 25 S.Ct. 539, 547 (1905):

> It [the Constitution] is made for people of fundamentally differing views, and the accident of our finding certain opinions natural and familiar, or novel, and even shocking, ought not to conclude our judgment upon the question whether statutes embodying them conflict with the Constitution of the United States....

The principal thrust of appellant's attack on the Texas statutes is that they improperly invade a right, said to be possessed by the pregnant woman, to choose to terminate her pregnancy. Appellant would discover this right in the concept of personal "liberty" embodied in the Fourteenth Amendment's Due Process Clause; or in personal, marital, familial, and sexual privacy said to be protected by the Bill of Rights or its penumbras...or among those rights reserved to the people by the Ninth Amendment.... Before addressing this claim, we feel it desirable briefly to survey, in several aspects, the history of abortion, for such insight as that history may afford us, and then to examine the state purposes and interests behind the criminal abortion laws....

Three reasons have been advanced to explain historically the enactment of criminal abortion laws in the 19th century and to justify their continued existence.

It has been argued occasionally that these laws were the product of a victorian social concern to discourage illicit sexual conduct. Texas, however, does not advance this justification in the present case, and it appears that no court or commentator has taken the argument seriously....

A second reason is concerned with abortion as a medical procedure. When most criminal abortion laws were first enacted, the procedure was a hazardous one for the woman.... Thus it has been argued that a State's real concern in enacting a criminal abortion law was to protect the pregnant woman, that is, to restrain her from submitting to a procedure that placed her life in serious jeopardy....

The third reason is the State's interest—some phrase it in terms of duty—in protecting prenatal life. Some of the argument for this justification rests on the theory that a new human life is present from the moment of conception. The State's interest and general obligation to protect life then extends, it is argued, to prenatal life. Only when the life of the pregnant mother herself is at stake, balanced against the life she carries within her, should the interest of the embryo or fetus not prevail. Logically, of course, a legitimate state interest in this area need not stand or fall on acceptance of the belief that life begins at conception or at some other point prior to live birth. In assessing the State's interest, recognition may be given to the less rigid claim that as long as at least *potential* life is involved, the State may assert interests beyond the protection of the pregnant woman alone....

It is with these interests, and the weight to be attached to them, that this case is concerned.

The Constitution does not explicitly mention any right of privacy. In a line or decisions, however, going back perhaps as far as [1891], the Court has recognized that a right of personal privacy, or a guarantee of certain areas or zones of privacy, does exist under the Constitution. In varying contexts the Court or individual Justices have indeed found at least the roots of that right in the First Amendment, *Stanley* v. *Georgia*, 394 U.S. 557, 564, 89 S.Ct. 1243, 1247 (1969); in the Fourth and Fifth Amendments, *Terry* v. *Ohio*, 392 U.S. 1, 8–9, 88 S.Ct. 1868, 1872–1873 (1968); *Katz* v. *United States*, 389 U.S. 347, 350, 88 S.Ct. 507, 510

(1967); *Boyd* v. *United States,* 116 U.S. 616, 6 S.Ct. 524 (1886), see *Olmstead* v. *United States,* 277 U.S. 438, 478, 48 S.Ct. 564, 572 (1928) (Brandeis, J., dissenting); in the penumbras of the Bill of Rights, *Griswold* v. *Connecticut,* 381 U.S. 479, 484–485, 85 S.Ct. 1678, 1681–1682 (1965); in the Ninth Amendment, *id.,* at 486, 85 S.Ct. at 1682 (Goldberg, J., concurring) or in the concept of liberty guaranteed by the first section of the Fourteenth Amendment, see *Meyer* v. *Nebraska,* 262 U.S. 390, 399, 43 S.Ct. 625, 626 (1923). These decisions make it clear that only personal rights that can be deemed "fundamental" or "implicit in the concept of ordered liberty," *Palko* v. *Connecticut,* 302 U.S. 319, 325, 58 S.Ct. 149, 152 (1937), are included in this guarantee of personal privacy. They also make it clear that the right has some extension to activities relating to marriage, *Loving* v. *Virginia,* 388 U.S. 1, 12, 87 S.Ct. 1817, 1823 (1967), procreation, *Skinner* v. *Oklahoma,* 316 U.S. 535, 541–542, 62 S.Ct. 1110, 1113–1114 (1942), contraception, *Eisenstadt* v. *Baird,* 405 U.S. 438, 453–454, 92 S.Ct. 1029, 1038–1039 (1972); *id.,* at 460, 463–465, 92 S.Ct. at 1042, 1043–1044 (White, J., concurring), family relationships, *Prince* v. *Massachusetts,* 321 U.S. 158, 166, 64 S.Ct. 438, 442 (1944), and child rearing and education, *Pierce* v. *Society of Sisters,* 268 U.S. 510, 535, 45 S.Ct. 571, 573 (1925), *Meyer* v. *Nebraska, supra.*

This right of privacy, whether it be founded in the Fourteenth Amendment's concept of personal liberty and restrictions upon state action, as we feel it is, or, as the District Court determined, in the Ninth Amendment's reservation of rights to the people, is broad enough to encompass a woman's decision whether or not to terminate her pregnancy. The detriment that the State would impose upon the pregnant woman by denying this choice altogether is apparent. Specific and direct harm medically diagnosable even in early pregnancy may be involved. Maternity, or additional offspring, may force upon the woman a distressful life and future. Psychological harm may be imminent. Mental and physical health may be taxed by child care. There is also the distress, for all concerned, associated with the unwanted child, and there is the problem of bringing a child into a family already unable, psychologically and otherwise, to care for it. In other cases, as in this one, the additional difficulties and continuing stigma of unwed motherhood may be involved. All these are factors the woman and her responsible physician necessarily will consider in consultation.

On the basis of elements such as these, appellants and some *amici* argue that the woman's right is absolute and that she is entitled to terminate her pregnancy at whatever time, in whatever way, and for whatever reason she alone chooses. With this we do not agree. Appellants' arguments that Texas either has no valid interest at all in regulating the abortion decision, or no interest strong enough to support any limitation upon the woman's sole determination, is unpersuasive. The Court's decisions recognizing a right of privacy also acknowledge that some state regulation in areas protected by that right is appropriate. As noted above, a state may properly assert important interests in safeguarding health, in maintaining medical standards, and in protecting potential life. At some point in pregnancy, these respective interests become sufficiently compelling to sustain regulation of the factors that govern the abortion decision. The privacy right involved, therefore, cannot be said to be absolute. In fact, it is not clear to us that the claim asserted by some *amici* that one has an unlimited right to do with one's body as one pleases bears a close relationship to the right of privacy previously articulated in the Court's decisions. The Court has refused to recognize an unlimited right of this kind in the past. *Jacobson* v. *Massachusetts,* 197 U.S. 11, 25 S.Ct. 358 (1905) (vaccination); *Buck* v. *Bell,* 274 U.S. 200, 47 S.Ct. 584 (1927) (sterilization).

We therefore conclude that the right of personal privacy includes the abortion decision, but that this right is not unqualified and must be considered against important state interests in regulation. . . .

Where certain "fundamental rights" are involved, the Court has held that regulation limiting these rights may be justified only by a "compelling state interest," . . . and that legislative enactments must be narrowly drawn to express only the legitimate state interests at stake. . . .

The District Court held that the appellee failed to meet his burden of demonstrating that the Texas statute's infringement upon Roe's rights was necessary to support compelling state interest, and that, although the defendant presented "several compelling justifications for state presence in the area of abortions," the statutes outstripped these justifications and swept "far beyond any areas of compelling state interest.".... Appellant and appellee both contest that holding. Appellant, as has been indicated, claims an absolute right that bars any state imposition of criminal penalties in the area. Appellee argues that the State's determination to recognize and protect prenatal life from and after conception constitutes a compelling state interest.... [W]e do not agree fully with either formulation.

A.   The appellee and certain *amici* argue that the fetus is a "person" within the language and meaning, of the Fourteenth Amendment. In support of this they outline at length and in detail the well-known facts of fetal development. If this suggestion of personhood is established, the appellant's case, of course, collapses, for the fetus' right to life is then guaranteed specifically by the Amendment. The appellant conceded as much on reargument. On the other hand, the appellee conceded on reargument that no case could be cited that holds that a fetus is a person within the meaning of the Fourteenth Amendment....

[T]he word "person," as used in the Fourteenth Amendment, does not include the unborn....

This conclusion, however, does not of itself fully answer the contentions raised by Texas, as we pass on to other considerations.

B.   The pregnant woman cannot be isolated in her privacy. She carries an embryo and, later, a fetus, if one accepts the medical definitions of the developing young in the human uterus.... The situation therefore is inherently different from marital intimacy, or bedroom possession of obscene material, or marriage, procreation, or education, with which *Eisenstadt, Griswold, Stanley, Loving, Skinner, Pierce,* and *Meyer* were respectively concerned. As we have intimated above, it is reasonable and appropriate for a State to decide that at some point in time another interest, that of health of the mother or that of potential human life, becomes significantly involved. The woman's privacy is no longer sole and any right of privacy she possesses must be measured accordingly.

Texas urges that, apart from the Fourteenth Amendment, life begins at conception and is present throughout pregnancy, and that, therefore, the State has a compelling interest in protecting that life from and after conception. We need not resolve the difficult question of when life begins. When those trained in the respective disciplines of medicine, philosophy, and theology are unable to arrive at any consensus, the judiciary, at this point in the development of man's knowledge, is not in a position to speculate as to the answer....

In view of...this, we do not agree that, by adopting one theory of life, Texas may override the rights of the pregnant woman that are at stake. We repeat, however, that the State does have an important and legitimate interest in preserving and protecting the health of the pregnant woman, whether she be a resident of the State or a nonresident who seeks medical consultation and treatment there, and that it has still *another* important and legitimate interest in protecting the potentiality of human life. These interests are separate and distinct. Each grows in substantiality as the woman approaches term and, at a point during pregnancy, each becomes "compelling."

With respect to the State's important and legitimate interest in the health of the mother, the "compelling" point, in the light of present medical knowledge, is at approximately the end of the first trimester. This is so because of the now established medical fact...that until the end of the first trimester mortality in abortion is less than mortality in normal childbirth. It follows that, from and after this point, a State may regulate the abortion procedure to the extent that the regulation reasonably relates to the preservation and protection of maternal health. Examples of permissible state regulation in this area are requirements as to the qualifications of the person who is to perform the abortion; as to the licensure of that person; as to the facility in which the procedure is to be performed, that is, whether it must be a hospital or may be a clinic or some other place of less-than-hospital status; as to the licensing of the facility; and the like.

This means, on the other hand, that, for the period of pregnancy prior to this "compelling" point, the attending physician, in consultation with his patient, is free to determine, without regulation by the State, that in his medical judgment the patient's pregnancy should be terminated. If that decision is reached, the judgement may be effectuated by an abortion free of interference by the State.

With respect to the State's important and legitimate interest in potential life, the "compelling" point is at viability. This is so because the fetus then presumably has the capability of meaningful life outside the mother's womb. State regulation protective of fetal life after viability thus has both logical and biological justifications. If the State is interested in protecting fetal life after viability, it may go so far as to proscribe abortion during that period except when it is necessary to preserve the life or health of the mother.

Measured against these standards, Art. 1196 of the Texas Penal Code, in restricting legal abortions to those "procured or attempted by medical advice for the purpose of saving the life of the mother," sweeps too broadly. The statute makes no distinction between abortions performed early in pregnancy and those performed later, and it limits to a single reason, "saving" the mother's life, the legal justification for the procedure. The statute, therefore, cannot survive the constitutional attack made upon it here. . . .

To summarize and to repeat:

1. A state criminal abortion statute of the current Texas type, that excepts from criminality only a *life saving* procedure on behalf of the mother, without regard to pregnancy stage and without recognition of the other interests involved, is violative of the Due Process Clause of the Fourteenth Amendment.

(a) For the stage prior to approximately the end of the first trimester, the abortion decision and its effectuation must be left to the medical judgment of the pregnant woman's attending physician.

(b) For the stage subsequent to approximately the end of the first trimester, the State, in promoting its interest in the health of the mother, may, if it chooses, regulate the abortion procedure in ways that are reasonably related to maternal health.

(c) For the stage subsequent to viability the State, in promoting its interest in the potentiality of human life, may, if it chooses, regulate, and even proscribe, abortion except where it is necessary, in appropriate medical judgment, for the preservation of the life or health of the mother. . . .

This holding, we feel, is consistent with the relative weights of the respective interests involved, with

lessons and example of medical and legal history, with the lenity of the common law, and with the demands of the profound problems of the present day. The decision leaves the State free to place increasing restrictions on abortion as the period of pregnancy lengthens, so long as those restrictions are tailored to the recognized state interests. The decision vindicates the right of the physician to administer medical treatment according to his professional judgment up to the points where important state interests provide compelling justifications for intervention. Up to those points the abortion decision in all its aspects is inherently, and primarily, a medical decision, and basic responsibility for it must rest with the physician. If an individual practitioner abuses the privilege of exercising proper medical judgment, the usual remedies, judicial and intra-professional are available. . . .

Mr. Justice DOUGLAS, concurring.

While I join the opinion of the Court, I add a few words. . . .

The Ninth Amendment obviously does not create federally enforceable rights. It merely says, "The enumeration in the Constitution of certain rights, shall not be construed to deny or disparage others retained by the people." But a catalogue of these rights includes customary, traditional, and time-honored rights, amenities, privileges, and immunities that come within the sweep of "the Blessings of Liberty" mentioned in the preamble to the Constitution. Many of them in my view come within the meaning of the term "liberty" as used in the Fourteenth Amendment.

First is the autonomous control over the development and expression on one's intellect, interests, tastes, and personality.

These are rights protected by the First Amendment and in my view they are absolute, permitting of no exceptions. . . .

Second is freedom of choice in the basic decisions of one's life respecting marriage, divorce, procreation, contraception, and the education and upbringing of children.

These rights, unlike those protected by the First Amendment, are subject to some control by the police power. Thus the Fourth Amendment speaks only of "unreasonable searches and seizures" and of "probable cause." These rights are "fundamental" and we have held that in order to support legislative action the statute must be narrowly and precisely drawn and that a "compelling state interest" must be shown in support of the limitation....

Third is the freedom to care for one's health and person, freedom from bodily restraint or compulsion, freedom to walk, stroll, or loaf.

These rights, though fundamental, are likewise subject to regulation on a showing of "compelling state interest."....

In summary, the enactment...is overbroad. It is not closely correlated to the aim of preserving prenatal life. In fact, it permits its destruction in several cases, including pregnancies resulting from sex acts in which unmarried females are below the statutory age of consent. At the same time, however, the measure broadly proscribes aborting other pregnancies which may cause severe mental disorders. Additionally, the statute is overbroad because it equates the value of embryonic life immediately after conception with the worth of life immediately before birth....

Mr. Justice WHITE, with whom Mr. Justice REHNQUIST joins, dissenting.

....With all due respect, I dissent. I find nothing in the language or history of the Constitution to support the Court's judgment. The Court simply fashions and announces a new constitutional right for pregnant mothers and, with scarcely any reason or authority for its action, invests that right with sufficient substance to override most existing state abortion statutes....

Mr. Justice REHNQUIST, dissenting.

...If the Court means by the term "privacy" no more than that the claim of a person to be free from unwanted state regulation of consensual transactions may be a form of "liberty" protected by the Fourteenth Amendment, there is no doubt that similar claims have been upheld in our earlier decisions on the basis of that liberty...But that liberty is not guaranteed absolutely against deprivation, only against deprivation without due process of law. The test traditionally applied in the area of social and economic legislation is whether or not a law such as that challenged has a rational relation to a valid state objective.... The Due Process Clause of the Fourteenth Amendment undoubtedly does place a limit, albeit a broad one, on legislative power to enact laws such as this. If the Texas statute were to prohibit an abortion even where the mother's life is in jeopardy,

I have little doubt that such a statute would lack a rational relation to a valid state objective.... But the Court's sweeping invalidation of any restrictions on abortion during the first trimester is impossible to justify under that standard, and the conscious weighing of competing factors that the Court's opinion apparently substitutes for the established test is far more appropriate to a legislative judgment than to a judicial one....

While the Court's opinion quotes from the dissent of Mr. Justice Holmes in *Lochner* v. *New York*, 198 U.S. 45, 74, 25 S.Ct. 539, 551 (1905), the result it reaches is more closely attuned to the majority opinion of Mr. Justice Peckham in that case. As in *Lochner* and similar cases applying, substantive due process standards to economic and social welfare legislation, the adoption of the compelling state interest standard will inevitably require this Court to examine the legislative policies and pass on the wisdom of these policies in the very process of deciding whether a particular state interest put forward may or may not be "compelling." The decision here to break pregnancy into three distinct terms and to outline the permissible restrictions the State may impose in each one, for example, partakes more of judicial legislation than it does of a determination of the intent of the drafters of the Fourteenth Amendment....

READING 64

Texas v. *Johnson* (1989)

William Brennan (Opinion of the Court) with Additional Concurrences and Dissents

One metric of a landmark Court ruling may be its extraordinary impact on the daily lives of millions (as surely was the case with Brown v. Board of Education*). Other critical decisions (such as* Roe v. Wade*) may affect fewer people directly, yet have an enormous tangible impact on the lives they do touch. Utilizing these criteria, it is difficult to see how* Texas v. Johnson, *dealing with a state statute prohibiting*

From *Texas* v. *Johnson*, 491 U.S. 397 (1989).

"desecrating a venerated object" (here, an American flag), rises to "landmark" status. Still, few Supreme Court rulings have resulted in as vocal and immediate mass condemnation as Texas v. Johnson, *coupled with passage of federal legislation seeking to overturn the decision, as well as efforts (continuing today) to pass a constitutional amendment banning flag burning. If, indeed, it is accurate to characterize the Supreme Court as an ongoing constitutional convention, because its decisions interpret the fundamental meaning of key constitutional words and phrases and apply them in a contemporary setting, then* Texas v. Johnson's *importance is quite evident.*

The case centers on the actions of Gregory Johnson who, during the 1984 Republican Convention in Dallas, protested the Reagan administration's policies by burning an American flag. The issue facing the Court was whether Johnson's actions constituted expressive behavior shielded by the First Amendment's free speech protections. In siding with Johnson for a highly divided (5–4) Court, Justice Brennan explores and defends eloquently the importance of free speech and political protest in a democratic society. It should be noted that in the ruling's aftermath Congress passed The Flag Protection Act of 1989, attempting to fine-tune an existing federal statute so that it, unlike the Texas law, would pass constitutional muster. In U.S. v. Eichman *(1990), however, the Court declared the federal law unconstitutional by the same 5–4 vote as in* Texas v. Johnson.

Justice Brennan delivered the opinion of the Court....

Johnson was convicted of flag desecration for burning the flag rather than for uttering insulting words. This fact somewhat complicates our consideration of his conviction under the First Amendment. We must first determine whether Johnson's burning of the flag constituted expressive conduct, permitting him to invoke the First Amendment in challenging his conviction. See, e.g., *Spence* v. *Washington,* 418 U.S. 405, 409–411, 94 S.Ct. 2727, 2729–31 (1974). If his conduct was expressive, we next decide whether the State's regulation is related to the suppression of free

expression. See, e.g., *United States* v. *O'Brien,* 391 U.S. 367, 377, 88 S.Ct., 1673, 1679 (1968)....

If the State's regulation is not related to expression, then the less stringent standard we announced in *United States* v. *O'Brien* for regulations of noncommunicative conduct controls.... If it is, then we are outside of *O'Brien's* test, and we must ask whether this interest justifies Johnson's conviction under a more demanding standard.... A third possibility is that the State's asserted interest is simply not implicated on these facts, and in that event the interest drops out of the picture....

The First Amendment literally forbids the abridgment only of "speech," but we have long recognized that its protection does not end at the spoken or written word. While we have rejected "the view that an apparently limitless variety of conduct can be labeled 'speech' whenever the person engaging in the conduct intends thereby to express an idea," *United States* v. *O'Brien, supra,* at 376, 88 S.Ct., at 1678, we have acknowledged that conduct may be "sufficiently imbued with elements of communication to fall within the scope of the First and Fourteenth Amendments." *Spence, supra,* at 409, 94 S.Ct., at 2730.

In deciding whether particular conduct possesses sufficient communicative elements to bring the First Amendment into play, we have asked whether "[a]n intent to convey a particularized message was present, and [whether] the likelihood was great that the message would be understood by those who viewed it." 418 U.S., at 410–411, 94 S.Ct., at 2730. Hence, we have recognized the expressive nature of students' wearing of black armbands to protest American military involvement in Vietnam, *Tinker* v. *Des Moines Independent Community School Dist.,* 393 U.S. 503, 505, 89 S.Ct., at 733, 735 (1969); of a sit-in by blacks in a "whites only" area to protest segregation, *Brown* v. *Louisiana,* 383 U.S. 131, 141–142, 86 S.Ct. 719, 723–24 (1966); of the wearing of American military uniforms in a dramatic presentation criticizing American involvement in Vietnam, *Schacht* v. *United States,* 398 U.S. 58, 90 S.Ct. 1555 (1970); and of picketing about a wide variety of causes, see, e.g., *Food Employees* v. *Logan Valley Plaza, Inc.,* 391 U.S. 308, 313–314, 88 S.Ct. 1601, 1605–06 (1968)....

Especially pertinent to this case are our decisions recognizing the communicative nature of conduct relating to flags. Attaching a peace sign to the flag, *Spence, supra,* at 409–410, 94 S.Ct., at 2729–30; saluting the flag, [*West Virginia State Board of Education* v.] *Barnette,* 319 U.S., at 632, 63 S.Ct., at 1182; and displaying a red flag, *Stromberg* v. *California,* 283 U.S. 359, 368–369, 51 S.Ct. 532, 535–36 (1931), we have held, all may find shelter under the First Amendment. See also *Smith* v. *Goguen,* 415 U.S. 566, 588, 94 S.Ct. 1242, 1254 (1974) (WHITE, J., concurring in judgment) (treating flag "contemptuously" by wearing pants with small flag sewn into their seat is expressive conduct). That we have had little difficulty identifying an expressive element in conduct relating to flags should not be surprising. The very purpose of a national flag is to serve as a symbol of our country....

The State of Texas conceded for purposes of its oral argument in this case that Johnson's conduct was expressive conduct.... Johnson burned an American flag as part—indeed, as the culmination—of a political demonstration that coincided with the convening of the Republican Party and its renomination of Ronald Reagan for President. The expressive, overtly political nature of this conduct was both intentional and overwhelmingly apparent. At his trial, Johnson explained his reasons for burning the flag as follows: "The American Flag was burned as Ronald Reagan was being renominated as President. And a more powerful statement of symbolic speech, whether you agree with it or not, couldn't have been made at that time. It's quite a just [juxtaposition]. We had new patriotism and no patriotism."... In these circumstances, Johnson's burning of the flag was conduct "sufficiently imbued with elements of communication," *Spence,* 418 U.S., at 409, 94 S.Ct., at 2730, to implicate the First Amendment.

The Government generally has a freer hand in restricting expressive conduct than it has in restricting the written or spoken word.... It may not, however, proscribe particular conduct *because* it has expressive elements. "[W]hat might be termed the more generalized guarantee of freedom of expression makes the communicative nature of conduct an inadequate *basis* for singling out that conduct for proscription. A law *directed at* the communicative nature of conduct must, like a law directed at speech itself, be justified by the substantial showing of need that the First Amendment requires." *Community for Creative Non-*

Violence v. *Watt,* 227 U.S. App. D.C. 19, 55–56, 703 F.2d 586, 622–623 (1983) (SCALIA, J., dissenting), rev'd sub nom. *Clark* v. *Community for Creative Non-Violence,* 468 U.S. 288, 104 S.Ct. 3065 (1984) (emphasis in original). It is, in short, not simply the verbal or nonverbal nature of the expression, but the governmental interest at stake, that helps to determine whether a restriction on that expression is valid.

Thus, although we have recognized that where " 'speech' and 'nonspeech' elements are combined in the same course of conduct, a sufficiently important governmental interest in regulating the nonspeech element can justify incidental limitations on First Amendment freedoms," *O'Brien, supra,* at 376, 88 S.Ct., at 1678, we have limited the applicability of *O'Brien*'s relatively lenient standard to those cases in which "the governmental interest is unrelated to the suppression of free expression".... In stating, moreover, that *O'Brien*'s test "in the last analysis is little, if any, different from the standard applied to time, place, or manner restrictions," *Clark, supra,* at 298, 104 S.Ct., at 3071, we have highlighted the requirement that the governmental interest in question be unconnected to expression in order to come under *O'Brien*'s less demanding rule.

In order to decide whether *O'Brien*'s test applies here, therefore, we must decide whether Texas has asserted an interest in support of Johnson's conviction that is unrelated to the suppression of expression. If we find that an interest asserted by the State is simply not implicated on the facts before us, we need not ask whether *O'Brien*'s test applies.... The State offers two separate interests to justify this conviction: preventing breaches of the peace and preserving the flag as a symbol of nationhood and national unity. We hold that the first interest is not implicated on this record and that the second is related to the suppression of expression.

Texas claims that its interest in preventing breaches of the peace justifies Johnson's conviction for flag desecration. However, no disturbance of the peace actually occurred or threatened to occur because of Johnson's burning of the flag. Although the State stresses the disruptive behavior of the protestors during their march toward City Hall...it admits that "no actual breach of the peace occurred at the time of the flagburning or in response to the flagburning."...

The State's emphasis on the protestors' disorderly actions prior to arriving at City Hall is not only somewhat surprising given that no charges were brought on the basis of this conduct, but it also fails to show that a disturbance of the peace was a likely reaction to Johnson's conduct. The only evidence offered by the State at trial to show the reaction to Johnson's actions was the testimony of several persons who had been seriously offended by the flag burning....

The State's position, therefore, amounts to a claim that an audience that takes serious offense at particular expression is necessarily likely to disturb the peace and that the expression may be prohibited on this basis. Our precedents do not countenance such a presumption. On the contrary, they recognize that a principal "function of free speech under our system of government is to invite dispute. It may indeed best serve its high purpose when it induces a condition of unrest, creates dissatisfaction with conditions as they are, or even stirs people to anger." *Terminiello* v. *Chicago,* 337 U.S. 1, 4, 69 S.Ct. 894, 896 (1949)....

Thus, we have not permitted the Government to assume that every expression of a provocative idea will incite a riot, but have instead required careful consideration of the actual circumstances surrounding such expression, asking whether the expression "is directed to inciting or producing imminent lawless action and is likely to incite or produce such action." *Brandenburg* v. *Ohio,* 395 U.S. 444, 447, 89 S.Ct. 1827, 1829 (1969) (reviewing circumstances surrounding rally and speeches by Ku Klux Klan). To accept Texas' arguments that it need only demonstrate "the potential for a breach of the peace,"... and that every flag burning necessarily possesses that potential, would be to eviscerate our holding in *Brandenburg.* This we decline to do.

Nor does Johnson's expressive conduct fall within that small class of "fighting words" that are "likely to provoke the average person to retaliation, and thereby cause a breach of the peace." *Chaplinsky* v. *New Hampshire,* 315 U.S. 568, 574, 62 S.Ct. 766, 770 (1942). No reasonable onlooker would have regarded Johnson's generalized expression of dissatisfaction with the policies of the Federal Government as a direct personal insult or an invitation to exchange fisticuffs....

We thus conclude that the State's interest in maintaining order is not implicated on these facts. The State

need not worry that our holding will disable it from preserving the peace. We do not suggest that the First Amendment forbids a State to prevent "imminent lawless action."... And, in fact, Texas already has a statute specifically prohibiting breaches of the peace...which tends to confirm that Texas need not punish this flag desecration in order to keep the peace....

It remains to consider whether the State's interest in preserving the flag as a symbol of nationhood and national unity justifies Johnson's conviction.

As in *Spence,* "[w]e are confronted with a case of prosecution for the expression of an idea through activity," and "[a]ccordingly, we must examine with particular care the interests advanced by [petitioner] to support its prosecution." 418 U.S., at 411, 94 S.Ct., at 2730. Johnson was not, we add, prosecuted for the expression of just any idea; he was prosecuted for his expression of dissatisfaction with the policies of this country, expression situated at the core of our First Amendment values....

Moreover, Johnson was prosecuted because he knew that his politically charged expression would cause "serious offense." If he had burned the flag as a means of disposing of it because it was dirty or torn, he would not have been convicted of flag desecration under this Texas law: federal law designates burning as the preferred means of disposing of a flag "when it is in such condition that it is no longer a fitting emblem for display," 36 U.S.C. § 176(k), and Texas has no quarrel with this means of disposal.... The Texas law is thus not aimed at protecting the physical integrity of the flag in all circumstances, but is designed instead to protect it only against impairments that would cause serious offense to others. Texas concedes as much: "[The stature] reaches only those severe acts of physical abuse of the flag carried out in a way likely to be offensive. The statute mandates intentional or knowing abuse, that is, the kind of mistreatment that is not innocent, but rather is intentionally designed to seriously offend other individuals."

Whether Johnson's treatment of the flag violated Texas law thus depended on the likely communicative impact of his expressive conduct....

We must therefore subject the State's asserted interest in preserving the special symbolic character of the flag to "the most exacting scrutiny." *Boos* v. *Barry,* 485 U.S., at 321, 108 S.Ct., at1164.

Texas argues that its interest in preserving the flag as a symbol of nationhood and national unity survives this close analysis. Quoting extensively from the writings of this Court chronicling the flag's historic and symbolic role in our society, the State emphasizes the "'special place'" reserved for the flag in our Nation.... The State's argument is not that it has an interest simply in maintaining the flag as a symbol of *something,* no matter what it symbolizes; indeed, if that were the State's position, it would be difficult to see how that interest is endangered by highly symbolic conduct such as Johnson's. Rather, the State's claim is that it has an interest in preserving the flag as a symbol of *nationhood* and *national unity,* a symbol with a determinate range of meanings.... According to Texas, if one physically treats the flag in a way that would tend to cast doubt on either the idea that nationhood and national unity are the flag's referents or that national unity actually exists, the message conveyed thereby is a harmful one and therefore may be prohibited.

If there is a bedrock principle underlying the First Amendment, it is that the Government may not prohibit the expression of an idea simply because society finds the idea itself offensive or disagreeable....

We have not recognized an exception to this principle even where our flag has been involved. In *Street v. New York,* 394 U.S. 576, 89 S.Ct. 1354 (1969), we held that a State may not criminally punish a person for uttering words critical of the flag. Rejecting the argument that the conviction could be sustained on the ground that Street had "failed to show the respect for our national symbol which may properly be demanded of every citizen," we concluded that "the constitutionally guaranteed 'freedom to be intellectually...diverse or even contrary,' and the 'right to differ as to things that touch the heart of the existing order,' encompass the freedom to express publicly one's opinions about our flag, including those opinions which are defiant or contemptuous." Id., at 593, 89 S.Ct., at 1366, quoting *Barnette,* 319 U.S., at 642, 63 S.Ct., at 1187. Nor may the Government, we have held, compel conduct that would evince respect for the flag. "To sustain the compulsory flag salute we are required to say that a Bill of Rights which guards the individual's right to speak his own mind, left it open to public authorities to compel

him to utter what is not in his mind." Id., at 634, 63 S.Ct., at 1183....

[T]hat the Government may not prohibit expression simply because it disagrees with its message, is not dependent on the particular mode in which one chooses to express an idea. If we were to hold that a State may forbid flag-burning wherever it is likely to endanger the flag's symbolic role, but allow it wherever burning a flag promotes that role—as where, for example—a person ceremoniously burns a dirty flag—we would be saying that when it comes to impairing the flag's physical integrity, the flag itself may be used as a symbol—as a substitute for the written or spoken word or a "short cut from mind to mind"—only in one direction. We would be permitting a State to "prescribe what shall be orthodox" by saying that one may burn the flag to convey one's attitude toward it and its referents only if one does not endanger the flag's representation of nationhood and national unity.

We never before have held that the Government may ensure that a symbol be used to express only one view of that symbol or its referents....

To conclude that the Government may permit designated symbols to be used to communicate only a limited set of messages would be to enter territory having no discernible or defensible boundaries. Could the Government, on this theory, prohibit the burning of state flags? Of copies of the Presidential seal? Of the Constitution? In evaluating these choices under the First Amendment, how would we decide which symbols were sufficiently special to warrant this unique status? To do so, we would be forced to consult our own political preferences, and impose them on the citizenry, in the very way that the First Amendment forbids us to do....

There is, moreover, no indication—either in the text of the Constitution or in our cases interpreting it—that a separate juridical category exists for the American flag alone. Indeed, we would not be surprised to learn that the persons who framed our Constitution and wrote the Amendment that we now construe were not known for their reverence for the Union Jack. The First Amendment does not guarantee that other concepts virtually sacred to our Nation as a whole—such as the principle that discrimination on the basis of race is odious and destructive—will go unquestioned in the marketplace of ideas.... We decline, therefore, to create for the flag an exception to the joust of principles protected by the First Amendment.

Our decision is a reaffirmation of the principles of freedom and inclusiveness that the flag best reflects, and of the conviction that our toleration of criticism such as Johnson's is a sign and source of our strength....

The way to preserve the flag's special role is not to punish those who feel differently about these matters. It is to persuade them that they are wrong.... And, precisely because it is our flag that is involved, one's response to the flag burner may exploit the uniquely persuasive power of the flag itself. We can imagine no more appropriate response to burning a flag than waving one's own, no better way to counter a flag burner's message than by saluting the flag that burns, no surer means of preserving the dignity even of the flag that burned than by—as one witness here did—according its remains a respectful burial. We do not consecrate the flag by punishing its desecration, for in doing so we dilute the freedom that this cherished emblem represents.

Justice KENNEDY, concurring....

The hard fact is that sometimes we must make decisions we do not like. We make them because they are right, right in the sense that the law and the Constitution, as we see them, compel the result. And so great is our commitment to the process that, except in the rare case, we do not pause to express distaste for the result, perhaps for fear of undermining a valued principle that dictates the decision. This is one of those rare cases....

With all respect to those views, I do not believe the Constitution gives us the right to rule as the dissenting members of the Court urge, however painful this judgment is to announce. Though symbols often are what we ourselves make of them, the flag is constant in expressing beliefs Americans share, beliefs in law and peace and that freedom which sustains the human spirit. The case here today forces recognition of the costs to which those beliefs commit us. It is poignant but fundamental that the flag protects those who hold it in contempt.

Chief Justice REHNQUIST, with whom Justice WHITE and Justice O'CONNOR join, dissenting....

The American flag...throughout more than 200 years of our history, has come to be the visible symbol embodying our Nation. It does not represent the views of any particular political party, and it does not represent any particular political philosophy. The flag is not simply another "idea" or "point of view" competing for recognition in the marketplace of ideas. Millions and millions of Americans regard it with an almost mystical reverence regardless of what sort of social, political, or philosophical beliefs they may have. I cannot agree that the First Amendment invalidates the Act of Congress, and the laws of 48 of the 50 States, which make criminal the public burning of the flag....

[T]he Court insists that the Texas statute prohibiting the public burning of the American flag infringes on respondent Johnson's freedom of expression. Such freedom, of course, is not absolute.... In *Chaplinsky* v. *New Hampshire*, 315 U.S. 568 62 S.Ct. 766 (1942), a unanimous Court said:

> "Allowing the broadest scope to the language and purpose of the Fourteenth Amendment, it is well understood that the right of free speech is not absolute at all times and under all circumstances. There are certain well-defined and narrowly limited classes of speech, the prevention and punishment of which have never been thought to raise any Constitutional problem. These include the lewd and obscene, the profane, the libelous, and the insulting or 'fighting' words—those which by their very utterance inflict injury or tend to incite an immediate breach of the peace. It has been well observed that such utterances are no essential part of any exposition of ideas, and are of such slight social value as a step to truth that any benefit that may be derived from them is clearly outweighed by the social interest in order and morality." Id., at 571–572, 62 S.Ct., at 769 (footnotes omitted).

The Court upheld Chaplinsky's conviction under a state statute that made it unlawful to "address any offensive, derisive or annoying word to any person who is lawfully in any street or other public place."... Chaplinsky had told a local Marshal, "You are a God damned racketeer" and a "damned Fascist and the whole government of Rochester are Fascists or agents of Fascists"....

Here it may equally well be said that the public burning of the American flag by Johnson was no essential part of any exposition of ideas, and at the same time it had a tendency to incite a breach of the peace. Johnson was free to make any verbal denunciation of the flag that he wished; indeed, he was free to burn the flag in private. He could publicly burn other symbols of the Government or effigies of political leaders. He did lead a march through the streets of Dallas, and conducted a rally in front of the Dallas City Hall. He engaged in a "die-in" to protest nuclear weapons. He shouted out various slogans during the march, including: "Reagan, Mondale which will it be? Either one means World War III"; "Ronald Reagan, killer of the hour, Perfect example of U.S. power"; and "red, white and blue, we spit on you, you stand for plunder, you will go under." For none of these acts was he arrested or prosecuted; it was only when he proceeded to burn publicly an American flag stolen from its rightful owner that he violated the Texas statute.

The Court could not, and did not, say that Chaplinsky's utterances were not expressive phrases—they clearly and succinctly conveyed an extremely low opinion of the addressee. The same may be said of Johnson's public burning of the flag in this case; it obviously did convey Johnson's bitter dislike of his country. But his act, like Chaplinsky's provocative words, conveyed nothing that could not have been conveyed and was not conveyed just as forcefully in a dozen different ways. As with "fighting words," so with flag burning, for purposes of the First Amendment: It is "no essential part of any exposition of ideas, and [is] of such slight social value as a step to truth that any benefit that may be derived from [it] is clearly outweighed" by the public interest in avoiding a probable breach of the peace. The highest courts of several States have upheld state statutes prohibiting the public burning of the flag on the grounds that it is so inherently inflammatory that it may cause a breach of public order....

The result of the Texas statute is obviously to deny one in Johnson's frame of mind one of many means of "symbolic speech." Far from being a case of "one picture being worth a thousand words," flag burning is the equivalent of an inarticulate grunt or roar that, it seems fair to say, is most likely to be indulged in not to express any particular idea, but to

antagonize others.... The Texas statute deprived Johnson of only one rather inarticulate symbolic form of protest—a form of protest that was profoundly offensive to many—and left him with a full panoply of other symbols and every conceivable form of verbal expression to express his deep disapproval of national policy. Thus, in no way can it be said that Texas is punishing him because his hearers—or any other group of people—were profoundly opposed to the message that he sought to convey. Such opposition is no proper basis for restricting speech or expression under the First Amendment. It was Johnson's use of this particular symbol, and not the idea that he sought to convey by it or by his many other expressions, for which he was punished....

Surely one of the high purposes of a democratic society is to legislate against conduct that is regarded as evil and profoundly offensive to the majority of people—whether it be murder, embezzlement, pollution, or flag burning.

Our Constitution wisely places limits on powers of legislative majorities to act, but the declaration of such limits by this Court "is, at all times, a question of much delicacy, which ought seldom, if ever, to be decided in the affirmative, in a doubtful case." *Fletcher v. Peck,* 10 U.S. (6 Cranch) 87, 128, 3 L.Ed. 162 (1810) (Marshall, C.J.). Uncritical extension of constitutional protection to the burning of the flag risks the frustration of the very purpose for which organized governments are instituted. The Court decides that the American flag is just another symbol, about which not only must opinions pro and con be tolerated, but for which the most minimal public respect may not be enjoined. The government may conscript men into the Armed Forces where they must fight and perhaps die for the flag, but the government may not prohibit the public burning of the banner under which they fight. I would uphold the Texas statute as applied in this case.

Justice STEVENS, dissenting.

As the Court analyzes this case, it presents the question whether the State of Texas, or indeed the Federal Government, has the power to prohibit the public desecration of the American flag. The question is unique. In my judgment rules that apply to a host of other symbols, such as state flags, armbands, or various privately promoted emblems of political or commercial identity, are not necessarily controlling. Even if flag burning could be considered just another species of symbolic speech under the logical application of the rules that the Court has developed in its interpretation of the First Amendment in other contexts, this case has an intangible dimension that makes those rules inapplicable....

[I]n my considered judgment, sanctioning the public desecration of the flag will tarnish its value—both for those who cherish the ideas for which it waves and for those who desire to don the robes of martyrdom by burning it. That tarnish is not justified by the trivial burden on free expression occasioned by requiring that an available, alternative mode of expression—including uttering words critical of the flag...be employed.

It is appropriate to emphasize certain propositions that are not implicated by this case. The statutory prohibition of flag desecration does not "prescribe what shall be orthodox in politics, nationalism, religion, or other matters of opinion or force citizens to confess by word or act their faith therein." *West Virginia Board of Education* v. *Barnette,* 319 U.S. 624, 642, 63 S.Ct. 1178, 1187 (1943). The statute does not compel any conduct or any profession of respect for any idea or any symbol.

Nor does the statute violate "the government's paramount obligation of neutrality in its regulation of protected communication." *Young* v. *American Mini Theatres, Inc.,* 427 U.S. 50, 70, 96 S.Ct. 2440, 2452 (1976) (plurality opinion). The content of respondent's message has no relevance whatsoever to the case. The concept of "desecration" does not turn on the substance of the message the actor intends to convey, but rather on whether those who view the *act* will take serious offense.... The case has nothing to do with "disagreeable ideas."... It involves disagreeable conduct that, in my opinion, diminishes the value of an important national asset.

The Court is therefore quite wrong in blandly asserting that respondent "was prosecuted for his expression of dissatisfaction with the policies of this country, expression situated at the core of our First Amendment values.".... Respondent was prosecuted because of the method he chose to express his dissatisfaction with

those policies. Had he chosen to spray-paint—or perhaps convey with a motion picture projector—his message of dissatisfaction on the facade of the Lincoln Memorial, there would be no question about the power of the Government to prohibit his means of expression. The prohibition would be supported by the legitimate interest in preserving the quality of an important national asset. Though the asset at stake in this case is intangible, given its unique value, the same interest supports a prohibition on the desecration of the American flag....

READING 65

U.S. v. *Nixon* (1974)
Warren Burger (Opinion of the Court)

The Supreme Court decisions we have presented in this chapter have all dealt with fundamental questions of rights and liberties. Our readings on Constitutional Interpretation, however, (such as Marbury *v.* Madison *and* McCulloch *v.* Maryland) *revealed the important role the Court can play in defining the structural distribution as well as the scope of governmental authority in the American system. In* U.S. *v.* Nixon *the Court was called on to address the scope and limits of the President's power of immunity from the compulsory processes of courts in an ongoing criminal investigation.*

Specifically at issue was the President's obligation to respond to a subpoena seeking access to a number of secret White House tapes of conversations with advisers under indictment for their role in Watergate. The President initially released a subset of edited materials, claiming that the judiciary had no power to compel him to release more because of his possession of "executive privilege." To accept such a claim would, in essence, place the President above the law.

From *U.S.* v. *Nixon,* 418 U.S. 683 (1974).

It has been well over two decades since Richard Nixon resigned from the presidency. With that passage of time, it is easy to overlook the fact that in U.S. v. Nixon the real possibility existed that the President would not submit voluntarily to a judgment rendered against him, bringing the country to the brink of constitutional crisis. When, in fact, Nixon acquiesced in the Court's order to release the disputed White House tapes, judicial "first principles" dating back to Marbury *were reasserted and the Court's successful challenge to the exercise of unchecked executive prerogatives, coupled with the actual content of the White House tapes, became the proximate "causes" of Nixon's resignation. Importantly, however, while executive privilege was denied to the President in this case, the Court hints broadly that in other circumstances and contexts such an executive prerogative could be validated.*

Mr. Chief Justice BURGER delivered the opinion of the Court. . . .

THE CLAIM OF PRIVILEGE

A

[W]e turn to the claim that the subpoena should be quashed because it demands "confidential conversations between a President and his close advisors that it would be inconsistent with the public interest to produce." . . . The first contention is a broad claim that the separation of powers doctrine precludes judicial review of a President's claim of privilege. The second contention is that if he does not prevail on the claim of absolute privilege, the court should hold as a matter of constitutional law that the privilege prevails over the subpoena *duces tecum.*

In the performance of assigned constitutional duties each branch of the Government must initially interpret the Constitution, and the interpretation of its powers by any branch is due great respect from the others. The President's counsel, as we have noted, reads the Constitution as providing an absolute privilege of confidentiality for all presidential communications. Many decisions of this Court, however, have

unequivocally reaffirmed the holding of *Marbury* v. *Madison,* 5 U.S. (1 Cranch) 137, 2 L.Ed. 60 (1803), that "it is emphatically the province and duty of the judicial department to say what the law is.". . .

No holding of the Court has defined the scope of judicial power specifically relating to the enforcement of a subpoena for confidential presidential communications for use in a criminal prosecution, but other exercises of powers by the Executive Branch and the Legislative Branch have been found invalid as in conflict with the Constitution. . . . In a series of cases, the Court interpreted the explicit immunity conferred by express provisions of the Constitution on Members of the House and Senate by the Speech or Debate Clause, U.S. Const. Art. I, § 6. *Doe* v. *McMillan,* 412 U.S. 306, 93 S.Ct. 2018 (1973); *Gravel* v. *United States,* 408 U.S. 606, 92 S.Ct. 2614 (1973); *United States* v. *Brewster,* 408 U.S. 501, 92 S.Ct. 2531 (1972); *United States* v. *Johnson,* 383 U.S. 169, 86 S.Ct. 749 (1966). Since this Court has consistently exercised the power to construe and delineate claims arising under express powers, it must follow that the Court has authority to interpret claims with respect to powers alleged to derive from enumerated powers.

Our system of government "requires that federal courts on occasion interpret the Constitution in a manner at variance with the construction given the document by another branch." *Powell* v. *McCormack,* 395 U.S., at 549, 89 S.Ct., at 1978. And in *Baker* v. *Carr,* 369 U.S., at 211, 82 S.Ct., at 706, the Court stated:

> "[D]eciding whether a matter has in any measure been committed by the Constitution to another branch of government, or whether the action of that branch exceeds whatever authority has been committed, is itself a delicate exercise in constitutional interpretation, and is a responsibility of this Court as ultimate interpreter of the Constitution."

Notwithstanding the deference each branch must accord the others, the "judicial power of the United State" vested in the federal courts by Art. III, § 1 of the Constitution can no more be shared with the Executive Branch than the Chief Executive, for example, can share with the Judiciary the veto power, or the Congress share with the Judiciary the power to override a presidential veto. Any other conclusion would be contrary to the basic concept of separation of powers and the checks and balances that flow from the scheme of a tripartite government.... We therefore reaffirm that it is "emphatically the province and the duty" of this Court "to say what the law is" with respect to the claim of privilege presented in this case. *Marbury* v. *Madison,* 5 U.S. (1 Cranch) at 177, 2 L.Ed. 60.

B

In support of his claim of absolute privilege, the President's counsel urges two grounds, one of which is common to all governments and one of which is peculiar to our system of separation of powers. The first ground is the valid need for protection of communications between high government officials and those who advise and assist them in the performance of their manifold duties; the importance of this confidentiality is too plain to require further discussion. Human experience teaches that those who expect public dissemination of their remarks may well temper candor with a concern for appearances and for their own interests to the detriment of the decision-making process. Whatever the nature of the privilege of confidentiality of presidential communications in the exercise of Art. II powers the privilege can be said to derive from the supremacy of each branch within its own assigned area of constitutional duties. Certain powers and privileges flow from the nature of enumerated powers; the protection of the confidentiality of presidential communications has similar constitutional underpinnings.

The second ground asserted by the President's counsel in support of the claim of absolute privilege rests on the doctrine of separation of powers. Here it is argued that the independence of the Executive Branch within its own sphere. *Humphrey's Executor* v. *United States,* 295 U.S. 602, 629–630, 55S.Ct. 869, 874–875 (1935); *Kilbourn* v. *Thompson,* 103 U.S. 168, 190–191 (1880), insulates a president from a judicial subpoena in an ongoing criminal prosecution, and thereby protects confidential presidential communications.

However, neither the doctrine of separation of powers, nor the need for confidentiality of high level communications, without more, can sustain an absolute, unqualified presidential privilege of immunity from judicial process under all circumstances. The President's need for complete candor and objectivity from advisers calls for great deference from the courts. However, when the privilege depends solely on the broad, undifferentiated claim of public interest in the confidentiality of such conversations, a confrontation with other values arises. Absent a claim of need to protect military, diplomatic or sensitive national security secrets, we find it difficult to accept the argument that even the very important interest in confidentiality of presidential communications is significantly diminished by production of such material for *in camera* inspection with all the protection that a district court will be obliged to provide.

The impediment that an absolute, unqualified privilege would place in the way of the primary constitutional duty of the Judicial Branch to do justice in criminal prosecutions would plainly conflict with the function of the courts under Art. III. In designing the structure of our Government and dividing and allocating the sovereign power among three coequal branches, the Framers of the Constitution sought to provide a comprehensive system, but the separate powers were not intended to operate with absolute independence.

> "While the Constitution diffuses power the better to secure liberty, it also contemplates that practice will integrate the dispersed powers into a workable government. It enjoins upon its branches separateness but interdependence, autonomy but reciprocity." *Youngstown Sheet & Tube Co.* v. *Sawyer,* 343 U.S. 579, 635, 72 S.Ct. 863, 870 (1952) (Jackson, J., concurring).

To read the Art. II powers of the President as providing an absolute privilege as against a subpoena essential to enforcement of criminal statutes on no more than a generalized claim of the public interest in confidentiality of nonmilitary nondiplomatic discussions would upset the constitutional balance of "a workable government" and gravely impair the role of the courts under Art. III.

C

Since we conclude that the legitimate needs of the judicial process may outweigh presidential privilege, it is necessary to resolve those competing interests in a manner that preserves the essential functions of each branch. The right and indeed the duty to resolve that question does not free the judiciary from according high respect to the representations made on behalf of the President. *United States* v. *Burr,* 25 Fed.Cas. 187, 190, 191–192 (No. 14,694) (CC Va. 1807).

The expectation of a President to the confidentiality of his conversations and correspondence, like the claim of confidentiality of judicial deliberations, for example, has all the values to which we accord deference for the privacy of all citizens and added to those values the necessity for protection of the public interest in candid, objective, and even blunt or harsh opinions in presidential decisionmaking. A President and those who assist him must be free to explore alternatives in the process of shaping policies and making decisions and to do so in a way many would be unwilling to express except privately. These are the considerations justifying a presumptive privilege for presidential communications. The privilege is fundamental to the operation of government and inextricably rooted in the separation of powers under the Constitution. In *Nixon* v. *Sirica,* 159 U.S. App.D.C. 58, 487 F.2d 700 (1973), the Court of Appeals held that such presidential communications are "presumptively privileged."... and this position is accepted by both parties in the present litigation. We agree with Mr. Chief Justice Marshall's observation, therefore, that "in no case of this kind would a court be required to proceed against the President as against an ordinary individual." *United States* v. *Burr,* 25 Fed.Cas. 187, 191 (No. 14,594) (CCD Va. 1807).

But this presumptive privilege must be considered in light of our historic commitment to the rule of law. This is nowhere more profoundly manifest than in our view that "the twofold aim [of criminal justice] is that guilt shall not escape or innocence suffer." *Berger* v. *United States,* 295 U.S. 78, 88, 55 S.Ct. 629, 633 (1935). We have elected to employ an adversary system of criminal justice in which the parties contest all issues before a court of law. The need to develop all relevant facts in the adversary system is both fundamental and comprehensive. The ends of criminal justice would be defeated if judgments were

to be founded on a partial or speculative presentation of the facts. The very integrity of the judicial system and public confidence in the system depend on full disclosure of all the facts, within the framework of the rules of evidence. To insure that justice is done, it is imperative to the function of courts that compulsory process be available for the production of evidence needed either by the prosecution or by the defense.

Only recently the Court restated the ancient proposition of law, albeit in the context of a grand jury inquiry rather than a trial,

> "'that the public...has a right to every man's evidence' except for those persons protected by a constitutional, common law, or statutory privilege, *United States* v. *Bryan,* 339 U.S. 323, 331, 70 S.Ct. 724, 730 (1949); *Blackmer* v. *United States,* 284 U.S. 421, 438, 52 S.Ct. 252, 255 (1932); *Branzburg* v. *United States,* 408 U.S. 665, 668, 92 S.Ct. 2646, 2660 (1972)."

The privileges referred to by the Court are designed to protect weighty and legitimate competing interests. Thus, the Fifth Amendment to the Constitution provides that no man "shall be compelled in any criminal case to be a witness against himself." And, generally, an attorney or a priest may not be required to disclose what has been revealed in professional confidence. These and other interests are recognized in law by privileges against forced disclosure, established in the Constitution, by statute, or at common law. Whatever their origins, these exceptions to the demand for every man's evidence are not lightly created nor expansively construed, for they are in derogation of the search for truth.

In this case the President challenges a subpoena served on him as a third party requiring the production of materials for use in a criminal prosecution on the claim that he has a privilege against disclosure of confidential communications. He does not place his claim of privilege on the ground they are military or diplomatic secrets. As to these areas of Art. II duties the courts have traditionally shown the utmost deference to presidential responsibilities. In *C. & S. Air Lines* v. *Waterman Steamship Corp.,* 333 U.S. 103, 111, 68 S.Ct. 431, 436 (1948), dealing with presidential authority involving foreign policy considerations, the Court said:

> "The President, both as Commander-in-Chief and as the Nation's organ for foreign affairs, has available intelligence services whose reports are not and ought not to be published to the world. It would be intolerable that courts, without the relevant information, should review and perhaps nullify actions of the Executive taken on information properly held secret."...

In *United States* v. *Reynolds,* 345 U.S. 1, 73 S.Ct. 528 (1952), dealing with a claimant's demand for evidence in a damage case against the Government the Court said:

> "It may be possible to satisfy the court, from all the circumstances of the case, that there is a reasonable danger that compulsion of the evidence will expose military matters, which, in the interest of national security, should not be divulged. When this is the case, the occasion for the privilege is appropriate, and the court should not jeopardize the security which the privilege is meant to protect by insisting upon an examination of the evidence, even by the judge alone, in chambers."

No case of the Court, however, has extended this high degree of deference to a President's generalized interest in confidentiality. Nowhere in the Constitution, as we have noted earlier, is there any explicit reference to a privilege or confidentiality yet to the extent this interest relates to the effective discharge of a President's powers, it is constitutionally based.

The right to the production of all evidence at a criminal trial similarly has constitutional dimensions. The Sixth Amendment explicitly confers upon every defendant in a criminal trial the right "to be confronted with the witnesses against him" and "to have compulsory process for obtaining witnesses in his favor." Moreover, the Fifth Amendment also guarantees that no person shall be deprived of liberty without due process of law. It is the manifest duty of the courts to vindicate those guarantees and to accomplish that it is essential that all relevant and admissible evidence be produced.

In this case we must weigh the importance of the general privilege or confidentiality of presidential communications in performance of his responsibilities against the inroads of such a privilege on the fair administration or criminal justice. The interest in preserving confidentiality is weighty indeed and entitled to great respect. However we cannot conclude that advisers will be moved to temper the candor of their remarks by the infrequent occasions of disclosure because of the possibility that such conversations will be called for in the context of a criminal prosecution.

On the other hand, the allowance of the privilege to withhold evidence that is demonstrably relevant in a criminal trial would cut deeply into the guarantee of due process of law and gravely impair the basic function of the courts. A President's acknowledged need for confidentiality in the communications of his office is general in nature, whereas the constitutional need for production of relevant evidence in a criminal proceeding is specific and to the fair adjudication of a particular criminal case in the administration of justice. Without access to specific facts a criminal prosecution may be totally frustrated. The President's broad interest in confidentiality of communications will not be vitiated by disclosure of a limited number of conversations preliminarily shown to have some bearing on the pending criminal cases.

We conclude that when the ground for asserting privilege as to subpoenaed materials sought for use in a criminal trial is based only on the generalized interest in confidentiality, it cannot prevail over the fundamental demands of due process of law in the fair administration of criminal justice. The generalized assertion of privilege must yield to the demonstrated, specific need for evidence in a pending criminal trial.

D

We have earlier determined that the District Court did not err in authorizing the issuance of the subpoena. If a president concludes that compliance with a subpoena would be injurious to the public interest he may properly, as was done here, invoke a claim of privilege on the return of the subpoena. Upon receiving a claim of privilege from the Chief Executive, it became the further duty of the District Court to treat the subpoenaed material as presumptively privileged and to require the Special Prosecutor to demonstrate that the presidential material was "essential to the justice of the [pending criminal] case." *United States v. Burr,* at 192. Here the District Court treated the material as presumptively privileged, proceeded to find that the Special Prosecutor had made a sufficient showing to rebut the presumption and ordered an *in camera* examination of the subpoenaed material. On the basis of our examination of the record we are unable to conclude that the District Court erred in ordering the inspection. Accordingly we affirm the order of the District Court that subpoenaed materials be transmitted to that court. . . .

Affirmed.

Mr. Justice REHNQUIST took no part in the consideration or decision of these cases.

FOOD FOR THOUGHT

1. Each of the case decisions presented in this chapter has been criticized by some analyst as being bad policy and/or bad law. Others, however, have argued equally strongly that the decisions represent good policy and, even more importantly, good law. First, what is the distinction between "law" and "policy" being made here. In your view, which of these decisions can be best defended as a matter of law? Which is least defensible? Why? Similarly, which of these decisions is most (and least) defensible as a matter of policy? Why?

2. The Court, in a part of its ruling in *Brown* v. *Board of Education* not reprinted here, delayed establishing a remedy for unconstitutional segregated public schooling to a second decision issued a year later. In *Brown II,* the Court announced its famous mandate that desegregation must occur "with all deliberate speed." Many analysts of the Court argue that the very existence of *Brown II* was a great mistake and, perhaps even more importantly, that the remedy the Court imposed for the constitutional violation found in *Brown I* made matters even worse. What, do you suppose, is the logic and justification for this argument? Do you agree?

3. The Supreme Court is, at bottom, a collegial decision making institution that values unanimity. Particularly in landmark cases such as *Brown* v. *Board of Education* and *U.S.* v. *Nixon,* the justices see a good deal to be gained by speaking through "one voice," particularly that of the Chief Justice, the "first among equals." Some analysts argue that obtaining unanimity can be bought at too high a price, with too much compromise and little definitive legal interpretation. Indeed, critics of the decision in *U.S.* v. *Nixon,* authored by Chief Justice Warren Burger, a Nixon appointee, have suggested that it is a very limited holding that does not go as far as it should in tempering presidential authority. From your reading of Burger's opinion, what is the basis for this characterization? Do you agree?